Pathways to Industrialization in the Twenty-First Century

UNU World Institute for Development Economics Research (UNU-WIDER) was established by the United Nations University as its first research and training centre and started work in Helsinki, Finland, in 1985. The purpose of the institute is to undertake applied research and policy analysis on structural changes affecting developing and transitional economies, to provide a forum for the advocacy of policies leading to robust, equitable, and environmentally sustainable growth, and to promote capacity strengthening and training in the field of economic and social policy-making. Its work is carried out by staff researchers and visiting scholars in Helsinki and via networks of collaborating scholars and institutions around the world.

UNU-WIDER
Katajanokanlaituri 6 B, 00160 Helsinki, Finland
www.wider.unu.edu

UNU-MERIT is a joint research and training centre of the United Nations University (UNU) and Maastricht University, the Netherlands. The joint institute was created on 1 January 2006 following the integration of the former UNU Institute for New Technologies (INTECH) in Maastricht and the Maastricht Economic Research Institute on Innovation and Technology, (MERIT) at Maastricht University. UNU-MERIT provides insights into the social political and economic factors that drive technological change and innovation. The Centre's research and training programmes address a broad range of policy questions relating to the national and international governance of science, technology, and innovation, with a particular focus on the creation, diffusion, and access to knowledge. In December 2010, UNU-MERIT merged with the Maastricht Graduate School of Governance, broadening its scope to include public policy analysis, social protection, and migration.

UNU-MERIT
Keizer Karelplein 19
6211 TC Maastricht, The Netherlands
www.merit.unu.edu

The United Nations Industrial Development Organization (UNIDO) is a specialized agency of the United Nations. Its mandate is to promote and accelerate sustainable industrial development in developing countries and economies in transition. Its activities focus on poverty reduction, inclusive globalization and environmental sustainability. Its services are based on two core functions: as a global forum, to generate and disseminate industry-related knowledge; as a technical co-operation agency, to provide technical support and implement projects. UNIDO's long-term vision is to aspire to a world of opportunity where progress is equitable, accessible, and sustainable, and where the alleviation of poverty is considered a common aim and global responsibility.

UNIDO
Vienna International Centre
Wagramerstrasse 5, 1400 Vienna, Austria
www.unido.org

Pathways to Industrialization in the Twenty-First Century

New Challenges and Emerging Paradigms

Edited by
Adam Szirmai, Wim Naudé, and Ludovico Alcorta

A study prepared by the World Institute for Development Economics Research of the United Nations University (UNU-WIDER), Maastricht Economic and Social Research Institute on Innovation and Technology of the United Nations University (UNU-MERIT), and the United Nations Industrial Development Organization (UNIDO).

OXFORD
UNIVERSITY PRESS

OXFORD
UNIVERSITY PRESS

Great Clarendon Street, Oxford, OX2 6DP,
United Kingdom

Oxford University Press is a department of the University of Oxford.
It furthers the University's objective of excellence in research, scholarship,
and education by publishing worldwide. Oxford is a registered trade mark of
Oxford University Press in the UK and in certain other countries

First Edition published in 2013

Impression: 1

British Library Cataloguing in Publication Data

Data available

ISBN 978–0–19–966785–7

Printed in Great Britain by
MPG Books Group, Bodmin and King's Lynn

Foreword

This book highlights the continuous relevance of industrial development and industrial policy in the national development strategies of developing countries. In the early post-war years it seemed that the recipe for development was a relatively straightforward one. Countries had to achieve structural change by shifting resources, especially labour, from agriculture to industry. Success in manufacturing was considered to be the key to economic development.

Some countries, particularly in East Asia, have indeed achieved economic success in this fashion. They started out with labour-intensive manufacturing based on low-cost labour and invested heavily in human and physical capital accumulation. In due course they also achieved technological upgrading and succeeded as industrial exporters. For example, in the course of two generations, countries such as the Republic of Korea or Singapore have transformed themselves from low-income to high-income economies. The industrial sector has also played a key role in the Chinese and Indian development experience. What about the prospects for the future?

The research presented here implies that manufacturing will continue to be important in the twenty-first century. This is the case in Brazil, China, and India and in a great variety of countries in Asia, Latin America, and Africa. There is also a rediscovery of the importance of manufacturing in the advanced service economies. There are many reasons for this. These include the central role played by technological progress, economies of scale and scope, and learning and industrial innovation in industrial activities. The importance of the many inter-sectoral linkages in industry is not only crucial in terms of employment, it is also crucial in terms of the development of human capital. Industry is characterized by numerous knowledge spillovers, both upstream and downstream, in terms of research, skills, and the continuous upgrading of inputs, ranging from raw materials and equipment to services. Industry will continue to play a key role in the development of most countries.

However, for developing countries wishing to achieve accelerated growth through industrialization, the situation has become more complicated. It is no longer clear whether the manufacturing sector can play the same dominant role as it did in the past and industrialization faces now a variety of new challenges. One of the most important new challenges is the need to achieve low-carbon growth paths in the face of climate change. Sustainable development and the greening of industrial activities raise fundamental yet common issues amongst the developing, emerging, and developed world. Other major challenges for newcomers include the strong competition from such established producers as China and India, and the need to participate actively in the global knowledge economy, create sufficient employment faced with jobless growth in manufacturing, and respond effectively to the emergence of fragmented global value chains.

Analysing past and present experiences with industrialization and industrial policy, this volume addresses these new challenges. It asks what can be learned from past experiences and tries to identify the responses needed in the light of new conditions facing countries that wish to industrialize in the twenty-first century. It provides essential reading for economists, policymakers, and scholars of development.

This book is the outcome of close collaboration between three United Nations Institutions, UNU-MERIT with its focus on the economics of innovation and technology, UNU-WIDER with its expertise in development economics, and the United Nations Industrial Development Organization (UNIDO) with its practical expertise in the industrial sector. In October 2009, these three institutions jointly organized a high-level workshop, bringing together a roster of international scholars from five continents. The editors, Adam Szirmai from UNU-MERIT, Wim Naudé from UNU-WIDER, and Ludovico Alcorta from UNIDO, made a careful selection from the studies presented at the workshop and brought them together to create a fluid, coherent, and balanced volume. Industrial policy, old or new, is back on the policy agenda—in developing countries, emerging countries, and in advanced economies. This book could not have been published at a better time.

Luc Soete, Director UNU-MERIT, Maastricht
Finn Tarp, Director UNU-WIDER, Helsinki
Kandeh K. Yumkella, Director-General UNIDO, Vienna

Acknowledgements

Industrial development is a complex process and industrial policies are notoriously difficult to get right. We were hence very fortunate to find that editing a book on these topics turned out to be stimulating, rewarding, and less daunting than we had thought. Although the three of us are passionate about the importance of industrialization, and believe that the challenges of industrial policy represent the cutting edge of economic policy, such passion is not enough to ensure publication of a book in itself. What made the difference for us was having supportive colleagues, committed and experienced contributors, and a superlative publication support team. We would like to acknowledge the roles that each of these groups have played.

First, this book reflects the joint vision and international collaboration of three institutions: UNU-WIDER (Finland), UNU-MERIT (The Netherlands), and UNIDO (Austria). We are grateful to our colleagues at these three institutions for their unwavering support. In particular a warm word of thanks goes to Luc Soete (director of UNU-MERIT), Tony Shorrocks and Finn Tarp (then and current directors of UNU-WIDER), and Kandeh K. Yumkella (director general of UNIDO). Wim Naudé, who joined the Maastricht School of Management (MsM) towards the later stages of the publication process, also wishes to thank his colleagues, in particular Peter de Gijsel (dean director of MsM), for their support.

Second, we were honoured in having the opportunity to work with a very distinguished set of contributors. Their insights, professionalism, and responsiveness to the issues under scrutiny meant that we could meet academic and publication standards with room to spare. We learned a lot from our interactions with our contributors. Readers can confirm for themselves that we were indeed lucky in having these experts on board.

Third, we wish to express our gratitude to our entire publication support team. The publication process started with the hosting of an international workshop in Maastricht on 22–23 October 2009. A selection of papers from this workshop formed the foundations of this book. Throughout the publication process a number of key individuals played critical roles. Here we cannot refrain from mentioning the names of Lorraine Telfer-Taivainen and Lisa Winkler at UNU-WIDER, and at UNU-MERIT the name of Eveline In de

Braek. Lisa Winkler was responsible for carefully checking and copy-editing the whole manuscript. We would also like to thank the staff at Oxford University Press, in particularly the commissioning editor Adam Swallow, for professionally and efficiently managing and overseeing a rigorous but sensible publication process.

Last but not least, we wish to gratefully acknowledge financial assistance that this endeavour has received. UNU-MERIT and UNIDO provided funding for the initial workshop in October 2009. UNU-WIDER provided financial assistance for the transformation of the workshop papers into working papers and chapters of the book. UNU-WIDER wishes to gratefully acknowledge contributions to its research programmes by the governments of Denmark (Royal Ministry of Foreign Affairs), Finland (Ministry for Foreign Affairs), Norway (Royal Ministry of Foreign Affairs), Sweden (Swedish International Development Cooperation Agency—Sida), and the United Kingdom (Department for International Development).

Adam Szirmai, Wim Naudé, and Ludovico Alcorta

Contents

List of Figures

List of Tables

List of Abbreviations

ABDI	Brazilian Industrial Development Agency
AGW	Anthropogenic global warming
BAT	Best available technologies
BNDES	National Economic and Social Development Bank
BTA	Border tax adjustment
COP15	Copenhagen Climate Change Conference
DIE	German Development Institute
ECLAC	Economic Commission for Latin American and the Caribbean
EPZ	Export processing zone
FE	Fixed effect
FDI	Foreign direct investment
FYP	Five-year plan
GATT	General Agreement on Tariffs and Trade
GDP	Gross national product
GEDI	Global Entrepreneurship Development Index
GFCF	Gross fixed capital formation
GGDC	Groningen Growth and Development Centre
GHG	Greenhouse gas
GLF	Great Leap Forward
GLS	Generalized least square estimator
GM	Genetically modified
GVC	Global value chain
HE	High-growth entrepreneurship
IBRD	International Bank for Reconstruction and Development
ICT	Information and communications technology
IEA	International Energy Agency
ILC	Industrially lagging country
ILO	International Labour Organization

IMF	International Monetary Fund
IPCC	Intergovernmental Panel on Climate Change
ISI	Import substitution industrialization
ISIC	International Standard Industrial Classification
LDC	Least developed country
LM	Lagrange multiplier
MDIC	Ministry for Development, Industry and Foreign Trade
MEF	Major Economies Forum
MENA	Middle East and North Africa
MNE	Multinational enterprise
NAFTA	North American Free Trade Agreement
NBS	National Bureau for Statistics
NIC	Newly industrialized country
NIE	Newly industrialized economy
NIS	National innovation system
NIFA	Newly increased fixed assets
NRC	National Resources Committee
OECD	Organisation for Economic Co-operation and Development
OEM	Original Equipment Manufacturer
OLS	Ordinary least square
PDP	Productive Development Policy (Brazil)
PET	Polyethylene terephthalate
PIM	Perpetual inventory method
PITCE	Guidelines for an Industrial, Technology and Foreign Trade Policy
POLS	Pooled OLS
PPP	Purchasing power parity
R&D	Research and development
RD&D	Research, development, and demonstration
SASID	South African standardized industry database
SE	Sensus Ekonomi
SEBRAE	Brazilian Service of Assistance to Micro and Small Enterprises
SI	Statistik Industri
SITC	Standard international trade classification
SME	Small and medium-sized enterprise
SOE	State-owned enterprise
SPC	State Planning Commission

SSA	Sub-Saharan Africa
TIFA	Total investment in fixed assets
TRIPS	Trade related intellectual property rights
TFP	Total factor productivity
TNC	Transnational corporations
TVET	Technical and vocational education and training
UNCTAD	United Nations Conference on Trade and Development
UNIDO	United Nations Industrial Development Organization
UNFCCC	United Nations Framework Convention on Climate Change
WTO	World Trade Organization

Notes on Contributors

Zoltan J. Ács is a university professor and director of the Center for Entrepreneurship and Public Policy (CEPP) at the School of Public Policy, George Mason University in Washington DC, former chief economist at the Office of Advocacy, US Small Business Administration and a visiting professor at Imperial College Business School London, UK. He developed the Global Entrepreneurship and Development Index (GEDI). He is also on the board of the World Entrepreneurship Forum, the Swedish Foundation for Small Business, the Corporate Research Board, and Eurasia Circle for Cultural Understanding and Prosperity EC-CUP.

Ludovico Alcorta is the Director of UNIDO's Development Policy, Statistics and Research Branch (DPR) in Vienna. He was a professor in economics of technology and innovation and Associate Dean for Research at Maastricht School of Management, The Netherlands. He was a research fellow at UNU-INTECH, and worked as economist for Latin America at the Economist Intelligence Unit and Midland Bank (part of the HSBC group) in London. He holds a bachelor's and a master's degree in economics from Universidad del Pacífico, Lima, as well as a master's in philosophy in development studies, and a PhD, both from the University of Sussex, Brighton, UK.

Tilman Altenburg is head of the Competitiveness and Social Development Department at the German Development Institute (DIE), Germany's think tank for development policy. Before joining DIE in 1995, Mr. Altenburg was a research fellow at Universities in Berlin and Marburg. He received his doctorate in Economic Geography from the University of Hamburg in 1991. Since 1986 Mr. Altenburg has done empirical research and published books and journal articles on issues of competitiveness, industrial and innovation policy, SME promotion, and value chain development. He regularly works as an adviser to the German government and international development agencies.

Haryo Aswicahyono is a researcher in the economics department of the Centre for Strategic and International Studies (CSIS), Jakarta, Indonesia. He specializes in trade and industry issues. Haryo Aswicahyono received his civil engineering degree at the Bandung Institute of Technology in 1983 and joined CSIS in 1985. In 1990, he continued his postgraduate study at the National Centre for Development Studies, Australian National University, Canberra. He received his doctoral degree in 2000, with the thesis 'Total Factor Productivity in Indonesia Manufacturing, 1975–1993'. After finishing his postgraduate study, he returned to work at CSIS.

Thomas Gries is a professor of economics at the Centre for International Economics, University of Paderborn in Germany. His research interest is international growth and development, both at micro and macro levels. In recent theoretical publications he has focused on entrepreneurship and the development of the modern sector. In recent empirical studies he concentrated on China.

Nobuya Haraguchi is an industrial research officer at the Development Policy, Statistics and Research Branch in the Strategic Research, Quality Assurance and Advocacy Division of UNIDO, conducting research on industrial structural change and drawing policy implications. Before joining UNIDO, he taught macroeconomics at St. John's University in the United States. He holds a PhD degree in development economics from the University of London.

Hal Hill is the H.W. Arndt Professor of South East Asian Economies, Arndt Corden Department of Economics, Crawford School, College of Asia and the Pacific, Australian National University. His general research interests are the ASEAN economies. He is the author or editor of 16 books and has written about 140 academic papers and book chapters. Current and recent book projects include a textbook on the ASEAN economies, and edited volumes on regional development dynamics in the Philippines, the Malaysian economy, the economy of East Timor, and foreign investment in the Asia-Pacific. He serves on the editorial board of 13 academic journals.

Mike Hobday is Visiting Professor at CENTRIM (Centre for Research in Innovation Management), Brighton University. He researches how firms in East and South East Asia catch up and overtake leading companies. He also works on innovation in high-value complex products and systems. Mike is the author of many publications, including *Innovation in East Asia: The Challenge to Japan*, Edward Elgar (1997); co-author with Andrew Davies of *The Business of Projects: Managing Innovation in Complex Products and Systems*, Cambridge University Press (2005); and co-editor with Andrea Prencipe and Andrew Davies of *The Business of Systems Integration*, Oxford University Press (2003).

Martin Medina received his PhD from Yale University. For 15 years, he has collaborated with governments, NGOs, academic, and international organizations in development projects in Africa, Asia, the Middle East, and Latin America, and the Caribbean. His main professional interests are: sustainable materials management, integrated waste management, and how waste management and recycling activities can reduce poverty, conserve resources, improve industrial competitiveness, and protect the environment. He has received several awards, and has published extensively, including the book *The World's Scavengers: Salvaging for Sustainable Consumption and Production*. He is currently senior international relations specialist at the US National Oceanic and Atmospheric Administration.

Dionisius Narjoko is a researcher at the Economic Research Institute for ASEAN and East Asia (ERIA). He was previously affiliated with the Jakarta-based think tank Centre for Strategic and International Studies and taught at the University of Indonesia. His research focuses on topics related to industrial organization, international trade, and industrialization.

Wim Naudé is Dean at Maastricht School of Management, and Professorial Fellow at UNU-MERIT and the Maastricht Graduate School of Management, University of

Maastricht, The Netherlands. Previously, he was Senior Research Fellow at UNU-WIDER, Professor and director of research at North-West University, South Africa, and Research Officer at the Centre for the Study of African Economies, University of Oxford.

John Page is a senior fellow in the Global Economy and Development Program at the Brookings Institution, Washington, DC, and a director at the International Growth Centre, London. From 1980 to 2008 he was a World Bank economist and manager. His senior positions included Director of Poverty Reduction, Director of Economic Policy, and Chief Economist of both the Middle East and North Africa and Africa regions. He has taught at Johns Hopkins, Princeton, and Stanford and has published widely on the economics of developing countries. His current research centers on industrial development and industrial policy in low-income countries.

Wilson Peres is Chief of the Innovation and ICT Unit at the UN Economic Commission for Latin America and the Caribbean (ECLAC). He has been a consultant to the OECD, the OAS, and the Mexican Government, as well as a visiting research fellow and lecturer at the University of California, San Diego (UCSD), and Professor of Industrial Organization at the Centro de Investigación y Docencia Económicas (CIDE) in Mexico. He has published widely on industrial policy, firm strategy, and ICT in Latin America. His current research interests are oriented towards industrial policy, the broadband system, and cloud computing.

Gorazd Rezonja is a consultant working for UNIDO's structural change research project since 2009. He obtained his university (BA) degree in Economics at the Faculty of Economics and Business of University of Maribor in Slovenia. He received his Master's degree in International Studies from the Diplomatic Academy of Vienna in Vienna, Austria.

Adam Szirmai is Professorial Fellow at UNU-MERIT and Professor of Development Economics at the Maastricht Graduate School of Governance of Maastricht University. His research focuses technological change, productivity, and growth in manufacturing in developing countries. His textbook *The Dynamics of Socioeconomic Development* was published by Cambridge University Press in 2005. A second edition is in preparation. Jointly with Wim Naudé and Micheline Goodhuys, he is editor of the book *Entrepreneurship, Innovation and Economic Development*, published by Oxford University Press in 2011.

Fiona Tregenna is an associate professor in the economics and econometrics department at the University of Johannesburg, South Africa. She holds a PhD in Economics from the University of Cambridge, a Master's degree in Economics from the University of Massachusetts (Amherst), and earlier degrees from the Universities of the Witwatersrand and Natal (now KwaZulu-Natal) in South Africa. Her research has been published in a number of peer-reviewed international journals and as chapters in several books. Her current research interests include: sectoral structure and growth, the relationship between the manufacturing and services sectors, poverty and inequality, unemployment, and deindustrialization.

John Weiss is Professor of Development Economics and Associate Dean in the School of Social and International Studies, University of Bradford. He specializes in industrial development, trade and cost-benefit analysis. Recent publications include the *Economics of Industrial Development*, Routledge (2011), *Poverty Strategies in Asia: Growth plus* (edited with H. A. Khan), Edward Elgar (2006), and *Poverty Targeting in Asia* (ed.) Edward Elgar (2005). He has worked as a consultant for, amongst others, the World Bank, the Asian Development Bank, and UNIDO. He was Director of Research at the Asian Development Bank Institute, Tokyo, 2001–6.

Harry X. Wu is a professor of economics at the Institute of Economic Research, Hitotsubashi University, Tokyo, and is Research Director at The Conference Board China Center, Beijing. Previously, he was a research fellow at Adelaide University and a senior economist at EAAU/DFAT, Canberra. He also taught at the Hong Kong Polytechnic University. His main areas of research include macroeconomic measurement, growth accounting, PPP-based international comparison and economics of transition, specialized in the Chinese economy. He has contributed extensively to the debate on China's growth and productivity performance.

Part I
Introduction

1

Introduction and Overview: The Past, Present, and Future of Industrialization

Adam Szirmai, Wim Naudé, and Ludovico Alcorta

1.1 The purpose of this book

This book is about the past, present, and future role of industrialization in economic development. Industrialization refers to the sustained structural transformation of a traditional economy into a modern economy driven by high-productivity activities in manufacturing. It has been the defining feature of the 'great take-off'; that is to say the period since the mid-eighteenth century, when first Britain, then other European countries and the USA underwent a historically rapid phase of economic development, followed in the twentieth century by Japan, the East Asian Tigers, and most recently China.

In the twenty-first century industrialization remains relevant for poor countries trying to catchup with more advanced economies and to provide increasing standards of living for their populations. Although the need for industrialization remains, the challenges it faces are perhaps more daunting than in the past. The emergence of global value chains (GVCs) has affected the nature of international competition. The prominence of multinational companies in the global economy influences access to knowledge and technology. The rise of China as a workplace of the world makes it harder for late industrializers to enter markets for manufactured products. Jobless growth in manufacturing may contribute to unemployment and social tensions. The challenge of climate change and global warming calls for new, more sustainable patterns of production, innovation, and energy use.

In a setting where poor countries wish to catchup through industrialization, while advanced economies struggle to maintain their competitiveness in a manner consistent with a reduction in CO_2 emissions and growing resource scarcity, the vector of national and international policies chosen to influence the direction and pace of industrialization across the world needs careful scrutiny. Such policies, subsumed under the term industrial policy, and referring to the processes whereby governments aim to deliberately affect the structural characteristics of their economies, are among the central concerns in this book. Focusing on new challenges and emerging paradigms with respect to industrialization, this book makes a case for carefully designed, well-co-ordinated, and appropriate industrial policies aiming to guide and shape the structural transformations of the twenty-first century.

The case for industrial policy is not one that is made lightly. Although there has always been a strong theoretical case for industrial policy based on market failures, the practical difficulties including the threat of government failure, survival of inefficient firms, rent-seeking, and misallocation of resources are considerable. The debate surfaces in various chapters in this book. Since the 1980s, these difficulties have generated a strong ideological opposition to industrial policy, especially with regard to more selective industrial policies.[1] But this may be changing. Ideological opposition to industrial policy is weakening, even in the USA.[2] Industrial policy has 'like a phoenix, risen from the ashes' (Evenett 2006: 1; see also Johnson 2009). In the EU much greater attention is now being given to industrial policy in the light of climate change[3] and concerns about a shrinking manufacturing base. In recent times, many developing countries have adopted new industrial policies or industrial development frameworks, including Botswana, India, South Africa, Uganda, Ethiopia, and countries in Latin America (ul-Haque 2007; Rodrik 2007a; Peres and Primi 2009). In the resurgence of industrial policy, there is a danger that the lessons from past policy failures are forgotten. This book gives careful consideration to past experiences with industrial policy focusing on lessons from successes as well as failures.

[1] Industrial policies range from extremely selective to non-discretionary (functional) policies. Selective policies attempt to pick winners, supporting specific firms, industrial champions, conglomerates, or investment projects. Functional policies do not 'pick winners' but promote the 'competitiveness' of the entire manufacturing sector, or even the entire supply side of the economy through educational investment, tax measures, or deregulation. At the intermediate level of sectors or technologies, selective industrial policies attempt to 'defy' a country's static comparative advantage and develop its 'latent' comparative advantage, for example through supporting selected industries through subsidies, tariffs, or quotas. Industrial policy as such is not limited to manufacturing. But in this book the focus is on the manufacturing sector.

[2] In the USA 'the term industrial policy has been taboo within the leadership of both major parties for many decades, carrying the taint of planned-economy socialism' (Pemberton 2008: 1).

[3] The Federal Government of Germany's Ecological Industrial Policy of 2006 calls for an 'ecological industrial policy that will adapt our industrial structures to the ecological and economic challenges.' And in October 2009 the European Trade Union Confederation adopted a resolution calling for an 'urgent need to launch the 3rd European Industrial Revolution based on green, sustainable and decent jobs'.

Given the important role that industrial policy can play in shaping twenty-first century industrialization, this book asks a number of questions regarding industrialization and the best policy responses to the challenges facing industrialization.

- Is industrialization still the most important engine of growth in light of the rise of the service sector? To what extent should manufacturing be the main focus of industrial policy in developing countries?
- What are the recent patterns of manufacturing structural change in the world economy?
- How big a threat to economic development is deindustrialization?
- What lessons can be learned from already successful industrializing countries in Asia?
- What lessons can be learned from past policy failures?
- What are the challenges facing industrial policy in Africa and Latin America?
- Can developing countries still industrialize after the rise of China?
- What about the least developed countries? Can industrial policy be successful when good governance is lacking?
- How should industrial policy take global climate change into account?
- What are the new directions and paradigms in thinking about industrial policy?
- How do the relationships between the state and entrepreneurs evolve across different stages of development and how does the nature of state–entrepreneurship relationships influence the choice of industrial policies?

The answers to these questions are explored—and further questions are raised—in the various chapters that follow. In the concluding chapter—Chapter 16—we will endeavour to summarize these answers. In the remainder of this chapter, we will first, in Sections 1.2 and 1.3, discuss industrialization and structural change in the world economy. In Section 1.4, we analyse the challenges for industrial policy in greater detail. Finally, in Section 1.5 we provide an overview of the chapters and summarize their contributions.

1.2 Background: the rise of manufacturing

Major technological breakthroughs in textile production and the application of steam power to production in Britain in the second half of the eighteenth century made a deep impression on contemporary and later observers. In the nineteenth century the term *Industrial Revolution* was coined to describe these developments in retrospect.[4]

In many respects the term Industrial Revolution is misleading. It disregards the incremental nature of increases in productive capacity in the eighteenth century, the continuity with earlier developments in northwest Europe (in particular in the low countries) as well as the importance of developments in other sectors of the economy. Also, the acceleration of British productivity growth only started in the early nineteenth century, rather than in the eighteenth century as widely perceived (Maddison 1982, 2007a; Crafts 1983).

In other respects, Industrial Revolution remains an apt term. It captures the introduction of radically new production technologies, which diffused across the globe and which have fundamentally affected the nature of global production. The emergence of modern manufacturing has led to dramatic changes in the structure of the world economy and to sustained increases in the growth of labour productivity and economic welfare (Maddison 2001, 2007a).

Britain was the first country to industrialize and it became the technological leader in the world economy. It was the exemplar for other countries. Manufacturing became the main engine of accelerating economic growth in the nineteenth century. A global race for industrialization had begun.

Industrialization should be seen as a single global process in which the industrial mode of production has diffused across the globe. Individual country experiences with industrialization can only be understood as part of this global and ongoing process of technological diffusion. But this does not mean that country experiences are identical. Individual countries follow different paths of industrial development depending on their initial conditions and the moment of their entry into the global race for industrialization (Pollard 1990). The first industrial followers were European countries such as Belgium, Switzerland, and France. Between 1815 and 1850, Belgium faithfully copied the British pattern of industrialization, based on coal mining, engineering, and textiles. It profited from rich mineral resources in the south of the country.[5] Switzerland was a landlocked economy with no coal, iron, or mineral resources and a limited internal market. It successfully concentrated on technologically advanced products such as fine silks, embroidery, and watchmaking. France followed the British model, but with variations based on its own initial conditions. It focused more on high-quality and luxury goods, made more use of its artisanal and artistic skills, and at the same time exploited

[4] In this section industrialization refers to the increasing importance of manufacturing. In international standard industrial classification, the industrial sector also includes mining, utilities, and construction.

[5] The foundations for Belgian industrialization were laid when Belgium was still a part of the Kingdom of the Netherlands from 1815 until 1830.

its cheaper labour (Crafts 1977; Bergier 1983; Pollard 1990; Von Tunzelmann 1995).

In the nineteenth century, the USA followed a radically different path towards industrialization based on primary exports, abundance of land and natural resources, and scarcity of labour. Labour scarcity encouraged highly capital-intensive production techniques. In the nineteenth century, technological leadership was taken over rapidly and creatively from the Britain and there was an inflow of skilled labour from Europe. Technological advance was labour-saving. Productivity growth in the USA was so rapid that it would overtake Britain by the end of the nineteenth century. The USA has retained its technological leadership ever since.

Famous latecomers to the process of industrialization were Germany, Russia, and Japan. As argued convincingly by Gerschenkron (1962), latecomers profit from the availability of modern technologies developed in the leading industrial economies, without bearing all the risks and costs involved in research and development (R&D). Gerschenkron referred to this as the 'advantages of backwardness'.[6] In modern economic terminology, latecomers profit from international technology spillovers. They do not pay for the full costs of R&D embodied in imported machinery,[7] equipment, and inputs (rent spillovers) and they can learn about international state-of-the-art knowledge and technology through copying, imitating, reverse engineering, and scientific, professional, and technological interaction (knowledge spillovers).

Gerschenkron reasoned that technological developments had increased the scale of industrial production in the nineteenth century. This required a larger scale of resource mobilization than before. Therefore, late industrialization would either not take place at all or it would be very dynamic. If the conditions were right and economic growth took off in a late-developing country, it would take the form of a growth spurt. Productivity growth in the late developer would be much more rapid than in the technologically leading country and the late developer would start catching up.

According to Gerschenkron, the role of government policy and large financial conglomerates was more important in late industrialization than in early industrialization. The self-financing of firms characteristic of early industrialization in Britain was incapable of raising sufficient resources to match the required scale of investment. Governments and financial institutions took over this role. They invested directly in industries and transport infrastructure.

[6] Earlier versions of this idea are to be found in the work of Veblen (1915), on imperial Germany, and the Dutch historian Romein (1937), who both tended to stress the disadvantages of technological leadership and its associated danger of lock in into technological trajectories that could become obsolete.

[7] These costs include the costs of R&D of failed innovation projects, which did not result in commercialized products and processes.

They played a crucial role in the mobilization of resources for investment and they were very active in education and technology acquisition.[8] Development-oriented governments set themselves the task of eliminating historical obstacles to industrialization and challenging the economic, political, and military dominance of the early industrializing countries.

What about the developing countries? From the middle of the nineteenth century onwards, the world economy had divided into industrial economies and agricultural economies (Lewis 1978a, 1978b; Maddison 2001, 2007a). Colonies and non-colonized countries in the tropics remained predominantly agrarian or mining economies, while the western world and the Asian latecomer Japan industrialized. Industrial growth in the West created an increasing demand for primary products from developing countries. Technological advances in transport, infrastructure, and communication expanded the opportunities for trade. Thus, the colonial division of labour came into being. Developing countries exported primary agricultural and mining products to the advanced economies, industrial economies exported their finished manufactured goods to the developing countries. Industrialization became synonymous with wealth, economic development, technological leadership, political power, and international dominance. The very concept of development came to be associated with industrialization. Industrialization was rightly seen as the main engine of growth and development.

In developing countries, moves towards industrialization were scarce and hesitant. Towards the end of the nineteenth century, one finds such beginnings in Latin American countries such as Brazil, Argentina, Chile, and Mexico, and large Asian countries such as India and China.[9] But developing countries still remained predominantly dependent on agriculture and mining. Lewis (1978a, 1978b) has argued that the sheer profitability of primary exports was one of main reasons for the specialization of developing countries in primary production. But colonial policies also played a negative role. For instance, in India, textile manufacturing suffered severely from restrictive colonial policies that favoured production in Britain.

Whatever the reasons, the groundswell of global industrialization, which started in Britain in the eighteenth century, swept through Europe and the USA and reached Japan and Russia by the end of the nineteenth century, subsided after 1900 (Pollard 1990). With a few exceptions, developing

[8] With the wave of mergers in the 1980s and 1990s, the role of government in resource mobilization has become again less important. The resources of the large multinational companies dwarf those of many of the smaller national states and they are able to mobilize financial resources for very large investment projects without any public support. However, policy incentives for investment and innovation are more important than ever.

[9] Around 1750, the Indian textile industry was producing around one quarter of global textile output (e.g. Roy 2010). However, the basis of production was more artisanal than industrial.

countries were bypassed by industrialization. The exceptions were countries such as Argentina, Brazil, and South Africa, which profited from the collapse of world trade in the crisis years of the 1930s to build up their own manufacturing industries, providing early examples of successful import substitution. In Asia, China and India experienced some degree of industrialization in the late nineteenth century, but industrialization only took off after these countries freed themselves from colonial influences and external domination. On the whole, the developing world remained overwhelmingly oriented towards primary production.

This started to change in 1945. After a pause of 50 years developing countries rejoined the industrial race in the post-war period (e.g. Balance, Ansari, and Singer 1982). Since the Second World War, manufacturing has emerged as a major activity in many developing countries and the shape and structure of global manufacturing production and trade has changed fundamentally. The colonial division of labour of the late nineteenth century has been stood on its head. Large parts of manufacturing have relocated to developing countries, which supply industrial exports to the rich countries. Some developing

Table 1.1. Catch-up since 1820

Country	Period[a]	Growth of GDP	Growth of GDP per capita	Rate of catch-up[b]
1820–1913				
USA	1820–1905	4.1	1.5	1.3
Germany	1880–1913	3.1	1.9	1.8
Russia	1900–1913	3.2	1.4	2.0
Japan	1870–1913	2.5	1.5	1.5
UK	1820–1913	2.0	1.1	
World average	1820–1913	1.5	0.9	
1946–2006				
China	1978–2006	8.1	6.9	3.6
West Germany	1950–1973	6.0	5.0	2.7
India	1994–2006	6.7	5.1	2.4
Indonesia	1967–1997	6.8	4.8	2.4
Ireland	1995–2006	6.2	6.2	2.8
Japan	1946–1973	9.3	8.0	3.6
Korea	1952–1997	8.2	6.3	3.0
Malaysia	1968–1997	7.5	5.1	2.6
Russia	1998–2005	7.2	7.2	3.9
Singapore	1960–1973	10.0	7.6	2.5
Taiwan	1962–1973	11.4	8.7	2.8
Thailand	1973–1996	7.6	5.8	3.2
Vietnam	1992–2005	7.6	6.1	2.9
World average	1950–1973	4.9	2.9	
World average	1973–1997	3.1	1.4	
World average	1997–2003	3.5	2.3	

Notes: [a]The periods have been chosen so as to maximize sustained high growth rates over an extended period; [b]ratio of growth of GDP per capita compared to growth in lead economy in corresponding period. Prior to 1913, the comparison is with the UK, after 1950 with the USA.

Sources: Country data 1990 and before, plus figures for world total from Maddison (2007b). Country data 1991–2006 and West Germany from: the Conference Board/GGDC (2007).

countries have experienced a process of rapid catch-up, which was invariably tied up with successful late industrialization (Szirmai 2008).

Table 1.1 summarizes catch-up experiences since the nineteenth century. Very rapid growth is the norm in catch-up economies since 1950.

Per-capita growth rates of GDP in the catch-up economies vary from 5 to 9 per cent per year. GDP growth varies from 6 to 11.5 per cent. With the exception of recent trends in the Russian Federation, all examples of catch-up are associated with the widespread and rapid emergence of manufacturing. Industrialization appears to be a key driver of catch-up.

One of the most interesting results in Table 1.1 is the way catch-up has accelerated since the nineteenth century, due to increased globalization, greater possibilities for international technology transfer, and increasing advantages of backwardness. In the nineteenth century, GDP per capita in the catch-up countries was growing at between 1.4 and 1.9 per cent per year, compared to the 5–9 per cent after 1950. The ratio of per capita GDP growth to that of the UK in the corresponding years prior to 1913 was between 1.3 and 2. After 1950, the catch-up countries were growing on average three times as fast as the world leader, the USA.

1.3 Background: the emergence of manufacturing in developing countries

The following tables document the process of structural change in developing countries and in the global economy in the period 1950–2005. Table 1.2 presents shares of agriculture, industry, manufacturing, and services for a sample of 29 larger developing countries and regional averages for a larger sample of 68 developing countries and 21 advanced economies. Table 1.3 presents more detailed trends in the share of manufacturing for the same 89 countries.

In 1950, 37 per cent of developing country GDP originated in the agricultural sector. The share of agriculture declined dramatically to 16 per cent in 2005. It is worth noting that the average share of services in 1950 was already 42 per cent of GDP, far higher than the total share of industry. Thus the pattern of structural change in developing countries differs radically from the traditional patterns of structural change, in which the rise of industry precedes that of the service sector. This is in line with the Gerschenkronian observation that latecomer patterns of structural change are not simple copies of earlier experiences.

In 1950, the share of manufacturing in developing countries was only 12 per cent of GDP compared to 29 per cent in the advanced economies. 12 per cent is low in comparative perspective, but much higher than one would have

Table 1.2. Structure of production, 1950–2005 (gross value added in agriculture, industry, and services as percentage of GDP at current prices, selected countries, and regional averages)

	1950[a]				1960[b]				1980				2005[c]			
	AG	IND	MAN	SERV	AG	IND	MAN	SERV	AG	IND	MAN	SERV	AG	IND	MAN	SERV
Bangladesh[d]	61	7	7	32	57	7	5	36	32	21	14	48	20	27	17	53
China	51	21	14	29	39	32	27	29	30	49	40	21	13	48	34	40
India	55	14	10	31	43	20	14	38	36	25	17	40	18	28	16	54
Indonesia	58	9	7	33	51	15	9	33	24	42	13	34	13	47	28	40
Malaysia	40	19	11	41	35	20	8	46	23	41	22	36	8	50	30	42
Pakistan	61	7	7	32	46	16	12	38	30	25	16	46	21	27	19	51
Philippines	42	17	8	41	26	28	20	47	25	39	26	36	14	32	23	54
South Korea	47	13	9	41	35	16	10	48	16	37	24	47	3	40	28	56
Sri Lanka	46	12	4	42	32	20	15	48	28	30	18	43	17	27	15	56
Taiwan	34	22	15	45	29	27	19	44	8	46	36	46	2	26	22	72
Thailand	48	15	12	37	36	19	13	45	23	29	22	48	10	44	35	46
Turkey	49	16	11	35	42	22	13	36	27	20	17	54	11	27	22	63
Argentina	16	33	23	52	17	39	32	44	6	41	29	52	9	36	23	55
Brazil	24	24	19	52	21	37	30	42	11	44	33	45	6	30	18	64
Chile	15	26	17	59	12	41	25	47	7	37	22	55	4	42	16	53
Colombia	35	17	13	48	32	23	16	46	20	32	24	48	12	34	16	53
Mexico	20	21	17	59	16	21	15	64	9	34	22	57	4	26	18	70
Peru	37	28	15	35	21	32	20	47	12	43	20	45	7	35	16	58
Venezuela	8	48	11	45	7	43	11	50	6	46	16	49	4	55	18	40
Congo, Dem. Rep.	31	34	9	35					27	35	15	38	46	27	7	28
Côte d'Ivoire	48	13		39	48	13		39	26	20	13	54	23	26	19	51
Egypt	44	12	8	44	30	24	14	46	18	37	12	45	15	36	17	49
Ghana	41	10		49	41	10		49	58	12	8	30	37	25	9	37
Kenya	44	17	11	39	38	18	9	44	33	21	13	47	27	19	12	54
Morocco	37	30	15	33	32	26	13	42	18	31	17	50	13	29	17	58
Nigeria	68	10	2	22	64	8	4	28	21	46	8	34	23	57	4	20

(continued)

Table 1.2. Continued

	1950[a]				1960[b]				1980				2005[c]			
	AG	IND	MAN	SERV	AG	IND	MAN	SERV	AG	IND	MAN	SERV	AG	IND	MAN	SERV
South Africa	19	35	16	47	11	38	20	51	6	48	22	45	3	31	19	67
Tanzania	62	9	3	20	61	9	4	30			12		46	17	7	37
Zambia	9	71	3	19	12	67	4	21	15	42	19	43	23	30	11	47
Averages																
Asia (15)	49	14	10	36	37	22	14	41	23	33	22	44	14	33	22	53
Latin America (25)	29	25	15	46	23	29	17	48	16	32	20	51	10	31	15	59
Middle East and North Africa (10)	31	23	9	46	23	27	11	49	12	39	14	49	11	33	13	52
Africa (18)	43	22	11	34	42	21	8	37	29	28	12	43	28	27	10	45
Developing countries (68)	37	22	12	42	31	25	13	44	21	32	17	47	16	31	15	53
Advanced economies (21)	16	40	29	45	12	41	30	47	4	35	23	60	2	27	16	71

Notes: [a]Earliest year for which data are available: 1950, except for Morocco, Taiwan, and Thailand: 1951; China and Tanzania: 1952; South Korea: 1953; Malaysia and Zambia: 1955; Ghana, Ivory Coast: 1960. Belgium: 1953, West Germany, Italy, and Norway: 1951, Japan: 1952; [b]China: 1962, proportions for 1960 not representative due to collapse of agriculture in Great Leap Forward 1958–60; Morocco: 1965, manufacturing share Tanzania: 1961; [c]Canada: 2003 instead of 2005, Venezuela: 2004, [d]Bangladesh: 1950–59, same data as Pakistan.

Source: Based on Szirmai (2009). This reference provides detailed source notes for the original sources used in this table.

Table 1.3. Shares of manufacturing in GDP in developing countries, 1950–2005 (at current prices)

	1950	1955	1960	1965	1970	1975	1980	1985	1990	1995	2000	2005
Average 15 Asian countries	9.8	12.0	14.3	15.9	18.9	19.9	22.1	21.7	20.8	20.8	21.7	22.0
Average 25 Latin America countries	14.7	15.2	16.6	18.0	19.2	20.1	19.9	19.6	18.7	17.0	16.4	15.4
Average 10 Middle East and North Africa	8.6	9.0	11.0	10.8	11.7	13.2	13.8	12.6	16.3	14.8	13.1	13.3
Average 18 African countries	10.9	8.7	8.3	9.9	10.7	11.5	11.7	11.8	12.9	11.1	10.7	10.0
Average 68 developing countries	12.1	12.4	13.2	14.3	15.8	16.8	17.4	17.1	17.3	16.0	15.6	15.2
Average 21 advanced economies	29.4	30.0	30.3	31.0	27.4	25.0	22.9	21.7	20.6	19.3	18.2	16.1

Source: Based on Szirmai (2009). This reference provides detailed source notes for the original sources used in this table, as well as the original country data for 89 countries.

expected for countries that are just embarking on a process of industrialization.[10] The only countries that really had negligible shares of manufacturing were Tanzania, Zambia, Nigeria, and Sri Lanka. Latin America was by far the most industrialized developing region in 1950.

The average share of manufacturing increased in all developing countries between 1950 and 1980, peaking at around 17.4 per cent in the early 1980s. China and Taiwan are the extreme cases with manufacturing accounting for, respectively, 40 and 36 per cent of GDP in 1980. Between 1980 and 2005, the share of manufacturing remained high and stable in many Asian economies, but there were processes of deindustrialization in Latin America and sub-Saharan Africa (SSA). This was most marked in Latin American countries where the average share of manufacturing declined from 20 per cent in 1980 to 15 per cent in 2005. In SSA the shares of manufacturing also declined by some two percentage points to 10 per cent in 2005. In the advanced economies, the share of manufacturing plummeted from 29.4 per cent in 1950 to 16 per cent in 2005. In 2005, the most important sector is the service sector, accounting for around 71 per cent of GDP, up from 44.6 per cent in 1950.

In comparative perspective we observe a long-run net increase in the shares of manufacturing in developing countries and a long-run net contraction in the shares of manufacturing in the advanced economies. By 2005, the average share of manufacturing in the developing world is only slightly lower than that in the advanced economies (15.2 against 16.1 per cent). The share in Asia is substantially higher than in the advanced economies.

There is no doubt that in the long run all economies are becoming more service-oriented. But statistics tend to exaggerate the increase in the shares of services for two reasons: outsourcing and price effects. First, many services that used to be produced in-house by manufacturing establishments—catering, financial accounting, transport and logistics, programming, consultancy, warehousing, distribution—have now been outsourced and are registered as service activities. Next, the price of services has tended to increase more rapidly than that of manufacturing goods. At constant prices, the share of services will be lower than at current prices.

The net increase in the share of manufacturing in developing-country value added and the net decline in the advanced economies expresses itself in an increasing share of developing countries in global manufacturing value added (see Table 1.4). At current prices, the share of developing countries increased from 13.7 per cent in 1980 to no less 32 per cent in 2007. Most of this change

[10] It is likely that the early national accounts for developing countries focus on the formal sector and thus will exaggerate the share of manufacturing. They tend to underestimate informal activities and the agricultural sectors, even though several of the national accounts present estimates for the non-monetary sectors.

Table 1.4. Developing country shares in world manufacturing value added, 1960–2007[a]

	Africa	West Asia and Europe	South and East Asia, excl. China	China	Latin America	Developing countries
Excluding China (constant 1990 prices)						
1960[a]	0.8	0.7	1.8		4.9	7.9
1970[a]	0.8	1.3	2.4		6.0	10.5
1980	0.9	1.7	3.7		6.9	13.2
1990	0.9	2.0	6.2		5.5	14.6
2000	1.0	2.2	9.4		5.5	18.0
2004	1.1	2.4	10.8		5.3	19.6
Including China (constant 1990 prices)						
1980	0.9	1.7	3.6	1.4	6.8	14.4
1990	0.9	1.9	6.0	2.6	5.4	16.8
2000	0.9	2.1	8.8	6.6	5.2	23.6
2004	1.0	2.2	10.0	8.5	4.9	26.6
Including China (current prices)						
1980[b]	0.9	1.6	2.4	1.7	7.1	13.7
1990	0.9	1.8	3.5	2.6	5.6	14.4
2000	0.9	1.2	8.4	6.7	6.6	23.8
2002	0.9	1.2	8.9	8.2	5.6	24.8
2005	0.8	1.6	9.7	10.0	5.9	28.0
2007[c]	0.9	1.7	9.4	12.9	7.0	31.9

Notes: [a]Extrapolated using the ratio of the shares of 1960 and 1970 to 1980 at 1980 constant prices;[b]China 1980 calculated using China South East Asia ratio for 1990;[c]the data for South and East Asia 2007 exclude those South Korea and Singapore but we have reincluded them for reasons of consistency with the earlier data. Korea and Singapore account for around 2.5 per cent of world value added. The UNIDO data for 2006 and 2007 no longer distinguish West Asia from Asia. Europe is added as a special category. Using ratios from the previous years, we have estimated figures for West Asia including Europe and South and Southeast Asia.

Source: Based on Szirmai (2009). Original Sources: Gosh (1984); UNIDO (1990, 1999); UNIDO, *International Yearbook of Industrial Statistics* (various years).

is due to a single country, China, which experienced an astonishing industrial transformation, increasing its share in global value added from less than 2 to 13 per cent. The rest of the increase is generated in South and South-East Asia. Latin America was the early manufacturing leader in the developing world, but its shares in global output have not changed since the 1980s. The shares of Africa and West Asia are insignificant and show little or no change.

One should realize that these estimates, derived from United Nations Industrial Development Organization (UNIDO) sources, seriously underestimate the share of developing countries in global value added, because they are calculated using exchange rates. A series of studies at the Groningen Growth and Development Centre show that industry-of-origin-based unit-value ratios in developing countries are often between 75 per cent and half of the exchange rates (e.g. Szirmai 1994; Szirmai and Ren 2000; Szirmai, Prins, and Schulte 2001; Yamfwa, Szirmai, and Lwamba 2002). If similar patterns apply

Table 1.5. Share of developing countries in world manufactured exports, 1963–2005

	1963	1973	1983	1993	2000	2005[c]
Asia (excl. advanced economies)	2.6	3.9	7.0	14.8	18.9	25.0
China				2.6	4.5	9.4
India	0.7	0.4	0.4	0.6	0.7	1.0
Latin America	0.8	1.6	1.7	2.7	3.6	3.8
Brazil	0.05	0.3	0.7	0.8	0.7	0.8
Argentina	0.1	0.2	0.1	0.2	0.2	0.2
Mexico	0.2	0.3	0.2	1.4	2.9	2.2
Africa, incl. South Africa	1.3	1.2	0.7	0.9	0.9	0.8
South Africa [a]	0.6	0.6	0.3	0.4	0.3	0.4
Middle East	0.1	0.3	1.2	0.6	0.6	0.9
Developing economies [b]	5.9	8.8	14.5	20.5	23.8	30.9
Advanced economies	75.3	79.0	69.5	75.3	69.3	66.4

Note: [a]Prior to 1993 South Africa refers to South African Customs Union;[b]Developing economies excluding former Soviet Asian Republics and economies in transition;[c]in recent years, Hong Kong, Taiwan, South Korea, and Singapore are classified as high-income economies. In the past they were developing economies and are therefore still included in the table as developing economies. Excluding these countries from developing Asia and developing economies total in 2005 of course results in much lower shares: 15.4% for Asia and 21.3 for developing economies.

Sources: WTO (1997, 2001) and World Bank (2002, 2012).

in 2007, the share of developing countries in global value added could well exceed 50 per cent.[11]

The change in the global structure of manufacturing is also manifest in Table 1.5, where developing countries have increased their share in world exports of manufactured goods from a marginal 6 per cent in 1963 to 31 per cent in 2005. Most of the increase is again generated in Asia, and in this case not exclusively in China. What is interesting in Table 1.5 is that in 2005 two-thirds of all manufactured exports still originate in the advanced economies. This runs counter to the common perception that South-East Asia has cornered the world market in manufactured exports.

Finally, Figure 1.1 provides a first impression of catch-up and falling behind in manufacturing for a selected number of countries in the post-war period. This figure uses binary industry-of-origin unit-value ratios to convert value added into US dollars for benchmark years. The productivity gaps for the benchmark years are subsequently extrapolated using time series of employment and constant-price value added. This provides a rough picture of comparative productivity trends—value added per person engaged—relative to the USA.

This figure highlights a number of important trends:

- Japan has experienced a spectacular period of catch-up, reaching 90 per cent of US productivity levels around 1990. But it then falls back, being

[11] The unit values tend to converge on the exchange rates as GDP per capita becomes higher. So, the adjustments for the richer developing countries would tend to be smaller than for the poorest ones.

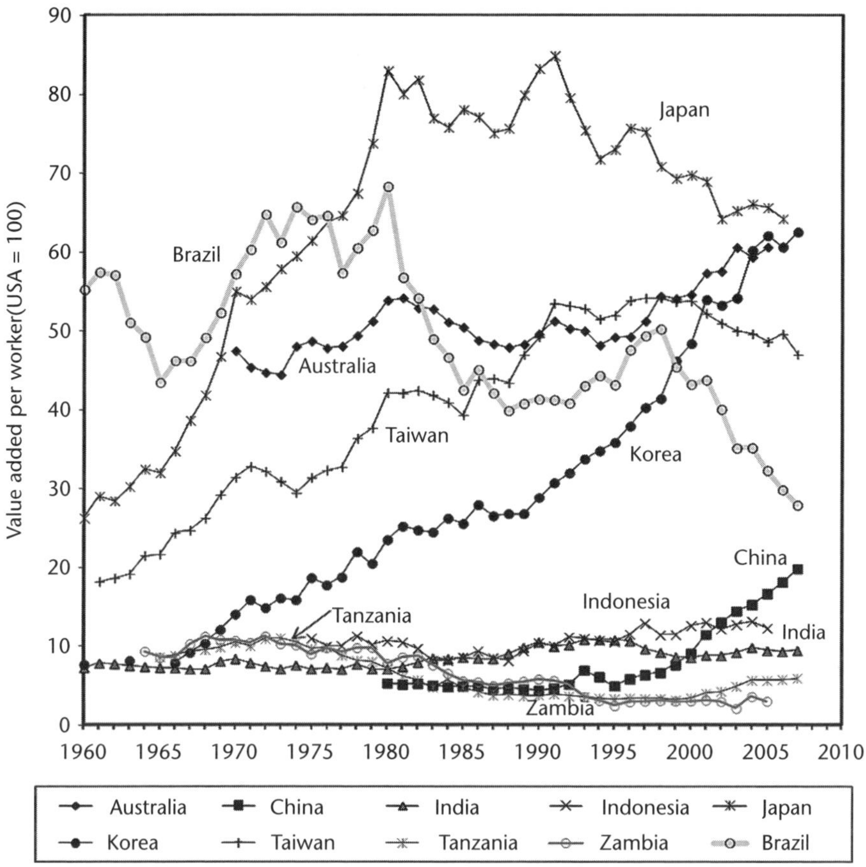

Figure 1.1. Comparative productivity trends, 1960–2007

Source: Based on Szirmai (2009), updated 2005–7. Authors' calculations from GGDC (2011a, 2011b) and GGDC country working papers, available at: http://www.rug.nl/feb/Onderzoek/Onderzoekscentra/GGDC/index For detailed sources, see Szirmai (2012).

unable to make a sustained shift from imitation to innovation at the technological frontier.

- Korea starts at low levels of productivity similar to those of the African countries Tanzania and Zambia, but achieves dramatic productivity catch-up, as does Taiwan, starting from a slightly higher level.
- Comparative productivity in the African economies of Zambia and Tanzania declines in line with the dismal manufacturing performance of Africa in general.
- Brazil experiences very high levels of comparative productivity till 1982, but after the debt crisis and the lost decade of the 1980s, its productivity

performance plummets from a peak of 65 per cent of the US level to around 25 per cent in 2003. The lost decade had similar impacts on industrial development in other Latin American countries.

- China starts at extremely low levels of comparative productivity in the 1980s—around 5 per cent of US productivity, even lower than the African economies. It dramatically improves its performance after the mid-1990s, reaching 20 per cent of the US level in 2007. However, China remains a highly labour-intensive economy and it will still take a long period of sustained high-productivity growth before it comes close to overtaking the productivity leader, the USA.

1.4 The policy challenge in the twenty-first century

1.4.1 *A variety of industrial policies and paradigms*

The aggregate trends in manufacturing performance discussed in Sections 1.2 and 1.3 obscure the variety of industrial experiences at the country level. These experiences are not only heterogeneous across countries, but also across policy choices and across time. Overall, it is clear that successful industrialization was rarely the result of accident or the unfettered operation of free markets. A variety of experiences attest to a pro-active role for industrial policy.

Perhaps the most famous case of industrialization is that of the (First) Industrial Revolution that took place in the UK in the eighteenth century, already mentioned in Section 1.2. The common perception of this period is that the role of the government and government policy was limited. Indeed the share of public expenditure in GDP was much lower than in the period since 1950. However, the Industrial Revolution was not just the fortunate outcome of the operation of free markets. Robinson (2009: 3) is even of the opinion that the Industrial Revolution was the result of 'the mother of all industrial policies' ...'a vector of policies which probably constitute one of the world's most successful, and most consequential industrial policies'.

Chang (2009) discusses the Walpole government's comprehensive infant industry protection programme that was implemented in 1721. Furthermore, the British government prohibited the exports of capital goods from the UK until 1843, and the emigration of skilled artisans until 1824, in order to protect and stimulate high-technology industries (De Araujo 1993). The focus on stimulating and protecting dynamic and technologically advanced sectors of manufacturing is still a key element of industrial policy in the advanced economies. Today the primary instrument for achieving this is an emphasis on protection of intellectual property rights and an acceptance and promotion of R&D subsidies and tax credits as valid and legitimate industrial policy measures, whilst opposing export subsidies for all but the least developed countries (LDCs).

Following Britain's rapid growth after the Industrial Revolution, industrial policies were adopted by other major European powers of the time, most notably France and Germany, and also in the next century by other European countries, the USA, and Japan. In Europe after the Second World War, selective industrial policy played an important part in reconstruction, as it did in Japan, with 'state ownership and economic planning as key industrial policy instruments. By the end of the 1970s, most western European states had nationalized substantial proportions of their industries' (Ulltveit-Moe 2008: 13).

Compared to Europe the USA was a latecomer to industrialization—but it very quickly caught up and even overtook the European economies in terms of productivity growth and technological leadership in the course of the nineteenth century (Szirmai 2009). This was again no accident of free markets. On the contrary, the USA made rigorous use of industrial policies, both in the nineteenth and twentieth century and presently (Lazonick 2009). Examples of industrial policy initiatives include the development of the steel-rail industry in the USA in the nineteenth century (Harrison and Rodriguez-Clare 2009) and the 'huge if somewhat wasteful industrial policy programme under the guise of R&D support for defence and public health' that was implemented between 1950 and 1980 (Chang 2009: 8). More recently, when faced by the 2008–9 financial crisis, the USA resorted strongly to industrial policies such as direct subsidies to ailing firms (bank and automobile manufacturing firms being bailed out), import protection (e.g. the imposition on tariffs on tyre imports), and domestic content measures (the 'buy American' clause in the Recovery Act). Furthermore Rodrik (2010) cites reports that the US Department of Energy announced plans after the 2008 financial crisis to invest more than US$40 billion to develop low-carbon technologies. The fact that industrial policy is back on the agenda, should not be taken to mean that all policies are uncontested. In particular, the bailout of General Motors in 2009 is sometimes seen as a revival of defensive industrial policies propping up non-viable and non-competitive firms.

In the second half of the twentieth century, the earlier catch-up experience of the USA and other Western offshoots was followed by the even faster catch-up and industrialization of Japan and the East Asian newly industrialized economies (NIEs) (as mentioned in Section 1.3, see also Szirmai 2009). The experiences of these countries, as well as those of China have become well-explored topics (e.g. Amsden 1989; Wade 1990; World Bank 1993; Nelson and Pack 1999; Chang 2002). Although Hobday (Chapter 5 in this book) cautions against the simplistic drawing of lessons from the successes of the NIEs, their experience again illustrates that catch-up industrialization is no accident left to unfettered free markets. All of these economies had in common industrial policies of varying degrees of selectivity (Chang 2009).

In both the UK's and USA's experience with industrialization and industrial policy, the role of technological innovation and technology leadership needs to be emphasized. Modern industrial policy also and importantly involves technology and innovation policy. Structural change and productivity growth require greater investments in learning, innovation, and the commercialization of innovations. This is confirmed by the experience of the East Asian 'Tigers' (see Chapter 5). In all explanations of why their industrial policies were more successful than in other regions, e.g. in Africa and Latin America, the role of education and skills formation and the absorption of foreign technology through the accumulation of knowledge and technological capabilities stand out. Thus industrial catch-up is fundamentally dependent on innovation[12] and capability accumulation (Fagerberg, Srholec, and Knell 2007; Lucas 2008; Dosi 2009). Successful innovation and capability accumulation in turn requires the development of 'national systems of production and innovation' (Nelson 1993), which involves learning, development of absorptive capacities, and an environment conducive to the commercialization of innovations (Cimoli et al. 2006). Industrial and innovation policies, together with the upgrading of the capabilities for adopting innovations, play a vital role as the accumulation of technological capabilities is far from automatic (Fagerberg, Srholec, and Knell 2007). Examples of industrial policies that resulted in successful innovation and capability accumulation include that of Finland (associated with the success of Nokia) (Toivanen 2011), Japan (associated for instance with the success of Toyota and Sony), and South Korea (associated with the success of Samsung and Posco). In these countries industrial policy was crucial to 'defy' the then current comparative advantage of the respective countries. As argued by Lin and Chang (2009: 497):

> ...the market gave Finland, Japan, and Korea unambiguous signals that they should not promote those industries; all the companies in those industries ran losses or earned profits on paper only because they were subsidized by profitable companies in the same business group and/or by the government.

The above examples are all of generally successful experiences with industrialization and industrial policy. But there are also cases where industrialization

[12] According to Lucas (2008: 1) the Industrial Revolution contributed to rapid economic transformation as it was made possible, and further enabled, the process of generating new knowledge: 'the Industrial Revolution involved the emergence of a class of educated people, thousands—now many millions—of people who spend entire careers exchanging ideas, solving work-related problems, generating new ideas'.

has not been as successful, and where industrial policy has been seen to have failed. This is largely the case for SSA.[13] Many countries in SSA adopted industrial policies where state-owned enterprises and import-substituting foreign direct investment (FDI) played a central role in the 1950s and 1960s—with little apparent success. Protection did not promote much learning, but simply kept non-competitive firms in existence. It is not surprising that these firms were not capable of surviving in a more competitive environment once the economies started opening up (Killick 1978; Pack 1993; Lall and Wangwe 1998; Jalilian, Tribe, and Weiss 2000; Szirmai and Lapperre 2001; Collier and Venables 2007; Robinson 2009). However, it needs to be pointed out that after industrial policies were rolled back in the 1980s and 1990s under structural adjustment and trade liberalization programmes of the World Bank and IMF, many African countries experienced significant deindustrialization of whatever manufacturing was built up under the previous policy regime (Carmody 2009). Today, the absence of effective policies in SSA is felt in the low levels of absorptive capacity, including skills and complementary technologies and infrastructure; the difficulty for firms to break into and benefit from GVCs; and the inability to compete with NIEs in Asia. In Chapter 9 of this book, Page revisits Africa's experience with industrialization and asks 'Should Africa Industrialize?'

In Latin America the situation is more complex—as Chapter 8 in this volume by Wilson Peres amply underscores. Three broad periods of industrialization can be discerned in Latin America: a period of industrial catch-up before the First World War; a period of consolidation and mixed successes after the war and up to the 1970s; and the experience after the 1970s when, as in SSA, IMF- and World Bank-led structural adjustment and liberalization de-emphasized industrial policies. Each period has its particular characteristics and drivers. Gómez-Galvarriato and Williamson (2009) document Latin America's experience with industrialization between 1870 and the First World War. They show that many countries in Latin America experienced a strong period of industrial growth between 1870 and 1910 and that by the latter date countries such as Brazil and Mexico were industrially more advanced than other developing countries in Asia, Africa, and the Middle East (see also Maddison et al. 1992). They explain this 'industrial lift-off' as the result of improvements in their terms of trade as well as effective industrial policies. The latter included tariff protection: 'Latin America was far more

[13] The exception is South Africa, where active industrial policies have been (and still are being) followed. Central to the country's industrial policy instruments were import substitution measures, export promotion assistance, and the creation of the largest venture capital fund for manufacturing on the African continent, the state-owned Industrial Development Corporation of South Africa, in 1940.

protectionist than anywhere else in the late nineteenth century' (Gómez-Galvarriato and Williamson 2009: 677).

Between the 1950s and 1980s, industrial policies are judged to have had mixed success in Latin America. In Brazil, Argentina, and Mexico growth continued to be rapid till around 1980, but import substituting industrialization (ISI) was running out of steam and inward-looking policies were continued for much longer than in East Asia. Imbalances in the economies continued to mount, resulting in the debt crisis of 1982 and adoption of structural adjustment policies. However, since the embarking on trade liberalization and privatization during the 1980s and 1990s there has been disagreement about whether industrialization prospects in Latin America have improved. Some see the recent changes as fostering improvements in technical efficiency and productivity while others find no positive impact. For instance, a recent study using longitudinal firm-level data from Brazil found that trade liberalization only benefited firms that also received government support to adjust and build their firm-level capabilities, suggesting that supporting industrial and technology policies remain important even when countries open up to international trade (Figueiredo 2008). There is also an ongoing debate on whether the disappointing performance in Latin America from 1980 to 2000 is due to excessive liberalization or whether it is determined by the negative legacy of the inward-looking and protectionist post-war policy regime. For instance, a study of Mexican car manufacturing points to the lack of sufficient learning and capability-building prior to liberalization. This made firms vulnerable to external competition when the Mexican economy opened up (Vallejo 2010).

Despite the failure of many industrial policies in the post-independence period, African and Latin American countries continue to pay attention to industrial policies. Rodrik (2007a) contains a discussion and examples of renewed industrial policy initiatives in El Salvador, South Africa, and Uruguay.

The contrast between the industrial successes and catch-up of relative latecomers to industrialization such China, Finland, Japan, the NIEs, and the industrial failures in SSA and parts of Latin America provides a good example that the *how* and *content* of industrial policies differed in important ways between regions and countries, and should be at the centre of the debate. For instance, in Latin America ISI policies were widely followed in the beginning (before widespread trade liberalization in the 1980s), but with little monitoring and generally little punishment for inefficient firms. Also, Latin America remained focused on domestic markets for too long and shifted to export orientation much later than the East Asian economies. In SSA, patronage and political interference resulted in low-productivity activities being sustained with large welfare losses as a consequence (Killick 1978; Robinson 2009). In both Latin America and SSA, macroeconomic imbalances (overvalued exchange rates and inflation) further constrained the performance of firms. In contrast, in East Asia continued protection of domestic firms was often accompanied by strict conditions (such as achieving a particular export target), encouragement of domestic competition, the political will to stop supporting unsuccessful firms and sunset industries (Pack 2000; Hodler 2009; Robinson 2009), and was characterized by flexibility when the domestic and/or international contexts changed (Kaplinsky 1997; Ulltveit-Moe 2008). These policies allowed much more rapid innovation and capability accumulation to take place in East Asia. Hence, Dosi (2009) argues that it was the differences in national systems of innovation between East Asia and Latin America that led to the variety of experiences and the different outcomes of industrial policies. Having said this, it should be noted that there is no single industrial policy model applicable to all East Asian countries. Despite commonalities, industrial policies differed considerably between countries—as the chapter by Hobday (Chapter 5) illustrates. This brings us to the conclusion of this section with the message that just as industrial policies differed in the past, they will differ in the future. Just as in the past industrial policy was influenced by national contexts and contemporaneous challenges, industrial policy today and in the future are and will be similarly informed. It is therefore necessary to consider some of the current contexts and challenges.

1.4.2 *New challenges and emerging paradigms*

The old challenges for industrial policy—how to build domestic capacities in the new Western offshoots in the eighteenth and nineteenth centuries, how to achieve reconstruction in post-Second World War Europe, and finally how to promote catch-up in developing countries since 1950—have increasingly given way to new challenges since 2000 (see also Chapter 15).

Major challenges of the twenty-first century include:

(i) how to achieve industrialization in an highly unequal and globalized world economy, dominated by large multinational companies and characterized by fragmented GVCs

(ii) the shrinking of the policy space for latecomers to industrialization in the present international economic order

(iii) the rise of the Asian driver economies (China and India) and its implications for the industrialization prospects of late entrants to industrialization (the Asian drivers also have implications for the continued industrial competitiveness of the advanced economies, but this will not be discussed here)

(iv) how to deal with jobless growth in manufacturing

(v) creating adequate systems of financial intermediation that ensure that the long-term funds needed for industrial investment are forthcoming
(vi) how industrial policies should respond to the threats of global warming and climate change (these challenges are taken up in detail in Parts II and III of this volume, respectively).

The first challenge is how to achieve industrialization in an unequal and globalized economy. The globalization of trade and investment, and the need for countries and regions to partake in international trade are not new challenges as such. Thus the world economy from 1870–1913 also experienced a dramatic increase in trade and financial flows. In terms of the stock of foreign capital as a percentage of developing country GDP, the world economy in 1914 was even more globalized than in 2000 (Maddison 2001). What is new in the present era of globalization is that industrially lagging countries (ILCs) now face new and different obstacles to partake in global supply chains and to benefit from these if they do. In the first place the very nature of globalization has changed. In the globalization era of 1870–1913, international trade focused on trade in final goods. Presently, international trade focuses on intermediate goods at different stages of the production process in GVCs. Production processes have become distributed across the globe, with different regions and countries specializing in different phases of production—research, design, intermediate inputs, semi-fabricated components, final assembly, marketing, post-sales services, and so forth.

The emergence of GVCs has been driven by two broad 'unbundling' forces (Baldwin 2011). The first unbundling was driven by improvements in transport and freight handling and the progressive liberalization of trade. It made it possible for production to be concentrated in specific places (to facilitate co-ordination) that were at a distance from final goods markets. The second was driven by improvements in information and communication technologies that made co-ordination across space easier and hence also alleviated the need for the physical bundling of production. Since the mid-1980s multinational enterprises (MNEs) used the opportunity created by these improvements to fragment production across the globe—described as the spatial 'disintegration of production' (Feenstra 1998). It hugely benefited these MNEs as they came to benefit by combining 'the high technology they developed at home with low-wage workers abroad' (Baldwin 2011: 7). Through this process, true GVCs[14] ('global production sharing') in production came into being (see for instance Hummels, Ishii, and Yi 2001; Yi 2003; Grossman and Helpman 2005; Nòrdas 2008; Houseman et al. 2010; Kaplinsky

[14] Defined as 'the break-up of a production process into vertically separated stages carried out in two or more countries' (Athukorala and Menon 2010: 1).

2011). International trade started to shift from 'trade in goods' to 'trade in tasks' (Bournakis, Vecchi, and Venturi 2011). World trade in parts and components increased from US$502 billion in 1992/3 to US$1,1762 billion by 2005/6 (Athukorala and Menon 2010).

The creation of these GVCs and the role of MNEs therein are discussed by Kaplinsky and Farooki (2010). It entails both benefits and costs for industrial development.[15] Discussions of these are contained in Altenburg et al. (2008); Saliola and Zanfei (2009); Gimet, Guilhon, and Roux (2010); Kaplinsky and Farooki (2010); Baldwin (2011); Fu, Pietrobelli, and Soete (2011). We will briefly mention some of the major issues that have been raised in this literature, and draw out some implications for industrial policy.

For industrially lagging countries the rise of global production sharing has radically changed the industrial policy instruments open to affect industrial development. This is because successful industrial development will require countries to be competitive not in the complete production of some good, but in the production only of a component ('trade in tasks'). Integrating a country's producers into GVCs may imply that the traditional focus of industrial policy on 'lumpy, complex industry' is not appropriate anymore.

This is seen by some as positive since it may open up a wide range of opportunities for poorer countries, which may be more likely to be able to find a niche in which to specialize rather than to be competitive along the entire production chain (Gimet, Guilhon, and Roux 2010). In other words, finding a comparative advantage in a 'slice' of the production chain may perhaps be easier than finding a comparative advantage in the entire production chain and can be shaped by industrial policies (Coxhead and Jayasuriya 2010). According to Baldwin (2011: 2) GVCs have made industrialization for lagging countries much easier and quicker, stating that GVCs have '... opened a new industrialization path. Today, nations can industrialize by joining a supply chain... there is no need to build a supply chain... the concept of a one-nation supply chain has disappeared'. Global production sharing has also been shown, at least in theory, to result in static and dynamic efficiency gains (Grossman and Rossi-Hansberg 2008; Rodriguez-Clare 2010; Bournakis, Vecchi, and Venturi 2011).

The challenge or problem today is that although industrialization may be easier, it may also be less 'meaningful' (Baldwin 2011). Thus we may not observe the same strong association between industrial exports and development as was the case in the twentieth century. As put by Baldwin (2011: 27)

15 China has been a key peg in global production sharing, having risen to become a 'premier assembly hub' (Athukorala and Menon 2010: 21). Kaplinsky and Morris (2008) deal in greater detail with the rise of China and India, the 'Asian drivers', and their impact on the industrialization prospects of industrially lagging countries. China's industrialization is discussed in greater depth by Harry Wu in Chapter 6 of this book.

'before the second unbundling a nation had to have a deep industrial base before it could export, e.g. car engines. Exporting engines was a sign of victory. Now it is a sign that the nation is located along a particular segment of an international value chain'. Meaningful industrialization, in other words reaping the benefits of industrialization as we discussed in Section 1.2 of this chapter, will require integration into GVCs and upgrading within the value chain. This twofold challenge has become an essential element of industrialization and industrial policy in the twenty-first century.

Integration into GVCs and upgrading within the value chain will require a greater emphasis than before on innovation, transport, and agglomeration effects, and less emphasis on the old industrial policy instruments such as tariffs, exchange rate policy, and quotas. Athukorala and Menon (2010), for instance, argue that if a country's ability to manufacture and deliver a particular component of a larger production chain is the determining factor of whether it will attract investment into that component production then exchange rate policy and tariff protection will be less effective in fostering industrialization. Rather, they argue, the emphasis needs to be on innovation, transport and agglomeration, and the creation of a domestic environment that is conducive to business.

The emphasis should also be on the upgrading of firms. As Kaplinksy and Farooki (2010: 4–5) note, meaningful industrialization with GVCs will ultimately require that developing country producers should be able to undertake four types of upgrading activity—process upgrading, product upgrading, functional upgrading, and chain upgrading. This has a number of implications for industrial policy.

The first is that a country's national innovation system (NIS) matters (Altenburg et al. 2008). A strong NIS can potentially reduce 'the risk of falling into a captive relationship or even of being captured by a leader' (Fu, Pietrobelli, and Soete 2011: 1209). This is because, as Kaplinsky and Farooki (2010: 4) note, 'suppliers of market requirements have their own interests to protect and will generally limit the upgrading path of their suppliers'. Being locked into such a captive relationship may lead to 'immiserising specialization' in developing countries, where a country's specializing in a particular component causes its relative real wages to fall and insufficient surpluses being generated to invest in higher value-added activities (Gimet, Guilhon, and Roux 2010).

The second implication concerns the type of GVCs that developing countries producers link into—according to Altenburg et al. (2008) the right type of GVC can encourage innovation and upgrading and not stifle it, and allow professional and personal networks to develop (Altenburg et al. 2008; Saxenian 2006). The latter has played a key role in China and India, where many skilled professionals have migrated (as return migrants) from advanced economies to work in the Chinese and Indian manufacturing and service sectors.

Hence an important goal of industrial policy becomes strategic integration into global trade: creating the capabilities to participate in, and subsequently to move to more profitable segments of, GVCs (Westphal 2002). This is an important difference to the inward-looking industrial policies of the 1950s and 1960s as well as the Washington Consensus era policies of the 1980s and 1990s.

Addressing these challenges through policy is particularly difficult in many industrially lagging countries, especially the LDCs and fragile states (Naudé, Santos-Paulino, and McGillivray 2011). Here, recent research has come to identify the upgrading of products, processes, and function and position in GVCs of indigenous producers (including of agricultural businesses) as of key importance for development—and has asked how a partnership approach (between MNEs, local firms, government, and donors) can provide an institutional vehicle when state capacity is lacking (Van Wijk, Vellema, and van Wijk 2010).

While strategic integration into world trade requires active government policies as well as the establishment of partnerships to fill institutional voids in this regard, latecomers to industrialization are threatened by a loss of policy space. 'This is the second challenge. The loss of policy space stems from two sources. First, the prominence of multinational companies in GVCs gives these companies a crucial role in controlling access to new technologies. The Japanese and Korean strategies for accessing technology while keeping multinational companies at an arm's length, no longer seems feasible (Lall and Narula 2006). Second, governance mechanisms serve to limit policy space. The loss of policy space in part stems from the fact that the current degree of globalization of trade and finance is so far reaching that it has necessitated certain (imperfect) governance mechanisms. These include the World Trade Organization (WTO) and related multilateral[16] and bilateral agreements. While these agreements have benefits for global trade they also restrict the options for industrial policy for developing countries. For instance the WTO prohibits adopting export subsidies or other incentives for export performance, the use of local content rules in government procurement or FDI, and utilizing quantitative restrictions or measures that discriminate against investors by origin (Rodrik 2004). The WTO also promotes the reduction and harmonization of tariffs (ul-Haque 2007). But many, if not all, of these

[16] These include the WTO agreements on the trade related aspects of intellectual property rights (TRIPS) dating from 1994, which stipulate minimum requirements for intellectual property protection, and on trade related investment measures (TRIMS), which aim to create a level playing field for foreign investors in member countries' domestic economies (for instance, TRIMS ban government policies that discriminate against foreign firms with stipulations on local-content, exports, and technology transfer, amongst others. According to Dosi (2009), developing countries should find ways around the TRIPS agreement and to promote the expansion of the domain of non-patentability, and work together for 'looser' intellectual property rights.

presently prohibited measures were actively applied by the present day industrialized countries during their own industrialization processes, causing Chang (2002, 2003) to accuse them of 'kicking away the ladder' for industrial upgrading in ILCs. Though many countries across the globe including India and China have experienced considerable degrees of liberalization since the 1980s, it should not be forgotten that all experiences of successful industrialization since 1870 have involved an inward-looking phase involving protection of and support for fledgling activities. WTO rules have also led to alternative forms of implicit industrial policies on the part of the advanced economies, such as the use of anti-dumping actions (ul-Haque 2007). Ludema (2007) notes, for instance, that the USA had no less than 274 anti-dumping duties in place in June 2005.

In addition to multilateral agreements such as WTO and TRIPS, many countries have negotiated bilateral trade and investment treaties or regional integration agreements that could erode their policy space even more (ul-Haque 2007). Due to this policy-space erosion, Dosi (2009) strongly argues against developing countries entering into bilateral agreements. Indeed, bilateral agreements have become one of the favoured instruments of industrial policy of the advanced countries to protect and support their own industries to the detriment of the development of industries in ILCs. For instance, in the USA the number of bilateral agreements increased from 3 to 29 between 2001 and 2006 (Ludema 2007). As Bhagwati (2005, as quoted in Ludema 2007: 1220) comments, 'the various lobbies in the USA have now shifted from multilateral trade negotiations to bilateral free trade agreements because they expect a much richer harvest for their own agendas'.

The challenges for the industrial policies of the ILCs are, then, to find ways to minimize the restrictions from multilateral agreements, and how to avoid being caught up unduly in unfavourable bilateral arrangements. It is also time to consider a return to the non-reciprocal arrangements under the general agreement on tariffs and trade (GATT), where advanced economies reduced the import tariffs, while emerging economies were allowed to engage in protection.

The third challenge is whether the option of entering the market for manufactured products and manufactured exports is still open to poor developing countries, in the face of the competition of Asian giants such as China and India. Thus textile industries across SSA have all but disappeared under the onslaught of Chinese competition. In Latin America, the manufacturing base has narrowed and manufacturing has shifted towards resource-based activities. On the other hand, the experiences of Vietnam, Cambodia, and Bangladesh have shown that even today countries can embark on industrialization in spite of Chinese competition. This involves a focus on exploitation of reserves of cheap labour, in combination with heavy investment in education and industrial policies supporting domestic industry and technological learning. One should also realize that the period of unlimited supplies of cheap labour in China is starting to come to an end, as the population starts to age and wages start increasing. This will create new windows of opportunity for African industrialization in the years to come. In addition, in recent times some Chinese FDI into Africa has also resulted in potential industrialization in certain corridors/special economic zones. For Latin America, Perez has argued for a shift towards resource-based industrialization, not as a second-best option, but as a deliberate policy to capitalize on the continent's advantages (Perez 2008).

A fourth challenge is the challenge of jobless growth in manufacturing, discussed among others in Chapter 3 by Fiona Tregenna. In many countries, the growth of employment in manufacturing has been slowing down under the influence of increasing capital-intensity and labour-saving technological change. Industrial development is no longer able to absorb large increases in labour supply. From a policy perspective, this will require a rethinking of the relationships between the industrial sector, the service sector, and the agricultural sector.

A fifth challenge is that of creating adequate systems of financial intermediation that can mobilize the funds needed for industrial investment in developing countries. Alternative models of financial intermediation include lending through a commercial banking sector with a sufficiently long-term horizon, the use of equity through venture capital schemes, and state-owned industrial development banks. This challenge is further elaborated by John Weiss in Chapter 15 of this volume.

One of the most important challenges for industrial policy relates to climate change (see the chapters in Part IV of this volume). In a world facing the spectre of climate change, low-carbon industrialization and green-growth paths have become imperatives. The industrial sector is responsible for around 30 per cent of global final energy demand and around 40 per cent of all energy-related emissions, with iron and steel, cement, chemicals and petrochemicals, pulp and paper, and aluminium production being the most carbon-intensive (IEA 2009). Naudé and Alcorta (2010: 1) stress that achieving low-carbon industrialization 'is going to require selective government intervention... neutrality towards all products and processes cannot be maintained. It has got to be driven by governments as co-ordination, subsidization, protection, information and large scale investments are at the core of the responses towards limiting the human impact on climate change'. The rationale for industrial policy is similar to that of the past—the need to stimulate a high volume of investments with positive externalities—but the environmental challenge is unprecedented. Promoting low-carbon industrialization and obtaining its accompanying developmental benefits may itself improve the ability of currently poor countries to adapt to climate change as it would raise per capita incomes and improve the knowledge base of the economy. According to Schelling 'the best defense against climate change is economic development' (Schelling 2009: 16).

Achieving low-carbon industrialization has a number of interrelated implications for industrial policy. The first is that it requires global policy co-operation. The second is that it will require innovation in and transfer of environmentally more sustainable technologies on an unprecedented scale. The latter may result in substantial entrepreneurial opportunities in low-carbon industrialization for developing countries. Many observers are already studying China's growing investments in low-carbon technologies as a way to reduce both energy costs, pollution, and provide new sources of growth and employment at the same time.

In meeting the challenges sketched above, the new pathways to industrialization in the twenty-first century will have to be based on new emerging paradigms for industrialization and industrial policy. Some principles for the design of new policies can now be identified.

Though there is a clear case for industrial policy interventions, the dangers of rent-seeking, corruption, imperfect and asymmetric information, and productive inefficiency, associated with industrial policy interventions are real threats that have to be taken into account. The long-term focus of future industrial policies is clearly on strategic integration into global trade, rather than a return to inward-looking policies aimed at self-sufficiency. We need to avoid beggar-thy-neighbour industrial policies and a resurgence of protectionism at a global level, which may hamper the growth of international trade, which is so crucial for catch-up. We need to take the lessons of past negative experiences into account and to seek ways in which such threats can be overcome, or at least reduced, through strengthening the basic institutions and improving transparency, political freedoms, and administrative capabilities. On the other hand, one should also realize that having no comprehensive industrial policy is not a guarantee that rent-seeking and corruption will be avoided. Indeed it has even been argued that in countries with weak institutions the *absence* of a coherent policy (implying incoherent protection) can be risky. Bayliss and Cramer (2001: 61) state that 'naïve privatization analysis and programme design may well encourage incoherent protection. Without a policy framework or rationale for selecting the beneficiaries of protection . . . it is more likely that weak developing country states will cave in haphazardly to pressure'.

Avoiding rent-seeking, therefore, depends clearly on the political context, as Robinson (2009) and Hodler (2009) also emphasize. More specifically, using a recent theoretical model that allows for both market and government failure, Hodler (2009) illustrates that a politically motivated government can increase welfare through industrial policy, but *only* if it has a small budget (i.e. the benefit from public support is low for entrepreneurs or firms with unprofitable projects). His model illustrates that government failures can be overcome, and confirms that in many East Asian NIEs, the government is able to exit sooner rather than later from the support of unproductive projects and sunset industries. The importance of political will in exiting from unproductive projects is emphasized by Pack (2000), as well as Ulltveit-Moe (2008), who terms this as the 'live and let die principle'.

Similarly the dangers of asymmetric information (a problem not just confined to industrial policy) can be overcome. Designing and using industrial policy as a learning process, as suggested by Rodrik (2007a, 2007b), offers opportunities to learn for both governments and their private sectors. The increased recognition of the importance of entrepreneurship for growth, innovation, and structural change requires that policies should provide sufficient scope for entrepreneurial behavior. Understanding entrepreneurship and small businesses and the relationship between business formation and business growth, including industrial dynamics, has also progressed to the point where policy-makers have a better understanding of the informational requirements for selective industrial support. Bos and Stam (2011), for instance, find that if sufficient data are available about young high-growth firms ('gazelles'), they may provide useful policy information on future industrial strengths and thus facilitate policies focusing on promising activities.

A second principle is that heterogeneity in policy approaches is advisable. In a Gerschenkronian world where the conditions for industrialization change, there are no general policy prescriptions irrespective of time and space (Rodrik 2007b). Among others, industrial policies should be tailored to the administrative capabilities of different countries, with the more selective policies requiring the highest levels of capability.

The example of the USA offers, perhaps ironically, a valuable lesson for latecomer industrializing countries on the importance of heterogeneity at subnational level. Ketels (2007) describes the USA as having very successful industries and industrial development policies, but without an overarching national industrial-policy framework. Instead, the USA's industrial development and support occurs on subnational, regional, and local level through state and local authority initiatives that are primarily aimed at facilitating the business environment. As a result the USA's regions 'are more specialized in particular clusters than their peers in Europe' (Ketels 2007: 163). Ketels (2007) ascribes this to the fact that subnational level policies in the USA come into being as a result of a strong process of local consultation between the private sector and local and state governments, which creates good environments for industrial clusters to emerge and develop, and provides an environment 'in which innovation and entrepreneurship policies can be more effective' (ibid.: 163). The decentralization of industrial policy, to subnational and local levels, is thus not only necessary to overcome informational problems and limit the benefits of rent-seeking associated with national overarching policies, it is required to reap the benefits of knowledge-driven growth (Nijkamp 2011). As has been pointed out by some observers, while the WTO restricts the policy space of developing countries at the national level, they may have more policy space at the subnational level, particularly in environmental and energy sectors (e.g. for green growth or low-carbon industrialization). An interesting example of heterogeneity at regional level is also provided by the Chinese experience, which allows for extensive policy experimentation in Chinese regions (Xu 2011).

The third principle is that of policy flexibility. Countries need to be flexible over time in their industrial policy. For the poorest countries for instance, a period of import protection may at first be justified in order that learning by doing takes place and dynamic economies of scale can be reaped. However, as the different experiences of countries in SSA and Latin America and Asia have shown (see Part III of this volume) the reliance on import protection needs to be modified over time—in a way that avoids inefficiency and economic stagnation on the one hand, and premature or too-rapid trade and financial liberalization on the other. Both Europe and India provide interesting examples of flexibility. At the end of the 1970s, industrial policy in Europe shifted towards privatization, deregulation, and the support of innovation (R&D) in order to facilitate further adjustment of industries after having reaped the benefits of state subsidies and state-owned enterprises for more than two decades after the war (Ulltveit-Moe 2008). In India, prior to 1991, the country's industrial policy involved high tariffs for more than 40 years. This was the era in which the foundations for India's industrial catch-up were laid and industrial capabilities were developed. Although the growth of manufacturing was slower than in East Asia, India performed better than many other developing regions (Kaplinsky 1997). In 1991, the country adopted a 'new' industrial policy that supported a substantial opening-up of the economy by removing most non-tariff barriers on imports, reducing tariff levels overall, as well as reducing the dispersal of tariff rates, abolishing investment licences, and cancelling many restrictions to FDI (see Kaplinsky 1997; Mani 2011). This succeeded in accelerating India's total factor productivity growth in manufacturing in the subsequent period (Milner, Vencappa, and Wright 2007).

1.5 Overview of this book

The chapters of this book have been grouped into six parts. Part I consists of the present chapter and provides the introduction and overview. Part II considers the need for and the challenge of industrialization. Part III sets out various pathways to industrial development, covering the experiences of East Asia, China, Indonesia, Latin America, and Africa. Part IV focuses specifically on the challenges posed by climate change and sustainability. Part V discusses the prospects of industrialization and industrial policy in the light of new challenges. Part VI draws together the various insights from the previous sections and offers answers to the questions raised in Section 1.1.

In Part II the case for industrialization is examined. This section consists of three chapters that analyse the relation between manufacturing and development and assess the importance of manufacturing as an engine of growth. The section details the patterns of manufacturing structural change across the world and deals with the threat of premature deindustrialization in developing countries.

In Chapter 2 'Manufacturing and Economic Development', Adam Szirmai asks why manufacturing deserves special attention from a development point of view. He puts forth eight arguments for the proposition that manufacturing acts as the main engine of growth and discusses them critically. These arguments are that:

(i) there is an empirical correlation between levels of manufacturing and economic development
(ii) there is a 'structural change bonus' from industrialization because productivity in manufacturing tends to be higher than in agriculture
(iii) opportunities for productivity growth may be more limited in services
(iv) there are more opportunities for capital accumulation in manufacturing
(v) there are more opportunities for realizing scale economies
(vi) manufacturing is the locus of technological change
(vii) manufacturing is a source of important spillover effects
(viii) as incomes increase, the relative demand for agricultural products will decline and the relative demand for manufactured goods will increase, creating dynamic opportunities for manufacturing.

Szirmai argues for manufacturing's benefits, but also points to mixed empirical findings and the need to maintain a balance between sectors. As he points out, manufacturing has been and still is of great importance but so are services, and agriculture, where productivity growth may in recent years have been even higher than in manufacturing.

In Chapter 3 'Deindustrialization, and Reindustrialization', Fiona Tregenna continues the comparative statistical analysis of the manufacturing sector across countries. Her concern is not so much with the contribution of manufacturing per se, but rather with the nature, measurement, and implications of deindustrialization. As shown in Section 3.3, after an initial period of industrialization many developing countries in Africa and Latin America are now experiencing deindustrialization. This may have negative consequences for their development prospects.

Tregenna argues that deindustrialization should be defined as a sustained decline in both the share of manufacturing in total employment and the share of manufacturing in GDP and not just as a decline in the former, as often is the case. She uses decomposition analysis to distinguish different types of deindustrialization. It makes a big difference whether or not a decline of manufacturing in employment is associated with rapid increases in labour productivity. If labour productivity increases very rapidly, the manufacturing sector is dynamic. A shrinking share of manufacturing in total employment can even be associated with an increasing share of manufacturing value-added in GDP. In such a case it does not make sense to speak of deindustrialization. If labour productivity in manufacturing is growing more slowly, the share of manufacturing value added may decline but less rapidly than the share of manufacturing employment. The worst type of deindustrialization is where declining shares in employment go hand in hand with labour productivity declines (e.g. Bolivia).

Based on her broader measure of deindustrialization, based on both employment and value-added shares, Tregenna shows that between 1985 and 2005 17 countries (in a sample of 20) experienced deindustrialization. These include both advanced economies such as the UK and Italy and developing countries at lower levels of GDP per capita. If deindustrialization takes place in a developing country context, Tregenna refers to this as premature deindustrialization. Countries experiencing premature deindustrialization include Argentina, Brazil, Chile, Peru, Venezuela, and South Africa. The issue of SSA countries' deindustrialization is taken up by John Page in Chapter 9.

The implication of these findings is that for many developing countries the challenge today is not just to industrialize, but to 'reindustrialize'. This challenge is complicated by the fact that 'reindustrialization after deindustrialization is likely to prove even more challenging than earlier industrialization'. According to Tregenna deindustrialization leads to deteriorations in market shares, fixed capital, networks, and tacit knowledge. Recovering these in the face of of growing competition from the Asian driver economies will be very hard indeed. Tregenna warns that industrialization in the twenty-first century 'cannot be business as usual. Decisive and effective industrial policies are required, along with a macroeconomic environment that does not contribute to the further emasculation of industry'.

Chapter 4 'Emerging Patterns of Structural Change in Manufacturing' by Nobuya Haraguchi and Gorazd Rezonja revisits the work of Chenery and his associates on structural change. Compared to the older work, the authors apply modern techniques of panel data analysis rather than ordinary least squares regressions and analyse a far larger sample of 159 countries over a far longer period of 45 years: 1963–2007. The dependent variables in the analysis are value added per capita in manufacturing sectors and the share of manufacturing in GDP. Explanatory variables include income per capita, population density, resources per capita, and climate. The analysis is performed for large and small countries. In small countries with less than 15 million inhabitants, the relationship between income level and manufacturing value added is more or less linear and positive. In large countries it tends to be curvilinear, with manufacturing growth slowing down or even declining at higher income levels, but the exact relationship differs from sector to sector. Another interesting difference between small and large countries is that population density has a positive effect on sectoral manufacturing growth in all sectors in large countries. In small countries this positive effect is only found for non-resource-based industries. Resource endowment per capita has a systematic negative effect on manufacturing growth in large countries for all but one sector. For small countries the results are more mixed. For seven sectors there is a positive effect, for four sectors there are negative effects.

An interesting contribution of the chapter is that the authors try to identify the importance of manufacturing sectors at different levels of income in order to identify the growth potential of sectors at different stages of development. Manufacturing sectors are classified by the income level (stage of development) at which their share in GDP peaks and by their overall growth rate (sustained growth, temporary growth, and low growth). Both in small and in large countries food and beverages and chemicals peak at early stages of development and show sustained growth. In later stages of development small economies only have a limited number of sectors with high development potential (sustained growth). Larger economies have many more such sectors. Late industries showing sustained growth are electrical machinery and equipment, precision instruments, machinery and equipment, and fabricated metals. This chapter provides a methodology that can be further developed to help us identify latent comparative advantage within manufacturing.

Part III of the volume consists of five chapters on the experiences with industrialization in East Asia, China, Indonesia, Latin America, and Africa. It focuses on past, present, and future pathways to industrialization, asking how some countries achieve successes, what current challenges they face, what lessons can be learned from successes and failures, and what their future prospects are.

What lessons can be learned from successful industrializing countries in East Asia is the topic of Chapter 5 'Learning from Asia's Success: Beyond Simplistic "Lesson-Making"' by Mike Hobday. The chapter starts with a discussion of the variety of experiences in Asia: differences in policies, differences in the respective roles of market and state, differences in firm size and structure, and different roles for FDI and multinational companies. Hobday warns that recommending other countries to follow the same policies as those of Asia is a 'grave mistake in policy thinking—and in the historical understanding of the nature and process of development'. He provocatively criticizes the lesson-making industry, which ignores the variety and change in policies in Asia. Instead, he argues for a Gerschenkronian perspective in which industrial policy should be aligned with a country's stage of development, its own resources and characteristics, and the changing international environment. This is a theme also dealt with in detail in the chapter by Zoltan Ács and Wim Naudé (Chapter 14).

Hobday argues that recognition of the importance of levels of development and varying local conditions are what all the successful East Asian industrializing countries had in common. To underpin locally grown, country-specific policies for industrialization and innovation, an approach of experimentation and trial-and-error learning is needed today as a pathway to industrialization in lagging countries. Such policies should complement, rather than copy the East Asian policies.

Chapter 6 by Harry X. Wu focuses on China, whose dramatic and remarkable experience in industrialization and dominance of global manufacturing has generated a large and growing literature. Entitled 'Rethinking China's Path of Industrialization', Wu's chapter contains both novel empirical analysis and novel interpretations of Chinese performance. Wu's new estimates of long-run Chinese performance show slower—though still impressive—growth rates than those derived from official estimates. He argues that extensive government intervention in the process of industrialization predates the communist period, having started early in the twentieth century. He shows that in post-war China periods of rapid growth and catch-up usually follow periods of catastrophic policy mistakes and political upheavals, such as the great leap forward or the Cultural Revolution, during which growth stagnates. He points to the inefficiencies of the Chinese state-driven model and argues that China could have achieved present levels of GDP per capita much earlier, if less erratic policies had been followed.

Chapter 7, 'Indonesian Industrialization: A Latecomer Adjusting to Crises', by Haryo Aswicahyono, Hal Hill, and Dionisius Narjoko provides an overview and analysis of the Indonesian pathway to industrialization since the 1960s. Indonesia provides a rich case study of the process of, and policies for, late industrialization. By the early 1960s the country was still an industrially lagging country—described by the authors as an 'economic basket case'. But then it quickly made up for the lag by high and sustained manufacturing growth until the late 1990s. Initially, Indonesia followed inward-looking import substitution policies, with a costly oil-driven heavy industrialization strategy. There was an important role for both state-owned enterprises and FDI. This was combined with highly orthodox macroeconomic policies. From the mid-1980s the economy turned outward, liberalized, and become a successful manufacturing exporter, based on labour-intensive production. The case of Indonesia is especially interesting, because Indonesia achieved export success in spite of its rich natural resource endowments (avoiding the 'natural resource curse').

After the Asian crisis of 1997, the growth of the economy and the manufacturing sector collapsed, taking over seven years to reach pre-crisis levels. Using a firm-level panel dataset, the authors examine the impact of the 1997 Asian crisis and how it affected post-crisis patterns of industrialization in the late 1990s and beyond. They show that industrial dynamism decreased after the crisis, with exit levels exceeding entry levels and small firms becoming less important. At the aggregate level, GDP growth did recover, but in the post-crisis period growth of output and employment in manufacturing were lower than in the economy as a whole. In line with the analysis of Tregenna in Chapter 4, Indonesia actually experienced premature industrialization, though the authors do not see this as very problematic, as other sectors such as agriculture and services are becoming more dynamic.

The authors argue that Indonesia's rapid industrialization between 1960 and 1990 was the result of a generally well-managed economy, and not so much of selective industrial policies. For them 'the fortunes of the manufacturing sector are closely linked to those of the economy as a whole'. The sustainability of industrialization and the fears of deindustrialization are valid for them only insofar as it is not caused by decreased competitiveness as a result of overregulation, insufficient investment, and greater political instability (especially since the Asian crisis). They conclude, and this is their lesson for other ILCs, 'that industrial policy may matter—although in Indonesia it has generally been ineffective—but the exchange rate, monetary policy, the state of infrastructure, openness to trade and investment, education outcomes, and labour market regulations are much more important'.

'Industrial Policies in Latin America' is the title of Chapter 8, written by Wilson Peres. Peres provides a historical overview of rise, fall, and subsequent resurgence of industrial policies in Latin America. Before summarizing the main message of the paper, it is useful to provide some further background on the patterns of industrialization in Latin America. The period before the 1980s, especially between 1950 and 1980, has been Latin America's most significant period of industrial development.[17] During this period its development was heavily influenced by what has been described as a 'state-led'

[17] There was also a significant period of industrialization in the nineteenth century (see Gómez-Galvarriato and Williamson 2009).

development strategy (Cimoli and Katz 2003). It consisted of exchange rate controls and ISI measures to promote demand for domestic goods; trade measures (protection and regional integration), and state-intervention in a number of areas such as development finance, research and development, and infrastructure (Ocampo and Ros 2011). Large and populous economies such as Brazil and Mexico recorded average annual growth rates of respectively 4.1 and 3.4 per cent between 1950 and 1980, as a result of which the region also experienced a significant period of poverty reduction (Ocampo and Ros 2011), although inequality remained very high. Mounting macroeconomic imbalances between 1973 and 1982 resulted in the 1982 debt crisis and a major turnaround in economic policy.

Chapter 8 opens with a discussion of these state-led (mainly ISI) policies of the 1950–80 period. Although Peres mentions some of the substantive criticisms levelled against ISI—its inward orientation, increasing distortions, and inefficiencies—his argument is that the opposition against industrial policies also included a strong ideological component. In the 1980s industrial policy came to be seen as a 'bad word' and the subsequent period from the late 1980s to the late 1990s can be described as one wherein 'market-oriented' development strategies dominated. They were characterized by a reduction in the role of the state, not only to eliminate the possible distortions this imparted to prices, but also to cut back on fiscal expenditures and deal with debt crises that had been a feature of the macroeconomic environment since 1982. As mentioned by Ocampo and Ros (2011: 17) the view was now widely held that 'the best industrial policy is not to have an industrial policy'. During this phase significant trade liberalization and opening up of the economies in Latin America took place. As described by Peres the focus was on 'horizontal' policy interventions aimed at increasing competitiveness, which did not target specific sectors or firms. In this period there was strong policy convergence in the region focused on five basic elements:

(i) increasing international trade competitiveness
(ii) horizontal or neutral instruments
(iii) support for small businesses, clusters and micro-enterprises
(iv) science, technology, and innovation policies for a knowledge-based economy
(v) focus on local or subnational economic areas.

By the end of the 1990s disappointment with market-oriented development strategies had set in. As we have already pointed out (see Tables 1.2 and 1.3), manufacturing shares in GDP have been shrinking and Latin America's share of global manufacturing value added has been declining since the 1980s. Manufacturing productivity gaps relative to the USA have been increasing (see Figure 1.1 for the case of Brazil, see also Lavopa and Szirmai 2011). According to Katz and Stumpo (2001) and Cimoli and Katz (2003) the post-1980 market-oriented period of industrial development in Latin America saw a mix of winners and losers and an overall pattern of industrial specialization in industries with lower knowledge-intensity and less innovation.

As far as countries are concerned, only Chile and the Dominican Republic achieved 'dynamic growth of productivity since the 1990s' (Ocampo and Ros 2011: 20) and only Argentina, Bolivia, Chile, and Uruguay achieved higher economic growth than in the earlier period. As far as industries are concerned, only industries based on natural-resource processing (especially in Argentina, Brazil, Chile, and Peru) and industries using cheap labour (such as in assembly plants in Mexico and Central America) improved their competitiveness and relative productivity. Technology and knowledge-intensive industries lost out to foreign competition and a massive surge in imported intermediates and inputs in high-technology sectors. Multinational firms and large conglomerates also appeared as winners, with small and medium-sized enterprises and state-owned firms as losers. Hence the structural reforms adopted since the 1980s resulted in a significant reallocation of resources—with overall results that ECLAC (2008: 59) characterized as 'disappointing'. Using the terminology of Tregenna, Latin America experienced premature deindustrialization. The region's firms did not benefit optimally from their position in GVCs; export-growth and FDI growth, although high, did not result in much stronger growth or in significant spillover effects (ECLAC 2008).

As a result, and as taken up in the discussion by Peres, since around 2000 there has been a re-emergence of policies focusing on strategic sectors or technologies. His chapter closes with a balanced critical discussion of these recent policies focusing on non-operational goals, lack of resources, poor institutional capabilities, and weak economic signals. Peres concludes with suggestions for policies, pointing out that 'industrial policies have been making a (slow) return in Latin America and have been able to operate, albeit on a small scale, in open economies and with orthodox macroeconomic policies—contrary to the previous conventional wisdom that they were incompatible.'

In Chapter 9 'Should Africa Industrialize?' John Page takes up the issue of deindustrialization, introduced by Fiona Tregenna in Chapter 3, with respect to SSA. Here, as Page reminds us, the share of industry in GDP has declined since 1980. Presently 'Africa's industrial sector is in many ways less advanced than in the first decade following independence'. Indeed the chapter shows how the importance, diversity, and product sophistication of African manufacturing has declined between 1975 and 2005. Page asks whether Africa should still consider industrializing at all, and if so, through which pathways?

The first question is answered positively. As Szirmai had shown in Chapter 2, industrialization is accompanied by rapid productivity growth. Hence Page argues that the lack of industrialization limits Africa's growth potential. Also, without industrialization African economies remain vulnerable to external shocks and adverse changes in long-term changes in terms of trade.

As for the second question—how Africa can industrialize—Page offers a critical discussion of a number of industrialization strategies, including agriculture-led industrialization, improvements in the general business climate, and firm-level assistance to encourage African firms to 'learn to compete'. He does not believe that agriculture can be the driver of African industrialization (or reindustrialization). Instead, he advocates business climate reform that 'shifts from a focus on stroke of the pen changes to regulations to embrace actions to close the infrastructure gap, create new skills, and achieve meaningful regional integration'. He also argues for a coherent strategic industrial policy to assist firm-level competitiveness, arguing that 'creating an export push, encouraging industrial clusters, and attracting task-based production offers an opportunity to give Africa a new start in industrialization'. Such an approach is also consistent with our previous discussion of the challenges of industrialization associated with the fragmentation of GVCs.

Part IV deals with the challenges of climate change and sustainability. This section consists of three chapters, one on the need for mitigation of climate change through low-carbon industrialization (Chapter 10), one on global co-ordination of industrial and climate policies (Chapter 11) and a final chapter on informal recycling and human development in developing countries (Chapter 12).

Chapter 10, by Wim Naudé is entitled 'Climate Change and Industrial Policy'. Adaptation and mitigation will have costs and opportunities for industrial development, but differ across the globe. Generally, the policy challenge is to ensure that the prospects for industrial development are not adversely affected by climate change and that industrial development takes place without worsening anthropogenic global warming (AGW)—ideally contributing towards moving global production, distribution, and consumption towards a low-carbon and eventually decarbonized economy. Moreover, industrialization itself could mitigate climate change and facilitate adaptation through providing the means to accelerate the transfer of employment from agriculture to industry—this could potentially reduce pressures on deforestation and clearing of land for agriculture, two important sources of greenhouse gas emissions. Thus this chapter explores the rationale for industrial policy due to climate change, and examines what it implies for the *how* of industrial policy. To achieve these objectives the chapter discusses the challenges facing both industrialized countries and industrially lagging countries in shifting towards a low-carbon economy. The central argument is that a low-carbon economy and environmental sustainability will require mitigation, explicit recognition of the relationship between adaptation and industrialization, and should be underpinned by international co-ordination. For the *how* of industrial policy it requires at a minimum a threefold approach, consisting of appropriate innovation and technological change, trade-policy alignment, and the prioritization of sustainable human development.

Chapter 11 by Thomas Gries is entitled 'Global Asymmetries and their Implications for Climate and Industrial Policies'. The chapter's concern is for the need for globally co-ordinated industrial policy in light of the climate change challenge. Based on a modelling exercise, Gries's chapter illustrates the complexities involved if ever a global 'deal' on such co-ordinated industrial policies could be reached. These complexities are due to major asymmetries and disparities between advanced countries in the north and developing countries in the south. Gries discusses six such disparities:

(i) huge income disparities
(ii) shift towards service production in the North and expansion of industrial production in the South
(iii) disparities in technological capabilities
(iv) disparities in current pollution emissions: since 2005 emissions from emerging economies exceed those of the advanced economies
(v) disparities in pollution stocks: two thirds of global warming can be traced back to the cumulative activities of advanced economies in the North
(vi) differential susceptibility to natural hazards.

With these asymmetries in mind, Gries argues that any global agreement on climate change policies—a 'global industrial policy' of sorts—will have to consider (1) the public good character of emissions, and (2) that pollution stocks accumulate and will exert an impact far into the future.

Using insights from environmental economics Gries proposes an analytical model to derive guidelines for global industrial policies to deal with climate change. He shows that there are two principles of an efficient policy. The first is that pollution reduction has to start where it can be achieved most easily. The second is that from a global point of view the most efficient measure to curb emissions is to implement efficiency-improving technologies in developing countries until they have reached the level of marginal resource efficiency of the advanced economies. Because a greater proportion of global pollution stocks are due to advanced economies they ought to carry a heavier burden in terms of the costs of the dissemination and implementation of such technologies.

An important implication of environmental sustainability is that the recovery of recyclable materials from waste has become a necessity—and also an opportunity. In Chapter 12 'Global Supply Chains in Chinese Industrialization: Impact on Waste Scavenging in Developing Countries', Martin Medina discusses the extent to which recycling has become a global business, driven by rapidly growing demand for recycled materials from India and China. Recyclables are also a driver for industrialization, According to Medina, 'it can be argued that Chinese industrialization has been fuelled by waste from the USA and other countries'. China is presently the world's largest importer of scrap metal.

While the potential for more sustainable manufacturing growth through extension of recycling is significant, Medina's chapter pays special attention to the poverty implications (or side effects) of recycling as a business. He notes that around 15 per cent of all China's imported recyclables come from developing countries. The demand for recyclables has resulted in more than 15 million scavengers in developing countries eking out subsistence by collecting waste. These scavengers tend to be stigmatized and relegated to the informal sector, where their unregulated living and working conditions are often terrible. For instance almost 50,000 people live and work on the municipal waste dumps of Calcutta, Manila, and Mexico City. Almost two centuries ago, writers as diverse as Charles Dickens and Karl Marx noted that rapid industrialization often results in serious social problems—with poverty, destitution, and exploitation as often-found ills. Recycling can make an important contribution to green growth, but not a sustainable one if the plight of scavengers is not addressed.

Medina therefore argues for the formalization, recognition, and destigmatization of scavenging—pointing out that it could bring a number of benefits including reduced smuggling, elimination of child labour, improvement in health outcomes, and reduced exploitation of scavengers. Such formalization is then clearly a prerequisite for recycling as a more appropriate pathway to industrialization in the twenty-first century.

Part V consists of three chapters on the prospects of industrial policy. Chapter 13 analyses institutional obstacles to industrial policies in Africa. In this chapter, Tilman Altenburg asks 'Can Industrial Policy Work under Neopatrimonial Rule?'. Neopatrimonial rule refers to the systems in many poor countries where ruling elites use patronage and political clientelism to stay in power. It poses an obstacle to industrial policies since under neopatrimonial rule the threat of political capture of the industrial policy process is very real. Hence in many industrially lagging countries, where the need for appropriate industrial policies may be acute, the capabilities of and incentives facing governments to craft and implement such policies may be lacking. Does this, however, rule out industrial policy completely? Altenburg attempts to answer this question by studying empirical evidence from a recent multi-country research project (focusing on four countries from SSA and three from the Middle East and North African region). He finds that 'neopatrimonialism is indeed pervasive in these countries and affects the way industrial policies are designed and implemented'. As a result industrial policy is largely unsuccessful. Only two cases stand out as positive exceptions—those of Ethiopia and Tunisia. Altenburg asks 'why did these two countries, despite weak governance and typical characteristics of neopatrimonialism manage to foster productive transformation better than the other countries?' The answer seems partly to be that in Ethiopia the industrial development approach managed to blend various ideological positions—becoming thus more pragmatic and generally supported—and avoided having government officials focusing too much on personal enrichment (Altenburg points out that corruption tends be lower in Ethiopia than in most SSA countries). In Tunisia the industrial policy thrust created a growing formal business sector and a middle class—which in itself further contributed to industrial development. However, this economic progress was not accompanied by political reform, hence the political upheavals in 2011 that overthrew the government.

Chapter 14, 'Entrepreneurship, Stages of Development, and Industrialization' by Zoltan Ács and Wim Naudé looks at entrepreneurship as a driver of industrialization. It analyses changes in the role of entrepreneurship at different stages of development and reflects on the implications of the changing relation between entrepreneurship and the state for the future of industrial policy. While Gries's chapter is concerned with public goods and the need for co-ordinated responses by governments, and the chapter by Naudé outlined the imperative for energy-efficient innovation in the light of climate change, Chapter 14 discusses 'how' such industrial policies can be realized. It argues for a shift in industrial policy from being government-centred towards being entrepreneur-centred, in a manner that takes a country's stage of economic development into consideration.

Ács and Naudé point out that there is as yet no substantial literature on the relationships between the stages of development, the evolving nature of entrepreneurship, and the orientation of the state. Indeed this chapter is one of the first to make this link, arguing that this, as yet emerging paradigm, is important for future pathways to industrialization. They distinguish three stages of economic development: a factor-driven stage, an efficiency-driven stage, and an innovation-driven stage. With reference to the Global Entrepreneurship Development Index (GEDI) they propose that the quantitative and qualitative levels of entrepreneurial activity across the nations and countries at different stages of development can be measured and that this can inform industrial policy. The different policy requirements needed to boost entrepreneurship and generate growth necessitate industrial policies that recognize the different kinds of entrepreneurial activity found at different stages of development. Thus, the GEDI rankings can be an indicator of whether a country needs to focus on improving its entrepreneurial attitudes, activity, or aspirations.

The last chapter in Part V (Chapter 15) is by John Weiss. Entitled 'Industrial Policy in the Twenty-first Century: Challenges for the Future' this chapter discusses five new challenges to industrialization and industrial policy:

(i) the need for and implications of financial sector reform
(ii) the difficulties for lagging countries to break into global production networks
(iii) the need to face competition from China and India
(iv) the complexities involved in dealing with climate change
(v) the need to avoid jobless growth.

This chapter provides a further elaboration of the challenges outlined in Section 1.4.2. In response to these challenges, Weiss argues for 'pragmatic and limited' industrial policies in developing countries, stressing the point that was also made by Tilman Altenburg in Chapter 13, namely that the countries where such industrial policies are most needed are also the countries where the capacity to implement them are weakest.

Part VI concludes with a synthesis chapter by Wim Naudé and Adam Szirmai (Chapter 16). Drawing on the insights from the preceding chapters, they discuss answers to the questions first posed in Section 1.1.

References

Altenburg, T., H. Schmitz, and A. Stamm (2008). 'Breakthrough China's and India's Transition from Production to Innovation'. *World Development* 36 (2): 325–44.

Amsden, A. (1989). *Asia's next Giant: South Korea's Late Industrialization*. Oxford: Oxford University Press.

Athukorala, P. C., and J. Menon (2010). 'Global Production Sharing Patterns and Determinants of Trade Flows in East Asia'. Working Paper Series on Regional Integration, No. 41. Manila: Asian Development Bank.

Balance, R., J. Ansari, and H. Singer (1982). *The International Economy and Industrial Development: Trade and Investment in the Third World*. Brighton: Wheatsheaf.

Baldwin, R. (2011). 'Trade and Industrialization after Globalization's 2nd Unbundling: How Building and Joining a Supply Chain are Different and Why it Matters'. Working Paper 17716. Cambridge, MA: NBER.

Bayliss, K., and C. Cramer (2001). 'Privatization and the Post-Washington Consensus: Between the Lab and the Real World?'. In B. Fine, C. Lapavitsas, and J. Pincus, J. (eds), *Development Policy in the Twenty-First Century. Beyond the post-Washington Consensus*. Milton Park: Routledge.

Bergier, J. F. (1983). *Die Wirtschaftsgeschichte der Schweiz: Von den Anfangen bis zur Gegenwart*. Zürich/Einsiedeln: Benziger Verlag.

Bhagwati, J. (2005). 'From Seattle to Hong Kong: Are We Getting Anywhere?' *Foreign Affairs*, 84 (7), special edition, December.

Bos, J., and E. Stam (2011). 'Gazelles, Industry Growth and Structural Change'. Working Paper 11-02. Utrecht: Utrecht School of Economics.

Bournakis, I., M. Vecchi, and F. Venturi (2011). 'Offshoring and Specialization: Are Industries Moving Abroad?', *Quaderni del Dipartimento di Economia, Finanza e Statistica* 98. Perugia: University of Perugia.

Carmody, P. (2009). 'An Asian-Driven Economic Recovery in Africa? The Zambian Case', *World Development*, 37 (7): 1197–207.

Chang, H.-J. (2002). *Kicking Away the Ladder*. London: Anthem Press.

——(2003). 'Kicking Away the Ladder: Infant Industry Promotion in Historical Perspective', *Oxford Development Studies*, 31 (1): 21–32.

——(2009). 'Industrial Policy: Can We Go Beyond an Unproductive Confrontation?'. Paper prepared for the Annual World Bank Conference on Development Economics, Seoul, South Korea, 22–24 June.

Cimoli, M., and J. Katz (2003). 'Structural Reforms, Technological Gaps and Economic Development: A Latin American Perspective', *Industrial and Corporate Change*, 12 (2): 387–411.

Cimoli, M., G. Dosi, R. Nelson, and J. E. Stiglitz (2006). 'Institutions and Policies Shaping Industrial Development. An Introductory Note'. Paper prepared for the Task Force on Industrial Policies and Development, Columbia University, New York, January.

Collier, P., and A. J. Venables (2007). 'Rethinking Trade Preferences: How Africa can Diversify its Exports', *The World Economy*, 30 (8): 1326–45.

Conference Board and Groningen Growth and Development Centre (2007). *Total Economy Database*. Available at: http://www.conference-board.org/data/economydatabase/ (downloaded November 2007).

Coxhead, I., and S. Jayasuriya (2010). 'China, India and the Commodity Boom: Economic and Environmental Implications for Low-Income Countries', *The World Economy*, 33 (4): 525–51.

Crafts, N. (1977). 'Industrial Revolution in England and France: Some Thoughts on the Question "Why Was England First?" ', *Economic History* Review, 30: 429–41; reprinted in 1985 in J. Mokyr (ed.), *The Economics of the Industrial Revolution*. Totowa, NJ: Rowman and Allanheld.

——(1983). 'British Economic Growth, 1700–1831: A Review of the Evidence', *Economic History Review*, 36 (2): 177–99.

De Araujo, J. T. (1993). 'The Scope for Industrial Policy in a Free Trade Environment', *Revista de Economia Politica*, 13 (3): 102–13.

Dosi, G. (2009). 'The Political Economy of Capabilities Accumulation: The Past and Future of Policies for Industrial Development', Paper presented at the DIE Workshop on Industrial Policy in Developing Countries, Bonn, 18–19 November.

Economic Commission for Latin America and the Caribbean (ECLAC) (2008). *Structural Change and Productivity Growth 20 Years Later: Old Problems, New Opportunities*. Chile: ECLAC.

Evenett, S. J. (2006). 'Does the Return of Industrial Policy Pose a Threat to Competition Law?'. Mimeo. St. Gallen: University of St. Gallen.

Fagerberg, J., M. Srholec, and M. Knell (2007). 'The Competitiveness of Nations: Why Some Countries Prosper While Others Fall Behind', *World Development*, 35 (10): 1595–620.

Feenstra, R. (1998). 'Integration of Trade and Disintegration of Production in the Global Economy', *Journal of Economic Perspectives*, 14 (4): 31–50.

Figueiredo, P. N. (2008). 'Industrial Policy Changes and Firm-Level Technological Capability Development: Evidence from Northern Brazil', *World Development*, 36 (1): 55–88.

Fu, X., C. Pietrobelli, and L. Soete (2011). 'The Role of Foreign Technology and Indigenous Innovation in the Emerging Economics: Technological Change and Catching-Up', *World Development*, 39 (7): 1204–12.

Gerschenkron, A. (1962). *Economic Backwardness in Historical Perspective*. Cambridge, MA: Harvard University Press.

Gimet, C., B. Guilhon, and N. Roux (2010). 'Fragmentation and Immiserising Specialization: The Case of the Textile and Clothing Sector'. Working Paper 1003. Lyon, St Etienne: Groupe d'Analyse et de Theorie Economique.

Gómez-Galvarriato, A., and J. G. Williamson (2009). 'Was It Prices, Productivity or Policy? Latin American Industrialization after 1870'. Paper presented at the XVth Economic History Congress, Utrecht, 3–7 August.

Gosh, P. L. (1984). *Industrialization and Development*, Westport, CT: Greenwood Press.

Groningen Growth and Development Centre (GGDC) (2011a). *Ten-Sector Database*. Available at: www.rug.nl/feb/Onderzoek/Onderzoekscentra/GGDC/data/10sector (downloaded 2011).

——(2011b). *EU KLEMS Database*. Available at: www.rug.nl/feb/Onderzoek/Onderzoekscentra/GGDC/data/eu-klems-iframe (downloaded 2011).

Grossman, G. M., and E. Helpman (2005). 'Outsourcing in a Global Economy', *Review of Economic Studies*, 72 (1): 135–59.

Grossman, G. M., and E. Rossi-Hansberg (2008). 'Trading Tasks: A Simple Theory of Offshoring', *American Economic Review*, 98 (5): 1978–97.

Harrison, A. E., and A. Rodriguez-Clare (2009). 'Trade, Foreign Investment, and Industrial Policy'. Paper 15561. Munich: MPRA.

Hodler, R. (2009). 'Industrial Policy in an Imperfect World', *Journal of Development Economics*, 90: 85–93.

Houseman, S., C. Kurz, P. Lengermann, and B. Mandel (2010). 'Offshoring and the State of American Manufacturing'. Working Paper 10-166. Kalamazoo, MI: Upjohn Institute.

Hummels, D., J. Ishii, and K. Yi (2001). 'The Nature and Growth of Vertical Specialization in World Trade', *Journal of International Economics*, 54: 75–96.

International Energy Agency (IEA) (2009). *Global Gaps in Clean Energy Research, Development and Demonstration*. Paris: IEA.

Jalilian, H., M. Tribe, and J. Weiss (2000). *Industrial Development and Policy in Africa: Issues of De-Industrialization and Development Strategy*. Cheltenham: Edward Elgar.

Johnson, S. (2009). 'The Quiet Coup', *The Atlantic*, May. http://www.theatlantic.com/magazine/archive/2009/05/the-quiet-coup/7364/

Kaplinksy, R. (1997). 'India's Industrial Development: An Interpretative Survey', *World Development*, 25 (5): 681–94.

——(2011). 'Commodities for Industrial Development: Making Linkages Work', Development Policy, Statistics and Research Branch Working Paper 01/2011. Vienna: UNIDO.

Kaplinsky, R. and M. Farooki (2010). 'What Are the Implications for Global Value Chains When the Market Shifts from the North to the South?'. Policy Research Working Paper 5205. Washington, DC: The World Bank.

Kaplinksy, R. and M. Morris (2008). 'Do the Asian Drivers Undermine Export-Oriented Industrialization in SSA?', *World Development*, 36 (2): 254–73.

Katz, J. and G. Stumpo (2001). 'Sectoral Regimes, Productivity and International Competitiveness', *CEPAL Review*, 75: 131–52.

Ketels, C. (2007). 'Industrial Policy in the United States', *Journal of Industry, Competition and Trade*, 7 (3): 147–67.

Killick, T. (1978). *Development Economics in Action: A Study of Economic Policies in Ghana*. London: Heinemann.

Lall, S., and R. Narula (2006). 'Foreign Direct Investment and its Role in Economic Development: Do We Need A New Agenda?'. In R. Narula and S. Lall (eds), *Understanding FDI-Assisted Economic Development*. Milton Park: Routledge.

Lall, S., and S. Wangwe (1998). 'Industrial Policy and Industrialization in Sub-Saharan Africa', *Journal of African Economies*, 7 (Supp 1): 70–107.

Lavopa, A., and A. Szirmai (2011). 'The Impact of Sectoral Heterogeneities in Economic Growth and Catching Up: Empirical Evidence for Latin American Manufacturing Industries'. Paper presented at the Globelics Conference, 15–17 November, Buenos Aires.

Lazonick, W. (2009). 'How American Capitalism Really Works: Some Lessons for Developing Countries', WIDER Angle April 2009. Helsinki: UNU-WIDER. Available at: http://www.wider.unu.edu/publications/newsletter/articles/en_GB/07-04-09/

Lewis, W. A. (1978a). *Growth and Fluctuations 1870–1913*. London: Allen and Unwin.

——(1978b). *The Evolution of the International Economic Order*. Princeton: Princeton University Press.

Lin, J., and H.-J. Chang (2009). 'Should Industrial Policy in Developing Countries Conform to Comparative Advantage or Defy it? A Debate between Justin Lin and Ha-Joon Chang', *Development Policy Review*, 27 (5): 483–502.

Lucas, R. E. (2008). 'Ideas and Growth', *Economica*, 76: 1–19.

Ludema, R. D. (2007). 'Allies and Friends: The Trade Policy Review of the United States, 2006', *The World Economy*, 30 (8): 1209–21.

Maddison, A. (1982). *Phases of Capitalist Development*. Oxford: Oxford University Press.

——(2001). *The World Economy: A Millennial Perspective*. Paris: OECD.

——(2007a). *Contours of the World Economy*. Oxford: Oxford University Press.

——(2007b). *Historical Statistics, World Population, GDP and Per Capita GDP, 1–2008 AD*. Available at: www.ggdc.net/MADDISON/oriindex.htm (downloaded August 2007).

Maddison, A., with A. Villela, V. Urquidi, and others (1992). *The Political Economy of Poverty, Equity, and Growth: Brazil and Mexico*. New York: Oxford University Press.
Mani, S. (2011). 'Promoting Knowledge Intensive Growth in India'. In A. Szirmai and W. A. Naudé (eds), *Entrepreneurship, Innovation, and Development*. Oxford: Oxford University Press.
Milner, C., D. Vencappa, and P. Wright (2007). 'Trade Policy and Productivity Growth in Indian Manufacturing', *The World Economy*, 30 (2): 249–66.
Naudé, W. A., and L. Alcorta (2010). 'Industrial and Environmental Sustainability: the Challenge after COP15'. WIDER Angle. Available at: www.wider.unu.edu/publications/newsletter/articles-2010/en_GB/01-2010-wider-angle/
Naudé, W.A., A. Santos-Paulino and M. McGillivray (eds) (2011). *Fragile States: Causes, Costs, and Responses*. Oxford: Oxford University Press.
Nelson, R. R. (1993). *National Innovation Systems. A Comparative Analysis*. New York: Oxford University Press.
Nelson, R. R., and H. Pack (1999). 'The Asian Miracle and Modern Growth Theory', *The Economic Journal*, 109 (457): 416–36.
Nijkamp, P. (2011). 'Entrepreneurship, Development and the Spatial Context: Retrospect and Prospects'. In W. A. Naudé (ed.), *Entrepreneurship and Economic Development*. Basingstoke: Palgrave Macmillan.
Nordås, H. K. (2008). 'Vertical Specialization and its Determinants', *Journal of Development Studies*, 44 (7): 1037–53.
Ocampo, J. A., and J. Ros (2011). 'Shifting Paradigms in Latin America's Economic Development'. In J. A. Ocampo and J. Ros (eds), *The Oxford Handbook of Latin American Economics*. Oxford: Oxford University Press.
Pack, H. (1993). 'Productivity and Industrial Development in Sub-Saharan Africa', *World Development*, 21 (1): 1–16.
——(2000). 'Industrial Policy: Growth Elixir or Poison?', *World Bank Research Observer*, 15 (1): 47–68.
Pemberton, M. (2008). 'A Climate Change Industrial Policy', *Foreign Policy in Focus*, 14 May. Available at: http://www.fpif.org/articles/a_climate_change_industrial_policy
Peres, W., and A. Primi (2009). 'Theory and Practice of Industrial Policy: Evidence from the Latin American Experience'. Desarrollo Productivo Serie 187. CEPAL: Santiago de Chile.
Perez, C. (2008). 'A Vision for Latin America: A Resource-Based Strategy for Technological Dynamism and Social Inclusion'. Paper for the ECLAC Program on Technology Policy and Development in Latin America. Chile: ECLAC.
Pollard, S. (1990). *Typology of Industrialization Processes in the Nineteenth Century*. Harwood: Academic Publishers.
Robinson, J. A. (2009). 'Industrial Policy and Development: A Political Economy Perspective'. Paper prepared for the 2009 World Bank ABCDE Conference, Seoul, Korea, 22–24 June.
Rodriguez-Clare, A. (2010). 'Off-shoring in a Ricardian World', *American Economic Journal: Macroeconomics*, 2 (2): 227–58.
Rodrik, D. (2004). 'Industrial Policy for the Twenty-First Century', Discussion Paper 4767. London: Centre for Economic Policy Research.

——(2007a). 'Normalizing Industrial Policy', Mimeo. Cambridge, MA: Harvard University, John F Kennedy School of Government. http://www.hks.harvard.edu/fs/drodrik/Research%20papers/Industrial%20Policy%20_Growth%20Commission_.pdf

——(2007b). *One Economics. Many Recipies. Globalization, Institutions and Economic Growth*. Princeton: Princeton University Press.

——(2010). 'The Return of Industrial Policy', Project Syndicate, 2010-04-12. Available at www.project-syndicate.org/commentary/rodrik42/English (accessed 16 November 2011).

Romein, J. (1937). De Dialectiek van de Voorutgang: Bijdrage Tot Het Ontwikkelingsbegrip in de Geschiedenis' [The Dialectics of Progress. A Contribution to the Concept of Development in History]. In J. Romein, *Het Onvoltooid Verleden; Cultuur-Historische Studies*. Amsterdam: Querido (First published in 1935).

Roy. T (2010). 'The Long Globalization and Textile Producers in India'. In L. Heerma van Voss, E. Hiemstra-Kuperus, and E. van Nederveen Meerkerk (eds), *The Ashgate Companion to the History of Textile Workers*, Farnham: Ashgate.

Saliola, F. and A. Zanfei (2009). 'Multinational Firms, Global Value Chains and the Organization of Knowledge Transfers', *Research Policy*, 38 (2): 369–81.

Saxenian, A. (2006). *The New Argonauts: Regional Advantage in a Global Economy*. Cambridge, MA: Harvard University Press.

Schelling, T. (2009). 'International Coordination to Address the Climate Challenge', *Innovations*, 4 (4): 13–21.

Szirmai, A. (1994). 'Real Output and Labor Productivity in Indonesian Manufacturing, 1975–1990', *Bulletin of Indonesian Economic Studies*, 30 (3): 49–90.

——(2008). 'Explaining Success and Failure in Development'. Working Paper 2008-013. Maastricht: UNU-MERIT.

——(2009). 'Industrialization as an Engine of Growth in Developing Countries, 1950–2005'. Working Paper 2009-10. Maastricht: UNU-MERIT.

——(2012). *Development Statistics*. Updated worksheets available at: www.dynamicsofdevelopment.com

Szirmai A. and P. Lapperre (eds) (2001). *The Industrial Experience of Tanzania*. Basingstoke: Palgrave Macmillan.

Szirmai, A., and R. Ren (2000). 'Comparative Performance in Chinese Manufacturing, 1980–92', *China Economic Review*, 11 (1): 16–53.

Szirmai, A., M. Prins, and W. Schulte (2001). 'Measuring Manufacturing Performance in Tanzania'. In A. Szirmai and P. Lapperre (eds), *The Industrial Experience of Tanzania*. Basingstoke: Palgrave Macmillan.

Toivanen, O. (2011). 'Innovation Policy, Entrepreneurship, and Development'. In A. Szirmai, W. A. Naudé, and M. Goedhuys (eds), *Entrepreneurship, Innovation and Development*. Oxford: Oxford University Press.

Ul-Haque, I. (2007). 'Rethinking Industrial Policy'. Discussion Paper 183. Geneva: UNCTAD.

Ulltveit-Moe, K. (2008). 'Live and Let Die: Industrial Policy in a Globalised World'. Expert Report 22. Stockholm: Sweden's Globalization Council.

UNIDO (1990). *Handbook of Industrial Statistics*. Vienna: UNIDO.

——(1999). *Handbook of Industrial Statistics*. Vienna: UNIDO.

UNIDO (various years). *International Yearbook of Industrial Statistics*. Cheltenham: Edward Elgar.

Vallejo, B. (2010). 'Innovation and Learning under Changing Market Conditions. The Auto Parts Firms in Mexico'. PhD Thesis. Maastricht: UNU-MERIT.

Van Wijk, J., S. Vellema and J. van Wijk, J. (2010). 'Institutions, Partnerships and Institutional Change: Towards a Theoretical Framework'. Working Paper 009. Rotterdam: The Partnerships Resource Centre.

Veblen, T. (1915). *Imperial Germany and the Industrial Revolution*. New York: Macmillan.

Von Tunzelmann, G. N. (1995). *Technology and Industrial Progress*. Cheltenham: Edward Elgar.

Wade, R. (1990). *Governing the Market: Economic Theory and the Role of Government in East Asian Industrialization*. Princeton: Princeton University Press.

Westphal, L. E. (2002). 'Technology Strategies for Economic Development in a Fast Changing Global Economy', *Economics of Innovation and New Technology*, 11 (4/5): 275–320.

World Bank (1993). *The East Asian Miracle. Growth and Public Policy*. New York: Oxford University Press.

——(2002). *World Development Indicators 2002*, CD-Rom, Washington, DC: World Bank.

——(2012). *World Development Indicators online*, http://databank.worldbank.org/ddp/home.do?Step=12&id=4&CNO=2 (accessed February 2012).

World Trade Organization (WTO) (1997). *Annual Report*, Volume II. Geneva: World Trade Organization.

——(2001). *International Trade Statistics 2001*. Geneva: World Trade Organization.

Xu, Ch. (2011). 'The Fundamental Institutions of China's Reforms and Development', *Journal of Economic Literature*, XLIX (4): 1076–151.

Yamfwa, F., A. Szirmai, and C. Lwamba (2002). 'Zambian Manufacturing Performance in Comparative Perspective'. Working Paper GD 53. Groningen: Groningen Growth and Development Centre.

Yi, K. M. (2003). 'Can Vertical Specialization Explain the Growth of World Trade?', *Journal of Political Economy*, 11 (1): 52–102.

Part II

The Need for and Challenge of Industrialization

2

Manufacturing and Economic Development

Adam Szirmai

2.1 Introduction[1]

Since the Industrial Revolution in the eighteenth century, manufacturing has been considered to be the main engine of economic growth and development. In development theory structural change was associated specifically with a shift of resources from the primary sector to the manufacturing sector. In recent years, however, the role of the manufacturing sector has been increasingly questioned. First, it is clear that the advanced economies are now predominantly service economies. Second, economic historians increasingly recognize the importance of service sectors such as trade, transport, and financial intermediation that have contributed to industrialization and development. Finally, the recent experiences of India and other emerging economies raise the question of whether services have become the key sector in economic development in the twenty-first century.

This chapter contributes to this debate by examining some of the theoretical and empirical evidence for the proposition that manufacturing has acted as the main engine of growth in developing countries in the period 1950–2005. The remainder of the chapter is structured as follows. Section 2.2 provides an overview of the main eight arguments for the hypothesis that manufacturing is the main engine of growth. In Section 2.3 these arguments are examined one by one on the basis of secondary literature and available secondary statistics. Section 2.4 concludes.

Before proceeding, however, we need to enter an important caveat. Even if we were to conclude that manufacturing has indeed been one of the most

[1] Earlier versions of this chapter were presented at seminars at UNU-MERIT, UNIDO, the Indian Institute of Sciences, Bangalore and the Globelics Conference in Dakar, 2009. I thank Angus Maddison and members of UNU-MERIT research group II for valuable comments and criticisms.

important engines of growth, this does not mean that other sectors of the economy such as agriculture or services should be neglected. One of the classic failures of post-war industrial policy has been the favouring of manufacturing and the discrimination against the agricultural sector in Latin America, Africa, and Asia. This has tended to retard agricultural development and indirectly has harmed industrial development and the overall rate of growth through the intersectoral linkages between agriculture and manufacturing (Szirmai 2005). Similar intersectoral linkages exist between manufacturing and services. From a policy perspective one should always keep the balance and the linkages between sectors in mind.

2.2 The case for manufacturing

There are powerful empirical and theoretical arguments in favour of industrialization as the main engine of growth in economic development. The arguments can be summarized as follows:

1. There is an *empirical correlation* between the degree of industrialization and the levels of per capita income in developing countries. More industrialized developing countries tend to be richer than less industrialized developing countries.
2. Productivity is higher in the manufacturing sector than in the agricultural sector. The transfer of resources from agriculture to manufacturing provides a *structural change bonus*. A dynamic version of the structural change bonus argument is that manufacturing has higher rates of productivity growth than other sectors.
3. The transfer of resources from manufacturing to services provides a *structural change burden* in the form of Baumol's disease. As the share of the service sector increases, aggregate per capita growth will tend to slow down.
4. Compared to agriculture, the manufacturing sector offers special *opportunities for capital accumulation*. Capital accumulation can be more easily realized in spatially concentrated manufacturing than in spatially dispersed agriculture. This is one of the reasons why the emergence of manufacturing has been so important in growth and development. Capital-intensity is high in manufacturing (and also in other industrial subsectors such as mining, utilities and construction). It is much lower in agriculture and services. Capital accumulation is one of the aggregate sources of growth. Thus, an increasing share of manufacturing and industry will contribute to aggregate growth.

5. The manufacturing sector offers special opportunities for *economies of scale*, which are less available in agriculture or services.
6. The manufacturing sector offers special opportunities for both *embodied and disembodied technological progress* (Cornwall 1977). Technological advance is concentrated in the manufacturing sector and diffuses from there to other economic sectors such as the service sector.
7. *Linkage and spillover effects* are stronger in manufacturing than in agriculture or mining. Linkage effects refer to the direct backward and forward linkages between different sectors. They create positive externalities to investments in given sectors. Spillover effects refer to the disembodied knowledge flows between sectors. Spillover effects are a special case of externalities referring to externalities of investment in knowledge and technology. Linkage and spillover effects are presumed to be stronger within manufacturing than within other sectors. Linkage and spillover effects between manufacturing and other sectors such as services or agriculture are also very powerful.
8. As per-capita income rises, the share of agricultural expenditures in total expenditures declines and the share of expenditures on manufactured goods increases (Engel's law). Countries specializing in agricultural and primary production will not profit from expanding world markets for manufacturing goods.

The arguments mentioned under points 4, 5, 6, and 7 refer to specific characteristics that supposedly make the manufacturing sector more productive and more dynamic than other sectors. Arguments 2 and 3 about the structural change bonus and burden depend on the assumption of higher productivity levels and growth rates in manufacturing. Point 7 points to the positive externalities that transmit growth from manufacturing to other sectors. Point 8 brings in the role of demand and suggests that the demand elasticities interact with supply effects to produce more rapid economic development. The first point is an empirical proposition about the relationship between industrialization and the level of development. Logically it follows from the arguments discussed under point 8.

2.3 Examination of the arguments for the engine of growth hypothesis

In this section, we provide a further elaboration of the debate on the role of manufacturing. We also examine some of the empirical evidence for the different propositions, using a mix of secondary data and secondary literature.

2.3.1 *Empirical correlations between industrialization and economic development*

The historical evidence points to the overall correlation between industrialization and the level of economic development. The presently advanced economies are the countries that first embarked on industrialization when the developing countries were still oriented towards primary production. Also, the more successful developing countries are invariably those that have been able to industrialize. The historical record provides strong support for this correlation.

Statistically the correlation is less easy to demonstrate, because the advanced economies have become service economies where service sectors account for over two-thirds of GDP. This makes the relationship between industrialization and per capita income a curvilinear one with a positive relationship between the share of manufacturing and GDP per capita at lower levels of per capita GDP and a negative relationship at higher levels (Rodrik 2009). Also, as discussed in Chapter 1, the sequence of structural change in developing economies is different from the earlier patterns of structural change in the presently advanced economies. In the earlier pattern of structural change, the shares of manufacturing in GDP and employment increased first, the shares of services increased later. In developing countries the share of services in GDP was usually already larger than that of the industrial sector in the 1950s and 1960s (see Chapter 1: Table 1.2 and Szirmai 2005).

Contributions of manufacturing to growth can be measured in different ways: using growth accounting techniques and econometric analysis (Bosworth, Collins and Chen 1995; Fagerberg and Verspagen 1999, 2002, 2007; Timmer and de Vries 2009). Growth accounting techniques analyse what proportion of a given growth rate of national income derives from growth of manufacturing. These techniques are straightforward and transparent. But they do tend to underestimate the contributions of dynamic sectors because they do not take various external effects and spillovers into account (argument 7). The role of manufacturing in nurturing technological advance and enhancing spillovers may make the net contribution of manufacturing to aggregate growth greater than found measuring direct sectoral contributions to growth. Such spillover effects are better captured with econometric techniques.

The evidence in the secondary literature is mixed. The older literature tends to emphasize the importance of manufacturing while the more recent literature finds that the contribution of service sector has increased. Also, in the more recent literature one finds that manufacturing tends to be more important as an engine of growth in developing countries than in advanced economies and also more important in the period 1950–73 than in the period after 1973.

Fagerberg and Verspagen (1999) regress real GDP growth rates on growth rates of manufacturing. If the coefficient of manufacturing growth is higher than the share of manufacturing in GDP, this is interpreted as supporting the engine-of-growth hypothesis. Fagerberg and Verspagen find that manufacturing was typically an engine of growth in developing countries in East Asia and Latin America, but that there was no significant effect of manufacturing in the advanced economies. In a second paper (Fagerberg and Verspagen 2002), the same authors examine the impact of shares of manufacturing and services on growth in three periods—1966–72, 1973–83, and 1984–95—for a sample of 76 countries. They find that manufacturing has much more positive contributions to growth before 1973 than after this year. The interpretation in both papers is that the period 1950–73 offered special opportunities for catch-up through the absorption of mass production manufacturing techniques from the USA. After 1973, information and communications technologies (ICTs) started to become more important as a source of productivity growth, especially in the 1990s. These technologies are no longer within the exclusive domain of manufacturing, but also operate in the service sector.

An article by Timmer and de Vries (2009) also confirms the increasing importance of the service sector. Using growth accounting techniques, they examine the contributions of different sectors in periods of growth accelerations, in periods of normal growth and in periods of deceleration. In periods of normal growth they find that manufacturing contributes most to growth. In periods of acceleration, this leading role is taken over by the service sector, although manufacturing continues to have an important positive contribution.

For India, Chakravarty and Mitra (2008) conclude, on the basis of vector autoregression analysis, that manufacturing is still one of the important drivers of growth, although more and more activities are becoming independent of the manufacturing sector. Kathuria and Raj (2009) focus on regional differences in growth in India. They analyse the relationship between manufacturing growth and output growth in Indian states (including the informal sector) and find support for the engine-of-growth hypothesis and conclude that manufacturing is still functioning as an engine of growth, even in India with its important and dynamic ICT service sectors.

Rodrik (2009) finds that rapid growth in developing countries since 1960 is strongly associated with structural change—the transfer of resources from traditional sectors to more modern industrial sectors. He explicitly concludes that transition to modern industrial activities acts as an engine of growth. But he is rather vague about what he means by 'modern' activities. They also include non-traditional primary activities such as horticulture in Ethiopia.

Recent research by Szirmai and Verspagen (2011) finds significant relationships between the shares of manufacturing in GDP at the beginning of five-year periods and average growth rates in five-year periods for a panel dataset of 90 countries for the period 1950–2005. However, when the sample is split into different subperiods or different groups of countries the relationship is much less straightforward.

In Table 2.1, we try to capture the empirical relationship between industrialization and development by focusing on the share of manufacturing in total commodity production (i.e. agriculture, mining, manufacturing, construction, and utilities) rather than in total GDP (for a similar approach see Balance, Ansari, and Singer 1982). The share of manufacturing in commodity value added is set out against a country's per capita gross national income in 2000. We find a highly significant positive correlation of 0.74 between a country's rank in terms of the logarithm of income per capita and its rank in terms of share of manufacturing in commodity production. Services are excluded from this table. Thus it cannot tell us whether manufacturing-led growth is more important than service-led growth. What we do learn is that the structure of commodity production is related to levels of per capita income and that manufacturing matters in this context.

In line with the argument in the previous section about different patterns of structural change and different initial conditions, the correlation is not a perfect one. Major exceptions among the advanced economies are primary exporters such as Norway, Canada, and Australia. Among the developing countries, Taiwan, Thailand, and Brazil rank higher in terms of industrialization than in terms of income. Nevertheless, the table illustrates the general point about industrialization. The poorest countries in the table are invariably those with the lowest shares of manufacturing and the highest shares of agriculture in commodity production. The more prosperous countries are the more industrialized ones.

2.3.2 *Structural change bonus*

A second argument in favour of industrialization states that labour productivity in agriculture is much lower than labour productivity in industry. A transfer of labour from low-productivity agriculture to high-productivity industry results in an immediate increase in overall productivity and income per capita. This transfer has been a major source of growth in developing countries. It is referred to as the structural change bonus (Lewis 1954; Fei and Ranis 1964; Chenery, Robinson, and Syrquin 1986; Fagerberg and Verspagen 1999; Timmer and Szirmai 2000; van Ark and Timmer 2003; Temple and Wößmann 2006; Rodrik 2009; Timmer and de Vries 2009).

Table 2.2 presents data on value added per worker for a selected number of developing countries for which data are available for longer periods. It is immediately clear from this table that value added per worker is much higher

Table 2.1. Industrialization and per capita gross national product in 2000 (45 countries)

	Share of manufacturing in total commodity production[(a)]		GNP per capita (2000 US$)	
	(%)[(b)]	Ranking		Ranking
Switzerland	72	2	38,140	1
Japan	64	11	35,620	2
Norway	26	40	34,530	3
USA	63	14	34,100	4
Denmark	60	17	32,280	5
Sweden	66	9	27,140	6
Austria	60	16	25,220	7
Finland	66	8	25,130	8
Germany	72	3	25,120	9
Netherlands	58	18	24,970	10
Belgium	69	4	24,540	11
UK	60	15	24,430	12
France	65	10	24,090	13
Canada	56	20	21,130	14
Australia	45	25	20,240	15
Italy	66	7	20,160	16
Taiwan	77	1	14,188	17
South Korea	66	6	8,910	18
Argentina	55	22	7,460	19
Mexico	63	12	5,070	20
Chile	36	32	4,590	21
Venezuela	35	34	4,310	22
Brazil	67	5	3,580	23
Malaysia	58	19	3,380	24
Turkey	36	30	3,100	25
South Africa	55	21	3,020	26
Peru	41	26	2,080	27
Colombia	31	36	2,020	28
Thailand	63	13	2,000	29
Egypt	38	29	1,490	30
Nigeria	38	28	1,180	31
Philippines	48	24	1,040	32
Sri Lanka	36	33	850	33
China	52	23	840	34
Côte d'Ivoire	36	31	600	35
Indonesia	41	27	570	36
India	31	38	450	37
Pakistan	31	37	440	38
Bangladesh	30	39	370	39
Kenya	34	35	350	40
Ghana	15	42	340	41
Zambia	25	41	300	42
Tanzania	12	43	270	43
Morocco	5	45	260	44
Congo, Dem. Rep.	6	44	100	45

Notes: (a) Value added in manufacturing as percentage of total value in commodity production (agriculture, forestry, fisheries, mining, manufacturing, construction and utilities).(b) Manufacturing share OECD countries, latest year in period 1998–2000.

Sources: GNP per capita and shares from World Bank (2002), except: (i) Zaire from World Bank, available at: www.worldbank.org/data/countrydata/countrydata.html; (ii) Canada, Norway, Sweden, Switzerland, Canada, and the USA: calculated with OECD Main Economic Indicators, 2010, available at: www.oecd.org/EN/document/0, EN-document-7-nodirectorate-no-1-5194-7,00.html) and UNIDO (2000).

Table 2.2. Value added per worker in agriculture and manufacturing (at constant prices)

	1950						1960						1970					
	Ag	Min	Ind	Man	Services	Tot	Ag	Min	Ind	Man	Services	Tot	Ag	Min	Ind	Man	Services	Tot
India							77	344	162	120	155	100	67	350	192	140	179	100
Indonesia																		
Malaysia																		
Philippines																		
South Korea													49	153	125	88	167	100
Taiwan													40	294	119	111	147	100
Thailand							46	238	326	283	287	100	38	134	300	294	274	100
Turkey																		
Argentina	29	94	113	98	134	100	39	142	91	86	135	100	43	242	115	114	110	100
Bolivia	31	783	334	205	235	100	32	799	298	229	231	100	25	621	268	194	183	100
Brazil	26	111	180	165	220	100	22	173	204	196	179	100	19	269	169	180	170	100
Chile	28	183	125	78	139	100	21	162	147	127	125	100	19	229	151	127	114	100
Colombia	54	262	160	134	160	100	50	277	171	147	140	100	53	385	159	129	118	100
Costa Rica	46	31	144	149	187	100	36	30	127	141	189	100	41	40	131	157	149	100
Mexico	30	166	139	130	237	100	27	121	131	127	208	100	26	96	115	112	180	100
Peru							26	452	173	137	198	100	23	481	159	142	169	100
Venezuela	11	1649	332	78	80	100	12	1950	313	90	61	100	18	2691	270	105	63	100
Average Asia													48	233	184	158	192	100
Average Latin America	32	410	191	130	174	100	30	456	184	142	163	100	30	562	171	140	139	100

	1980						1990						2000					
	Ag	Min	Ind	Man	Services	Tot	Ag	Min	Ind	Man	Services	Tot	Ag	Min	Ind	Man	Services	Tot
India	57	555	222	158	206	100	50	458	221	175	190	100	41	446	169	142	219	100
Indonesia	42	2909	320	165	110	100	39	1253	243	193	119	100	40	1099	217	196	96	100
Malaysia	61	1013	169	120	97	100	64	1737	149	126	91	100	54	1981	123	115	98	100
Pakistan																		
Philippines	49	304	274	261	95	100	54	287	248	278	95	100	56	333	243	271	89	100
South Korea	41	172	131	113	130	100	48	160	132	115	95	100	57	427	181	192	69	100
Taiwan	36	258	98	96	135	100	31	398	92	95	126	100	27	392	88	96	118	100
Thailand	33	167	249	259	206	100	24	479	246	263	187	100	28	1110	220	243	122	100
Turkey																		
Argentina	46	327	112	115	105	100	67	480	123	127	96	100	76	700	166	161	85	100
Bolivia	32	312	198	181	133	100	40	438	236	229	112	100	49	462	155	170	108	100
Brazil	17	205	173	190	140	100	28	372	154	143	116	100	37	646	182	166	95	100
Chile	25	316	149	130	104	100	39	268	151	125	93	100	63	625	175	145	79	100
Colombia	55	137	169	162	107	100	61	329	165	138	98	100	67	401	165	143	93	100
Costa Rica	42	52	127	151	123	100	47	111	115	126	126	100	62	72	140	163	95	100
Mexico	26	153	106	104	145	100	32	179	105	107	131	100	37	322	110	120	113	100
Peru	18	362	180	169	144	100	31	384	167	145	118	100	32	689	224	173	111	100
Venezuela	36	1545	190	131	71	100	43	1393	201	155	71	100	38	1759	213	137	66	100
Average Asia	46	768	209	167	140	100	44	682	190	178	129	100	43	827	177	179	116	100
Average Latin America	33	379	156	148	119	100	43	439	157	144	107	100	51	631	170	153	94	100

Notes: At constant prices. The base-year varies per country, but all base-years are in the mid-1990s.

Sources: Groningen Growth and Development Centre (2009).

in manufacturing than in agriculture. This is in line with the structural bonus argument. There will be a positive static shift effect, when workers relocate to manufacturing.

It is also not surprising that labour productivity in the capital-intensive mining sector is far higher than that in manufacturing. The results with regard to services in Latin America are more puzzling. Between 1950 and 1970, labour productivity in the service sector in Latin American countries is much higher than in manufacturing. If this is not due to measurement error, this would suggest that transfer of resources to services would provide a higher static shift effect than to manufacturing, which is counter-intuitive. From 1980 onwards, however, productivity in manufacturing is substantially higher than in services, which is more in line with our expectations.[2]

A second aspect of the structural change bonus argument focuses on the dynamics of sectors. If productivity growth in manufacturing is more rapid than in other sectors, a transfer of resources to this sector will result in more rapid aggregate growth (this is referred to as the dynamic shift effect). Here the evidence is more mixed. In the world's richest countries growth of labour productivity in agriculture in the post-war period was higher than in industry—particularly due to bio-technological innovation (see Maddison 1991). However, in most developing countries productivity growth in manufacturing was more rapid than in the agricultural sector between 1950 and 1973.

In Table 2.3, we present a comparison of growth rates in manufacturing and agriculture in a sample of developing countries (derived from the GGDC 10-sector database). These are compared with sectoral growth rates in advanced economies in the post-war period. This table provides some interesting findings that provide a more nuanced picture of the role of manufacturing in growth. Between 1950 and 1973, the growth rate of labour productivity in manufacturing is substantially higher than in agriculture and also higher than that in the total economy. This is even more pronounced if we look at growth of output (8.6 per cent versus 3.9 per cent). Manufacturing is clearly a very dynamic sector contributing to overall growth performance. Between 1950 and 1973, productivity growth in manufacturing was higher than in agriculture in 10 out of 14 countries. In the case of value added, all countries show higher growth in manufacturing in this period.

After 1973, the picture becomes more complicated. Our sample of developing countries starts looking more like the advanced economies, in that productivity growth in agriculture is systematically higher than in manufacturing. This is true for 12 out of the 16 developing countries in Table 2.3. However, in

[2] The use of constant prices with a base year in the 1990s of course overestimates the share of services in value added in the early years, as manufacturing prices increase less than service prices. But a similar table with current values—not reproduced here—shows very similar patterns.

Table 2.3. Growth of output and productivity in agriculture and manufacturing, 1950–2005

	1950–1973						1973–2005					
	Labour productivity			Value added			Labour productivity			Value added		
Country	Agric.	Manu.	Total	Agri.	Manu.	Total	Agri.	Manu.	Total	Agri.	Manu.	Total
Argentina	2.8	2.6	1.3	1.9	3.6	2.6	3.0	1.5	0.5	1.9	0.7	1.8
Bolivia	1.9	2.1	2.7	1.2	3.3	3.0	2.5	-1.3	-0.4	2.7	2.6	2.4
Brazil	2.1	4.9	4.1	3.8	8.8	7.5	3.9	0.2	0.9	3.4	2.4	3.2
Chile	0.1	4.0	2.0	0.4	6.3	3.6	5.7	2.5	1.5	5.7	2.9	4.1
Colombia	2.3	3.8	1.0	3.4	6.5	3.5	1.3	0.3	0.7	2.6	3.0	3.7
Costa Rica	3.6	3.9	3.5	5.0	8.7	7.0	1.8	1.0	0.5	2.8	4.7	4.1
India	0.4	3.7	1.9	2.3	5.4	3.5	0.9	3.0	2.9	2.7	6.1	5.3
Indonesia	2.1	1.6	3.7	3.1	6.8	5.9	2.3	4.9	2.9	3.1	9.2	5.4
Korea	3.1	7.3	4.6	3.8	15.9	6.1	4.8	8.4	4.9	1.6	11.2	7.3
Malaysia							3.8	3.5	3.8	2.6	9.0	6.7
Mexico	2.8	3.0	3.6	3.6	7.7	6.2	1.7	0.6	0.4	1.8	3.5	3.4
Peru	5.4	19.3	16.6	3.2	7.4	5.9	1.5	0.7	0.1	2.9	1.8	2.3
Philippines							1.0	0.3	0.6	2.5	2.8	3.4
Taiwan	10.9	11.1	12.4	12.2	22.2	17.2	7.6	6.9	8.8	4.3	9.1	11.0
Thailand	3.1	5.6	4.9	4.7	9.4	7.1	2.6	2.9	3.5	3.2	8.1	6.1
Venezuela	5.3	3.5	2.1	5.3	8.9	5.5	1.1	0.7	-1.2	2.1	2.1	1.7
Australia							3.4	2.5	1.6	2.8	1.3	3.2
Austria							3.5	3.6	2.2	1.1	2.4	2.4
Belgium							3.7	4.1	1.7	1.6	2.0	2.1
Czech Republic							7.1	5.0	2.5	1.4	4.7	2.1
Denmark							6.3	1.9	1.5	2.9	0.4	1.8
Finland							4.5	4.8	0.0	0.7	3.9	0.0
France							4.7	3.1	1.7	1.4	1.5	2.2
Germany							4.1	2.4	1.5	0.7	1.0	2.0
Greece							3.4	2.5	1.6	2.8	1.3	3.2
Hungary							10.8	7.7	4.0	1.6	5.5	2.9
Ireland							4.2	6.8	2.9	1.8	7.4	4.8

(continued)

Table 2.3. Continued

	1950–1973						1973–2005					
	Labour productivity			Value added			Labour productivity			Value added		
Country	Agric.	Manu.	Total	Agri.	Manu.	Total	Agri.	Manu.	Total	Agri.	Manu.	Total
Italy							5.7	2.4	1.5	1.5	2.0	2.1
Japan	5.7	8.3	6.4	2.4	12.5	8.4	2.6	4.5	2.7	-0.6	3.6	3.1
Netherlands							3.7	3.1	1.2	3.3	2.1	2.5
Poland							1.4	7.2	4.0	1.7	5.0	3.6
Spain							6.0	1.9	1.4	2.5	2.1	2.7
Sweden							3.6	4.4	1.9	0.4	3.0	2.2
UK							2.9	2.9	1.6	1.2	0.3	2.0
USA							5.3	3.7	1.3	4.9	2.8	2.9
Average:												
Developing countries	3.3	5.4	4.6	3.9	8.6	6.1	2.8	2.3	1.9	2.9	5.0	4.5
Advanced economies							4.6	3.9	1.9	1.8	2.8	2.5

Source: Own calculations using data from the following sources: Advanced economies plus South Korea, 1973–2005: Groningen Growth and Development Centre (2008); Developing countries, 1950–2005 and South Korea, 1953–73: Groningen Growth and Development Centre (2009).Developing countries with data which do not cover the full period 1950–2005 include the following: Bolivia (lab 50–03); India (lab, 60–04); Indonesia (lab 61–05; va, 60–05); Korea (lab, 63–05; VA, 53–05); Malaysia (lab 75–05; VA, 70–05); Peru (Lab, 60–05); Philippines (Lab 63–05; VA 51–05); Taiwan (Lab 63–05; VA 51–05); Thailand (Lab 60–05; VA 51–05).

terms of value added the growth rate in manufacturing is still much higher in 10 out of 16 developing countries in the table. This is consistent with a shrinking share of agriculture in total value added. The same pattern can be seen in the sample of advanced economies. In terms of productivity per person engaged, the agricultural sector systematically outperforms the manufacturing sector and the total economy. A smaller fraction of the total labour force is producing more and more output per person in agriculture. The only real exceptions are the European catch-up economies, Poland and Ireland, where productivity growth in manufacturing is much higher than in agriculture.

However, in terms of value added, growth in manufacturing and growth in the total economy is much more rapid than in agriculture. Agriculture's share in valued added has systematically been shrinking. Summarizing the information in Table 2.3, we may conclude that in developing countries manufacturing is indeed one of the more dynamic sectors in terms of productivity and output growth, especially in the period 1950–73. In the period 1973–2003, productivity growth in agriculture surpasses that of manufacturing, but manufacturing still dominates in terms of output growth.

2.3.3 *Structural change burden*

In many service sectors, the possibilities for productivity growth are limited due to the inherently labour-intensive nature of service production. This implies that an increasing share of services results in a productivity slowdown (Baumol's law; Baumol 1967). Such service sectors include personal services, restaurants and hotels, health care and medical services, and government. What productivity improvement there is often takes the place of reducing quality of output or simply providing less services for the same price, so it would not show up in productivity indices if these were correctly measured using hedonic price indices.

Baumol's law has recently come under fire, because there are some very important market service sectors such as the financial sector, software services, transport and logistics, and retail sales and distribution where there are major productivity improvements, often based on ICTs (Triplett and Bosworth 2003; de Vries 2010). Nevertheless, the working hypothesis is that countries with very large service sectors will tend to grow at a slower rate than countries with a smaller service sector. Advanced economies are predominantly service economies and these are all characterized by slower aggregate growth rates (Nordhaus 2008; Hartwig 2011). This creates new possibilities for catch-up in developing countries, where the industrial and the manufacturing sector have a proportionately larger shares in output.

On the other hand, developing countries are characterized by a rather large share of the service sector at rather early stages of development in the 1950s. They did not follow the traditional linear sequence of a shift from agriculture to manufacturing, followed by a shift from manufacturing to services. As much of the large service sector in post-war developing countries consisted of large, inefficient, and extremely unproductive government sectors, developing countries suffered from a structural change burden at early stages of development. Other parts of the service sector consisted of activities of 'survival entrepreneurs' in the informal sector, which are also not very productive or dynamic. But, in recent years in countries such as India, larger parts of the service sector have consisted of dynamic activities such as IT services, which would tend to reduce or even eliminate the structural change burden.

Unfortunately, it is hard to test these hypotheses using regression analysis, because of endogeneity issues. Rich countries have larger service sectors because the demand for services increases at higher levels of income. So, even if the service sector acts as a brake on growth, service sector shares will not be negatively correlated with per capita income levels.[3]

2.3.4 *Opportunities for capital accumulation*

The reasons for high labour productivity and rapid labour productivity growth in manufacturing are manifold. Important reasons included capital accumulation, economies of scale, and technological progress. Spatially concentrated activities such as manufacturing offer better possibilities for capital accumulation and capital-intensification than spatially dispersed agriculture. The most capital-intensive sectors in the economy are manufacturing, mining, construction, and utilities.

Internationally comparable data on capital stocks are scarce, especially for developing countries. In Table 2.4, we have put together data for a selected number of developing countries from a World Bank database compiled by Larson et al. (2000). We compared these with data for advanced economies from the EUKLEMS database. This table provides some very interesting results

- In developing countries, capital intensity in manufacturing is much higher than in agriculture (as expected).[4] The shift from agriculture to manufacturing is important in the process of aggregate capital accumulation.

[3] A better approach is to analyse the impact of the sectoral shares at the beginning of a period on growth rates of income per capita in that period (cf. Fagerberg and Verspagen 1999).

[4] The same is true for mining and utilities (figures not reproduced here).

Table 2.4. Capital-intensity in agriculture and manufacturing (Sectoral capital intensity as % of total)[a,b]

	1970		1980		1990		2000	
	Agric.	Manuf.	Agric.	Manuf.	Agric.	Manuf.	Agric.	Manuf.
India	25	199	24	210	20	206		
Indonesia	3	114	3	65	10	57		
Pakistan	34	93	27	120	22	134		
Philippines	42	138	14	166	9	168		
South Korea	18	159	25	100	42	87		
Sri Lanka			7	53	4	31		
Taiwan	32	131	29	85	27	77		
Turkey	26	188	22	173	16	88		
Argentina	59		52		52			
Chile	48	88	67	70	77	37		
Colombia	19	89	15	90	11	70		
Peru	13	133	14	130	16	97		
Venezuela	63	109	40	88	28	87		
Egypt	33	166	25	186	27	181		
Morocco					6			
Average developing countries	32	134	26	118	24	102		
Australia	114	50	125	55	112	71	105	81
Austria			59	69	60	81	62	90
Czech Rep.							59	64
Denmark	141	53	177	65	207	69	235	84
Finland	44	98	77	81	114	95	151	94
West Germany	71	61	83	68	97	74		
Germany							110	85
Italy	52	85	69	95	107	100	137	108
Japan	67	114	72	97	93	93	118	105
Netherlands	106	67	125	69	135	80	146	90
Portugal							33	95
Sweden							119	106
UK	207	76	226	84	205	95	178	98
USA	151	81	173	89	145	96	114	104
Average advanced economies	106	76	119	77	127	85	121	93

Notes: [a]capital-intensity total calculated excluding real estate for advanced economies. Real estate refers to the residential capital stock. We assume the totals for developing countries from Larson et al. (2000) also exclude real estate. [b]Agricultural capital stock in developing countries refers to gross fixed capital stock excluding tree stock and cattle stock. In the advanced economy data, agricultural capital stock includes tree stock and cattle stock. This results in an upward bias in the estimates of agricultural capital-intensity.

Source: own calculations from the following sources, capital stock developing countries, Larson et al. (2000); persons engaged developing countries, Groningen Growth and Development Centre (2009), except Egypt, Morocco, Pakistan from ILO, Labour Statistics Database (2008). Advanced economies: Groningen Growth and Development Centre (2008).

- Between 1970 and 1990, capital intensity in manufacturing as a percentage of the total economy capital-intensity declines. Other sectors become more capital intensive. The importance of manufacturing as the sector driving capital accumulation declines.
- In the advanced economies the roles of agriculture and manufacturing have been reversed with regard to capital intensity. Capital intensity in the small sector of agriculture is much higher than in manufacturing. This has to do with the 'industrialization of agriculture'. In the advanced economies the share of agricultural labour and value added has declined enormously, but agriculture has become much more productive due to the application of very capital-intensive technologies such as greenhouse farming, intensive pig, cattle, and poultry farming, use of combines, and so forth. But there is also a measurement problem. The EUKLEMS data seem to include tree stocks and cattle stocks. This overstates the capital intensiveness of agriculture, because tree stocks and cattle stocks do not refer to capital accumulation in the modern technological sense. In the case of the developing countries, we have been able to exclude tree and cattle stocks.
- The advanced economy data illustrate that manufacturing has become one of the less capital-intensive sectors of the economy. The EUKLEMS data indicate that mining, utilities and transport are the most capital-intensive sectors. Agriculture also has above average capital intensity. Manufacturing has become much less important as a key sector where capital accumulation takes place. There are again measurement issues. The data in the table refer to total fixed capital formation, including fixed structures. It is very likely that in terms of machinery and equipment the data would show a more important role for manufacturing.

In economic growth accounting studies, the contribution of growth of physical capital to growth of output in post-war advanced economies turns out to be less important than previously thought. Other factors such as growth of employment, growth of human capital, and disembodied technological change are very important as well (Maddison 1987; Thirlwall 1997). However, for developing countries, physical capital accumulation still seems to be of great importance because they start with so much less capital per worker (Hoffmann 1965; Nadiri 1972; Pilat 1994; Bosworth, Collins, and Chen 1995; Thirlwall 1997).

2.3.5 *Opportunities for scale economies*

Historically the industrial sector (including mining, manufacturing, construction, and utilities) profited more from economies of scale, compared to service sectors and agriculture. This is partly due to the nature of the technologies that are most productively applied in large-scale production. But it also has to do with learning by doing. Expansion of production expands the scope for learning (Fagerberg and Verspagen 1999). Thus the rate of growth of productivity in manufacturing depends positively on the rate of growth of output (Verdoorn 1949; Kaldor 1966, 1967).

With the rise of ICTs this may have changed from the 1990s onwards. In certain service sectors, scale effects have become overwhelmingly important, as the marginal costs of providing an additional unit of service have come close to zero. The question is justified whether the role of manufacturing in future growth may become less important than in the past 60 years. The service sector might become the new engine of growth. It is too early to say whether this is indeed the case. Many service sectors—such as government, medical services, education, and personal care—still suffer from the Baumol's disease. In the case of digitized services, the marginal costs may be close to zero, but there is an increasing problem of appropriation of revenues from these services, as the flow of services becomes impossible to control and valorize.

2.3.6 *Technological change*

The manufacturing sector offers special opportunities for both embodied and disembodied technological progress. Rapid capital accumulation is associated with embodied technological progress, as new generations of capital goods embody the latest state-of-the art technology.

Disembodied technological progress refers to changes in the knowledge of product and process technologies in firms and in the economy as a whole. Since the Industrial Revolution, technological advance has been concentrated in the manufacturing sector and diffuses from there to other economic sectors such as the service sector. Cornwall (1977) in particular has argued that manufacturing is the locus of technological progress. Even in the IT sector, advances in software applications are dependent on advances in hardware chip technologies and information transmission technologies such as fibre optics and satellite technologies.

Some brief remarks need to be made here about the difficulties in unscrambling capital accumulation and technological change. From the perspective of a developing country, the use of more capital goods per worker in itself represents an important kind of technological change. The mode of production changes dramatically, and the mastering of new, usually imported, technologies requires major innovative efforts on behalf of developing countries and their firms. In this sense, all capital accumulation in developing countries represents technological change. It involves the diffusion of machinery from the advanced economies and diffusion of the technologies embodied in them.

However, one needs to distinguish between the increase in the pure volume of existing capital goods (more of the same) and the shift over time from technologically less sophisticated to technologically more advanced capital goods. This is called *embodied technological change*, still a form of international diffusion of technology through capital imports, but now with the emphasis on the upgrading of the capital stock.

Next, in the course of economic development, output per unit of input (total factor productivity) can increase due to various factors—shifts from one economic sector to another, economies of scale, and more efficient allocation of resources within sectors. One of the most important factors, which can cause increases in output per unit of input, is so-called *disembodied technological change*. Disembodied technological change refers to general advances in science, technology, and the state of knowledge; changes in the stocks of knowledge available to firms, sectors, or countries; improvements in the level of knowledge absorbed by employees and managers in educational institutions and on the job (Maddison 1987); learning-by-doing by workers and managers on the job; improvements in the collective technological capabilities of firms or the social capabilities of countries and finally positive external effects of investment in knowledge and new technologies, through spillovers from firm to firm or from country to country.

2.3.7 *Linkage and spillover effects*

Linkage effects refer to the direct backward and forward linkages between different sectors or firms. Linkages are direct physical relations of intersectoral supply and demand. The positive external effect of linkages is that they can create economies of scale in the domestic economy. Spillover effects refer to the disembodied knowledge and technology flows between economic actors and economic sectors. Actors learn from each other, so that investment in technological knowledge or increased efficiency in one firm has positive external effects on the economy as a whole.

Intersectoral backward and forward linkages in manufacturing are perceived to be much stronger than in mining or agriculture, which are typically characterized by weak linkages (Hirschman 1958; Cornwall 1977; Myint 1980). Investment in one branch of manufacturing can have strong positive external effects on other sectors.

Spillover effects between manufacturing and other sectors are also very powerful. As indicated above, the manufacturing sector is one of the primary sources of technological advance in the economy as a whole. It is here that most product and process technologies are developed. One of the important spillover effects in modern economies is that from the industrial sector to other sectors, such as the service sector. Thus advances in ICT hardware technologies produced in the manufacturing sector (silicon chips, glass fibre cables) fuel technological change in the software-producing and software-using service sectors.

2.3.8 *Engel's law*

The argument in the previous paragraph was couched in terms of supply factors. But demand relationships and factors are also relevant for the debate about the role of manufacturing. The lower the per capita income of a country, the larger the proportion of that income will be spent on basic agricultural foodstuffs—this is known as the Engel's law (Engel 1857). As per capita incomes increase, the demand for agricultural products will decline and the demand for industrial products will tend to increase. Economic development creates a mass market for industrial products. This creates dynamic opportunities for manufacturing. If a country remains focused on agriculture and fails to develop its domestic manufacturing industry, it will have to import increasing amounts of manufactured goods.

However, a similar argument could be made for services at higher levels of per capita income. At higher levels of economic development, the income elasticity of service consumption is quite high (Chakravarty and Mitra 2009). This is an argument in favour of service-led growth at higher levels of development. However, one has to distinguish between real changes in the composition of demand and price effects. Due to Baumol's law, productivity in services will lag behind that of manufacturing. If service wage levels follow manufacturing wage levels, then the price of services will increase, leading to higher proportions of income being spent on services.

2.4 Conclusion

This chapter has presented an overview of theoretical arguments and empirical evidence for the proposition that in the past 50 years, manufacturing has functioned as an important engine of growth in developing countries. There is no doubt that manufacturing has been an important driver of growth and catch-up. But not all expectations of the engine of growth hypotheses are supported by the statistical evidence, in particular not with regard to the presumed higher capital intensity in manufacturing and the productivity dynamics of manufacturing. In more recent years, productivity growth in agriculture has even been higher than in manufacturing.

The review of the secondary literature also presents a mixed picture. The older literature tends to emphasize the importance of manufacturing, the more recent literature finds that the contribution of service sectors has increased. Manufacturing is definitely important, especially in the period 1950–73 and much more so in developing countries than in advanced economies. It continues to act as a vehicle of catch-up after 1973. But in the advanced economies the contribution of the service sector has become more and more important and the share of services in GDP is now well above 70 per cent.[5]

The more general historical evidence provides stronger support for the engine-of-growth hypothesis. There are no important examples of success in economic development in developing countries since 1950 that have not been driven by industrialization. All the Asian catch-up stories are stories of successful industrialization. Neither tourism, nor primary exports, nor services have played a similar role, with the possible exception of IT services in India since 2000. But even in India manufacturing has been and still is of great importance.

Sub-Saharan African countries are underrepresented in most statistical exercises and statistical databases. With the exception of South Africa, Mauritius, Botswana, and Namibia, they all have very low per capita incomes, disappointing long-run growth performance and they have all failed to industrialize. Their development experiences provide further support for the engine-of-growth hypothesis.

What can one conclude with regard to the future role of manufacturing in the twenty-first century? The answers can at best be somewhat speculative, but let us nevertheless try to formulate some expectations.

1. Given the sheer size of the service sector in the advanced economies, productivity advances and technological change in the service sector have inevitably become more important in explaining differences in growth performance between the advanced economies. Thus in recent years, more rapid productivity growth in key service sectors in the USA is one of the factors explaining the productivity gap between the USA and Europe (van Ark, O'Mahoney, and Timmer 2008).
2. Manufacturing will continue to be important in accelerating growth and achieving catch-up in developing countries, especially in countries at lower levels of per capita income.

[5] As prices of services have increased far more than those of industrial goods, the share of the service sector in constant prices has increased far less and the contribution to growth will also be less than when measured at current prices.

3. Compared to the past 60 years, market service sectors will become relatively more important as potential sources of growth and catch-up.
4. As developing countries become richer and their economic structure becomes more similar to that of the presently advanced economies, the importance of manufacturing will tend to decline. But as developing countries come closer to the technological frontier, their rates of growth will also tend to slow down as a consequence of the structural change burden.
5. With the exception of small island economies, which are a special case, it is hard to imagine sustained growth spurts in less-developed countries exclusively driven by the primary sector, by the construction sector, or by market services alone.
6. One of the most important lessons from past experiences is that industrial policy should not overemphasize the importance of a single sector, however important it seems to be. Linkages between agriculture and manufacturing, between services and industry, have been important in the past and will continue to be so in future patterns of economic development.

References

Balance, R., J. Ansari, and H. Singer (1982). *The International Economy and Industrial Development: Trade and Investment in the Third World.* Brighton: Wheatsheaf.

Baumol, W. J. (1967). 'Macro-economics of Unbalanced Growth: The Anatomy of Urban Crises', *American Economic Review,* 57 (3): 415–26.

Bosworth, B, S. M. Collins, and Y. Chen (1995). 'Accounting for Differences in Economic Growth'. Paper for Conference on 'Structural Adjustment Policies in the 1990s: Experience and Prospects', Institute of Developing Economies, Tokyo, Japan, 5–6 October.

Chakravarty, S., and A. Mitra (2009). 'Is Industry still the Engine of Growth? An Econometric Study of the Organized Sector Employment in India', *Journal of Policy Modeling,* 31: 22–35.

Chenery, H., S. Robinson, and M. Syrquin (1986). *Industrialization and Growth a Comparative Study.* Oxford: Oxford University Press for the World Bank.

Cornwall, J (1977). *Modern Capitalism. Its Growth and Transformation.* New York: St. Martin's Press.

de Vries, G. (2010). 'Productivity, Firm Heterogeneity, and Policy Reforms in Latin America'. PhD Thesis. Groningen: Groningen University.

Engel, E. (1857). 'Die Produktions- und Consumptionsverhältnisse des Königreichs Sachsen', *Zeitschrift des Statistischen Bureaus des Königlich Sächsischen Ministeriums des Innern,* November.

Fagerberg, J., and B. Verspagen (1999). 'Modern Capitalism in the 1970s and 1980s'. In M. Setterfield (ed.), *Growth, Employment and Inflation*. Basingstoke: Palgrave Macmillan.

——(2002). 'Technology-Gaps, Innovation-Diffusion and Transformation: An Evolutionary Interpretation', *Research Policy*, 31: 1291–304.

——(2007). 'Innovation, Growth and Economic Development: Have the Conditions for Catch-up Changed?', *International Journal of Technological Learning, Innovation and Development*, 1 (1): 13–33.

Fei, J. C. H., and G. Ranis (1964). *Development of the Labor Surplus Economy. Theory and Policy*. Homewood, IL: Irwin.

Groningen Growth and Development Centre (2008). *EU KLEMS database*, http://www.rug.nl/feb/Onderzoek/Onderzoekscentra/GGDC/data/eu-klems-iframe (downloaded July and September 2008).

——(2009). *Ten Sector Database*, http://www.rug.nl/feb/Onderzoek/Onderzoekscentra/GGDC/data/10sector GGDC (downloaded February 2009).

Hartwig, J. (2011). 'Testing the Baumol–Nordhaus Model with EU-Klems Data', *Review of Income and Wealth*, 57 (3): 471–89.

Hirschman, A. O. (1958, reprinted 1988). *The Strategy of Economic Development*. Boulder and London: Westview Press.

Hoffmann, W. G. (1965). *Das Wachstum der Deutschen Wirtschaft seit der Mitte des 19. Jahrhunderts*, Berlin: Springer.

ILO (2008). *Labour Statistics Database*. Available at http://laborsta.ilo.org/, accessed 2008.

Kaldor, N. (1966). *Causes of the Slow Rate of Economic Growth of the United Kingdom. An Inaugural Lecture*. Cambridge: Cambridge University Press.

——(1967). *Strategic Factors in Economic Development*. Ithaca: Cornell University, New York State School of Industrial and Labor Relations.

Kathuria V., and R. S. N. Raj (2009). 'Is Manufacturing an Engine of Growth in India? Analyis in the Post Nineties'. Paper for the UNU-WIDER/UNU-MERIT/UNIDO Workshop, Pathways to Industrialisation in the 21st Century. New Challenges and Emerging Paradigms, Maastricht 22–23 October.

Larson, D. F., R. Butzer, Y. Mundlak, and A.Crego (2000). 'A Cross-Country Database for Sector Investment and Capital', *The World Bank Economic Review*, 14 (2): 371–91.

Lewis, A. (1954). 'Economic Development with Unlimited Supplies of Labour', *The Manchester School of Economic and Social Studies*, 22: 139–91.

Maddison, A. (1987). 'Growth and Slowdown in Advanced Capitalist Economies', *Journal of Economic Literature*, XXV, June: 649–98.

——(1991). *Dynamic Forces in Capitalist Development*. Oxford: Oxford University Press.

Myint, H. (1980). *The Economics of the Developing Countries*, 5th edition. London: Hutchinson.

Nadiri, M. (1972). 'International Studies of Factor Inputs and Total Factor Productivity. A Brief Survey', *Review of Income and Wealth*, 18 (2): 129–154.

Nordhaus, W. D. (2008). 'Baumol's Diseases: A Macroeconomic Perspective'. *The B. E. Journal of Macroeconomics*, 8 (1): 1–37.

OECD (2010). *Main Economic Indicators, 2010*. Available at: www.oecd.org/EN/document/0, EN-document-7-nodirectorate-no-1-5194-7,00.html

Pilat, D. (1994). *The Economics of Rapid Growth: The Experience of Japan and Korea*. Aldershot: Edward Elgar.

Rodrik, D. (2009). *Growth after the Crisis*. Cambridge, MA: Harvard University, John F. Kennedy School of Government.

Szirmai, A. (2005). *Dynamics of Socio-Economic Development*. Cambridge: Cambridge University Press.

Szirmai, A., and B. Verspagen (2011). 'Manufacturing and Economic Growth in Developing Countries, 1950–2005'. Working Paper Series, 2011–69. Maastricht: UNU-MERIT.

Temple J., and L. Wößmann (2006). 'Dualism and Cross-country Growth Regressions', *Journal of Economic Growth*, 11: 187–228.

Thirlwall, A. P. (1997). *Growth and Development, with Special Reference to Developing Economies*, 6th edition. Basingstoke: Palgrave Macmillan.

Timmer, M. P., and A. Szirmai (2000). 'Productivity in Asian Manufacturing: The Structural Bonus Hypothesis Examined' *Structural Change and Economic Dynamics*, 11 (4): 370–91.

Timmer M. P., and G. J. de Vries (2009). 'Structural Change and Growth Accelerations in Asia and Latin America: A New Sectoral Data Set', *Cliometrica*, 3 (2): 165–90.

Triplett, J. E., and B. P. Bosworth (2003). 'Productivity Measurement Issues in Service Industries: "Baumol's Disease" Has Been Cured', *Economic Policy Review*, September: 23–33.

UNIDO (2000). *Industrial Statistics Database*. Available at: www.unido.org/Regions.cfm?area=GLO

Van Ark, B., and M. P. Timmer (2003). 'Asia's Productivity Performance and Potential: The Contribution of Sectors and Structural Change'. Groningen: University of Groningen and the Conference Board.

Van Ark B., M. O'Mahoney, and M. P. Timmer (2008). 'The Productivity Gap between Europe and the United States: Trends and Causes', *Journal of Economic Perspectives*, 22 (1): 25–44.

Verdoorn, P. J. (1949). 'Fattori che Regolano lo Sviluppo della Produttivita del Lavoro', L'Industria. Translated by A. P. Thirlwall in D. Ironmonger, J. Perkins, and T. Hoa (eds), *National Income and Economic Progress: Essays in Honour of Colin Clark*. Basingstoke: Palgrave Macmillan.

World Bank (2002). *World Development Indicators*. Washington, DC: World Bank.

3

Deindustrialization and Reindustrialization

Fiona Tregenna

3.1 Introduction[1]

The challenge of industrialization in the twenty-first century differs in several ways from the experiences of developed countries when they initially industrialized in the nineteenth century, as well as developing countries that rapidly industrialized in the twentieth century. One important difference is that many countries have in fact experienced *deindustrialization* in recent times. Deindustrialization has occurred in most upper-income countries over the past few decades, but it has become increasingly prevalent in middle-income countries as well. The challenge of industrialization in the twenty-first century is thus, in reality for many countries, actually a challenge of *reindustrialization*.

Industrialization, deindustrialization, and reindustrialization refer here to changes in the share of the manufacturing sector in GDP and/or employment. Manufacturing is of course not synonymous with 'industry' (which includes mining and usually construction as well). However, it is the manufacturing sector specifically which is regarded in some economic schools of thought as having particular characteristics that make it important as an 'engine of growth' and hence make industrialization important for growth. (Furthermore, the share of mining in countries' employment and GDP is, to a significant extent, outside their control given that it derives in part from a country's mineral endowments.) The analysis here is thus specifically of the manufacturing sector and of changes in its share in employment and GDP.

[1] The methodology and background for this chapter draws on Tregenna (2009). Helpful comments and suggestions were received from Wim Naudé, Adam Szirmai, and other participants at the UNU-WIDER, UNU-MERIT, and UNIDO international workshop, held in Maastricht, October 2009, as well as Gabriel Palma. The usual disclaimers apply.

In recent decades there has been a significant decline in the share of manufacturing in GDP—and even more so of the share of manufacturing in employment—especially in advanced economies. The fall in the share of manufacturing in employment has been characterized in the literature as deindustrialization. The levels of manufacturing employment corresponding to particular levels of GDP per capita have fallen over time in upper- and middle-income economies (Palma 2005), and there is increasing evidence of deindustrialization in some middle-income developing countries, especially in Latin America. International value added and employment data clearly show a generalized trend towards a relative decline in manufacturing and a relative increase in services, particularly in the case of employment.

Does this matter at all for growth? From Kaldorian (Kaldor 1978, 1980), and structuralist (see Blankenburg, Palma, and Tregenna 2008) perspectives, manufacturing has special properties as an engine of growth. In this thinking, characteristics that are particularly strongly associated with the manufacturing sector include: dynamic economies of scale in manufacturing; strong backward and forward linkages between manufacturing and other sectors of the domestic economy; strong properties of learning-by-doing; innovation and technological progress; and the importance of manufacturing for the balance of payments.[2] According to Kaldor's laws, faster growth in manufacturing is (causally) associated with faster aggregate growth, productivity growth in manufacturing is endogenous to the growth of manufacturing output, and aggregate productivity growth is positively related with the growth of manufacturing output and employment. Chapter 2 discusses in more detail what have been regarded as the 'special properties' of manufacturing and empirical evidence concerning the relationship between the relative size of the manufacturing sector and economic growth. To the degree that these properties are indeed especially pronounced for the manufacturing sector, this would imply that deindustrialization could negatively affect economic growth.

A number of empirical studies, using various techniques and testing across a range of countries and time periods, have found support for the validity of Kaldor's laws and/or for the role played by the manufacturing sector as an engine of growth.[3] Szirmai, in Chapter 2 in this volume, finds that statistical evidence for the argument that manufacturing has been an engine of growth is mixed, but that there is some broad historical support for the

[2] See Tregenna (2009) for further discussion of these characteristics.

[3] Some recent studies include those by Bairam (1991); Drakopoulos and Theodossiou (1991); Atesoglu (1993); Bernat (1996); Hansen and Zhang (1996); Felipe (1998); Fingleton and McCombie (1998); Harris and Lau (1998); Harris and Liu (1999); Necmi (1999); Pons-Novell and Viladecans-Marsal (1999); Leon-Ledesma (2000); Diaz Bautista (2003); Wells and Thirlwall (2003); Knell (2004); and Beheshti and Sadighnia (2006).

engine-of-growth hypothesis. This chapter does not empirically investigate the validity of Kaldor's laws and the extent to which there is evidence for a special role of manufacturing in the growth process, as the focus is on the dynamics of deindustrialization and the prospects of reindustrialization. To the extent that the existing evidence supports the role of manufacturing as an engine of growth, deindustrialization would be of concern from a growth perspective and reindustrialization could be seen as desirable.

This chapter analyses episodes of deindustrialization and considers the prospects of reindustrialization. The next section reviews some of the literature on deindustrialization. Section 3.3 is an empirical analysis of periods of deindustrialization internationally. This emphasizes the diversity of deindustrialization experiences internationally, and focuses in particular on trends in labour productivity in manufacturing. Section 3.4 considers the challenge of moving from deindustrialization to reindustrialization. Section 3.5 concludes and draws out some broad policy implications.

3.2 Literature on deindustrialization

The literature on deindustrialization emerged primarily in the UK, and was concerned with explaining the slowdown in growth. A prominent early contribution was that of Singh (1977), who conceptualizes deindustrialization in terms of an 'efficient' manufacturing sector, in the sense of it being 'able to provide (currently and potentially) sufficient net exports to meet the country's overall import requirements at socially acceptable levels of output, employment and exchange rate' (1977: 134). On this basis Singh identifies a structural disequilibrium in the UK in that the competitive position of manufacturing was deteriorating despite increasing productivity and increasing cost and price competitiveness. Singh argues that 'deindustrialization is a symptom or a consequence of this "inefficiency" or of disequilibrium, rather than its cause' (ibid). Singh thus regards deindustrialization as problematic insofar as it is a manifestation of structural disequilibrium in the economy, in the sense of manufacturing being unable to not only satisfy domestic demand at least cost but also to export enough to pay for the full employment level of imports (at a 'reasonable' exchange rate).

Rowthorn and Wells (1987) is a seminal study on deindustrialization. They distinguish between positive and negative deindustrialisation. The former is conceptualised as:

> ...the normal result of sustained economic growth in a fully employed, and already highly developed, economy. It occurs because productivity growth in the manufacturing sector is so rapid that, despite increasing output, employment

> in this sector is reduced, either absolutely or as a share of total employment. However, this does not lead to unemployment, because new jobs are created in the service sector on a scale sufficient to absorb any workers displaced from manufacturing. Paradoxically, this kind of deindustrialization is a symptom of economic success. (Rowthorn and Wells 1987: 5)

Negative deindustrialization, by contrast, is defined by the authors as 'a product of economic failure and occurs when industry is in severe difficulties... labour shed from the manufacturing sector—because of falling output or rising productivity—will not be reabsorbed into the service sector. Unemployment will therefore rise' (ibid.). Note that their typology actually brings in two different issues: the cause of the relative decline in manufacturing employment, and whether or not displaced workers are absorbed into the services sector. There could thus be permutations of these two dimensions other than the ones that they include in their definitions. Rowthorn and Wells also identify a third type of deindustrialization, in which 'the pattern of net exports shifts away from manufactures towards other goods and services', which can 'lead to a transfer of labour and resources from manufacturing to other sectors of the economy' (ibid.: 6).

Several recent studies have empirically analysed the causes of deindustrialization in developed countries. Saeger (1997) finds evidence that imports from the south contributed to lower manufacturing employment in 23 OECD countries between 1970 and 1990. In contrast, Rowthorn and Ramaswamy (1997) find that deindustrialization in 18 OECD countries between 1963 and 1994 is primarily explained by the systematically higher productivity growth in manufacturing than in services; furthermore, they argue that deindustrialization is a natural result of industrial dynamism in advanced economies. Rowthorn and Ramaswamy find that trade accounts for a quite small proportion of deindustrialization. In an updated and extended analysis for 23 OECD countries over the period 1963–2002, Rowthorn and Coutts (2004) find that trade with less-developed economies contributed significantly to deindustrialization in the North, although domestic factors such as productivity growth and shifting patterns of demand were even more important. Alderson (1999) finds an outflow of direct investment, as well as import penetration from the South, to have contributed to deindustrialization in OECD countries between 1968 and 1992. Kucera and Milberg (2003) attribute deindustrialization in ten OECD countries between the late 1970s and the mid-1990s primarily to North–South trade.

Palma (2005, 2008), in analysis that includes both developed and developing countries, identifies four 'sources' of deindustrialization, drawing on Rowthorn's earlier work. First, an inverted-U relationship between manufacturing employment and income per capita, referring to the decline in the share of manufacturing as economies mature. Second, a declining relationship over time between income per capita and manufacturing employment. Third, changes in the level of income per capita at which the share of manufacturing employment is expected to decline (i.e. changes in the turning point of the income per capita–manufacturing employment regression). Fourth, Palma suggests that Dutch disease could be considered an additional form of deindustrialization. This refers to an additional degree of deindustrialization in cases where a country discovered significant natural resources, developed export finance or tourism, or as a result of policy 'liberalization' in middle-income countries.

Rowthorn and Coutts (2004) summarize five explanations of deindustrialization that have been advanced in the literature. The first of these is specialization, referring to the domestic outsourcing of activities, previously performed in-house in manufacturing businesses, to specialized service providers, resulting in an apparent decline in manufacturing employment that is a 'statistical artefact' rather than real. Second, a fall in the relative prices of manufactures means that they account for a smaller share of consumer expenditure. Third, the higher rate of productivity growth in manufacturing relative to services is associated with slower employment growth in manufacturing than in services, even if output increases at the same rate. Fourth, international trade might negatively affect manufacturing employment in advanced economies by increasing productivity through higher competitive pressures, eliminating low-value added activities or inefficient firms, and by replacing relatively labour-intensive activities subject to import pressures with less labour-intensive activities producing sophisticated exports. Finally, decreases in the rate of investment will tend to decrease the share of manufacturing (in both employment and GDP), since a disproportionately large share of investment expenditure is accounted for by manufactures. To these explanations we might add Palma's explanation of Dutch disease, as discussed above.

3.3 Empirical analysis of changes in manufacturing employment internationally

This section is an analysis is of periods of deindustrialization internationally, with the aim of getting a better understanding of the dynamics involved. In particular, we investigate the role of changes in labour productivity in manufacturing. There are two steps of the empirical analysis: a two-way dynamic decomposition of changes in the level of manufacturing employment, and a three-way decomposition of changes in the share of manufacturing in total employment.

Data are drawn from the Groningen Growth and Development Centre 10-sector database, which provides standardized data on countries' employment and (real) value added by sector over the period 1950–2005 (see Timmer and De Vries 2009). South Africa was added to the sample, with data extracted from the South African standardized industry database (SASID) produced by Quantec. The sample for the analysis thus includes 12 high-income countries (of which 10 are OECD members), 11 upper-middle-income countries, and 5 lower-middle-income countries. Geographically, 10 of the countries are from Asia, 7 from Europe, 9 from Latin America and the Caribbean, 1 from North America, and 1 from Africa. The sample includes both countries that did and did not experience deindustrialization during the period of analysis. The focus of the analysis is on the period 1985–2005.

Table 3.1 summarizes the trends in value added (level and share in total value added), employment (level and share in total employment), and productivity in the manufacturing sectors of the sample countries. In 23 out of the

Table 3.1. Summary of trends in manufacturing performance among sample countries, 1985–2005

	%Δ level manuf. VA	%Δ level manuf. employment	Δ share manuf. VA	Δ share manuf. employment	%Δ manuf. productivity
Argentina	44	−22	−3	−7	84
Bolivia	105	204	1	6	−32
Brazil	38	23	−2	−2	13
Chile	156	43	−3	−2	79
Colombia	77	73	−1	−0	2
Costa Rica	176	92	1	−2	44
Hong Kong	−4	−75	−7	−29	287
Indonesia	317	106	10	3	102
India	264	73	2	2	111
Japan	42	−21	−1	−6	79
Korea	416	21	14	−5	327
Mexico	77	40	1	−2	27
Malaysia	526	166	12	8	136
Peru	64	21	−0	−2	35
Philippines	103	58	−1	−0	28
Singapore	355	55	5	−4	194
Thailand	432	165	16	7	101
Taiwan	175	9	−5	−6	152
Venezuela	26	−0	−4	−7	26
South Africa	43	0	−2	−2	42
Denmark	−3	−26	−6	−6	32
Spain	65	31	−3	−4	26
France	44	−25	−1	−7	91
Italy	22	−10	−3	−5	35
Netherlands	54	−10	−2	−6	71
Sweden	116	−26	7	−5	191
UK	22	−37	−6	−10	94
USA	80	−19	0	−7	123

Note: %Δ refers to net changes in percentage points over the whole period 1985–2005; VA is value added.
Source: derived from Groningen Growth and Development Centre data and Quantec South African Standardised Industry Database (http://www.ggdc.net/databases/10_sector.htm http://www.quantec.co.za/data/easydata-rsa-standardised-industry).

28 countries manufacturing declined as a share of total employment—these are the instances which would be classified as deindustrialization as conventionally defined. The exceptions in this regard are the relatively low-income cases of Bolivia, India, Indonesia, Malaysia, and Thailand. In 17 of the 23 cases this decline in the share of manufacturing in total employment was accompanied by a decline in the share of manufacturing in total value added. There are no instances in which the share of manufacturing in total value added declined concomitant with an increase in the share of manufacturing in total employment. In the majority of these cases in which manufacturing declined as a share of total value added and total employment, the absolute level of manufacturing employment (though not of manufacturing value added) also fell. Declines in manufacturing as a share of total employment and value added were particularly strong and generalized among the developed countries of the sample, as would be expected. However, Argentina, Brazil, Chile, Colombia, Hong Kong, Peru, Philippines, Taiwan, Venezuela, and South Africa are the developing countries in the sample in which manufacturing declined both as a share of value added and employment. These might be regarded as instances of 'premature deindustrialization' in that they are deindustrializing at levels of income per capita that are significantly lower than the levels at which advanced countries deindustrialized earlier.

In analysing changes in manufacturing employment internationally, we begin by decomposing changes in the level of manufacturing employment into two components: changes in the value added of the sector, and changes in the labour-intensity of that sector. The object is to understand how much of each country's change in manufacturing employment is associated with changes in the overall size of manufacturing, and how much with changes in the labour-intensity of that production. The separation of these two vectors is useful in distinguishing different types of deindustrialization where it has occurred. For instance, a given fall in manufacturing employment could be associated with either a falling labour-intensity of production or with a shrinkage of manufacturing as a whole (or, of course, with a combination of these factors). These two processes would be very different, even if associated with the same change in manufacturing employment.

Let L_{ijt} be the employment in sector *i* in country *j* at time *t*, i.e. $L_{jt} = \sum_{i=1}^{n} L_{ijt}$, where sector *i* is manufacturing throughout. Then as an identity, $L_{ijt} \equiv \phi_{ijt} Q_{ijt}$, where Q_{ijt} is manufacturing value added, and ϕ_{ijt} is the labour-intensity of manufacturing, measured as $\frac{L_{ijt}}{Q_{ijt}}$. This is the inverse of the labour-productivity in the manufacturing sector (that is, labour-productivity in terms per person and not per hour). Then the change in employment in a given sector over a given period *h* is given as follows

$$\Delta L_{ij} = \phi_{ijt}Q_{ijt} - \phi_{ijt-h}Q_{ijt-h}$$

$$= \underbrace{(\phi_{ijt} - \phi_{ijt-h})\left(\frac{Q_{ijt-h} + Q_{ijt}}{2}\right)}_{\text{labour-intensity effect}} + \underbrace{(Q_{ijt} - Q_{ijt-h})\left(\frac{\phi_{ijt-h} + \phi_{ijt}}{2}\right)}_{\text{sector growth effect}}.$$

The labour-intensity effect is the change in the number of manufacturing jobs associated with the changing labour-intensity of manufacturing. Since labour-intensity is defined as the inverse of labour-productivity, this is equivalent to the change in manufacturing employment associated with changes in productivity in manufacturing. The sector growth effect is the change in the level of manufacturing employment that is associated with a change in the level of manufacturing value added. Where $\Delta L_{ij} < 0$, the labour-intensity and the sector growth effects can be thought of as the two components of 'absolute deindustrialization' (referring to a fall in the level of manufacturing employment).

Deindustrialization associated predominantly (at least in this 'accounting' sense) with one or other of the two effects could have different causes and implications. On the one hand, a loss of manufacturing jobs associated primarily with the sector growth effect might suggest that the issue is primarily one of the manufacturing sector as a whole and its lack of dynamism. On the other hand, a loss of manufacturing jobs associated primarily with the labour-intensity effect might suggest that the manufacturing sector as a whole is not necessarily in decline, but that the 'problem' pertains more to its labour-absorbing capacity.

The cross-country results from this decomposition are summarized graphically in Figure 3.1. Each point in the scatterplot denotes the combination of the labour-intensity effect (x-coordinate) and sector growth effect (y-coordinate) for a particular country. Two points are shown for each country: the initial point, indicated with a square marker, is for the period 1985–95, while the second point is for the period 1995–2005. It should thus be noted that the length of a line of course does not indicate the size of the effects (these can be observed from the coordinates of the points), but just the extent of how different the country's dynamics are between the two periods. The values are normalized in terms of the country's manufacturing employment at the beginning of the period, meaning that the coordinates of each point represent the contribution of that effect to the percentage change in manufacturing employment for that country. That is, the labour-intensity effect is shown as $(\phi_{ijt} - \phi_{ijt-h})\left(\frac{Q_{ijt-h} + Q_{ijt}}{2}\right)\left(\frac{100}{L_{ijt-h}}\right)$ and the sector growth effect

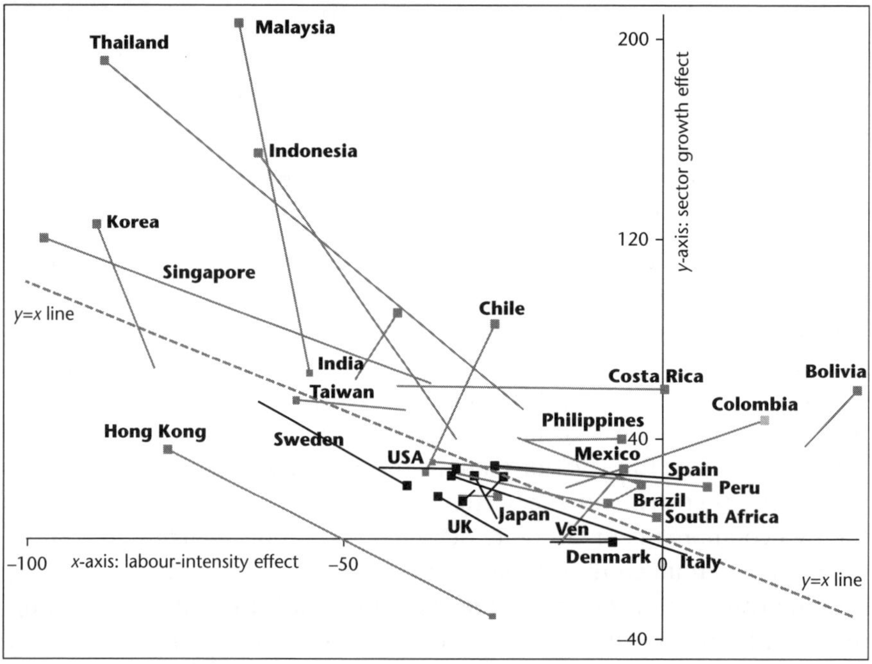

Figure 3.1. Decomposition of change in the level of manufacturing employment: 1985–95 and 1995–2005

Note: Square marker refers to 1985–95; end of line refers to 1995–2005. Argentina, France, and the Netherlands are included in the chart, but are not labelled for reasons of space; these are the short lines located nearby the UK and Japan. Ven denotes Venezuela.
Source: author's illustration.

as $(Q_{ijt} - Q_{ijt-h})\left(\frac{\phi_{ijt-h}+\phi_{ijt}}{2}\right)\left(\frac{100}{L_{ijt-h}}\right)$, summing to the percentage change in sectoral employment $\frac{100\,\Delta L_{ij}}{L_{ijt-h}}$. Developed countries are shown in black and developing countries in grey.

The results shown in the chart can be elucidated with the example of Korea. The initial coordinates of Korea (–89; 126) indicate that between 1985 and 1995 the fall in manufacturing labour-intensity accounted for a 89 per cent fall in the level of Korea's manufacturing employment, and the growth of manufacturing value added accounted for a 126 per cent increase in manufacturing employment. The sum of these two effects, 37 per cent, is the actual percentage increase in the level of manufacturing employment in Korea over the period 1985–95. The coordinates of Korea for the period 1995–2005, denoted by the end point of the line for Korea, are (–80; 68). Korea experienced a 12 per cent decline in the level of manufacturing jobs over this period, which is the sum of these coordinates. Decomposing this decline, the reduction in the labour-intensity of manufacturing accounted for an 80 per cent decline in Korea's manufacturing employment, which was mostly mitigated by a 68 per cent increase in employment associated with growth in manufacturing value added.

The position of a point in the north-east quadrant indicates that both the labour-intensity and sector growth effects were positive, such that the change in the labour-intensity of manufacturing and the growth in manufacturing value added each accounted for manufacturing employment creation, with unambiguously positive manufacturing employment growth. Conversely, the location of a point in the south-west quadrant indicates that the change in labour-intensity and the change in manufacturing sector size each accounted for negative manufacturing employment growth, with an unambiguously negative change in manufacturing employment. A point in the north-west quadrant indicates that the drop in labour-intensity accounted for a negative change in manufacturing employment while the sector growth accounted for a positive change in manufacturing employment. The position of a point in this quadrant lying above the diagonal $y = x$ line would indicate that the positive sector growth effect outweighed the negative labour-intensity effect, hence net manufacturing job creation, as with the example of the initial point of Korea (1985–95). Below the line in this quadrant indicates the reverse, and thus net manufacturing job loss, as with Korea in the period 1995–2005. Finally, a point in the south-east quadrant points to a case where the rise in labour-intensity accounted for a positive change in manufacturing employment while the change in sector size accounted for a negative change in manufacturing employment. A country in the quadrant above the diagonal $y = x$ line would have had net manufacturing employment creation, with the positive labour-intensity outweighing the negative sector growth effect, with a country below the diagonal line having had net manufacturing employment loss. Overall, any point falling below/to the left of the dashed diagonal line shows manufacturing employment loss for that country, while any point above/to the right of the diagonal line shows manufacturing employment growth.

Bolivia is the only country in which both the labour-intensity and sector growth effects were positive in both 1985–95 and 1995–2005. That is, both an increase in labour-intensity in manufacturing and growth in manufacturing value added contributed to growth in the level of manufacturing employment. Note that Bolivia has the second lowest levels of income per capita in the sample. Both components were positive in the first period, but not the second in Colombia, Peru, and (marginally) in Costa Rica. Somewhat surprisingly, Spain is the only country in which both components were positive in the second period, but not the first.

The paucity of observations in the north-east quadrant suggests that, as a stylized fact, it is unusual for manufacturing to grow (in real value added) while simultaneously becoming more labour-intensive. This is especially the case at higher levels of income per capita. This may be related to the fact that labour-intensity is essentially the inverse of labour-productivity, and high and increasing labour-productivity is central to sustainable growth in manufacturing value added. A possible policy implication arising out of this observation, where countries wish to maximize job creation in manufacturing, may be that a focus on accelerating value added in manufacturing may be a preferable route to go rather than trying to maximize the labour-absorbing capacity of any given level of manufacturing value added. This could have implications, *inter alia*, for the specific types of manufacturing activities that a country may choose to prioritize, given the typically high degree of heterogeneity among manufacturing subsectors.

There is a clustering of points in the north-west quadrant, for both periods and among both developed and developing countries. For points in this quadrant, there was real growth in manufacturing value added, but manufacturing became less labour-intensive. Within this quadrant, most developing countries fall above the dotted diagonal line, indicating that the positive sector growth effect outweighed the negative labour-intensity effect such that there was net growth in the level of manufacturing employment—with the reverse evident for developed countries.

A clear regional clustering is evident. Developing Asian countries are grouped towards the top left of the chart, with large and positive sector growth effects and large and negative labour-intensity effects. This is indicative of their strong manufacturing performance, both in value added and in productivity. Apart from Japan, the one Asian country that is an exception to this pattern is the Philippines. The Philippines has been dubbed an 'honorary Latin American country' due to its economic structure and development trajectory being more akin to Latin America than Asia, and indeed here the Philippines fits in well with most Latin American countries. A common trend is also evident when comparing the two periods for Asian countries. Recall that the square point marks each country's observation for the initial period. In the second period (1995–2005), the sector growth and labour-intensity effects are both relatively smaller (as a percentage of the initial level of employment in each period) than in the first period (1985–95). While India—the lowest income and least industrialized Asian country in the sample—fits the general pattern of the Asian countries, the only difference is that in the second period the labour-intensity effect becomes a bit more negative than in the first period (note how the line for India slopes down and to the left, whereas the lines for the other Asian countries slope down and to the right). A further commonality to the developing Asian countries (excluding the Philippines) is in the magnitude of the difference between the two periods, as shown by their relatively lengthy lines.

Latin American countries are clustered towards the right. Compared to the developing Asian countries, they have relatively low sector growth effects and the labour-intensity effects are either positive or less negative than in the case of Asian countries. Recall that the labour-intensity effect can be thought of as an inverse labour-productivity effect. The difference between the results for Asia and Latin America fits in with the fact that the former generally had higher growth in both value added and productivity in manufacturing than the latter. The contrast between Latin American and Asian countries can be illustrated with a comparison of manufacturing performance in Korea and Venezuela. As can be seen from Table 3.1, these two countries experienced roughly similar trends in the level of manufacturing employment between the two periods. However, the performance is vastly different when it comes to manufacturing value added and productivity, with growth of these variables several times higher in the case of Korea than in the case of Venezuela. South Africa—the only African country in the sample, and with a level of income per capita and economic structure similar to Brazil—is similar to the Latin American countries.

Unlike most developing countries, all developed countries in both periods (except Spain) fall below the dotted diagonal line, indicating an absolute contraction in manufacturing employment. For all these countries—except Denmark and Italy in the second period where even the sector growth effect was negative—the positive sector growth effect was outweighed by a larger negative labour-intensity effect. This would be associated with the generally more advanced deindustrialization at higher levels of income per capita. Although the inverted-U relationship between manufacturing employment and income per capita refers to the share of manufacturing in total employment, in advanced deindustrialization even the level of manufacturing employment is likely to fall, as is evident amongst almost all developed countries shown here.

Next, we analyse changes in the *share* of manufacturing in total employment, by decomposing changes in manufacturing employment share into components associated with changes in manufacturing labour-intensity, share of manufacturing in GDP, and aggregate labour-productivity. As noted earlier, deindustrialization is conventionally defined as a decline in the share of manufacturing in total employment.

Therefore, we define σ_{ijt} as the share of manufacturing in total employment and with the following terms as previously defined: L_{ijt} and Q_{ijt} as employment and value added respectively (in sector i manufacturing) in country j and at time t, and ϕ_{ijt} is the labour-intensity of manufacturing, measured as $\frac{L_{ijt}}{Q_{ijt}}$. We further define $\theta_{jt} = \frac{Q_{jt}}{L_{jt}}$, the aggregate labour-productivity, δ_{ijt}, the share of manufacturing in total value added in country j at time t, measured as $\frac{Q_{ijt}}{Q_{jt}}$, and Q_{jt}, the total value added (which can be a proxy for GDP) of country j at time t.

Next, the following identity can be set up to express the share of manufacturing in total employment as a product of the labour-intensity of manufacturing, the share of manufacturing in total value added, and aggregate (economywide) labour-productivity

$$\sigma_{ijt} \equiv \frac{L_{ijt}}{L_{jt}} \equiv \phi_{ijt}\delta_{ijt}\theta_{jt}$$

This allows for a separation of changes in the share of manufacturing in total employment into components associated with changes in manufacturing labour-intensity, share of manufacturing in total value added, and economy-wide labour-productivity respectively, as follows:[4]

$$\sigma_{ijt} \equiv \underbrace{\frac{1}{6}(\phi_{ijt} - \phi_{ijt\ h})\{(\delta_{ijt-h}\theta_{jt\ h} + \delta_{ijt}\theta_{jt}) + (\theta_{jt-h} + \theta_{jt})(\delta_{ijt\ h} + \delta_{ijt})\}}_{\text{labour–intensity effect}} +$$

$$\underbrace{\frac{1}{6}(\delta_{ijt} - \delta_{ijt\ h})\{(\phi_{ijt\ h}\theta_{jt-h} + \phi_{ijt}\theta_{jt}) + (\theta_{jt-h} + \theta_{jt})(\phi_{ijt-h} + \phi_{ijt})\}}_{\text{sector–share effect}} +$$

$$\underbrace{\frac{1}{6}(\theta_{ijt} - \theta_{ijt\ h})\{(\phi_{ijt-h}\delta_{jt-h} + \phi_{ijt}\delta_{jt}) + (\delta_{jt-h} + \delta_{jt})(\phi_{ijt-h} + \phi_{ijt})\}}_{\text{aggregate labour–productivity effect}} .$$

The labour-intensity effect measures the contribution of changes in the labour-intensity of manufacturing (that is, the inverse of labour-productivity in manufacturing) to changes in the share of manufacturing in total employment. The sector-share effect measures changes in the share of manufacturing in total value added to changes in the share of manufacturing in total employment. The aggregate labour-productivity effect measures the contribution of changes in aggregate labour-productivity to changes in the share of manufacturing in total employment. This is something of a residual in this decomposition and the results are not of primary interest here.

The labour-intensity and sector-share effects of the sample countries and shown in Figure 3.2, in percentage form. Each point shows the combination of the labour-intensity effect (x-coordinate) and sector-share effect (y-coordinate) for a country. For each country, the initial point, denoted with a square marker, is for the period 1985–95, while the second point is for the period 1995–2005. As in Figure 3.1, the length of a line shows the change for a

[4] See the Appendix for the derivation of these terms.

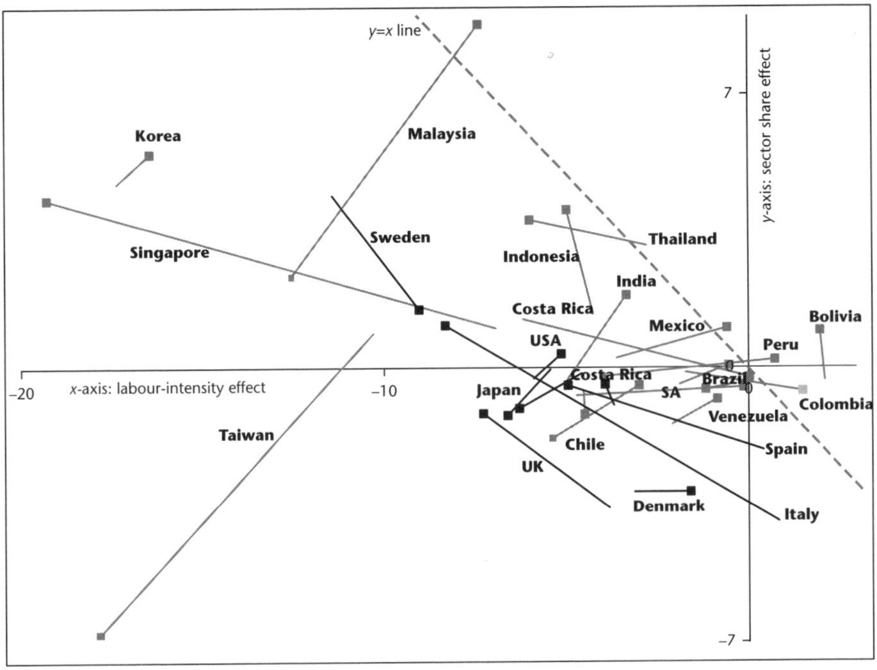

Figure 3.2. Partial results from decomposition of changes in the share of manufacturing employment: 1985–95 and 1995–2005

Note: Only the labour-intensity and sector-share effects are shown here, not the aggregate labour-productivity effect. Square marker refers to 1985–95; end of line refers to 1995–2005. The Philippines is included in the chart but is not labelled for reasons of space.
Source: author's illustrations.

country between the two periods and not the size of the two effects, it is the coordinates of the two points that indicate the relative size of the effects in each period. Again, developed countries are shown in black and developing countries in grey.

For example, in the UK during the period 1985–95, the labour-intensity effect was –7.3, the sector-share effect was –1.2, and the aggregate labour-productivity effect was 4 (all in percentage points). These sum to –4.5; this is the actual decline in the share of manufacturing in total employment this period (from 21 per cent to 16.5 per cent of total employment). The values of the labour-intensity and sector-share effects can be read off the coordinates in Figure 3.2: for the UK for the period 1985–95, the coordinates of the square marker are (–7.3; –1.2) indicating the labour-intensity and sector-share effects, respectively. For the period 1995–2005, as can be seen from the terminal point of the line of the UK, the labour-intensity and sector-share effects were –3.8 and –3.6 respectively. Combined with the aggregate labour-productivity effect of 2.1, these sum to −5.3, which is the percentage points by which manufacturing declined as a share of total employment in the UK during this period.

Since the decomposition of employment shares is three-dimensional, the location of a point in this two-dimensional figure (which excludes the aggregate labour-productivity effect) cannot be as neatly interpreted as in the first decomposition, which decomposed changes in the level of manufacturing employment into just two dimensions. In Figure 3.2, the location of a point in the north-east quadrant indicates that both the labour-intensity and sector-share effects contributed positively to growth in the share of manufacturing in total employment. The net change in the share of manufacturing in total employment would, however, depend on the sign and relative magnitude of the aggregate labour-productivity effect as well.[5] Only in Peru and Bolivia—which are two of the lowest-income countries in the sample—and only for the first period 1985–95 are points located in the north-east quadrant. This is indicative of the low probability of a country's manufacturing sector simultaneously becoming more labour-intensive and growing as a share of total value added, especially at higher levels of income per capita.

A location in the north-west quadrant indicates that, for that country and time period, manufacturing grew as a share of total value added but became less labour-intensive. Where the point falls to the right of the $y = x$ line, the positive share effect outweighs the negative labour-intensity effect, and conversely to the left of the line. Both the sector-share and labour-intensity effects are negative in the south-west quadrant, and unless their sum were outweighed by a positive aggregate labour-productivity effect there would have been a fall in the share of manufacturing in total employment for that country and time period. For a point located in the south-east quadrant, manufacturing became more labour-intensive but shrank as a share of total value added. In this quadrant, for a point to the right of the diagonal $y = x$ line the positive labour-intensity effect outweighed the negative sector-share effect, and vice versa.

The overwhelming majority of points are located either in the south-west quadrant, where manufacturing became less labour-intensive while shrinking as a share of total value added, or in the north-west quadrant to the left of the $y = x$ line, where manufacturing became less labour-intensive but grew as a share of total value added. Although the latter category comprises primarily developing countries, an interesting exception is that of Sweden, in which

[5] Note that the aggregate labour-productivity effect is positive in all cases except for the following: Mexico in the first period, Venezuela in both periods, and Spain (marginally) in the second period.

manufacturing grew as a share of total value added, in particular between 1995 and 2005.

The results also show up an interesting contrast between Asian and Latin American middle-income countries. With the exception of Taiwan in the first period, all the Asian newly industrialized countries (NICs) in both periods are in the north-west quadrant, with manufacturing becoming less labour-intensive (i.e. more productive) and growing as a share of value added. In middle-income Latin American countries such as Venezuela, Chile, Colombia in the second period, and Brazil, by contrast, both the labour-intensity and sector-share effects were negative in both periods. Despite the fact that manufacturing was generally a lower share of total value added in these countries than in the Asian NICs at the beginning of the period of analysis, manufacturing shrank as a share of total value added in the Latin American countries while growing further in the Asian NICs. It is also striking that the Asian NICs are located far out from the origin, indicating the size of both the sector-share and labour-intensity components, in contrast to the Latin American countries, Venezuela and Brazil in particular. These differences are surely not unrelated to the divergent growth performances of these two groups of middle-income countries during these periods of time.

Reflecting on the results from the decompositions, both of changes in the level and share of manufacturing employment, a fall in manufacturing employment (whether level or share) associated primarily with changes in the labour-intensity of production, is very different from a fall in manufacturing employment associated primarily with a declining level/share of manufacturing output. These two types of falling manufacturing employment are quite different phenomena, likely to have different causes, different implications for growth, and to require different policy interventions (should they be deemed undesirable). Given that labour-intensity refers here to the labour-intensity of value added, which is simply the inverse of labour-productivity, a decline in labour-intensity amounts to an increase in labour-productivity.

If a decrease in manufacturing employment share is primarily accounted for by falling labour-intensity of manufacturing, this calls into question the extent to which 'deindustrialization' is an appropriate characterization. This is especially relevant in cases where the manufacturing sector is growing in real terms as well as increasing its share of GDP. There could be various underlying economic causes behind falling labour-intensity in manufacturing, which might relate to the subsectoral composition of manufacturing and/or to processes within subsectors (including as a defensive response to cheap manufacturing imports from lower-wage countries). In an 'optimistic' scenario, falling labour-intensity could essentially amount to exogenous increases in labour-productivity, driven by factors such as improved skills or technology. Alternatively, falling labour-intensity could be caused by labour-displacing capital intensification. The actual causes of falling labour-intensity would vary across countries and time periods, and are not the focus of this study. The point is that a fall in the share of manufacturing employment that is mostly accounted for by falling labour-intensity of manufacturing (i.e. increasing labour-productivity of manufacturing) would not necessarily have a negative impact on growth. The impact on growth would be contingent on various conjunctural factors, including the causes of the fall in labour-intensity.

This is very different from the case where the fall in the share of manufacturing employment is associated primarily with a decline of the manufacturing sector as a share of GDP (and especially in cases such as the latter two, where manufacturing shrank in real terms as well). In such a scenario, an economy would be particularly at risk of losing out on the growth-pulling effects of manufacturing. This could be associated with a diminution of long-term growth prospects (although of course this would be contingent on the country's stage of development, on the nature of the manufacturing sectors in decline, of the sectors whose share of GDP is growing and so on). This strongly suggests the need to go deeper into the black box of falling share of manufacturing employment—as this chapter has attempted to do—before the effects on growth can be assumed.

One insight that emerges from this analysis is the significant heterogeneity of experiences that would be characterized as 'deindustrialization' when considered exclusively in terms of the share of manufacturing in total employment (as with the conventional denotation of deindustrialization). We would argue that a case in which the sector growth effect, sector-share effect, and aggregate labour-productivity effects are all positive and the decline in manufacturing employment level and/or share is accounted for entirely by a negative labour-intensity effect should not be characterized as deindustrialization in any real sense. If labour-productivity rises more rapidly in manufacturing than in the rest of the economy—as might be expected if manufacturing does indeed have the Kaldorian properties attributed to it—and if manufacturing does not increase its share of GDP commensurately, then the share of manufacturing in total employment would of course fall.

However, it does not seem meaningful to characterize such a process as deindustrialization, particularly when associating deindustrialization with negative implications for growth. Rather than defining deindustrialization in terms of the single dimension of falling share of manufacturing in total employment, as in the current literature, we propose that deindustrialization should be regarded as occurring when there is a sustained decline in both the share of manufacturing in total employment and the share of manufacturing in GDP.

3.4 From deindustrialization to reindustrialization?

In considering pathways to industrialization in the twenty-first century, the reality that there has been, and continues to be, deindustrialization in many countries needs to be taken into account. This implies that the challenge of industrialization may thus also entail 'reindustrialization'.

We have suggested that deindustrialization should appropriately be defined as a sustained decline in both the share of manufacturing in total employment and the share of manufacturing in GDP. Reindustrialization might be thought of as a sustained increase in both the share of manufacturing in total employment and the share of manufacturing in GDP. Naturally, this is not simply a case of 'inverse deindustrialization' as there would be different dynamics at work. It is likely that there is an asymmetry, in that reindustrialization is less likely to 'just happen' than is the case with a similar magnitude of deindustrialization.

We briefly review recent international experiences in which countries have experienced an increase in their share of manufacturing in GDP, and thereafter where manufacturing has increased as a share of total employment.

There are 52 countries in which manufacturing has increased as a share of GDP since 2000.[6] These are listed in Table 3.2, excluding the 15 countries in which the increase was less than one percentage point. Almost all of these are low- or middle-income countries. In 18 of these 52 countries, the increase in the share of manufacturing in GDP followed increases in the share of manufacturing in GDP in the preceding decade (1990–2000), while for the other 34 countries the recent increase followed a fall in the preceding decade. This latter group might be cases of reindustrialization, at least on the value added side, but they could also be cases of manufacturing simply partially bouncing back from a previous decline without a structural reversal. In fact, there only appear to be about seven countries in which manufacturing declined as a share of GDP in the 1990s but increased by a greater magnitude since 2000. These are almost all low-income countries: Pakistan, Myanmar, Equatorial Guinea, Sudan, Mali, Liberia, and Burkina Faso.

The apparent paucity of cases in which manufacturing increases as a share of GDP, outweighing previous declines, is to some extent a result of the somewhat arbitrary points in time chosen here. Manufacturing would have grown in other countries over periods spanning these points. Nevertheless, this does underline how difficult it is for manufacturing to recover (as a share of GDP) after an earlier decline.

[6] All value added data here sourced from UN National Accounts database (http://unstats.un.org/unsd/snaama/Introduction.asp).

Table 3.2. Countries in which manufacturing increased as % GDP, 2000–7

Country	Change in manufacturing as % GDP	
	2000–7	1990–2000
Uruguay	6.5	−8.7
Uzbekistan	5.6	−8.4
Argentina	5.4	−9.0
Equatorial Guinea	4.9	−1.4
Oman	4.6	2.4
Mozambique	3.7	0.8
Pakistan	3.7	−1.2
Myanmar	3.6	−0.6
Lao	3.6	7.0
Suriname	3.2	4.6
Bangladesh	2.7	2.8
Belize	2.7	−4.4
Sudan	2.6	−1.9
Mali	2.5	−1.0
Madagascar	2.3	−4.3
Qatar	2.3	−7.3
Congo	2.2	−4.8
Vietnam	2.2	6.3
Jordan	2.1	−2.3
Zimbabwe	1.9	−10.6
Lesotho	1.9	4.1
Liberia	1.9	−1.7
Turkey	1.9	−2.8
Cambodia	1.8	8.1
Yemen	1.7	−2.6
Burkina Faso	1.6	−1.2
Swaziland	1.6	0.8
Nicaragua	1.5	−2.1
Lithuania	1.4	2.0
Ukraine	1.3	−15.5
North Korea	1.3	−14.1
Greece	1.2	−4.5
Thailand	1.2	8.7
Saint Lucia	1.1	−3.1
Albania	1.0	4.8
Syria	1.0	−4.0
Angola	1.0	−2.1

Note: Sample limited to countries in which the 2000–7 increase exceeds one percentage point.

Source: Data sourced from UN National Accounts (http://unstats.un.org/unsd/snaama/Introduction.asp).

Next, we briefly review some recent international experiences of employment creation in manufacturing. The focus is on employment creation in the decade up to the latest consistently available data (which does not extend beyond 2003). A decade is used for consistency (unless there is a specific reason to use a different period) and in order to look at sustainable manufacturing employment creation rather than short spurts of employment growth.

All data is derived from the ILO.[7] The figures cited should be treated as indicative. Furthermore, it should be noted that most low- and lower-middle-income countries are excluded from the data, although it is in these categories of countries that most manufacturing growth (particularly in terms of the share of total employment) would be expected.

Unusually for a developed country, Canada has seen increases in both the level and share of manufacturing employment from the early to the late 1990s (the latest available data is for 1998), although the share is not as high as it had been in the 1980s. In Ireland the level of manufacturing employment has grown steadily at a rate of 2.2 per cent per annum between 1993 and 2003 (there is a break in the series in 1998 and the effects of this are unclear), although it has declined as a share of total employment. In Italy the share of total employment in manufacturing has remained roughly steady since the mid-1980s, and although the level of manufacturing employment had earlier declined it has since been increasing from the mid 1990s onwards (data up to 2003).

There have been steady increases in the level of manufacturing employment but falls in the share of total employment in the decade up to 2003; in Ecuador (data up to 2002), Honduras (2.3 per cent manufacturing employment growth per annum from 1995–2002), and El Salvador (3.8 per cent growth per annum from 1992–2001). In Guatemala (up to 2002), both the level and share of manufacturing employment have been increasing. The Bahamas has experienced an almost continuous growth of manufacturing employment over the period for which data is available (2.8 per cent per annum for 1991–99), although it has remained low and stable as a percentage of total employment.

Brazil, surprisingly given the poor performance of its manufacturing sector, shows increases in both the level and share of manufacturing employment in the decade up to 2002 (although the share is not as high as it was in the 1980s), with an annual increase of 2.2 per cent in the period 1992–2002. There is however a break in the series in 2002 which may have artificially inflated this increase; if the year 2002 is excluded, the annual increase from 1992–2001 is 1.2 per cent per annum In Trinidad and Tobago the level of manufacturing employment has been increasing at a rate of 2.8 per cent per annum in the decade up to 2002, while the share has been fluctuating around a fairly constant level. In Nicaragua both the level and share of employment have been increasing (at a rate of 9.4 per cent per annum from 1993–2003, but excluding the years 2002 and 2003 where there are breaks in the series, just 2.8 per cent per annum). One consideration to be borne in mind regarding the figures from Latin America and the Caribbean is that some or all of the manufacturing jobs created (notably in countries such as Nicaragua, Mexico, Guatemala, and Honduras) is due to

[7] See: http://www.ilo.org/empelm/what/lang–en/WCMS_114240.

'maquila' production, which has less of the positive effects associated with manufacturing than would be the case in most non-maquila manufacturing.

In Egypt, data is only available up to 1995, but up to that point the level of manufacturing employment is increasing, but the share is fluctuating around a fairly constant level. The level of manufacturing employment in Mauritius has been increasing (2 per cent per annum in the five years up to 1999, the latest available date), but roughly steady as a share. Data for Hungary are available only up to 1998, but the couple of preceding years saw small increases in both the level and share.

Indonesia has seen significant and steady increases in both the share and level (4.4 per cent per annum from 1992–2002). The level of manufacturing employment in Malaysia has been on a general upward trend (2.4 per cent annual increases from 1992 to 2002) although declining a bit as a share since the mid-1990s. In Myanmar, data is available only up to 1998, but until that point both the level and share of manufacturing employment have been increasing (the former at 2 per cent per annum). In Pakistan the level of manufacturing employment has been increasing at 4 per cent per annum (1992–2002); the share had earlier fallen, but has since increased back to the high shares of the 1980s.

In the Philippines the level of manufacturing employment has been increasing (by 2.1 per cent per annum during 1991–2001) while the share has been fluctuating around a fairly constant level for some time. In Sri Lanka the level of manufacturing employment has been increasing though in a volatile fashion (data up to 1998) but the share falling. In Thailand both the level and share of manufacturing employment have been rising, with the number of manufacturing jobs increasing at 2.5 per cent per annum from 1993–2003. There is, however, a break in the series in 2002; if measured only up to 2001 the annual increases are 2.3 per cent. Both the level and share of manufacturing employment have also been increasing in Turkey: the level by 3.3 per cent per annum from 1990 to 2000 (the latest available), and the share from 14.2 per cent to 16.9 per cent.

There are thus a number of countries, especially in Asia, that have been experiencing increases in manufacturing employment—particularly in the level, less commonly in the share—in recent years. The annual rates of increase cited are (generally) for the most recent decade for which data is available, and faster rates of increase are of course evident for shorter periods, as well as in earlier periods. Of course, there are bound to be many more countries whose employment in services has grown than for manufacturing. As would be expected, these are particularly but not exclusively upper-middle- and higher-income countries.

3.5 Conclusions

The empirical analysis of changes in the level and share of manufacturing employment internationally over the period 1985–2005 brought out the heterogeneity of what could conventionally be characterized as deindustrialization. This heterogeneity relates in particular to the dynamics of manufacturing productivity. In some cases, decline in manufacturing employment is accounted for in the main by decreasing labour-intensity in manufacturing, which is equivalent to increasing labour-productivity. This is so particularly in fast-growing economies. Increasing labour-productivity in manufacturing was an important dynamic in the growth experiences of the East Asian NICs. This is a very different situation from where the manufacturing sector as a whole is in decline with contracting output.

A stylized fact that emerges is that it is highly unusual for manufacturing to grow (in terms of real value added) while simultaneously becoming more labour-intensive. This holds true especially at higher levels of income per capita. This observation again underlines the importance of increasing labour-productivity in manufacturing for manufacturing growth. It also poses a challenge for the role of manufacturing in labour absorption, especially in countries facing a problem of high rates of unemployment.

Reindustrialization after deindustrialization is likely to prove even more challenging than the earlier industrialization. Re-raising the share of manufacturing in a country's total employment (or GDP) in the twenty-first century would take greater 'effort' than was the case in the initial increase.

Developing countries that have deindustrialized may, in some ways, face the most acute challenges. Deindustrialization in developing countries can be considered 'premature', in the sense of commencing at lower levels of income per capita than was generally the case for deindustrialization in advanced economies. Furthermore, deindustrialization in developing countries could be associated with policy shifts—in particular trade and financial liberalization—rather than just with the 'maturation' of their economic structure; see Palma (2005, 2008) for more on this. Premature deindustrialization is likely to have particularly severe negative effects on long-term growth, as less of the benefits of industrialization would already have been captured. Competition from China and other low-cost manufacturers in Asia tends to affect developing countries especially hard, as they are more likely to be competing in the manufacture of similar types of goods. Developing countries can be in a situation of being unable to compete with China on cost grounds, yet lacking the technology, skills, and market access to compete higher up the value chain with developed countries.

Reindustrialization may be particularly necessary, as well as viable, in countries where 'premature' deindustrialization has been triggered or exacerbated by policy-related factors such as trade or financial liberalization. Policy interventions might be able to reverse some of such premature deindustrialization. However, it needs to be recognized that it is generally difficult to build up lost production capacity, because of micro-level factors such as loss in market share, fixed capital, networks both in input sourcing and output markets, skills, tacit knowledge, and the other institutional qualities that are built up over time. Moreover, where the international market structure has changed since deindustrialization—for instance, due to the increasing dominance of low-cost producers in labour-intensive activities—this can make re-entry much more difficult than earlier entry would have been. Even maintaining a market position can be difficult in the current global environment.

These challenges, along with the stylized facts of the changes in sectoral composition internationally, do not detract from the importance of developing the manufacturing sector and of the desirability of (re)industrialization, especially in middle- and lower-income countries. They do, however, underline how difficult this can be. The types of policies relevant to meeting these challenges are beyond the scope of this chapter. What we can say is that, if countries want to pursue (re)industrialization in the twenty-first century, it cannot be 'business as usual'. Decisive and effective industrial policies are required, along with a macroeconomic environment that does not contribute to the further emasculation of industry

Appendix 3.1 Technical details of decomposition

This appendix sets out the derivation of the three components in the decomposition of the share of manufacturing in total employment presented in Section 3.3; all terms are as defined there.

$$\sigma_{ijt} \equiv \frac{L_{ijt}}{L_{jt}} \equiv \phi_{ijt}\delta_{ijt}\theta_{jt}$$

hence $\Delta\sigma_{ij} = \phi_{ijt}\delta_{ijt}\theta_{jt} - \phi_{ijt-h}$

$$= \underbrace{(\phi_{ijt} - \phi_{ijt-h})\left(\frac{\delta_{ijt\ h}\theta_{jt\ h} + \delta_{ijt}\theta_{jt}}{2}\right)}_{\text{labour-intensity effect}_1} + \underbrace{(\delta_{ijt} - \delta_{ijt\ h})\left(\frac{\theta_{jt-h} + \theta_{jt}}{2}\right)\left(\frac{\phi_{ijt-h} + \phi_{ijt}}{2}\right)}_{\text{sector-share effect}_1} +$$

$$\underbrace{(\theta_{jt} - \theta_{jt-h})\left(\frac{\delta_{ijt-h} + \delta_{ijt}}{2}\right)\left(\frac{\phi_{ijt-h} + \phi_{ijt}}{2}\right)}_{\text{aggregate labour-productivity effect}_1}$$

$$= \underbrace{(\phi_{ijt} - \phi_{ijt-h})\left(\frac{\delta_{ijt-h} + \delta_{ijt}}{2}\right)\left(\frac{\theta_{jt-h} + \theta_{jt}}{2}\right)}_{\text{labour–intensity effect}_2} + \underbrace{(\delta_{ijt} - \delta_{ijt\ h})\left(\frac{\theta_{jt-h}\phi_{ijt-h} + \theta_{jt}\phi_{ijt}}{2}\right)}_{\text{sector–share effect}_2} +$$

$$\underbrace{(\theta_{jt} - \theta_{jt\ h})\left(\frac{\delta_{ijt-h} + \delta_{ijt}}{2}\right)\left(\frac{\phi_{ijt-h} + \phi_{ijt}}{2}\right)}_{\text{aggregate labour–productivity effect}_2}$$

$$= \underbrace{(\phi_{ijt} - \phi_{ijt\ h})\left(\frac{\delta_{ijt-h} + \delta_{ijt}}{2}\right)\left(\frac{\theta_{jt-h} + \theta_{jt}}{2}\right)}_{\text{labour–intensity effect}_3} +$$

$$\underbrace{(\delta_{ijt} - \delta_{ijt-h})\left(\frac{\theta_{jt-h} + \theta_{jt}}{2}\right)\left(\frac{\phi_{ijt-h} + \phi_{ijt}}{2}\right)}_{\text{sector– share effect}_3} + \underbrace{(\theta_{jt} - \theta_{jt\ h})\left(\frac{\delta_{ijt-h}\phi_{ijt\ h} + \delta_{ijt}\phi_{ijt}}{2}\right)}_{\text{aggregate labour–productivity effect}_3}$$

Taking the means of each of the three terms from the three alternative formulations, the labour-intensity effect = $\frac{1}{6}(\phi_{ijt} - \phi_{ijt-h})\{(\delta_{ijt-h}\theta_{jt-h} + \delta_{ijt}\theta_{jt}) + (\theta_{jt-h} + \theta_{jt})(\delta_{ijt-h} + \delta_{ijt})\}$ the sector-share effect = $\frac{1}{6}(\delta_{ijt} - \delta_{ijt-h})\{(\phi_{ijt-h}\theta_{jt-h} + \phi_{ijt}\theta_{jt}) + (\theta_{jt-h} + \theta_{jt})(\phi_{ijt-h} + \phi_{ijt})\}$ and the aggregate labour-productivity effect = $\frac{1}{6}(\theta_{ijt} - \theta_{ijt-h})\{(\phi_{ijt-h}\delta_{jt-h} + \phi_{ijt}\delta_{jt}) + (\delta_{jt-h} + \delta_{jt})(\phi_{ijt-h} + \phi_{ijt})\}$.

These three components sum exactly to the change in the share of employment in sector in the total employment of country *j* over the period *h*.

References

Alderson, A. (1999). 'Explaining Deindustrialization: Globalization, Failure, or Success?', *American Sociological Review*, 64 (5): 701–21.

Atesoglu, H. (1993). 'Manufacturing and Economic Growth in the United States', *Applied Economics*, 25 (1): 67–9.

Bairam, E. (1991). 'Economic Growth and Kaldor's Law: The Case of Turkey, 1925–78', *Applied Economics*, 23 (8): 1277–80.

Beheshti, M., and R. Sadighnia (2006). 'Testing Kaldor's Engine of Growth Hypothesis in Iran's Economy', *Quarterly Iranian Economic Research*, 28: 39–60.

Bernat, G. (1996). 'Does Manufacturing Matter? A Spatial Econometric View of Kaldor's Laws', *Journal of Regional Science*, 36 (3): 463–77.

Blankenburg S., J. G. Palma, and F. Tregenna (2008). 'Structuralism'. In L. Blume and S. Durlauf (eds), *The New Palgrave: A Dictionary of Economics*, 2nd edition. Basingstoke: Palgrave Macmillan.

Diaz Bautista, A. (2003). 'Mexico's Industrial Engine of Growth: Cointegration and Causality', *Momento Economico*, 126: 34–41.

Drakopoulos, S., and I. Theodossiou (1991). 'Kaldorian Approach to Greek Economic Growth', *Applied Economics*, 23 (10): 1683–89.

Felipe, J. (1998). 'The Role of the Manufacturing Sector in Southeast Asian Development: A Test of Kaldor's First Law', *Journal of Post Keynesian Economics*, 20 (3): 463–85.

Fingleton, B., and J. S. L. McCombie (1998). 'Increasing Returns and Economic Growth: Some Evidence for Manufacturing from the European Union Regions', *Oxford Economic Papers*, 50 (1): 89–105.

Hansen, J., and J. Zhang (1996). 'A Kaldorian Approach to Regional Economic Growth in China', *Applied Economics*, 28 (6): 679–85.

Harris, R., and E. Lau (1998). 'Verdoorn's Law and Increasing Returns to Scale in the UK Regions, 1968–91: Some New Estimates Based on the Cointegration Approach', *Oxford Economic Papers*, 50 (2): 201–9.

Harris, R., and A. Liu (1999). 'Verdoorn's Law and Increasing Returns to Scale: Country Estimates Based on the Cointegration Approach', *Applied Economics Letters*, 6 (1): 29–33.

Kaldor, N. (1978). *Further Essays on Economic Theory*. London: Duckworth.

—— (1980). *Essays on Economic Stability and Growth*, 2nd edition. London: Duckworth.

Knell, M. (2004). 'Structural Change and the Kaldor-Verdoorn Law in the 1990s', *Revue d'Economie Industrielle*, 105: 71–83.

Kucera, D., and W. Milberg (2003). 'Deindustrialization and Changes in Manufacturing Trade: Factor Content Calculations for 1978–1995', *Review of World Economics*, 139 (4): 601–24.

Leon-Ledesma, M. (2000). 'Economic Growth and Verdoorn's Law in the Spanish Regions, 1962–91', *International Review of Applied Economics*, 14 (1): 55–69.

Necmi, S. (1999). 'Kaldor's Growth Analysis Revisited', *Applied Economics*, 31 (5): 653–60.

Palma, G. (2005). 'Four Sources of "De-Industrialisation" and a New Concept of the "Dutch Disease". In J. A. Ocampo (ed.), *Beyond Reforms: Structural Dynamics and Macroeconomic Vulnerability*. New York: Stanford University Press and World Bank.

—— (2008). 'Deindustrialisation, Premature Deindustrialisation, and the Dutch Disease'. In L. Blume and S. Durlauf (eds), *The New Palgrave: A Dictionary of Economics*, 2nd edition. Basingstoke: Palgrave Macmillian.

Pons-Novell, J., E., and E. Viladecans-Marsal (1999). 'Kaldor's Laws and Spatial Dependence: Evidence for the European Regions', *Regional Studies*, 33 (5): 443–51.

Rowthorn, R., and K. Coutts (2004). 'Commentary: Deindustrialisation and the Balance of Payments in Advanced Economies', *Cambridge Journal of Economics*, 28 (5): 767–90.

Rowthorn, R., and R. Ramaswamy (1997). 'Deindustrialization: Causes and Implications'. Working Paper 97/42. Washington, DC: IMF.

Rowthorn, R., and J. Wells (1987). *De-industrialization and Foreign Trade*. Cambridge: Cambridge University Press.

Saeger, S. (1997). 'Globalization and Deindustrialization: Myth and Reality in the OECD', *Review of World Economics*, 133 (4): 579–608.

Singh, A. (1977). 'UK Industry and the World Economy: A Case of De-industrialisation?', *Cambridge Journal of Economics*, 1 (2): 113–36.

Timmer M., and G. J. de Vries (2009). 'Structural Change and Growth Accelerations in Asia and Latin America: A New Sectoral Data Set, *Cliometrica*, 3 (2): 165–90.

Tregenna, F. (2009). 'Characterising Deindustrialisation: An Analysis of Changes in Manufacturing Employment and GDP Internationally', *Cambridge Journal of Economics*, 33 (3): 433–66.

Wells, H., and A. P. Thirlwall (2003). 'Testing Kaldor's Laws Across the Countries of Africa', *African Development Review*, 15 (2–3): 89–105.

4

Emerging Patterns of Structural Change in Manufacturing

Nobuya Haraguchi and Gorazd Rezonja

4.1 Introduction[1]

What did it take for rich countries to become economically more developed than others? One explanation can be found in the strand of growth literature linking the level of economic development with industrialization, which contends that changes in the structure of production (structural change) are accompanied by economic growth.

Referring to Simon Kuznets, Syrquin states that

> ...growth and structural change are strongly interrelated. Once we abandon the world of homothetic preferences, neutral productivity growth with no systematic sectoral effect, perfect mobility, and markets that adjust instantaneously, structural change emerges as a central feature of the process of development and an essential element in accounting for the rate of pattern of growth. It can retard growth if its pace is too slow or its direction inefficient, but it can contribute to growth if it improves the allocation of resources.... Syrquin (2007: 4)

The term 'structural change' most commonly refers to long-term changes in the composition of an aggregate, which may be attributable to changes in the relative significance of sectors of the economy,[2] to changes in the location of economic activity (urbanization) and to other concomitant aspects of industrialization, which are jointly referred to as structural change.

[1] We thank Niki Rodousakis for stylistic revision and Walliya Premchit for helpful advice on econometrics.

[2] In this chapter, 'sector' describes economic activities at the level of agriculture, industry, and services (or in the primary, secondary, and tertiary sectors). Manufacturing, which belongs to the industrial sector, is divided into subsectors termed 'manufacturing industries' in this chapter.

Studies on changes in the structure of production gained attention over half a century ago, especially with the work of Kuznets (1957), which linked manufacturing development with rising per capita income. Other frequently cited studies on structural change are those of Fisher (1939), Clark (1940), Chenery and Syrquin (1975), and Kader (1985). Although Chenery (1960) and Chenery and Taylor (1968) focused on development patterns in the manufacturing sector, structural change within the manufacturing sector has since then not been studied in depth. On account of renewed interest in industrial policy for economic development in recent years (see Chapter 1 of this volume), revisiting the work of Chenery (1960) and Chenery and Taylor (1968) may be timely. As argued by Lin (2010), a country's optimal industrial structure will differ according to its stage of development and its given characteristics. Countries at different development stages have comparative advantages in different industries. Identifying latent comparative advantages and understanding their evolution helps countries pursue welfare-enhancing industrial structural change, something many developing countries have been struggling to achieve (McMillan and Rodrik 2011). This chapter will demonstrate the likely evolution of industrial structure in countries with different characteristics.[3] The aim is to provide countries with a reference point to identify their comparative advantages.

The motivation of this chapter is twofold. First, improvements in data availability and estimation methods make possible the identification of benchmark growth patterns for manufacturing sectors given a given country's stage of economic development (indicated by the proxy measure of GDP per capita). This reflects that for a given income level, there may be a corresponding production level of a specific manufacturing industry, which tends to rise with income growth. However, when income level rises to a certain point, steady-state production will be reached and the production level may begin to decline. Hence, structural change is reflected in emergence of new types of industries to the detriment of previous ones. Based on this analysis, we identify the growth potential of different manufacturing industries at different development stages and classify the manufacturing industries accordingly.

The second motivation for this chapter is to classify manufacturing industries based on the timing of their contribution to the economy, their growth potential, the influence of given country characteristics on their development patterns, and the reliability of such patterns.

[3] A distinction is made between country characteristics over which a government has little or no control, such as population size, geographic area, climate, or availability of natural resources, and other country-specific characteristics such as policies and institutional reforms over which the government does have control. The first set of characteristics are referred to as country-given characteristics, the second set as country-specific characteristics.

Once the general growth patterns of manufacturing industries are established for countries with different characteristics, they can be used to examine the development patterns of countries with comparable characteristics for policy purposes. Any deviations of the actual developments from the benchmarks can then be explained by future research, possibly by looking into policy, historical, and institutional factors.

From this viewpoint, Section 4.2 reviews the seminal work of Chenery and others and conceptually and empirically examines their work in light of available data and econometric techniques that have improved significantly over the past four decades. In Section 4.3 an alternative model for assessing patterns of industrial development is proposed that takes account of the universal effects associated with income levels, the effect of country-given features such as market size or natural resources, as well as other country-specific characteristics such as policy regimes. In Section 4.4, we present the results of the regression analysis and construct benchmark growth patterns. By developing an industrial typology based on our results, policy implications are derived. Section 4.5 concludes by providing directions for future research.

4.2 Review of past models for estimating manufacturing value added

This section discusses the theoretical background of the analysis and derives an estimating equation for capturing the structural transformation for different manufacturing industries. Our methodology builds on Chenery's basic explanation of structural change in which the growth of a manufacturing industry depends on:

(i) the normal effect of universal factors that are related to the levels of income[4]

(ii) the effect of other general factors such as market size or natural resources over which the government has little or no control[5]

[4] The income effect includes both the supply and demand effect. The demand effect is usually associated with the fact that rising income leads to changes in the composition of demand, of which the decline in the share of food (Engel's law) is the most notable feature. The supply effect, on the other hand, entails two factors of general importance: (i) the overall increase in capital stock per worker; and (ii) the increase in education and skills of all kinds. Since the production in which labour, capital, and skills can be combined varies from industry to industry, a change in factor supplies causes a systematic shift in comparative advantage as the per capita income rises (Chenery 1960).

[5] We refer to these as a country's given features, over which the government has no, or at minimum, limited control in the short- to medium-run. The aim is to control for these features by establishing benchmark growth patterns, on the one hand, and to isolate them from country-specific features that are related to a country's given historical evolution, on the other.

(iii) the effects of the country's individual history, its political and social objectives, and the specific policies the government has followed to achieve these (Chenery and Syrquin 1975).

Chenery's (1960) model, which uses value added per capita for manufacturing industries as a dependent variable, was able to capture the universal effects of income and country size (effects (i) and (ii)). In their subsequent work, Chenery and Syrquin (1975) applied a similar analysis at a more aggregated level and looked at the changes in the share of manufacturing value added in gross domestic product (GDP) as their dependent variable.[6]

The authors could not, however, present a full picture of structural transformation at the manufacturing level based on the three aforementioned components due to:

- data limitations at a more detailed level within manufacturing
- data limitations with regard to country-given features
- lack of data over longer periods of time, which can capture a full development cycle, indicating periods of industrialization as well as deindustrialization.

Chenery (1960) argued that supply and demand factors embedded in the level of income contribute to different patterns across sectors and thus provide a benchmark of structural transformation. The sectoral growth function contained in Chenery's original work (1960)—based on the general equilibrium model of Walras—estimated the level of production as a function of demand side variables as follows

$$X_i = D_i + W_i + E_i - M_i \tag{1}$$

where X_i is domestic production of product i, D_i is domestic final use of i, W_i is the intermediate use of i by other producers, E_i is the export of i, and M_i is the import of i.

Since Chenery felt it was necessary to have a sufficiently large sample size and since each demand component is a function of income level, he later decided to adopt single functions of income and population instead. This

[6] Value added per capita is more industry-specific, therefore it is more appropriately used when studying industrial capacity potential. It can either be related to industrial productivity or to respective industrial concentration in manufacturing. Value added share in GDP, on the other hand, is used to study changes in the composition of the aggregate and is more appropriately used for studying the significance of an industry within an economy, which is subject to the industry's own growth and decline, as well as that of other industries, which in turn changes the composition of an aggregate.

allows viewing the effects of income level and country size by using a linear logarithmic regression equation to estimate the value added level as follows

$$\log V_i = \log \beta_{i0} + \beta_{i1}\log Y + \beta_{i2}\log N \qquad (2)$$

where V_i is per capita value added for manufacturing industry i and β_{i1} andβ_{i2} represent growth elasticity and size elasticity, respectively. Cross-section data of 38 countries available for any year between 1950 and 1956 were used for this single equation. Equation (2) became the basis for subsequent structural change research and its modifications have been widely used in later studies. For example, Chenery and Taylor (1968) included a quadratic term for income as the decline in elasticities with rising income became apparent. In later years, Chenery and Syrquin applied a more general equation, as shown below, allowing a non-linear effect for population and including dummy variables to identify period effects (Chenery and Syrquin 1975; Syrquin and Chenery 1989)

$$x = \alpha + \beta_1 \ln y + \beta_2(\ln y)^2 + \gamma_1 \ln N + \gamma_2(\ln N)^2 + \sum \delta_i T_i \qquad (3)$$

where x is a dependent variable, covering different aspects of structural change (usually expressed as a share in GDP), y is per capita GNP in 1980 US\$, N is population in millions, and T is a dummy variable for time periods taking a non-zero value for different periods.

It is worth mentioning the contributions of our work to the research tradition initiated by Chenery (1960). The first contribution concerns the estimation method applied to our analysis. Instead of using cross-sectional ordinary least squares (OLS) regressions, we apply standard linear-panel data techniques, which are known to be able to control for potential endogeneity problems encountered in OLS regressions. Therefore, with respect to previous empirical approaches, we expect our methodology to provide consistent and robust results. The second contribution is the reformulation of the estimation model itself. This provides for the possibility to more accurately disentangle those factors that influence structural change. The third contribution relates to the quality of our dataset, which covers a set of longer time series and more countries (a maximum of 45 years and 159 countries).

In order to illustrate the inefficiency of OLS estimations in cross-sections, we take Chenery's baseline equation (2) and re-estimate it using panel data techniques and compare the results with the standard OLS method. We argue that due to the potential endogeneity bias of the dependent variable in the model, the usual OLS may yield biased and inconsistent coefficient estimates, which, however, can be avoided by using panel data methods. In the scope of our empirical model, the endogeneity bias may arise from two sources (see a review of all potential sources in Wooldridge 2002). The first one comprises omitted, unobserved, country-specific effects, which refer to any country characteristic not included in the regression. The second source of endogeneity is attributable to a reverse-causality relationship between GDP and manufacturing value added, as value added is itself part of GDP, yet GDP level also relates to a country's level of industrial activity. Taking these endogeneity aspects into account, we apply new estimation methods to panel data to improve the forecast quality of Chenery's baseline model. We also apply an instrumental variable estimation technique to the panel data (IV estimation) to control for the reverse-causality problem. Lastly, due to the long coverage of data over the 45-year period, it is also necessary to control for time-fixed effects in our regressions. Hence, our panel specification of equation (2) is re-expressed in the equation (2′) below:

$$\ln VAPC_{it} = \beta_0 + \beta_t + \beta_1{}^{*}\ln RGDPC_{it} + \beta_2{}^{*}\ln POP_{it} + u_{it} \qquad (2')$$

with β_0 being a constant term translating any effects common to all years and countries, β_t being effect-specific to year t but common to all countries in order to capture common shocks in time (e.g. oil crisis), and u_{it} being the error term specific to each country and year and assumed to be log-normally distributed. We follow Chenery (1960) and use manufacturing value added per capita (*VAPC*) as a dependent variable while the income effect is captured by real GDP per capita (*RGDPC*) and the size effect by population level (*POP*). Results of the regressions are reported in columns (1)–(5) in Table 4.1, along with the applied estimators indicated beneath the column numbers.

The regression in column (1) replicates the estimation strategy used by Chenery (1960) by applying a pooled OLS estimation (POLS) without controlling for time-fixed effects. The estimates in column (2) differ from this regression when time-fixed effects are controlled for. However, real GDP per capita and population may be correlated with country-specific effects, and the statistic of the Lagrange multiplier (LM) test in column (3) also confirms the existence of these effects in our model. Hence, the generalized least square estimator (GLS) depicted in column (3) is more consistent compared to the POLS estimator. However, modelling the country-specific effects as fixed as in column (4) is more appropriate since we reject the Hausman test with the null hypothesis that the GLS provides consistent estimates. Lastly, continuing with fixed-effects regressions (FE), when controlling for the endogeneity of RGDPC, the statistics of the overidentification test reveal the consistency of the FE–IV estimator compared to the FE-within. Hence, in the remainder of this chapter, we will apply country-fixed effect regressions using IV to control for potential endogeneity problems.

Table 4.1. Comparison of estimators at the overall manufacturing level

Dependent variable:	(1)	(2)	(3)	(4)	(5)
ln(VAPC)	POLS	POLS	GLS	Within	IV
ln(RGDPC)	1.778***	1.704***	1.281***	1.215***	4.809***
	(0.061)	(0.065)	(0.013)	(0.015)	(0.163)
ln(POP)	0.160***	0.134***	0.208***	0.279***	2.523***
	(0.036)	(0.037)	(0.015)	(0.025)	(0.108)
N	55184	55184	55184	55184	46947
R^2	0.612	0.633	—	0.606	0.186
Country-specific effects	No	No	Random	Fixed	Fixed
Test of time-fixed effects	No	25***	12590***	19***	3465***
		F(44,138)	$chi^2(44)$	F(44,138)	$chi^2(44)$
Test of specific effects[(a)]	—	—	400000***	—	—
Hausman test W vs. GLS[(b)]	—	—	—	2865***	—
Hausman test IV vs GLS[(c)]	—	—	—	—	2270***
Test of over-identification[(d)]	—	—	—	—	1704***

Notes: *** Significant at 0.1% level. The time dummy variables and the constant are not reported to save space. Life expectancy is used as an instrument for RGDPC in the IV regression.
(a): $Chi^2(1)$ statistic from Breusch and Pagan LM (Lagrange multiplier) test for random effects;
(b): $Chi^2(2)$ statistic from Hausman test applied to the differences between Within and GLS estimators, without time effects;
(c): $Chi^2(2)$ statistics from Hausman tests applied to the differences between IV and GLS estimators, without time effects;
(d): $Chi^2(2)$ statistics from Hausman tests applied to the differences between IV and Within estimators, without time effects.

Source: Calculated by the authors based on regression estimations (Equation 2) using INDSTAT data.

4.3 Alternative model for assessing patterns of manufacturing development

This section discusses the theoretical background of the analysis and derives the equation to be estimated to obtain an accurate picture of structural transformation. Based on Chenery's methodology, our model tries to capture the effect of the three aforementioned factors. For each manufacturing industry, we estimate the following equation

$$\begin{aligned}\ln X^{i}_{ct} = & \alpha_1 + \alpha_2 \text{*}\ln RGDPL_{ct} + \alpha_3 \text{*}\ln RGDPL^{2}_{ct} + \alpha_4 \text{*}\ln POPD_{ct} \\ & + \alpha\text{*}\ln RPC_{ct} + TROPICAL_c + e^{i}_{ct}\end{aligned} \quad (4)$$

The subscripts c and t denote country and year, respectively, whereas i indicates the respective manufacturing industry, where X is our dependent variable. We will base our analysis on estimating and establishing industrial benchmark growth patterns on real value added per capita (*RVAPC*) as a main dependent variable, and will also apply this method to value added share in GDP in order to classify the industries according to their corresponding significance within an economy at different income development stages.

As for the right-hand side variables, *RGDPL* stands for real GDP per capita (Laspeyres adjusted), $RGDPL^2$ for real GDP per capita squared, *POPD* for population density, *RPC* for resource per capita, *TROPICAL* is a dummy variable equal to one if a country belongs to a tropical zone and zero otherwise and $e^{i}{}_{ct}$ stands for country-fixed effect. Dependent and explanatory variables are expressed in logarithmic terms in order to measure the elasticity of each variable.

Four remarks must be added with regard to the above specification. First, we assume that income effect is a non-linear function, i.e. real value added per capita increases at a diminishing rate with a country's development level. Second, we consider three country-given characteristics, which capture the effects of population density, natural resource endowment, and climatic condition on industrial growth, aware that countries have no or little influence on these characteristics in the short- to medium-run. Third, we divide countries into two subsamples of 'small' and 'large' countries according to their population size. Following the practice of past studies (Chenery and Taylor 1968; Chenery et al. 1986; Syrquin 1988), population size is not included in the equation, but equation (4) is applied to two sub-groups of small and large countries. When a variable, in this case size, has overarching effects on other country characteristics, it is better to estimate separate patterns that are representative of more homogenous groups of countries (Chenery and Taylor 1968). A country is classified as small if its population size in the year 1983 was less than 15 million and is considered large if its population size was larger than 15 million in 1983. Note that we are aware of this arbitrary division and that population growth is not taken into account, but this threshold offers a plausible division of countries in our dataset.

4.3.1 *Estimation issues, data, and variable descriptions*

Section 4.2 discussed the superiority of the fixed-effect IV method compared with other estimators. Specifically, due to the time constant variable in the model (*TROPICAL*) we will use the Hausman–Taylor IV method, which generally allows an estimation of time constant regressors while also controlling for the endogeneity problem in the same way as within the estimator.

The model is estimated for up to 159 countries over a period of 45 years from 1963–2007, with a subset of 107 small countries and 52 large countries. The data are taken from three sources. Industrial data are obtained from UNIDO's Industrial Statistics Database at the 2-digit level of ISIC Rev. 3 (UNIDO 2009). Series of national income data are derived from Penn World Tables, while country characteristic variables come from the World Bank's World Development Indicator and Global Development Finance database (available at: http://databank.worldbank.org/ddp/home.do). UNIDO's INDSTAT2 dataset has the advantage of providing a long-term series of industrial data for 22 manufacturing sectors from 1963–2006, with historical data being converted from ISIC Rev. 2. However, as many countries report industrial data as a combination of two or more sectors of ISIC Rev. 3 at the 2-digit level, we merge these sectors in our dataset and end up with 18 sectors in total. Table 4.2 lists all the sectors that have been merged and used in our analysis.

In the literature on structural change it has been established that country size has a significant effect on patterns of industrial development because economies of scale, natural resource endowments, and scale of domestic demand often vary with country size (Chenery and Taylor 1968; Chenery and Syrquin 1975; Syrquin 1988; Perkins and Syrquin 1989). Past empirical evidence shows that the manufacturing industry has more weight in large countries' economies at an earlier stage of development than in smaller countries. Also, the manufacturing growth of large countries usually slows down before that of smaller countries, which has more linear growth patterns across different income levels.

As for the variables required in our regressions, they are calculated as follows:

- *RVAPC* is calculated by dividing the real value added of the observed country by its population size. We calculate real value added from value

Table 4.2. ISIC Revision 3 classification

ISIC description	ISIC abbreviation	ISIC code
Food and beverages	Food and beverages	15
Tobacco products	Tobacco	16
Textiles	Textiles	17
Wearing apparel, fur and leather products, and footwear	Wearing apparel	18, 19
Wood products (excluding furniture)	Wood products	20
Paper and paper products	Paper	21
Printing and publishing	Printing and publishing	22
Coke, refined petroleum products, and nuclear fuel	Coke and refined petroleum	23
Chemicals and chemical products	Chemicals	24
Rubber and plastic products	Rubber and plastic	25
Non-metallic mineral products	Non-metallic minerals	26
Basic metals	Basic metals	27
Fabricated metal products	Fabricated metals	28
Machinery and equipment n.e.c. and office, accounting, computing machinery	Machinery and equipment	29, 30
Electrical machinery, apparatus and radio, television, and communication equipment	Electrical machinery and apparatus	31, 32
Medical, precision and optical instruments	Precision instruments	33
Motor vehicles, trailers, semi-trailers, and other transport equipment	Motor vehicles	34, 35
Furniture, manufacturing n.e.c.	Furniture, n.e.c.	36

Source: UNIDO (2009).

added in benchmark years extrapolated with the industrial index of production.

- In the model, *RGDPL* indirectly reflects the interaction between the demand effects of rising income and the supply effects of changes in factor proportions and technology. Therefore, it is assumed that rising income ought to bring about relatively uniform patterns in structural transformation. Data on GDP per capita based on 2005 prices are adjusted in accordance with purchasing power parity and are retrieved from the Penn World Tables.
- Keesing and Sherk (1971) show that population density plays an important role on patterns of trade and development. In particular, densely populated areas appear to have a greater impact on increased exports of manufactured goods relative to primary products. This relationship suggests that only the most densely populated, small developing countries can look forward to early successful export specialization in the manufacturing industries. Population density is determined by simply dividing a country's population size by the country's total area.

- Although Chenery (1960) recognized that natural resource endowments affect the process of industrialization, he was not able to find a statistical measure of resource supply for a large number of countries and therefore excluded it from his regression equation (Chenery 1960). *RPC* is calculated as the difference between exports and imports of relevant resource commodities expressed in per capita terms. The commodities included as reported in the standard international trade classification (SITC) revision 1 are SITC2: crude materials, inedibles except fuels; SITC32: coal, coke, and briquettes; SITC331: petroleum, crude and partly refined; SITC3411: gas, natural gas.
- Tropical climate is likely to create adverse conditions for economic development either directly or indirectly through institutions (Sachs 2001; Easterly and Levine 2003). To control the effects of this given country condition as well as to measure such effects on manufacturing performance, a dummy variable separating countries with or without tropical conditions (*TROPICAL*) is included in the equation.

The underlying purpose of our model is to attain a relatively accurate picture of structural transformation at the detailed manufacturing level. As already indicated, the country variables included in the model, namely natural resources per capita, population density, and tropical climate, are the conditions on which countries have no or limited influence. This implies that any policy approach a country might undertake is unlikely to bring about rapid changes in those variables. Once such benchmark patterns are obtained, research can focus on explaining the deviations of a country's industrial development patterns from the benchmarks by examining policy-related, institutional, and historical factors. Below we present the results based on our regressions.

4.4 Results

4.4.1 *Drivers of development patterns*

In Tables 4.3 and 4.4, we summarize the results of the regression analysis and show the marginal effect of the variables included in the model for small and large countries, respectively. In Tables 4.5 and 4.6 for small and large counties, we summarize the effect (negative or positive) of income level, population density, and resource endowments. The manufacturing industries in each column of Tables 4.5 and 4.6 are ranked and sorted in ascending order based on the marginal effect of the explanatory variable on real value added per capita in an industry.

Table 4.3. Regression estimations based on equation 4 for small countries

ISIC Rev.3	Abbreviation	*C*	ln*RGDPL*	ln*RGDPL*^{2}	ln*POPD*	ln*RPC*	*TROPICAL*	*N*	*RHO*
15	Food and beverages	−5.88***	1.89***	−0.08***	0.06	−0.04	−0.9/1**	1146	0.96
16	Tobacco	−14.99***	3.40***	−0.17***	−0.01	0.18	−1.3/1*	1073	0.98
17	Textiles	−33.74***	7.49***	−0.39***	0.2/1**	0.14	−1.47***	1212	0.95
18/19	Wearing apparel	−51.08***	10.43***	−0.52***	1.23***	−0.14	−1.44	1270	0.98
20	Wood products	−38.39***	9.06***	−0.50***	−1.09***	0.56***	−1.93	1225	0.99
21	Paper	−24.70***	5.15***	−0.22***	−0.28***	0.07	−0.9	1182	0.96
22	Printing and publishing	−19.48***	4.12***	−0.17***	0.34***	−0.2/1**	−1.46***	1133	0.95
23	Coke and refined petroleum	−35.58***	7.28***	−0.35***	−0.1	0.2/1*	0.52	585	0.99
24	Chemicals	1.7	−0.04	0.05	0.34***	−0.46***	−1.2/1*	1111	0.97
25	Rubber and plastic	−41.87***	9.56***	−0.49***	−0.2/1**	0	−1.66	1113	0.99
26	Non-metallic minerals	−39.56***	8.96***	−0.45***	−0.31***	0.1/1*	−1.16	1141	0.98
27	Basic metals	−41.09***	9.11***	−0.47***	−0.43***	0.24***	−1.37	839	0.99
28	Fabricated metals.	−40.04***	8.43***	−0.43***	−0.03	0.3/1**	−1.9/1*	1061	0.97
29/30	Machinery and equipment	−19.44***	3.71***	−0.1/1**	0.2/1*	−0.16	−1.6/1**	1097	0.96
31/32	Electrical machinery and apparatus	−37.53***	8.77***	−0.40***	−0.41***	−0.58***	−1.02	1156	0.98
33	Precision instruments	−35.62***	6.14***	−0.28***	−0.11	0.70***	−3.16	877	0.99
34/35	Motor vehicles	−37.62***	8.20***	−0.38***	0.2/1**	−0.3/1**	−1.9/1**	1096	0.95
36	Furniture, n.e.c.	−31.61***	8.49***	−0.42***	−1.63***	−0.06	−0.84	979	0.99

Notes: * p<0.10,** p<0.05,*** p<0.01.

Source: Calculated by the authors based on regression estimations for small countries (Equation 4).

Table 4.4. Regression estimations based on equation 4 for large countries

Isic Rev. 3	Abbreviation	*C*	ln*RGDPL*	ln$RGDPL^2$	ln*POPD*	ln*RPC*	*TROPICAL*	*N*	*RHO*
15	Food and beverages	1.38	2.12***	−0.08***	0.30***	−1.29***	−0.86	973	0.99
16	Tobacco	−10.24***	4.86***	−0.24***	0.06	−1.32***	−0.9	918	0.97
17	Textiles	−16.13***	4.29***	−0.20***	0.15	−0.37	−0.90**	998	0.92
18/19	Wearing apparel	−25.37***	6.49***	−0.30***	0.11	−0.58	−0.97*	981	0.93
20	Wood products	−12.22***	2.95***	−0.14***	−0.11	0.02	−2.24**	934	0.98
21	Paper	−5.00*	3.49***	−0.13***	−0.32***	−1.36***	−0.79*	926	0.94
22	Printing and publishing	3.11	1.27**	−0.04	−0.56***	−0.7	−2.03**	913	0.97
23	Coke and refined petroleum	−13.09***	3.03***	−0.11***	1.22***	−0.80***	−0.98	742	1
24	Chemicals	−5.46**	0.91**	0.03	1.20***	−0.68***	−0.47	906	0.99
25	Rubber and plastic	−6.13**	2.20***	−0.08***	0.08	−0.58**	−1.13*	921	0.97
26	Non−metallic minerals	−13.45***	4.09***	−0.17***	1.20***	−1.20***	−0.73	960	0.99
27	Basic metals	9.20**	0.62	0.04	2.25***	−2.74***	−0.52	783	1
28	Fabricated metals.	−9.67**	1.76***	−0.01	1.32***	−0.78**	−0.93	881	0.99
29/30	Machinery and equipment	−10.62*	−5.18***	0.41***	1.61***	2.65***	−0.99	948	0.98
31/32	Electrical machinery and apparatus	0.07	2.73***	−0.04	1.26***	−2.69***	−0.1	968	0.98
33	Precision instruments	−12.14**	1.01	0.05	0.93***	−0.26	−2.42	795	0.99
34/35	Motor vehicles	14.96***	−4.55***	0.38***	2.26***	−1.07**	−0.29	951	0.99
36	Furniture, n.e.c.	−13.50***	3.47***	−0.15***	−0.14	−0.22	−2.15**	815	0.97

Notes: * $p<0.10$,** $p<0.05$,*** $p<0.01$.

Source: Calculated by the authors based on regression estimations for large countries (Equation 4).

Table 4.5 reveals that the marginal income effect in small countries is positive and significant in all manufacturing industries, with the exception of the chemicals industry. Similarly in Table 4.3, apart from the chemicals industry, the non-linear term (ln$RGDPL^2$) is negative and significant, indicating that along with the growth of GDP per capita, manufacturing value added per capita initially grows and then begins to decline after reaching a peak. The marginal income effect is lowest in the food and beverages industry and highest in the rubber and plastics industry.

As indicated above, population density, natural resources, and tropical variables are characterized by country-given features, indicating that countries cannot exert any, or only minimal, influence on those variables through policy measures in the short- to medium-run. The marginal effect of population density is significant and positive for textiles, machinery and equipment, motor vehicles, printing and publishing, chemicals and wearing apparel, and negative for furniture, n.e.c.,[7] wood products, basic metals, electrical machinery and apparatus, non-metallic minerals, paper and rubber and plastic. The level of natural resource endowments is significant and positively associated with the value added level of non-metallic minerals, coke and refined petroleum, basic metals, fabricated metals, wood products, and precision instruments, while negatively associated with that of electrical machinery and apparatus, chemicals, motor vehicles, and printing and publishing. As expected, the impact of the tropical dummy on value added is negative across all industries. It is significant only in industries such as food and beverages, chemicals, tobacco, printing and publishing, textiles, machinery and equipment, fabricated metals, and motor vehicles.

When it comes to large countries (Table 4.6), apart from basic metals and precision instruments, the income effect is positive and significant. The non-linear term of income is negative for those industries, yet non-significant for chemicals, printing and publishing, fabricated metals, and electrical machinery and apparatus. This may indicate a linear growth trajectory and with possible decline only at very late stages of development. The marginal effect of income is lowest in the chemicals and highest in the wearing apparel sectors. The impact of population density on industries' value added is significant in the food and beverages, paper, printing and publishing, precision instruments, chemicals, non-metallic minerals, coke and refined petroleum, electrical machinery and apparatus, fabricated metals, machinery and equipment, basic metals, and motor vehicles sectors. The marginal effect is negative in the paper and printing and publishing industry and positive in the other industries. The marginal effect of natural resource endowment is significant in

[7] Not elsewhere classified.

Table 4.5. Marginal effect of explanatory variables on value added per capita for small countries

	Income effect	Population-density effect	Resource effect	Tropical effect
Negative		Furniture, n.e.c. Wood products Basic metals Electrical machinery and apparatus Non-metallic minerals Paper Rubber and plastic	Electrical machinery and apparatus Chemicals Motor vehicles Printing and publishing	Motor vehicles Fabricated metals Machinery and equipment Textiles Printing and publishing Tobacco Chemicals Food and beverages
Positive	Food and beverages Wearing apparel Tobacco Machinery and equipment Printing and publishing Paper Precision instruments Coke and refined petroleum Textiles Motor vehicles Fabricated metals. Furniture, n.e.c. Electrical machinery and apparatus Non-metallic minerals Wood products Basic metals Rubber and plastic	Textiles Machinery and equipment Motor vehicles Chemicals Printing and publishing Wearing apparel	Non-metallic minerals Coke and refined petroleum Basic metals Fabricated metals. Wood products Precision instruments	

Source: Calculated by the authors based on regression estimations for small countries (Equation 4).

Table 4.6. Marginal effect of explanatory variables on value added per capita for large countries

		Population density effect	Resource effect	Tropical effect
Negative		Printing and publishing Paper	Basic metals Electrical machinery and apparatus Paper Tobacco Food and beverages Non-metallic minerals Motor vehicles Coke and refined petroleum Fabricated metals. Chemicals Rubber and plastic Machinery and equipment	Wood products Furniture, n.e.c. Printing and publishing Rubber and plastic Wearing apparel Textiles Paper
Positive	Chemicals Printing and publishing Fabricated metals. Food and beverages Rubber and plastic Electrical machinery and apparatus Wood products Coke and refined petroleum Furniture, n.e.c. Paper Non-metallic minerals Textiles Motor vehicles Tobacco Machinery and equipment Wearing apparel	Food and beverages Precision instruments Chemicals Non-metallic minerals Coke and refined petroleum Electrical machinery and apparatus Fabricated metals. Machinery and equipment Basic metals Motor vehicles		

Source: Calculated by the authors based on regression estimations for large countries (Equation 4).

the rubber and plastic, chemicals, fabricated metals, coke and refined petroleum, motor vehicles, non-metallic minerals, food and beverages, tobacco, paper, machinery and equipment, electrical machinery and apparatus, and basic metals sectors, but it is positive only in the machinery and equipment sector. Similarly, as for small countries, the tropical variable has a negative marginal effect on value added for all manufacturing industries and is significant in the paper, textiles, wearing apparel, rubber and plastic, printing and publishing, furniture, n.e.c., and wood products sectors.

Comparisons between small and large countries reveal that, in general, higher population density supports the industrialization of large countries while it tends to mostly support the development of non-resource-based industries in small countries. In contrast, natural resource endowment usually has a negative effect on the development of manufacturing industries in large countries, except for the machinery and equipment sector. On the other hand, this factor can be conducive to the growth of resource-based industries in small countries. Finally, tropical climate hampers manufacturing development in both small and large countries. This condition, in the case of large countries, particularly affects those industries that usually emerge at an early stage of a country's development, whereas in small countries, the negative effects may also be felt in some late industries.

4.4.2 *Benchmark growth trajectories*

Chenery's original estimation (1960) included countries with a GDP per capita of up to around US$9,300 (US$1,300 in 1960 prices). Figure 4.1 indicates that the pattern of industrial development is indeed more or less linear up to such a low income level. This may explain why Chenery's linear model (1960) resulted in relatively high adjusted R^2 values, which convinced him that the model could be considered for assessing patterns of industrial development. The availability of long-term time series and diverse cross-section data with income per capita including both low- and high-income economies allows presentation of more accurate patterns of industrial development, indicating when and how growth in value added per capita is likely to begin slowing down before decreasing.

Figure 4.1 presents the growth and decline of 18 manufacturing industries in relation to GDP per capita in small and large countries. The bar charts in Figure 4.1 are based on regression results from Tables 4.3 and 4.4 and allow us to illustrate the evolution of individual industries relative to the rise in GDP per capita up to US$38,000. Four different elasticity thresholds are calculated in relation to GDP per capita. The first stage is characterized by the rapid growth of value added per capita, with an elasticity larger than 2. At this stage, 10 per cent growth in GDP per capita would lead to more than 20 per

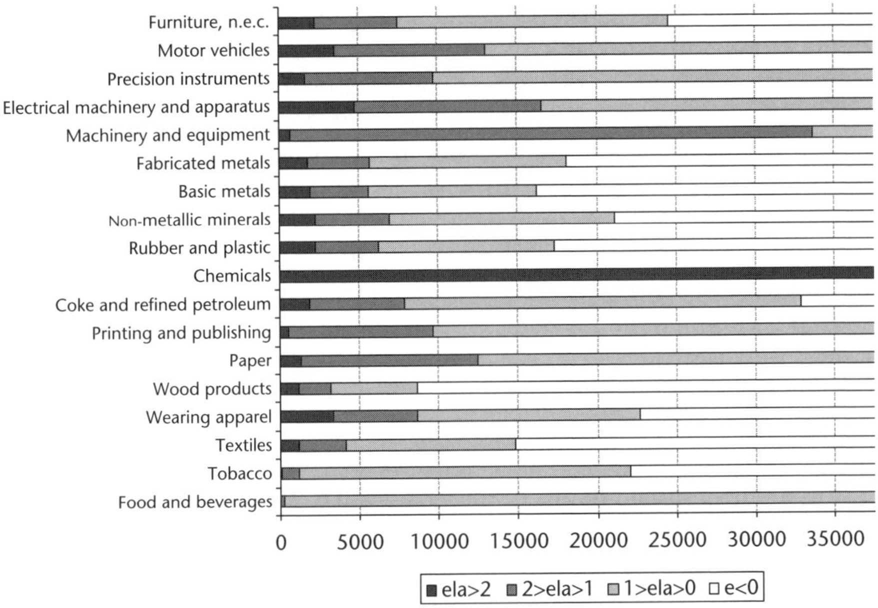

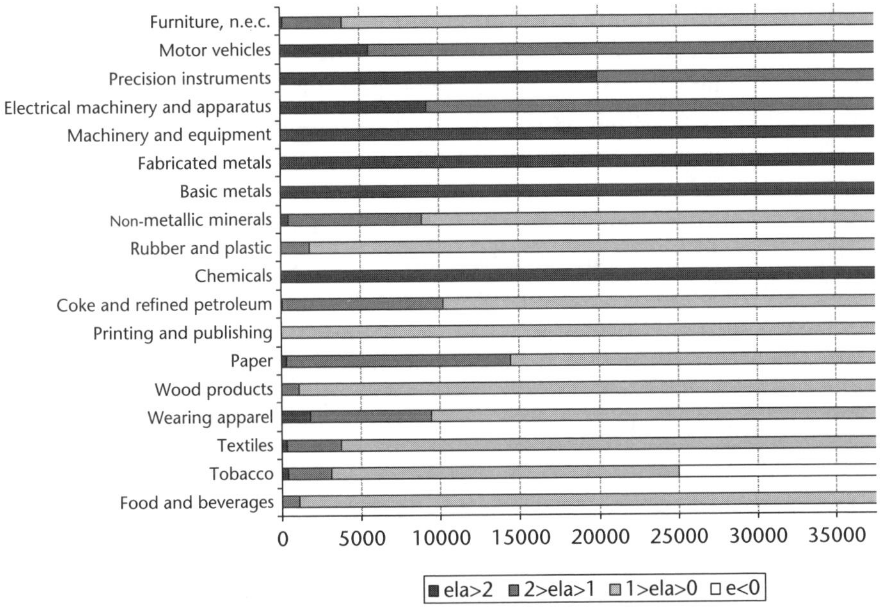

Figure 4.1. Growth elasticities for manufacturing industries in small and large countries

Source: Developed by the authors based on regression estimations of Tables 4.3 and 4.3.

cent growth of value added per capita. In the second stage, value added per capita grows with an elasticity between 2 and 1, and in the third stage, between 1 and 0, value added continues to grow but less than the growth rate of GDP per capita. In the fourth stage, with an elasticity smaller than 0, industries experience absolute declines in their value added per capita. The value added per capita of industries reaches its peak when elasticity reaches zero and subsequently begins to decline.

Unlike other industries that emerge at an early stage of a country's development, the value added per capita of the food and beverages industry does not show a declining trend for both small and large countries and continues to grow until a very high income level is reached. Although the result seems to confirm evidence from earlier studies (Chenery 1960; Chenery and Taylor 1968; Maizels 1968) which estimated that the income elasticity of demand for the *food and beverages* industry was around or less than 1, the significance of this industry should not be dismissed as it makes a sustained contribution to the economy for a long period of time.

Figure 4.2 shows fitted curves that are based on scatter plots of estimation results for selected industries representing low-tech, resource-based, medium- and high-tech industries using UNIDO's technological classification (UNIDO 2002). It reveals that differences in growth patterns do indeed exist between small and large countries. Overall, manufacturing industries of large countries start at a higher level of value added per capita than those of small countries and tend to demonstrate largely linear development patterns. Industries in small countries experience faster growth, albeit starting from a lower level of value added per capita, and reach their peak and begin declining earlier than in large countries. Hence, their industrial development patterns are more concave, as illustrated below. These results contradict those of an earlier study, which suggested linear patterns for small countries and concave ones for large countries (Taylor 1969). Due to the limited availability of time-series data, the earlier study may have only depicted half of the industrialization process, primarily showing the take-off and rapid-growth periods of manufacturing industries, and excluding the deindustrialization part of the process.

4.4.3 *Identification of the most relevant industries at different development stages*

A summary of the above discussion is presented here, in which industries are classified (Tables 4.7 and 4.8) by the stage and growth potential of their development in order to determine shifts in comparative advantages. In the first column, the headings for early, middle and late industries refer to the stage of development at which each industry makes its greatest contribution to the economy over the span of its development. Specifically, using the share

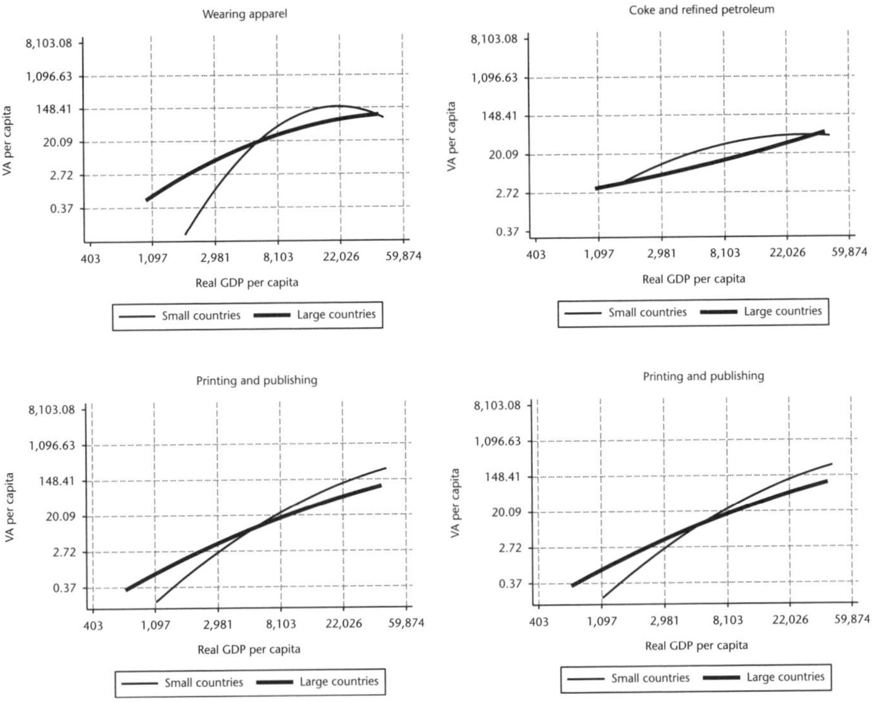

Figure 4.2. Development patterns of manufacturing industries in small and large countries (fitted lines)

Source: Developed by the authors based on regression estimations for small and large countries (Equation 4).

of an industry's value added in GDP as a measure of the industry's significance within an economy, we divide industries into early, middle and late industries based on the per capita income range at which each industry reaches its peak share in the economy. Within each category, industries are listed in chronological order from the industry that reaches the point of highest share in the economy first. Second, an industry is classified under 'sustained growth' if it is estimated to exceed the value added per capita level of US$150 during its development. If the industry is estimated to reach a level between US$20 and US$150, it is classified under 'temporary growth'. Industries that are not very likely to reach the value added per capita level of US$20 are listed under 'low growth'. To determine the reliability of their development paths, those industries where GDP per capita accounts for less than 70 per cent of changes in manufacturing value added per capita are shown in italics. In other words, country-given features and country-specific effects have a relatively high influence on the development paths of those industries.

A comparison between Tables 4.7 and 4.8 shows that small countries have a limited number of industries with high development potential (sustained

Table 4.7. Industrial classifications by stage of development and growth for small countries

	Sustained growth	Temporary growth	Low growth
Early industries			*Tobacco*
	Chemicals		
	Food and beverages		
		Rubber and plastics	
			Wood products
		Textiles	
Middle industries		Paper	
		Basic metals	
		Non-metallic minerals	
		Coke and refined petroleum	
		Fabricated metals Wearing apparel	
		Furniture, n.e.c.	
Late industries	Electrical machinery and apparatus		
		Motor vehicles	
	Printing and publishing		
	Machinery and equipment	*Precision instruments*	

Source: Developed by the authors based on regression estimations for small (Equation 4).

Table 4.8. Industrial classifications by stage of development and growth for large countries

	Sustained growth	Temporary growth	Low growth
Early industries	Food and beverages		
		Coke and refined petroleum	
		Wood products	
	Chemicals	*Textiles*	
			Tobacco
		Non-metallic minerals Wearing apparel	
Middle industries		Furniture, n.e.c.	
	Paper		
		Rubber and plastic	
	Printing and publishing		
		Basic metals	
	Motor vehicles		
Late industries	Electrical machinery and apparatus		
	Precision instruments Fabricated metals Machinery and equipment		

Source: Developed by the authors based on regression estimations for large countries (Equation 4).

growth). In general, country-given features and country-specific effects tend to exert a high influence on a large number of industries, indicating a higher uncertainty of their path of industrialization. During the early stage of development, the food and beverages and chemicals sectors play an important role in small countries. Even though their contribution to the economy relative to other industries is highest before countries reach US$5,000 GDP per capita, these industries continue to support industrialization by sustaining their growth. Their sustained contributions to the economy are realized as these broad industrial classifications allow continuous changes in their product mix to take place within the same industry classifications. For example, in the case of chemicals, at an early stage the industry focuses on the production of basic chemicals, such as fertilizers, but shifts to the manufacture of more capital-intensive products, such as pharmaceuticals, as it develops.

Compared to food and beverages, the development of the chemicals industry is influenced more by country-given features. In addition to tropical climate, which negatively affects both the food and beverages and chemicals industry, higher levels of natural resource endowments generally lower the industry's value added across income levels, while higher population density works favourably for the development of the chemicals industry. Thus, keeping in mind the importance of developing these two industries, countries need to carefully evaluate how their given features affect the development of the early industries, including the temporary growth industries, rubber and plastics and textiles. The latter industry's development is highly dependent on country-specific factors, so countries have to study their given features as well as the policy, institutional, and other conditions necessary to successfully develop it.

Among the industries whose contribution to the economy peaks in the next stage of economic development, only the paper and furniture n.e.c industry can be expected to develop, with a relatively high degree of certainty, along with the income increase in small countries. Given that there is no manufacturing sector with 'sustained growth' at this stage and the uncertainty of other industries, small countries will continue to face the precarious situation of having to undertake special efforts to identify sectors that are appropriate for their country characteristics rather than leaving industrialization to spontaneous development through market forces.

As small countries' GDP per capita reaches a substantially high level of more than US$10,000, those industries referred to as late industries in Table 4.7 should become relevant in the country's economy. In other words, without the successful transformation of manufacturing industries to establish those late sectors, it is unlikely for small countries to reach a high income level. Thus for successful industrialization, small countries need to start nurturing the development of late industries long before the 'late' stage is reached. Among the late industries, the electrical machinery and apparatus, printing and publishing, and machinery and equipment industries in particular will be important for the economy as they are likely to sustain their growth even when most other industries begin to decline at a very high income level. Small countries with a relatively high population density have a better chance of developing the printing and publishing and machinery and equipment industries rather than the electrical machinery and apparatus industry. The opposite is true for countries with a low population density. Furthermore, as shown in Table 4.5, the electrical machinery and apparatus industry is an industry that is highly subject to the effects of the 'resource curse', although climatic conditions do not prevent the industry's development. Of the three industries, the development of the printing and publishing and the machinery and equipment industries are more predictable in relation to GDP per capita increases. Country-given features account for a relatively large share of changes in the value added per capita of the electrical machinery and apparatus industry. Therefore, for the development of the latter, small countries have to evaluate how their geographic and demographic conditions affect the industry's development in light of the results of Table 4.7, and any possible negative effects such as high resource endowments have to be compensated by country-specific effects, such as improved policies and institutions over which governments have control.

In contrast to small countries, the manufacturing industries in large countries develop with a much higher degree of certainty along with the rise of income. Large countries have more industries with 'sustained growth' and fewer industries with 'low growth' than small countries, and each stage of development has at least one industry of 'sustained growth', which makes the manufacturing transformation process smoother. Accordingly, it is probably more effective for large countries to focus on removing obstacles to the functioning of the market and provide functional support to educational, skills, and institutional development rather than focusing exclusively on the unique needs of each sector.

One caveat to large countries is the importance of properly managing their natural resources if endowed with a relatively high level. As demonstrated in Table 4.6, the level of natural resource endowments negatively affects value added per capita for many industries in large countries. In particular, key industries, whose development is crucial for deepening and advancing industrialization after the early stage of development, are especially affected by an abundance of natural resource endowments. Countries such as Canada and Mexico have industrialized their economies despite their relatively high natural resource endowments. Large countries with similar conditions can learn from these and other successful examples.

The development classifications in Tables 4.7 and 4.8, together with changes in the growth elasticities illustrated in Figure 4.1, indicate when, how fast, how far, and how reliably manufacturing industries develop in countries with different geographic and demographic characteristics. The analysis of this information indicates that certain paths of manufacturing development are preferable over others, depending on country characteristics, and there seems to be room for industrial planning, policy, and coordination for successful industrialization.

Overall, small countries begin their manufacturing development later than large countries. However, once small countries' manufacturing industries take off, they tend to grow faster than those of large countries during most of the middle-income stage, before large countries once again overtake small countries in terms of the manufacturing industries' value added per capita. Thus, small countries experience a relatively rapid growth and decline of their manufacturing industries while large countries are likely to see slow yet more sustainable growth. These development patterns are likely to be attributed to the difference in the weights of exports as a source of demand for their manufacturing products. The heavier reliance of small countries on external markets allows a rapid expansion of the manufacturing industries—disproportionate to their country size—when they have comparative advantages in manufacturing industries, but leads to rapid declines once they lose the advantages in the international market. As small countries reach between US$7,000 and US$12,000 GDP per capita, they lose the advantages in many of their manufacturing industries and cannot extend their development further, because their small domestic market does not constitute a significant source of demand to sustain their development. On the other hand, due to the importance of the domestic market as a source of demand, manufacturing industries in large countries develop more commensurately with the country's economic growth. The large domestic market gives their manufacturing industries the scale advantage, and it also buffers against the loss of competitiveness in the international market, thus extending the period of their development.

These general patterns of manufacturing development indicate that small countries, relative to large ones, need to have more detailed strategies for their manufacturing development, accompanied by contingency plans. They must carefully manoeuvre manufacturing transitions from one growth industry to another based on an understanding of their development patterns (Table 4.7) and the impact of country-given features on the patterns (Table 4.5). This conclusion is based on the three findings of our chapter. First, as described above, the window of opportunity for manufacturing development is only open for a relatively short period for small countries. As Figure 4.2 shows, the value-added trend lines of small countries are often more curvilinear. Figure 4.1 shows that most industries reach the stage of relative decline (in which elasticity becomes less than 1) faster than those of large countries once the fast growth period ends (when elasticity becomes less than 2 but greater than 1).

Second, as the comparison of Tables 4.7 and 4.8 reveals, there is a larger number of industries in small countries whose value added changes are explained more by country-given features and country-specific characteristics. This implies that the universal effect of income level is a less reliable determinant for industrial output levels (on average, 0.67 R-square for small countries versus 0.80 R-square for large countries). It is therefore more important for small countries than large ones to undertake efforts to determine how their country characteristics are likely to work as an advantage or disadvantage for the development of industries they aim to establish and, if necessary, how they can create conditions conducive for such development.

Finally, as the typologies in Tables 4.7 and 4.8 show, the fact that small countries have fewer 'sustained-growth' and more 'low-growth' industries means that their paths of industrialization have to be supported by shifting from one temporary-growth industry to another, perhaps by pro-actively facilitating manufacturing transformation. For small countries, the food and beverages, chemicals, electrical machinery, printing and publishing, and machinery and equipment industries will be cornerstones of the sustained industrialization needed to bring the economy to a high per capita GDP level. While understanding the significance and supporting the development of these industries early on is essential, the electrical machinery and apparatus, printing and publishing, and machinery and equipment industries will only have a significant weight in the economy at a later stage of industrialization. To bridge the early and late stages, even very small countries would need to establish at least a few successful manufacturing industries from the 'middle industries' in Table 4.7 to sustain their industrialization processes. However, there are no 'middle industries' that could sustain growth up to a high level of value added, and most of their development patterns are uncertain due to the significant influence of country-given features and country-specific effects.

Thus in order to increase the likelihood of advancing their industrialization, small countries need to assess how their country characteristics could affect the development of the 'middle industries' based on data such as that provided in Tables 4.5 and 4.7. For example, if a small, densely populated, resource-poor country is to strategically promote industrialization, the country will benefit from the information provided by Table 4.7, even if an in-depth country assessment is still necessary. As demonstrated in the table, in addition to the chemicals and food and beverages industries, a country, on average, probably has a better chance of success in developing its textile and/or wearing apparel industry than its mineral industries, such as the basic metals and non-metallic minerals industries or resource-based industries such as paper, rubber and plastics, and coke and petroleum refining. However, both the textiles and wearing apparel industries' growth rates will slow down relatively quickly and reach a period of relative decline (a growth rate less than the GDP per capita growth) at a per capita income of about US$4,500 for textiles and US$8,500 for wearing apparel after the end of the rapid growth period, with a GDP per capita of approximately US$1,000–3,000. Hence, small countries need to foster the emergence, if not the successful establishment, of late industries long before reaching such income levels, whereby the machinery and equipment industry is the best candidate in light of the country's given characteristics. As these descriptions suggest, understanding the general characteristics of manufacturing industries, such as their timing, speed, and length of development and the country conditions conducive for their growths, will provide policy-makers with a rough benchmark of their country's long-term manufacturing transformation and will help elaborate policies to support industrialization.

4.5 Concluding remarks

Chenery and others made a seminal contribution to the conceptualization of factors that affect structural change. Their empirical studies, however, usually focused on the universal effect of income on structural change, mostly at a broad aggregation of a three-sector classification, paying little attention to country-given features, over which the government has little or no control, and other country-specific effects. Building on their conceptual framework, this chapter first contributed to the statistical analysis to account for the income effect on manufacturing transformation. The level of income explains most of the output variations for the sectors of large countries. Its explanatory power is lower for small countries, but is the most important determinant of sectoral development, accounting for two-thirds of the variations, on average. This chapter also showed how country-given features influence the development of individual sectors. The country-given features account less for changes in value added per capita than income does. However, depending on the industry, these features do show statistically significant influences on their development paths. In short, a detailed analysis of income, country-given features, and their combined information allow us to present the patterns of manufacturing transformation before the influence of other country-specific factors for which our model was able to control.

The in-depth analysis of the manufacturing industry at the disaggregated level reveals the basic characteristics of manufacturing sectors with regard to their timing, speed, and stage of development. What these country-specific effects are will be a topic for future research.

References

Chenery, H. B. (1960). 'Patterns of Industrial Growth', *The American Economic Review*, 50 (4): 624–54.

Chenery, H. B., and M. Syrquin (1975). *Patterns of Development 1950–1970*. Oxford: Oxford University Press.

Chenery, H. B., and M. Syrquin (1989). 'Patterns of Development, 1950 to 1983'. Discussion Paper 41. Washington, DC: World Bank.

Chenery, H. B., and L. Taylor (1968). 'Development Patterns: Among Countries and Over Time', *The Review of Economics and Statistics*, 50 (4): 391–416.

Chenery, H. B., S. Robinson, and M. Syrquin (1986). *Industrialization and Growth: A Comparative Study*. Oxford: Oxford University Press.

Clark, C. (1940). *The Conditions of Economic Progress*. London: Macmillan.

Easterly, W., and R. Levine (2003). 'Tropics, Germs and Crops: How Endowments Influence Economic Development', *Journal of Monetary Economics*, 50: 3–39.

Fisher, A. G. B. (1939). 'Production, Primary, Secondary and Tertiary', *Economic Record*, 15: 24–38.

Kader, A. (1985). 'Development Patterns among Countries Reexamined', *The Developing Economies*, 23 (3): 199–220.

Keesing, D. B., and D. R. Sherk (1971). 'Population Density in Patterns of Trade and Development', *American Economic Association*, 61 (5): 956–61.

Kuznets, S. (1957). 'Quantitative Aspects of the Economic Growth of Nations: II. Industrial Distribution of National Product and Labor Force', *Economic Development and Cultural Change*, 5 (4) Supplement: 1–111.

Lin, J. (2010). 'New Structural Economics: A Framework for Rethinking Development'. Policy Research Working Paper 5197. Washington, DC: World Bank.

Maizels, A. (1968). *Exports and Economic Growth of Developing Countries*. Cambridge: Cambridge University Press.

Perkins, D., and M. Syrquin (1989). 'Large Countries: The Influence of Size'. In H. Chenery and T. N. Srinivasan (eds), *Handbook of Development Economics*, Volume II. North Holland: Elsevier Science Publishers.

McMillan, M., and D. Rodrik (2011). 'Globalization, Structural Change, and Productivity Growth'. Mimeo. Boston, MA: Harvard Kennedy School.

Sachs, J. (2001). 'Tropical Underdevelopment'. Working Paper Series 8119. Cambridge, MA: National Bureau of Economic Research.

Syrquin, M. (1988). 'Patterns of Structural Change'. In H. B. Chenery and T. N. Srinivasan (eds), *Handbook of Development Economic*, Volume I. North Holland: Elsevier Science Publishers.

——(1988). 'Structural Change and Economic Development: The Role of the Service Sector', *Journal of Development Economics*, 28 (1): 151–4.

——(2007). 'Kuznets and Pasinetti on the Study of Structural Transformation: Never the Twain shall meet?'. Working Paper 46. Prague/Torino: International Centre for Economic Research.

Taylor, L. (1969). 'Development Patterns: A Simulation Study', *The Quarterly Journal of Economics*, 83 (2): 220–41.

UNIDO (2002). *Industrial Development Report 2002/2003*. Vienna: UNIDO.

Wooldridge, J. (2002). *Econometric Analysis of Cross Section and Panel Data*. Cambridge, MA: MIT Press.

Part III

Pathways to Industrial Development: Past, Present, and Future

5

Learning from Asia's Success: Beyond Simplistic 'Lesson-Making'

Mike Hobday

5.1 Introduction

Many governments, international organizations, consultancy companies, and academic observers look to Asia's economic success, recommending that other developing countries follow similar models and paths of development. Indeed, generating lessons from Asia is quite an industry—and a major contributor to the Washington Consensus analysis of the 1990s and early 2000s. However, Asian 'lesson-making' usually represents a grave error in policy-thinking and in the historical understanding of the nature and process of development.

This chapter examines the paths of successful growth of East and South East Asia, to identify what we can and cannot learn from the Asian experience. The chapter argues that there are no models to imitate and no direct lessons for other developing countries in other regions. It asks the question: if there are no direct lessons or models to imitate, what can other developing countries learn from Asia's success, if anything?

There are some very general things that can be learned from the Asian experience, but these can probably be learned from all forms of successful capitalist development (e.g. the role of education, the need for a stable macroeconomy, the importance of building an infrastructure for development, policies that incentivize rather than penalize entrepreneurship and enterprise). However, the particular paths, models, and specific policies of Asian development cannot—and should not—be copied by other developing countries. The fast-growing Asian economies followed highly unusual and distinctive paths of growth and there was considerable variety across Asia. They did not copy or follow other more developed countries (with the partial exception of Japan)—nor should today's poorer countries. In fact, Asian governments often rejected the 'conventional wisdom' of the day regarding development.

To justify these arguments, Section 5.2 begins by examining some of Asia's paths of development, showing how variety and innovation in organization and technology played a central role. Section 5.3 looks at the typical lessons often drawn from the Asian experience. Section 5.4 turns to some of the great development thinkers of the past, arguing that 'lesson-making' is a common, but incorrect feature of development thinking. Section 5.5 looks at some of the general development insights that can usefully be gleaned from Asia's successful progress. The conclusion summarizes the main arguments.

5.2 Paths and patterns of Asian innovation

When we look at Asia's growth over the past 30 years or so we can see obvious similarities, such as export-led growth, a commitment to education, and economically progressive government policies that enable rather than restrict business. However, beneath these similarities lie a great deal of diversity supported by innovation in policy, institutions, and technology. Indeed, the paths forged by the Asian economies have no obvious historical parallel but were distinctive, innovative, largely unplanned, and unpredictable.

For example, instead of following the conventional economic wisdom of the day (based on comparative advantage theory) the four Asian 'dragons'—Korea, Taiwan, Singapore, and Hong Kong—looked for inspiration to the Japanese export model for lessons and insights. In the case of Korea, there was considerable institutional policy-learning and collaboration with Japan. There was also a widespread rejection of the conventional Western policies of the day. Both Korea and Taiwan rejected free-market comparative-advantage policies and often ignored the recommendations of conventional economists (Vogel 1991). Instead, policy makers, with business leaders, began to deliberately engineer development and invested in the education and infrastructure needed to go beyond low-cost manufacturing based on cheap labour.

The export-led success of the region is well-documented. In 1962, Taiwan and Korea had gross national product per capita levels close to those of the poorer African nations. By 1986 the two countries had moved up the rankings by 47 and 55 places respectively, with average gross domestic product growth of 8 per cent to 10 per cent per annum. Firm-level growth rates were extremely high, often reaching 20 per cent to 30 per cent per annum for sustained periods of time.[1] Hong Kong and Singapore also grew at around 10 per cent annually in the 1960s by expanding their manufacturing industries. As a result of these rapid growth rates, the newly industrializing countries achieved near full employment, with rising wages and higher technology levels. Assembly activities gradually shifted out to Malaysia, Indonesia, Thailand, Vietnam, the Philippines, and China, producing an export-led growth ripple effect in the region. By the early 1990s a significant proportion of world trade and manufacturing had shifted to East and South East Asia.

When we examine how the local exporting firms of East Asia grew, we see both similarities and differences in approaches to technology acquisition and catching-up. These so-called latecomer firms faced considerable developing country disadvantages. They were dislocated from international sources of technology and research and development (R&D) and 'cut off' from Western markets. Unlike leaders and 'followers' based in advanced markets, they confronted formidable challenges, much like firms today in the poorest countries of Africa and Latin America.

Samsung, perhaps the most successful Korean latecomer firm, reveals an incredible story of catch-up via technological learning and innovation from 'behind the technology frontier'. The firm entered the export market through the assembly of simple, low-cost transistor radios and black and white TVs in a joint venture with Sanyo in 1969. Prior to this, its main activities were in insurance, property, paper, and other low-technology products for the local market. By the mid-2000s Samsung Electronics had become one of the most successful electronics producers in the world. In 2007 it registered 2725 patents in the USA, nearly as many as the world leader IBM with 3148. In 2006 Samsung spent US$5.6 billion on R&D, employed around 123,000 workers, operated 17 R&D centres around the globe, and had become a world leader in semiconductors, mobile phones, laptop computers, and several other high-tech electronic goods.

Electronics was, and still is, the main export industry of the Asian region. Samsung's strategy in catching up in electronics provides an insight into how many firms approached the electronics industry, although only a very few, such as Hyundai and L-G of Korea, and Acer and Tatung of Taiwan, have achieved anything like the progress of Samsung. From the early 1960s to the mid-1970s these firms concentrated mainly on basic assembly, beginning the manufacture of standard, simple goods, often supplying foreign transnational corporations (TNCs), mostly from the USA and Japan, under the sub-contracting arrangement called original equipment manufacturer (OEM). Within OEM the foreign TNC buyer supplied the design, technology, and necessary

[1] Information for this section is from Hobday (1996), unless otherwise stated.

training and then distributed the product in the developed country markets under its own brand name. This manufacturing service was of great competitive value to the TNCs in their efforts to lower their production costs. OEM began in basic consumer electronics, components, and simple computing and telecommunications products, as well as electrical appliances such as fans and microwave ovens.

OEM was an important institutional innovation which began in the 1960s and then evolved and expanded considerably. From the mid-1970s to the mid-1990s, Samsung and others learned not only to master the manufacturing process but also to innovate with manufacturing and product improvement. Learning the techniques of product design fed back into the manufacturing processes, enabling 'design-for-manufacture', which improved yields and quality. Following on from improvements to design, the firms learned to design new products and begun offering their own ranges to TNC buyers who would then sell under the TNC brand name. The TNCs benefited from low-cost design and manufacture and often gained much of the value added.

From the mid-1990s onwards, firms learned how to produce original product designs from scratch, and they began to rely more on their own R&D to innovate. Firms like Samsung had invested in design and R&D for many years, both to support manufacturing and to realize the long-term vision of competing as a leader. Its depth of skills in design engineering, R&D and, increasingly, distribution and marketing, enabled Samsung to build up its own brand products and international brand image. Today, Samsung has caught up with world leaders in most of its leading products, including sophisticated DRAM semiconductors, TFT–LCDs, mobile phones, and PCs.

The OEM system was extremely important because it allowed Samsung and others to engage in a long-term, highly organized 'hard slog' of technological learning, in a way that removed the risk of attempting to compete with its own products and brands at the start. By beginning gradually, with simple mechanical assembly, these firms overcame the barriers to entry mentioned above and embarked upon a path of low-cost innovation, whilst at the same time engaging with world markets and technology via foreign customers and technology suppliers.

While analysts and academics at the time promoted the linear model of innovation, which relied on local public research institutes and local universities, these firms built up their capabilities with foreign buyers. To give some idea of its importance, OEM accounted for 70–80 per cent of total Korean electronics exports as recently as the early 1990s. It provided a huge channel for technology transfer from abroad, economies of scale and technological learning at home, and a mechanism for generating large-scale exports and foreign exchange earnings. Often the TNCs, in competition with each other, would provide advice on capital equipment, design engineering, and management training.

This unusual sequence of events allows us to compare the Asian innovation path (see Figure 5.1) with that of 'normal' Western innovation models, which starts with R&D and product creation and leads eventually to manufacturing and product maturity. In contrast to the Western model, Samsung and the others began with mature (i.e. manufacturing-intensive and high-volume) products and technologies and moved 'backwards' along the normal cycle of innovation, from assembly to manufacturing to design, and ultimately to R&D-intensive, low-volume products. This reverses the typical Schumpeterian path, which is supposed to begin with R&D and new products.

This Asian innovation path was highly unusual and innovative in terms of business strategy. Japan had also pursued this type of strategy in some respects (e.g. via sub-contracting to US firms), but was much more developed technologically and economically and had a large internal market. Poor developing countries had never embarked on this type of path on such a scale. Indeed, the economic development 'wisdom' of the day was to develop local industry under the protection of import substitution policies.

Despite innovation similarities, there were in fact many significant differences in paths of development in relation to ownership, industry structure,

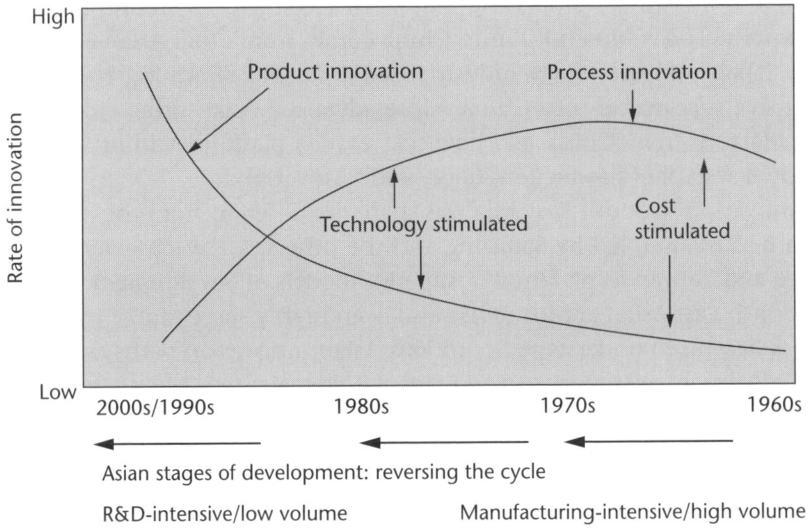

Figure 5.1. Comparing Asian firms with the standard (MIT)* model

Note: *MIT = Massachusetts Institute of Technology.
Source: Derived from the four-country study of Asian electronics (Hobday 1995: 188 and 194); for the standard MIT model see Utterback and Abernathy (1975); for similar models that compare Asian with leadership paths covering a range of industries, see Kim (1997: 89, based on Kim 1980; and Lee et al. 1988).

government policy, firm size, and so on. One broad difference was between East Asia (i.e. Korea, Taiwan, and Hong Kong) and South East Asia. The latter (e.g. Singapore, Malaysia, and Thailand) depended on foreign direct investment (FDI) and the subsidiaries of TNCs to lead export growth, rather than local firms. In Singapore, for example, the government believed that local capitalists were not capable enough to lead industrialization. The government therefore invited foreign TNCs to lead industrialization—a very unpopular policy among developing nations, academics, and international development institutions at the time. However, this policy proved highly successful, with TNCs exporting huge amounts of electronics from special economic zones.

The experimentation that was taking place in South East Asia was leading to a very different trajectory to East Asia (e.g. South Korea and Taiwan). At the time, TNC-led development was a major policy innovation. Today, competing for FDI is almost the new conventional wisdom. Singapore's strategy led to imitation by nearby Malaysia and then Thailand, and later Indonesia, the Philippines, Vietnam, and China. All these countries began by pursuing the innovation path of the East Asian countries, but rather than relying on local firms they relied on foreign subsidiaries. In China, foreign affiliates are today responsible for a large proportion of exports of electronics. Gaulier, Lemoine and Unal-Kesenci (2004) have shown that in 2003 FDI accounted for more than 55 per cent of total Chinese exports, compared with only 20 per cent in 1992. Within China's processing zones, FDI accounted for around 80 per cent of exports. Today, much FDI into China comes from other Asian economies, with Japan and the newly industrialized countries relocating their labour-intensive production into China. More advanced Asian firms today benefit considerably from China as a low-cost export platform within a complex regional system of production, trade, and innovation.

Innovation in South East Asia was therefore different from the innovation path in East Asia, led by Samsung and the others. Many observers point to Korea and Taiwan as preferred or superior models of development. However, the South East Asian approach has also been highly successful.

It is helpful to understand South East Asian innovation paths through the lens of the global strategies of individual TNCs. Figure 5.2 presents the main technological activities carried out by a TNC and its subsidiaries, ranging from basic research at the tip of the triangle through to simple technical improvement activities at the base of the triangle. R&D and core product design tends to be conducted within the TNC home country. Although R&D is often stressed, it amounts usually to the 'tip of the iceberg', usually well under 15 per cent of corporate turnover and often less than 10 per cent. Other vital technological activities include design, engineering, and technician and manufacturing tasks. In the case of subsidiaries in South East Asia (e.g. the Malaysian example in Figure 5.2) this manufacturing-centred profile is also

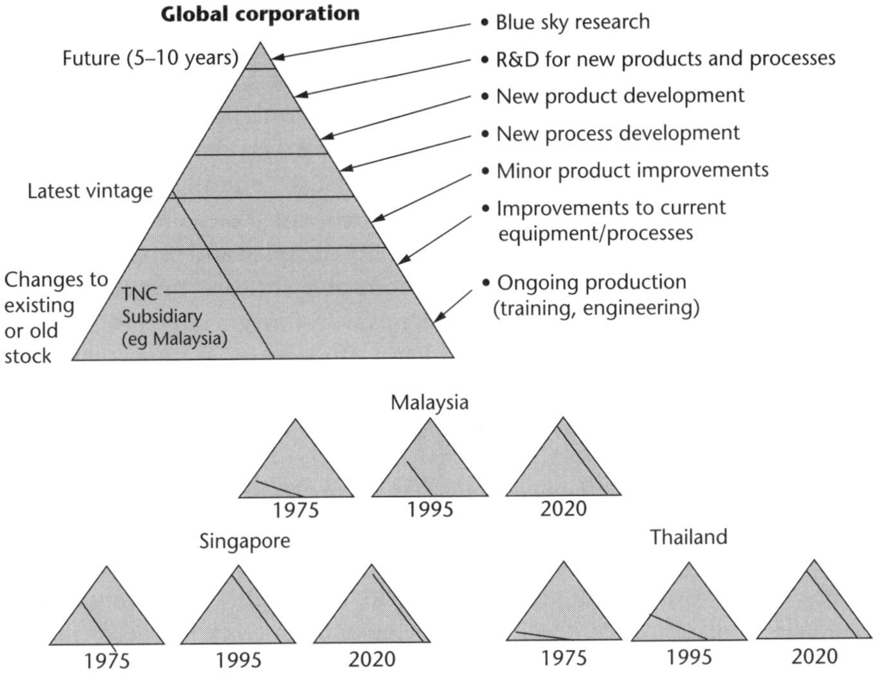

Figure 5.2. TNC subsidiaries: South East Asian model of technology catch-up

Source: Adapted from Hobday (1996: 78) which provides evidence in support of this interpretation.

very important for corporate competitiveness, and is essential for achieving productivity and quality for the TNC.

To put the TNC subsidiary activities in context, they not only form an essential part of the overall operation or 'technology triangle' but also, through time, they have progressed from basic assembly through to higher stages of technological activity, such as process engineering and minor product design, as a result of investments in capital goods technology, skills, and training. Malaysian and Thai subsidiaries are typically situated between higher technology operations in countries such as the USA and the UK and lower-cost operations in China and other less-developed nations. The next stage for TNC subsidiaries in Malaysia and Thailand is to build up further capabilities in precision engineering, product design, and R&D.

The evidence shows that Singapore leads in South East Asia, followed by Malaysia and Thailand, with others still at the basic assembly stage (Hobday 1996, 2000). Over time, technology activities in all countries have gradually extended outwards as the subsidiaries graduate from cheap labour assembly tasks to higher technology activities. Firms such as Motorola and Intel in Malaysia and Seagate in Thailand have made substantial progress in advanced manufacturing technology in areas such as semiconductors and hard disk drives, supplying demand mainly from the USA and Western Europe.

China is very special case. It is following a similar path, but combining local firm (East Asian) *and* TNC-led (South East Asian) growth paths. China has also managed to exploit its unusual advantages of a very large local market, coupled with an immense reservoir of low-cost, technically sound labour. The relatively late entrance of China compared with Korea and Taiwan has allowed it to benefit from an increased mobility of capital and people as well as ideas and business models. China has been able to learn from the earlier developers, sometimes forming partnerships with foreign TNCs keen to gain shares of the expanding local market. China appears to be compressing the earlier 'stages' of technological catch-up by moving more swiftly across the triangle than the earlier entrants and by rapid imitation on the part of local exporting firms.

As well as the broad differences between East and South East Asia and China, the evidence shows considerable variety in policy mechanisms, industrial structures, and firm size, as individual countries intelligently adapted themselves to the export-led growth model to suit their circumstances and resources. Regarding the level of direct government involvement, in the early stages of development (i.e. in the 1960s and 1970s) South Korea and Singapore showed far greater intervention than Taiwan or the laissez-faire approach adopted in Hong Kong. The government in South Korea financially supported and pushed the large *chaebol*[2] into specific export areas with both penalties and privileges (Amsden 1989). In Singapore, the government supported the large foreign TNCs with tax holidays and other incentives through the idea of export processing zones (Yue 1985).

Policy innovation, experimentation, and adaptation occurred across the region. Compared with South Korea and Singapore, Taiwan's initial export path depended on small and medium-sized companies who exported via local and foreign traders (Chou 1992). In Taiwan, many firms were suspicious and fearful of the government, with some operating in the underground economy for many years (Chaponniere and Fouqin 1989). Later on, after the export success in electronics the Taiwanese government became directly involved through large-scale investments in Hsinchu and other industrial parks.

Variety can also be seen in the degree of economic openness of each economy. Korea and Taiwan remained fairly closed to FDI during the 1960s, 1970s, and 1980s, compared with the open economies of Singapore and Hong Kong. Between 1980 and 1988 period, total FDI from Japan and the USA was US$14.3 billion in the four dragons, Hong Kong receiving US$6.3 billion and

[2] *Chaebol* refers to a South Korean form of business conglomerate.

Singapore US$3.6 billion. By contrast South Korea, a much larger economy, only received US$2.3 billion and Taiwan only US$2.1 billion (James 1990: 15). FDI policies differed considerably, with Singapore and Hong Kong having very few restrictions while Taiwan and South Korea enforced tightly controlled FDI regimes, protecting local industries and negotiating each investment in favour of domestic firms and against foreign competitors in local markets. South Korea simply banned many consumer goods and raw materials imports that could be produced locally. The Taiwanese government negotiated the terms of FDI and tied TNC investments to export targets and local-content rules.

We also see great variety in company size, with Taiwan and Hong Kong relying on small (and a few large) ethnic Chinese-owned family businesses, while the South Korean government supported the large local *chaebol*. Taiwan's SMEs tended to rely on speed and flexibility, whereas the *chaebol* of South Korean focused on very high-volume, process-intensive electronics. The South Korean conglomerates learned lessons from the Japanese *keiretsu*,[3] to which many Korean firms were connected through OEM and joint ventures. Many Korean directors spoke Japanese rather than English in the early stage of their business development. Like the Japanese they emphasized large-scale and very high degrees of vertical integration.

Variety and innovation in paths of development were key features of government policy and corporate strategy because each country began with its own distinctive resources and capabilities so that policies needed to be adapted to initial starting conditions. Each country had to develop a strong local capitalist class in slightly different ways, with Korea relying on its local 'tycoons', Singapore on the subsidiaries of foreign TNCs, and Taiwan and Hong Kong on waves of immigrants, rich and poor, fleeing communist China.

5.3 The lesson-making industry

Directly and indirectly, many observers draw lessons from the Asian 'model', ignoring the evidence of the variety and policy innovation in evidence across Asia. Much of the conventional wisdom of the pre-Obama 'Washington Consensus' relies on lessons arising from perceptions of Asian growth. Frequently, agencies such as the World Bank, IMF, EU, OECD, individual governments, academics, and consultancy companies draw on the Asian experience to recommend export-led growth paths, open markets, privatization, high-technology (e.g. biotechnology, new materials, or information and communication technologies (ICT)) production, as well as government support for

[3] *Keiretsu* is a set of Japanese companies with interlocking business relationships and shareholding.

industrial clusters. Not only is it analytically wrong to draw lessons in this way, even worse, many of these policies had little or nothing to do with Asian development. For example, government support for high-tech and knowledge-based industries are very recent phenomena, which have nothing to do with the take-off and rapid growth described in Section 5.2. Often, policy analysts argue that the developing countries of Latin America and other regions should learn lessons from the experiences of successful Asian economies (especially Korea, Taiwan, Singapore, and China) and engage in export-led growth and open markets, ignoring the fact that countries such as Korea and Taiwan often banned imports of 'non-essential' items and placed heavy restrictions on FDI.

Simple follow-the-leader catch-up theory and 'common sense' not only draws on the Asian experience, but also perceived 'best practices' from the currently developed nations, leading to a hotchpotch of policy recommendations (e.g. see Table 5.1) that have no analytical basis and are impossible to follow in practice. For example IBRD (2008) is a major study commissioned by the Commission on Growth and Development sponsored by The International Bank for Reconstruction and Development, part of The World Bank Group. This report develops lessons from 13 successful economies, nine of which are Asian (the others are, curiously, Botswana, Brazil, Malta, and Oman). The report argues that modern institutions and good practices (e.g. privatization, liberalization, modern property rights, and enforceable contract law) are prerequisites for growth and development (rather than a consequence, as in much of Asia). The report also assumes the standard historical 'agriculture to manufacturing' model still applies (e.g. ibid.: 6), whereas, for example, recent Indian growth has been fuelled by domestic services rather

Table 5.1. Rules of good behaviour for promoting economic growth

Original Washington Consensus	'Augmented' Washington Consensus: the previous 10 items, plus
1. Fiscal discipline	11. Corporate governance
2. Reorientation of public expenditures	12. Anti-corruption
3. Tax reform	13. Flexible labour markets
4. Interest rate liberalization	14. Adherence to WTO disciplines
5. Unified and competitive exchange rates	15. Adherence to international financial codes and standards
6. Trade liberalization	16. 'Prudent' capital-account opening
7. Openness to DFI	17. Non-intermediate exchange rate regimes
8. Privatization	18. Independent central banks/inflation targeting
9. Deregulation	19. Social safety nets
10. Secure property rights	20. Targeted poverty reduction

Source: Rodrik (2004: 20). Table reproduced with the permission of Dani Rodrik.

than manufacturing or exports (Singh 2005; Gordon and Gupta 2004; Hansda 2001).

Similarly, the World Bank's 'Doing Business' programme argues that poorer countries should adopt the policies of the leading nations of the world, including the most advanced Asian countries, in areas such as owning property, starting-up businesses, and the liberalization of markets. The programme argues that more than 2 per cent could be added to the growth of the 'most difficult countries to do business' if they adopted the practices of the leading nations (World Bank 2004: 3).

The Doing Business approach can be seen as a subset of the Washington Consensus's conventional wisdom, presented as 'rules of good behaviour for promoting economic growth' (Rodrik 2004: 20). Typical policy recommendations include: export-led growth paths; more open markets (i.e. to foreign investment and imports), privatization, deregulation and business friendly policies, high-tech production (e.g. ICT, bio-technology, and new materials), government support for knowledge-based industries and industrial clusters, and the construction of science and technology parks.

This kind of lesson-making reflects a deeply flawed and ahistorical understanding of how latecomer development occurs. Perhaps even worse, many of the 'lessons' run contrary to the Asian evidence. Some of the 'explanations' and 'best practices' occurred well after the take-off (e.g. science and industrial parks and policies towards clusters). In contrast to high-technology and knowledge-intensive production, the focus of exporting for at least the first 20 years was on 'low-technology' products with fairly simple manufacturing processes. Even today, electronics hardware is the main Asian export staple, rather than software, capital goods, or knowledge-based services, where developing Asia remains conspicuously weak.

Rodrik (2004) provides a lucid critique of the modern lesson-making approach, noting that the Washington Consensus has now been augmented to include new 'rules of good behaviour for promoting economic growth' as shown in Table 5.1. The 'Doing Business' reforms described above are included in items 8 to 13 in the list.

Referring to the 'laundry list' of reforms, Rodrik makes the obvious point that these are based on what the successful country *already* looks like. This may have taken decades or even centuries to achieve. Furthermore, the agenda comes without any mechanism for determining priorities nor any appreciation of the administrative capacity, human resources, and political will and ability required to implement the vast agenda of reforms, which may simply not exist in many developing countries (Rodrik 2004: 6).

Rodrik's arguments mirror those made by Gerschenkron (1962, 1963), discussed in Section 5.4. In his debate with Rostow (1960) Gerschenkron argued that it was intellectually flawed in the extreme to derive policy lessons from the stages of development of the now-developed countries. Gerschenkron contended that industrial development experiences of the past could not provide a model for today's developing countries. In particular, he argued that Rostow's process of identifying the preconditions for development that were missing in a particular country (e.g. investment, modern institutions, and technology)—and then installing them—was not a logical strategy for achieving a take-off to sustained growth. Instead, he argued that it was an example of historical determinism and flawed thinking. Gerschenkron argued that each developing country would need to create its own development agenda based on its existing institutional resources and stage of development. Of course, some things could be learned from earlier industrializers but no direct model could apply (Gerschenkron 1962: 356–8).

A key problem with the Washington consensus reforms applies equally to the myriad of 'lessons' from Asia. As Rodrik (2004: 6–7) puts it:

> Yet the agenda comes without a way of determining priorities. Too often, the result is that policy effort is spread too thinly over too many different areas: governments are overwhelmed with the range of things that need to be done, copies of Western legislation or 'best-practice' codes are adopted without much consideration of their suitability and adaptability, and too little effort is made to render the reforms politically popular and ultimately sustainable . . . The implicit, and sometimes explicit, approach seems to be to say: 'well, we know that all of these things cannot be done at once, but more is better than less, and the more countries can do the better'. So they and the governments they advise proceed opportunistically, and try to complete the enlarged agenda as best as they can, as completely as they can, and as quickly as they can . . . After much effort, governments may find that economic performance has hardly improved . . . Finally, there is something intellectually worrisome about the Augmented Washington Consensus, in that it is entirely unfalsifiable. Such is the nature of the agenda that if a country adopts it and fails to grow, it is always possible to find something wrong with what the government did. So in the end it is the policymakers who end up being chastized for the 'incompleteness' of their reforms. And if enough countries find themselves in this predicament, then it must be time to augment the list further by adding yet other needed reforms.

Rodrik and his colleagues provide their own historical study of spurts of growth over the last 50 years (Hausmann et al. 2004). They show that the vast majority of growth take-offs are not preceded or produced by significant economic reforms. Equally, most significant economic reforms do not produce growth take-offs. Like Gerschenkron (1962), Rodrik argues for a country-specific 'diagnostic' approach to growth. A poor country needs to identify and address the 'binding constraint' or most significant bottleneck to growth, which could be a lack of investment funds, high costs of capital, or the inability of firms to appropriate returns on investment. Other barriers to development might include macroeconomic instability, internal political conflict, war, corruption, and a lack of obvious opportunities for achieving dynamic comparative advantage through specialization.

5.4 Learning from the classic development debates: the fallacy of lesson-making

The modern lesson-making problem is a new version of an old debate highlighted in the argument between Rostow and other leading development economists, most notably Gerschenkron, in the 1960s. W. W. Rostow (1916–2003), like today's policy-makers, also proposed a 'follow the leader' approach. His classic text *The Stages of Economic Growth: A Non-Communist Manifesto* (1960) sold more than 260,000 copies in the first edition and became the conventional policy wisdom of the day, taught in many universities. Rostow's main contribution was a prescriptive growth model for developing countries, based on stages of economic development and take-off of the then developed countries. Rostow argued:

> It is useful, as well as roughly accurate to regard the process of development now going forward in Asia, the Middle East, Africa, and Latin America as analogies to the stages of the preconditions and take-off of other societies in the late eighteenth, nineteenth, and early twentieth centuries.... (Rostow 1960: 153)

This is a remarkably similar agenda to that of today's policy imitators, i.e. the lessons of past industrializers (e.g. Asia) should be applied directly to the developing countries of today.

However, several other economists at the time were highly sceptical of this approach. Alexander Gerschenkron (1904–78) a Russian-born, Austrian-trained Harvard economic historian, completely rejected the ideas of Rostow as ill-conceived and ahistorical. Gerschenkron researched European latecomer industrialization and also viewed industrialization as a 'stagelike' process but disagreed fundamentally with Rostow, arguing that: (i) there were (and could be) no automatic stages of development; and (ii) latecomers did not/could not pass through the same stages as previous industrializers, precisely because others had passed through them, changing the market and technological circumstances facing new industrializers.

Gerschenkon argued that each country has its own distinctive resources, related to its own particular stage of backwardness, which would strongly influence any potential growth path. He found the idea of identifying previous states of growth useful, but not for imitation or policy purposes. In his text of 1962, *Economic Backwardness in Historical Perspective: A Book of Essays*, he argued:

> ... this [Gerschenkron's interpretation of stages] differs essentially from the various efforts in 'stage making', [typified by Rostow] the common feature of which was the assumption that all economies were supposed regularly to pass through the same individual stages as they moved along the road of economic progress ... Thus, Rostow was at pains to assert that the process of industrialization repeated itself from country to country. ... (Gerschenkron (1962: 355)[4]

Simon Kuznets (1958, 1966) made similar points. Kuznets argued that the developing economies of his era possessed characteristics distinct from earlier developers, disputing the conventional view that countries tended to go through the same stages in their development history. He argued that:

> Examination of similarities and differences [of industrialization experiences] should be particularly instructive [for today's developing countries] since it would suggest the different role of various factors as the conditions, set by the changing world scene and the historical heritages of each country, modify the process of adjustment to the industrial system. (Kuznets 1958: 152)

Kuznets' cross-sectional and time-series empirical evidence on the characteristics of developing countries showed that they possessed very different structural characteristics compared with the industrialized countries at the time they developed. There could be no simple predictable paths or stages. As a result, he helped establish the field of development economics, the main task of which was to illustrate the distinctive paths and experiences of contemporary developing countries.

Similarly, in his celebrated paper, 'Catching Up, Forging Ahead and Falling Behind', Moses Abramovitz (1986: 405–6) stressed the shaping role of the initial conditions of developing nations in their growth and development potential, arguing that the prevailing institutions and educational attainment levels were key factors governing the diffusion of knowledge and the mobility of resources in any particular country. He argued that:

> The state of a country's capability to exploit emerging technological opportunity depends on a social history that is particular to itself and that may not be closely bound to its existing level of productivity. And there are changes in the character of technological advance that make it more congruent with the resources and institutional outfits of some countries but less congruent with those of others. (ibid.: 405)

More recently Richard Nelson (1998) argued the case for more sophisticated and history-friendly growth models to reflect observed historical patterns. In his paper, 'The Agenda for Growth Theory: A Different Point of View', Nelson criticizes evidence and history-free modern growth models. He reflects on the

[4] For a full discussion, see Hobday (2003).

need to understand and differentiate between different kinds of national systems of innovation in developing countries, again stressing variety. To be of value, theories need to understand the nature of institutions and technological processes as well as the different capabilities of firms. Nelson makes the point that growth and technological advance are disequilibrium processes, which are not (and perhaps cannot be) captured in existing formal growth models. Again we see variety and distinctiveness as key features of growth.

From a theoretical perspective, these insights suggest the need for a resource-based conceptualization of economic development, perhaps similar to, and drawing from, the firm-level theory of growth introduced by Penrose (1959), which was later extended to embrace the idea of 'dynamic capabilities' (Teece and Pisano 1997). Such a theory could conceptualize the rare and distinctive resources required for latecomer countries to develop, and compare these with the resources prevalent in already-developed economies, illustrating paths and processes of development.

Returning to Gerschenkron, there are several other highly instructive insights from his analysis of European latecomer development: '... the industrial development of Europe appears not as a series of mere repetitions of the "first" industrialization but as an orderly system of graduated deviations from that industrialization' and '... the higher degree of backwardness, the more discontinuous the development is likely to be' (Gerschenkron 1962: 44 and 45), suggesting variety and discontinuity in patterns of development. This idea of graduated deviation in Europe conforms closely to the experience of Asian industrialization. Japan was the first to develop, followed by the four 'dragons'—South Korea, Taiwan, Hong Kong, and Singapore—with significant differences. The four dragons were then followed by the second-tier countries of South East Asia (including Malaysia, Thailand, Indonesia, and Thailand). China's economy took off, combining many of the 'old' strategies of East and South East Asia (e.g. exports via foreign multinationals and large-scale subcontracting through locally owned firms), but with radical new features, including the exploitation of a very large local market and its huge supplies of cheap technical labour. China's development must also be viewed in the context of the latest phase of increasingly fluid internationalization of capital, managerial labour, and productive and innovative activity, which was quite different from the conditions facing the four dragons in the 1960s and 1970s.

Regarding imitation, Gerschenkron proposed that, rather than proceeding to imitate prior industrializers, modern latecomers should engage in the 'substitution of missing prerequisites'. Contesting Rostow's view, Gerschenkron held that latecomers should not invest in some standard set of prerequisites or preconditions but, instead, to *substitute* for missing prerequisites. Indeed, European history should be seen as a pattern of substitution of missing prerequisites, governed by the prevailing and changing degree of backwardness.

In substituting for missing prerequisites, Gerschenkron stressed the importance of innovation and learning through trial and error. 'The very concept of substitution is premised upon creative innovating activity, that is to say, upon something that is inherently unpredictable with the help of our normal apparatus of research' Gerschenkron (1962: 359–60). As far as using this analytical method for developing policy lessons was concerned, Gerschenkron was very cautious:

> There is no intention to suggest that backward countries necessarily engaged in deliberate acts of 'substitution' for something that had been in evidence in more advanced countries. Men in a less developed country may have simply groped for and found solutions that were consonant with the existing conditions of backwardness. Gerschenkron. (1962: 359)

In the context of 'lessons' from Asia, this discussion has two important implications. First, it points to the intrinsically unpredictable and innovative nature of latecomer paths to development. Second, it indicates that the 'normal' apparatus of research cannot easily grapple with or shape contemporary latecomer development.

5.5 What can be learned?

Most Asian research suggests the importance of basic and technical education, a relatively stable macroeconomy for business planning, entrepreneurial culture, a reasonably efficient infrastructure, fairly effective government, and the need for gradually upgrading the technological base of the economy. Export-led growth played a major role in most of the Asian countries, but has been less important in Indian growth, which has been largely driven internally (Handa 2001; Singh 2005). According to some, Chinese growth is also 'turning inwards' as the export source of growth (perhaps temporarily) declined due to the economic crisis (STRATFOR 2009). However, despite Western recommendations that China should rely more on its domestic market, it is unclear whether this will in fact take place and over what time period such a major adjustment would occur. These basic features of Asian growth are highly 'general' statements, which provide little policy guidance even if other countries wanted to follow the old Asian model, which may now have run its course as the Asian countries move towards middle- and high-income levels.

Furthermore, the specific ways in which Asian countries pursued their growth—their paths of 'graduated deviation'—are most definitely the lessons of the past, relating to yesterday's development battles. They are highly unlikely to provide a guide to the future for other developing regions or countries.

Indeed, at a prescriptive detailed policy level, there are few (if any) direct historical lessons or models to imitate from Asia or, indeed, from other successful cases. For example, the Asian export focus on electronics hardware may well now be a 'boat that has passed' (or a window of opportunity that has closed) and other countries would be wise not to try and imitate or compete with the Asian nations, which now collectively represent a formidable world centre for production and innovation in this sector.

So, what should other poor developing countries do? To begin with, in Gerschenkron's terms, it may well be useful to think of the 'missing prerequisites' facing specific countries and how they can be substituted for using local resources, capabilities, and skills. This might require 'out-of-the-box' thinking. For example, if government capabilities are missing—or if government bureaucracy is a barrier to development (as argued generally by de Soto 2000 and, for India, Das 2006)—then development may have to rely on the private sector and business-led development, as appears to be the case for the Indian software industry (Athreye and Hobday 2009). If export-led growth is no longer an option for most countries (given the collapse in Western demand and the strength of China and other Asian exporters), then local demand, regional markets, and other developing countries might provide alternative targets, as in the case of some recent Brazilian successes (Teixeira 2008).

This kind of approach may assist in developing possible future scenarios for experimentation and learning. This accepts the major differences between developing countries and suggests that nations should look to their own distinctive resources and capabilities to chart their own road to development.

For example, as Perez (2008) argues in her 'Vision for Latin America', the region's natural resource endowments are a potential platform for a technologically dynamic future. By identifying the distinctive capabilities and resources of individual nations through a mixture of empirical research and creative thinking about possible futures, new paths may be identified. This approach rejects 'follow-the-leader' policy-thinking and focuses on the search for new innovative growth paths that build on each country's history, capabilities, and opportunities. Unpredictable forms of innovation might be expected to be a core dimension of any successful growth path.

This is in fact a key, if implicit, 'lesson' from Asia. In Asia, the process of exploiting export-led growth in electronics occurred out of experimentation and trial-and-error learning. There is no evidence that planners or government agencies chose the sectors or technologies in advance, only that they were determined to overcome their natural resource limitations, problems of poverty and unemployment and local market constraints in any way possible.

Electronics 'emerged' from small beginnings after other sectors such as foodstuffs, clothing, apparel, toys, and electrical goods had shown the value of low-cost assembly activities for gaining export earnings.

In Asia, different policies emerged from the varied local endowments and capabilities and a great deal of graduated deviation took place. The Asian development take-off in the 1950s and 1960s occurred largely in the dark, through trial-and-error learning. No other developing nation had grown in the way these countries did, using large-scale OEM and TNC-led export production. The latter were genuine institutional innovations that engaged local firms in foreign technology acquisition and export marketing. Today, it may be possible to go beyond Gerschenkron's notion of groping forward to find solutions (1962: 354). Perhaps key groups could agree a broad 'sense of direction' and develop innovative projects based on local advantages, and which might stimulate further experimentation and entrepreneurial activity in a variety of potentially dynamic areas of development.

The Asian growth experience *complemented* the take-off in world demand for electronics hardware, which was itself fuelled by innovations in ICT. This suggests that rather than imitate or compete with Asia, the most appropriate approach is to *complement, rather than copy* the Asian economies (and for that matter the most successful developed countries). By identifying untapped potential where a developing nation has a comparative advantage over fast-growing Asia—and which complements Asian growth—the country in question could benefit from the success of Asia. This is a very different 'mindset' from Washington Consensus, IBRD, and World Bank thinking, which looks to Asia and advanced countries for 'lessons'. In fact, this kind of complementary specialization has already occurred, as some Latin American and African nations supply raw materials to support China's recent growth.

Korea, Taiwan, and Singapore are densely populated countries with low endowments of natural resources. Other Asian countries such as China, Malaysia, and Indonesia are abundant in some natural resources but still require imports to enable rapid growth. We know from the Asian manufacturing export experience that the key to turning this opportunity into a long-term, sustainable growth path is to ensure that initial entry is followed by progressive, step-by-step, deliberate technological and economic upgrading. However, we often find, for example in the case of Latin America, that natural resource upgrading has not been the core of the growth strategy, and suppliers remain technologically weak. Latin America, as Perez (2008) argues, is rich in natural resources and relatively weak in manufacturing export industry. Because many Latin American firms have long experience in natural resource development—these 'complementary' positions give Asia the advantage in labour- and technology-intensive manufacturing, while Latin America has a potential dynamic comparative advantages in resource-based processing industries. Latin American nations have extremely varied resource endowments and capabilities so that, within this broad thrust of development, specialization can be achieved within and between economies.

Perez's vision for Latin America is a good example of the 'complement not copy' approach to thinking about development. Her strategy entails a rapid technological upgrading of specific resource-based activities in particular countries, aimed at improved export performance through continuous innovation in products, processes, technology, and services. Recent research by Teixeira (2008) on Brazil shows that this type of upgrading has already begun in some industries (not only process industries), leading to strong Brazilian export performance in sectors as diverse as cosmetics, toilets and fragrance, food and beverages, textiles, machines and equipment, automotive production, veterinary products (including animal health products), and the medical industry equipment (including magnetic resonance equipment). In each of these industries, Brazil now competes with world leaders and local firms have upgraded and transformed their innovation and marketing capabilities. This process of transition from import-substitution to export-led growth in Brazil was characterized by continuous technological innovation and the growth of robust export-market competencies.

However, Teixeira's work also shows that these achievements are limited to a fairly small number of leading firms and that policy makers have not understood or supported progress in this area. So far, relatively few private sector companies have participated so, despite some islands of growth, there has been no 'bandwagon' effect as yet and the economy-wide impact is limited. Other research on successful high-technology capital goods exporting from Argentina (Papa 2009) and software exports from India (Athreye and Hobday 2009) shows that despite a lack of government understanding and, in some cases, government barriers and hurdles, businesses may still innovate and thrive.

The issue of sustainability must also be considered. Today, 'growth for its own sake' is increasingly being questioned and becoming less viable in a world of instant mass communication and corporate scrutiny by the media. Growth without environmental responsibility, energy conservation, and social inclusion is rightly criticized and offending corporations can suffer dramatic brand damage, along with loss of reputation and a decline in share value. Forms of growth capable of addressing unemployment, underemployment, and poverty need to be sought out in poor countries. In much of the developing world 'trickledown' alone has seldom brought about wide social benefits. Therefore, new approaches to development should not only focus on growth opportunities but also somehow address poverty, unemployment, and the environment (see Chapter 12).

Responsible growth is most likely to occur with some kind of socially and politically shared vision, supported by an effective institutional framework capable of consensus building among groups in government, business, universities, and non-governmental organizations. Creative and clear policy measures, which avoid bureaucracy and induce the right kind of market behaviour and entrepreneurialism, are needed. In today's mass communications environment, deliberate consensus building among social groups may be more plausible than in previous eras, creating a positive-sum growth-development strategy that builds on local capabilities.

Today, despite Gerschenkron's reservations concerning the 'normal apparatus of research' (1962: 359–60), research may be able to play a useful role in developing specific research agendas. For example, research can identify cases where growth processes are already occurring, perhaps in embryonic ways, illustrating how firms confront and overcome barriers to growth and learn how to innovate and export (Teixeira 2008; Athreye and Hobday 2009). Different kinds of specialization routes and strategies may be identified by research and learned from, preparing the ground for an expansion of such activities. Research evidence may help promote new policies and strategies that bring about small practical changes that contribute to a shared vision.

There is also potential for developing and applying practical tools and processes that are able to convert research-based ideas, models, and examples into strategies and visions. Tools and ideas developed by leading companies in the private sector could potentially be modified and integrated into more traditional academic research and applied to strategy development. For example, de Geus (1988, 1999) shows how Royal Dutch Shell used their planning process to learn about and shape possible futures; this work helped to develop the idea of the learning organization. Schwartz (1991) developed a range of tools for engagement with different organizations in order to help shape future opportunities. Pfeffer and Sutton (2000) provide methods for turning research knowledge into action, arguing that there is little purpose for the accumulation of research for its own sake.

However, any such action-research experiments need to be co-developed with development practitioners through all their stages, not just at the end of the research as academics typically do. In other words, such research needs to be carried out with decision makers in government, business, and other social groups who might contribute to development. The latter must be fully engaged in the vision process, as they are responsible for bringing about change.

5.6 Conclusion

This chapter argues that it is both analytically wrong and empirically flawed to draw direct policy lessons or to develop models from Asia for other developing countries to imitate. In contrast to the recommendations of many experts, developing nations should not attempt to imitate the paths of the successful Asian economies, and they certainly should not chose similar sectors or technologies in which to compete with them directly.

When we examine paths of Asian development through the lens of successful exporting industries we see a great deal of variety, not only in policy-making, but also in industrial structure, corporate ownership, firm strategy, size of business, and so on. Often the innovation in policy, institutions, technology, and business approach we observe in Asia is ignored in lesson-making. Sometimes the underpinning 'success factors' identified are simply incorrect or occurred long after the growth take-off.

However, even if the Asian diagnosis was correct it would still be a grave mistake to draw policy lessons that imitate the paths of the successful Asian economies, or indeed the 'best practices' of other advanced nations. This is because technological and market circumstances have now changed and any sensible strategy for development must be based on the resources, stage of development, challenges, and external circumstances now facing the particular country in question. There can be no standard list of development prerequisites or 'best practices'. Each case must be treated on its own merits, taking into account its public- and private-sector institutional structures and competencies.

The basic mistake of 'follow the leader' catch-up policy has a long tradition in development thinking. Indeed, in our examination of an earlier version of this debate that occurred in the post-war period, the use of growth stages and prerequisites for lesson-making was heavily criticized by leading economists of the time, a fact which seems to have been overlooked, forgotten, or ignored by many observers today. Kuznets (1958, 1966), Gerschenkron (1962, 1963), and Abramovitz (1986) all argued that development processes and strategy must be based on the resources, capabilities, institutions, and external conditions facing individual nations, not on the paths or models of previous industrializers.

However, developing nations cannot ignore the rise of Asia. And there may well be some subtle and useful insights from the Asian experience. In building on their own unique sets of capabilities and institutions developing countries should (like Asia did) seek to complement, not copy, the growth paths of more successful economies, including Asian ones. One of the insights to be gained from each of the Asian nations is the importance of identifying and building a distinctive path of development, supported by policies that encourage these paths. This will probably require, as it did with Asia, significant innovation and creativity in business organization, wider institutional structures, and technology. Today's developing nations, like Asia, need to forge their own distinctive and, by definition, novel development paths.

In discussing government policy, the capability, experience, and track record of the particular government must also be taken into consideration. Some governments erect hurdles and barriers to development and wittingly or unwittingly suffocate entrepreneurship and innovation through their policies (de Soto 2000). Certainly, some governments are more capable than others and in the absence of competent government alternative pathways to development need to be sought. In this chapter we pointed to several cases where business and export growth occurred without the knowledge or support of government and, in some cases, despite the efforts of government (Athreye and Hobday 2009; Papa 2009). In short, while there can be no direct or specific lessons or models to be imitated, other developing countries can learn many interesting and useful things from Asia's success.

References

Abramovitz, M. (1986). 'Catching Up, Forging Ahead and Falling Behind', *The Journal of Economic History*, 46 (2): 385–406.

Amsden, A. (1989). *Asia's Next Giant: South Korea and Late Industrialization*. New York: Oxford University Press.

Athreye, S., and M. Hobday (2009). 'Overcoming Development Adversity: How Entrepreneurs Led Software Development in India', *Journal of Technological Learning, Innovation and Development*, 3 (1): 36–46.

Chaponniere, J. R., and M. Fouquin (1989). 'Technological Change and the Electronics Sector—Perspectives and Policy Options for Taiwan'. Report prepared for a Development Centre Project. Paris: OECD.

Chou, T. C. (1992). 'The Experience of SMEs' Development in Taiwan: High Export-Contribution and Export-Intensity', *Rivista Internazionale di Scienze Economiche e Commerciali*, 39 (12): 1067–84.

Das, G. (2006). 'The India Model', *Foreign Affairs*, 85 (4): 2–16.

de Geus, A. (1988). 'Planning as Learning', *Harvard Business Review*, 66 (2): 70–4.

——(1999). *The Living Company: Growth, Learning and Longevity in Business*. London: Nicholas Brealey Publishing.

de Soto, H. D. (2000). *The Mystery of Capital: Why Capitalism Triumphs in the West and Fails Everywhere Else*. New York: Basic Books.

Gaulier, G., F. Lemoine, and D. Unal-Kesenci (2004). 'China's Integration in Asian Production Networks and its Implications'. Paper prepared for the Conference

'Resolving New Global and Regional Imbalances in an Era of Asian Integration', CEPII, Tokyo, 17–18 June.
Gerschenkron, A. (1962). *Economic Backwardness in Historical Perspective: A Book of Essays*. Cambridge, MA: The Belknap Press of Harvard University Press.
——(1963). 'The Early Phases of Industrialisation in Russia'. In W. W. Rostow (ed.), *The Economics of Take-off into Sustained Growth*. Basingstoke: Palgrave Macmillan.
Gordon, J., and P. Gupta (2004). 'Understanding India's Services Revolution'. Working Paper WP/04/171. Washington, DC: IMF.
Hansda, S. (2001). 'Sustainability of Services-Led Growth: An Input Output Analysis of the Indian Economy'. Reserve Bank of India Occasional Paper, 22 (1, 2, and 3). Mumbai: Reserve Bank of India.
Hausmann, R., D. Rodrik, and A. Velasco (2004): 'Growth Diagnostics'. Unpublished Manuscript. Cambridge, MA: Harvard University. Available at http://ksghome
Hobday, M. (1995). *Innovation in East Asia: The Challenge to Japan*. Cheltenham: Edward Elgar.
——(1996). 'Innovation in South East Asia: Lessons for Europe?', *Management Decision*, 34 (9): 71–82.
——(2003). 'Innovation in Asian Industrialisation: A Gerschenkronian Perspective'. *Oxford Development Studies*, 31 (3): 293–314.
International Bank for Reconstruction and Development (IBRD) (2008). 'The Growth Report: Strategies for Sustained Growth and Inclusive Development'. Washington, DC: IBRD and World Bank, Commission on Growth and Development.
James, W. (1990). 'Basic Directions and Areas for Cooperation: Structural Issues of the Asia-Pacific Economies'. Asia Pacific Cooperation Forum, Session 2, Korea Institute for International Economic Policy, Seoul, 21–22 June.
Kim, L. (1980). 'Stages of Development of Industrial Technology in a Less Developed Country: A Model', *Research Policy*, 9 (3): 254–77.
——(1997). *Imitation to Innovation: The Dynamics of Korea's Technological Learning*. Boston, MA: Harvard Business School Press.
Kuznets, S. (1958). 'The Pre-Industrial Phase in Advanced Countries: an Attempt at Comparison'. In A. N. Agarwala and S. P. Singh (eds), *The Economics of Underdevelopment*. Oxford: Oxford University Press.
——(1966). '*Modern Economic Growth: Rate, Structure, and Spread*. New Haven, CO: Yale University Press.
Lee, J., Z. T. Bae, and D. K. Choi (1988). 'Technology Development Processes: A Model for a Developing Country with a Global Perspective', *R&D Management*, 18 (3): 235–50.
Nelson, R. R. (1998). 'The Agenda for Growth Theory: A Different Point of View', *Cambridge Journal of Economics*, 22: 497–520.
Papa, J. (2009). 'Catching up in Capital Goods and High Technology Services: The Unusual Case of an Argentinean Latecomer Firm'. Unpublished MSc Thesis. Sussex: University of Sussex, SPRU.
Penrose, E. T. (1959). *The Theory of the Growth of the Firm*. Oxford: Basil Blackwell.

Perez, C. (2008). 'A Vision for Latin America: A Resource-Based Strategy for Technological Dynamism and Social Inclusion'. Paper presented to the ECLAC Programme on Technology Policy and Development in Latin America, Santiago, Chile.

Pfeffer, J., and R. I. Sutton (2000). *The Knowing Doing Gap: How Smart Companies Turn Knowledge into Action.* Boston, MA: Harvard Business School Press.

Rodrik, D. (2004). 'Rethinking Growth Policies in the Developing World', Locu d'Agliano Lecture in Development Economics, Torino, Italy.

Rostow, W. W. (1960). *The Stages of Economic Growth: a Non-Communist Manifesto.* Cambridge: Cambridge University Press.

Singh, A. (2005). 'The Past, Present and Future of Industrial Policy in India: Adapting to Changing Domestic and International Environment'. Paper presented at New Delhi Industrial Policy Meeting, University of Cambridge, Faculty of Economics, 13–14 December.

Schwartz, P. (1991). *The Art of the Long View: Paths to Strategic Insight for Yourself and Your Company.* New York: Currency Doubleday.

Strategic Forecasting, Inc. (STRATFOR) (2009). 'China's Internal Divisions, Economic Crisis and the Stimulus Plan'. Economics/China Economy, 24 February.

Teece, D. J., and G. P. Pisano (1997). 'Dynamic Capabilities and Strategic Management', *Strategic Management Journal*, 18 (7): 509–33.

Teixeira, A. (2008). 'Latecomer Transition Capabilities: The Case of Brazilian Export Firms'. Unpublished PhD Thesis. Sussex: University of Sussex, SPRU.

Utterback, J. M., and W. J. Abernathy (1975). 'A Dynamic Model of Process and Product Innovation', *OMEGA, The International Journal of Management Science*, 3 (6): 639–56.

Yue, C. S. (1985). 'The Role of Foreign Trade and Investment in the Development of Singapore'. In W. Galenson (ed.), *Foreign Trade and Investment: Economic Development in the Newly Industrialising Asian Countries.* Wisconsin: University of Wisconsin Press.

Vogel, E. F. (1991). *The Four Little Dragons: the Spread of Industrialisation in East Asia.* Cambridge, MA: Harvard University Press.

World Bank (2004). *Doing Business in 2005.* Washington, DC: World Bank.

6

Rethinking China's Path of Industrialization

Harry X. Wu

6.1 Introduction

Economic theory can logically explain how a preindustrialization economy may grow out of its traditional or agrarian constraints, and hence start an industrialization process that will go through a sequence of stages as described by 'stylized facts' in textbooks. However, economic history shows that there has never been a universal path of industrialization among countries (Maddison 1995, 2001).[1] One of the factors that make countries significantly diverge in their paths of industrialization is the role of the state; that is, *how* and *to what extent* the government has influenced or intervened in the allocation of resources through policy instruments and hence has transformed and shaped the course of economic development.[2]

Though much has been written about the uniqueness of China's industrialization, the literature still lacks an integrated view—conceptually as well as empirically—on China's experiences, with more than 100 years of industrialization prior to the market-oriented industrial reforms in the mid-1980s.[3] Most studies focus on the post-reform period's unprecedented growth spurt, which was driven by a series of policy changes and institutional rearrangements, using the performance of the planning era as a reference. The poorer

[1] Also see Maddison (1970) for the role of government in driving and shaping the courses of economic development among countries through various industrial policies.

[2] Of course, as correctly put by Mason (1960), the government, as part of society or history, and inevitably shaped by it, cannot go and shape the course of the society's development as far as it likes. Ultimately, how far it can go depends on how the government intervenes in the principle of cost and benefit of the economy and the society.

[3] Although popularly used in official documentation and by researchers, the year of 1978 can be accepted as the timeline to distinguish China's reform period from its planning past; nationwide agricultural reform only began in 1979–80 and industrial reform in 1985, along with a dual-track price system.

productivity performance under central planning is widely considered as a fiasco resulting from an imported Soviet model of industrialization that completely ignored China's comparative advantage (see Lin, Cai, and Li 1996). However, I would argue that China's path of industrialization is not unique because of its distinct resource endowments as the world most populous country, its cultural and ideological heritages, or its institutional traditions. What distinguishes China is the unique role of the state throughout China's long pursuit for modernization since the mid-nineteenth century, when Western powers forced the country to open up. Chinese governments, under different regimes in the past one and a half centuries, intervened, engineered, and hence shaped the course of China's industrialization at almost every vital stage. This not only laid important foundations for, but also created constraints on its subsequent development. Heavy government intervention on such a large scale is not only inherently inefficient but is also likely to have made China's industrialization path-dependent. This will be explored further in this chapter.

Collecting, organizing, and interpreting historical evidence on the role of the state in China's industrialization is unavoidably subjective and cannot easily be done in a systematic way. Here I will rely on a more objective approach to analyse the role and impact of the state, using a newly constructed dataset designed to tackle major data shortcomings in standard growth accounting analysis. The data covers the Chinese aggregate economy and its major sectors since 1949 (Wu 2011). The industrial part of the dataset will be linked, in a preliminary fashion, with an earlier series going back to 1912, the time when the Republican Revolution ended China's Qing Dynasty and set off a new wave of investment in modern industries.

To outline this chapter, Section 6.2 briefly discusses the key factors explaining government intervention in the modern economic development in general. Section 6.3 attempts to use a novel graphical approach to explore the role of the government in China's post-1949 industrialization, using India's growth path as a reference. Then, Section 6.4 attempts to identify the driving forces of China's industrial production since the beginning of the twentieth century to substantiate my path-dependence conjecture. Section 6.5 sets out the new dataset to be used. Based on this data Section 6.6 presents a systematic analysis of the growth, sectoral change, and productivity performance of the Chinese economy throughout both the planning and the reform periods, against the background of major policy regime shifts. The Section 6.7 concludes the main findings with a deeper discussion of the nature of the 'China model' problems, which will shed light on how to break the inefficient path that has been sustained and developed by strong state interests.

6.2 Why do governments intervene in economic development?

The direct reason for governments to intervene or even engage in economic activities lies in state interests, ranging from a concern for national security to a desire to catch up with the advanced countries. However, the root cause of intervention is economic backwardness that is essentially determined by the time when a country begins its course of industrialization. Gerschenkron (1962), who was one of the first authors to introduce the concept of backwardness, relates an increasing role of the state to the degree of backwardness found in the society in which the process of industrialization is being initiated. By influencing the goals of the society and the motivations of its political elites, backwardness can shift the responsibility of development to government because it can play an important role in the transfer of new technologies and the establishment of new industries as well as their required institutions. In this sense, backwardness may result in a government-facilitated process of accelerated catch-up in which a country can skip some of the earlier or unnecessary stages of technological development.

Government intervention is widely observed among the post-Second World War late-industrializers that were pressured to pursue rapid catch-up. Amongst these, the newly industrialized countries in East Asia have been studied most thoroughly, in order to identify the causes of their successes, especially with regard to the role of government. However, researchers still remain divided on how to relate various government interventions to the unprecedented growth performance of these countries.[4] The active role of the state is not only confined to the late industrializers but can also be observed in the countries that industrialized earlier. Concerns about technological backwardness, national security, and welfare improvement were the main driving forces. As shown by Aubrey (1949) with ample evidence, the adoption of new English innovations by the French was stimulated by the Continental Blockade of the Napoleonic Era in Europe (1799–1815). The struggle for independence (1775–83), the self-imposed embargo (1807), and its war aftermath (1812–15) in the USA had similar functions. Governments took deliberate actions to foster the formation of national industries, typically by establishing machinery industries, promoting mechanical production, and encouraging the widest possible diffusion of new technologies because 'most governments were reluctant to see their industries decline under the impact of increased foreign productivity and to risk subsequent domestic shortages' (Aubrey 1951: 266–7). Government intervention became accentuated in the Schumpeterian gales of technological innovations and international competitions in the second wave of

[4] For example, see different views in a NBER East Asia volume edited by Ito and Krueger (1995), see also Hobday in this volume.

the Industrial Revolution that began in the 1850s, because of an ever-increasing need for the state to quickly facilitate entrepreneurial initiatives by setting up venture capital support and by distributing the latest technical knowhow.

The nature of the prevailing technological stage also matters. As argued by Amsden (1991), who conducted a thorough investigation into the determinants of South Korea's industrialization in 1989, the main reason for government intervention becoming indispensable in East Asia was that late industrialization was driven by *imitating* existing technologies rather than *innovating*. This is because

> ... [in] the absence of pioneering technology, low wages even in labor intensive sectors usually fail to provide a cost advantage at market determined prices. Persistent problems of competitiveness... have compelled the state to play a more active role than in the past. (ibid.: 1991: 285)

In essence, the nature of the government intervention is subsidization, explicit or implicit, to help establish, strengthen, or maintain a cost advantage.

I would argue that the timing of industrialization and the nature of technology determined by the timing of industrialization are still insufficient to explain the active role of the state. We should not disregard the role of the economies of scale caused by the size of a country.[5] This argument is related to resource constraints. It is very costly for small countries to build up their own producer goods industries due to the lack of economies of scale.[6] Instead, small countries can benefit from exchanging goods and services in which they have a comparative advantage (typically natural resources or related services) for imports of manufactured goods from other countries. A small economy is necessarily more dependent on trade than a large economy (Kuznets 1958). Since it is small enough to be a price taker and hence has little influence on world market prices, it presents no threat to other countries and can rely on international alliances for purposes of national security. Since a small country can achieve modernization without going through a typical industrialization process involving the establishing of its own capital goods sector, it is not necessary for the state to play an active role, even in a

[5] See empirical evidence about the effect of country size on growth and structural change in Chenery and Syrquin (1975) and Perkins and Syrquin (1989), as well as in Haraguchi and Rezonja in this volume.

[6] How to define the 'size' of a country can be controversial. It depends on the purpose of the researcher. Resource-wise, both the size of population and the land area are important. If considering market power (price taker or price maker), per capita income has to be taken into account. The type of available natural resources may also be considered for atypical cases (e.g. oil-rich countries). Both the cross-country means and standard deviations should be considered when defining 'size'. For example, I would define large (small) countries to be above (below) one standard deviation from the mean, thus the rest of the countries are considered average in size. Such an empirical exercise is not pursued in this study. However, by any standard, China unquestionably falls into a large country category.

latecomer country. This is not the case for large countries. Obviously, it is too risky for a large country to rely on other countries for the supply of key technologies, the main producer goods, and basic needs as suggested by the free trade argument. This is because such supplies have to be in large quantities and hence, if interrupted, they can significantly obstruct the operation of the economy.[7] Equally important, large size can help reduce the high initial cost of the development of heavy industry (benefiting from economies of scale). With much more resources and potentially a much larger market than a small country, it is appealing for the government of a large country to engineer industrialization through a planned allocation of resources in which heavy industries are prioritized.

Although all these considerations may well explain why a government has to intervene for the sake of economic catch-up, they tell us little about the likely consequences of the intervention. Perhaps economic efficiency is the foremost consideration in assessing the consequences of government intervention, though efficiency as such is rarely an integral part of government objectives. If we argue that efficiency is one of the ultimate constraints that determine how and to what extent the state can play an active role in economic development, this implies that there is endogeneity between the intervention and its consequences. In fact, the efficiency issue is at the core of the recently revitalized debate on whether the government industrial policy should be comparative-advantage conforming or defying (Lin 2009; Lin and Chang 2009). The issue of the efficiency of government intervention will be examined empirically in this study of the Chinese case, using a newly constructed time series.

6.3 Exploring the role of government in China's post-1949 development

Studies of China's post-1949 industrialization are generally concerned with policy issues and in assessing the role of government in development. They can be roughly divided into two categories: policy-focused and measurement-oriented studies. Policy-focused studies tend to document the details of important policy changes and then speculate about their likely impacts—benefits or mistakes that may have important implications for future policy

[7] There is also a latent unfavourable factor for very large countries that are engaged in trade. Large countries in international trade can induce self-enhanced deteriorating terms of trade that harm themselves, i.e. what large countries can produce and hence export tends to lower international prices and what they have to import tends to push up international prices.

changes or institutional reforms. The historical roots of the prevailing policies may be traced but the analysis is mostly ad hoc in nature.

On the other hand, the measurement-oriented studies are mostly data-driven and tend to put industrial policy or the role of government in industrialization under a kind of 'consequence test', typically in a production function framework. Scholars in this camp have also pursued more detailed breakdowns of economic performance, such as by industry, region, or ownership type. Data inadequacies have, however, remained as a major source of differing and sometimes contradictory findings among researchers in terms of the real growth rates, structural changes in, and productivity performance of the economy, either as a whole or by the various breakdowns of it.[8]

In what follows, I first explore the role of government in China's post-1949 development using India as a benchmark. Instead of comparing per capita income growth, structural change, and productivity performance between the two economies as is often done in existing studies, I first use a simple 'trend-benchmarking' approach to examine the *actual growth path* of each country over the long run against a *hypothetical trend* based on its own growth experience at an earlier period in its growth path. The growth trend of the 1950s in each country is set as the hypothetical trend because the 1950s can be considered the first decade of peaceful development after the Second World War, independence in India (1947), and the civil war in China (1949).

Based on the trend-benchmarking I then make a comparison between the two economies. Despite some obvious incompatibilities between the world's two most populous countries, India is best suited to benchmark China, not only because of its comparable size and stage of development, but also because both countries adopted Soviet-style central planning in the 1950s. However, in contrast to China, India did not completely close down the market and eliminate the private sector, which allows us to explore the role of government.

Based on Maddison's (2003) estimates, in the 1870s both China's population size and the level of GDP were about 40 per cent larger than those of India. After conversion into 1990 purchasing power parity (PPP) dollars, the two countries had almost the same level of per capita GDP.[9] However, their subsequent social and economic development paths diverged. As shown in Figure 6.1, by the early 1950s, China's per capita GDP was only about 60 per cent of that of India (US$380 versus US$620 in 2010 PPPs, see TCB 2011). This

[8] In a review of studies measuring China's total factor productivity. I show how contradictory results could be caused by severe data problems in measuring labour, capital, and output (Wu 2011).

[9] Measured in 1990 Geary–Khamis dollar (see Maddison 2003).

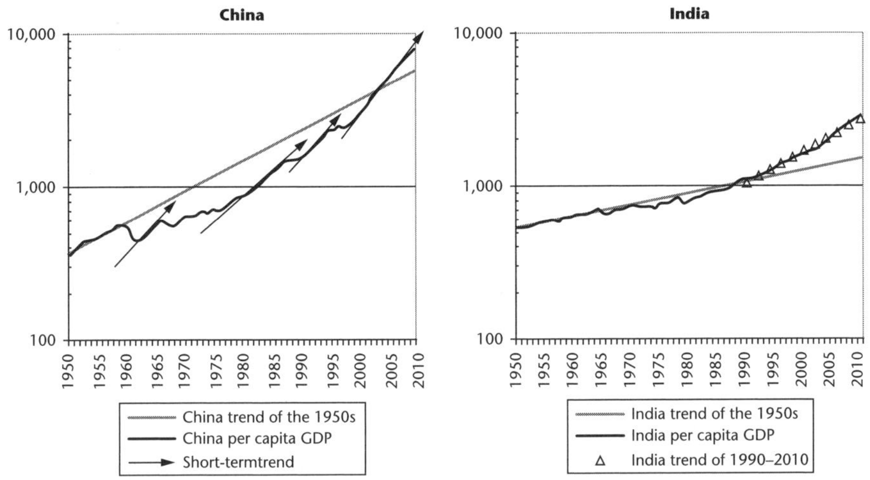

Figure 6.1. Chinese and Indian per capita GDP level and growth trends, 1950–2010 (in 2010 PPP dollar and logarithmic scale)

Notes: The TCB-TED measure of per capita GDP is in 2010 EKS PPP dollars. The pre-2003 TCB series for China is largely based on Maddison and Wu (2008) which used the Geary-Khamis PPP approach. The values for 2010 are preliminary. The trends are obtained by regression approach.

Source: Based on Maddison and Wu (2008), Wu (2011), and TCB (2011).

income gap can be used to represent the differences in the initial conditions for the post-war growth in the two economies.

The evolution of Chinese and Indian per capita GDP over the long period 1950–2010 is depicted in Figure 6.1 (on a logarithmic scale), with an estimated trend for each country based on the performance in the 1950s. Note that the trend implicitly assumes a growth path that the initial conditions were able to support. Here, I propose the following working hypothesis: if the 1950s' growth trend was mainly determined by market forces or underlying fundamentals rather than by government intervention, in subsequent years the economy would basically be able to follow the trend extrapolation, experiencing normal economic cycles, but not substantially deviating from the trend.

Strikingly enough, despite a much lower starting level of per capita income, hence less ability to save and invest, China's trend growth rate in the 1950s was much higher than that of India: 4.6 against 1.6 per cent per annum. Nonetheless, China's growth path was much more volatile than that of India. A more important observation is that in spite of episodes of faster growth as revealed by the short-term growth trends, China underperformed relative to its 1950s trend for most of the period, and only returned to the extrapolated trend around 2005. By contrast, India basically followed its 1950s trend extrapolation till about the end of the 1980s, when, at an income level of about US$1,270 per capita (taking the annual average of per capita incomes of 1988–90 from Figure 6.1), it embarked on an unprecedented acceleration, which seemingly established a new trend with an annual growth rate of 4.8 per cent (indicated by the triangles in the figure). Interestingly, this new trend more or less replicates the growth rate that China had achieved in the 1950s (4.6 per cent) starting from a much lower initial level of income of US$380. This observation clearly suggests that there were stronger non-market forces affecting the course of industrialization in China than in India.

The initial income level of China and India at the beginning of the 1950s was very low by international standards, only 17 and 28 per cent of the world average of US$2,200 (an average of 1950–2), respectively. Compared to the rest of Asia (excluding Japan, China, and India), with a level of per capita income of US$730 at the beginning of the 1950s and an annual growth rate of 2.2 per cent over the 1950s (TCB 2011), India's annual growth of 1.6 per cent does not look atypically slow, even taking its low initial income level (US$620) into account. In comparison, China's much higher annual growth rate of 4.6 per cent, starting at an even lower initial income level (US$380), implying less capability to save and invest, does not seem plausible without pre-existing production capacity (to be discussed below) and/or state-engineered investment through forced savings.[10] If we follow neo-classical convergence theory, a country's saving rate is one of the conditions that needs to be controlled for poorer economies to grow faster than richer ones (Barro and Sala-i-Martin 1992; Mankiw, Romer, and Weil 1992). Indeed, such high-growth performance in China was achieved at the time when the state closed the market and mobilized resources through radical nationalization, confiscation, land reform and collectivization, in other words by forced savings, to facilitate a Soviet-type, ambitious heavy-industry-oriented five-year plan (FYP) (1953–7).

Undoubtedly, China's growth drive in the 1950s was already overstretched given the prevalent conditions. Therefore, it was almost impossible for China to achieve an even faster growth rate subsequently without a more active role for the state to mobilize the required resources. Of course, one should not forget that the nature of the central planning also matters in understanding the effectiveness of the government in resource mobilization. In China, the central planning system was adopted as a coherent part of the Marxist ideology that laid the very foundations of the regime. Thus, industrial policies were implemented with strong political reasoning and underpinning, and hence

[10] Taking into account the initial income level at the beginning of the 1950s, China's high growth rate over the 1950s also seems incompatible with that of its Eastern European socialist counterparts. Of those with similar economic structures or based on an even more agrarian economy, Albania grew by 3.6 per cent a year but with an initial income of US$1,300 and Bulgaria grew by 3.7 per cent a year with an even higher initial income of US$2,400 (TCB 2011).

were unchallengeable. By contrast, in India a democratic constitution was implemented and maintained. The central planning system was adopted mainly as the means to achieve faster industrialization. The government's industrial policies could still be debated and challenged without fear of political persecution. It was less likely to implement an unrealistic high-growth or leap-forward plan at any expense. In China, the ideology-underpinned central planning system was all-embracing and far-reaching and replaced the market system. Resources, including consumer goods, were administratively allocated according to national plans, leaving little room for private activities. Although the planning authorities in India also had tight controls over resource allocation, the market still functioned although subject to some degree of distortion, and there was still room for private initiatives.

My question is whether such a scale of domestic resource mobilization was sufficient for implementing an ambitious heavy industrialization plan so successfully (as suggested by China's high performance of the 1950s). In this regard, studies often emphasize the importance of Soviet assistance in 156 key heavy-industry projects (e.g. Lin, Cai, and Li 1996). Nevertheless, the financing of those projects was not through aid but through loans, and they were fully paid for by Chinese exports by the early 1960s (Zeitz 2010). In other words, these projects were supported by Chinese savings. To have successfully implemented and operated these ambitious projects in a huge war-torn country, there must have existed an industrial base in China, not only in terms of infrastructure and complementary industries, but also in terms of human capital stock. Admittedly, the Soviet Union also provided engineers for implementing the imported plants (these were part of the loans), but there must already have been a large number of skilled workers and technicians who were able to work in those modern capital- and technology-intensive factories. Besides, even more importantly, there must have also been sufficient numbers of professionals, ranging from administrators, managers, and accountants to scientists, engineers, and technicians, whose training and experience satisfied the basic requirements of a comprehensive planning system operating in a large country like China. Before I go further with this inquiry, let us again look at Chinese and Indian growth performance over the entire period (Figure 6.1).

Intuitively, China's high-growth path appeared to be less 'natural' than that of India. Remarkably, each of the subsequent greater efforts to achieve more rapid growth in China had to make up for the losses caused by the previous shocks apparently caused by policy mistakes or political instabilities. This implies that China had to save and invest more in order to achieve the given rate of growth, something which can clearly be seen by zooming in on the Chinese growth path of per capita real income in Figure 6.1. For example, a faster annual growth rate of 7.6 per cent obtained in 1963–6, a period that saw a significant policy retreat from the feverish Maoist Great Leap Forward

(GLF) campaign. This growth rate somehow compensated for the high cost of a significant decline in per capita GDP of 5.7 per cent a year in the disastrous GLF aftermath in 1959–62. In fact, the average growth rate from 1959 to 1968 was virtually zero.

Another almost equally rapid yet shorter-lived growth spurt was achieved in 1969–70, with an average growth at 7.1 per cent per annum, seemingly engineered to support Mao's triumph over his political enemies after vital struggles in 1967–8 (the most chaotic period of the Cultural Revolution), which had caused a decline of 5 per cent a year in per capita income. Next, the period 1971–9 witnessed an average growth rate of 3.2 per cent per annum, which was also highly volatile. It included a long period of stagnation between 1971 and 1976 when GDP per capita grew by merely 1.5 per cent a year as a result of the prolonged political struggles that ended with Mao's death, and a neo-GLF campaign period in 1977–8 when the growth rate jumped to 6.9 per cent a year to economically proclaim Deng's victory over Madame Mao's elite group (the Gang of Four).

Since the late 1980s the duration of slowdowns has become shorter and the duration of the growth episodes has become longer, thanks to Deng's reforms and opening-up. However, there have still been policy-induced shocks that slowed down growth. For example, the forced retreat from the neo-GLF slowed down the growth to 3.3 per cent per annum in 1980–1; the Tiananmen movement (1989) and its aftermath reduced the annual growth rate to 1.1 per cent in 1989–90; and an overdose of austerity in 1996 forced China into a hard landing, resulting in merely 1 per cent growth, down from 13 per cent in 1995. This was followed by the Asian financial crisis, which caused negative growth in 1998.[11] Again, these downturns were followed by two fast growth periods, one growing by 9.4 per cent a year in 1992–5 when Deng decreed bolder reforms and another one growing by 10.2 per cent a year in 2001–10, which is the fastest and longest growth spurt in the history of Chinese industrialization, mainly attributed to a new type of government support that aimed to facilitate China's entry into the World Trade Organization (WTO) and into competition in the world market, an issue that will be revisited at the end of this chapter.

Some simple 'what-if' calculations suggest that China has indeed paid a very high price for disastrous policy mistakes and institutional shocks. Just before the global financial crisis at the end of 2008, China's per capita GDP

[11] There is a controversy about the real growth rate of 1998 when China was badly hit by the Asian financial crisis, though this is denied by the authorities. While the official growth rate is reported as 7.8 per cent, conjectures (e.g. Rawski 2001) and alternative estimates (Maddison and Wu 2008) suggest it possibly to be around zero or even negative, which is further confirmed by my recent work (Wu 2011). Nonetheless, a substantial revision of the national accounts for the period 1992–2004 following China's First National Economic Census left 1998 untouched (Wu 2007).

was about twice that of India (about US$6,200 versus US$3,000 in 2010 PPP$, TCB 2011). The Chinese path is seemingly superior to the Indian path if judged in this way. However, had the 1950s' trend been closely followed, China could have surpassed India by the early 1960s at a level of US$1,080 per capita rather than two decades later (around 1984). Putting it a different way, if China had not swung like a roller coaster, it could have grown steadily by 3.4 per cent a year till it overtook India. Nonetheless, my purpose here is not to gauge the cost of China's government-engineered industrialization, but to address the question why China seems willing to stick to a costly and inefficient track? Or to put it differently: was the course of China's industrialization so heavily path-dependent that breaking away from that path was even more costly than continuing it?

6.4 History matters

Assuming that present practice is path-dependent, we argue that past choices and their outcomes along the way influence the present and hence alter the course of history (David 1985). What happens at the beginning may only be a small initial advantage or a few minor random shocks that result in an initial advantage. However, subsequent increasing returns from that initial advantage induce more choices to be made or more actions to be taken, hence creating a set of forces and complementary institutions that encourage and facilitate the sustaining of the earlier choices (North 1990; Page 2006). A path is then shaped in such a process and becomes self-reinforcing. In this sense, history matters (Page 2006).

China's industrialization and modernization did not begin in 1949, neither did government intervention in China's economic development. Admittedly, government intervention may take different forms under different regimes in history. However, there is clear evidence that even with regard to central government industrial planning there was no sharp change in 1949. Thanks to Kirby's (1984, 1990) careful studies with convincing facts, we now know that it is incorrect to completely attribute China's post-1949 planned industrialization to the influence of the Soviet Union (Eckstein 1975) or to the onset of the communist system (Cheng 1963), as widely believed by scholars in this field. Thus the assumption that the assembling of China's planning machine only began in the north-east region (Manchuria) during the civil war period (1946–9) also implies that government-engineered industrialization began with the communist system in China (Donnithorne 1967; Levine 1987). It is also historically incorrect to relate China's post-1949 development mainly to the pre-1949 private sector, which assumes that the role of the state in the China's modern economic development was insignificant prior to the communist regime (Rawski 1980). Equally important, as put by Bian (2005)

> ... [t]he basic institutional arrangement of China's state-owned enterprise—the bureaucratic governance structure, the distinctive management and incentive mechanisms, and the provision of social services and welfare—took place during the Sino-Japanese War and was not derived from the Soviet model as is conventionally believed. (ibid.: 213)

Taking a historical view, the first and foremost pre-1949 legacy for China's post-1949 industrialization consists of the state-owned and state-controlled industries that were created under the National Resources Committee (NRC) of the nationalist government. The NRC was established in 1932[12] as a state agency that was mandated to 'develop, operate and control' all the nation's basic industries and mines, as well as 'such other enterprises as designated by the government' (Kirby 1990: 127). Notably, it performed a role similar to that of the post-1949 State Planning Commission (SPC) under the communist government.[13] By August 1947, after a significant wartime development and an equally important post-war expansion and restructuring that integrated the existing state establishments with the confiscated enterprises formerly under the control of the Japanese occupation authorities or the Chinese puppet government during the war, the NRC had employed about 33,000 staff members (including scientific and engineering professionals as well as administrators and managers) and 230,000 workers (more than 500,000 if we include joint ventures with provincial governments). It accounted for 67.3 per cent of China's total industrial capital.[14] These numbers seem to have been growing without a significant break throughout the civil war period and over the time when the communist forces took power in 1949, thanks to the collaboration of the NRC senior management and staff members (Shao and Sun 1994).

By the end of 1949, based on my data, which was reconstructed from official sources, there were already 3.15 million workers engaged in the state industrial sector, half of whom were engaged in heavy industries (Wu and Yue 2010). This estimate is close to another source of information that gives an estimate for 1949 of there being 1.29 million workers who came from the former NRC system and its nationwide industrial network and from the

[12] Originally, the NRC was set up as the Defence Planning Committee under the General Staff Headquarters. In May 1935, it was brought under the administration of the National Military Committee as NRC. In March 1938, it was relocated to the Ministry of Economy, and in March 1946, it was put under the administration of the Executive Yuan (State Council).

[13] Indeed, two of the prominent members of NRC, Qian Changzhao and Sun Yueqi, who were also the last two NRC chairmen, served as vice-chairmen of the Central Financial and Economic Planning Bureau under the State Council's Financial and Economic Commission, which was founded in 1951 and the direct predecessor of the SPC set up two years later (Kirby 1990: 135).

[14] See Kirby (1990: 132, footnote 32) for sources of information.

enterprises owned by the nationalist party, military, and various government ministries (Wang 2010). The rest come from other sources such as enterprises seized by the communists in the north east (which were not all included in the NRC network and statistics), enterprises confiscated as a result of the civil war, and foreign enterprises purchased through forced acquisition (Wang 2010). By the end of 1952, or just before Soviet technical assistance and loans became available, the state industrial sector was already employing 4.33 million staff and workers and was producing 18.8 billion yuan of output (gross value added at 1990 prices), which accounted for about 45 and 60 per cent of the national totals, respectively (estimate based on Wu 2011).

These simple figures suggest something very important, namely that China must have already developed a physical and human capital foundation by 1949 that was capable of accommodating the state-driven heavy industrialization introduced under the new regime. Soviet assistance and loans were undoubtedly important for China to recover and to expand with the implementation of the first FYP in 1953–57, but it was more like compensation for the destruction of the war rather than a change of the underlying path. To explore this conjecture, I have made an attempt to construct China's path of industrialization over the past century by linking my new estimates for industrial value added (Wu 2011) to those of Chang (1969) for the earlier period.[15] The result is astonishingly supportive of the notion of continuity between the pre-1949 and post-1949 periods, as shown in Figure 6.2. Despite all abnormal shocks because of war and regime shifts, the underlying growth path does not seem to have changed as suggested by the estimated exponential trend.[16]

In the first place, Figure 6.2 reveals that the underlying path might have started no later than the beginning of the 1900s (as far as the data extend) and then developed steadily until being interrupted by the Japanese invasion in 1937. In the second place it shows that the post-war recovery began in 1947 and, despite a major interruption in 1948 due to the impact of the civil war, by 1952 it had brought the industrial growth back to the track established earlier.

[15] Chang's work is perhaps the best of a limited number of the existing studies that have attempted to construct China's industrial production index for the pre-1949 period. Chang's index covers the entire economy including Manchuria in 1931–45 and the other Japanese occupied areas of China during the Sino-Japanese war in 1937–45 (Chang 1969). His index is based on 15 carefully constructed factory-produced commodity series in five key industry groups: coal mining, other mining products, ferrous metals, power generation, and consumer goods. He has provided evidence that the exclusion of other commodities, especially consumer goods, due to poor data, does not significantly affect the trend of the index. Chemicals and machinery industries are also not included due to data problems as well as insignificant development before the war. But he argues that their trends were probably captured by other heavy industries included in the index.

[16] The approach used here is very different from the one in Figure 6.1 in which the growth trend extrapolation of one period, i.e. the 1950s, is used to benchmark China's per capita GDP growth over the period 1950–2010. In Figure 6.2 China's real industrial growth over the period 1912–2009 is depicted against an estimated underlying trend.

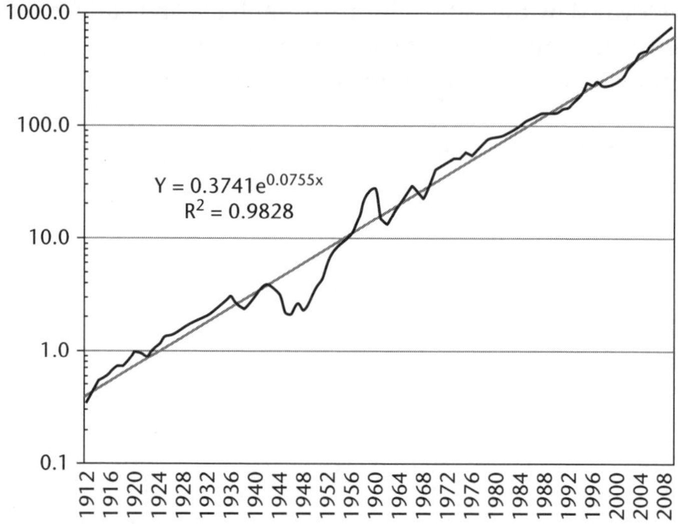

Figure 6.2. China's century-long industrial development (real industrial output, 1984 = 100)

Notes: The original data are two separate series covering 1912–48 and 1949–2008, respectively. The data series for 1912–48 is constructed using commodity-based estimates of industrial net value added (NVA) by Chang. The data series for 1949–2008 is also based on commodities but conforming to the SNA concept of gross value added (GVA). The two data series are linked assuming that the change of capital consumption was similar to the change of NVA. The trend is estimated by an exponential function.

Sources: Based on Chang (1969) and Wu (2011).

This implies that the strong performance figures of the state industrial sector in 1949–52 cited above may largely and logically reflect the result of a post-war recovery that made good use of the unemployed industrial capacities caused by the war and idle human resources, including the accumulated knowledge and experience of pre-war industrialization. Third, China's post-1949 high-growth path, often considered as beginning with China's first FYP and attributed to the Soviet Union's assistance, still closely followed the underlying path that began at least in the beginning of the twentieth century. In other words, there was no such thing as a 'revolutionary path' established and sustained by the new regime. The first FYP, the GLF drama, and the post-1978 reforms did not create a new path that deviated from the underlying long-run path.

The fact that history matters does not mean that all history is relevant. What matters in history is the sequencing of events that change the course of the future (Page 2006). If we argue that China's post-1949 state-planned and state-engineered industrialization is path-dependent, we need to consider which pre-1949 events in China induced or led to the subsequent events and hence shaped the course of China's industrialization after 1949. As discussed earlier, whether government plays an active role in a country's industrial development is determined by two key factors: the timing of industrialization and the size of the country. I have argued that the catch-up pressures on a latecomer could be enhanced if industrialization is motivated by the need for national or regime security. This was very much the case for China.

China's modern industries were initially bred by the state in the second half of the nineteenth century, especially during the government's self-strengthening movement (*yang wu yun dong*) of 1861–95. The movement was primarily motivated by China's series of military defeats and concessions to the Western powers after the First Opium War (1839–42), as well as several devastating domestic uprisings, of which the Taiping Rebellion (1850–64) was most regime-threatening and damaging. The main purpose of the self-strengthening movement was to catch up with the West by modernizing and industrializing the economy. Because of increasing domestic and foreign threats to the regime, the state's industrialization projects were essentially defence-oriented, stressing capital goods industries and supportive infrastructures. Powerful provincial governor-generals, rather than the weak imperial government, played a key role in early industrialization. However, driven by strong local interests, competition among provincial governments enhanced the role of the state and speeded up the industrialization process. Government power was used to mobilize resources to build arsenals throughout coastal China in the 1860s and to develop supportive infrastructure and industries in the 1870s. Government power was also used to promote and adopt Western technologies and practices. In 1876, China's first modern coal mine company and first telegraph company were established, followed by the first railway, first iron and steel works, and modern textile factories. These burgeoning industries were administered by a principle called *guan du shang ban* (literally 'government supervision with merchant operation') in which, while the day-to-day running of the companies was in the hands of merchants, all major decisions were handled by officials. Importantly, this movement also helped nurture the development of state economic agencies that were responsible for planning, financing, and supporting the industrial projects.

The defeat of the Qing Imperial Navy in the first Sino-Japanese War in 1894 was the final blow to the Qing Dynasty. It also exacerbated the new regime's sense of national crisis and encouraged Chinese national elites to believe in an active role for the state in China's modernization. This is clearly reflected in the *Industrial Plan* (1922) of the founder of republican China, Sun Yat-sen.[17] In Kirby's view

[17] The Industrial Plan was originally distributed in Chinese as *Shiye Jihua*, and later published in English as *The International Development of China* in 1922, and a new edition in 1953.

> ...the most 'statist' reading of Sun's economic thought was the prevalent interpretation during the mainland period of the Nationalist rule, which stressed Sun's commitment to the state-planned development of all basic heavy industries and infrastructure. (Kirby 1990: 125)

The pursuit of central-government-planned industrialization began soon after the establishment of the Nanjing regime in 1927. Prior to the set-up of the NRC, various government ministries had already begun proposing different versions of national plans in line with Sun's blueprint, such as the reconstruction ministry's ten-year plan in 1928, the industry ministry's ten-year plan in 1930, their four-year plan in 1932, and the National Economic Council's three-year plan in 1931. It appears that to compete for limited resources, all these government ministries did was to make appealing plans—the more detailed and ambitious, the better. In fact, rising national security concerns encouraged ambitious plans for fast industrialization. Kirby (1990) noted that

> ...planning agencies and personnel expanded significantly after the Manchurian Incident [1931, plotted by the Japanese], stressing the rapid growth of military-related state capitalism...The greatest progress occurred under the National Resources Commission (NRC), the technical and managerial agency that came to dominate state industry. (ibid.: 125)

Nevertheless, Figure 6.2 does not convincingly show that the ambitious heavy industrialization plan that was implemented and managed under the NRC created a new path. Rather, the so-called nationalist 'golden decade' in China's industrialization in 1927–37 was a fairly smooth continuation of the earlier development that was rooted in the late Qing's self-strengthening movement.[18] In the light of the absolute size of the country, the heavy-industry projects undertaken during that movement might be considered insignificant. But they were momentous if one takes the limited availability of national savings at that time into account. As argued by Page (2006):

> ...any constraint, be it a budget constraint, a spatial constraint, or a time constraint, imposes negative externalities [on other options] and...the exclusion of other options drives the path dependence. (ibid.: 90)

Given a high resource constraint in the late Qing period, the industrial initiatives of the state inevitably created increasing returns in the selected industries while imposing costs upon other activities that could be more in line with China's comparative advantage. In this situation, the government aiming at accelerated catch-up was no longer just a provider of public goods that was supposed to ensure that any external costs must be paid (through taxes). Instead, it reaped the benefits. Beneficial opportunities not only retained the

[18] My hypothesis here is preliminary and requires further empirical exploration.

resources already invested in the industries selected by the state, but also attracted even more physical and human capital investment to those industries. Consequently, supportive institutions grew, private businesses fought for government projects or procurement opportunities, and foreign investors pursued preferential treatment from or joint ventures with the government. Frequent foreign invasions and internal threats pressured the government to expand its role and hence enhanced the process. All these factors helped sustain and strengthen the path rather than furthering deviations from it. This path-dependence perspective helps provide insight into the state-engineered nature and the inefficiency problems of China's subsequent industrialization in both the pre-1949 nationalist regime and the post-1949 communist regime.

6.5 Data issues

Data inadequacy has been a major obstacle to a proper assessment of China's post-1949 growth and productivity performance. Official output and employment data contain serious flaws (Maddison and Wu 2008; Wu and Yue 2010) and official estimates on capital stocks are lacking (Wu 2008). Recently, I improved Maddison and Wu's earlier estimates of real output (gross value added), reconstructed employment for three broad sectors (primary, secondary, and tertiary), and estimated net capital stocks for the Chinese economy as a whole. In the following paragraphs the shortcomings of previous datasets are discussed, and the generation of new estimates is explained.

6.5.1 *Employment*

The new employment data used in this study is the result of two major adjustments. The first was to fix a structural break in the official employment series that show a substantial jump of over 17 per cent or 94.2 million workers between 1989 and 1990. This jump subsequently created a huge discrepancy between total national employment and the sum of sectoral- and industry-level employment figures (Maddison and Wu 2008). The second adjustment was to improve Maddison's earlier estimates for employment of the so-called 'non-material/non-market services'[19] (Maddison 2007).

[19] The term of 'non-material services' refers to service activities that are excluded from the 'material product' in the old Soviet-style national accounts or MPS (material product system). They include both market and non-market services: banking, insurance, housing services, administration of real estate, social services, health, education, entertainment, personal services, R&D activities, the armed forces, police, government, and party organizations. They are now incorporated in the Chinese accounts, but the estimates are not shown explicitly. Official

My hypothesis for the 1990 structural break is that it was created by a gap or inconsistency between the 1990 population census, which captured the informal sector's activities, and the regular statistical reporting system, which only focused on the employment of the formal sector. If this is true, the gap should have appeared at the time when the planned employment system began to change. I investigated the earlier 1982 population census—the first comprehensive population census in almost two decades—and compared it with later censuses and annual estimates. My discovery supported the hypothesis. It suggests that the break could have already appeared in 1982 because the annual estimates did not take into account the employment emerging outside the labour planning and administration system as a result of policy changes in the early 1970s, which encouraged small, collective enterprises to employ surplus labour, especially in rural areas. In the adjustment, I first made an interpolation between 1982 and 1990 using the 1987 1 per cent population survey as the mid-point. Thus the 1990 break was 'shifted' back to 1982. Then, using a 'trend deviation' method, I estimated the employment trend for 1970–82 using the 1970 official estimate as the beginning point and the re-estimated 1982 figures at the end point, so as to account for the additional (outside-planning) employment. Finally, the additional numbers of employed in 1971–89, estimated as a result of the exercise, were allocated to major sectors according to the adjusted sectoral weights.[20]

The second adjustment is based on newly gathered information on military service and makes the inclusion of military personnel from 1949 to 1990 reflect annual changes.[21] This has improved Maddison's earlier work, which simply added a fixed 3 million military personnel to each year's 'non-material service' employment (Maddison 2007: 168). The results have a significant impact on the early 1950s, when the size of the military personnel was much larger than in later periods. This provides a new employment base for improving Maddison's earlier real output estimates for this sector (Maddison 2007).

In addition to these two major adjustments, at the aggregate level of the economy, I made a further adjustment to the estimated workforce

estimates show an estimate for the 'tertiary' sector as a whole, and a breakdown for two 'material' component sub-sectors (transport-telecommunication and commerce).

[20] Since the additional labourers are the least skilled and educated ones, they will be mainly engaged in labour-intensive manufacturing and services. Thus, at the broad sectoral level, I allocated them into agriculture, industry, construction, and so-called material services according to their weights, excluding 'non-material/non-market services' (see the proceeding footnote). However, given the situation of underemployment in the farm sector, I adjusted the agricultural share downward by 40 per cent (Wu 2011).

[21] From 1990 onwards military personnel have been included in the official employment estimates (Wu 2011).

representing 'quality change', using educational attainment as a proxy.[22] The quality-adjusted estimates of labour input have been used in the growth accounting exercise in this study.

6.5.2 *Value added*

The new estimates of China's value added are the results of two major adjustments. The first was to improve Maddison's value added estimates of 'non-material services' and the second was to improve my earlier value added estimates for industry.[23] My work on the value added by 'non-material services' is also labour-productivity-based, but it allows for annual labour-productivity growth since the reform period rather than adopting Maddison's 'zero labour-productivity growth' hypothesis for the entire period. My closer examination has shown that there was indeed zero labour-productivity growth in 'non-material services' from the early 1950s to the early 1980s, but the growth that followed became abnormally fast. This suggests that the zero labour productivity growth hypothesis is implausible relative to other services in China (Maddison and Wu 2008) and compared with the experiences of other countries (van Ark 1996). The adjustment used my new employment estimates for 'non-material services' with an assumption of zero labour-productivity growth in 1952–77, 1 per cent annual growth in 1978–92 and 2 per cent annual growth afterwards.

My latest work (Wu 2011) to improve China's industrial value added is not a simple update of my earlier work, which investigated the upward bias hypothesis[24] for the official estimates (Wu 2002; Maddison and Wu 2008). It is still based on the physical output of commodities, but instead of using single-benchmark weights and assuming a constant value-added–output ratio, it incorporates multiple input–output table weights and time-variant value-added–output ratios. A clear Gerschenkron effect is revealed in this new exercise, which suggests the existence of substitution bias in my earlier estimates based on 1987 input–output table weights, hence overestimating

[22] For the initial stock, I assume a level 500 million years of primary level-equivalent schooling, equivalent to about 15 years of education production after 1949. Following Maddison (1998), I derive primary school equivalent annual flows. However, similar to Wang and Yao (2001), I use the number of annual graduates rather than annual enrollment as in Barro and Lee (2001) and Maddison (1998), which depend on a strong assumption of the completion rate of each level of education (Wu 2011).

[23] For agriculture, I adopted and updated Maddison's quantity output-based value added estimates as he showed that the official statistics were basically reliable (Maddison 1998). For construction and 'material services' I simply accepted the official value added estimates because there is no useful information for any adjustment, the same treatment as that in Maddison and Wu (2008).

[24] See Perkins (1988); Keidel (1992); Ren (1997); Maddison (1998); Woo (1998); and Rawski (2001, 1993). The upward bias hypothesis states that official Chinese estimates systematically overestimate Chinese rates of economic growth.

growth after 1987, as explained by Gerschenkron (1951).[25] This finding supports the shift from the single 1987 output weights to multiple output weights based on three Chinese full input–output tables for 1987, 1992, and 1997.[26]

Next, based on the available Chinese input–output tables including full tables and reduced forms since 1981, when the first material product system (MPS)-type input–output table was constructed, and earlier work by Wu and Yue (2000), I can show that reform was accompanied by a declining value-added ratio in industry, from 38 per cent in 1978 to 23 per cent in 2007 (the most recent available input–output table) whereas the ratio stayed at 38–40 per cent in the pre-reform period. This means that my earlier estimates based on a fixed (1987) value-added ratio still exaggerated China's real industrial growth.

The results of the new exercise further confirmed my previous finding that the alternative estimates suggest a slower but more volatile growth rate of industrial value added than the official estimates. For the planning period 1953–78, the annual growth rate of the alternative estimates for the industrial sector is 9.54 per cent per year compared to the 10.89 per cent of the official estimates, while for the reform period 1979–2009, the corresponding figures are 7.48 and 10.87 per cent per year, respectively. For the whole period, the coefficient of variation of the annual growth rate is 1.72 for my estimates and only 1.18 for the official estimates. The new results look more plausible than my earlier work, not only because they have highlighted the effects of policy shocks on China's industrialization, but also because they have revealed an underlying path for the post-1949 period that can be integrated well with the pre-1949 path, as shown in Figure 6.2.[27]

[25] Since changes in prices are negatively correlated with changes in quantities of commodities (assuming that buyers are rational), a quantity index based on a later benchmark year would show less growth than a quantity index based on an earlier benchmark year. In other words, the fixed-weight quantity index will overstate the growth rates after the benchmark year and understate the growth rates prior to the benchmark year.

[26] Input–output weights refers to the input and output relationships or the ratios of GVA to gross value of output that can be derived from national input–output tables. Multiple input–output table weights as in the new exercise are better than single input–output table weights because they better capture structural changes over time.

[27] One of the main criticisms of my commodity-based output index is that it underestimated the effect of quality change, i.e. the quality change was miscounted as a price effect and hence removed (Holz 2006a; Rawski 2008). To see if there was an obvious underestimation of the growth rate due to insufficient representation of quality change, I derived a gap series by subtracting my rates from the official rates and then estimated a trend to filter out the noise. If the criticisms were correct and the gap indeed captured mainly the unobserved quality change, China's industrial development seemed to have experienced a continuous quality improvement from the mid-1960s to the mid-1980s but a significant quality deterioration since the industrial reform from the mid-1980s. This did not look plausible at all (Wu 2011).

6.5.3 *Net capital stock*

Estimates of net capital stock are required to examine China's total factor productivity (TFP) performance. Unlike other studies, I used the National Bureau for Statistics (NBS) gross fixed capital formation (GFCF) rather than more problematic indicators such as total investment in fixed assets (TIFA) and newly increased fixed assets (NIFA) as the investment variable.[28] I estimated a depreciation rate based on service life and declining balance measures at industry level rather than taking an arbitrary rate as in many existing studies, and constructed an alternative deflator rather than sticking to the official deflator for fixed asset investment.

There are three major steps in my capital stock construction (Wu 2011). In the first step the GFCF series from the expenditure accounts is deflated by two alternative deflators, i.e. the official implicit investment deflator derived from the expenditure accounts and my deflator based on producer prices for capital goods (machinery and building materials). In the second step the initial stock for 1952, K_0, is estimated assuming that $K_0 = I_0/(\delta + \bar{g}_T)$, where I_0 denotes the initial GFCF, $\bar{g}_T$ stands for the average annual GDP growth rate of the selected period T (here set as 1952–5) and δ stands for a geometric depreciation rate.[29] In the last step, the estimates of China's net capital stock are obtained by applying the perpetual inventory method (PIM) $K_t = I_t + K_{t-1}(1 - \delta)$ to the constructed variables.

The results are approximately reconcilable with my estimates of industry-level capital stock, which are independent from the estimation for the aggregate economy (Wu 2008). As correctly put by Chow (2006), one of the important assessments of the estimated capital stock is the rate of return to capital implied by the capital stock. It follows that, for 1954, Chow's (1993)

[28] There has been controversy concerning which investment indicator should be used. Wang and Szirmai (2012) provide a good review of the literature on this topic. As explained in Wu (2008 and 2011), while both TIFA and NIFA have coverage problem, TIFA contains significant double counting and it has been worsening since the property bubble in the mid-2000s, which increased land transaction costs, and to some extent TIFA blurred the line between fixed capital formation and inventory (see Chow 1993). Frankly, many studies have misunderstood these concepts, especially Holz (2006b). Wang and Szirmai (2011) have made a good effort in adjusting NIFA and brought our attention to the concept of productive NIFA. However, due to long price distortions of residential housing, I opt for the indicator of GFCF. GFCF is part of the official GDE (gross domestic expenditure) estimates. Strictly speaking, if GDP has been revised as in this study and in Maddison and Wu (2008), GFCF should then be adjusted to the revised GDP. Given the complexity of the capital stock estimation (also see Footnote 30), I would like to leave it to the next stage of the data work.

[29] The assumed geometric decay function follows an age-efficiency argument supported by clear empirical evidence (Hulten and Wykoff 1981), rather than hyperbolic function as used in Wang and Szirmai (2011). Choosing a more proper decay function for economic depreciation in the context of the Chinese economy is certainly an important issue that deserves further study. As for the value of δ, since it is found to be from 5.7 to 6.6 per cent over time in my work on industries (Wu 2008), alternative estimates are therefore made as 5, 6, and 7 per cent, as well as multiple rates assuming accelerated depreciation along with market-oriented reforms (Wu 2011).

estimated capital stock implies a rate of return to capital of 0.22, whereas Holz's (2006b) work implies a rate of 0.993. Based on a market economy assumption for the Chinese economy in the early 1950s, Chow (2006) considers Holz's result to be implausible. Although there are conceptual problems in Holz's work (Wu 2011), the assumption that the economy in the early 1950s was a typical market one can also be questioned given our clear evidence that the state already owned and controlled the majority of the economy. Thus, an abnormally high rate of return to capital may be reasonable though it may not be as high as what Holz's results have implied.[30] For a comparison, the rate implied by my estimated capital stock is 0.763 and by Wang and Szirmai's work is 0.673, both lower than that of Holz but still much higher than that of Chow.[31]

6.6 Growth, structural change, and productivity performance

This section uses my newly constructed dataset (Wu 2011) to examine China's post-1949 industrialization in terms of growth, structural change, and productivity performance. The focus of the examination is the aggregate economy and its major sectors, instead of the industrial sector alone, in order to see the effect of the industrialization on other sectors.

Path dependence is by no means efficient simply because it rules out alternatives and market-based competition, particularly if the state is a main factor determining and sustaining the path. My working hypothesis is that if the state sector is generally less efficient than the private sector, as both economic theory and empirical evidence have suggested, and if China's course of industrialization has indeed followed a path that has been developed and sustained by strong government interests, the Chinese economy would have been inherently inefficient.

[30] Another very likely reason for the abnormally high return to capital in the early 1950s could be due to an underestimate of the initial capital stock K_0. Recalling the formula $K_0 = I_0/(\delta + \overline{g}_T)$ that I used in the estimation of K_0, it implicitly assumes that the given I is sufficient to generate the observed (average) g (the rate of GDP growth) after compensating for the capital consumption (δ). It would be wrong if g in the early 1950s was actually achieved by a much larger K_0. This deserves a further investigation.

[31] All of these estimates conform to the 'diminishing return to capital' theorem, though their implied diminishing rates vary substantially. Using 1998 as an example, to follow Chow's timeframe, the estimated rate of return to capital is ranged from 0.122 by Holz (2006b), 0.158 by Chow (1993), 0.162 by Wu (2011), and 0.279 by Wang and Szirmai (2012). Compared to the corresponding rates in 1954 (see text), this suggests that the decline of the rate of return to capital between 1954 and 1998 was 2, 0.7, 3.5, and 4.7 per cent, respectively.

6.6.1 *Periodization*

Given the available data, the examination focuses on the period 1953–2009. The whole period is first divided into planning and reform periods, each further divided into several subperiods to capture the effects of major policy-regime shifts on the Chinese economy. More detailed events in each subperiod are given in Appendix Table 1.

In the following analysis the planning period is divided into four subperiods: the implementation of the Soviet-style central planning system through the first FYP in 1953–7; the feverish Maoist GLF campaign and its disastrous aftermath in 1958–65, the defence industry-oriented 'Great Third Front' campaign together with the chaotic time of the Cultural Revolution in 1966–71, and the new policy efforts including the neo-GLF, which attempted to get the economy out of the shadow of the Cultural Revolution in 1972–8.

As for the reform period, it is also split into four subperiods: the initial agricultural reform in 1979–84; a nationwide industrial reform through a dual-track price system in 1985–91; the state-sector reform following the adoption of 'socialist market' system in 1992–2001; and China's emergence as the 'world factory' following its WTO entry in 2002–9.

6.6.2 *Growth and structural change*

With this new dataset, let us first examine the growth performance at the sector level and hence the structural changes of the Chinese economy against policy-regime shifts as reported in Tables 6.1 and 6.2. The following observations are noteworthy. In terms of the real output growth, first, the period of the GLF and its aftermath exhibited the slowest growth, while China's post-WTO period showed the most rapid growth in the entire period in question.[32] Under central planning, it is not surprising that the industrial sector (mining, manufacturing, and utilities) was the fastest growing sector, contributing 50 per cent to the aggregate growth whereas only 4 per cent was contributed by construction, 18 per cent by agriculture, and 28 per cent by services.[33] In the reform period, services outpaced industry on average. As a result, the contribution by services to the aggregate growth rose to 41 per cent and the contribution by construction rose to 7 per cent, whereas the contributions by agriculture

[32] Of course, the fastest and largest ever money injection in 2009 to fight the global financial crisis helped sustain this period's strong growth. However, even if the two crisis-hit years of 2008–9 are removed, China's post-WTO period still exhibited the fastest growth in history.

[33] Sectoral contribution to aggregate growth rate is derived based on the growth rates in Table 6.1 and GVA weights (at 1990 prices) in Table 6.2. There are small discrepancies between the aggregate growth rate and the sum of the weighted sectoral growth rates due to the underlying index number problems.

Table 6.1. Growth of output and employment by major sector, 1953–2009 (per cent per annum)

	Growth value added (at 1990 Prices)					Employment				
	Total	A	I	C	S	Total	A	I	C	S
Planning:										
1953–1957	5.6	3.7	16.0	17.2	3.7	2.5	1.6	4.1	25.5	2.9
1958–1965	3.5	0.6	7.2	2.3	5.2	2.4	2.5	3.0	−6.8	3.4
1966–1971	4.8	3.1	10.3	8.4	1.9	3.7	3.3	9.6	4.7	2.4
1972–1978	4.4	2.2	6.9	3.6	4.0	3.1	1.2	12.0	4.0	5.8
1953–1978	***4.4***	***2.2***	***9.5***	***7.0***	***3.8***	***2.9***	***2.2***	***7.2***	***5.0***	***3.7***
Reform:										
1979–1984	7.4	7.1	5.4	9.7	9.7	3.4	2.1	4.6	9.3	7.1
1985–1991	4.7	3.5	4.8	8.6	5.2	2.5	1.6	2.2	7.7	4.8
1992–2001	7.0	3.8	6.6	9.6	8.9	1.1	−0.7	0.4	5.2	5.0
2002–2009	9.2	4.3	12.4	12.4	7.7	0.9	−2.3	4.0	2.0	3.3
1979–2009	***7.1***	***4.5***	***7.5***	***10.1***	***7.9***	***1.8***	***0.0***	***2.5***	***5.7***	***4.9***

Notes: A: Agriculture, I: Mining, manufacturing and utilities, C: Construction, S: Services.
Source: Based on estimates in Wu (2011), updated using *China Statistical Yearbook 2010* (NBS 2010), with adjustments.

Table 6.2. Structural changes of output and employment, 1953–2009 (Total = 100)

	GVA (at 1990 prices)				Employment			
	A	I	C	S	A	I	C	S
Planning:								
1953–1957	51.2	14.0	2.2	32.6	81.0	6.2	2.5	10.3
1958–1965	36.3	21.2	2.5	40.0	72.9	9.0	4.2	13.9
1966–1971	39.0	25.8	2.5	32.6	79.9	7.1	2.0	11.0
1972–1978	33.9	34.1	2.9	29.1	74.0	12.8	2.0	11.3
1953–1978	***39.1***	***24.4***	***2.6***	***33.9***	***76.4***	***9.0***	***2.8***	***11.8***
Reform:								
1979–1984	29.5	35.5	3.1	31.9	64.9	18.3	2.4	14.4
1985–1991	27.1	33.6	4.1	35.2	59.9	17.6	4.3	18.2
1992–2001	22.4	33.4	5.3	39.0	52.7	17.2	5.6	24.6
2002–2009	15.6	39.5	6.0	39.0	44.7	18.0	6.2	31.1
1979–2009	***23.1***	***35.4***	***4.8***	***36.7***	***54.6***	***17.7***	***4.8***	***22.9***

Notes and source: See Table 6.1.

and industry declined to 15 and 37 per cent, respectively. Effects of policy and institutional changes are clearly evident, especially in:

- the high-growth performance of industry and construction in the first FYP period (1953–7)
- the first phase of the so-called 'Third Front' campaign (1966–70, Appendix Table 1) and in the period following China's WTO entry
- the strong growth of agriculture during the initial period of the agricultural reform (1979–84)

- the significant improvement of services in the early reform and following the official adoption of the so-called 'socialist market system' (1993, Appendix Table 1).

Moreover, the substantial resource mobilization to support industrial development had a strong negative impact on the growth of agriculture during the GLF period and on services during the 'Third Front' campaign.

Second, changes of employment over the planning and reform periods also suggest strong policy and institutional effects. Industry and construction exhibited the most volatile employment growth among all sectors, although in general this growth was slower than sectoral real output growth. In particular, the post-GLF retrenchment resulted in a very slow growth in industrial employment and negative growth in construction employment during the period 1958–65, while the promotion of local and especially rural enterprises in 1972–8 resulted in the most rapid growth in industrial employment, which outpaced the growth in industrial real output. During the planning period, agriculture and services maintained an approximate balance between the real output and employment growth, which to a large extent 'reduced' the pressures on job creation. However, in spite of the economy's four decades of high growth and rapid structural change, China's agriculture did not experience an absolute decline in employment until the 1990s. As shown in Table 6.1, the post-WTO period was accompanied by the fastest decline in agricultural employment, of 2.3 per cent a year, thanks to the WTO-induced new round of industrial expansion that enhanced China's export-oriented labour-intensive manufacturing.

Third, as Table 6.2 shows, different growth performances across sectors also resulted in structural changes in output and employment. The share of the industrial sector in the real output increased over the 1950s–60s, remained almost unchanged over the 1970s–90s, and then rose further following China's WTO entry. It should also be noted that the change of the real output structure in agriculture and services in the 1960s usually reversed: the share of agriculture increased rather than continued to decline, and the share of services declined rather than continued to rise. In fact, for services this usual decline continued over the last planning period 1972–8.

In terms of employment structure, this regress was even more evident. In 1966–71, both industry and services moved back almost to their initial shares in employment in the 1950s. In the same period, the significant decline of industry's share in employment along with the rise of its share in real output apparently reflected misallocation of labour. During the reform period, deregulation in the labour market and the growth of labour-intensive industries and services started a correction to the distortion and triggered China's most significant labour transformation in history, from agriculture to industry, construction, and services. From the early 1980s to the end of the 2000s, the share of agriculture in employment declined from 65 to 45 per cent while the share of services in employment rose from 14 to 31 per cent. However, in the most recent period China still had to use 45 per cent of its workforce in agriculture to produce 16 per cent of GDP, suggesting that the post-reform industrialization has not yet achieved the most efficient allocation of resources.

6.6.3 *Productivity performance*

We now examine China's industrialization from a productivity perspective. Table 6.3 presents a decomposition of annual changes of aggregate labour productivity into the contribution of sectoral labour-productivity change and the effect of resource reallocation across sectors in terms of percentage points. The latter measures the contribution of resources that have moved from sectors with slower labour productivity growth to sectors with faster labour productivity growth.[34]

For the aggregate economy, labour-productivity growth in the reform period was on average more than double that of the planning period (5.3 versus 2.3 per cent per annum). Before the reform, 35 per cent of labour-productivity growth was attributable to industry, 5 per cent to construction and 60 per cent to the reallocation effect, leaving agriculture and services making no contribution at all. A closer examination of the subperiods of the planning period in Table 6.3 shows that the first FYP period appeared much 'healthier' than other periods, with the highest labour-productivity growth (4.5 per cent) and a positive reallocation effect (1 percentage point or ppt). In 1958–65, however, a significant labour productivity decline in agriculture (−0.7 ppts) and almost nil gain in the allocation effect offset about 40 per cent of labour-productivity gain in other sectors. Inefficiency was also evident in the period 1972–8, during which more than 50 per cent of the gain from resource reallocation (3.7 ppts) was offset by the drop in labour productivity in industry (−2.1 ppts).

Table 6.3 also shows that the growth of labour productivity during the reform period was 5.3 per cent per year, of which 2 ppts were attributable to industry, 0.2 ppts to construction, 1 ppt to agriculture and services, respectively, and 1.2 ppts to the reallocation effect. The fastest labour-productivity growth during the reform era was observed in 2002–9 at 8.7 per cent per year following China's WTO entry, of which 3.5 ppts were attributable to industry, 0.6 ppts to construction, 0.8 ppts to agriculture, 1.8 ppts to services, and 2 ppts

[34] To measure the reallocation effect, sectoral labour productivity needs to be weighted by nominal output (GVA). Therefore, the sum of so-weighted sectoral labour productivity is not equal to the aggregate labour productivity measured in real terms. That is, the growth rate of total labour productivity in Table 6.3 is not simply a result of subtracting the growth rate of total employment from the growth rate of total GVA in Table 6.1.

Table 6.3. Sectoral contribution to labour productivity growth and reallocation effect, 1952–2009 (per cent per annum)

	Labor productivity growth	Sectoral contribution and reallocation effect (percentage point/ppt)				
		A	I	C	S	Reallocation
Planning:						
1953–1957	4.5	0.9	2.6	−0.3	0.2	1.0
1958–1965	1.8	−0.7	1.4	0.4	0.5	0.2
1966–1971	1.6	−0.1	0.2	0.1	−0.1	1.5
1972–1978	1.5	0.3	−2.1	0.0	−0.4	3.7
1953–1978	***2.3***	***0.0***	***0.8***	***0.1***	***0.0***	***1.4***
Reform:						
1979–1984	3.6	1.6	0.3	0.0	0.6	1.1
1985–1991	2.2	0.5	1.0	0.0	0.1	0.6
1992–2001	6.0	0.8	2.5	0.3	1.4	1.0
2002–2009	8.7	0.8	3.5	0.6	1.8	2.0
1979–2009	***5.3***	***1.0***	***2.0***	***0.2***	***1.0***	***1.2***

Notes: The sectoral contribution and reallocation effect estimates are calculated using the formula: $\Delta \ln y_t = \sum_i \bar{\omega}_{i,t} \Delta \ln y_{i,t} + (\sum_i \bar{\omega}_{i,t} \Delta \ln L_{i,t} - \Delta \ln \sum_i L_{i,t}) = \sum_i \bar{\omega}_{i,t} \Delta \ln y_{i,t} + R_t$, where y and L stand for labor productivity and employment, respectively, whose annual growth rate is defined as log difference; $\bar{\omega}_{i,t}$ stands for sectoral output weight in nominal terms with a bar denoting an average of two adjacent periods; and R stands for the reallocation effect across sectors.

Source: See Table 6.1.

to the reallocation effect. The reform of 1979–84 brought about perhaps the most rapid labour-productivity growth in agriculture in China's post-1949 history. In this period, the aggregate labour productivity grew by 3.6 per cent per year, of which 40 per cent (1.6 ppts) came from agriculture. Since the 1990s, services have enjoyed high labour-productivity growth thanks to the government's promotion of the so-called 'socialist market economy' and more rapid industrialization and urbanization, especially after China's WTO entry. During the periods 1992–2001 and 2002–9 the total labour productivity grew by 6 and 8.7 per cent per annum, respectively, of which over 20 per cent came from services.

Labour productivity is only a partial measure of productivity because it incorporates the effect of changing capital–labour ratios. Besides, labour productivity, which is measured by numbers employed, also improperly assumes that the human capital embodied in the workforce is constant. Obviously, efficiency will deteriorate if an increase in physical or/and human capital does not bring about the same increase in the real output. A full picture of the Chinese economy's efficiency and productivity performance is presented in Table 6.4, including the contribution of measured inputs, i.e. employment, physical and human capital, and TFP for each period. The results are also depicted in Figure 6.3 for an intuitive examination. The TFP is estimated by

Table 6.4. Sources of growth of the Chinese economy, 1953–2009 (per cent per annum)

	Growth of gross value added	Factor contribution (percentage point)			
		Employment	Human capital	Physical capital	TFP
Planning:					
1953–1957	5.6	0.7	0.4	3.6	0.9
1958–1965	3.5	0.6	0.7	3.7	−1.6
1966–1971	4.8	0.9	1.0	3.6	−0.7
1972–1978	4.4	0.7	1.4	4.8	−2.6
1953–1978	***4.4***	***0.7***	***0.9***	***3.9***	***−1.2***
Reform:					
1979–1984	7.4	0.8	0.4	4.6	1.7
1985–1991	4.7	0.6	0.1	4.9	−0.9
1992–2001	7.0	0.3	0.4	7.0	−0.7
2002–2009	9.2	0.2	0.4	7.1	1.5
1979–2009	***7.1***	***0.4***	***0.3***	***6.1***	***0.3***

Notes: The estimates are obtained by the standard growth accounting approach using input–output table factor income weights as explained in the text. The underlying neo-classic framework imposes strong institutional and behavioural assumptions (such as free mobility of factors and profit maximization of firms), which may not be appropriate to an economy like China. However, to compare with many existing studies these assumptions are accepted in this study. Since the Chinese economy may not be operating on the production possibility frontier, TFP growth may capture both technological progress and efficiency improvement.

Source: See Table 6.1.

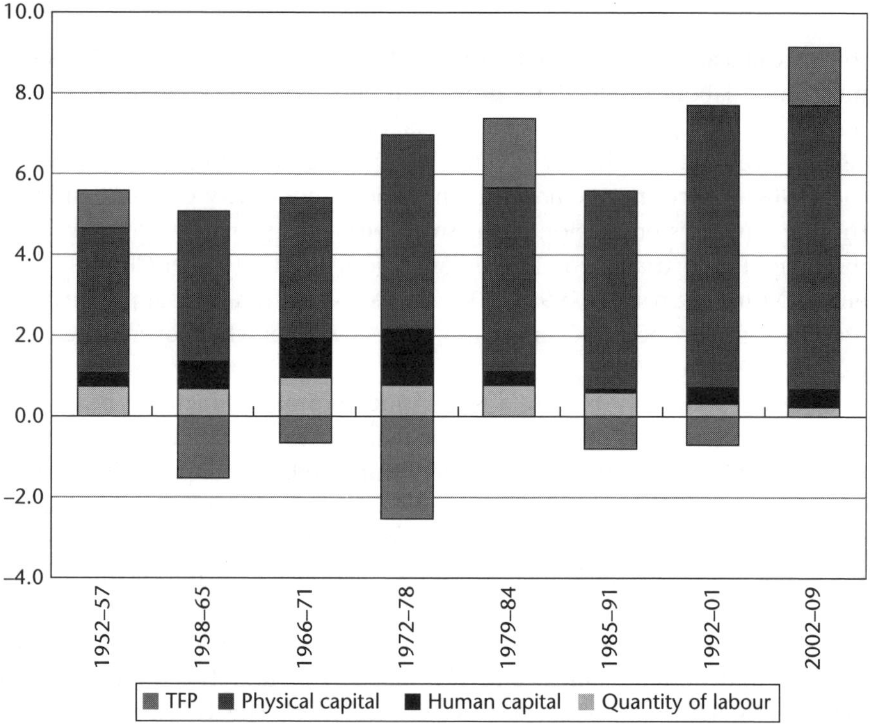

Figure 6.3. Sources of growth of the Chinese economy (per cent per annum; period average)

Note and sources: See Table 6.4.

using time-variant factor income shares based on available Chinese input–output tables since 1987 and estimates for the period prior to 1987 (Wu 2011).

The estimated TFP performance suggests that there has been no stable improvement of efficiency or sustained productivity growth for the entire period. The central planning period saw TFP decline by 1.2 per cent per year while the reform period exhibited TFP growth of merely 0.3 per cent per year. It also appears that the investment in physical capital was the primary driving force of the Chinese economy in all periods, contributing about 83 per cent of the annual growth in the planning period and 86 per cent in the reform period.

Comparing the TFP performance over different periods, one may be convinced that policy and institutional shocks are the best candidates to explain the variations of China's TFP growth. Interestingly, two significant positive TFP gains are somewhat 'related' to the central planning system: one with China's shift to the central planning system in 1953–7 and the other with China's departure from the planning regime in 1979–84. However, I would argue that the most significant TFP gain, in 1953–7, is mainly attributable to the re-employment of the idle production capacity (in terms of both physical and human capital) rather than the implementation of the first Soviet-style FYP. Besides, positive incentives because of the arrival of the long-awaited peace might also have contributed to the TFP growth. On the other hand, the TFP gain in 1979–84 was mainly caused by the *de facto* privatization of agriculture, which improved farmers' incentives, as well as initial reform measures in the rest of the economy. This was, not surprisingly, only a one-off gain.

All major political and ideological campaigns in the pre-reform era, whether or not aiming at economic growth, resulted in severe TFP decline. The period 1972–8 experienced the most rapid growth in investment and employment under central planning, but it was extremely inefficient because of wasteful investment together with long-deteriorating incentive problems. In fact, during this period nearly 40 per cent of the real income growth vanished because of inefficient use of inputs (based on Table 6.4).

On the other hand, perhaps contrary to what many observers believed, the reform measures introduced between the mid-1980s and the beginning of the 2000s were not TFP growth-promoting. The industrial reform that began in 1985 brought about a shock to the existing system as reflected by a negative TFP growth in 1985–91. Although the following period 1992–2001 saw the fastest-ever growth in physical investment that resulted in the most rapid economic growth since 1949, the TFP growth still remained in the negative zone (Figure 6.3).

China's WTO entry at the end of 2001 was followed by a significant positive TFP growth, although not as high as estimates in many other studies that used

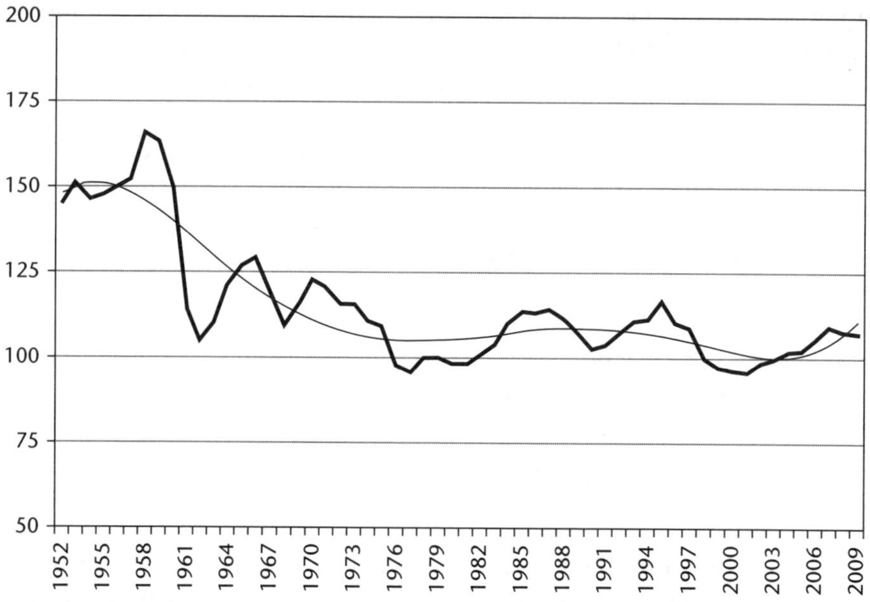

Figure 6.4. Total factor productivity index of the Chinese economy (1978 = 100)

Note and sources: See Table 6.4.

unadjusted official data (Wu 2011). However, this may not simply suggest that China benefited from its comparative advantage in labour-intensive manufacturing through a substantially enlarged external market. In fact following the WTO entry, China found itself in a favourable position because the investment in the 1990s had built up a huge production capacity, of which a large part was under-utilized, evidenced by China's long deflation from 1996 to 2002 in which producer prices declined by 1.3 per cent per year (NBS 2010).[35]

To show a cumulated productivity effect for the Chinese economy as well as its long-run trend, I constructed a TFP index and present it in Figure 6.4. The index is based on 1978 to highlight the impact of the reform. A closer examination of China's TFP locus shows that, compared with the 1978 level, China's initial level of TFP was 50 per cent higher. This simply means that the planning period suffered from a continuous productivity deterioration. The GLF caused a huge damage to productivity and the economy had not yet emerged from its shadow by the time of the reform. The policy retreat in 1963–5 only resulted in a short-term turnaround in productivity performance. It then entered another long decline over most of the 1970s until the agricultural reform in 1978. The initial reform was

[35] Note that business cycle effect is not removed in this type of growth accounting. Therefore, an expansion with underutilized capital stock can 'generate' positive TFP growth, ceteris paribus.

TFP-promoting. However, the industrial reform, with the dual-track price system of 1985, was accompanied by a significant decline in TFP. Deng's push for bolder reform in the early 1990s produced a short spell of positive TFP growth before China entered the longest TFP decline in the reform period in 1995–2001, which was ended by its WTO entry. The post-WTO TFP growth was halted again by the global economic crisis in 2008.

The trend line (estimated by a polynomial function) in Figure 6.4 helps 'filter out' most short-term fluctuations and noise—hence the effect of changes in capacity utilization can be more or less 'observed'. The figure thus depicts China's productivity growth over the long term, reflecting the country's inefficient path of industrialization under the communist government. This productivity trend shows that although the reforms since 1978 reversed a long period of productivity deterioration that begun with the collapse of the GLF, it will still take a long time before the country can make up for its productivity losses due to past policy mistakes and institutional shocks.

6.7 Concluding remarks

In this chapter I started out by exploring the role of the government in China's industrialization by comparing China and India in their post-Second World War growth paths. Following path-dependence theory, I then took an even longer historical perspective to show that China's industrialization was initiated and engineered by the state from the very beginning. It was motivated by the pressing needs to secure the regime's position and to enhance national security in the period from the 1860s to the 1890s. I also showed how industrialization was subsequently sustained by the nationalist government using even more ambitious heavy-industry-oriented plans from the mid-1920s to mid-1930s, and how it was further enhanced during the war, motivated by the state's mounting national defence needs. My empirical evidence shows that China's post-1949 state-led industrialization, strongly motivated by the urge to achieve a fast catch-up with the West, has closely followed an underlying path that began at least in the beginning of the twentieth century. Contrary to conventional wisdom, neither the new communist regime in 1949 nor the reform in 1978 created a new path for China.

I have argued that if the state sector is generally less efficient than the private sector or if government intervention tends to distort the incentives of economic agents hence reducing efficiency, as both economic theory and empirical evidence have suggested, and if China's course of industrialization has indeed followed a path that has been developed and sustained by strong government interests, the Chinese economy must be inherently inefficient. My hypothesis is well supported by an analysis of China's post-1949 productivity growth using a newly constructed dataset for the total economy with a breakdown of major sectors. The findings show that there has been almost no steady and continuous productivity growth or efficiency improvement since 1949. Reform efforts through policy and institutional instruments to improve efficiency have, after some initial gains, been virtually ineffective.

The key factor behind such an inefficient path is not the inefficient use of the resources that have sustained and developed the path, but lies in the interest groups, nurtured by the state-led industrialization, which have influenced the allocation of resources. These interest groups in many cases are deeply rooted in the communist party and the government bureaucracy. They will fight to defend their interests if any reform is seen as a potential threat to them. Although deteriorating inefficiency from time to time forced the government to retreat from comprehensive and rigid planning controls and eventually forced it to adopt market-oriented reforms by the end of the 1970s, the state interests in the economy and their influences have never been weakened. For the government, reform is in essence only a means not a goal. Most of the reform measures have been searching for a better way to speed up the growth of GDP, albeit at the expense of high inequality. This explains why the state-selected industries can continuously enjoy cheap credit, easy access to scarce resources, and protected markets.

As a result, the market-oriented reforms that have allowed the private sector and foreign enterprises to play a role and opening up to international competition are still subject to state interests and government interventions that are highly growth-motivated without any efficiency concern. Indeed, Wu and Shea (2008) show that it is the government factor rather than the development of market institutions that has played a key role in driving China's growth while maintaining stability in the reform era. Their findings have answered the great 'China puzzle' of high-growth and low volatility in the absence of healthy market institutions. Inefficiency problems become worse when growth is increasingly driven by competitions between local governments following the fiscal decentralization measures. While some Chinese economists have praised the role of such inter-governmental competition in promoting fast growth (Zhang and Zhou 2008), they have virtually ignored the fact that government bureaucracies do not act to maximize profits or minimize costs.

China's WTO entry appears to be the best chance for China to break the long inefficient path through institution-building that is efficiency improving and international competition. However, I have been convinced that it is too naïve to believe this. The main obstacle to efficiency improvement is still the interests of the party and the government. As Wu and Shea put it (2008)

> ...the collapse of the communist governments in the Eastern Bloc had further convinced the Chinese communists that the legitimacy of their regime would only be secured by maintaining social stability and delivering economic growth. Ironically, this endeavor to safeguard its legitimacy has compromised the government's commitment to the market-oriented reform and created strong incentives for the government to engage in or interfere with business decisions, especially regarding financial resource allocation, even if it requires the sacrifice of market efficiency and institution building. From government officials' perspective, direct intervention in business decisions could help protect their vested interests..., while building up strong institutions would certainly do the opposite. (ibid.: 126)

WTO accession may act as a counterforce to the ideological and political constraints. It can encourage the government to strengthen the financial institutions in order to facilitate smooth integration with the global economy. However, in the case of China uncertainty about the consequences of further opening up to global competition due to ideological and political constraints increases the government's preoccupation with growth and stability, which waters down the efficiency-improvement effects of WTO entry.

China's post-WTO emergence as the world's manufacturing power house is not an archetypal market fairytale but a story of how the government has successfully manipulated various policy instruments to make the market serve its best interests. To a growth-motivated local government inefficiency is an unobservable, external cost (negative externality) born by other localities, by the general public, or by future generations. To attract investment, no matter whether foreign or domestic, land costs can be lowered or waived, environmental charges can be bypassed or postponed thus raising national health costs, low wage rates can be maintained for a long period, and water and energy can be subsidized. In doing so, these governments are actually rewarding current growth while incurring costs for the future. This is, however, not the end of the story. The unpaid or underpaid costs will artificially raise profits and then encourage overinvestment and overproduction. Consequently, it will intensify competition, which in turn calls for further government support. When this goes on, both the Chinese producers who produce consumer goods for export and foreign consumers in high-income countries are 'subsidized' by the Chinese government. In my view, such a dual-subsidization is to some extent responsible for the existing global imbalances.

The 'success' of the Chinese model cannot be easily replicated under any type of true democracy. Breaking away from this inefficient path requires a genuine political reform in China—an important stage that China cannot bypass prior to achieving modernity. In such a process the state has to substantially withdraw from business and to become the real public goods provider. It should help build up institutions that can enhance market competition, remove barriers to factor mobility that can enhance efficiency improvement, and ensure all external that costs of production are paid or externalities are sufficiently internalized.

Appendix: China's major economic and political events in 1953–2009

Period	Economic plans and policies	Political and institutional events
Planning:		
1953–7	The 1st FYP; Soviet financial loans and technical assistance; Soviet-type central planning	Socialist transformation in industry, handicrafts, and services (1953–6); collectivization in agriculture (1955–56); the 'Anti-Rightists' movement (1957)
1958–65	The GLF (1958–9); the 2nd FYP (1958–63); the Great Famine (1960–2); the first decentralization (1958); the post-GLF retrenchment (1960–2); recentralization (1961–5)	Communization in agriculture (1958–9); 'Anti-Rightist Wing' campaign within the Communist Part of China (CPC) (1959); Sino-Soviet breakup (1960); policy retreat (1960–5)
1966–71	The 3rd FYP (1966–70), i.e. the first five years of the 'Great Third Front' construction (1966–75); the second decentralization (1970)	The chaotic period of the Cultural Revolution (1966–8); Mao's triumph over the 'capitalist roaders' (1969)
1972–8	The 4th and 5th FYPs (1971–5; 1976–80); promotion for local and rural enterprises; the neo-GLF campaign (1976–8)	Sino-US rapprochement (1972); Mao's death (1976); the fall of the Gang of Four (Madam Mao's elite group) (1976)
Reform:		
1979–84	Agricultural reform; abolishment of the 'Great Third Front' construction; fiscal decentralization; special Economic Zones (1980); experimental industrial reform; the 6th FYP (1981–5)	The beginning of Deng's era (at the end of 1978); rehabilitation of the 'Rightists' (1979); decollectivization in rural China (1982–3)
1985–91	Nationwide industrial reform (1985); dual-track price reform; trade and foreign exchange regime reform; the 7th FYP (1986–90); legal developments for foreign direct investment (1986–8)	Crackdown of the Tiananmen Movement (1989); CPC's debate of the nature of the reform (socialism or capitalism?) (1990–1)
1992–2001	Deepening state-owned enterprises (SOE) reform; de facto privatization of small SOEs (1997); the longest deflation since the reform (1997–2002); the 8th and 9th FYPs (1991–5; 1996–2000)	Deng's push for bolder reform and opening up (1992); CPC's adoption of Deng's 'Socialist Market Economy' (1993)
2002–9	China's WTO entry (at the end of 2001); Strategic adjustment and advancement of the state sector; abolition of agricultural tax (2006); the 10th and 11th FYPs (2001–5; 2006–10)	CPC's adoption of Jiang's more capitalist philosophy ('three represents') (2002); Hu's new ideological promotion for a 'harmonious society' (2005); Adoption of the controversial PRC's first Property Law (2007)

Sources: Based on information and materials in Wang (2010).

References

Amsden, A. H. (1991). 'Diffusion of Development: The Late-Industrializing Model and Greater East Asia', *American Economic Review*, 81 (2): 282–6.

Aubrey, H. G. (1949). 'Deliberated Industrialization', *Social Research*, June: 159–74.

——(1951). 'The Role of the State in Economic Development', *American Economic Review*, 41 (2): 266–73.

Barro, R. J., and J. W. Lee (2000). 'International Data on Educational Attainment: Updates and Implications'. Working Paper 42. Cambridge, MA: Harvard University, Center for International Development.

Barro, R. J., and X. Sala-i-Martin (1992). 'Convergence', *Journal of Political Economy*, 100 (2): 223–51.

Bian, M. L. (2005). *The Making of the State Enterprise System in Modern China: The Dynamics of Institutional Change*. Cambridge, MA: Harvard University Press.

Chang, J. K. (1969). *Industrial Development in Pre-Communist China, 1912–1949*. Edinburgh: Edinburgh University Press

Chenery, H. B., and M. Syrquin (1975). *Patterns of Development 1950–1970*. Oxford: Oxford University Press.

Cheng, C.-Y. (1963). *Communist China's Economy, 1949–1962: Structural Changes and Crisis*. South Orange, NJ: Seton Hall University Press.

Chow, G. C. (1993). 'Capital Formation and Economic Growth in China', *Quarterly Journal of Economics*, 108 (3), 809–42.

——(2006). 'New Capital Estimates for China: Comments', *China Economic Review*, 17, 186–92.

David, P. (1985). 'Clio and the Economics of QWERTY', *American Economic Review*, 75 (2): 332–7.

Donnithorne, A. (1964). 'China's Economic Planning and Industry'. In C.-M. Li (ed.), *Industrial Development in the Twentieth Century*. Ann Arbor, MI: University of Michigan Press.

Eckstein, A. (1975). *Chinese Economic Development: The Interplay of Scarcity and Ideology*. Ann Arbor, MI: University of Michigan Press.

Gerschenkron, A. (1951). *A Dollar Index of Soviet Machinery Output, 1927–28 to 1937*. Santa Monica CA: Rand Corporation.

——(1962). *Economic Backwardness in Historical Perspective, A Book of Essays*. Cambridge, MA: Belknap Press of Harvard University Press.

Holz, C. A. (2006a). 'China's Reform Period Economic Growth: How Reliable Are Angus Maddison's Estimates?', *The Review of Income and Wealth*, March: 85–119.

——(2006b). 'New Capital Estimates for China', *China Economic Review*, 17: 142–85.

Hulten, C. R., and F. C. Wykoff (1981). 'The Measurement of Economic Depreciation'. In C. R. Hulten (ed.), *Depreciation, Inflation, and the Taxation of Income from Capital*. Washington, DC: The Urban Institute Press.

Ito, T., and A. O. Krueger (eds) (1995). *Growth Theories in Light of the East Asian Experience*, NBER-EASE Volume 4. Chicago: University of Chicago Press.

Keidel, A. (1992). 'How Badly do China's National Accounts Underestimate China's GNP?', Paper E-8042. Bloomington, IN: Rock Creek Research Inc.

Kirby, W. C. (1984). *Germany and Republican China*. Palo Alto, CA: Stanford University Press.

——(1990). 'Continuity and Change in Modern China: Economic Planning on the Mainland and on Taiwan, 1943–1958,' *The Australian Journal of Chinese Affaires*, 24: 121–41.

Kuznets, S. (1958). 'Economic Growth of Small Nations'. In A. Bonne (ed.), *The Challenge of Development*. Jerusalem: Hebrew University.

Levine, S. I. (1987). *Anvil of Victory: The Communist Revolution in Manchuria, 1945–1948*. New York: Columbia University Press.

Lin, J. Y. (2009). *Economic Development and Transition: Thought, Strategy, and Viability*. Marshall Lectures, 2007/8. Cambridge: Cambridge University Press.

Lin, J. Y., F. Cai, and Z. Li (1996). *The China Miracle: Development Strategy and Economic Reform*. Hong Kong: The Chinese University Press.

Lin, J. Y., and H.-J. Chang (2009). 'Should Industrial Policy in Developing Countries Conform to Comparative Advantage or Defy It? A Debate between Justin Lin and Ha-Joon Chang', *Development Policy Review*, 27 (5): 483–502.

Maddison, A. (1970). *Economic Progress and Policy in Developing Countries*. London, Norton, and New York: Allen and Unwin.

——(1995). *Explaining the Economic Performance of Nations: Essays in Time and Space*. Cheltenham: Edgar Elgar.

——(1998). *Chinese Economic Performance in the Long Run*. Paris: OECD. Out of print, available at: www.ggdc.net/Maddison

——(2001). *The World Economy: A Millennial Perspective*. Paris: OECD.

——(2003). *The World Economy: Historical Statistics*. Paris: OECD.

——(2007). *Chinese Economic Performance in the Long Run, 960–2030*. Paris: OECD.

Maddison, A., and H. X. Wu (2008). 'Measuring China's Economic Performance', *World Economics*, 9 (2): 13–44.

Mankiw, N. G., D. Romer, and D. N. Weil (1992). 'A Contribution to the Empirics of Economic Growth', *Quarterly Journal of Economics*, 107 (2): 407–37.

Mason, S. E. (1960). 'The Role of Government in Economic Development', *American Economic Review*, 50 (2): 636–41.

National Bureau of Statistics, China (NBS) (2010). *China Statistical Yearbook*. Beijing: China Statistics Press.

North, D. C. (1990). *Institutions, Institutional Change, and Economic Performance*. Cambridge: Cambridge University Press.

Page, S. E. (2006). 'Path Dependence', *Quarterly Journal of Political Science*, 1: 87–115.

Perkins, D. H. (1988). 'Reforming China's Economic System', *Journal of Economic Literature*, 26: 601–45.

Perkins, D. H., and M. Syrquin (1989). 'Large Countries: The Influence of Size'. In H. Chenery and T. N. Srinivasan (eds), *Handbook of Development Economics*, Volume II. North-Holland: Elsevier Science Publishers.

Rawski, T. G. (1980). *China's Transition to Industrialism: Producer Goods and Economic Development in the Twentieth Century*. Ann Arbor, MI: University of Michigan Press.

——(1993). 'How Fast has the Chinese Industry Grown?'. Policy Research Working Paper 1194. Washington, DC: World Bank.

——(2001). 'What is Happening to China's GDP Statistics?', *China Economic Review*, 12: 347–54.

——(2008). 'Can China Sustain Rapid Growth Despite Flawed Institutions?'. Paper for The Sixth International Symposium of the Center For China-US Cooperation, University of Denver, 30–31 May.

Ren, R. (1997). *China's Economic Performance in International Perspective*. Paris: OECD.

Shao, L., and J. Sun (1994). 'Sun Yueqi and Shao Lizi—An Interview with Sun Yueqi, the Former President of National Resource Committee, the Godfather of Chinese Modern Industry', *Nanjing History Record* 1.

TCB (2011). *The Conference Board Total Economy Database*, The Conference Board, January 2011 Release, New York. Available at: http://www.conference-board.org/data/economydatabase/

Van Ark, B. (1996). 'Sectoral Growth Accounting and Structural Change in Postwar Europe'. In B. van Ark and N. Crafts (eds), *Quantitative Aspects of Post-war European Economic Growth*. Cambridge: Cambridge University Press.

Wang, H. (2010). *Industrial Economic History of Modern China, 1940–2009*. Shanxi: Shanxi Economic Press.

Wang, L., and A. Szirmai (2012). 'Capital Inputs in the Chinese Economy: Estimates for the Total Economy, Industry and Manufacturing', *China Economic Review*, 23 (1): 81–104.

Wang, Y., and Y. Yao (2002). 'Sources of China's Economic Growth, 1952–99: Incorporating Human Capital Accumulation', *China Economic Review*, 14 (1): 32–52.

Woo, W. T. (1998). 'Chinese Economic Growth: Sources and Prospects'. In M. Fouquin and F. Lemonie (eds), *The Chinese Economy*. Paris: Economica Ltd.

Wu, H. X. (2002). 'How Fast has Chinese Industry Grown?—Measuring the Real Output of Chinese Industry', *The Review of Income and Wealth*, 48 (2): 179–204.

——(2007). 'The Chinese GDP Growth Rate Puzzle: How Fast Has the Chinese Economy Grown?', *Asian Economic Papers*, 6 (1): 1–24.

——(2008). 'Measuring Capital Input in Chinese Manufacturing and Implications for China's Industrial Growth Performance, 1949–2005'. Paper presented at 'The 2008 World Congress on National Accounts and Economic Performance Measures for Nations', Washington, DC, 12–17 May.

——(2011). 'Accounting for China's Growth in 1952–2008—China's Growth Performance Debate Revisited with A Newly Constructed Data Set. Discussion Paper/11-E-003. Tokyo: RIETI.

Wu, H. X., and E. Y. P. Shea (2008). 'The 'China' Chapter—Institutions, Domestic Financial Architecture and Macro Volatility'. In José M. Fanelli (ed.), *Macroeconomic Volatility, Institutions and Financial Architecture*. Basingstoke: Palgrave Macmillan.

Wu, H. X., and X. Yue (2000). 'Reconstructing the Post-War Chinese Industrial GDP with a Laspeyres' Quantity Index Approach: A Further Inquiry'. In K. Odaka, Y. Kiyokawa, and M. Kuboniwa (eds), *Constructing A Historical Macroeconomic Database for Trans-Asian Regions*. Tokyo: Hitotsubashi University, Institute of Economic Research.

Wu, H. X., and X. Yue (2010). 'Accounting for Labor Input in Chinese Industry, 1949–2005'. Paper presented at the 31st IARIW General Conference, St. Gallen, Switzerland, 22–28 August.

Zeitz, P. (2010). 'Trade in Equipment and Technological Development: Evidence from the Sino-Soviet Split'. Mimeo. Palo Alto, CA: Stanford University.

Zhang, J., and L. Zhou (eds) (2008). *Competition for Growth—Political Economy of Growth in China*. Shanghai: Shanghai People's Press.

7

Indonesian Industrialization: A Latecomer Adjusting to Crises

Haryo Aswicahyono, Hal Hill, and Dionisius Narjoko

7.1 Introduction

Indonesia, the fourth most populous nation in the world and the largest economy in South East Asia, has an unusual economic and industrial history, with its post-1945 independent history dominated by three major episodes. Through to the mid-1960s, it had barely commenced the process of modern industrialization. It lagged behind its Asian neighbours, experiencing neither the state-orchestrated heavy industrialization of China and India, nor the export-oriented growth then getting under way in the Asian newly industrialized economies. Its modern industrial sector, such as it was, was dominated by a few large state-owned enterprises, which in most cases had been established by Dutch commercial interests before the Pacific War, and subsequently taken over by the state as part of the 1957–8 nationalizations.

Then, in a sudden reversal of fortunes, the country began to experience very rapid industrialization from the late 1960s, with the manufacturing sector growing at more than 10 per cent per annum for most of the subsequent three decades. Initially this growth was import-substituting in nature, but from the mid-1980s a successful transition to export-orientated industrialization was engineered. That rapid growth was brought to an abrupt halt in 1997–8 with the Asian financial crisis, which resulted in a peak-to-trough growth collapse of more than 20 percentage points. Subsequently, growth recovered, but the effects on the nature and drivers of industrial growth appear to be profound.

The purpose of this chapter is to provide an analytical narrative and interpretation of Indonesia's industrialization outcomes and policies, and to draw attention to the general lessons for late industrializers. The country's industrial experience is of general interest not only because of its size but also the lessons from its unusual history, particularly its pronounced episodes in development, its management of natural resource abundance, the continuing ambivalence towards globalization, adjustment to large external shocks, and major political and institutional transitions. These episodes of economic development and industrial policies also provide insights into how firms develop and respond to major events. The effects of the deep crisis of 1997–8, for example, can be examined with reference to an unusually rich firm-level panel dataset. The dramatic events of this crisis and its aftermath, presaging major institutional changes, have also altered the country's industrial growth dynamics.

We organize the chapter as follows: Section 7.2 provides a brief analytical narrative of Indonesian economic development, highlighting its generally strong economic performance since the late 1960s, in the context of pronounced variations in economic outcomes, policy environments, and external circumstances. In Section 7.3 we discuss the key features of its industrialization record, including rapid growth, structural change, the switch to export orientation in the 1980s, and its unusual ownership features. Section 7.4 examines how major economic crises impact on the industrial sector, with special reference to firm-level impacts and responses in the wake of the Asian financial crisis. Section 7.5 investigates the phenomenon of 'jobless industrialization' during the period since 1998. The finally section sums up and assesses some broader implications from the Indonesian experience.

7.2 Indonesian economic development

The focus of this chapter is industrialization, but it is important to understand the broader context of economic history. By the mid-1960s, Indonesia was an economic basket-case. Inflation was out of control and the left-leaning government had withdrawn from most international organizations, preferring instead to be part of the Beijing–Pyongyang–Hanoi–Phnom Penh–Jakarta axis of 'new economic forces'. Rudimentary national accounts estimates suggest that the country's per capita income was about three-quarters of that half a century earlier (van der Eng 2002). The standard development economics textbook of the time, authored by one of the leading foreign authorities on the country, portrayed Indonesia as a 'chronic economic dropout' (Higgins 1968). Then, in one of the most remarkable reversals of fortune in recent economic history, the regime change in 1966 ushered in a period of rapid economic growth, with per capita income approximately quadrupling over the next three decades (Figure 7.1). This growth was largely fuelled by the

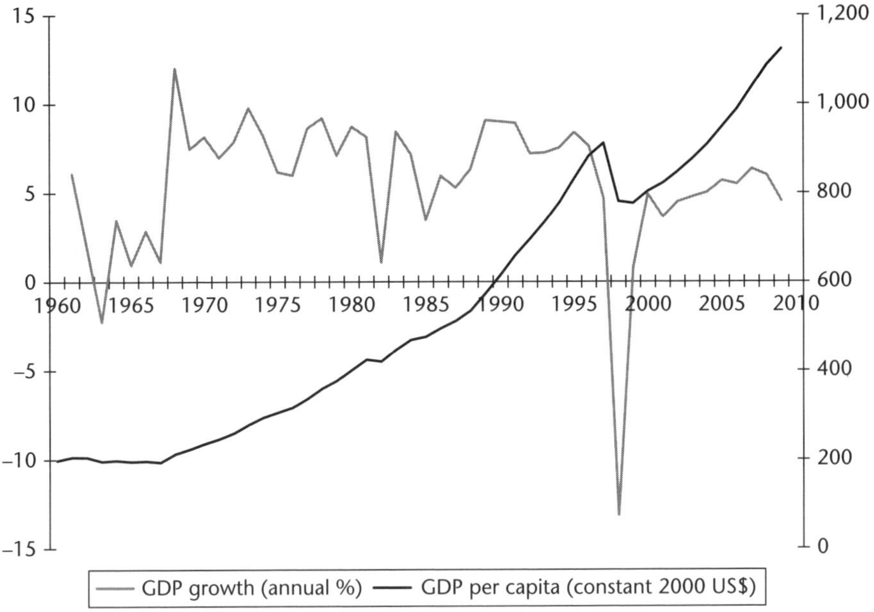

Figure 7.1. GDP per capita and economic growth, 1960–2010
Note: GDP per capita measured on the right axis, GDP growth on the left axis.
Source: computed from World Bank World Development Indicators, online database.

adoption of broadly orthodox policies, including the restoration of macroeconomic stability, more open trade and investment policies, encouragement of the private sector, and investments in infrastructure and education. The 1970s oil boom, large overseas aid flows, the vigorous implementation of the green revolution and rural development more generally, and strong synergies with the then emerging regional superpower, Japan, greatly facilitated this rapid economic growth (Hill 2000).

Indonesia's rapid growth came to a sudden and unanticipated halt in 1997, with the Asian financial crisis. Its economic contraction in 1998, of over 13 per cent, was the sharpest among the four crisis-affected East Asian economies, and one of the most severe in the modern era. The formal banking sector imploded and the currency fell to less than one-fifth of its pre-crisis value. Moreover, the country experienced 'twin crises', in the sense that the economic crisis was accompanied by, and indeed precipitated by, regime collapse, resulting in the departure of President Soeharto in May 1998 after 32 years of authoritarian rule, and ushering in a period of political instability. Its territorial integrity was, for a period, threatened, and there were very serious ethnic and social disputes. From 1998 to 2004 there were five presidents and there was a major reworking of its political institutions. As a result, the once

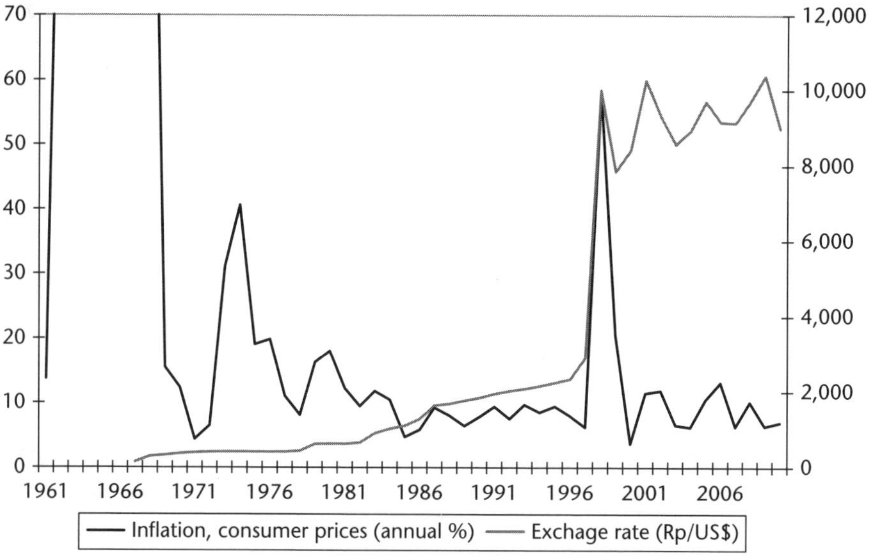

Figure 7.2. Inflation and the exchange rate, 1960–2009
Note: inflation is measured on the left axis, exchange rate on the right axis.
Source: computed from World Bank World Development Indicators, online database.

stable and predictable commercial environment became much less certain. Nevertheless, and contrary to widespread expectations at the time given the magnitude of the 1998 growth collapse, Indonesia recovered moderately quickly, following the pattern of its East Asian neighbours. Its per capita income and most social indicators recovered to pre-crisis levels by around 2004.

Reflecting these developments, Indonesia also has an unusual macroeconomic history, experiencing two episodes of hyper-inflation (Figure 7.2). The most serious was in the mid-1960s, when inflation peaked at over 1000 per cent. In 1998, a shorter episode saw inflation reach almost 100 per cent. Both events were associated with regime change and had their origins in the loss of fiscal discipline, in turn caused by deep political instability. However, for the rest of recent history, macroeconomic policy has been more prudent, with fiscal deficits rarely exceeding 3 per cent of GDP and inflation, while typically above that of the country's major trading partners, in single digits apart from the 1970s' resource booms. Exchange-rate movements have largely reflected these inflation outcomes, in addition to the special case of the 1997–8 capital flight that triggered the exchange-rate collapse and periods of high commodity prices that have resulted in a stronger nominal or real exchange rate.

Since the impact of and response to the crisis are a significant part of our story, it is useful to provide a brief narrative of the major institutional and political economy changes that occurred in response to the crisis (Hill and

Shiraishi 2007). There were seven in total. First, in contrast to the Soeharto era, there is now a weakened (though now directly elected) presidency, subject to a variety of checks and balances. Second, cabinet unity is significantly weakened, with a 'rainbow coalition' of disparate voices and interests. Third, the legislature has become much more powerful, in contrast to the Soeharto era when it was essentially a rubber stamp for all government legislation. In the new arrangements, the president's party is in the minority, and members of parliament need to be persuaded or bought off. Fourth, civil society has become much more active. Long suppressed under Soeharto, think tanks have proliferated, a free press has flourished, and street protests are common and occasionally influential. Fifth, the role of the bureaucracy has changed; it is no longer an arm of the president, accountable directly to him and subject to few pressures from the parliament and civil society. A sixth feature is that the historically underdeveloped legal system now formally has greatly enhanced independent power and authority, but not yet the capacity or resources to undertake its commercial law responsibilities. Finally, a major decentralization programme was introduced in January 2001, shifting substantial power and resources from the central government to the second level districts.

As we will argue below, these changes have profound implications for economic policy settings, for the conduct of economic policy, and for institutional development more generally. We provide illustrations below on how they have affected the pattern of industrialization since the late 1990s.

7.3 Indonesian industrialization: a broad overview

Turning now to the industrialization story, four key features characterize outcomes and the policy environment (Hill 1997). First, after decades of stagnation, Indonesia began to experience very rapid industrialization following the major political changes and economic reforms of 1966–7. Annual industrial growth was at least 9 per cent in all but two of the 27 years, 1970–96 (Figure 7.3). Initially, catch-up and import substitution were the principal drivers. There was a decade of oil-driven growth, and the beginnings of a brief and costly heavy-industry strategy. From the mid-1980s, labour-intensive exports became a significant engine of growth. This growth came to an abrupt halt with the crisis of 1997–8. The contraction in the manufacturing sector was about the same as for the economy as a whole, at 13 per cent. Thereafter, positive growth has been recorded from 1999, but at lower rates than pre-crisis. For reasons we discuss below, the Asian financial crisis appears to have been a turning point for the industrial sector, with its growth falling below the economy-wide average for the first time since the 1960s. As a result of this rapid growth, from 1965 to 1997 the share of the

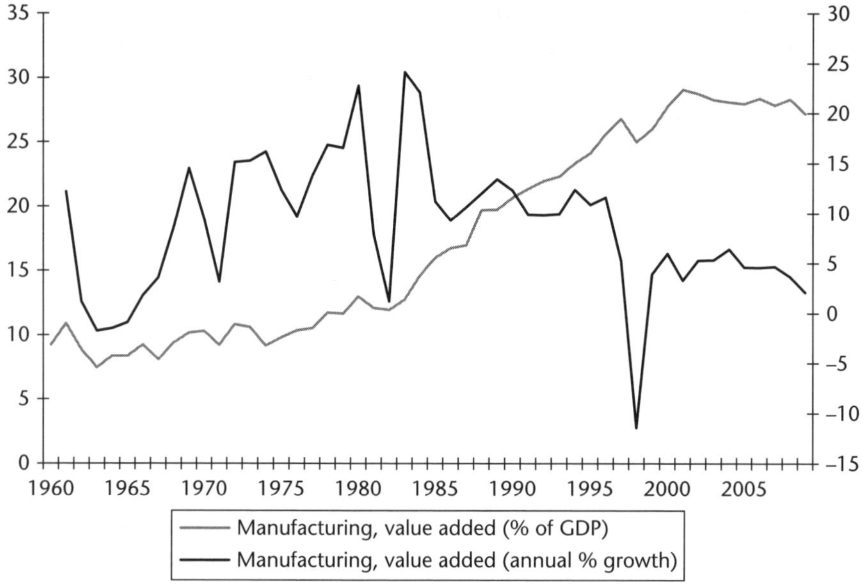

Figure 7.3. Manufacturing growth and share of GDP, 1960–2009
Note: manufacturing growth measured on the right axis, manufacturing share on the left axis.
Source: computed from World Bank World Development Indicators, online database.

manufacturing sector in GDP more than trebled (Figure 7.3). Since the crisis, the share of manufacturing has tended to decline slightly, triggering fears of a premature 'deindustrialization'.

Second, within manufacturing, structural change has been equally rapid (Table 7.1). Since the 1970s, there has been a shift towards a more diversified industrial structure, away from the earlier dominance of simple consumer goods and resource processing. The major labour-intensive and footloose industries grew rapidly during the switch towards export orientation in the mid-1980s. Textiles, garments, and footwear were the major drivers of this export growth. Wood products expanded quickly in response to the prohibition on the export of unprocessed timber, before encountering environmental constraints in the 1990s. Heavy industry grew quickly through to the mid-1980s in response to protection and major state investments. Within machinery and equipment, the automotive industry grew rapidly under the impetus of prohibitive protection for most of the Soeharto period, but collapsed in 1998–99. Electronics has become increasingly important and export-oriented, but never as prominent as in neighbouring East Asian economies.

Third, Indonesia became a significant industrial exporter from the mid-1980s (Figure 7.4). In retrospect, the 1980s were a crucial period in Indonesian economic history. At the beginning of the decade, as oil prices first tapered off

Table 7.1. The changing structure of manufacturing output

	(Percentage of value added, firms with 20+ workers)							
	1975	1980	1985	1990	1995	2000	2005	2009
Food, beverage, and tobacco	44.4	38.2	32.6	23.0	22.3	21.2	24.7	25.3
Textile, leather products, and footwear	10.7	13.3	14.0	19.7	17.8	16.1	11.9	12.6
Wood and wood products	2.4	5.7	8.7	12.1	8.2	5.4	3.9	2.3
Paper and printing	4.7	4.0	3.8	4.7	4.8	6.3	7.7	6.8
Fertilizers, chemicals, and rubber	22.4	18.0	16.0	12.8	13.1	14.8	17.2	20.5
Cement and non-metallic mineral	2.6	4.2	5.0	3.8	3.6	3.5	5.1	5.0
Iron and basic steel	0.7	3.1	7.2	8.0	7.5	3.6	2.7	3.4
Transport equipment machinery, and apparatus	12.1	13.4	12.5	15.5	21.9	27.0	24.8	21.9
Other manufacturing products	0.1	0.1	0.2	0.5	0.7	2.1	1.9	2.2

Source: computed from unpublished data from Badan Pusat Statistik, Central Board of Statistics, Indonesia, Statistik Industri.

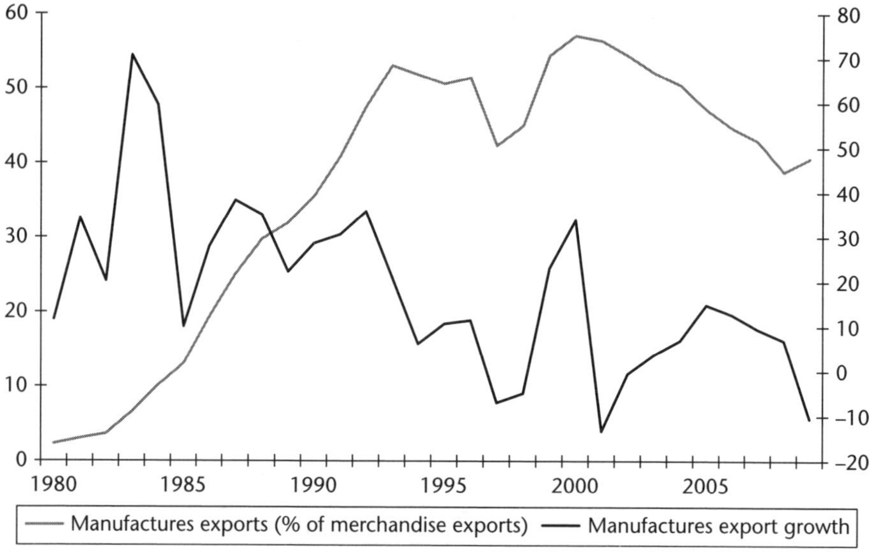

Figure 7.4. Manufacturing export growth and share, 1980–2009

Note: manufacturing growth measured on the left axis, manufacturing share on the right axis.
Source: Badan Pusat Statistik, Central Board of Statistics, Indonesia (exports) annual.

and then fell sharply, the country was highly exposed to the international oil market. Oil, gas, and related minerals provided about two-thirds of government revenue and almost three-quarters of merchandise exports. Indonesia could well have followed other major developing OPEC members—notably Mexico and Nigeria—into a debt crisis.[1] Instead, the decline in oil prices triggered a major reassessment of trade and industry policy. The political economy pendulum swung in favour of the technocrats and their supporters, who advocated a more liberal economic agenda, including reduced protection, a more open posture towards foreign investment, and simplified export procedures (Basri and Hill 2004).

Initially, manufactured exports were concentrated in resource-based activities, especially plywood, reflecting the country's natural-resource endowments and the prohibition of unprocessed commodities (Table 7.2). Its industrial export base began to widen significantly as the reforms took hold, with textiles, garments, footwear, electronics, furniture, sporting goods, and toys also registering rapid growth. The share of labour-intensive products in

[1] See Gelb and Associates (1988) for a comparative assessment of the management of the 1970s oil boom in selected developing countries. Indonesia emerges as the country that most effectively recycled its windfall oil-boom revenues, and which adjusted most quickly to the downturn in prices.

Table 7.2. Manufactured exports by factor-intensity, 1980–2009

	1980	1985	1990	1995	2000	2005	2009
Unskilled labour-intensive	170.9	663.3	4201.4	10573.3	13429.4	13786.8	14945.9
	34.2	*32.5*	*46.5*	*46.1*	*38.1*	*34.3*	*32.0*
Resource-based, labour-intensive intenintintenintensive	77.0	957.2	3083.6	4722.0	3413.6	2904.6	2043.0
	15.4	*46.8*	*34.1*	*20.6*	*9.7*	*7.2*	*4.4*
Resource-based, capital-intensive	115.4	241.8	997.9	2406.0	4749.4	5975.0	8516.2
	23.1	*11.8*	*11.0*	*10.5*	*13.5*	*14.9*	*18.2*
Electronics	97.1	80.9	205.4	2944.3	9072.2	10050.2	9545.3
	19.5	*4.0*	*2.3*	*12.8*	*25.7*	*25.0*	*20.4*
Footloose capital-intensive	38.6	100.6	552.7	2311.2	4576.1	7448.0	11717.6
	7.7	*4.9*	*6.1*	*10.1*	*13.0*	*18.5*	*25.1*
Total	499.0	2043.8	9040.8	22956.8	35240.7	40164.6	46768.0
	100.0	*100.0*	*100.0*	*100.0*	*100.0*	*100.0*	*100.0*

Note: the first row for each series refers to totals in US$ millions, while the second refers to its percentage share of the total.

Source: computed from unpublished data from Badan Pusat Statistik, Central Board of Statistics, Indonesia, Statistik Industri.

total manufactured exports increased in the wake of the 1980s reforms, from about 45 per cent in the mid-1980s to 61 per cent by 1996. These reforms 'worked' in the sense that there was the strong and immediate export response observed above. Indonesia grew quickly out of the early 1980s recession and, although external debt rose sharply in the mid-1980s, debt/GDP ratios remained comfortable and began declining at the end of the decade. The reforms were also good for equity, as employment expanded significantly in the new export-oriented factories on Java. For the first time in its history, Indonesia became 'East Asian' in the sense of emerging as a major industrial exporter. Since around 1990, export performance has been more erratic. Growth began to slow in the early 1990s as a result of increased competition in export markets, a slackening in the reform momentum, slower productivity growth, and the real Rupiah appreciation. In the post-crisis era, export growth has also generally slowed, around an increasingly volatile trend, for reasons to be discussed shortly.

A fourth feature is the country's ownership patterns, which are unusual in some respects. Reliable estimates are now dated, and relate to the pre-1997 period, but are still broadly indicative of the patterns. There are high levels of ownership concentration, both in the sense of corporate conglomeration and seller concentration. Claessens, Djankov, and Lang (2000) have documented the former, finding that Indonesia exhibited the highest level of corporate concentration in East Asia in 1996, with the top ten families owning 57.7 per cent of listed corporate assets, but many were short-lived operations reflecting their rent-seeking origins.[2] In terms of plant-level industrial concentration, Bird (1999) found high levels of concentration, typical of those in relatively small, late-industrializing economies. Over the period 1975–93, concentration levels were declining steadily, though in the latter year the simple average four-firm concentration ratio was still 54 per cent. Concentration ratios were significantly lower once allowance was made for imports.

Indonesia's industrial ownership patterns reflect the interplay of history, policy, and industrial organization factors (Table 7.3). In the mid-1960s, no foreign capital was present, and the 'commanding heights' of the economy were in state hands. The state-owned enterprises (SOE) sector continued to be important throughout the Soeharto era. The oil boom period financed a major expansion in the SOE sector, initially in heavy industry, and later in several costly high-tech projects. Meanwhile, foreign investment returned to the country from the late 1960s in response to the newly liberal policy regime and generous fiscal incentives. As is the case in most countries, domestic firms

[2] That is, in terms of the shares of its leading conglomerates in output and capitalization. Note, however, that the mid-1990s data were dominated by Soeharto-linked conglomerates that have since been largely dismantled, and thus the figure would be lower now.

Table 7.3. Concentration and foreign ownership by sector, 1990–2005

		Concentration (CR4)					
		1990	1993	1996	1999	2002	2005
31	Food, beverages, and tobacco	59	69	59	57	56	60
32	Textile, clothes, and leather industry	29	32	28	29	30	42
33	Wood and wood products	22	24	26	25	29	33
34	Paper and paper products	61	57	61	70	73	64
36	Non-metallic mineral products	61	59	59	63	66	66
37	Basic metal industries	80	73	79	79	74	66
38	Fabricated metal, machinery, and equipment	74	75	74	67	69	71
39	Other manufacturing industries	61	66	61	62	73	79
1-ULI	Unskilled, labour-intensive	30	33	29	30	32	43
2-RLI	Resource-based, labour-intensive	48	57	51	50	51	57
3-RCI	Resource-based, capital-intensive	65	62	64	67	66	61
4-ELE	Electronics	74	68	68	57	55	67
5-FCI	Footloose capital-intensive	73	78	78	75	72	72
	Non-oil and gas manufacturing	54	56	56	54	57	58
Foreign ownership (share, in %)							
		1990	1993	1996	1999	2002	2005
31	Food, beverages, and tobacco	8.5	9.7	14.0	15.8	9.4	24.9
32	Textile, clothes, and leather industry	17.8	21.8	29.3	37.4	32.1	32.8
33	Wood and wood products	10.1	11.7	22.9	15.8	11.6	11.2
34	Paper and paper products	30.2	14.9	33.8	23.5	46.4	29.0
35	Chemicals and chemical products	33.1	36.6	43.0	44.8	29.7	26.3
36	Non-metallic mineral products	18.0	23.3	33.4	34.6	28.3	35.9
37	Basic metal industries	24.8	35.3	24.3	43.1	29.4	30.5
38	Fabricated metal, machinery, and equipment	46.1	36.4	42.4	58.0	67.6	68.3
39	Other manufacturing industries	19.5	44.4	51.9	56.1	33.7	46.9
1-ULI	Unskilled labour-intensive	16.2	21.1	27.3	35.4	28.8	30.0
2-RLI	Resource-based, labour-intensive	9.0	10.2	16.8	15.9	9.8	22.8
3-RCI	Resource-based, capital-intensive	29.5	32.5	35.9	40.0	34.9	29.9
4-ELE	Electronics	41.7	43.0	48.7	82.4	71.5	68.9
5-FCI	Footloose capital-intensive	47.2	34.7	39.5	44.0	66.0	68.1
	Non-oil and gas manufacturing	21.9	23.4	30.9	35.5	33.5	37.2

Source: computed from unpublished data from Badan Pusat Statistik, Central Board of Statistics, Indonesia, Statistik Industri.

are the major players in Indonesian industry, accounting for more than 50 per cent of manufacturing value added in most two-digit industries. Among domestic firms, SOEs are important in certain 'strategic' industries, such as fertilizer, steel, and cement, together with some firms that were inherited from the pre-1966 nationalizations (e.g., sugar processing) and never subsequently relinquished. During the Asian financial crisis, the SOE sector in general contracted, especially in the case of the prestige projects, which were heavily dependent on direct government support. Foreign ownership has risen steadily since the economy was opened up in the late 1960s. The share of these firms in non-oil manufacturing value added rose from about 23 per cent in 1975 to 37 per cent in 2005 (Table 7.3). The share rose higher still in the wake of the crisis, in response to policy liberalizations and the opportunity for foreign firms to buy distressed local assets. Moreover, as we will document below, foreign firms have been better able to endure the crisis. As is evident in the two-digit ownership data, and consistent with industrial organization theory, multinational enterprises are important in the international standard industrial classification (ISIC) 38, dominated by electronics and the automotive industry. They are also important in basic metals (principally steel and related products), the chemical industries, and a few labour-intensive activities (textiles, garments, footwear, and miscellaneous manufactures) where knowledge of export markets is important.

7.4 Economic crises: firm-level impacts and responses[3]

We referred above to the general impacts of the 1997–98 economic crisis, including the deep but short-lived growth collapse, the general slowdown in the manufacturing sector, and indifferent export performance. In this and the following section, we examine first in more detail the firm-level impacts and second, the employment effects.

A feature of rapid industrialization and well-functioning product and factor markets is high levels of firm mobility across size groups. In an earlier study of Indonesian industrialisation (Aswicahyono, Bird, and Hill 1996), we found there was considerable evidence of this mobility, in particular of firms 'graduating' to larger size groups. We were able to examine this phenomenon through very detailed firm-level analysis, made possible by the fact that each firm in the annual survey is identified by a consistently designated code that enables it to be traced over time. One of the results of this earlier analysis was to demonstrate that the widely discussed phenomenon of the apparent

[3] This section draws on Aswicahyono, Hill, and Narjoko (2010).

decline of the share of small firms in industrial output could actually be interpreted positively, not as a sign that these firms were being pushed out in the process of the rapid industrialization—the commonly held perception at the time—but rather that they were vacating the smaller size groups and graduating to larger groupings. This result was shown by comparing the share of total output by firm-size at the 'current year', the basis for the gloomy conclusion, and the 'initial year', the basis for the positive interpretation.

In this chapter, we repeat the exercise through to the year 2005. That is, we trace each firm over the period 1990–2005, and assign it to a firm-size grouping. These are groupings are chosen arbitrarily but plausibly as firms with 20–99 workers, 100–499 workers, and more than 500 workers.[4] We then estimate output (and employment, though not shown here) by the three size groups, based on each firm's size in the current year and the initial year, with the latter being either 1990 or the year the firm commenced operation. The results are presented in Table 7.4. There is little change in the size share based on current size, with the share of small firms rising slightly pre-crisis, then falling somewhat, while the largest firms were most affected by the economic crisis. However, based on size in the initial year, the small-firm share rose quite quickly through to the crisis, but then began to decline from 2001.

Thus the crisis and its immediate aftermath appear to have marked a turning point in this process of firm mobility. Until the crisis, smaller firms continued to display the dynamism evident in the pre-crisis period. However, after the crisis, the pace of graduation slowed and the small-firm share in both series declined. These results are not necessarily cause for concern, as they could simply reflect a longer-term process of industrial consolidation. They may also reflect the effects of the crisis, from which smaller firms experienced greater adjustment difficulties, or the increased competitive pressures that occurred as firms sought to survive.

There are no general data to support the latter proposition. But there is presumptive evidence to advance the hypothesis that the barriers for smaller firms increasing their scale have risen since the crisis, particularly in access to finance. This arises due to the credit-rationing devices that are commonly put in place after crises, which invariably support larger firms with better collateral and credit histories (Stiglitz and Weiss 1981). The underlying argument is that banks have more difficulty differentiating between 'good' and 'bad' loan applicants after the crisis and, as a result, banks are more likely to adopt more stringent lending policies, favouring those who were able to provide more collateral and/or an established credit history. There is some evidence

[4] That is, approximately corresponding to small, medium, and large firms respectively. Experimentation with different size groups revealed that the general conclusions are not sensitive to the definition of size groups.

Table 7.4. Manufacturing output by size group, 1990–2005

	Current size (percentage of value added)		
	Small L = 20–99	Medium L = 100–499	Large L = 500+
1990	7	27	66
1991	6	28	66
1992	7	28	64
1993	7	23	70
1994	7	23	70
1995	7	22	71
1996	7	21	73
1997	8	27	65
1998	8	24	68
1999	7	25	68
2000	7	24	68
2001	9	24	68
2002	7	24	69
2003	6	23	70
2004	6	25	69
2005	5	25	70
	Initial size (percentage value added)		
	Small L = 20–99	Medium L = 100–499	Large L = 500+
1990	7	27	66
1991	7	28	65
1992	10	31	59
1993	10	31	58
1994	11	29	60
1995	13	29	59
1996	12	31	57
1997	14	38	48
1998	14	32	54
1999	12	33	54
2000	13	31	56
2001	15	31	54
2002	13	31	56
2003	13	31	56
2004	13	32	55
2005	12	33	55

Source: computed from unpublished data from Badan Pusat Statistik, Central Board of Statistics, Indonesia, Statistik Industri.

from East Asia in the late 1990s supporting this view. As Gosh and Gosh (1999) and Ding, Domac, and Ferri (1998) have argued, not only was there credit rationing during the crisis, but also small and medium-sized firms were more adversely affected than larger ones.

Indonesia's banking sector was the most severely affected among the East Asian crisis economies, resulting in a significant renationalization of banks and reform of the regulatory regime. However, as Rosengard et al. (2007) note, these reforms have had the unintended consequence of limiting the access of

Table 7.5. Transition matrices: distribution of plants for 1992 and 1996, and 2001 and 2004

1996				
1992		S = 20–99	M = 100–499	L = 500+
	S = 20–99	90.6	8.8	0.6
	M = 100–499	13.1	75.4	11.5
	L = 500+	1.9	13.1	85.1
2004				
2001		S = 20–99	M = 100–499	L = 500+
	S = 20–99	96.1	3.7	0.1
	M = 100–499	10.9	84.3	4.8
	L = 500+	0.9	11.8	87.3

Source: computed from unpublished data from Badan Pusat Statistik, Central Board of Statistics, Indonesia, Statistik Industri.

small enterprises to formal-sector financial institutions. Based on the questionable premise that larger financial institutions are less likely to fail than smaller ones, the country's small, community-based institutions have been instructed to merge with larger, centralized units, and among the latter '... innovative microfinance services were viewed with suspicion and hostility' (ibid.: 87).

Transition matrices of the size distribution of firms support the conclusion that the speed of firm mobility slowed after the crisis. These matrices are computed for the pre- and post-crisis periods, defined here as 1992–6 and 2001–4 (Table 7.5). They show the distribution of firms for the same three size groups according to the initial and final year of each subperiod. Thus, of the small firms in 1992, by 1996 90.6 per cent were still small, while 8.8 per cent and 0.6 per cent had graduated to the medium and large groups respectively. A clear result over the two sub-periods is that there is less mobility: more small firms remained small after the crisis than before it. A similar conclusion holds for the medium-sized firms.

We can further extend the analysis of firm-level dynamics by examining two additional aspects: the patterns of firm-level entry and exit, and the rates of expansion and contraction for 'surviving' firms. Here, too, we undertake this analysis by tracking the history of each firm enumerated in the survey. An earlier study by Narjoko (2006) examined these patterns in the pre-crisis and crisis periods. This analysis extends the examination through to 2004, by which time manufacturing output had returned to pre-crisis levels and was growing moderately strongly. Specifically, we examine two interrelated phenomena: the entry and exit rates of firms over time and, among the survivors, expansion and contraction rates.

First, with respect to entry and exit rates, the analysis can be conducted with reference to number of plants, employment, or value added. The story is

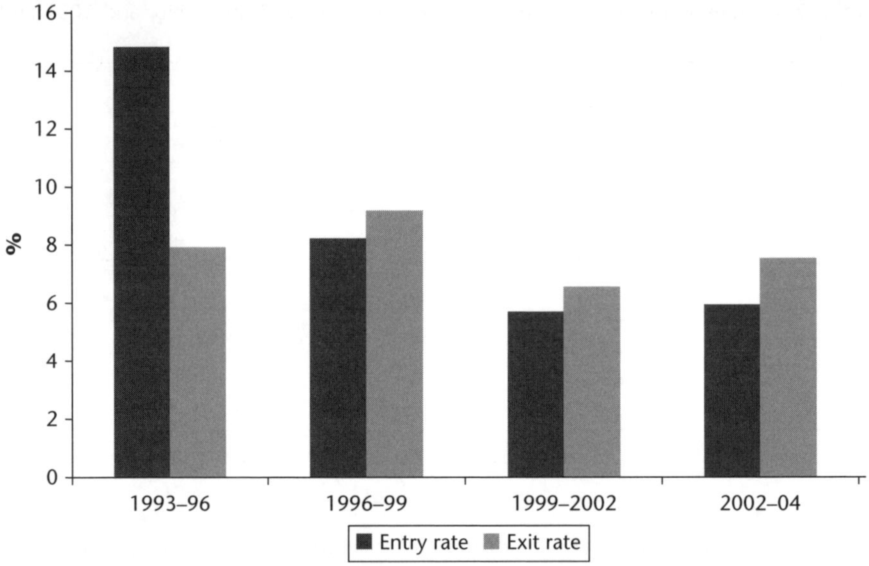

Figure 7.5. Entry and exit rates in manufacturing, 1993–2004

Note: percentage based on number of plants.

Source: computed from unpublished data from Badan Pusat Statistik, Central Board of Statistics, Indonesia, Statistik Industri.

broadly similar, and so we present results only for the rates by number of firms.[5] The following definitions are used for entry and exit rates, for industry j and time periods t and $t-1$:

$$\text{Entry rate}_{j,t} = \frac{NEP_{j,t}}{NTP_{j,t-1}}$$

$$\text{Exit rate}_{j,t} = \frac{NXP_{j,t}}{NTP_{j,t-1}},$$

where $NEP_{j,t}$ = total number of plants that enter industry j between t and $t-1$, $NXP_{j,t}$ = total number of plants that exit industry j between t and $t-1$, and $NTP_{j,t-1}$ = total number of plants in industry j in $t-1$.

We identify four separate subperiods: pre-crisis (1993–6), crisis (1996–9), early post-crisis (1999–2002), and return to growth (2002–4). Before the crisis, as would be expected, there were high plant-entry rates, and these were almost double the exit rates (Figure 7.5). Note also, however, and consistent with industrial dynamism, that the exit rates were not insignificant. As the crisis hit, entry rates fell to approximately half the pre-crisis figure, while

5 The additional data for other variables are available from the authors on request.

exit rates rose and began to exceed entry rates. These trends applied to practically all industry groups, but especially to textiles, clothing and footwear, wood products, and non-metallic minerals (respectively ISIC 32, 33, 36). They also apply to most firm and ownership groups, though with considerable variations (see Narjoko (2006) and for a summary Narjoko and Hill (2007)).

While this response is as would be expected, some trends are puzzling. In particular, the immediate crisis response of exit rates exceeding entry rates has persisted through to 2004, by which time positive economic growth had been under way for four years. Moreover, entry rates have continued to decline, in contrast to what might have been the expected outcome of a sharp decline during the crisis and recovery thereafter. At least two possible conjectures are plausible here. One is that there is a delayed response of firms: the initial adjustment is to reduce output, switch output composition, extend credit lines, live off past capital and so on, in the hope that firms can trade through the difficulties. Especially for well-established firms, such strategies can endure for several years, hence the exit rates are spread out over several years, as illustrated in Figure 7.5, rather than a single large reduction in the crisis period. The second conjecture relates to the extended decline in entry rates for five years after the crisis. Here the likely explanation is that potential new entrants were holding back, observing the continuing exit process, in addition to the fact that there were high levels of excess capacity following the crisis. The difficulties in accessing finance and rising competitive pressures, as noted above, have arguably resulted in increased barriers to entry.

What happened to firms that survived the crisis? We follow the usual definitions of expansion and contraction rates (see for example Davis, Haltiwanger, and Shuh 1996), with reference to employment in industry j and time period t

$$\text{Expansion rate}_{j,t} = \frac{EMPL\_POS_{j,t}}{EMPL\_T_{j,t-1}}$$

$$\text{Conraction rate}_{j,t} = \left| \frac{EMPL\_NEG_{j,t}}{EMPL\_T_{j,t-1}} \right|$$

where $EMPL\_POS_{j,t}$ = total employment of plants that expanded between t and $t-1$, $EMPL\_NEG_{j,t}$ = total employment for plants that contracted between t and $t-1$, and $EMPL\_T_{j,t}$ = total employment in year t.

Here too, as would be expected, expansion rates exceeded contraction rates prior to the crisis (Figure 7.6). During the crisis, expansion rates declined, but contraction rates increased and the two rates converged. Thereafter, the pre-crisis pattern of expansion exceeding contraction resumed, although the gap between the two narrowed; that is, the net expansion rate was lower. There are also differences among major industry groups, with a similar division as for

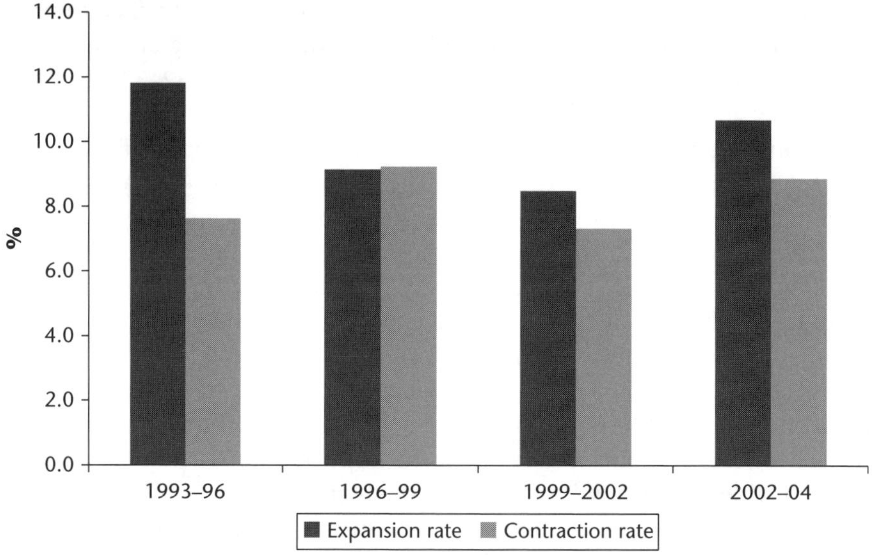

Figure 7.6. Expansion and contraction rates in manufacturing, 1993–2004

Note: percentage based on employment.

Source: computed from unpublished data from Badan Pusat Statistik, Central Board of Statistics, Indonesia, Statistik Industri.

the entry and exit rates. In particular, growth has originated more from the expansion of existing plants than the entry of new ones in the resource-based and capital-intensive industries, such as food products and processing, paper products, chemicals, and machinery and equipment (respectively ISIC 31, 34, 35, and 38).

The picture for firm dynamics can be summarized by decomposing employment growth into that due to entry/exit on the one hand and expansion/contraction on the other. We conduct the analysis with reference to employment effects rather than plants, and thus the terms are referred to as 'entry rate 2' and 'exit rate 2' to differentiate them from those above. That is

$$\text{Entry rate } 2_{j,t} = \frac{EMPL\_EN_{j,t}}{EMPL\_T_{j,t-1}}$$

$$\text{Exit rate } 2_{j,t} = \frac{EMPL\_EX_{j,t}}{EMPL\_T_{j,t-1}}$$

where $EMPL\_EN_{j,t}$ = total employment of plants that entered industry *j* between *t* and *t*–1, $EMPL\_EX_{j,t}$ = total employment of plants that exited industry *j* between *t* and *t*–1.

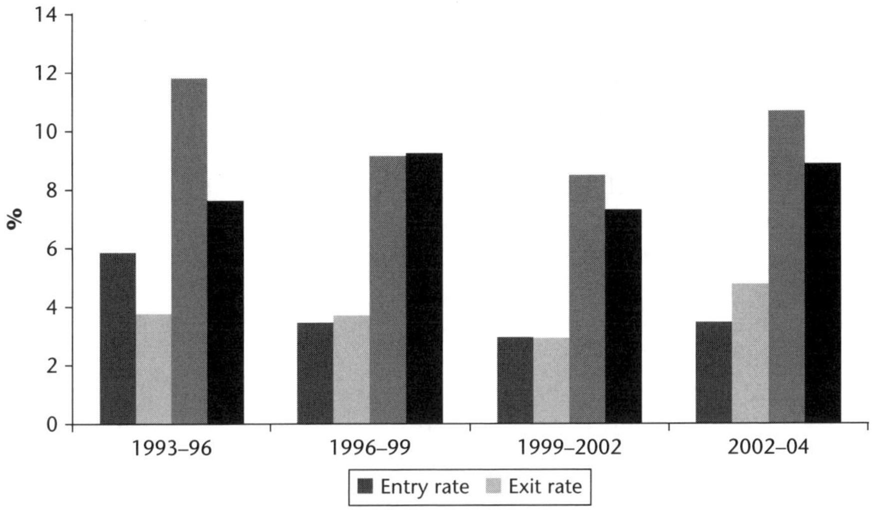

Figure 7.7. Decomposition of employment growth, 1993–2004

Note: The four shaded bars for each time period refer respectively to (reading from left to right) entry rate, exit rate, expansion rate, and contraction rate (see text for the definitions of each of these terms).

Source: computed from unpublished data from Badan Pusat Statistik, Central Board of Statistics, Indonesia, Statistik Industri.

So,

$$\text{employment growth decomposition}_{j,t} = \text{entry rate } 2_{j,t} + \text{expansion rate}_{j,t} + \text{exit rate } 2_{j,t} + \text{contraction rate}_{j,t}$$

Figure 7.7 presents the results of the decomposition. The results show that, since the crisis, expansion has become more important than entry for employment over time. The inference is therefore that, in the wake of the crisis, most of the growth originated from what may be termed 'insiders'; that is, firms who were able to survive the crisis and adapt more quickly to the significantly altered policy and commercial environment. As Narjoko (2006) demonstrates for the period through to 2000, specific firm attributes were commonly associated with these outcomes, in particular prior export orientation and foreign ownership. In addition, firms that maintained credit lines or had low debt generally survived and were able to respond more quickly to the economic recovery from 2000. Potential new entrants were apparently deterred by real or perceived barriers to entry, including the more unpredictable business and political environment and a much more cautious financial sector.

7.5 Jobless industrialization?[6]

At the same time as firm mobility and dynamics appeared to have declined, output growth since the crisis has become considerably less employment-elastic, resulting in the formerly major engine of Indonesian employment growth becoming much less significant. To probe this relationship, we undertake three sets of calculations: the relationship between output and employment growth in Indonesia by sector before and after the Asian financial crisis, the Indonesian employment manufacturing record in comparative Asian perspective, and Indonesia's industrial employment dynamics among the major firm-size groups.[7]

We commence with the observation that employment growth is the outcome of a simple identity; that is, it is the product of output growth and the elasticity of employment growth with respect to output growth. Hence,

$$\triangle N = \triangle Y(\triangle N/\triangle Y)$$

To understand employment growth, the left-hand variable in the equation, we therefore need data on the two right-hand variables. Our analysis commences with the aggregate picture for the major sectors in Indonesia, pre- and post-crisis, followed by a comparison of the industrial sectors for Indonesia and several neighbouring economies. Since we are focusing on longer-term trends, and the crisis years were so atypical, we present data for two sub-periods, 1990–6, corresponding to the later years of the long Asian boom, and 2000–8, by which time the immediate crisis impacts had been resolved and economic growth had resumed, but before the global financial crisis had any major impact.

Table 7.6 shows output and employment growth for the two periods, together with the implied output elasticities.[8] We also present for each sector the differences between the two periods for the three series, and the rankings of these differences.

Aggregate *output growth* was considerably slower in the second period, at about two-thirds of that in 1990–6. However, the slowdown was not uniform across sectors. In fact, the data point to major changes in the drivers of Indonesian economic dynamism pre- and post-crisis. Two sectors actually grew faster: agriculture, reflecting generally buoyant commodity prices and

[6] This section draws on Aswicahyono, Hill, and Narjoko (2011).

[7] In the paper on which this section draws, we also present estimates of employment–output and employment–wage elasticities. These results generally confirm those from the more aggregated sectoral estimates.

[8] Henceforth for convenience we will refer to output–employment elasticities as 'output elasticities' and employment–wage elasticities as 'wage elasticities'.

Table 7.6. Indonesia: sectoral output and employment growth, 1990–2008

	1990–6	2000–8	Change	Ranking
GDP growth (%)				
Agriculture	3.1	3.9	0.8	2
Mining and utilities	5.3	1.5	−3.8	5
Manufacturing	11.2	5.2	−6	6
Construction	13.7	6.5	−7.3	7
Wholesale trade	8.9	5.8	−3	4
Transport	8.2	10.1	1.9	1
Other activities	6.4	5.8	−0.7	3
Total	7.9	5.3	−2.6	
Employment growth (%)				
Agriculture	−1.7	0.2	1.9	1
Mining and utilities	6	3.7	−2.3	3
Manufacturing	6	0.9	−5	5
Construction	10.8	5.7	−5.1	6
Wholesale trade	6.5	1.7	−4.8	4
Transport	9.4	3.9	−5.5	7
Other activities	4.6	3.6	−1	2
Total	2.3	1.7	−0.6	
Implied output elasticities				
Agriculture	−0.56	0.05	0.6	2
Mining and utilities	1.14	2.56	1.4	1
Manufacturing	0.53	0.18	−0.4	5
Construction	0.78	0.88	0.1	3
Wholesale trade	0.74	0.3	−0.4	6
Transport	1.14	0.38	−0.8	7
Other activities	0.71	0.62	−0.1	4
Total	0.29	0.32		

Source: ADB statistical database system (https://sdbs.adb.org/sdbs/index.jsp).

competitive exchange rates, and transport and telecommunications, driven by technological changes and substantial deregulation.

By contrast, there was a major slowdown in three sectors—mining and utilities, manufacturing, and construction—with growth rates in the second period less than half those of the first. The explanations for these outcomes are both sector-specific and economy-wide. Construction growth pre-crisis was at unsustainable levels and was hard hit by the crisis. Growth since then has been subdued, owing in part to financing constraints and reduced public-sector investment. The latter factors also explain slower utilities growth, while mining growth has been slow as a result of the uncertain exploration and taxation environment, and notwithstanding historically high commodity prices.

The slowdown in manufacturing growth, from well above the economy-wide average to just below it, is the most puzzling result. As a tradable goods sector, like agriculture, it benefited from the competitive boost of a depreciating exchange rate in the wake of the Asian financial crisis. Moreover, the sector faced no significant demand-side constraints until the recent global financial crisis. Global manufacturing growth was rapid, there was a continuous relocation of the industry to developing economies, and unlike agriculture there have been no major external trade barriers.

The picture is similarly varied for employment growth, except that the slowdown was less pronounced as compared to output. That is, employment growth in the second period was about three-quarters of that in the first, and this in a context where aggregate labour supply is anyway gradually beginning to decline. Here too, there is considerable variation across sectors. The two major differences are the turnaround in agriculture, to slightly positive growth compared to the earlier contraction, and the collapse in manufacturing growth. Employment in all the other sectors grew more slowly, in some cases by a significant margin. Some of these outcomes reflect a continuation of significant labour-saving technological changes, such as the major transformation in trade patterns, from traditional petty trade to modern malls and retail outlets, in addition to the ubiquitous mobile telecommunications revolution, and the rapid growth of civil aviation and motorized land transport.

The bottom panel presents the implied output elasticities. These indicate whether the slowdown in non-agricultural employment is due mainly to slower output growth or less employment-elastic output growth. The aggregate picture is that output elasticity rose slightly. However, the increase is almost entirely due to the change in agriculture, from labour-shedding to slightly positive growth. With the exception of mining and utilities, which employ few workers, and a slight increase in construction, the general picture is less elastic employment growth. In particular, the elasticities fell sharply for three major employers of labour—manufacturing, trade, and transport and communications. The explanation in the case of the latter two is clear: there was a major change in the technology with which the service was provided; that is, owing to the proliferation of modern shopping malls, rapidly expanding civil aviation, and so on. Even in a low-wage economy like Indonesia, all these activities are much more capital-intensive than the services they replaced. However, there was no such exogenous labour-displacing technology sweeping through manufacturing. The explanation for the declining output–employment elasticities in manufacturing therefore has to lie elsewhere, in the commercial environment and factors affecting the willingness of employers to hire labour.

To sum up on the Indonesian employment picture, growth in aggregate was marginally slower after the crisis. But this conceals major sectoral differences. Agriculture returned to positive growth, reflecting Indonesia's diverse natural-resource advantages in the context of high commodity prices. Construction employment growth fell sharply, but this was entirely due to lower output growth. Employment growth slowed significantly in some of the service

Table 7.7. East Asian manufacturing output and employment growth, 1988–2008

	1988–96	2000–8	Change	Reverse ranking
GDP growth (%)				
Indonesia	11.3	4.7	−6.5	2
Malaysia	13.9	4.3	−9.7	1
Philippines	3	4.2	1.2	5
Thailand	11.2	6	−5.1	3
Korea	7.5	6.3	−1.2	4
Employment growth (%)				
Indonesia	7.6	0.9	−6.7	3
Malaysia	8.6	−1.4	−10	1
Philippines	2.4	0.7	−1.7	4
Thailand	9.9	2	−7.9	2
Korea	0.2	−1	−1.1	5
Implied output elasticities				
Indonesia	0.67	0.2	−0.47	4
Malaysia	0.62	−0.32	−0.94	1
Philippines	0.78	0.17	−0.62	2
Thailand	0.88	0.33	−0.55	3
Korea	0.02	−0.16	−0.18	5

Source: ADB statistical database system (https://sdbs.adb.org/sdbs/index.jsp).

sectors experiencing rapid technological change, even though output growth was strong. Manufacturing is unique in that it is the only major sector to experience more than a halving in both its output growth and its output elasticity.

It is useful to compare these results to outcomes in neighbouring developing economies, to ascertain whether any of these trends are evident. Here also we conduct the analysis for the pre- and post-crisis periods, with respect to output and employment growth, and the implied elasticities. Table 7.7 presents the results.

In the pre-crisis period, the pace of Indonesian industrialization was similar to its rapidly industrializing neighbours, Malaysia and Thailand, and much faster than Korea and the Philippines. Industrial growth in the three South East Asian growth economies—Indonesia, Malaysia, and Thailand—slowed sharply after the crisis, most of all in Malaysia and the least in Thailand. The Philippine growth rate accelerated slightly, from a weak base, while Korean growth slowed somewhat. Thus from a growth perspective, Indonesia is well within South East Asian norms.

The employment picture is also broadly similar. The three South East Asian economies experienced a very sharp growth slowdown. Malaysian manufacturing employment actually shrunk, reflecting the fact that this higher-wage economy has been progressively shedding its labour-intensive segments. Employment growth in Thailand was slightly stronger, but the absolute growth decline was sharper than in Indonesia. Korean and Philippine employment growth was anaemic throughout, contracting in the former case since 2000. Thus, here also, Indonesia does not emerge as a regional outlier.

The output elasticities declined significantly in all five economies. As noted, they turned negative for Korea and Malaysia. The rates of decline are broadly similar for Indonesia, the Philippines, and Thailand. In fact, although Thailand's output elasticity remains the highest of the five, the rate of decline in Indonesia is the lowest among the South East Asian sample.

To sum up so far, on the basis of the aggregated sectoral data Indonesia has experienced a pronounced slowdown in industrial employment growth since the Asian financial crisis. Manufacturing was the only sector to experience both a marked deceleration in output growth and a major decline in output elasticity. This therefore suggests that there were sector-specific factors at work in the country's industrial labour market. However, in comparative East Asian terms, the Indonesian industrial record is not an outlier. Other fast-industrializing middle-income developing countries registered similar declines in both output growth and output elasticities.[9] Among the four comparators, the Thai experience is arguably the most relevant. Korea has clearly moved out of the labour-intensive phase of industrialization, while Malaysia is in transition. In both cases, very low or even negative employment-output elasticities are not surprising. Growth in the Philippines has been slower throughout. The widespread presumption in Indonesia is that the tightening of the labour market regulations since 2000 is the principal explanation for the sharp drop in its output elasticity. Yet, although Thailand's output and employment growth remain somewhat higher, its output elasticity has fallen just as fast. This is in spite of the fact that the Thai labour market is not as heavily regulated as Indonesia's, and has not been subject to the regulatory tightening since the Asian financial crisis. In other words, there appear to be more general factors at work affecting the patterns of South East Asian industrialization and employment, in addition to labour market policies.

We now turn to the more disaggregated Indonesian industrial census data to shed light on these issues. Indonesia has two main industrial statistics series, the annual survey of establishments with at least 20 employees, known as *Statistik Industri* (SI), and the decennial economic census of all industrial establishments (*Sensus Ekonomi*, henceforth SE). We present results from the SE series which, although conducted only once every decade, are more comprehensive in scope, covering all firms with at least five employees, as compared to the SI cut-off of 20 employees. The SE data are probably also more reliable, since it is a census and therefore there was a more concerted attempt to collect data for all firms.

[9] See also Tregenna in this volume for a general discussion of these issues.

The SEs were conducted in 1986, 1996, and 2006. These periods thus neatly coincide with major sub-periods. That is, 1986–96 was the decade of reform and rapid growth, while 1996–2006 encompasses the crisis and return to slower growth. To investigate the impacts across firms of different size, we classify establishments into three (arbitrary) groups, 'large' (100+ employees), 'medium' (20–99), and 'small' (5–19). Alternative size classifications do not affect the results. The disaggregation by size is relevant to our chapter since we conjecture that scale may influence firm responses to economic events and regulations. For example, smaller firms may be more resilient to adverse economic shocks, and they may fall outside the regulatory net. We examine the industrial statistics at the two-digit ISIC level of industrial classification. We further combine the industries into a broader factor intensity grouping, 'labour-intensive' (ISIC 32, 33, 39), 'resource-based' (ISIC 31, 34, 35), and 'capital-intensive' (ISIC 36–38), since industries within these groupings share some similar characteristics and response patterns.[10]

The raw data on manufacturing employment are revealing. Table 7.8 summarizes the results for the three SE by size groups. Employment grew quite rapidly over the whole period 1986–2006, by 7.3 per cent per annum. However, there was a marked slowdown between the two subperiods, with growth declining from 10.1 per cent in the first decade to just 4.6 per cent in the second. There were also some significant compositional shifts. In both 1986 and 1996, the large firms accounted for just over half of the employment, whereas by 2006 the small firms had become the dominant employer. The medium-firm share declined throughout the period. Employment in both the large and small firms grew rapidly in the first decade, by 10.3 per cent and 11.4 per cent respectively. But from 1996 to 2006, large-firm employment barely increased, at just 1 per cent per annum, whereas small-firm employment continued to expand quickly, by 8.8 per cent. Medium-firm employment growth also declined, but not to the same extent as the large firms.[11]

[10] The labour-intensive industries are textiles, garments and footwear, wood products and furniture, and miscellaneous manufactures. The resource-based are food and related products, paper products, and chemical, rubber, and plastic products. The capital-intensive group includes non-metallic minerals, steel products and metal and machine goods, electronics and automobiles. More elaborate classifications could be employed, but they are unlikely to affect our results significantly. If Indonesia were a major participant in global electronics production networks (which it is not), then strictly speaking the components assembly industry should be classified as labour-intensive.

[11] One caveat to be attached to these results is that the employment data are all 'head-count' estimates. We do not have data on the intensity of work, that is hours worked, by firm-size. While the estimates for L and M firms are likely to closely resemble some 'full-time equivalent' employment figure, that for the S firms could well be lower, owing to seasonality factors and more variable output and work patterns. Hence, it is possible, but not certain, that the rising S share is an overstatement.

Table 7.8. Indonesian manufacturing employment by firm size, 1986, 1996, and 2006

Total (000)	Large	Medium	Small	Total
1986	1,331	345	770	2,446
1996	3,545	609	2,273	6,427
2006	3,921	823	5,297	10,041
Composition (% of total)				
1986	54	14	32	100
1996	55	10	35	100
2006	39	8	53	100
Growth (annual average, %)				
1986–96	10	6	11	10
1996–2006	1	3	9	5
1986–2006	6	4	10	7

Source: computed from unpublished data from Badan Pusat Statistik, Central Board of Statistics, Indonesia, Sensus Ekonomi (1986, 1996, and 2006).

Thus there has clearly been a sharp slowdown in Indonesia's industrial employment growth since the Asian financial crisis, especially compared to the 'reform decade', 1986–96. This has occurred because of the slower industrial growth and most particularly because of the much lower output–employment elasticity. Among the sectors, manufacturing is unusual in this respect, in that there has been both slower output growth and lower employment elasticity. This growth slowdown appears to have occurred across all major manufacturing sectors. There have also been significant compositional shifts since the Asian financial crises, with almost all of the industrial employment growth coming from small firms. Firms in the 'factory sector', with 20 or more workers, seem to have virtually stopped hiring over this period.

Linking these conclusions back to the discussion in Section 7.2, the explanation for these outcomes is broadly as follows. In the intermediate aftermath of the crisis, there was a major boost to competitiveness from the rapidly depreciating nominal exchange rate. But this did not translate into employment growth since much of the formal sector of the economy was incapacitated by corporate debt workouts, the exodus of foreign investors, and the freezing up of financial markets. Also, regulatory and policy uncertainty increased in the transition from authoritarian to democratic rule and the major decentralization initiative of 2001. The latter especially affected access to natural resources, on which several Indonesian manufacturing activities depend. Intensified labour market regulations and infrastructure constraints emerged as serious problems after 2000. From about 2003, rising commodity prices and the return of foreign capital began to put pressure on the exchange rate, with a significant real appreciation commencing around 2005. By then, all the earlier competitiveness advantages from the exchange rate depreciation had been eroded. These events occurred in the context of intensified international competition, particularly from China, but also other lower-wage competitors, notably Vietnam.

These factors operated as economy-wide influences, in addition to sector-specific effects. For example, tighter labour market regulations had an adverse effect on the traditional labour-intensive sectors, textiles, clothing and footwear, in addition to the breakdown in the formerly effective operation of the import drawback facility for export-oriented firms. The more cumbersome export–import procedures and a less inviting foreign investment regime meant that Indonesia has been a relatively minor participant in rapidly expanding global production networks centred on 'fragmentation trade'. Natural-resource-based activities were affected by interruptions to reliable raw material supplies.

Does this slower manufacturing employment growth matter? The answer to this question depends on the explanation for the slower growth. It is of concern to the extent that a major link in the transmission mechanism from growth to poverty alleviation has been weakened. That is, fewer Indonesian workers are now drawn into the relatively better-paid jobs in the manufacturing sector. Moreover, most of the industrial jobs now being created are in small firms, where employment conditions are generally inferior to those of the larger units, especially to the extent that smaller firms are able to evade labour-protection measures. As argued above, the much slower employment growth is principally the result of Indonesia's declining international competitiveness, underlining again the crucial link between macro-level economic reform and poverty alleviation.

Nevertheless, it is important not to overstate the problems, for at least three reasons. First, the Indonesian record is not that different from its neighbours, including the traditionally dynamic Thai economy, where intensified labour market regulation has not occurred. This suggests that the changes observed in this chapter are part of a generalized regional phenomenon, in which rising competition from China and the demise of very labour-intensive segments are important factors explaining slower employment growth.

Second, we have shown that more jobs are being created in other sectors. The fastest growth has occurred in several service sectors, reflecting technological advancement, deregulation, and at the margin the switch to non-tradables as a result of the appreciating real exchange rate since around 2003. Agriculture has reversed the earlier decline, reflecting buoyant commodity prices, and reminding us of Indonesia's resource-based economic diversity. It is an overstatement to assert, as some have, that Indonesia is experiencing premature deindustrialization, but there is certainly an industrial deceleration evident, and it seems to have become a permanent feature of Indonesia. Is this structural shift in employment patterns a cause for concern? 'Industrial fundamentalists' would assert that it is, on the grounds that there are greater externalities associated with industrialization, such as inter-industry linkage creation and skill formation. But such views are of dubious validity, as shown by the existence of many high-income service and resource-based economies in the world.

7.6 Summing up and lessons

Indonesia's industrialization experience is of interest for a number of reasons. It has industrialized rapidly since the late 1960s. There have been pronounced episodes in its industrialization outcomes and policy orientation. It managed the transition from import-substituting to export-oriented industrialization quite successfully. It has had to navigate through a series of large external shocks, some positive (such as rising commodity prices for its abundant natural-resource endowments) and others negative (downside terms of trade movements and economic crises). Analysis of these various events is greatly facilitated by its good industrial statistical base, including firm-level data over time.

Two major turning points are clearly evident in its industrial history. The first is a straightforward story of a dramatic change in policy direction in the mid-1960s, ushering in mostly rapid industrial growth over the past four decades. This is a conventional episode of a well-managed policy reform producing the dividend of rapid socioeconomic development, including a significant industrial transformation.

The second turning point, of 1997–8, is a more complex story. The economy in aggregate recovered quite quickly from the exceptionally severe economic crisis. But the effects on industry have been mixed. Although manufacturing output growth has recovered, the industrial dynamics have been altered quite profoundly. Growth has been slower than the economywide average, and manufacturing is no longer the leading growth engine it was prior to the crisis. Manufacturing employment growth has also slowed appreciably, and in the formal manufacturing sector it is now anaemic. Firm dynamism also appears to have declined significantly.

The general implication from our analysis is that the fortunes of the manufacturing sector are closely linked to those of the economy as a whole, and in turn to the macroeconomic policy environment. Industry policy may matter—although in Indonesia it has generally been ineffective—but the exchange rate, monetary policy, the state of infrastructure, openness to trade and investment, education outcomes, and labour market regulations are much more important. Moreover, it is not obvious that the changing relative fortunes of the country's manufacturing sector are cause for concern, except to the extent that the root cause may be a problem of competitiveness related to excessive regulatory policies and under-investment in key supply-side inputs. But these are also economywide issues, and they need to be addressed through economywide, not sectoral, approaches.

References

Aswicahyono, H. H., K. Bird, and H. Hill (1996). 'What Happens to Industrial Structure when Countries Liberalise? Indonesia since the mid-1980s', *Journal of Development Studies*, 32 (3): 340–63.

Aswicahyono, H. H., H. Hill, and D. Narjoko (2010). 'Industrialisation after a Deep Economic Crisis: Indonesia', *Journal of Development Studies*, 46 (4): 1084–108.

——(2011). 'Indonesian Industrialization: Jobless Growth?'. In C. Manning and S. Sumarto (eds), *Indonesia Update 2011*. Singapore: Institute of Southeast Asian Studies.

Basri, M. C., and H. Hill (2004). 'Ideas, Interests and Oil Prices: The Political Economy of Trade Reform during Soeharto's Indonesia', *World Economy*, 27 (5): 633–56.

Bird, K. (1999). 'Industrial Concentration in Indonesia', *Bulletin of Indonesian Economic Studies*, 35 (1): 43–73.

Claessens, S., S. Djankov, and L. H. P. Lang (2000). 'The Separation of Ownership and Control in East Asian Corporations', *Journal of Financial Economics*, 58 (1–2): 81–112.

Davis, S. L., J. C. Haltiwanger, and S. Shuh (1996). *Job Creation and Destruction*. Cambridge, MA: MIT Press.

Ding, W., Domac, I., and Ferri, G. (1998). 'Is there a Credit Crunch in East Asia?'. Policy Research Working Paper 1959. Washington, DC: World Bank.

Gelb, A. and Associates (1988). *Oil Windfalls: Blessing or Curse?*. New York: Oxford University Press for the World Bank.

Gosh, S. R., and A. R. Gosh (1999). 'East Asia in the Aftermath: Was there a Crunch?'. Working Paper 38. Washington, DC: IMF.

Higgins, B. (1968). *Economic Development*, 2nd edition. New York: W.W. Norton.

Hill, H. (1997). *Indonesia's Industrial Transformation*. Singapore: Institute of Southeast Asian Studies.

——(2000). *The Indonesian Economy*, 2nd edition. Cambridge: Cambridge University Press.

Hill, H., and T. Shiraishi (2007). 'Indonesia after the Asian Crisis', *Asian Economic Policy Review*, 2 (1): 123–41.

Narjoko, D. A. (2006). *Indonesian Manufacturing and the Economic Crisis of 1997/98*. PhD Thesis. Canberra: Australian National University.

Narjoko, D. A., and H. Hill (2007). 'Winners and Losers during a Deep Economic Crisis: Firm-level Evidence from Indonesian Manufacturing', *Asian Economic Journal*, 21 (4): 343–68.

Rosengard, J., R. Patten, D. Johnston, and W. Koesoemo (2007). 'The Promise and the Peril of Microfinance Institutions in Indonesia', *Bulletin of Indonesian Economic Studies*, 43 (1): 87–112.

Stiglitz, J. E., and A. Weiss (1981). 'Credit Rationing in Markets with Imperfect Information', *American Economic Review*, 71 (3): 393–410.

van der Eng, P. (2002). 'Indonesia's Growth Performance in the Twentieth Century'. In A. Maddison, D. S. Prasada Rao, and W. F. Shepherd (eds), *The Asian Economies in the Twentieth Century*. Cheltenham: Edward Elgar.

8

Industrial Policies in Latin America

Wilson Peres

8.1 Introduction: industrial policy during import-substitution industrialization[1]

Industrial Policies seek to change a country's production structure, which necessarily implies the creation of new industries (ECLAC 2007). In Latin America import-substitution industrialization (ISI) prioritized the creation of new sectors and the diversification of the production structures, with the objective of changing the prevalent specialization pattern and increasing the weight of technology-intensive activities in the production structure. ISI also responded to the need of endogenizing the effects of domestic demand growth, channelling it to productive investments and avoiding fuelling imports, which would have deteriorated the trade balance.

In the 1970s most industry analysts highlighted that investment had two complementary effects on the economy. On the one hand, there was a supply effect through the creation of production capacity (capital accumulation). On the other hand, there was a demand effect on the production of capital goods. Given that the domestic supply of these goods was insufficient, the demand effect was mostly transferred abroad through increasing imports. Such processes generated stop-and-go cycles derived from recurring trade imbalances. This, together with the recognition of potential knowledge and productivity spillovers derived from technical progress embedded in capital goods production, were the rationale behind programmes to foster the domestic production of such goods in the largest countries of the region, mainly Brazil and Mexico.

[1] This chapter updates the analysis presented by the author in Cimoli, Dosi, and Stiglitz (2009) and is a product of a research endeavour developed continuously for almost two decades (Peres 1993, 1997, 2006, and 2009). The opinions presented in this document are the author's and may not represent those of ECLAC.

During the ISI, industrial policies combined trade protection with investment promotion (both state and foreign investments were supported) and national development banks were the main financing agents. Two of the most notable examples of industrial policies in the region during the 1970s were the Second National Development Plan of Brazil and the National Industrial Development Program 1979–82 of Mexico, which coincided with its boom in oil exports.

Industrial policies programmed the expansion of domestic supply in an effort to change the prevailing specialization pattern of the production structure. Three interrelated factors were at the basis of the strength of those policies:

(i) the organization of the public sector development apparatus according to sectoral and even sub-sectoral structures[2]

(ii) the existence of sectoral business associations (chambers) representing the interests of private enterprises, which were the principal defenders of trade protection

(iii) the existence of negative or positive sectoral preference lists in international trade negotiations, such as those carried through under the Latin American Integration Association, the Central American Common Market, the Caribbean Community, or the Andean Pact.

Although policies tended to focus both on the agricultural and the manufacturing sectors, the weight of the latter was such that the term 'sectoral policy' tended to be associated with policy for the manufacturing industry.

However, during the debt crisis and the 'lost decade' of the 1980s the ISI model was the object of serious critiques and industrial policies lost their leading role. There were several reasons for this:

- public enterprises that had traditionally invested directly in new sectors were either privatized or closed, reflecting the new view that the state should play only a subsidiary role in economic growth
- the need to balance public finances meant eliminating subsidies, particularly fiscal ones and the subsidy components of credit operations
- there was a (sometimes controversial) perception that many investments suffered from bad planning, poor project management and corruption, and in some cases implied high inefficiencies—the so-called 'white elephants'.

[2] For example, ministries of industry, agriculture, mining, and others, and the corresponding general directorates for food, metal manufactures and machinery, chemicals, capital goods, and so forth.

Beyond these implementation problems, which had already weakened the standing of industrial policies by the 1970s, orthodox analyses insisted that these policies were bad per se and that the ISI strategy had been a big mistake that substituted (usually wrong) policy decisions for market signals. Thus, resources were misallocated—too much capital and too little labour were used in economies with scarce capital and an almost unlimited labour supply.

In this context, industrial policy became a sort of 'bad word', that it was better not to pronounce in 'correct' political discourse. Hence industrial policy, at least in its more strict formulation, ended up being practically excluded from the new economic model that was established by market-friendly economic reforms. This loss of legitimacy of industrial policy, however, did not occur homogeneously in all the regions of the world. It was much pronounced in Latin America. For example, in several countries of East and South East Asia, active sectoral policies, sometimes even with targeting at the firm level, remained in force until the mid-1990s—fading gradually, and at different rates, as domestic production and technological capabilities gained competitiveness.

Apart from the orthodox economic arguments against industrial policy, political opposition to the new economic model came from agents who supported the previous paradigm, thereby consolidating the 'developmentalist-vs-neoliberal' stereotype. Agents in favour of the economic reforms portrayed sectoral industrial policies as distortions in resource allocation and accused them of being at the origin of recurrent fiscal deficits that fuelled inflationary pressures and trade imbalances. Although most governments in the region shared this negative stance towards industrial policy,[3] such an extreme view did not always coincide with de facto policy measures. Even strongly reformist governments, such as those of presidents Menem in Argentina, Collor de Melo in Brazil, and Salinas de Gortari in Mexico, maintained certain sectoral policies, in particular for the automotive industry, beyond their plain support of the market-led economic model.

8.2 Industrial policy after the economic reforms

8.2.1 *National strategies*

Much of the region's experience in industrial policy during the Washington Consensus era is summarized by the term 'competitiveness policies' (Peres 1997). In the mid-1990s, almost all countries in the region designed

[3] In the early 1990s, it was frequent to hear high-ranking macroeconomic policy officials propounding the view that 'the best industrial policy is no industrial policy'. Although simplistic, that phrase aptly reflected their position on the subject.

programmes to support the competitiveness of their economies. In this respect we can identify three groups of countries. First, countries such as Brazil, Mexico, and some of the English-speaking Caribbean (e.g. Jamaica), elaborated policy documents specifically targeted to the manufacturing sector, analysing its role in national competitiveness and highlighting its linkages with technological development and with an efficient participation in international trade.[4] These documents constituted working agendas elaborated by the government together with the private sector, but had neither the form nor the contents of former industrial development plans. Critics accused them of being 'programmes without targets' and, what was even worse, 'without resources'.

The focus on competitiveness pervaded also the Andean and the Central American countries. In this second group, the predominant approach was to enhance competitiveness of the economy as a whole, without explicitly targeting the manufacturing industry. The national competitiveness strategies were based on the cluster methodology, albeit under a variety of names, mainly, industrial agglomerations or 'conglomerates'.[5] From the policy implementation standpoint, those activities resulted in the negotiation and implementation of sectoral agreements between private agents and the government for specific value chains, where the latter played the role of catalyst or 'facilitator'.

Cluster development policies expanded quickly throughout the region. In some countries, they became the core of national competitiveness strategies; e.g. in Colombia, whose very pro-active and sustained strategy is strongly cluster-based,[6] or in El Salvador, which has made significant efforts to design policies to support small and micro firms within specific clusters (Ministerio de Economía 2005). Policies to promote clusters have also been extensively implemented at the subnational level, and countries such as Mexico and Brazil built up strong capabilities to support local development. Incentives for the

[4] Pérez Caltendey (2003) highlights the intensity of sectoral incentives in the Caribbean economies, particularly in member countries of the Association of Eastern Caribbean States, and in Barbados and Guyana, the latter having the broadest package of incentives in the region. Those incentives basically targeted the manufacturing and service sectors, particularly hotels and tourism.

[5] This approach was developed on the basis of Porter (1990), and was materialized in policy proposals by *Monitor Company* in the Andean countries in the early 1990s, and in the project 'Central America in the twenty-first century: an agenda for competitiveness and sustainable development', coordinated by INCAE/CLADS (Costa Rica) in the middle of that decade. In these countries, in the second half of the decade of 2000, the approach suggested by Hausmann and Rodrik (2003) and Rodrik (2004) to view development as a process of self-discovery contributed to the debate on industrial policy.

[6] Colombia's 2008 National Competitiveness and Productivity Policy focuses on five strategies: development of world class clusters, acceleration of productivity and employment creation, reduction of the informal economy, support to science, technology and innovation, and horizontal actions to foster competition and investment (Gómez Restrepo 2009).

footwear cluster in the state of Guanajuato or the electronics industry in the state of Jalisco (Mexico) are two relevant examples (Dussel Peters 1999; Unger 2003). In Brazil the main player has been the Brazilian Service of Assistance to Micro and Small Enterprises (SEBRAE), which implemented programmes throughout the country—one of its most extensive programmes has been the one to develop local clusters (*arranjos produtivos locais,* APL). The legitimacy enjoyed by cluster policies, especially among international financial organizations, has facilitated their acceptance by governments. At the same time, the general consensus on cluster policies led to the inclusion under this category of a mixed series of public support programmes, which indeed have neither a production chain nor a geographic conglomerate scope.

The third group of countries includes those that did not implement any formal industrial policy or selective national competitiveness strategy, focusing basically on horizontal interventions.[7] Argentina, Chile, and Uruguay privileged neutral interventions that did not discriminate between sectors and which were basically oriented by firms' demand (contrary to the previous supply-side-oriented model). However, those countries managed their horizontal programmes in a pragmatic way, introducing a sectoral focus every time that there was a 'sectoral' problem. Thus, in Chile the supposed neutral character of the policies did not prevent the government from directly supporting the forestry and the mining (coal) sectors and some key export activities for a long time (Moguillansky 2000).

Chile's approach to competitiveness began to change around 2005. The National Strategy of Innovation for Competitiveness presented in 2007 put special attention to actions aimed at developing some clusters, basically related to natural-resources processing. This new strategy showed that policymakers were changing their perspective and accepting policies beyond horizontal or neutral ones, an approach which had prevailed in the country for decades (Agosín, Larraín, and Grau 2009). Early in 2010, this strategy was complemented by the Innovation and Competitiveness Agenda 2010–20 that defined priorities at the cluster level and some horizontal 'bases' to foster innovation at the firm level and production diversification, all this supported by science, technology, and human capital development (Consejo Nacional de Innovación para la Competitividad 2007–08 and 2010).

[7] The term 'neutral' or 'horizontal' policy, which is widely used in the region, conceals the fact that any policy is bound to favour some sectors more than others ex post. This is because such policies aim to enhance the operating efficiency of markets for factors of production that are used with varying intensity according to the sector or product in question. In some cases, policies are presented as neutral to gain greater legitimacy, despite being aimed at specific sectors from the outset. This frequently happens with technological development policies.

8.2.2 *Policy lines and instruments*

Regional policies, even those with sectoral scope, have focused much more on enhancing the efficiency of existing sectors than on creating new ones (Peres 1997; Melo 2001; Melo and Rodríguez-Clare 2006). This is consistent with the search for greater penetration in international markets, grounded essentially on the pursuit of static comparative advantages (unskilled labour and natural resources). This has been the case both in countries with a diversified production structure, such as Brazil and Mexico, as well as in those whose production structures are concentrated in few activities. In the more diversified countries, it could be argued that there are few non-existent sectors, so a sectoral policy could only be detected at the level of specific products. Although this might be true, the evidence, especially in Mexico and to a lesser extent in Brazil until the 2008 industrial policy, suggests that sectoral measures have focused on strengthening and expanding existing sectors; the clearest example being the automotive industry.

The creation of new activities appeared sporadically as a policy objective, mainly related to international trade negotiations aimed at increasing market access and to the attraction of foreign direct investment (FDI). Policy initiatives resulted in the expansion of Mexico's export platform in the framework of the North American Free Trade Agreement between Mexico, Canada, and the USA (automobiles and transport equipment components, electronics and clothing); the promotion of the basic assembly activities (*maquiladoras*) in a number of Central American and Caribbean countries (clothing); and investments in privatized firms in the services and primary sectors in South American countries. Different combinations of sectoral policies and transnational corporations' strategies induced a certain level of production diversification. Nonetheless, this strategy had limitations, such as low value-added in the assembly activities, weak linkages to the domestic economy, and the consequent scant generation of endogenous technological capabilities (Peres and Reinhardt 2000; Mortimore 2002).

Three types of instrument have been used to attract FDI: direct incentives—basically export free zones and special tax regimes; creation of business friendly environments—rule of law, transparency, access to international markets, infrastructure, etc.; and development of specialized production factors, particularly skilled labour (Mortimore and Peres 1998). Most Latin American countries applied these three types of instrument, but the first and the second were the most frequent. Rather similar tools have been used to promote investment in general, both domestic and foreign. Besides fiscal and credit incentives, governments tried to develop competitive environments (defence of competition and regulation of highly concentrated sectors), to reduce transaction costs (e.g. through deregulation), and to create conditions to attain economies of scale (sectoral agreements along value chains, support to network and cluster creation, etc.).

Policy instruments in the region enjoy different degrees of legitimacy. Thus, according to this criterion, we can identify three groups of industrial policies: winning, losing, and emerging (Peres 1997).

Winning policies include those that are generally accepted by governments, i.e. they enjoy strong legitimacy. In addition to the policies for export promotion and FDI attraction, this group also includes policies to foster science, technology, and innovation,[8] human resources development, support to small and micro firms—generally through establishment or consolidation of networks or clusters[9]—and local development, the latter two being closely linked. Acceptance of these policies stems from their assumed neutrality, since they operate on factor markets (technology and labour), or because of their (also supposed) positive impact on job creation, basically at the subnational or local levels.

Losing policies, in contrast, are clearly contrary to the prevailing free-market approach. They include direct fiscal subsidies, targeted credits with subsidized interest rates, trade tariffs, and government procurement. In terms of the latter, the situation varies from one country to another: while some, such as Brazil, use it nationally or subnationally, in others it is out of the policy agenda because its use is deemed contrary to the goals of expenditure efficiency and transparency.

Emerging policies, which, among other things, encompass competition policy, improvement of corporate governance regimes, regulation of infrastructure sectors where markets do not operate efficiently, or corporate social responsibility, enjoy increasing legitimacy, but have not yet reached consensus and do not have a strong constituency. Some countries have modern legislation and relatively strong institutions to enforce them, whereas in others, they are still at the discussion and decision stages. Usually such policies are not a significant item on the policy agenda.

Beyond the different approaches to sectoral policies, the region displays a strong convergence in terms of policy design over the last decade, centred around five basic elements:

[8] A few years ago, most science and technology policies were concentrated in the largest or richest countries in the region; recently such efforts expanded to smaller economies such Nicaragua and Panama in Central America, and Bolivia, Ecuador, and Paraguay in South America.

[9] A case in point is Bolivia, whose 2008 Constitution establishes that small and micro firms will be protected and promoted by the State (Article 318, II). See Ministerio de Desarrollo Productivo y Economía Plural (2009).

(i) emphasis on increasing international trade competitiveness
(ii) generalization of the legitimacy of horizontal or neutral instruments, which, as mentioned above, are not horizontal or neutral ex post
(iii) support for small businesses and micro-enterprises, basically for reasons linked to their job creation capacity
(iv) efforts to design science, technology, and innovation policies aimed at advancing towards knowledge-based economies
(v) focus on sub-national or local economic areas.

The boom of cluster support programmes provides the clearest example of the combination of these elements; the SEBRAE programmes to support clusters in Brazil, which were mentioned above, are the most important in the region.

This convergence has been extremely stable in the long run, which is an indication that the region accumulated capabilities and experience in policy formulation. Moreover, changes of government, even when there entailed a significant break with the countries' past policies, such as in Mexico in 2000 or Uruguay in 2005, have not produced major changes in attitudes towards industrial policies. The set of countries belonging to the three above mentioned categories is sticky. Two examples, albeit in different directions, are the constant marginal relevance of sectoral policies in Chile, and use of cluster policies to support competitiveness in Colombia for almost two decades.[10] This progress in institutional development should not be overstated, because cases of programme design just to overcome or muddle through short-term competitiveness problems are still frequent.[11] Even in Brazil, the policy for the automotive industry in the 1990 contained elements that pointed more to the rescue of a sector in crisis (unable to face external competition) than to a long-term policy for supporting a leading sector (Bonelli and Motta Veiga 2003).

8.2.3 *The reemergence of sectoral policies*

Unlike other policies, which are considered winning, losing, or emerging in almost all countries of the region, there is no consensus on sectoral policies. Whereas some countries have a discourse that clearly rejects such policies, despite providing some ad hoc sectoral support in practice, other countries

[10] Such agreements encompassed 41 production chains and sectors accounting for 86 per cent of all non-traditional exports. Of these, 31 are national and 10 regional, 29 correspond to goods and 12 to services. Not all of them are programmes for clusters strictly defined; some target specific sectors (potatoes, farmed shrimp, tuna, trawled shrimp, flowers, coffee, and bananas). The relatively loose application of the productive chain concept reflects the fact that most of the agreements were signed for pragmatic reasons aimed at mobilizing entrepreneurs (Velasco 2003).

[11] See Scarone (2003) on policies in Uruguay and Villagómez (2003) on the 2002–10 electronics industry programme in Mexico.

recognize the validity of targeted policies for increasing the competitiveness of activities with strong growth or export potential, or that are facing strong competition from imports. There is a double standard with respect to sectoral policies: some countries deny their usefulness, especially when they support the manufacturing sector, but when it comes to the support of agricultural, mining, and service sectors (e.g. tourism) the same countries use them openly, without facing any pressure to legitimize them.

The return of sectoral industrial policies has been a slow process. In this direction, after the 2001 crisis, Argentina selected nine production chains to be supported by the National Forum for Industrial Competitiveness and Production Chains.[12] The following year, Mexico launched its 2002 Economic Policy for Competitiveness, which defined 12 branches to be promoted through sectoral programmes. Four of these were formulated after a short period (textiles and garments, leather and footwear, electronics and high tech, and software), while others took much longer or were not formulated. More recently, the Mexican government defined 'Ten Guidelines to Increase Competitiveness 2008–12', which included promoting the upgrading of the automotive, electrical and electronics, steel, and aeronautics industries, and restructuring of mature industries such as textiles and garments, leather and footwear, furniture, toys, chemicals, pharmaceuticals, and agribusiness, as well as support for biotech, nanotech, and mechatronics (Secretaría de Economía 2007).

As mentioned above, even Chile moved, in 2007–10, from pure horizontal policies towards a new approach to innovation, this time based on the selection of a set of priority clusters: selected foodstuffs, mining, tourism, logistics and transportation, financial services, outsourcing, construction, and broadband internet (Consejo Nacional de Innovación para la Competitividad 2007–8 and 2010). Other countries, such as Costa Rica, Peru, and Uruguay, targeted development actions in even greater detail, supporting individual projects in given firms. Examples included investment incentives in megaprojects in the Peruvian mining sector,[13] measures taken by the government of Costa Rica to encourage INTEL to establish operations in the country (Alonso 2003), or tax exemptions in support of projects declared to be in national interest in Uruguay.[14]

[12] The sectors are wood and furniture, leather and leather products, textiles and apparel, agricultural machinery, building materials, software, biotechnology, natural gas for automobiles, and cultural industries.

[13] In Peru, the main policies implemented in support of the mining sector in the 1990s were as follows: promotion and guarantees for FDI, privatization of state-owned enterprises, approval of a framework law guaranteeing free enterprise and private investments, tax, exchange rate and administrative stability, modernization of the mining concessions process, tax benefits (reinvested profits are exempt from income tax); tax incentives for investment in megaprojects (income tax exemptions and advance drawback of the general sales tax). See Fairlie (2003).

[14] The 1998 Investments Act allows the government to promote specific investments by declaring a project to be of national interest. Benefits can be general or specific to a given project

Beyond these cases, the comeback of sectoral policies is best exemplified by Brazil. In November 2003, the government announced the 'Guidelines for an Industrial, Technology and Foreign Trade Policy' (PITCE), which set out its strategic sectoral alternatives in four knowledge-intensive activities: semiconductors, software, pharmaceuticals and medicines, and capital goods.[15] This policy was accompanied by the creation of a new institution in charge of the coordination and implementation of that policy, the Brazilian Industrial Development Agency (ABDI). The PITCE marked the return of industrial policies to the country's development agenda.

As mentioned above, in 2008, Brazil launched its 'Productive (i.e. Production) Development Policy: Innovate and Invest to Sustain Growth' (PDP), which has an even stronger sectoral focus. Beyond horizontal, basically fiscal, measures and six strategic technological programmes under the control of the Ministry of Science and Technology,[16] this policy includes seven programmes targeted to leading sectors under the control of the National Economic and Social Development Bank (BNDES): aeronautics, oil, natural gas and petrochemicals, bio-ethanol, mining, steel, pulp and paper, and meat, and twelve industrial competitiveness programmes, under the direct control of the Ministry for Development, Industry and Foreign Trade (MDIC): automobiles, capital goods, textiles and garments, wood and furniture, cosmetics, civil construction, services, shipbuilding, leather, footwear and leather goods, agribusiness, biodiesel, plastics, and other sectoral programmes (Government of Brazil 2008; Ferraz, Nassif, and Oliva 2009). Up to now, this is the most advanced and ambitious industrial policy undertaken in the region.

Implementation of the PDP faced an immediate challenge: four months after its launch the international financial crisis changed most of the parameters this policy was based upon. The task then was much more to prevent a deep economic fall than to sustain investment and growth. However, Brazil's rapid recovery in 2009 and very fast growth in 2010 reopened space for the PDP. In August 2011, the government that had taken office in January issued a

(e.g. tax exemption for real estate property). General benefits can be automatic (e.g. exemption from the wealth tax on movable property destined for the productive cycle), or discretionary (not regulated as of mid-2003). See Scarone (2003).

[15] Those sectors were selected because (i) they display sustained and increasing dynamism, (ii) they account for significant proportions of international investments in research and development, (iii) they open up new business opportunities, (iv) they are directly related to innovations in processes, products and modes of use, (v) they increase the density of the productive fabric, and (vi) they are important for the future of the country and have potential for the development of dynamic comparative advantages (MDIC 2003). These guidelines were strengthened by the Growth Acceleration Program, enacted in February 2007, which relies mainly on fiscal incentives.

[16] The technological programs (health, ICT, defense, nuclear energy, bio- and nanotechnologies) prioritize areas of strategic importance for the medium- and long-term, and actually point, in some cases, to the very *creation of a sector* and not to its strengthening, as it is for the nanotechnology.

new industrial policy (the *Plano Brasil Maior*), which implies a move towards a stronger role for horizontal policies, keeping some of the main instruments aimed at supporting labour- and technology-intensive sectors. The new plan has a wider scope than the PDP and includes policies not only to foster investment, innovation, and foreign trade, but also to protect the domestic market and local manufacturing. This is particularly important in a context in which the big appreciation of the local currency puts domestic production under much competition from imports.[17]

8.3 Implementation and evaluation

Latin American countries have made significant progress regarding industrial policy formulation. Most market-distorting policy instruments were eliminated or phased out, and subjects such as technological innovation, clusters and small and medium-sized enterprises (SME) were included, or became more important, in the policy agenda. Besides, governments now tend to approach industrial policy from a much more systemic view than in the past. In all these aspects, the reemergence of industrial policies in the region is not just the revamping of ISI policies, but a combination of new and old objectives and instruments, such as cluster development and structural change, or technology funds and state procurement, respectively.

Conversely, the implementation and evaluation of impacts are still weak in the region. Although there are some data on the funding allocated to certain policies (actually programmes or projects), the information is insufficient to evaluate implementation overall. Despite this, it has been shown that, with some exceptions, the degree of policy implementation in the region has been low, as already indicated in Peres (1997). Particularly clear results are provided by Alonso (2003) concerning the situation of the five Central American countries and Fairbanks and Lindsay (1997) concerning the Andean countries that designed competitiveness strategies based on clusters development.

The situation in terms of policy evaluation is also unsatisfactory. Although there are assessments of a number of specific programmes,[18] together with general assessments or aggregate results of what happened *after* policy implementation or aggregate results (not always determined by the policy being evaluated), impact evaluation in the region is sparse and not robust. It hardly ever identifies and tests cause–effect mechanisms. Lack of information

[17] See: http://www.brasilmaior.mdic.gov.br/images/data/201204/c29cf558d29f0293eae88bbb 2a21fd16.pdf

[18] Two examples are Silva and Sandoval (2003), for SME support policies in Chile, and Baz et al. (2010), for a set productive development programmes in Mexico.

frequently hampers policy evaluation. In addition, the instruments seldom explicitly establish the criteria and mechanisms for follow-up and evaluation. Also, there is a lack of consensus on how to evaluate complex policies with multiple targets, objectives, and lines of action.

Even though the discussion usually focuses on the lack of evaluation of past and ongoing programmes, policies seldom reach the stage in which they need to be evaluated. Countries dispose of policies that have been formulated, approved and announced, but which are not always implemented. Various factors are responsible for widespread implementation failures and for the consequent shortfall between design and execution; among them we highlight the following.

8.3.1 *Non-operational or unachievable goals*

Objectives specified through declarative statements without setting clear, measurable goals, and without effective mechanisms for financial resource allocation, hamper policy evaluation. An evaluation of success factors in the 41 Colombian sectoral agreements shows that:

- those with well-structured, quantifiable commitments and specific time horizons were easier to monitor and fulfil
- agreements with few and simple commitments tended to be more successful
- the leadership and decision-making power of the individuals who negotiated the agreements played a fundamental role
- production chains in which support was carried out prior to the agreements achieved better results (Velasco 2003).

Given that practice in the region often makes no attempt to take these success factors into account, policy documents tend to be shopping lists of needs and objectives. Although the multiplicity of goals may reflect the involvement of many stakeholders in complex societies, it also indicates an inability to choose priorities and build consensus around a small number of attainable goals.

8.3.2 *Lack of human and financial resources to implement policies*

This issue is particularly relevant in small and poor countries, which often depend on external aid (loans or grants) to design and implement their programmes. In addition to a lack of resources, policies are usually announced without considering their cost and the corresponding required financing, assuming once again that 'first we decide and then we see what can be done and with what resources'. Moreover, given that financial and fiscal subsidies necessary for the implementation of the *winning* policies are themselves *losing* policies, a sharp contradiction arises. Thus, policy implementation deteriorates when governments that want to support industrial development through winning policies are unable to implement them because of the lack of effective fiscal and financial instruments.

8.3.3 *Poor institutional capabilities*

Nearly all of the countries of the region lack institutional capacity for policy management and implementation. This shortcoming is greater when policies aim to replicate international best practices rather than responding to the needs of the countries interested in applying them. This tendency results in policy designs that are disconnected from reality, often promoted by institutions of scant political weight in the structure of governments, or by business associations that are unrepresentative and have little economic and political clout.[19] The problem is further aggravated by the tendency to separate the policy design from the implementation. Although countries can increase their institutional capacity over time, and some have done so in the region, institution-building requires stability of objectives for longer periods than the time horizon of a government (between four and six years). Also, the wide range of the fiscal pressure between countries, from less than 10 per cent to over 30 per cent of GDP, introduces differences in terms of public resources available to support policies.

8.3.4 *Weak economic signals*

There is a proliferation of plans and programmes designed merely to respond to political pressures from economic stakeholders, for complying with conditionality to access international funding, or to fulfil legal or constitutional provisions. The will and strength the private sector showed to support the ISI is not present anymore. Business associations have scarcely supported most of the recent efforts to diversify the production structure beyond competitiveness programmes.[20] Actually, tariff protection used during the ISI was a most powerful economic signal ('invest in a new sector and get rich'); nowadays many policies must be disguised under a 'market-friendly' non-discriminatory approach. At best, the entrepreneur is offered a package that is complex to conceptualize and operate, and whose impact on profitability is uncertain and

[19] For example, in a recent evaluation of the implementation of several programs in Mexico, Baz et al. (2010) indicate that PDPs are often uncoordinated, redundant, or even incongruent with each other.

[20] Moreover, differences between the government and the private sector, although less than before, are far from having disappeared, as shown by Alonso (2003) for Guatemala and Scarone (2003) for Uruguay.

far from clear. It is hardly surprising that there is a perception that 'policies do not work'.

Despite these limitations, in some countries there were significant efforts in institution-building for policy design and implementation. Thus, the Colombia National Competitiveness Commission or the Chilean National Council on Innovation for Competitiveness strengthened their operations, while Brazil put in place a complex institutional structure to implement and follow up the 2008 Production Development Policy. Under strategic guidelines determined by a National Industrial Development Council (CNDI)[21] and the general coordination of the MDIC, an executive secretariat—integrated by the Treasury (Ministerio da Fazenda), BNDES, and ABD—is the core policy operator. This sui generis institution aims at overcoming organizational bottlenecks within the government, where some powerful agencies operate with overreaching autonomy, not always paying attention to strategies designed at the highest hierarchical levels (Suzigan and Furtado 2006).

Moreover, in the last two decades many countries of the region increased their capabilities to create spaces for debate between public authorities and business chambers about policy design and, in a few cases, about implementation. Significant progress has been made in developing public–private dialogue. The process has reached a stage in which the leadership of policy proposals has often been exercised by business associations.[22] Business chambers have participated actively in consultative forums discussing measures in support of competitiveness, such as the National Competitiveness Council in Colombia, the Production Development Forum in Chile, or the 'sectoral chambers' and National Industrial Development Council in Brazil.[23]

On the other hand, policy coordination with other civil society organizations has been much weaker. Although labour unions have participated in discussion forums, in general their presence has not been decisive for the dynamics of such mechanisms. An exception, however, is the role played by unions in Brazil, especially in the 'sectoral chamber' of the automotive industry. Other stakeholders played a marginal role, with the exception of the academic sector, which was directly involved in the efforts of the National

[21] CNDI was created in 2006 and includes representatives of 13 sectoral ministries, the BNDES, and 14 business associations. It is chaired by the MDIC.

[22] Examples include the Asociación Nacional de Industriales of Colombia, the Confederación de Cámaras de la Industria de Transformación in Mexico, the Asociación de Industriales in the Dominican Republic, the Cámara de Industrias in Costa Rica, or the Federación de Cámaras Industriales de Centroamérica, which promoted an Industrial Modernization Agenda in Central America. In these countries and elsewhere, it is even possible to speak of public–private co-responsibility in policy formulation, rather than policy consensus (Peres 1997).

[23] In Brazil, the expression 'sectoral chamber' (*cámara sectorial*) refers to a tripartite government–entrepreneurs–workers negotiation space.

Competitiveness Council in Colombia and which participated in the design and management of the sectoral technology funds in Brazil.

Implementation failures and the perception that 'policies do not work' undermine their legitimacy and their acceptance, especially among their main beneficiaries: the entrepreneurs. This gives rise to the paradox that business people bemoan the lack of resources available for policies, while at the same time they fail to make full use of what is available. Overcoming these implementation failures and making sure that instruments designed actually function are some of the key challenges for industrial policies nowadays. What can be done to close the gap between what is decided and announced and what is actually done and evaluated? Three lines of action, which are not mutually exclusive, look promising and should be followed up.

First, policy design should be accompanied, not followed, by explicit consideration of the institutions that will have to implement them. This means involving industrial policy stakeholders and creating institutions that allow this participation on a continuing basis. Although reform of the state and organizational development are not issues that are close to the industrial organization specialist, they need to be addressed to reduce implementation failures. Second, there is a need to increase the amount and the quality of human resources specialized in policy design and implementation, prioritizing the latter, even through transfer of qualified personnel. A third line of action is to develop and strengthen the institutions and the individuals that link policy design and implementation. Three courses of action are available for that purpose: strengthen public institutions, search for leaders in the private sector, and strengthen intermediate implementation agents, such as business associations.

The countries of the region accumulated long experience in terms of policy management in the areas of macroeconomic policy and central banks; such experience could and should be replicated in areas linked to industrial development. Private leadership of policies has been efficient in some cases (e.g. in the development of local clusters), and should be used whenever possible, but experience shows that this approach is hard to replicate and it is not distributed according to implementation needs. Thus, economically weak areas that need major efforts from policy operators tend also to have weak private leaderships. The strengthening of intermediate implementation bodies has been a successful strategy in countries such as Chile, where it has been used to carry through programmes to promote SME networks, although they suffer from the predictable problems of adverse selection and moral hazard. Different arrangements are possible. None of them is a panacea or easy to implement, but they do open up alternatives and deserve to be explored from perspectives that combine the economic, institutional, and management dimensions.

8.4 Conclusions

Industrial policies are the core of specialization or diversification strategies. There are five key points in elaborating an industrial development strategy:

(i) the criteria for targeting production sectors
(ii) the mix of policy instruments associated to each objective
(iii) the constraints imposed by endogenous capabilities
(iv) political will
(v) the institutional capabilities to manage that strategy and the amount and continuity of financial resources available for implementation.

Regarding targeting production activities and sectors, the policy should recognize that, while there are no blueprints for prioritizing sectors, history shows that countries have in fact chosen and continue to choose sectors on the basis of a few more-or-less precise criteria. The knowledge-intensity of the activities in question, their dynamism in the international market as a result of high elasticity with respect to world income, and their potential for productivity growth, are some of the general criteria used by countries to identify sectors to promote structural change. These criteria are supported by others related to the strategic nature of certain activities, which basically reflect their importance in output, exports, or employment, usually at the national level, but also with a local or subnational dimension.

From the 1980s, the technological 'dimension' has increasingly been used to define the scope of industrial policies. Although we can define industries or production sectors as sets of goods with high cross-price elasticity of demand, it is also possible to define as sectors sets of activities that share a technological path (Robinson 1953; Dosi 1988). One can therefore speak of the aerospace, biotechnology, or ICT sectors. To promote activities encompassed by a given technology, there are as many experiences centred on horizontal policies as others involving direct intervention at the level of firms, market segments, or knowledge networks. In practice, policies to promote clusters are frequently inseparable from innovation or technological development policies.

As policies acquire systemic scope, their impact on competitiveness in the economy at large requires special attention. The higher costs associated with the initial stages of learning curves should not be so high that they endanger the competitiveness of firms that use the new goods or services that are being incorporated into the basket, particularly when those firms have a strong foreign-trade orientation. The balance between supporting the diversification of the domestic production structure and taking advantage of opportunities to import cheaper capital goods or better technology is not easy to strike—it can only be found through experimentation and trial and error, i.e. we need pragmatic rather than ideological policies. As pragmatic policies are frequently of a reactive type, a major challenge for the region is to combine pragmatism with much more proactive policies.

In Latin America and the Caribbean, the tools available to implement industrial policies are well-known and present in the policy discourse. The big difference with respect to past experience in the region and elsewhere stems from the current open-economy scenario, in which it is impossible to use instruments involving widespread and permanent trade protection. This constraint weakens the economic signal (expected profitability) sent to potential investors in new activities, and causes a significant portion of the cost of development activities to fall on the fiscal area. This leads to problems, both in setting priorities for the allocation of budgetary resources, and for the stability of those resources at times of fiscal constraint.

The sustaining of long-term development instruments, possibly spanning more than one government term, remains a challenge that the countries of the region have so far been unable to tackle successfully. Another powerful tool of sectoral policy—direct investment by the state—is off the policy agenda in most countries, but the degrees of freedom in this subject are large, as shown by various experience, particularly at the local level. Experience in the region suggests that the policy packages applied so far have not had the force to induce the specific investment behaviour that protection had in the past, although the cumulative effects remain to be evaluated.

In the case of small economies, apart from these constraints, it has been argued that they not only should not develop sectoral policies, but in fact cannot do so. Without ignoring the importance of the domestic market to achieve economies of scale and learning, it should be remembered that the issue is less important in open economies, as shown by numerous small countries that operate as highly competitive export platforms. Although institutional capacity can also be a major constraint, especially in the short-run, this does not mean that it is impossible to implement industrial policies, rather that their scope should be in accordance with those capacities. In other words, the alternative is to focus efforts downward rather than shooting wildly into the air.

Despite these considerations, from the standpoint of political will, sectoral measures face ambivalence in the region, enjoying high levels of legitimacy in some countries, although always less than during the ISI period, but very low levels in others. Nonetheless, even in countries that do not consider themselves legitimate, actual practice is far more ad hoc, and specific measures are often implemented to support sectors in crisis. Given the need for these policies to move development forward in the region, it is worth asking what needs to be done to increase their legitimacy.

There are two priority areas of action. First, implementation capacity needs to be improved to narrow the gap between policy design and institutional capacity for effective implementation, the persistence of which undermines the credibility of policy makers and hence the policies themselves. Second, significant progress also needs to be made in evaluating the impact of the initiatives implemented in terms of their ultimate objectives: economic growth, technological progress, and increased productivity. When public resources are scarce, only sound evaluations can create space to divert resources from other policy areas to these ones.

Although these points are not new, they are crucial. Some progress has been made on this issue, examples being Mexico's Business Development Program 2001–6 or Brazil's 2008 industrial policy, which explicitly mention quantitative targets, improving previous practice. Nonetheless, progress in the region as a whole is insufficient. This is very serious for policies that have to justify their own raison d'être and compete for fiscal resources with others that enjoy greater legitimacy, such as basic education, public health, or citizen safety. As industrial policies are crucial for diversifying the production structure and raising the pace of productivity growth, they need to regain their legitimacy by demonstrating their impact.

From a broader perspective, some crucial questions remain unanswered. If, in the late 1990s, an analyst who advocated industrial policies had been asked to design an ideal political scenario for their acceptance and implementation in the region, they could hardly have hoped for a better environment than that which exists today. At present, political parties or coalitions of parties that based much of their long-term platforms on the rejection of 'economic neoliberalism' are in power in Argentina, Brazil, Bolivia, Chile, Ecuador, Nicaragua, Uruguay, and Venezuela. Industrial policies had frequently been mentioned by these parties as a substantive part of their strategic guidelines for achieving sustainable development with greater social justice.

Reality appears not to have fulfilled those expectations. Even in the most advanced example of policy development and actions (Brazil), the perception is that a lot has to be done in terms of what is needed to change the production structure of the country. In short, there has been no significant action in most of the countries mentioned above to change the current economic model, in terms of its pattern of production specialization, through the application of industrial policies.

Two explanations may be attempted. The first is that the discourse of the opposition was rapidly constrained, upon its rise to power, by the pressure of global financial markets and the existing consensus as to what constitutes a 'responsible' macroeconomic policy, and that, as part of the same move toward international acceptance, the discourse of structural change was relegated to second or third place. Naturally, once countries showed they held 'responsible' policies, their degrees of freedom increased, and, if they wanted to do so, they were able to undertake bolder actions to diversify their production structure. The most notorious case is Brazil's, and the most recent Uruguay's, where the administration that took office in March 2010 almost immediately began the formulation of an industrial policy for 2010–15, which includes significant sectoral components (Torres 2010).

Another explanation might be that, without denying the significance of the factors mentioned above, the structural change or industrialist discourse lacked the strength to show that it could be translated into specific operational proposals, capable of yielding at least a few results that were attainable within the space of a single administration. If the second explanation is correct, one might conclude that the main concern of structural policy analysis should be to pay attention to governments that wish to carry out such policies, as they might not know how to do so and, if they did, would scarcely have the time needed for those policies to yield results that strengthen their position and allow them to remain in office.

Even if policies to diversify the production structure can technically demonstrate their capacity to generate positive impacts, it is by no means clear which stakeholders would be interested in generalizing them in the countries of the region. In other words, which stakeholders are likely to put their economic and political resources behind initiatives that go beyond support for cluster development, the great majority of which are in any case far from well-funded? Industrial policies have been making a (slow) return in Latin America and have been able to operate, albeit on a small scale, in open economies and with orthodox macroeconomic policies—contrary to the previous conventional wisdom that they were incompatible. Enhancing their, if not minimal then at least marginal, status requires stakeholders, including the state, to take ownership of them and commit their power and resources behind them.

References

Agosín, M., C. Larraín, and N. Grau (2009). 'Industrial Policy in Chile'. Santiago: University of Chile, Department of Economics.

Alonso, E. (2003). 'Políticas para el Fomento de los Sectores Productivos en Centroamérica'. Santiago: ECLAC, DDPE.

Baz, V., M. C. Capelo, R. Centeno, and R. Estrada (2010). 'Productive Development Policies in Latin America and the Caribbean: The Case of Mexico'. Working Paper IDB-WP-168. Washington, DC: IDB.

Bonelli, R., and P. Motta Veiga (2003). 'A Dinâmica das Políticas Setoriais no Brasil na Década de 1990: Continuidade e Mudança'. Santiago: ECLAC, DDPE.

Cimoli, M., G. Dosi, and J. E. Stiglitz (eds) (2009). *Industrial Policy and Development: The Political Economy of Capabilities Accumulation*. Oxford: Oxford University Press.

Consejo Nacional de Innovación para la Competitividad (2007–8). *Estrategia Nacional de Innovación*, Volumes I and II. Santiago: Consejo Nacional de Innovación para la Competitividad.

——(2010). *Agenda de Innovación y Competitividad 2010–20*. Santiago: Consejo Nacional de Innovación para la Competitividad.

Dosi, G. (1988). 'Sources, Procedures and Microeconomic Effects of Innovation', *Journal of Economic Literature*, 26 (3): 1120–71.

Dussel Peters, E. (1999). 'La Subcontratación como Proceso de Aprendizaje: El Caso de la Electrónica en Jalisco (México) en la Década de los Noventa'. Series Desarrollo Productivo 55. Santiago: ECLAC.

Economic Commission for Latin America and the Caribbean (ECLAC) (2007). 'Progreso Técnico y Cambio Estructural en América Latina'. Series Documento de Proyecto 136. Santiago: ECLAC.

Fairbanks, M., and S. Lindsay (1997). *Plowing the Sea: Nurturing the Hidden Resources of Growth in the Developing World*. Boston: Harvard Business School Publishing.

Fairlie, A. (2003). 'Políticas Sectoriales y Cadenas Productivas en el Perú Reciente'. Santiago: ECLAC, DDPE.

Ferraz, J. C., A. Nassif, and R. Oliva (2009). 'Avanços, Desafios e Oportunidades para Políticas de Desenvolvimento Produtivo na América Latina'. Rio de Janeiro: Banco Nacional de Desenvolvimento Econômico e Social.

Gómez Restrepo, H. J. (2009). 'Prioridades de la Agenda Competitiva y Políticas a Desarrollar'. Presentación en el INALDE, Consejo Privado de Competitividad, Bogotá, April 21.

Government of Brazil (2008). 'Política de Desenvolvimento Produtivo: Inovar e Investir para Sustentar o Crescimento'. Rio de Janeiro: ABDI, BNDES, MF, and MDIC.

Hausmann, R., and D. Rodrik (2003). 'Economic Development as Self-Discovery', *Journal of Development Economics*, 72 (2): 603–33.

Melo, A. (2001). 'Industrial Policy in Latin America and the Caribbean at the Turn of the Century'. Working Paper 459. Washington, DC: Inter-American Development Bank.

Melo, A., and A. Rodríguez-Clare (2006). 'Productive Development Policies and Supporting Institutions in Latin America and the Caribbean'. Washington, DC: Inter-American Development Bank.

Ministerio de Desarrollo Productivo y Economía Plural (2009). *Plan Sectorial de Desarrollo Productivo con Empleo Digno*. La Paz: Ministerio de Desarrollo Productivo y Economía Plural.

Ministerio de Economía (2005). *Propuesta de la Política Industrial 2005–09*. San Salvador: Ministerio de Economía.

Ministério do Desenvolvimento, Indústria e Comércio Exterior (MDIC) (2003). 'Diretrizes de Política Industrial, Tecnológica e de Comércio Exterior'. Brasilia: Ipea.

Moguillansky, G. (2000). *La Inversión en Chile. El Final de un Ciclo de Expansión?*. Santiago: Fondo de Cultura Económica.

Mortimore, M. (2000). 'Corporate Strategies for FDI in the Context of Latin America's New Economic Model', *World Development*, 28 (9): 1611–26.

Mortimore, M., and W. Peres (1998). 'Policy Competition for Foreign Direct Investment in the Caribbean Basin: Costa Rica, Jamaica, and the Dominican Republic'. Desarrollo Productivo 49. Santiago: ECLAC.

Peres, W. (1993). 'Industrial Policy: Where Do We Stand?'. *CEPAL Review*, 51: 35–47. Santiago: ECLAC.

——(coordinator) (1997). *Políticas de Competitividad Industrial en América Latina y el Caribe en los Años Noventa*. Mexico: Siglo XXI Editores.

——(2006). 'The Slow Comeback of Industrial Policies in Latin America'. *CEPAL Review*, 88: 67–83. Santiago: ECLAC.

——(2009). 'The (Slow) Return of Industrial Policies in Latin America and the Caribbean'. In M. Cimoli, G. Dosi, and J. E. Stiglitz (eds), *Industrial Policy and Development: The Political Economy of Capabilities Accumulation*. Oxford: Oxford University Press.

Peres, W., and N. Reinhardt (2000). 'Latin America's New Economic Model: Micro Responses and Economic Restructuring', *World Development*, 28 (9): 1543–66.

Pérez Caltendey, E. (2003). *Policies for Productive Development in Caribbean Economies*. Santiago: ECLAC.

Porter, M. (1990). *The Competitive Advantage of Nations*. New York: The Free Press.

Robinson, J. (1953): 'Imperfect Competition Revisited', *Economic Journal*, 63 (251): 579–593.

Rodrik, D. (2004). 'Industrial Policy for the Twenty-first Century'. Background Paper. Vienna: UNIDO.

Scarone, C. (2003). 'Las Políticas Sectoriales en Uruguay 1998–2002'. Santiago: ECLAC, DDPE.

Secretaría de Economía (2001). *Programa de Desarrollo Empresarial de México, 2001–06*. Mexico: Secretaría de Economía.

——(2007). 'Decálogo Estratégico de la Secretaría de Economía', Mexico: Secretaría de Economía.

Silva, I., and C. Sandoval (2003). 'Políticas de Desarrollo Productivo en Chile, con Especial Referencia al Nivel Local y Regional'. Santiago: ECLAC, DDPE.

Suzigan, W., and J. Furtado (2006). 'Industrial Policy and Development'. CEPAL Review 89. Santiago: ECLAC.

Torres, S. (2010). 'Políticas Industriales y Agendas Regionales Sur-Sur: Próximos Pasos'. *Encuentro de Especialistas en Política Industrial e Integración Productiva*, 89: 69–84. Brasilia: ABDI-UNCTAD.

Unger, K. (2003). 'Clusters Industriales en México: Especializaciones Regionales y la Política Industrial'. Santiago: ECLAC, DDPE.

Velasco, M. P. (2003). 'Una Evaluación de las Políticas de Competitividad en Colombia'. Regional Project 'Una Estrategia de Desarrollo de Clusters Alrededor de Recursos Naturales: Sus Implicaciones Sobre Crecimiento, Distribución y Medio Ambiente'. Santiago: ECLAC, DDPE.

Villagómez, A. (2003). 'Una Revisión de la Política Sectorial en México: 1995–2003'. Santiago: ECLAC, DDPE.

9

Should Africa Industrialize?

John Page

9.1 Introduction[1]

> *Industry . . . is the means by which rapid improvement in Africa's living standards is possible . . .*
>
> *Kwame Nkrumah (1965)*

Africa's post-independence leaders—like many developing country policy makers in the 1960s and 1970s—looked to industrialization as the key to rapid economic growth. However, the state-led, import-substituting industries they created were frequently uncompetitive and unsustainable. Efforts to spur industrial development in Africa largely vanished with the economic collapses and adjustment programmes of the 1980s and 1990s.[2]

While the last two decades of the twentieth century were boom times for industrial development in low- and middle-income countries, industry was moving *out* of Africa. Between 1995 and 2008, while manufacturing growth in developing economies was more than 6 per cent per year, in Africa it was about 3 per cent. Since 1980 industry in Africa has declined in its share of both global production and trade (UNIDO 2009), and today, Africa's industrial sector is in many ways less advanced than in the first decade following independence. In contrast to much of the rest of the developing world Africa has 'deindustrialized'.[3]

[1] Comments of the workshop participants and the editors of this volume are gratefully acknowledged. I am indebted to Nick Krafft and Jessica Smith for helpful research assistance.

[2] The international community—a key partner in Africa's economic story—also virtually abandoned interest in growth in pursuit of the Millennium Development Goals.

[3] For further discussion of deindustrialization, see Fionna Tregenna's contribution to this volume.

This paper addresses the questions: should Africa industrialize and how? Section 9.2 takes up the question of why Africa should industrialize. The post-1995 growth turnaround notwithstanding, lack of structural change—the shift of resources from low-productivity to higher-productivity sectors—limits Africa's long-term growth prospects. Industry is most often the leading high-productivity sector, and recent research indicates that economies with more diverse and sophisticated industrial sectors tend to grow faster. Africa, however, is moving in the opposite direction. Manufacturing value added has declined as a share of GDP since the mid-1980s. New evidence on changes in industrial production and export sophistication for 18 African economies shows that between 1975 and 2005 the diversity and sophistication of industrial production and exports have declined in most African economies.

Section 9.3 begins the discussion of how to industrialize. Agriculture remains the largest employer in many of Africa's economies, and it therefore must play a role in the region's industrialization. One view of that role argues that an agricultural transformation is a necessary precursor to an industrial transformation. Two factors suggest that this type of agriculture-led industrialization strategy is of limited relevance to contemporary Africa: lack of technological innovation in African agriculture and globalization. An alternative way in which agriculture can support industrialization is via agro-industry-specific value chains. This approach appears to hold more promise as an industrialization strategy, but the strategic and policy interventions needed to boost value-chain-based agro-industrial production are similar to those needed for an industrialization strategy in general.

Section 9.4 presents an industrialization strategy for Africa. It outlines two broad areas of public action. The first is the less controversial: continuing the investment-climate reforms urged by the international financial institutions, but with greater emphasis on public action in infrastructure, skills, and regional integration. The second is more likely to provoke debate: Africa must learn to compete through strategic actions to create an export push, to develop industrial clusters, and to attract task-based production. Section 9.5 concludes.

9.2 Why industrialize?

After stagnating for much of its post-colonial history, economic performance in Africa markedly improved after 1995. Between 1994 and 2008, average economic growth was close to 5 per cent per year. And, while Africa did not escape the global crisis of 2008–9, its impact was relatively mild. The region managed to avoid a contraction in 2009, growing by 2 per cent, and it grew by about 5 per cent in 2010. Growth is projected to accelerate to 6 per cent in

2011 (IMF 2010). However, Africa's growth, both before and after the crisis, is fragile. In a series of papers Arbache and Page (2007, 2008, 2009) use a new approach to the analysis of 'growth episodes' to assess Africa's growth turnaround.[4] They find that the improvement in economic performance in Africa after 1995 was due largely to avoiding the catastrophic economic policy mistakes of the 1980s. This resulted in a substantial reduction in the frequency and severity of growth collapses. Growth accelerations were confined mainly to mineral-rich economies.

What is missing from Africa's growth story is structural change. There is little evidence that significant changes in structural variables underpinned more rapid growth between 1995 and 2005 (Go and Page 2008; Arbache and Page 2009). Like the 1995–2005 growth turnaround, the region's post-crisis recovery has been driven primarily by fewer mistakes, commodity prices, and the recovery of domestic demand. Without major changes in economic structure Africa remains vulnerable to shocks and to a long-run decline in commodity prices.

9.2.1 *What Africa makes matters: structural change, diversity, and sophistication*

The 1980s and 1990s were marked by a shift of manufacturing production out of Africa. Excluding South Africa, the region's share of global manufacturing production fell from 0.4 per cent in 1980 to 0.3 per cent in 2005, and its share of world manufactured exports from 0.3 to 0.2 per cent (UNIDO 2009). Table 9.1 compares selected indicators of industrial development for Africa and all developing countries in 2005. The share of manufacturing in GDP is about one third of the average for developing countries, and in contrast with developing countries as a whole, it is declining.[5] Per capita manufactured output and exports are less than 20 and 10 per cent of the developing country average, respectively. The region has low levels of manufactured exports in total exports and of medium- and high-tech goods in manufactured exports. Particularly worrying is the fact that these measures have changed little since the 1990s (UNIDO 2009).

That Africa has experienced so little structural change through industrialization is worrying in itself, but recent research on structural change within industry points to two further threats to the region's long-run growth, lack

[4] Important contributions to this literature on growth episodes—focused on growth accelerations only—include Hausmann, Pritchett, and Rodrik (2005) and Jones and Olken (2005).

[5] In this volume, Adam Szirmai documents the processes of deindustrialization in sub-Saharan Africa between 1950 and 2005.

Table 9.1. Selected indicators of industrial development, 2005

	Mfg exports per capita 2005 (US$)	Growth of per capita mfg exports 2000–05 (%)	Share of mfg exports in total (%)	Share of medium/high-technology in total mfg exports (%)	Mfg. value added p 2005 (US$)	Share of mfg in GDP 2005 (%)	Change in mfg share of GDP 2000–05
Africa average	39.0	1.65	54.9	13.3	63.6	07.6	0.45
All developing countries	487.2	10.05	75.8	57.3	372.9	21.7	1.14

Source: Author's calculations based on UNIDO (2009).

of diversity, and sophistication. Globally, countries with more diversified production and export structures have higher incomes per capita, and countries that produce and export more sophisticated products—those that are primarily produced by countries at higher income levels—tend to grow faster. Both of these stylized facts suggest that what Africa makes, matters.

Poor countries tend to specialize in a fairly narrow range of activities. Across a wide range of incomes, however, the diversity of what a country produces increases with the level of per capita income (Imbs and Wacziarg 2003). The relationship between diversity in production and income per capita is not solely a product of structural change between primary production and manufacturing. Within the manufacturing sector new product lines are introduced and new activities are taken up in existing sectors until countries reach quite high levels of income. At that point specialization in production again increases, resulting in a U-shaped relationship between specialization and per capita income. Other research indicates that the same U-shaped relationship holds for export diversification (Cadot, Carrère, and Strauss-Kahn 2011). As per capita incomes rise, exports diversify within existing product lines and through the introduction of new products.

Two empirical studies also find a strong, positive relationship between the level of 'sophistication' of a country's industrial production and export structure and its subsequent growth (Hausmann, Hwang, and Rodrik 2007; UNIDO 2009). In this work the degree of sophistication of a product or export is measured by the per capita incomes of the countries that 'intensively' produce (export) it. If mostly high-income countries produce (export) a product, the income level associated with the product is high and the product is classified as sophisticated. Products mainly produced (exported) by low-income countries are classified as unsophisticated. Developing countries that produce and export a high proportion of products that are mainly produced by richer economies grow faster.[6]

Figure 9.1 plots the relationship between the production sophistication of the manufacturing sector of each country in the UNIDO database (on the vertical axis) and per capita GDP (on the horizontal axis). The index of production sophistication is constructed in two steps. First, the sophistication of each International Standard Industrial Classification (ISIC) three-digit manufacturing sector is measured by the weighted average of the per capita GDP of all countries producing goods in the sector. The weights are the production intensities of the sector—the ratio of the value added share of the sector in a country's total manufacturing value added relative to the sector's value added share in world manufacturing value added—in each producing country (normalized to 1).[7] Next, country-level manufacturing production sophistication is calculated as the weighted average of each country's individual sectoral sophistication indices, where the weights are the share of manufacturing value added of each sector. Figure 9.2 repeats the exercise for export sophistication, where the weights now refer to export intensities and export shares.

The regression line indicates the cross-section 'average' level of manufacturing production sophistication associated with a given level of development. By the nature of its construction, the country measure of sophistication shows a high positive correlation with aggregate per capita income levels. OECD countries cluster around the regression line in the upper right of each graph. The African economies in the sample are concentrated in the lower left corner of each figure.

Because the indices of production sophistication are measured in current US$ it is not possible to compare sophistication levels from year to year directly, since they are affected by price changes. The relevant comparison in the figures is the distance from the predicted relationship. Countries substantially above or below the regression line are of considerable interest. Positive outliers produce goods more typical of countries at higher levels of income. Countries below the regression line produce goods that are less sophisticated than would be predicted by their levels of income.

Moving between the figures from earliest to latest traces the path of economic development and manufacturing sophistication for individual

[6] Hausmann, Hwang, and Rodrik (2007) argue that their econometric evidence points to the relationship running from greater sophistication to growth. The relationship is robust to a number of specifications and treatments for two-way causality. UNIDO (2009) uses a different approach to address the endogeneity problem and arrives at similar results.

[7] Production intensity indicates whether a country's production in a sector is more or less concentrated than the world average. Hence, changes in production intensity indicate whether an economy is entering or leaving a sector relative to the evolving structure of global production. This approach is analogous to the use of revealed comparative advantage for exports by Hausmann, Hwang, and Rodrik (2007).

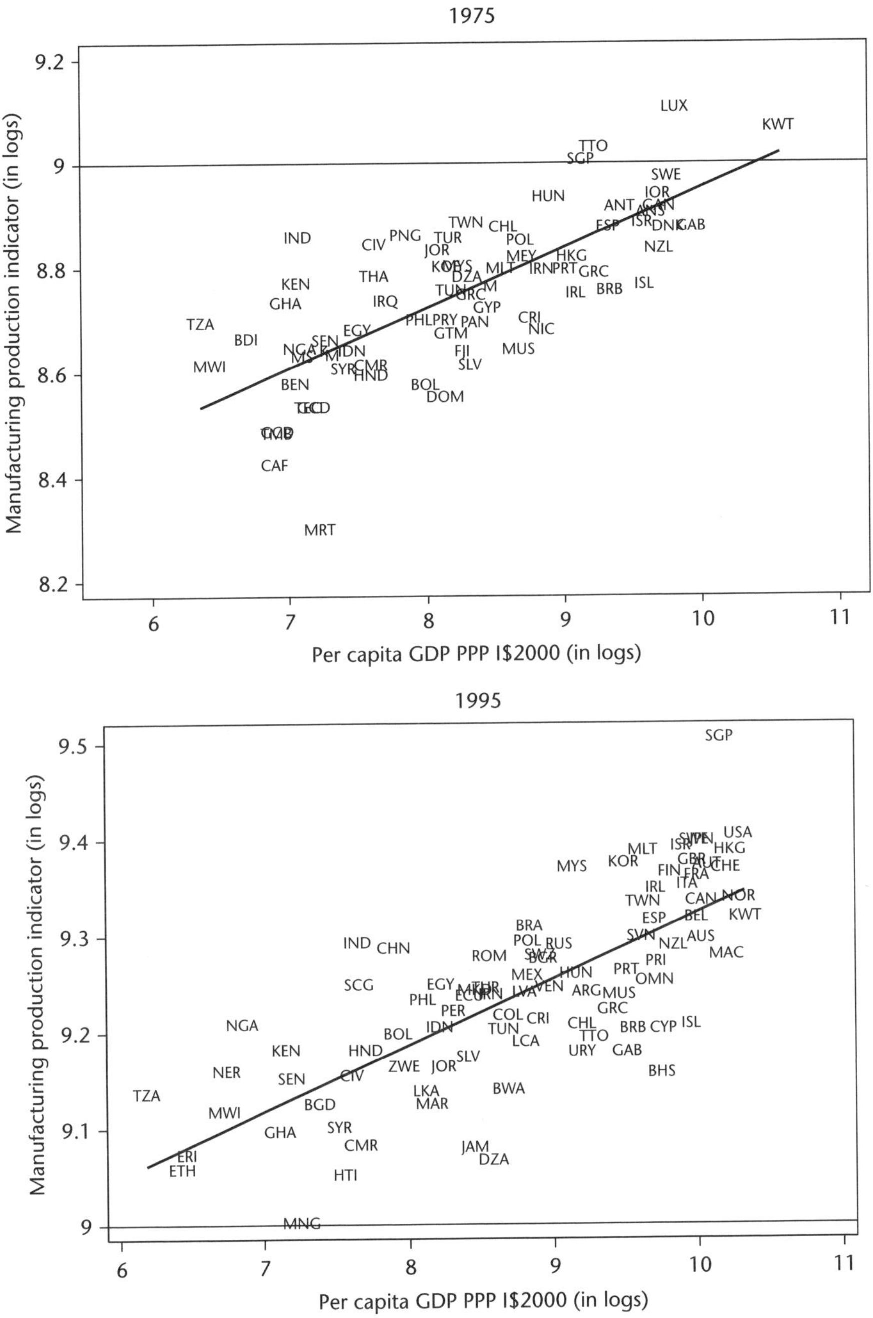

Figure 9.1. Production sophistication and per capita income, 1975 and 1995

Source: UNIDO (2009).

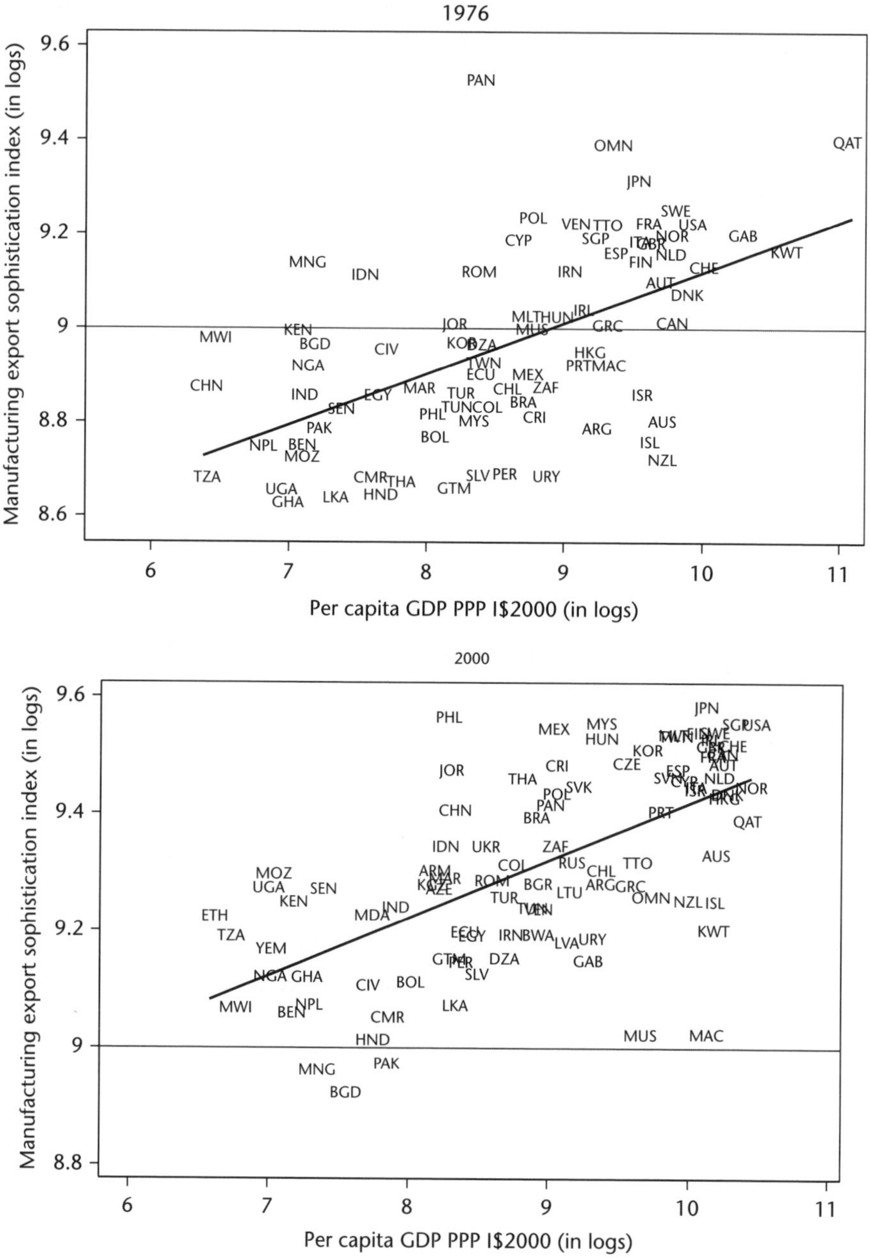

Figure 9.2. Export sophistication and per capita income, 1976 and 2000

Source: UNIDO (2009).

economies. The paths taken by such successful industrializing economies as Hong Kong, Malaysia, Singapore, and South Korea move up and to the right in these figures, reflecting the positive association between product and export sophistication and per capita income growth. China and India stand out among the low-income countries. Early on both economies had structures of manufacturing production that were significantly more sophisticated than those associated with their level of per capita income. In India's case, however, its manufactured export sophistication was more in line with predicted values.

The concept of sophistication combines the more traditional idea of technological sophistication based on process technology with 'firm capabilities', the tacit knowledge and working practices embodied in the firm's work force, into a single measure of productivity.[8] Sophisticated products embody advanced-country productivity levels along both dimensions. The ability of firms in lower-income economies to produce and, especially, export sophisticated goods indicates that they have mastered both the 'hardware' (process technology) and the 'software' (management practice, quality control, and value-chain management) required to produce such goods at an earlier level of development than might be expected. Low-income economies with a high concentration of such firms are likely to exhibit more rapid productivity growth in manufacturing.[9]

The UNIDO (2009) study represents a first attempt to look simultaneously at the impact of both diversity and sophistication on growth. Tracing the evolution of industrial structure over time for economies classified by initial level of income and growth performance, UNIDO finds that fast-growing low- and middle-income countries both diversified and increased the sophistication of their production and export structures between 1975 and 2005. Slowly growing low- and middle-income countries in contrast were less successful at diversifying, and performed especially poorly in terms of increasing product and export sophistication.

9.2.2 *Diversity and sophistication have declined in Africa*

Since the middle of the 1970s Africa has been making fewer of the kinds of industrial products that matter for its growth. Between 1975 and 2005, the sophistication of the manufacturing sector in 16 of the 18 African economies in the UNIDO database declined relative to predicted values. The results are more mixed for exports. About half of the African countries in the sample increased the sophistication of their export bundle relative to their level of

[8] UNIDO (2009) discusses the ranking of products by sophistication of process technology. For an introduction to the concept of firm capabilities, see Sutton (2005).

[9] For further discussion, see UNIDO (2009).

income while the other half moved in the opposite direction. None of the African countries in the sample had the movement up and to the right that is characteristic of successful industrializers. In contrast with more rapidly growing countries, the diversity and sophistication of the region's manufacturing sectors and its per capita incomes stagnated.

Figure 9.3 shows how two classes of industrial activity—low-sophistication products and high-sophistication products—have evolved in Africa between 1975 and 2003 relative to several comparators.[10] The average production intensity for the country–product group is plotted along the vertical axis. The beginning point of each arrow in the figure marks the average production intensity for the country–product group in 1975–80. The tip of the arrow marks the average production intensity for the period after 1995.[11] A value of 0, marked by the horizontal line, indicates that the average production intensity for the country–product group is equal to the global average.

In the period since 1975 fast-growing low-income countries—Africa's most relevant comparator—captured an increasing share of global production in both high-sophistication and, driven mainly by the explosive growth of apparel manufacturing, low-sophistication sectors. Thus the fast-growing low-income countries have become increasingly diversified and sophisticated. Africa in contrast failed to keep pace with the fast-growing low-income countries in low-sophistication sectors and was exiting high-sophistication production. Production intensities increased marginally in low-sophistication sectors and declined in high-sophistication sectors. The region's manufacturing base was becoming less diverse and at the same time less sophisticated. The decline in manufacturing sophistication was especially sharp in the region's early industrializers—Kenya, Ghana, Tanzania, and Zambia.

Figure 9.4 repeats the analysis for exports. Here again there is little structural change and the contrast between the fast-growing low-income countries and the sample of African countries is equally stark. Fast-growing low-income countries increased export intensities in both low-sophistication and high-sophistication sectors, indicating increasing revealed comparative advantage in both categories of exports. The African economies increased export intensities in low-sophistication goods, but much more slowly and had virtually unchanged export intensities in high-sophistication sectors. Relative to the fast growers, African manufactured exports were also becoming more concentrated and less sophisticated.

[10] Manufacturing activities are classified as 'sophisticated' if they have an index value of US $13,500 or above for the period after 1995 (regardless of their values in the earlier periods). Unsophisticated activities are classified as those with values below US$10,000 in 1995. The omitted category of products lies between those two bounds. See the notes to Figures 4 and 5 for the sectoral breakdown.

[11] The final year of the series is 2003 in the case of production and 2005 in the case of exports.

Putting the production and export stories together, what appears to have taken place in Africa during the 1980s and 1990s was a narrowing of the production and export structure in manufacturing and a shift toward less sophisticated activities. This is consistent with the closure of non-competitive, import-substitution industries—many of them state owned—following the trade liberalizations and privatizations of the adjustment period. At the high-sophistication end African manufacturers were not able to compete

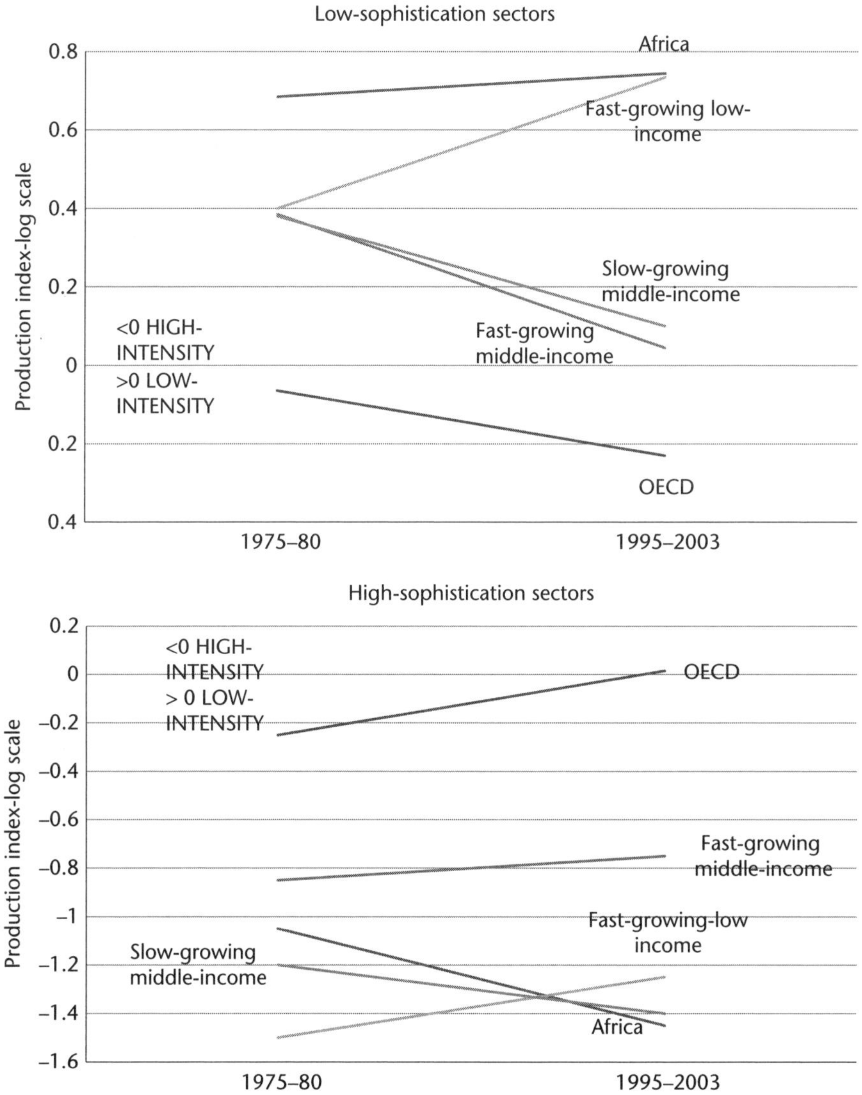

Figure 9.3. Production intensities by level of sophistication

Source: Author's calculations based on UNIDO (2009).

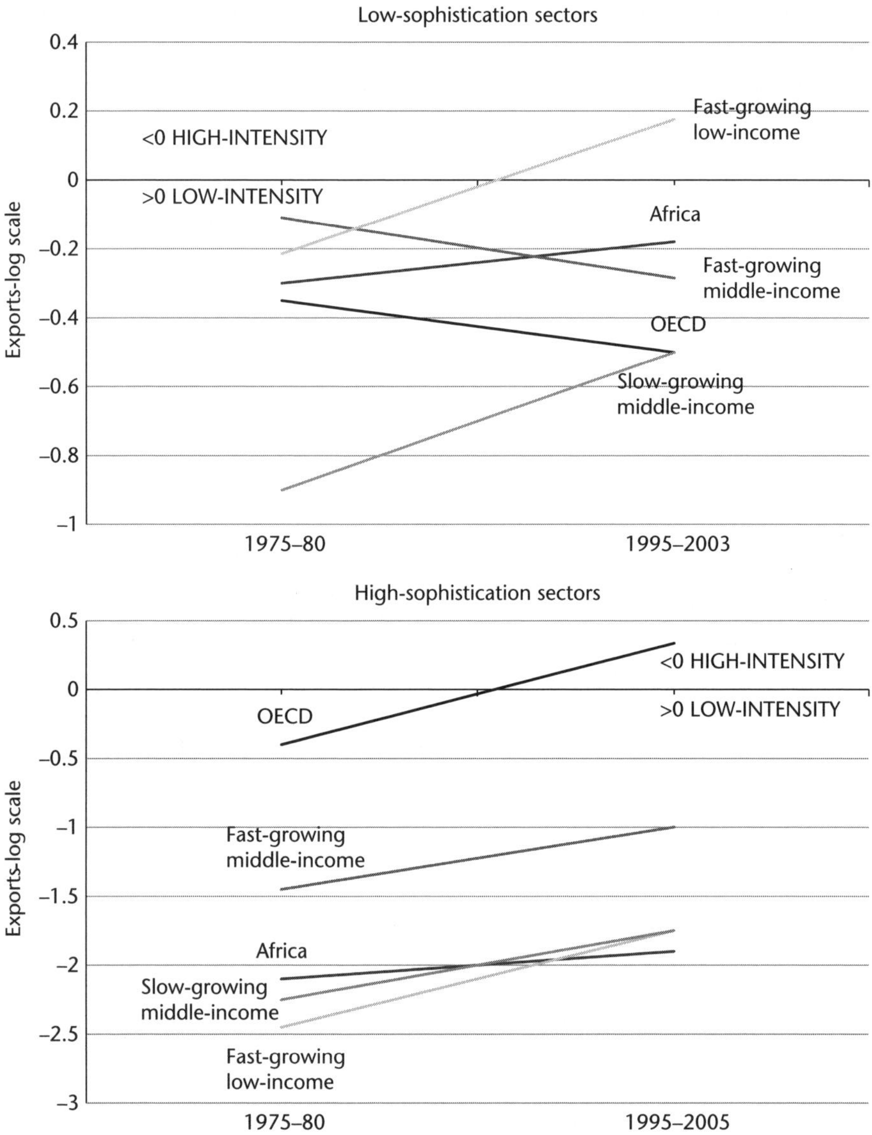

Figure 9.4. Export intensities by level of sophistication

Notes to Figures 9.3 and 9.4: The vertical axis represents the logarithm of production intensity, such that a value of zero indicates world average intensity. A value of 0.5 (1) is equivalent to 165% (265%) of world average, while a value of −0.5 (−1) equates to 61% (37%) of world average intensity The division between low- and high-sophistication is based on the sector rankings presented in UNIDO (2009). The 'high-sophistication' group is made up of the Fabricated Metals (381), Machinery (382), Electrical Machinery (383), Transport (384), Equipment (385), Furniture (332) and Printing & Publishing (342) sectors. The 'low-sophistication' group is made up of the Food (311), Beverages (312), Tobacco (313) Textiles (321), Leather (323), Footwear (324) and Rubber (355) sectors.

Source: Authors' calculations based on UNIDO (2009).

with OECD and middle-income developing country suppliers. Africa lost ground in high-sophistication sectors. Those manufacturing activities that remained following trade liberalization were more competitive internationally. As a consequence, revealed comparative advantage in low-sophistication goods increased somewhat. That was the good news. The bad news was that competitive pressure from Asia—as a global supplier of such products as clothing and footwear—meant that low-sophistication production and exports from Africa grew very little relative to the evolving global structure of production and exports.

9.3 Agriculture and industrialization

A majority of Africans continue to work in agriculture, and any new approach to industrialization must consider its relevance to industrial development. There is a large literature that argues that successful cases of industrialization are rare in the absence of a prior agricultural transformation.[12] This section examines two perspectives on the relationship between industry and agriculture in Africa. The first argues that an agricultural transformation is needed before industrial growth can take off. For the majority of Africa's economies there are two reasons to be sceptical of such an agricultural-led industrialization strategy: the limited range of technological innovations available to transform African agriculture and the globalization of both agriculture and manufacturing. A second, and more promising, view is that productivity change in agriculture can boost industrial development by supporting global value chains in agro-industrial products.

9.3.1 *Agriculture-led industrialization*

Since the early 1970s John Mellor and others have championed the concept of agriculture-led industrialization, based mainly on their interpretations of the Industrial Revolution in Britain and the East Asian miracle.[13] The intellectual architecture of agriculture-led industrialization is grounded in the closed, dual-economy model. In its simplest form the story follows these lines. Agricultural growth is driven by productivity improvements in smallholder agriculture, either in the form of new technologies for the production of existing crops, as in the Green Revolution, or the introduction of new higher value added crops, such as fruits and vegetables. The increases in agricultural

[12] For a survey, see World Bank (2008).

[13] The cases of Hong Kong and Singapore are dismissed by these authors as city states and therefore unique.

productivity raise farm household incomes and in turn lead to higher expenditures on non-agricultural goods, stimulating the growth of the industrial and services sectors. In the absence of international trade, productivity growth is also needed to restrain increases in the price of food, the urban wage good, as the urban economy expands. The evidence in support of agriculture-led industrialization comes largely from research showing that the consumption multipliers from growth in agriculture are higher than from other sectors (Mellor 1995; World Bank 2008).

This view of the role of agriculture in industrial development leads to seemingly paradoxical policy advice. For industrialization to succeed it is necessary first to focus on an agricultural transformation, raising land productivity and creating more efficient market links between urban and rural areas. Only after these public actions have taken place should governments turn to industrial development. In Africa this approach to industrialization has found concrete expression in Ethiopia, where, since 1993, the growth and development strategy has been built on 'agricultural development-led industrialization'.[14]

For an agriculture-led industrialization strategy to succeed, Africa would need a 'double green revolution', combining new agricultural technologies with adaptation to its huge diversity of ecosystems (Otsuka 2008). The need for new innovations is made even more urgent by climate change, which is likely to pose a significant threat to African agriculture. The Stern Review (Stern 2006) points to some potentially dramatic shifts in agricultural productivity due to global warming. Agriculture in higher-latitude developed countries is likely to benefit from moderate warming (2–3°C), while even small amounts of warming in tropical regions will lead to yield declines. Stern estimates that impacts of global warming will be highest in Africa. This is because crops are already close to critical temperature thresholds and most of the countries have limited adaptation potential in agriculture.

However, the innovations on which an agriculture-led industrialization strategy could be based are not likely to be available. Although modern agricultural biotechnology has the potential to transform African agriculture, Africa has banned the use of genetically modified (GM) crops. Therefore, very little research will be conducted on the biotechnology innovations most relevant to the region. Even if the GM ban were lifted within the next few years, because the lead time between research and application is around 15

[14] For a large, landlocked agrarian economy such as Ethiopia the logic of the agriculture-first strategy cannot be dismissed out of hand, although as Dercon and Zeitlin (2009) point out the evidence supporting such an approach is not wholly persuasive. Even in Ethiopia rapid increases in agricultural yields over more than ten years have failed to generate corresponding increases in industrial production. Recently, the government in Ethiopia has modified the strategy to include more activist industrial development policies.

years, new technologies would not become available until around 2030 (Collier 2010). The lack of appropriate technologies for African agriculture is exacerbated by the collapse of agricultural innovation and extension systems across the continent (Oyelaran-Oyeyinka and Gehl Sampath 2010).

Openness to trade fundamentally changes a key assumption underpinning the agriculture-led industrialization strategy. Over the past 25 years multilateral and bilateral trade agreements have opened all of Africa's economies and those of its major markets to international trade in both manufactured and agricultural products. These global changes mean that industry no longer needs a growing domestic market for its continued growth. Exports provide a far larger market. Rural–urban migration and rising urban demand no longer need result in sustained increases in the relative price of food; imports can substitute for domestic production.

The fact that an agriculture-led industrialization strategy may be inappropriate for contemporary Africa does not mean, however, that it is possible to ignore agricultural development. Given the large relative size of Africa's rural economy, productivity growth in agriculture is needed to raise rural incomes and reduce poverty. In a world of increasing food-price volatility it also represents a means to dampen food-price inflation. Moreover, improvements in the productivity and quality of high-value agricultural crops can make it possible to enter global agro-industrial value chains. Rather than leading industrial development, it is essential that productivity growth and greater market integration in agriculture proceed together with industrialization.

9.3.2 *Entering global value chains*

The idea of 'adding value' to agricultural commodities prior to export has a long history in Africa. It continues to have relevance today. Modern agro-industry covers a broad range of activities. At one extreme agricultural processing can involve the transformation of agricultural raw materials into a variety of processed products. This traditional linkage between agriculture and industry remains underexploited in Africa in part due to deficiencies in the supply of agricultural inputs and in part due to cascading tariffs in importing countries—particularly in Asia—that discriminate against the export of higher-stage processed goods. At the other extreme there is the expanding global trade in horticultural products and flowers. Keeping products fresh (maintaining the cool chain) and transferring them quickly from farm to shelf adds value. Value is also added through packaging, preparation, and innovation.

Global markets for agro-industrial products have become more challenging in recent years for two reasons:

- *Standards*: both the range of items covered by mandatory standards and the stringency of standards have increased, and compliance with standards has become more complicated because of a shift from product standards, largely enforced through testing at borders, towards controls over the way that products are grown, harvested, processed, and transported.
- *Product requirements*: global buyers' requirements include volume, speed, and reliability of delivery, customization of products through processing and packaging, and product safety.

Because of these challenges, global agro-industry is increasingly dominated by value-chain relationships in which lead firms coordinate the vertical supply chain (World Bank 2003). These lead firms have taken on many of the characteristics associated with modern manufacturing, including driving product differentiation and innovation, quality assurance based on risk management, and process control (Humphrey and Memedovic 2006).

In agro-processing, cut flowers, and horticultural exports the coordination, management, and control challenges posed by entering global value chains are closer to those of manufacturing than traditional agriculture, and the policy actions needed to spur their growth are the same as those needed to meet the industrialization challenge more generally. Successful agro-industrial exporting calls for development of a logistics capability. Physical infrastructure is critical at points of export (airports and seaports) and in connecting production centres to ports (roads and rail). Value-chain coordination puts a premium on effective communication. This requires investment in information and communication technology. The standards infrastructure is particularly important for success in global markets. Finally, given the importance of business service requirements in agro-industrial value chains, the support services needed by agricultural producers are closer to business development services than to agricultural extension (Humphrey and Memedovic 2006).

9.4 Toward an industrial development strategy

The state-led, import-substitution strategies of the 1960s and 1970s produced industry without efficiency. The distortions to the price system and the subsidies from the public purse were simply too great for the region's industrial enterprises to be sustainable in the long run. The adjustment policies of the 1980s and 1990s, however, produced efficiency without industry. Liberalized international trade benefited the consumers of industrial products, weeded out obviously non-competitive firms, and improved the allocation of investment, but industry failed to grow, even in the product lines that remained competitive following the economic reforms. Restoring industrial growth in Africa will require a new set of policies and public actions. This section sets out two elements of an industrialization strategy.

9.4.1 *Improving the investment climate*

Reacting to the unsuccessful and sometimes disastrous results of Africa's early experiment with industrialization, policy attention since the mid-1990s—especially from the international donor community—has tended to focus on the costs of doing business. These have been well-documented in a decade of comparative research sponsored by the World Bank and the World Economic Forum and are summarized in the report of the Commission on Growth and Development (2008). Much of the difference in industrial performance between Africa and other developing countries can be traced to differences in the 'investment climate'—the physical, institutional, and regulatory environment within which private investors make their decisions. Overall, the cost of doing business in Africa is 20–40 per cent above that for other developing regions.[15]

The reform agenda for the investment climate has centred on economy-wide reforms in trade, regulatory, and labour market policies, designed to reduce the role of government in economic management. While these policy and institutional reforms are perhaps necessary, they have not proved to be sufficient to increase investment and growth, especially in Africa.[16] At a minimum the government and donor view of the investment climate needs to be broadened to encompass three critical business environment factors that constrain industrialization in Africa: infrastructure, skills, and regional integration.[17]

9.4.1.1 INFRASTRUCTURE

Firm-level studies of productivity in Africa highlight infrastructure deficiencies as a significant barrier to greater competitiveness (Eifert, Gelb, and Ramachandran 2005; Yoshino 2008). Although indicators of infrastructure access rose between the 1990s and 2000s this was mainly in communications

[15] See for example the Doing Business surveys by the World Bank or the Africa Competitiveness Report by the World Economic Forum, the World Bank, and the African Development Bank.

[16] The relationship between 'doing business' reforms and investment, industrial development, and growth has not been well established empirically. Doing Business (2011) asserts that 656 articles have been published in peer-reviewed academic journals and about 2,060 working papers have been written using the eight years of available data. It is notably selective, however, in reviewing the evidence presented in these papers. Notably, a number of rapid industrializers in South East Asia and Central America score as badly on the Doing Business surveys as many African economies (see Page 2012).

[17] For a fuller exposition of these arguments, see Page (2012).

Table 9.2. Impact of unreliable infrastructure services on the productive sector

Service problem	SSA	Developing countries
Electricity		
Delay in obtaining electricity connection (days)	79.9	27.5
Electrical outages (days per year)	90.9	28.7
Value of lost output due to electrical outages (per cent of turnover)	6.1	4.4
Firms maintaining own generation equipment (per cent of total)	47.5	31.8
Telecommunications		
Delay in obtaining telephone line (days)	96.6	43.0
Telephone outages (days per year)	28.1	9.1

Source: Based on World Bank (2007a).

technology, water supply, and sanitation. Sub-Saharan Africa (SSA) continues to lag at least 20 percentage points behind the average for low-income countries on almost all major infrastructure measures.[18] In addition, the quality of service is low, supplies are unreliable, and disruptions are frequent and unpredictable (Table 9.2).

There has been little strategic orientation of Africa's infrastructure investments to support industrial growth and little willingness on the part of Africa's development partners to finance infrastructure investments (World Bank 2007a; Page 2012). Road infrastructure has received scant attention, and although concessions have been awarded to operate and rehabilitate many African ports and railways and some power distribution enterprises, financial commitments by the concessionaire companies are often small. Access to communications services has increased dramatically, thanks to the cellular revolution, but high-speed data transmission critical to exporting lags badly.

9.4.1.2 SKILLS

Africa's skills gap with the rest of the world is large and growing. While East Asian countries increased secondary enrolment rates by 21 percentage points and tertiary enrolment rates by 12 percentage points between 1990 and 2002, Africa raised its secondary rates by seven percentage points and its tertiary rates by only one percentage point. Real expenditure on tertiary education in Africa fell by about 28 per cent between 1990 and 2002, and expenditure per pupil declined from US$6,800 in 1989 to US$1,200 in 2002. Staff student ratios in West African universities increased from 1:16 in 1990 to 1:32 in 2007 (World Bank 2007b).

The skills gap poses a major potential constraint on Africa's industrial development. Employer surveys report that African tertiary graduates are

[18] An important exception is the penetration of fixed-line and mobile telephones, where SSA leads low-income countries by as much as 13 per cent. The largest gaps are for rural roads (29 percentage points) and electricity (21 percentage points).

weak in problem solving, business understanding, computer use, and communication skills (World Bank 2007b). Cross-country research indicates that there is a strong empirical link between export sophistication and the percentage of the labour force that has completed post-primary schooling (World Bank 2007b). There is also some evidence to suggest that enterprises managed by university graduates in Africa have a higher propensity to export (Wood and Jordan 2000; Clarke 2005), and more robust evidence shows that among firms owned by indigenous entrepreneurs, those with university-educated owners tend to have higher growth rates (Ramachandran and Shah 2007).

9.4.1.3 REGIONAL INTEGRATION

The small size of Africa's economies and the fact that many are landlocked make regional approaches to the common problems that affect trade and industrialization—infrastructure in trade corridors, institutional and legal frameworks (customs administration, competition policy, and regulation of transport) and trade-related services—imperative. For exporters in landlocked countries poor infrastructure in neighbouring coastal economies, incoherent customs and transport regulations, inefficient customs procedures, and 'informal taxes' in transport corridors slow transit times and raise costs.

Tangible progress on trade logistics in Africa's regional groupings has been slow. Investments in regional infrastructure are hampered by the technical complexity of multi-country projects and the time required for decisions by multiple governments. Institutional reforms—such as common standards, regulations, and one-stop border facilities—have also failed to materialize. Africa's development partners have also not been helpful, preferring to deal with individual countries rather than regional organizations and limiting financial commitments to transborder projects.

9.4.2 Learning to compete

It is not surprising, given Africa's past experiments with industrialization, that African governments and the international development community have chosen to focus on the regulatory environment. Reforms to reduce the role of government in economic decision making are easily measured and understood.[19] They may not, however, correctly identify the binding constraints to industrial development in Africa. Shifting focus to the obvious deficiencies in infrastructure, skills, and regional integration is an important first step toward accelerating the pace of industrialization. But public actions to improve the

[19] The annual World Bank Doing Business report goes so far as to publish a league table of the 'cost of doing business' and a list of 'top reformers'.

investment climate may not be sufficient to reverse Africa's increasing marginalization in global manufacturing.

In low-income countries there are large differences in productivity levels across firms, even in the same industry. While poorer countries have some firms that achieve world-class productivity levels, they also have a higher percentage of low-productivity firms.[20] Closing the productivity gap between African industry and the rest of the world will be essential, if Africa has any hope of breaking into global markets for manufactured goods. Today, new entrants to manufacturing are no longer only competing with the high-wage OECD, as China was when it entered the market. They are competing with 'factory Asia', and in the absence of more rapid firm-level productivity growth, the differences in wages between East Asia and Africa may not be sufficiently large to offset Asia's productivity advantage.

The problem of breaking in raises an old policy question with a contentious history: can public policy help African firms learn to compete? The debate about what, if anything, governments can do to increase firm-level productivity is at the heart of the decades-long controversy over industrial policy. Advocates of selective policies to promote productivity growth emphasize the success of some East Asian economies including China. Sceptics remain unconvinced.[21] However, an industrialization strategy for Africa need not confront the choice between 'picking winners' and 'levelling the playing field'. Rather, it can deploy the existing arsenal of public policies—including those related to the investment climate—towards three broad strategic objectives focused on learning to compete: creating an export push, encouraging industrial agglomerations, and attracting task-based production.

9.4.2.1 CREATING AN EXPORT PUSH

There is substantial evidence that African manufacturing firms improve their productivity by exporting (Söderbom and Teal 2003; Mengistae and Pattillo 2004; Milner and Tandrayen 2006). Bigsten et al. (2004) find that, controlling for self-selection, African firms enhance their productivity by around 9 per cent per year if they export. The public-policy implications of learning by exporting are straightforward but powerful. An 'export-push' strategy,

[20] Hsieh and Klenow (2009) for example show that these gaps are larger in China and India than in the USA, and that they have the potential to explain between a quarter and a third of the differences in aggregate productivity between the USA and China and India in the manufacturing sector.

[21] The report of the Commission on Growth and Development (2008) tries to have it both ways, concluding that the balance of the evidence suggests that proponents of selective industrial policies have failed to establish their general efficacy, but that some policy interventions have yielded positive results in individual country or institutional settings.

involving a concerted set of investments, and policy and institutional reforms designed to increase the share of manufactured exports in GDP, can generate higher levels of economy-wide total factor productivity and more rapid growth.

Creating an export push will require coordinated action across government to succeed. Trade reforms have brought tariffs down in Africa, and its trade regimes discriminate against exports to about the same degree as those of other regions worldwide, but a number of at-the-border reforms—especially to trade-related institutions—still remain to be undertaken to reduce anti-export bias. Duty drawback and tariff-exemption schemes are often complex and poorly administered, resulting in substantial delays. Export procedures—including certificates of origin, quality and sanitary certification, and permits—are also burdensome (Clarke 2005).

Beyond the border, surveys of manufacturing firms in African countries highlight—in addition to the obvious deficiencies in infrastructure—a number of areas of trade logistics that impose penalties on exporters: port transit times are long, customs delays on both imported inputs and exports are significantly longer for African economies than for China, and markets for transport services and handling are often insufficiently competitive (Yoshino 2008).

Africa's success in boosting non-traditional exports may, however, ultimately depend as much on the actions of its international partners as on its own efforts. Aid agencies will need to support strategic investments in trade-related infrastructure and institutions, mainly under the aegis of an adequately funded WTO 'Aid for Trade' initiative. In addition more advanced economies can reduce escalating tariffs directed at higher-stage processing of Africa's commodity exports and could offer a measure of trade preferences for its non-traditional exports.[22]

9.4.2.2 ENCOURAGING INDUSTRIAL CLUSTERS

Manufacturing and service industries tend to concentrate in geographical areas, driven by common needs for inputs and access to markets, knowledge flows, and the need for specialized skills (Fujita, Krugman, and Venables 1999; Sonobe and Otsuka 2006). There are significant productivity gains to firms from industrial agglomeration, making the public-policy challenge posed by agglomeration daunting (Glaeser et al. 1992; Henderson 1997; Bigsten, Gebreeyesus, Siba and Söderbom 2012). Starting a new industrial location is a form of collective-action problem: if a critical mass of firms can be persuaded to

[22] See Collier and Venables (2007) for such a proposal.

locate in a new area, they will realize agglomeration economies, but no single firm has the incentive to locate in a new area in the absence of others. Because Africa has few modern industrial clusters, it is both more difficult for existing African firms to compete and more difficult to attract new industry to Africa.

Given the low level of industrial export dynamism in most of Africa, linking export promotion and spatial policies in an export processing zone (EPZ) may be an attractive way of encouraging agglomeration. The main benefit of an EPZ is that it provides a clear focus for government investments and institutional reforms designed to encourage the location of firms in a specific area. It is also subject to an efficiency test—firms located in the cluster must be able to export. Case studies suggest that concentrating investment on high-quality infrastructure in a limited physical area is crucial. They also suggest that improving social services in an industrial zone to levels above national standards is highly desirable (UNIDO 2009).

9.4.2.3 ATTRACTING TRADE IN TASKS

In some manufacturing activities the production process can be decomposed into a series of distinct steps or tasks (Grossman and Rossi-Hansberg 2006). As transport and coordination costs have fallen, it has become efficient for the production of different tasks to be located in different countries, each working on a different step in the process. Task-based production has expanded dramatically in the past 20 years. In 1986–90 imported intermediates constituted 12 per cent of total global manufacturing output and 26 per cent of total intermediate inputs. By 1996–2000 these figures had risen to 18 per cent and 44 per cent, respectively. Exports use a substantially higher share of imported intermediate inputs than production for the domestic market, a ratio of about 2 to 1 (UNIDO 2009).

For countries that have failed to industrialize, task-based production is a potential lifeline. It is easier to specialize in a single task than in the entire range of tasks needed to produce a product. But trade in tasks has also amplified the importance of trade logistics. Countries at the final stages in the production chain of a task-traded good are unlikely to be competitive if their trade logistics costs on imported intermediates are high, and countries hoping to enter upstream in a global value chain cannot afford to have high trade logistics costs for their exports. End-stage tasks are highly mobile, and African economies can gain a foothold in task-based production through concerted programmes of investment promotion, provision of infrastructure, and improvements in trade-related institutions, beginning with the creation of world-class EPZs.

9.5 Conclusions

This chapter began by asking, should Africa industrialize? The answer to whether to industrialize is relatively straightforward: for the vast majority of the region's economies the lack of structural change, industrial diversity, and sophistication are powerful constraints to growth. The answer to how to industrialize is more complex. For several reasons agriculture is unlikely to lead industrialization in Africa, but it has important links to a successful industrial transformation. Improvements to the investment climate—the physical, institutional, and policy environment within which firms operate—are still needed, but public policy needs to shift from a focus on stroke-of-the-pen changes to regulations to embrace actions to close the infrastructure gap, create new skills, and achieve meaningful regional integration.

To break into global markets Africa must raise the productivity of its enterprises. Here the role of public policy is more controversial. Africa's past experiments at industrialization were largely unsuccessful, and there has been a tendency to dismiss the idea of industrial policy as inappropriate or unworkable in Africa. This view of industrial policy as 'picking winners' misses the point. What is missing in Africa beyond the investment climate is a coherent, strategic set of public actions to support productivity growth. Creating an export push, encouraging industrial clusters, and attracting task-based production offer an opportunity to give Africa a new start on learning to compete.

References

Arbache, J. S., and J. Page (2007). 'More Growth or Fewer Collapses? A New Look at Long Run Growth in Sub-Saharan Africa'. Policy Research Working Paper 4384. Washington, DC: World Bank.

——(2008). 'Patterns of Long Term Growth in Sub-Saharan Africa'. In D. Go and J. Page (eds), *Africa at a Turning Point? Growth, Aid and External Shocks*. Washington, DC: World Bank.

——(2009). 'How Fragile Is Africa's Recent Growth?', *Journal of African Economies*, 19: 1–24.

Bigsten, A., et al. (2004). 'Do African Manufacturing Firms Learn from Exporting?', *Journal of Development Studies*, 40 (3): 115–41.

Bigsten, A, M. Gebreeyesus, E. Siba, and M. Soderbom (2012). 'Enterprise Agglomeration, Output Prices and Physical Productivity: Firm-Level Evidence from Ethiopia', Gothenburg: University of Gothenburg available at: http://www.soderbom.net/bgss_AC_june12_wp.pdf (accessed 16 August 2012).

Cadot, O., C. Carrère, and V. Strauss-Kahn (2011). 'Export Diversification: What's behind the Hump?', *Review of Economics and Statistics*, 93 (2): 590–605.

Clarke, G. R. G. (2005). 'Beyond Tariffs and Quotas: Why Don't African Manufacturers Export More?'. Policy Research Working Paper 4317. Washington, DC: World Bank.

Collier, P. (2010). *Plundered Planet*. New York: Oxford University Press.

Collier, P., and A. J. Venables (2007). 'Rethinking Trade Preferences: How Africa Can Diversify its Exports', *World Economy*, 30 (8) 1326–45.

Commission on Growth and Development (2008). *The Growth Report: Strategies for Sustained Growth and Development*. Washington, DC: World Bank.

Dercon, S., and A. Zeitlin (2009). 'Rethinking Agriculture and Growth in Ethiopia: A Conceptual Discussion'. Mimeo. Oxford: University of Oxford, Department of International Development. Available at: http://www.economics.ox.ac.uk/members/Stefan.Dercon/ethiopia%20paper%202_v2.pdf (accessed 16 August 2012).

Eifert, B., A. H. Gelb, and V. Ramachandran (2005). 'Business Environment and Comparative Advantage in Africa: Evidence from the Investment Climate Data'. Working Paper 56. Washington, DC: Center for Global Development.

Fujita, M., P. Krugman, and A. J. Venables (1999). *The Spatial Economy: Cities, Regions and International Trade*. Cambridge, MA: MIT Press.

Glaeser, E. L., H. D. Kallal, A. Scheinkman, and A. Shleifer (1992). 'Growth in Cities', *Journal of Political Economy*, 100: 1126–52.

Go, D., and J. Page (eds) (2008). *Africa at a Turning Point? Growth, Aid and External Shocks*. Washington, DC: World Bank.

Grossman, G., and E. Rossi-Hansberg (2006). 'The Rise of Offshoring: It's Not Wine for Cloth Anymore', Federal Reserve Bank of Kansas City's *Proceedings*, 59–102.

Hausmann, R., J. Hwang, and D. Rodrik (2007). 'What you Export Matters', *Journal of Economic Growth*, 12 (1): 1–25.

Hausmann, R., L. Pritchett, and D. Rodrik (2005). 'Growth Accelerations', *Journal of Economic Growth*, 10: 303–9.

Henderson, J. V. (1997). 'Externalities and Industrial Development', *Journal of Urban Economics*, 42 (3): 449–70.

Hsieh, C.-T., and P. Klenow (2009). 'Misallocation and Manufacturing TFP in China and India', *Quarterly Journal of Economics*, 124 (4): 1403–48.

Humphrey, J. and O. Memedovic (2006). 'Global Value Chains in the Agrifood Sector'. Working Paper. Vienna: UNIDO.

Imbs, J., and R. Wacziarg (2003). 'Stages of Diversification', *American Economic Review*, 93 (1): 63–86.

IMF (2012). 'Regional Economic Outlook Sub-Saharan Africa: Back to High Growth?' Washington, DC: International Monetary Fund.

Jones, B. F., and B. A. Olken (2005). 'The Anatomy of Start-Stop Growth'. Working Paper 11525. Cambridge, MA: NBER.

Mellor, J. (1995). 'Introduction'. In J. Mellor (ed.), *Agriculture on the Road to Industrialization*. Baltimore, MD: Johns Hopkins University Press.

Mengistae, T., and C. Patillo (2004). 'Export Orientation and Productivity in Sub-Saharan Africa', *IMF Staff Papers*, 51 (2): 327–53.

Milner, C., and V. Tandrayen (2006). 'The Impact of Exporting and Export Destination on Manufacturing Wages: Evidence for Sub-Saharan Africa', *Review of Development Economics*, 11 (1): 13–30.

Nkrumah, K. (1965). Neo-Colonialism: The Last Stage of Imperialism Leiden: Brill Academic Publishers.

Oyelaran-Oyeyinka, B., and P. Gehl Sampath (2010). 'Technology Innovation and Africa's Industrialization'. Tunis: AfDB (processed).

Otsuka, K. (2008). 'Strategy for Agricultural Growth in Ethiopia'. Briefing Note. Oxford: University of Oxford. Available at: http://www.economics.ox.ac.uk/members/Stefan.Dercon/Brief_KOtsuka%20_rev_.pdf (accessed 16 August 2012).

Page, J. (2012). 'Can Africa Industrialize?', *Journal of African Economies*, 21 (Supplement 2): ii86–ii124.

Ramachandran, V., and M. Shah (2007). 'Why Are There So Few Black-Owned Firms in Africa? Preliminary Results from Enterprise Survey Data'. Working Paper 104. Washington, DC: Center for Global Development.

Söderbom, M., and F. Teal (2003). 'Are Manufacturing Exports the Key to Economic Success in Africa?', *Journal of African Economies*, 12 (1): 1–29.

Sonobe, T., and K. Otsuka (2006). *Cluster-Based Industrial Development: An East Asian Model*. Basingstoke: Palgrave Macmillan.

Sutton, J. (2005). 'Competing in Capabilities: An Informal Overview'. Mimeo. London: London School of Economics. Available at: http://info.worldbank.org/etools/docs/library/139596/sutton.pdf (accessed 16 August 2012).

Stern, N. (2006). *The Economics of Climate Change: The Stern Review*. New York: Cambridge University Press.

United Nations Industrial Development Organization (UNIDO) (2009). *Industrial Development Report, 2009 Breaking in and Moving Up: New Industrial Challenges for the Bottom Billion and the Middle Income Countries*. Vienna: UNIDO.

Wood, A., and K. Jordan (2000). 'Why Does Zimbabwe Export Manufactures and Uganda Not?', *Journal of Development Studies*, 37 (2): 91–116.

World Bank (2003). 'Modernizing Africa's Agro-Food Systems: Analytical Framework and Implications for Operations'. Africa Region Working Papers 44. Washington, DC: World Bank.

——(2007a). 'Accelerating Development Outcomes in Africa: Progress and Change in the Africa Action Plan'. Development Committee Paper. Washington, DC: World Bank.

——(2007b). 'Expanding the Possible in Sub-Saharan Africa: How Tertiary Institutions Can Increase Growth and Competitiveness'. Washington, DC: World Bank.

——(2008). *World Development Report: Agriculture for Development*. Washington, DC: World Bank.

Yoshino, Y. (2008). 'Domestic Constraints, Firm Characteristics, and Geographical Diversification of Firm-Level Manufacturing Exports in Africa'. Policy Research Working Paper 4575. Washington, DC: World Bank.

Part IV
Climate Change and Sustainability

10

Climate Change and Industrial Policy

Wim Naudé

10.1 Introduction[1]

Industrial policy is vital for sustainability in its broadest sense: both environmental as well as societal sustainability depend on industrial policy. In a world characterized by growing inter- and intra-country inequality, industrialization offers scope for providing job opportunities, incomes, and the chance for industrially lagging countries (ILCs) to catch up. In a world facing the spectre of climate change, low-carbon industrialization and green growth paths have become imperatives. Altenburg (2009) describes climate change as one of the most important challenges facing industrial policy. Naudé and Alcorta (2010) stress that achieving low-carbon industrialization

> ...is going to require selective government intervention...neutrality towards all products and processes cannot be maintained. It has got to be driven by governments as coordination, subsidization, protection, information and large scale investments are at the core of the responses towards limiting the human impact on climate change. The need for making the right choices will become even more apparent as the world's population increases to more than 9 billion people by 2050. A growing population with increasing purchasing power will demand new and more products and ways of making them that will not only have a heavy toll on the environment but will also put heavy pressure on the availability of natural resources to produce them. (ibid.: 1)

Moreover, promoting low-carbon industrialization and obtaining its accompanying development benefits (Szirmai 2009) will itself improve the ability of currently poor countries to adapt to climate change. It is the case that

[1] This chapter is a slightly revised version of a paper published in 2011 in *Sustainability*, 3 (7): 1003–21.

'the best defence against climate change is economic development' (Schelling 2009: 16).

Although the Earth's climate has always been changing there is now wide agreement that the climate is warming and that human emission of greenhouse gases[2] (GHGs)—anthropogenic global warming (AGW)—is a contributing factor. 'Every company, every farm, every household emits some greenhouse gases' (Tol 2010: 29). One of the most significant sources of greenhouse gases is industrial activity. Industry demands around 30 per cent of global final energy demand and is responsible for around 40 per cent of all energy-related emissions, with iron and steel, cement, chemicals and petrochemicals, pulp and paper, and aluminum production being the most carbon intensive (IEA 2009b). The human-emitted component of GHGs in the atmosphere has risen considerably since the first Industrial Revolution. It poses a challenge for human well-beings as a warmer climate is expected to have many negative (although also some positive) impacts on society.

When the current industrially advanced countries underwent their rapid industrialization process starting in the eighteenth and nineteenth centuries, and even when China started its economic reform in 1978, the potential threat of climate change, and in particular the threat from anthropogenic global warming, was unknown. Over the past two decades, however, it has become one of the most talked about global challenges of our times.

Climate change is predicted to have particular economic and social impacts through various channels. Moreover, these are expected to differ geographically, and as the next section will detail, developing countries are expected to be worst affected. These impacts and consequences will require *adaptation* to climate change as well as actions to *mitigate* anthropogenic global warming. They mean that active and selective industrial policy will have to be used by both advanced as well as developing countries to achieve the balancing act of reducing GHG emissions and ensuring that industry (manufacturing in particular) remains an engine of growth and employment.

Adaptation and mitigation will have costs and opportunities for industrial development, but differing across the globe. Generally, the challenge is to ensure that industrial development and the prospects for industrial development are not adversely affected by climate change and that industrial development takes place without worsening anthropogenic global warming—ideally contributing towards moving global production, distribution, and consumption towards a low-carbon and eventually decarbonized economy. Moreover, industrialization itself could mitigate climate change and facilitate adaptation through providing the means to accelerate the transfer of

[2] Including carbon dioxide, CO_2, and methane, CH_4.

employment from agriculture to industry, which could potentially reduce pressures on deforestation and clearing of land for agriculture, two important sources of GHG emissions.[3]

The purpose of this chapter is to further explore the need or rationale for industrial policy due to climate change, and to determine what it implies for the how of industrial policy. To achieve these objectives the remainder of the chapter will discuss the challenges facing both industrialized and industrially lagging countries in contributing towards a low-carbon economy. The central argument of the chapter is that a low-carbon economy will require mitigation, explicit recognition of the relationship between adaptation and industrialization, and should be undergirded by international coordination. For the *how* of industrial policy it requires at a minimum a threefold approach, consisting of:

(i) appropriate innovation and technological change
(ii) trade policy alignment
(iii) the prioritization of sustainable human development.

Before discussing the elements of this threefold approach, the basics of climate change economics as it pertains to industrialization and industrial policy is discussed in Section 10.2. This is to provide an adequate frame of reference and to stress the daunting obstacles in the path of low-carbon industrialization. Then, in Section 10.3, the three implications for the how of industrial policy (innovation, trade, and sustainable human development) with respect to mitigation and adaption and industrialization are discussed. Section 10.4 concludes.

10.2 Climate change and industrialization

10.2.1 *Greenhouse gas emissions and industrialization*

Before proceeding it may be necessary to deal briefly with the question of how anthropogenic global warming occurs? The answer, as alluded to in the introduction, is that human activity gives rise to GHGs (especially carbon dioxide, CO_2, and methane, CH_4). The so-called Kaya Identity (see Girod et al. 2009) is used to depict the main links between human activity and GHG emission:

$$GHG\,emissions = population \times \left\{ \left(\frac{GDP}{Population} \right) + \left(\frac{Energy\,Use}{GDP} \right) + \left(\frac{GHG\,emissions}{Energy Use} \right) \right\}$$

[3] According to estimates deforestation in developing countries is currently the source of up to 25 per cent of all GHG emissions (Martin 2010).

The Kaya Identity shows that GHG emissions arise from human activity, through increases in incomes, and energy and carbon intensity, all which rise with population growth. Industrialization therefore contributes towards GHG emissions through:

(i) contributing to general GDP growth
(ii) having a dramatic overall impact on energy demand and use
(iii) using carbon-intensive production methods.

Based on the Kaya identity, given forecasts of economic development, population growth, and given assumptions on energy demand and carbon intensity of production and consumption, it is possible to predict GHG emissions caused by human activity. Such predictions are provided by the Intergovernmental Panel on Climate Change (IPCC)[4] and the International Energy Agency (IEA). According to the IEA's recent estimates, CO_2 emissions are currently increasing by about 1.5 per cent annually. As a result it predicts emissions will rise from 28.8 Gt (gigaton) in 2007 to 40.2 Gt by 2030 (IEA 2009a). Faster industrialization in the developing world will, *ceteris paribus*, raise these emissions and contribute to further anthropogenic global warming.

10.2.2 *Economic impacts of global warming*

What are the consequences of global warming, and hence the consequences of industrialization? The overall assessment is that global warming will be detrimental to economic development and contribute to greater poverty (Ojha 2008). Various studies, using quantitative modelling techniques involving computable general equilibrium models, have, since the early 1990s, been used to estimate the economic impact of global warming. Most studies have assumed an increase in global mean temperature of either 1°C or 2.5°C—which is assumed would occur if the amount of GHGs in the atmosphere doubles. Table 10.1, adapted from Tol (2010), summarizes the key peer-reviewed studies in this regard.

Table 10.1 indicates that most peer-reviewed estimates of the economic impacts of climate change ranges between −11.4 and +2.3 per cent of global GDP. It can also been seen that some regions are net losers—in many cases Africa or Asia—and some net winners—mostly Russia and the countries of the former Soviet Union.

One of the most quoted (and criticized) estimates on the impacts and costs of climate change and its mitigation comes from the Stern Review (Stern 2006). The Stern Review estimated that climate change's economic damages

[4] For a discussion of the criticisms against the IPCC's scenarios, see Girod et al. (2009).

Table 10.1. The global economic impact of climate change: estimates from the literature

Authors	Impact on global GDP (%)	Worst affected region	Best off region
Fankhauser (1995)	−1.4%	China	Eastern Europe and former Soviet Union
Tol (1995)	−1.9%	Africa	Eastern Europe and former Soviet Union
Nordhaus and Yang (1996)	−1.7%	Developing Countries	Former Soviet Union
Plambeck and Hope (1996)	−0.5% to −11.4%	Asia	Eastern Europe and former Soviet Union
Mendelsohn, Schlesinger, and Williams (2000)	0.0% to 0.1%	Africa	Eastern Europe and former Soviet Union
Nordhaus and Boyer (2000)	−1.5%	Africa	Russia
Tol (2002)*	2.3%	Africa	Western Europe
Maddison (2003)	−0.1%	South America	Western Europe
Rehdanz and Maddison (2005)	−0.4%	Africa	South Asia
Hope (2006)	0.9%	Asia	Eastern Europe and former Soviet Union

Note: *Assumes a 1°C warming only.
Source: Adapted from Tol (2010: 31).

would amount to around 12 per cent of global GDP, and that the costs of mitigation—moving to a low-carbon economy—would be much lower, around 1 per cent of global GDP. Hence the key message of the Stern Review was that the impact of climate change is likely to be severe but the costs of avoiding it relatively small, if the world acted without delay.

Key criticisms against the Stern Review were that too low a discount rate was used to value future damages, thereby overstating future damages, and that mitigation costs were underestimated (see e.g. Tol and Yohe 2006; Nordhaus 2007).

The World Bank's 2010 World Development Report focused on climate change. According to the World Bank (2010) global climate change will have disproportionate negative impacts on developing countries, in particular on agricultural productivity in Africa, South Asia, and parts of Latin America. The World Bank also expected that Russia and Canada and parts of Western Europe may benefit through improving agricultural productivity. The potential out-migration of people from agriculture in Africa, South Asia, and Latin America has accordingly been raised as a concern (Martin 2010), and emphasizes the importance for structural change—industrialization—to assist in providing alternative employment to out-migrants from agriculture.

Predicting the economic impacts of global warming is however, a contentious issue—as is the case generally with climate modelling or weather forecasting—with Prins et al. (2010: 18) complaining that assumptions and simplifications used in such models can 'undergird just about any view of the future that one prefers', and Tol (2010: 30) stating that 'the uncertainties about climate change are vast indeed, so vast that the standard tools of decision making under uncertainty and learning may not be applicable'. He provides a discussion of some of the methodological challenges in estimating the economic impacts of climate change such as the difficulties of :

(i) assigning uncertainties (i.e. discount rates)
(ii) modelling adaptation
(iii) putting values on environmental services
(iv) estimating the marginal costs of GHG emissions.

Given the acknowledgement that, despite uncertainties in estimating the impact of climate change, it remains a significant threat and that reducing GHG emissions are warranted, economists have asked what the social costs of GHG emissions are, with a view of establishing a price on carbon (through taxes, emission trading, or regulation). This approach is based on the economic view that the cost of a negative externality, such as a carbon emission, needs to be internalized by the party responsible.

Tol (2010: 41) considered estimates from 232 published scientific studies and concluded that 'the uncertainty about the social costs of climate change is very large'. The mean estimate from these studies is US$105 per ton of carbon, with the modal estimate around US$13 per ton and the median US$29 per ton.

Industrialization, given its high contribution to emissions, thus clearly carries a price. Although the extent of the ultimate price is still subject to uncertainty, what is certain is that poorer countries will be worst affected, and that unless industrialization can proceed in a way that reduces GHG emissions, the eventual price will be higher, both in terms of damages to GDP and the social costs of emissions. Indeed, as the IEA (2009b: 21) notes, 'total industrial energy consumption and CO_2 emissions are rising and progress in industrial efficiency and CO_2 intensity has been more than offset by growing industrial production'.

10.3 Implications for industrial policy

Achieving low-carbon industrialization has a number of interrelated implications for industrial policy. These will be discussed in the following sub-sections.

10.3.1 *International coordination of industrial policy*

A piecemeal, country-by-country approach is likely to be sub-optimal. In the past, industrial policy was very much nationally-oriented with little cooperation and coordination between countries. Now, however, a transition to a low-carbon economy will require global cooperation and coordination. This raises issues of the appropriate and effective institutional mechanisms to achieve such coordination. Is it through the UN, the G20, regional initiatives like the EU, or perhaps some other sovereign, non-state actor? And how will compliance be ensured and monitored? Before coming to these issues, the case for international coordination of industrial policies needs to be stressed.

It has been estimated that in order to limit average global warming to 2°C by 2100, with a 50 per cent probability, that concentrations of CO_2 should be stabilized at 450 ppm (parts per million) by 2030 (IEA 2009a). It is, at the time of writing (2010), around 389 ppm and rising by 2 ppm per year—growing at around 1.5 per cent annually (IEA 2009a; Prins et al. 2010).

The challenge in achieving this reduction in CO_2 seems almost too enormous to achieve. Barrett (2009) reports that CO_2 should be reduced, not to 450 ppm, but to 350 ppm to limit global warming—a level already exceeded. He refers to the need therefore for a 'global climate-technology revolution' to aim at this target, while the IEA (2009a: 8) calls for a 'low-carbon revolution'. It expects that, at current rates, CO_2 emissions will continue to rise from 28.8 Gt (gigatonnes) in 2007 to 40.2 Gt in 2030. This is estimated to push average global temperatures up by 6°C and result in CO_2 levels of more than 1000 ppm.

Currently, and since the first Industrial Revolution, most developing countries have not been major GHG emitters—even large emerging economies like China, Brazil, and India emit relatively little in per capita terms—although due to the size of their populations and economies their total emissions are significant (Ojha 2008). However, as far as the future is concerned, the IEA (2009a) expects that *all* of the projected increase in CO_2 emissions between now and 2030 will come from developing countries—mainly China, India, and the Middle East. Around 75 per cent of the predicted 12 Gt increase in annual emissions is set to come from China alone, with the country expected to become the world's largest importer of oil by 2025 (IEA 2009a). The growth in CO_2 will be driven not only by the growing prosperity and rising demand from rising industrial giants such as China and India, but also from the need to meet the, as yet unmet, demand of around 1.5 billion people around the world who lack access to electricity. The majority of these live in sub-Saharan Africa (SSA) (IEA 2009a).

Developing countries will, however, in many cases also be the worst affected by climate change, as was discussed in Section 10.2. And most of the current industrially-generated stock of carbon in the atmosphere has been caused by advanced economies, where most of the technological capability, know-how, human skills, and financial resources needed to mitigate climate change and adapt to its impacts reside. This suggests that a low-carbon revolution requires global coordination. Many questions have arisen and remain relevant. How can this change be accomplished? Is it possible? What will be the costs? Is globally coordinated action towards a low-carbon economy possible? There are currently no clear answers. What is clear at the time of writing is that the multilateral (UN-mediated) negotiations route, which has characterized global coordination attempts for almost two decades, has not yet resulted in definitive success. The process, which started with the Rio Declaration and includes the flawed Kyoto Protocol, has not been a total failure as some would suggest. There have in fact been hugely important milestones—but they have not yet brought the world significantly closer towards containing global warming.

The 'Hartwell Paper' (see Prins et al. 2010) is particularly critical of the multilateral UN-mediated route to achieve a reduction in CO_2 emissions, claiming that it is putting carbon reductions before human development, that it is being overly top-down in its approach—working through 'set-piece conferences'—and that it obscures varying 'interests and agendas within utopian talk of global and universal solutions' (ibid.: 12).

What bedevils global coordination with respect to achieving a low-carbon economy are a number of conflicting incentives arising out of the nature of the climate change challenge. The first is that developing countries have potentially much to gain from carbon-intensive industrialization. This issue will be discussed in greater depth in the next section, as it has a bearing on the objectives of industrial policy.

The second problem is that climate change and the move to a low-carbon economy creates both potential losers and winners—it has unequal benefits and costs so that countries face an incentive structure that 'resembles a multiplayer prisoner's dilemma game' (Brandt and Svendsen 2003: 10). These create potential benefits for countries with low-carbon technologies and/or the knowledge to be a producer and exporter of such technologies—indeed they could corner the market. In other words a first-mover advantage in low-carbon technology and products could be valuable. How should countries with such an advantage exploit it? The answer is through industrial policies that ensure that a sufficiently large number of countries would want to adopt such technologies—for instance through committing to binding agreements on CO_2 reductions and increasing the share of non-renewable energy. Such a country-level strategy could, however, be counterproductive from the point of view of obtaining binding agreements on CO_2 reductions if there are countries who do not want, for competitiveness reasons, to allow others to exploit their first-mover advantage.

However, according to Brandt and Svendsen (2003), this is exactly the position the EU and USA find themselves in, and could explain part of the USA's reluctance to commit to the Kyoto Protocol. Their thesis is that the EU has a first-mover advantage in some renewable energy technologies, for instance wind turbines,[5] and is therefore quite keen to push for wide

[5] Brandt and Svendsen (2003) discuss the case of Denmark, where government subsidizing of the wind turbine industry (following the oil crisis of 1973) has resulted in the country gaining a lead in the production of windmills.

international agreements that will see a rise in the price of carbon and targeted share of renewable energies in future energy consumption.[6] See also Helm (2009), who states that the EU is projecting a leadership role for itself in setting GHG emissions targets. However, for countries without this advantage, such agreements will result in them having to spend more on importing such renewable energy technologies from the EU. Brandt and Svendsen (2003) argue that this may be a reason why countries such as the USA have been reluctant to commit to such globally-binding agreements, and may perhaps also explain why the EU's climate policy over the past two decades has 'probably not made as much as one part per million difference . . . the rhetoric, the plethora of initiatives, directives, and interventions has not been matched by outcomes' (Helm 2009: 1).

International coordination of industrial policy is thus needed for low-carbon industrialization, but faces daunting challenges in dealing with strategic and opportunistic national behaviour.

10.3.2 *Objectives of low-carbon industrial policy*

A second implication of the need for low-carbon industrialization for industrial policy is for the fundamental objective of a low-carbon industrial policy and the cooperation and coordination to underpin it. Should it be, first and foremost, (as has been the case in current global climate negotiations) about carbon reduction, or on human development (as growing numbers of commentators have been arguing)?

However such coordination is achieved, it might mean that industrial policies will face certain (more) international constraints (policy space for supporting carbon-intensive manufactured goods may for instance increasingly shrink), but will have to balance global pressures for climate change mitigation against national pressures for job creation and infrastructure.

In Section 10.3.1 the difficulty of reaching a substantial international agreement on climate change was discussed. There was noted that many developing countries potentially have much to gain from carbon-intensive industrialization, particularly as they face struggles for job creation and provision of basic services, including electricity.

The IEA (2009a) estimates that more than 1.5 billion people worldwide lack access to electricity. High unemployment is critical in emerging regions such as Africa and Latin America, and industrial development remains one of the engines of job creation. As put by Ojha (2008: 324), for most developing countries 'the

[6] The EU's 20-20-20 Climate Change Package adopted in January 2008 aims to reduce EU emissions to 20 per cent below 1990 levels by 2020 and raise the proportion of energy from renewable to 20 per cent by 2020 (Helm 2009).

more pressing need obviously is achieving poverty reduction rather than controlling carbon emissions'. This should be seen against the background of coal remaining one of the most abundant and cheapest sources of energy in developing countries. For instance, in India it accounted for over 47 per cent of energy supply in 2005 (Ojha 2008), and South Africa started the construction of a huge coal-fired power station only months after it became a party to the Copenhagen Accord of December 2009 (which is, however, not legally binding).

It is not that these countries are not concerned with the impacts of climate change. Rather it is a question of addressing the challenge without compromising on demands for development and rising living standards; the latter demands are likely to win in any 'contest'. As recognized by Helm (2009: 6):

> The key challenge for climate change policy is how the developing world can raise its standards of living towards those of the developed countries and at the same time global carbon emissions, and other environmental damage, can be reduced.

With this in mind, many have criticized the United Nations Framework Convention on Climate Change (UNFCCC) multilateral-type of approach of putting carbon reductions ahead of people's development, and see the failure of the Copenhagen Climate Change Conference (COP15) in December 2009 as a result of this misplaced emphasis. As was put forcefully by the Hartwell Paper:

> Climate change is better understood as a persistent condition that must be coped with and can only be partially managed more-or-less well . . . it is not straightforwardly an environmental problem either. It is axiomatically as much an energy problem, or a land use problem, and may be better approached through these avenues than as a problem of managing the behaviour of the Earth's climate. (Prins et al. 2010: 16)

Similarly, Bondre (2010: 16) saw the failure of the COP15 meeting as due to the singular focus on GHG reduction, stating that climate change is a 'multi-pronged challenged' and should not just have 'a singular focus on global warming' as it would drive polarization. Tol (2010, 2002a, 2002b) and others have argued that, because poverty is a fundamental cause of climate change, that the best strategy is to speed up economic growth and development—it is seen in these quarters as even better than emissions reduction. Also, it has been argued that developed countries may find it 'cheaper to compensate poorer countries for the climate change damages caused, rather than to pay for reducing their own greenhouse gas emissions' (Tol 2010: 36).

Some have also asked about the effectiveness of advanced regions, such as the EU, trying to adopt expensive measures to reduce their GHG emissions. According to Helm (2009: 6) '. . . there may be much cheaper ways, for example by preserving tropical rainforests or decarbonizing China and India's rapid coal-based economic growth'.

The implication is that once the objective of low-carbon industrial policy is to promote sustainable human development, issues such as these raised above become important, and start to shift to centre stage in the debate, resulting not only in different approaches to industrial policy (more internationally coordinated), but also in industrial policy with different content (such as compensation and transfers from advanced to emerging countries).

10.3.3 *Innovation-driven industrial policy*

Achievement of a low-carbon revolution is clearly impossible without innovation and technological change. Innovation is a complex process, and requires a systems approach—as is seen on a country basis in governments' efforts to enhance their national systems of innovation and on an international level by the promoting of research, development, and demonstration (RD&D) by the UNFCCC, the Major Economies Forum (MEF),[7] and the IEA. It is also a process wherein entrepreneurship plays a leading role. Entrepreneurship is vital for innovation (Schumpeter 1911) and entrepreneurial innovation has already played an important role in reducing CO_2 emissions. The Soviet Union and Maoist China were examples of large economies that had little prospect of declining emissions—indeed these countries saw very rapid CO_2 emissions during their industrialization in the twentieth century.

Innovation can be a gradual progress, and as far as low-carbon industrial policies are concerned, this will have to be taken into consideration. It poses, however, difficult questions in terms of capital investments and returns on these. For instance, as discussed by Prins et al. (2010), moving to a low-carbon economy will require industrial policy measures towards innovation and technological change that have different outcomes over the short, medium, and long term. Over the short term the emphasis needs to be on improving energy efficiency; over the medium term, on phasing in the greater use of renewable energy and energy diversification; and over the longer term on introducing more path-breaking technologies for low-carbon production. The remainder of this subsection discusses energy efficiency, renewable energy and energy diversification, and low-carbon production technologies.

10.3.3.1 ENERGY EFFICIENCY

Energy efficiency entails using less energy in production and consumption. Examples include development of 'smart grids', improvements in building energy efficiency, industrial energy efficiency, and vehicle efficiency, including the promotion of electric/hybrid and hydrogen-based vehicles (IEA

[7] An objective of the MEF is to double expenditures on RD&D for low carbon technologies by 2015 (IEA 2009b).

2009b). Energy efficiency in industrial processes can contribute significantly to reduced GHG emissions—Trudeau and Tam (2009) estimate that energy savings in the industry could contribute to a reduction of up to 5.7 Gt in CO_2 emissions by 2050. Globally coordinated industrial policy and cooperation in industrial policy is required, since developing countries can reduce their industrial emissions significantly over the short to medium term through adoption of currently existing best available technologies (BAT). Prins et al. (2010) for instance report that BAT in the steel industry is globally diffused; it would reduce CO_2 emissions annually by around 340 million tons. Similarly, significant reductions may be obtained if coal-powered plants could adopt best-available practice (IEA 2009b). Industrial policies facilitating learning, copying, adopting, and experimentation on a sector-by-sector basis (the nature, needs, and requirements for improving energy efficiency differs substantially between industrial sectors) will be needed (Trudeau and Tam 2009).

It should be noted that though improvement in industrial energy efficiency can make an important short-term contribution, it may not necessarily lead to significantly lower energy demand or reduced GHG emissions. This is because of the income-effect of energy savings—people may channel their energy savings into increased consumption on other, more carbon-intensive goods. This means that carbon taxes may be needed as an industrial policy measure to facilitate longer-term reductions in GHGs from energy efficiency (Helm 2009). And industries may expand faster than the savings they establish.

10.3.3.2 ENERGY DIVERSIFICATION

Energy diversification requires clear industrial policy initiatives to increase the share of non-fossil fuels in energy demand. Energy diversification would mean greater use of nuclear and renewable energy sources—clean energy. Such diversification is enjoying high priority in many countries, not just based on concerns about climate change, but also about energy security and the possible opportunities it may hold for industrialization and job creation. For instance, in the latter regard the South African government estimates that 300,000 new jobs could be created in the country through renewable energy production over a period of ten years. The country's Industrial Development Corporation envisages a US$10 billion investment in renewable energies between 2010 and 2015 (Creamer 2010). Diversifications of energy towards renewable and nuclear sources are therefore set to continue for these reasons.

The main sources[8] of renewable energy include wind, solar, bioenergy, geothermal, and wave (marine) energy, although at present most RD&D into

[8] Nuclear power is not a renewable source of energy because it is dependent on uranium supplies. However, it can provide substantial non-carbon energy over the medium term, subject to risks (Barrett 2009).

renewable energy is going into solar power (see Table 10.2). Marine and hydroelectricity is relatively neglected, as also noted in the IEA (2009b) reports on renewable energy initiatives.

According to Barrett (2009), the main task is to reduce the relative cost of these sources—currently they are much more expensive than carbon sources of energy and thus uneconomical. He points out that lowering their costs will involve not only technological innovation in the energy generation process itself, but also in complementary technologies in the transmission and storage—especially of wind and solar energy, where the resource is often located at some distance from where the energy is demanded. It will also require a high and rising price of carbon. Carbon can be priced through putting a tax on it or using a market-based mechanism such as a permits or trading scheme. A large literature has appeared on the pros and cons of various ways of pricing carbon. Many argued that taxes are better than permits or trading schemes (e.g. Helm 2009; Nordhaus 2009).

The major trading schemes that have so far been created for pricing carbon include the Regional Greenhouse Gas Initiative in the north eastern USA and the European Union's Emission Trading Scheme (ETS). Carbon-pricing mechanisms, in particular cap and trade proposals and carbon taxes, have generated substantial criticism. Prins et al. (2010: 9) claim that:

> The huge efforts that have been invested in elaborating complex top-down regulatory regimes and in particular the ambitions for regional—let alone global—cap and trade regimes to regulate carbon by price can now be seen to have been barren in their stated aims although profitable for some in unexpected and unwelcome ways.

There have also been concerns that energy demand is highly inelastic, so that a higher price for carbon will have little impact—apart from hurting the poor.

Other criticisms concern the difficulties in establishing a price for carbon (see Helm 2009), reflected in the fact that governments have so far been unsuccessful in cooperating to increase the price of carbon (Barrett 2009). Indeed many have pointed to the volatility of carbon prices in the ETS as creating uncertainty. Helm (2009) provides extensive criticism of the EU's ETS, arguing that it is has been a failure due to political compromises and lobbying by polluters—a typical problem of any industrial policy. As Helm describes, 'a tradable permits regime creates new markets, which in turn create rents for participants. There is now a rapidly growing set of vested financial interests with every incentive to lobby for the retention and development of the EU ETS' (ibid.: 9).

The challenge for low-carbon industrial policies is how the incentive problem for getting entrepreneurial investment into developing and rolling out low-carbon technologies can be successfully overcome. Fundamentally, there may be substantial entrepreneurial opportunities in low-carbon industrialization for developing countries. Many are already looking at China's example to provide the lead and create further incentives and opportunities for industrially lagging countries to use low-carbon technologies as a way to catch up—similar to the way that it provided opportunities for catching up in conventional manufacturing. China, the world's largest energy consumer, is already a world leader in wind power and solar energy, and is making strides in expanding nuclear energy generation.

10.3.3.3 CARBON CAPTURE, STORAGE, AND SEQUESTRATION

Over the longer term more path-breaking technologies for low-carbon production and energy diversification are needed. How can industrial policy promote these? One answer is that industrial policy should invest in mechanisms for directly removing, storing, and sequestering carbon from the atmosphere (Barrett 2009). As put by Helm (2009: 21), 'unless coal can be burnt in a less harmful way... there will be little or no progress in abating global emissions'. Such carbon capture and storage (CCS) mechanisms are currently expensive, ranging from US$25 per ton of CO_2 to US$90 per ton of CO_2 (Barrett 2009). Stimulating further investment in these will also require, as in the case of energy-efficiency measures, that a positive and increasing price of carbon be established to underpin industrial policy for a low-carbon economy.

But carbon pricing will in itself not be sufficient to stimulate investment in CSS. In addition, subsidies to low-carbon technologies and goods will be required (greater spending on RD&D), as well as industrial policy measures to reduce carbon leakage.

Consider RD&D: IEA (2009b) provides a discussion of current RD&D expenditures of mainly OECD countries and the aims of these expenditures across ten categories of RD&D in low-carbon technologies.[9] These expenditures are summarized in Table 10.2.

Table 10.2 indicates that, based on available data, by far the most significant bulk of RD&D expenditures to promote low-carbon economies takes place in the area of advanced vehicle technologies—almost twice as much as on the second most sizeable area, CCS.

According to the IEA (2009b), advanced vehicle technology RD&D is particularly focused on the development of plug-in vehicles, hybrid-electric vehicles, lightweight materials, energy storage systems, hydrogen fuel cell

[9] There are a number of efforts to globally coordinate RD&D efforts. These include initiatives by the MEF, the UFCCC, and the IEA. The MEF aims to double expenditures on RD&D for low carbon technologies by 2015. Other major initiatives for low-carbon technological RD&D include the Carbon Sequestration Leadership Forum, the International Partnership for the Hydrogen Economy, and the International Thermonuclear Experimental Reactor.

Table 10.2. Estimated RD&D expenditure on low-carbon industrialization in selected countries, 2009 (in US$ million)

Country	Advanced vehicles	Bioenergy	CCS	Building energy	Industrial energy	Lower coal emissions	Smart grids	Solar energy	Wind energy
USA	539.4	287.6	594.0	85.4	79.9	217.2	60.2	190.3	31.7
Japan	319.6	18.7	36.8	139.0	143.9	78.9	94.4	1.0	1.9
Australia	189.9	6.9	123.5	22.7	26.4	100.2	20.8	39.0	5.7
France	135.8	40.2	38.8	32.8	16.7		12.2	47.9	2.5
EC	94.0	19.2	31.9	—	—	43.0	18.9	44.4	15.9
Korea	73.4	4.7	12.2	8.0	81.9	16.9	27.7	58.3	18.4
Italy	62.9	17.5	11.7	83.3	13.2	16.1	90.6	93.6	4.4
Germany	57.4	34.7	8.3	31.6	11.0	47.2	57.4	79.0	49.9
Canada	36.1	43.2	19.0	19.2	12.6	17.1	12.2	13.6	8.3
UK	19.0	24.8	6.5	8.2	1.8	2.0	15.6	40.0	30.9
Russia	15.2	14.5	0.9	22.6	23.4	5.0	9.6	6.9	
Brazil		62.8							
India		10.5						20.6	4.3
China		5.1						29.3	11.7
Totals	1542.7	590.4	883.6	452.8	410.8	543.6	419.6	663.9	185.6

Source: Compiled from IEA data (2009b).

vehicles, and low-rolling-resistance tyres. These can be seen as energy-saving technologies.

The second largest category in terms of RD&D spending is on CCS. According to the IEA (2009b), most research here is focused on direct capture of CO_2 from the air, on development of CO_2 storage facilities, on CO_2 pipeline transport, and on using CO_2 in enhanced oil recovery methods and cement production. This is followed by RD&D expenditure on solar energy, with the USA, Italy, and Germany leading the field. Most solar energy applications aim at providing electricity through photovoltaic or concentrated solar power (IEA 2009b). Solar energy is seen by many as providing particular opportunities for green growth to developing countries, particularly those in Africa.

Industrial policy for innovation-driven low-carbon industrialization will, in addition to carbon pricing and subsidized RD&D, also have to deal with carbon leakage. Carbon leakage refers to the practice whereby firms and factories can migrate to countries where carbon prices are lower. Dealing with carbon leakage will require industrial policy, but also trade policy and an alignment of trade and industrial policies. This is discussed again in detail below in Section 10.3.5. For now, it can be mentioned that industrial policy may deal with carbon leakage through industry-level agreements on the global scale—hence again requiring coordination of industrial policies. In this regard sector approaches, agreements, and mechanisms have been called on to support low-carbon industrialization. These would entail sector-level agreements—for instance in the steel industry—to move towards particular emission standards, working towards adopting and spreading the best available technologies in this regard, and policing of the agreements (Prins et al. 2010; Wooders 2010).

10.3.4 *Aligning industrial policy with trade*

Industrial policies aimed at fostering a low-carbon economy will have important repercussions for trade and foreign direct investment (FDI)—and hence trade policies. Hence a paper on industrial policy and climate change cannot omit a discussion of the foremost trade issues that may arise. Note, however, that a comprehensive discussion of the relationship between climate change and trade falls outside the scope of this paper—the interested reader is referred to Hufbauer, Charnovitz, and Kim (2009) for a recent overview.

One of the central global issues that has spilled over from the industrial low-carbon debate onto the trade arena is related to concerns about 'carbon leakage', as was already mentioned in Section 10.3.3.3. The fear is that regions that take the lead in moving to a low-carbon industrial base could become competitively disadvantaged. Some have even added to this the fear the possibility that the overall impact of such carbon leakages could be that global emissions *increase*, as they may create huge incentives for carbon production in other regions (Helm 2009). UNCTAD (2010:36) stresses the incentive this would create for many developing countries, stating that 'for poor countries in dire need of expanding their productive capacities such foreign investment could potentially generate large development gains'.

In the absence of globally binding agreements on low-carbon regulations and a global price of carbon, two alternative mechanisms have been mooted to deal with this potential problem. The one is border tax adjustments (BTAs)—tariffs on the carbon content of imported goods. The other is the development of emission trading schemes requiring importers to buy emission rights domestically to offset imported emissions.

BTAs currently appear to be the most favoured approach, at least politically. The approach boils down to getting industrial and trade policies consistent. But can it be effective? While there are proponents, a growing number of economists have in recent times cast doubt on the desirability and feasibility of BTAs.

Dong and Whalley (2008) discuss some of the difficulties with using BTAs to affect emissions. First, they note that it is growth rather than trade that is the major contributor to emissions. Second, emissions differ more substantially between countries than products, posing the problem of whether trade policy should discriminate against products, or countries—and conflict with the non-discrimination clauses of the WTO. Third, WTO-based tariff measures are likely to have a small impact on emissions because most emissions are in a small number of sectors where output is not directly traded, such as electricity generation and transport. Fourth, it is difficult to define and agree on what could be regarded as 'environmentally sensitive' goods and services to treat separately in trade. Moreover, as UNCTAD (2010) also indicates, it is difficult to measure or agree to measure the carbon intensity of individual goods. Fifth, the administration of BTAs based on the carbon content of imports will be a very costly process and difficult to implement. Finally, Dong and Whalley (2008) also point to the danger that once BTAs are used governments may want to engage in further 'strategic' trade policies to try to offset other perceived sources of competitive disadvantage, which could herald a new era of retreating from freer global trade to protectionism. In other words BTAs could be misused for protectionism—or 'old' industrial policies.

Hence in the context of climate change industrial policies should guard against being usurped by strategic trade policies due to misuse of BTA. Careful alignment with trade is needed; moreover, the pitfalls yet again emphasize the importance of globally coordinated industrial policies.

10.3.5 *Funding industrial policies for a low-carbon economy*

There is recognition that all of the above will require huge amounts of investment—by both private and public sector. Financial resources would need to be made available for developing countries. From whom and how such funds should be channelled remain largely unresolved global questions. Proposals include the reform of the Clean Development Mechanism and the establishment of international funding pools. More FDI into low-carbon projects in developing countries are needed (UNCTAD 2010).

At COP15 member states agreed (as part of the Copenhagen Accord) to create a funding mechanism to support mitigation of climate change in developing countries. It has subsequently been estimated that in order to achieve the targets in GHG reductions contained in the Copenhagen Accord, at least US$440 billion in additional annual investment will be needed between 2010 and 2015, and that this would rise to US$1.2 trillion per year by 2030 (Creamer 2010). Other estimates of the investment required for climate change mitigation have come from the IEA. According to the IEA (2009a), in order to limit CO_2 levels to 450 ppm by 2030 will require additional investment in energy infrastructure and capital to the amount of US $10.5 trillion. Half of this would be in transport and around US$1.5 trillion would be specifically needed in industrial and second generation biofuel production. Developing countries are estimated to require around US$197 billion in extra investment by 2020 (IEA 2009a).

For developing countries, international transfers will be a key source of funding a low-carbon economy, as well as adaptation. However, taxation of CO_2—broadening the resource-base and providing incentives for switching from carbon will also be important. And developing countries seem to be taking such taxes seriously—e.g. in 2010 South Africa introduced a carbon tax on vehicles (Van der Merwe 2010a, 2010b).

Generally though, especially coming after the financial crisis, many developing (and advanced) countries will find it hard to scrape together substantial funds for supporting mitigation efforts and particularly low-carbon industrialization. Here the entrepreneurial perspective comes into play again. As UNCTAD (2010: 24) stress, 'the financial contribution of the private sector is essential for achieving progress in making economies worldwide more climate-friendly, particularly in view of the huge public deficits worldwide'.

These efforts will need to be supported on a global level by much more FDI into low-carbon production in developing countries. Such FDI is seen as an important channel for transferring knowledge about low-carbon technology and for limiting carbon leakage (UNCTAD 2010) According to UNCTAD (2010), the estimated FDI in 2009 into renewable, recycling, and low-carbon manufacturing was around US$90 billion, with around 40 per cent of this going to developing countries. Private funding will thus be an important source of funds for mitigating climate change in developing counties. There are some encouraging signs of such funding already emerging in SSA. For instance, private investors have established, at the time of writing, at least two funds for developing and rolling out low-carbon technologies on the continent, including a technology development fund and a technology deployment fund (Van der Merwe 2010b). With aid to developing countries shrinking, and aid perhaps being diverted to climate change funds, and in view of the many practical difficulties in making operational the planned global funds for addressing climate change, the need for industrial policy to engage with the private sector and elicit private funding is likely to be crucial in getting low-carbon industrialization efforts financially supported.

10.4 Concluding remarks

More than fifty years ago Raul Prebisch pointed out that 'industrialization of the periphery has always been a controversial subject, not only in the centers, but also in the peripheral countries themselves' (Prebisch 1959: 251). Given rising global inequalities, the failure of industrialization in the poorest countries, particularly in SSA, and the challenges of climate change, the industrialization of the periphery will undoubtedly become an even more controversial subject in times to come.

This chapter started out by pointing to industry as a major emitter of GHG, contributing to global climate change. It is also a major driver of economic growth and development. The benefits of industrialization are sorely needed in a very unequal world, where more than a billion people still live in absolute poverty. But in light of the likely economic impact of climate change, industrialization needs to take place in a way that mitigates climate change and facilitates adaptation.

Industrialization in the coming decades will face clear costs and benefits. This chapter made the case why selected policies needed to deal with such industrialization in the midst of the climate change challenge. The costs implied by climate change will be incurred because countries' entrepreneurs need to shift their firms onto a different production technology frontier—changing the way goods are produced. Investment in new techniques and processes as well as shifts to lower-carbon energy sources are required. These all imply costs, and hence the guidance of industrial policies to minimize costs. Carbon itself will have to be priced, and will have to become gradually more expensive. This will result in more costly production, at least over the medium term.

However, a transition to a lower-carbon industrialization process also offers benefits and opportunities. These include opportunities for producing low-carbon products. Many developing countries could benefit from this green growth if they could marshal the adequate and timely responses through industrial policies. These could also generate substantial savings in the cost of using fossil fuels, if successful. In addition to these direct benefits, achieving a sustainable low-carbon industrialization path would result in indirect spill-over benefits such as a cleaner environment and health improvements.

There are many pitfalls in applying industrial policy. From past debates about industrial policy most of these are known—they revolve around the imperfect information possessed by governments and the potential for industrial policies to be captured by special interest groups. Avoiding such government failures remain importants. In the context of climate change, however, perhaps the most important prerequisite for avoiding pitfalls is that industrial policies need greater international coordination and cooperation than ever before. This has been the central argument of this chapter. Achieving such international coordination is perhaps, given the possible adverse impacts of climate change, one of the greatest challenges facing global development. This chapter noticed a number of stumbling blocks, including the fact that developing and advanced economies face different objectives and challenges in low-carbon industrialization. For developing countries, job creation and the extension of energy to their populations are key issues; for advanced economies it is job creation and energy security. Industrial policies for low-carbon industrialization need to be designed and coordinated around these imperatives.

The most likely path forward for low-carbon industrialization that will be consistent with the needs of human development may be one supported by use of nuclear power, that also uses coal, but that uses carbon capture and storage technologies as far as possible to reduce carbon in the atmosphere. These need to be accompanied by a diversification into renewable energy sources over the medium to longer term. Hence industrial policies need to have different short- and long-term goals. Cooperation—between the big emerging powers of China and India on the one hand and the USA and EU on the other—in reducing carbon emissions would afford ILCs some leeway to achieve growth from cheaper supplies of coal, while moving at an appropriate tempo to a carbon-free economy. Of course, this leeway should be supported by the large emerging powers and advanced countries by transfers of technology and climate funding.

For SSA and large parts of Latin America, the fundamental challenge is not to make a short- or medium-term contribution to the mitigation of global warming, but to adapt industrialization to the consequences of global warming. SSA industrial development can not be divorced from agriculture. More research is needed to draw out the implications for industrial policies in Africa, where the base will be agriculture, which is the livelihood of a majority of the population, and will, according to most estimates, be severely affected by global warming. Hence the best response in Africa could be to promote job-intensive growth, the rolling out of social security nets, and the encouragement of entrepreneurship—in other words generally increase the resilience of the population to adapt to climate changes and climate shocks. For this, sociopolitical stability and continued improvements in governance will be required from African governments. Advanced countries should support and rewards such improvements, inter alia by coordination of their own policies (such as scrapping expensive subsidies for farmers in advanced economies) with that of developing countries. Ultimately, international coordination of industrial policies leading to a change in the nature of development cooperation—moving it from donor-driven aid towards partnerships—will be required if the climate change challenge is to be credibly shouldered. Partnerships that are consistent with local needs, conditions, and abilities, and that give developing-country policy-makers, through their industrial policies, a driving-seat role in their countries' development.

References

Altenburg, T. (2009). 'Industrial Policy for Low and Lower-Middle Income Countries'. Paper presented at the UNU-WIDER, UNU-MERIT, and UNIDO Workshop on 'Pathways to Industrialization in the 21st Century: New Challenges and Emerging Paradigms', Maastricht, The Netherlands, 22–23 October.

Barrett, S. (2009). 'The Coming Global Climate-Technology Revolution', *Journal of Economic Perspectives*, 23 (2): 53–75.

Bondre, N. (2010). 'Whence Climate Skepticism?, *Global Change*, 75:16–19.

Brandt, U. S., and G. T. Svendsen (2003). 'Fighting Windmills? EU Industrial Interest and Global Climate Negotiations'. IME Working Paper 37/03. University of Southern Denmark, Department of Environmental and Business Economics.

Creamer, T. (2010). 'Yearly Green Investments of $440bn Needed to Meet Climate Target', *Engineering News*, 23 July. Available at http://www.engineeringnews.co.za/article/yearly-green-investments-of-440bn-needed-to-meet-climate-target-2010-07-23 (accessed 14 August 2012).

Dong, Y., and J. Whalley (2008). 'Carbon, Trade Policy, and Carbon Free Trade Areas'. Trade Working Paper 1847. East Asian Bureau of Economic Research.

Frankhauser, S. (1995). *Valuing Climate Change: The Economics of the Greenhouse*. London: Earthscan.

Girod, B., A. Wiek, H. Mieg, and M. Hulme (2009). 'The Evolution of the IPCC's Emission Scenarios', *Environmental Science Policy*, 12 (2): 103–18.

Helm, D. (2009). 'EU Climate-Change Policy—A Critique'. In D. Helm and C. Hepburn (eds), *The Economics and Politics of Climate Change*. Oxford: Oxford University Press.

Hope, C.W. (2006). 'The Marginal Impact of CO2 from PAGE2002. An Integrated Assessment Model Incorporating IPCC's Five Reasons for Concern', *Integrated Assessment Journal*, 6 (1): 19–56.

Hufbauer, G. C., S. Charnovitz, and J. Kim (2009). *Global Warming and the World Trading System*. Washington DC: Peterson Institute.

International Energy Agency (IEA) (2009a). *World Energy Outlook 2009*. Paris: IEA.

——(2009b). *Global Gaps in Clean Energy Research, Development and Demonstration*. Paris: IEA.

Maddison, D. J. (2003). 'The Amenity Value of the Climate: The Household Production Function Approach', *Resource and Energy Economics*, 25 (2): 155–75.

Martin, P. (2010). 'Climate Change, Agricultural Development, and Migration'. GMF Study Team on Climate-Induced Migration. Washington DC.

Mendelsohn, R. D, M. E. Schlesinger, and L. J. Williams (2000). 'Comparing Impacts across Climate Models', *Integrated Assessment*, 1 (1): 37–48.

Naudé, W. A., and L. Alcorta (2010). 'Industrial Policy and Environmental Sustainability: The Challenge after COP15'. WIDER Angle January 2010. Available at: www.wider.unu.edu/publications/newsletter/articles-2010/en_GB/01-2010-wider-angle/ (accessed 29 July 2012).

Nordhaus, W. D. (2007). 'A Review of the Stern Review on the Economics of Climate', *Journal of Economic Literature*, 45 (3): 686–702.

Nordhaus, W. D., and Z. Yang (1996). 'RICE: A Regional Dynamic General Equilibrium Model of Optimal Climate Change Policy', *American Economic Review*, 86 (4): 741–65.

Ojha, V. P. (2008). 'Carbon Emissions Reduction Strategies and Poverty Alleviation in India', *Environment and Development Economics*, 14: 323–48.

Plambeck, E. L., and C. W. Hope (1996). 'PAGE95—An Updated Valuation of the Impacts of Global Warming', *Energy Policy*, 24 (9): 783–93.

Prebisch, R. (1959). 'Commercial Policy in Underdeveloped Countries', *American Economic Review*, 49 (2): 251–73.

Prins, G., I. Galiana, C. Green, R. Grundmann, A. Korhola, F. Laird, T. Nordhaus, R. Pielke S. Rayner, D. Sarewitz, M. Shellenberger, N. Stehr, and H. Tezuko (2010). 'The Hartwell Paper: A New Direction for Climate Policy after the Crash of 2009'. London/Oxford: University of Oxford and London School of Economics. Available at: www.lse.ac.uk/collections/mackinderProgramme/theHartwellPaper/ (accessed August 6, 2010).

Schelling, T. (2009). 'International Coordination to Address the Climate Challenge', *Innovations*, 4 (4): 13–21.

Schumpeter, J. A. (1911). *The Theory of Economic Development*. Cambridge, MA: Harvard University Press (1934 trans. R. Opie).

Stern, N. (2006). *The Economics of Climate Change (The Stern Report)*. Cambridge: Cambridge University Press.

Szirmai, A. (2009). 'Industrialization and an Engine of Growth in Developing Countries, 1950–2005', Paper presented at the UNU-WIDER, UNU-MERIT and UNIDO Workshop on 'Pathways to Industrialization in the 21st Century: New Challenges and Emerging Paradigms', Maastricht, The Netherlands, 22–23 October.

Tol, R. S. J. (2002a). 'Estimates of the Damage Costs of Climate Change—Part I: Benchmark Estimates', *Environmental and Resource Economics*, 21 (1): 47–73.

——(2002b). 'Estimates of the Damage Costs of Climate Change—Part II: Dynamic Estimates', *Environmental and Resource Economics*, 21 (2): 135–60.

——(2010). 'The Economic Effects of Climate Change', *Journal of Economic Perspectives*, 23 (2): 29–51.

Tol, R. S. J., and G. Yohe (2006). 'A Review of the Stern Review', *World Economics*, 7 (4): 233–50.

Trudeau, N., and C. Tam (2009). 'Energy Technology Perspectives Transition for Industry' Presentation. Paris: IEA.

UNCTAD (2010). *World Investment Report 2010: Investing in a Low Carbon Economy*. New York and Geneva: United Nations.

Van der Merwe, C. (2010a). 'SA Business Should Investigate Carbon Tax Implications', *Engineering News*, 20 July. Available at http://www.engineeringnews.co.za/article/sa-business-should-investigate-carbon-tax-implications-webber-wentzel-2010-07-20 (accessed on 14 August 2012).

——(2010b). 'Private Investors Make $200m available for Clean Energy Projects', *Engineering News*, 19 July. Available at http://www.engineeringnews.co.za/article/private-investors-make-200m-available-for-clean-energy-projects-2010-07-19 (accessed 14 August 2012).

Wooders, P. (2010). 'International Sectoral Approaches and Agreements: Case Studies of the Steel Sector in China, India and Japan—Policy Recommendations', *Climate Strategies*, July 27th. Available at www.climatestrategies.org/

World Bank (2010). *World Development Report 2010: Development and Climate Change*. Washington DC: The World Bank.

11

Global Asymmetries and their Implications for Climate and Industrial Policies

Thomas Gries

11.1 Introduction

In today's globalized world there is a complex relationship between economic activity and the environment. In addition, there is a feedback mechanism from the environment to economic activity and welfare. Besides the fact that economic development is a driving force for climate change, policies that aim to mitigate global warming may also impact negatively on the speed of global development processes. We aim to demonstrate that there can be no global-scale solution for the problem of global warming that does not account for the effects that climate policy has on economic development, especially for less-developed countries. Moreover, the causal interdependencies are highly asymmetric. Looking at the variety of countries in the world, we observe major asymmetries and heterogeneities. There are asymmetries in welfare, technology, industrial structure, pollution, the accumulation of a pollution stock, and in the way countries are affected by climate change. The effects of these asymmetries in the world economy are neither adequately understood nor taken into account. This chapter seeks to highlight the main effects of global asymmetries on the efficiency of a global climate and industrial policy, and to illustrate the distribution problems that arise from such a policy. Since economic theory is well developed with respect to environmental economics we can use the associated findings as a starting point for analysing the asymmetry issue.

11.2 Global asymmetries

An important step towards understanding the relationship between economic development and global climate policy is to understand the enormous

Table 11.1. Income and population in the world economy

	Population share (p_i)	Mean income (μ_i)	Gini (G_i)	Overlapping index (O_i)
Third world (poorer than or equal to Brazil)	0.76	1,171	0.494	0.89
Middle class	0.08	4,609	0.462	0.54
First world (equal or richer than Italy)	0.16	10,919	0.344	0.25
World	1.00	3,031	0.659	
Between-group Gini			0.449 (68%)	
Within-group Gini $\sum_i s_i G_i O_i$			0.210 (32%)	

Source: based on Milanovic and Yitzhaki (2002: table 16).

asymmetries and heterogeneities in the global economy. We consider the six most important of these.

11.2.1 *Income: poor versus rich*

It is only possible to comprehend what happens in international talks on climate policy and to understand the positions of the different countries if one understands the major income asymmetries and wealth disparities in the participating countries. Milanovic and Yitzhaki (2002) provide a good overview of existing disparities and income inequalities in the global economy. Table 11.1 shows these disparities using mean income, Gini coefficients and the overlapping index. A simple comparison of the mean incomes in this table reveals that at the beginning of this century three-quarters of the world's population earned less than 10 per cent of the incomes of the richest 16 per cent of the world's population.

Only 16 per cent of the world's population live in the rich countries.[1] They produce and enjoy 58 per cent of world income. By contrast, 76 per cent of the world's population live in poor countries and generate only 29 per cent of world income. During the last 150 years of growth the richest 16 per cent of the world's population were able to accumulate an estimated share of over 80 per cent of the world's wealth. In other words, these 16 per cent own the main share of real world capital and, in turn, most of the world's firms and corporations. This affluent population group also participates in 60 per cent of international trade and an even greater proportion of international financial transactions. So, on the one hand, the richest 16 per cent of today's population have been able to generate the technological and economic growth that

[1] According to Milanovic and Yitzhaki (2002) this group consists of the G7 or G7-equivalent states, the latter having at least the per capita income of the G7.

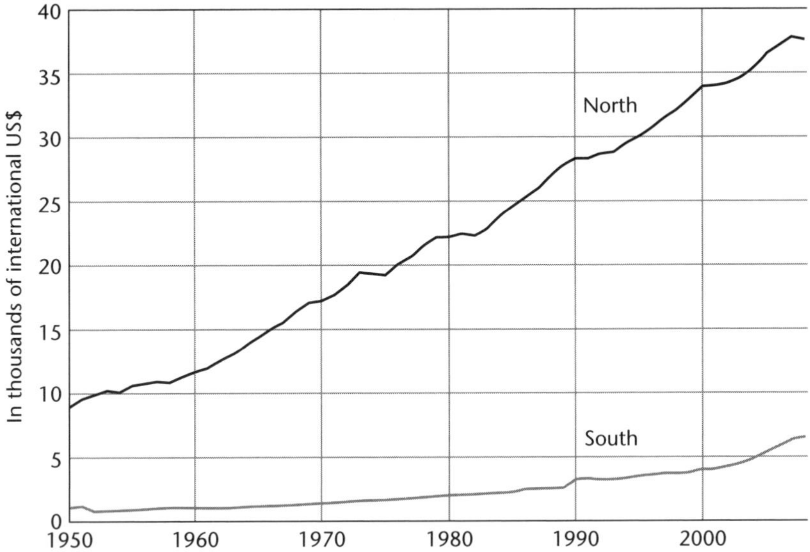

Figure 11.1a. Income per capita, North and South

Notes: *The rich northern countries of the G20, or the North, are Australia, Canada, France, Germany, Italy, Japan, the UK and the USA. **The poor southern countries of the G20, or the South, are Argentina, Brazil, China, India, Indonesia, Mexico, Russia, Saudi Arabia, South Africa, South Korea, and Turkey. *** GDP data for (a) China and South Korea (South) is included since 1952, (b) Indonesia (South) is included since 1960, (c) Germany (FRG and GDR) (North) is included since 1970, (d) Saudi Arabia (South) is included since 1986, and (e) Russia (South) is included since 1990. Data for the former USSR are not included.

Source: Penn World Table 7.0.

has led to progress in human development, but also to the major disparities we observe today. On the other hand, even if the disparities in per capita income remain drastic, absolute economic activity, which can be an indicator for political power, indeed shows that the developing world has not only started to grow more rapidly, but has already undergone a considerable catching-up process. These developments, described in Figures 11.1a to 11.3b, have clear effects on the functioning and mechanisms of global governance. Because most of the economically successful countries are in the northern hemisphere we refer to these countries as the rich North,[2] in contrast to the poor South.[3] To simplify the discussion we do not take all countries into account but rather focus on the G20 states. The G20 represent by far the largest share of global economic activity, and using them we can demonstrate the asymmetries in

[2] The rich countries of the G20, or the North, are the USA, Germany, Japan, the UK, France, Italy, Canada, and Australia.

[3] The poor countries of the G20, or the South, are China, Brazil, Russia, India, South Korea, Mexico, Turkey, Indonesia, Saudi Arabia, South Africa, and Argentina.

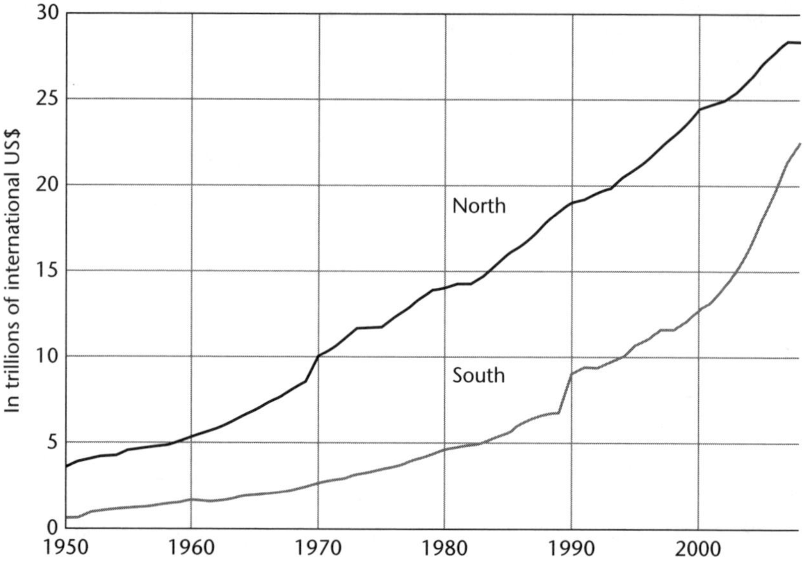

Figure 11.1b. Total income, North and South

Note: *For a definition of the country sets 'North' and 'South' and for a note on specific difficulties with the data, see Figure 11.1a.

Source: Penn World Table 7.0.

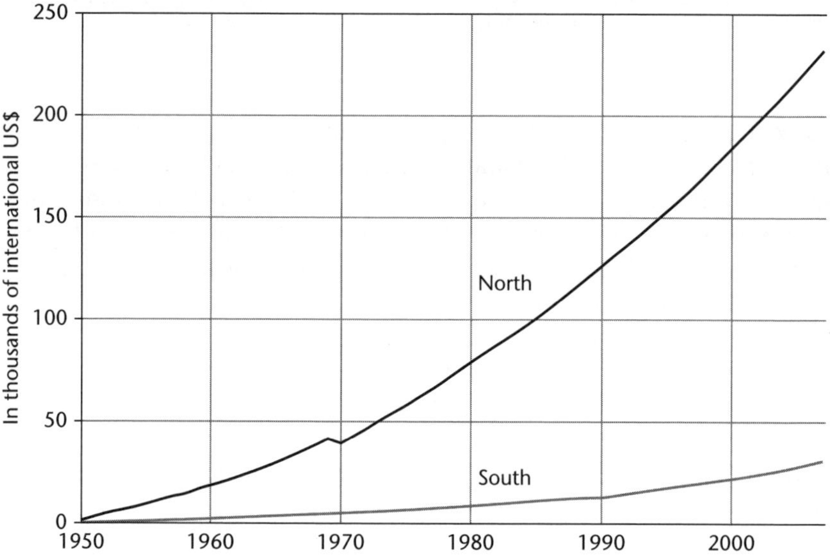

Figure 11.2a. Real capital stock per capita, North and South

Note: *For a definition of the country sets 'North' and 'South' and for a note on specific difficulties with the data, see Figure 11.1a.

Source: Penn World Table 7.0.

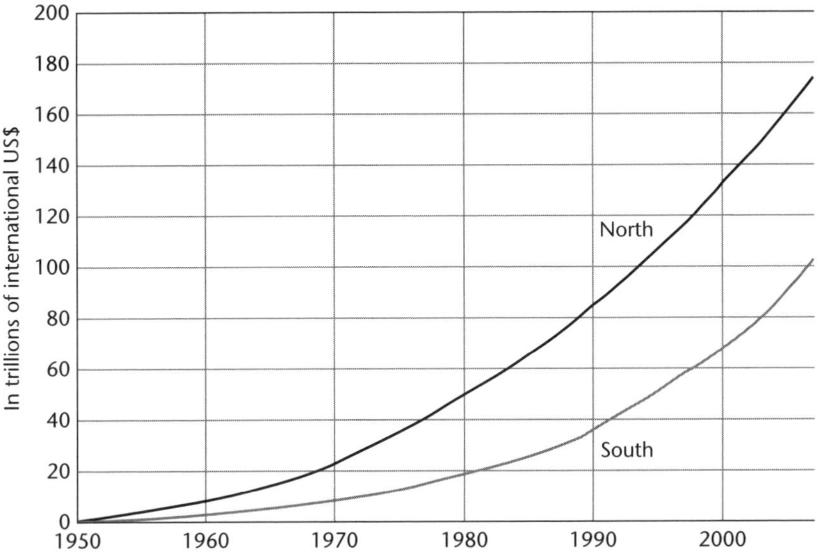

Figure 11.2b. Total real capital stock, North and South

Note: *For a definition of the country sets 'North' and 'South' and for a note on specific difficulties with the data, see Figure 11.1a.

Source: Penn World Table 7.0.

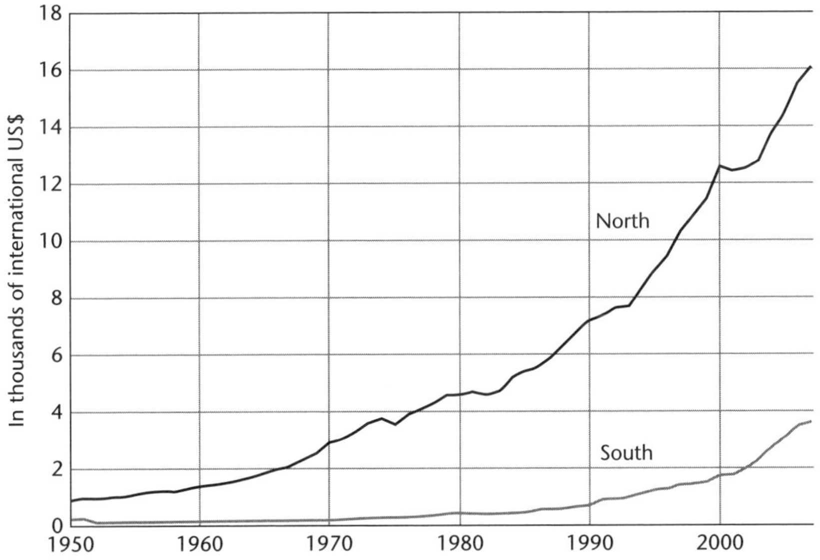

Figure 11.3a. Trade per capita, North and South

Note: *For a definition of the country sets 'North' and 'South' and for a note on specific difficulties with the data, see Figure 11.1a.

Source: Penn World Table 7.0.

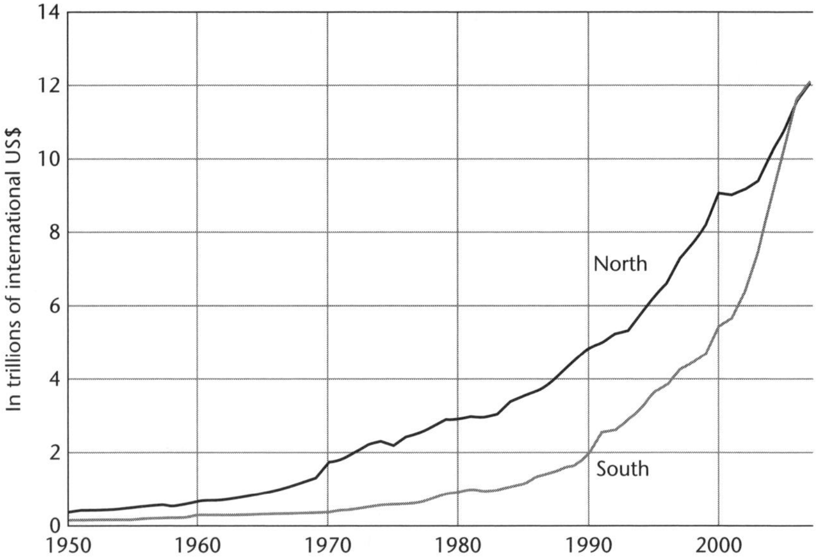

Figure 11.3b. Total trade, North and South

Note: *For a definition of the country sets 'North' and 'South' and for a note on specific difficulties with the data, see Figure 11.1a.

Source: Penn World Table 7.0.

the world most vividly. Hence, we split the G20 group into Northern and Southern countries.

Looking at Figures 11.1a to 11.3b it becomes apparent that the North is no longer by far the dominant part of the world economy. The world economy faces a 'global shift'[4] in relative weights, with important effects on both the North and the South. The reasons for these differences in development are complex and go far beyond the scope of this chapter. Nevertheless, identifying these enormous heterogeneities and asymmetries is a prerequisite for understanding the global climate debate and the various positions taken by the countries in developing an appropriate policy.

11.2.2 *Industry structure: physical production versus value added in services*

Income disparity is not the only factor to contribute to the range of positions and conclusions when negotiating a global environmental, industrial, and climate policy. Equally important are asymmetries in industry structure. Per capita income in the South accelerated thanks to rapid modernization and structural change. There is no sustainable development process that is not directly

[1] For a more detailed discussion of this shift in the global economy, see Gries (2007).

connected with a structural shift away from agriculture towards the modern industrial or service sector. Indeed, there is an ongoing debate about the role of industrialization in the process of development. Some evidence for Latin America and Africa even seems to indicate a process of deindustrialization since the 1980s. A direct shift from an agriculture-dominated towards a service-driven economy seems possible. However, the most impressive development processes, particularly in Asia, are fuelled by massive industrialization and hence an expanding industrial sector. Comparative advantages in labour-intensive, standardized-production processes clearly point less to the importance of the service sector, and more to a rapid expanding manufacturing industry within an internationally-oriented outward-looking development strategy. Due to the emergence of industrial sectors in the South and a shift in comparative advantage between the South and the North, a large part of today's global industrial production takes place in the South. However, industrialization in the South is beneficial not only for the successful emerging markets; the North also benefits via international trade. Many of the goods produced in the South are eventually consumed in the North. Northern consumers benefit in particular from low prices, which increase real purchasing power in the North. In other words, the development process undergone by the South also affects the North very positively.

However, international integration has led to acceleration in the economic division of production processes all over the world. The late take-off of developing economies, and the process of industrialization that goes along with development, means that developing countries are currently passing through the stages of industrialization that advanced economies went through long ago. Typically this process begins with a massive expansion of industrial production. Value added is created in the shape of physical production using standardized technologies and labour-intensive production processes. As products become more complex and sophisticated, technologies become commonplace and the value-adding processes change. The proportion of standardized physical production declines in favour of high-value-adding, high-quality services. This represents yet another structural change, which brings with it another substantial change in resource intensity. Whereas physical production during the first phase of industrialization is characterized by high resource and energy intensity, we observe declining resource and energy intensity in advanced countries as technology and human-capital intensity increases.

Generally speaking, the stage of development at any one time partly determines (a) the production structure; and, in turn, (b) resource and energy intensity. This has two implications for the current negotiations on a global climate policy. First, high-income countries are fortunate enough to no longer have a dominant physical industrial production sector. In these countries the less-energy-intensive service sector is responsible for about 70 per cent of value added, so they have a production structure with high energy and resource efficiency. Second, since emerging economies are in the relatively early stages of development their production structures are undergoing increasing physical industrialization. The success of these countries is driven by the fact that they are responsible for a rising share of the world's physical production. Their development is an industrialization process driven by the alignment of their production structures with their comparative advantages. Thus the North–South structural asymmetry is the result of international integration and a successful, export-driven development strategy.[5] Whereas in the North successful development goes hand in hand with ongoing deindustrialization and a growing technology and service sector, the South is growing through industrial modernization.

11.2.3 *Technologies: high-tech versus backward technology*

The third considerable asymmetry relates to the technological differences between the North and the South and partly to the developmental asymmetries mentioned above. There are enormous technological differences between the North and the South in all dimensions and areas of economic activity. In addition to the structural advantages of the industry of the North (with a less energy-intensive structure), energy efficiency in the North (with the exception of the USA) is far better than in the South. In this section we focus on the differences in the use of fossil energy resources.

Figure 11.4 illustrates this difference. Germany and Japan are two examples of Northern countries with high efficiency in avoiding pollution. China is an example of a Southern emerging economy with low energy efficiency, while the USA is a rich and developed country with an efficiency in avoiding the pollution similar to that of a developing economy. CO_2 emissions per unit of output in the North are far lower than in the South for two reasons. First, higher per capita income in the North seems to influence the preferences towards a cleaner environment. Second, this shift in preferences encourages the development of technologies that reduce pollution from production processes. Energy-efficient technologies are in demand. In particular, more efficient electrical power plants are leading to a significant reduction in pollutant emissions. While technologies with low CO_2 emissions are available, most of them are implemented only in the North and hence asymmetrically. Even if many of these technologies were developed with high public subsidies, property rights are often privatized. Today, most of these technologies are owned

[5] On developmental and catching-up processes, international integration, and structural changes, see also Gries (1995) and Gries and Jungblut (1997a, 1997b).

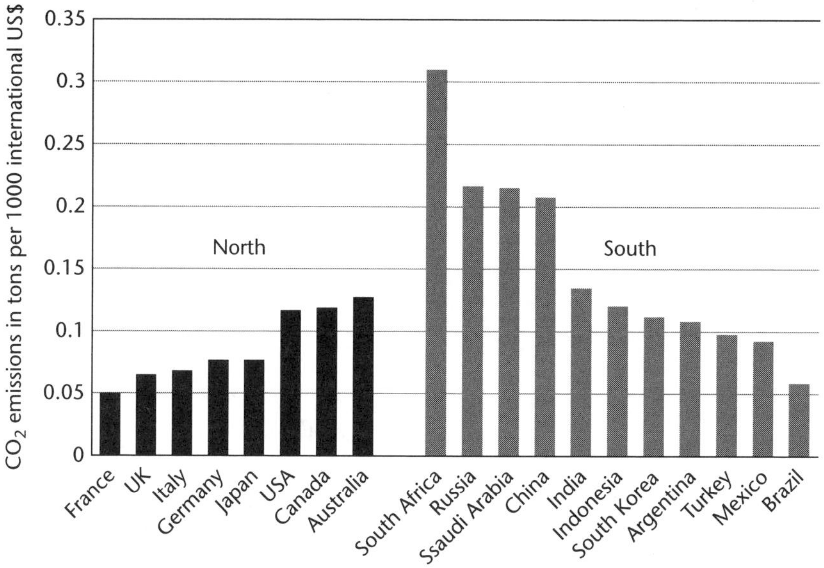

Figure 11.4. CO_2 efficiency 2008, North and South
Source: Boden, Marland, and Andres (2011), Penn World Table 7.0.

by private firms in the North. These asymmetries in availability and ownership have to be taken into account as well when negotiating a global climate policy.

11.2.4 *Current pollution emissions*

The fourth global asymmetry is based on the differences in economic development and emissions efficiency. As shown in Figure 11.5a most of today's global pollution is generated by the two country groups under review. On the one hand, there are the rich countries of the North; on the other, there are the emerging economies of the South. Interestingly, in Figure 11.5a we can observe that since 2005 emerging markets have contributed more pollution than the Northern countries.

However, for both country groups it is clear that pollution is linked to the level of economic activity. A high absolute level of economic activity leads to a high absolute level of pollution. Because the advanced countries still account for the largest absolute share in world production they still have high pollution, despite their structural advantages. This becomes especially apparent when we convert absolute pollution to per capita pollution. Thus most of today's global pollution is due to income- and welfare-generating activities in the rich countries, even though some successful emerging

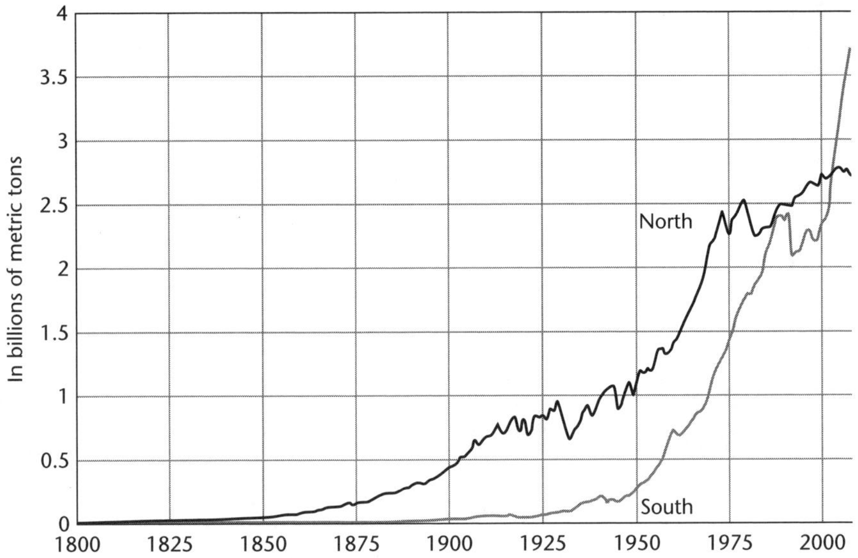

Figure 11.5a. Total CO_2 emissions, North and South

Note: *For a definition of the country sets 'North' and 'South', see Figure 11.1a. ** Emission data for all countries excluding Russia (South) are available since the onset of the individual countries' industrialization. Emission data for Russia are available since 1992. As a substitute for the unavailable Russian emission dataset the former USSR was introduced for the time before 1992.

Source: Boden, Marland, and Andres (2011).

countries like China, India, and Indonesia do contribute a considerable amount of pollution.

11.2.5 *Historical pollution (pollution stock)*

These asymmetries in pollution become even more dramatic if we not only consider today's pollution flows but also the pollution that has accumulated over time. Figure 11.5b displays current accumulated levels of pollution responsible for global warming. Although emerging markets are catching up fast and generate a noteworthy amount of pollution themselves, most of today's pollution can be traced back to more than two-thirds of the Northern countries. Hence some of today's prosperity and wealth in the advanced countries has been virtually paid for with global pollution and global warming. Assuming inter-generational responsibility is an accepted principle, the Northern countries ought to—and owing to their prosperity, are able to—contain the damage they have caused in an adequate way. This basic consideration becomes even more drastic when absolute values are converted to per capita values. As is shown in Figure 11.7a and b, not only is the North by far

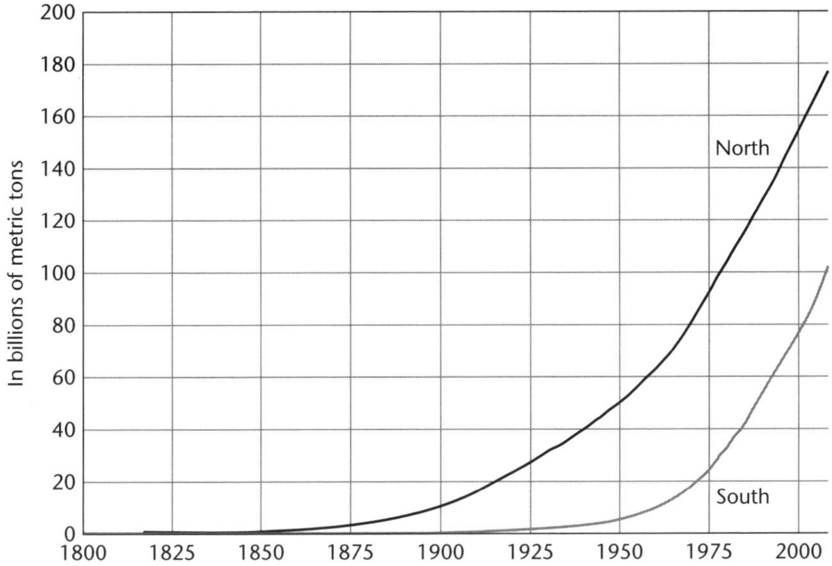

Figure 11.5b. Accumulated CO^2 emissions, North and South

Note: *For a definition of the country sets 'North' and 'South', see Figure 11.1a and for a note on specific difficulties with the data see Figure Figure 11.5a.

Source: Boden, Marland, and Andres (2011).

the biggest polluter in absolute terms, but these countries are also the greatest beneficiaries in terms of the use of fossil resources for the sake of wealth development, expressed in accumulated per capita pollution.

11.2.6 *Natural disasters and resulting damage*

The final asymmetry affects the vulnerability of the North and South to future climate change-induced effects. Of all the asymmetries discussed above this is the most theoretical one, in particular because to this day we have no reliable forecasts concerning the impact of global warming on different regions in the North and South. There are some clear indications of growing desertification, a rising number of extreme weather events and an increase in weather-related disasters. There are also indications that sea levels are rising and that ocean currents may shift, yet all of these statements involve so much uncertainty and coincidence that it is impossible to make stylized predictions. Statements about potential exposure vary depending on the likelihood of that exposure, ranging from the predominant exposure of the Southern countries (in particular because of their proximity to the equator and the resulting desertification issues and extreme weather conditions) to a rising vulnerability of Northern countries (for example due to changes in the great marine conveyor belt causing extreme weather and wind phenomena). In this regard, there are asymmetries in both regions. Which of these asymmetries will occur or whether there will be any asymmetries at all is completely unclear, as it stands today. Maybe this uncertainty about the future symmetric or asymmetric exposure offers the greatest chance of reaching an agreement. As for the cost of global climate-change-induced damage, Stern (2006) assumes that it equates to between 5 and 11 per cent of global GDP each year.

11.3 Climate change and the global efficiency problem

Since using the environment as an absorbent for pollution affects welfare and quality of life, pollution-producing activities have to be closely monitored. To consider the environment as a resource implies an economization of the environment. The economic objective is to find a reasonable, ideally even an optimal, way to manage this resource in order to improve global welfare. How can we manage the 'environment resource' in the best possible way? So far the global climate policy debate has not appropriately tackled the issue of global efficiency and global fairness, in particular with regard to the strong North–South asymmetry. While references to the asymmetries between these are made once in a while, they do not form part of a comprehensive proposal for global policy implementation.[6]

To solve the problem of finding a global environmental policy for an asymmetric world, special consideration must be given to two characteristics that arise from the use of the environment as a resource. The first one is the global 'public good characteristic' of CO_2 pollution. Emissions, no matter where they are produced, cause global warming that can potentially affect everyone. Hence, pollution causes damage for potentially everyone and correspondingly also reduces universal wealth. Second, pollution accumulates to become a more and more serious problem. The enormous pollution stock accumulated slowly over time has created today's global warming problems.

These two characteristics have to be taken into consideration when finding ways to treat the current emissions problems effectively. In the following we will describe some stylized thoughts that may lead to a more efficient solution of the pollution stock problem that is causing climate change. We will do so in two steps. In the first step we assume a homogeneous world: our approach towards the problem of developing an efficient environmental policy involves 'assuming away' all the asymmetries in the global economy as described in

[6] For a comparison of different proposals, see, for example, Agrawala (2005) and OECD (2009a, 2009b).

Section 2, an experiment that will shed light on the fundamental and economically useful aspects of a global environmental policy. In a second step we consider the existing asymmetries in the global economy. We identify the special challenges of an asymmetric world, again within a stylized discussion, with the aim of illustrating a global environmental policy under asymmetric conditions.

All lines of argumentation are based on the model described in the next section and the version of this model of a asymmetric world is given in the Appendix 11.1

11.3.1 *A simple global pollution-stock model in a homogeneous world*

This contribution cannot claim to present a fully developed model for an optimal global policy with asymmetric world regions. However, what it can do is to outline an optimal environmental policy in a homogeneous world and, in the Appendix 11.1 present a first extension of this model for the asymmetric world.

In this first reference model,[7] we assume that these asymmetries do not exist. There are no differences between agents, technologies, or countries. Hence we assume a representative agent consuming C from world production. Pollution causes damage all over the world. This damage E enters the agent's utility function causing disutilities $U\ (C,E)$. Hence *welfare* W of the society, including future generations, is defined as:

$$W = \int_0^\infty U(C,E)e^{-\rho\tau}d\tau \quad U_c > 0 \quad U_E < 0$$

Environmental damage E is generated by two components: the consumption of fossil energy resources R and the existing state (stock) of pollution A.

$$E = E(R,A) \quad E_R > 0, \quad E_A > 0$$

World product Q is produced using the flow of extracted exhaustible energy resources R and accumulated capital K. Since environmental damage E is a negative public good it also affects the production process as a negative externality:

$$Q = Q(R,K,E), \quad Q_R > 0, \quad Q_K > 0, \quad Q_E < 0$$

While pollution causes damage, there is also a clean-up technology F. While the production technology determines how efficiently resources are used, the

[7] As a starting point this simple model is closely based on the standard descriptions of this problem given in e.g. Perman et al. (2003: chapter 16). Further theoretic models are presented by Farzin (1996) and Lieb (2004).

clean-up technology reduces existing damage. With V being the cost of applying the clean-up technology, we improve the effectiveness of this technology by spending more:

$$F = F(V) \quad F_V > 0$$

The effects of economic activity on resource stocks S and accumulated pollution R are

$$\dot{S} = -R$$

and for exhaustible resources

$$\dot{A}(t) = M(R) - \alpha A - F(V)A(t) = \int_0^t \Big(M(R) - \alpha A - F(V)\Big)d\tau$$

As for stock pollution dynamics we assume that stock pollution changes as a function of the current use of resources $M(R)$ less the natural regeneration rate indicated by rate α and less the effects of the clean-up technology F.

The model is closed by considering the budget constraint for the representative agent

$$\dot{K} = Q - C - V$$

To solve this problem we use optimal control theory as described in Appendix 11.1. From the first-order condition concerning resource use we obtain the efficient price path as

$$P^{net} = \omega Q_R = P - U_E E_R - \omega Q_E E_R - \lambda M_R \tag{1}$$

where P^{net} is the net price that corrects for negative externalities of resource use to obtain an efficient allocation of resources. We discuss the message of this efficiency condition in the following section.

In Figure 11.6 we see the price path for a fossil resource causing flow and stock pollution effects. The fact that the resource is exhaustible and not easy to completely substitute leads to a generally rising price. However, the damage caused by the pollution requires a price adjustment to reduce the use of the resource and cut down the damage. There are two flow externalities: one damage affects consumers and another producers. For both effects a price correction could reduce the damage towards an efficient use of the resource. A third effect is the one generated by the accumulated stock of pollution. Since the accumulated stock of pollution together with today's additional pollution causes further future negative effects, this stock pollution effect also requires a price correction.

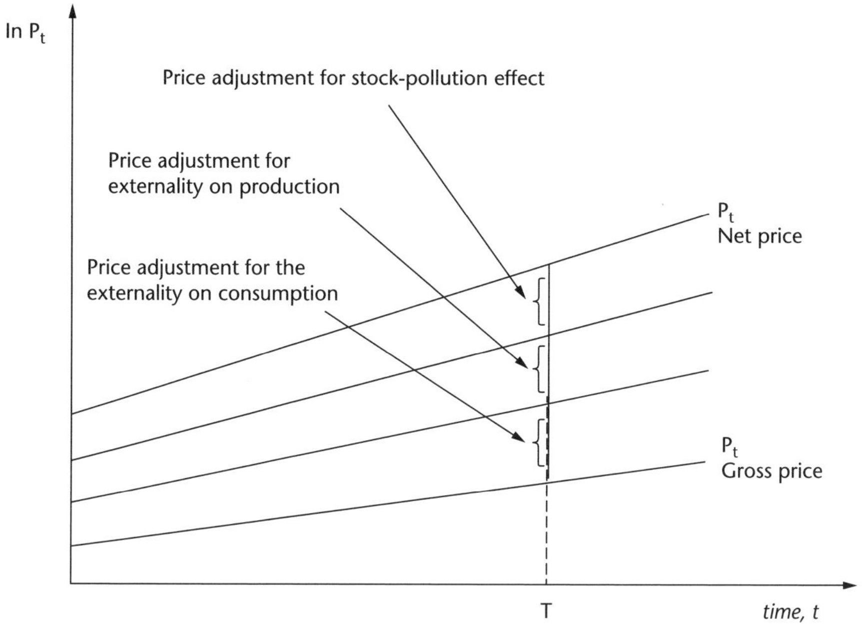

Figure 11.6. Price adjustments towards an efficient price path, North and South
Source: based on Perman et al. (2003).

11.3.2 *A global environmental policy in a homogeneous world*

Based on the theoretical concept discussed in the previous section we now discuss a world with no differences between North and South. In this world, wealth is positively affected by consumption and negatively affected by pollution—both pollution flows and pollution stocks—already accumulated. In this model the pollution comes from burning fossil fuels to generate electricity. Hence they are major factors of production. If burning fossil resources is necessary for production, on the one hand, but generates welfare-reducing pollution on the other, one can find an optimal level of use. From equation (1) in the above model we learn that under free-market conditions the resource is used too intensively and the pollution caused by burning fossil resources is too high. Figure 11.6 shows the theoretical price path of the resource that arises without an environmental policy, as well as the efficient price path that should be taken via policy instruments to guarantee efficient resource use.

The condition reflects well-established insights from the economics of externalities and public goods. First, Figure 11.6 shows that the gross price ought to increase by the marginal values of all three kinds of damage, namely the direct marginal effect on utility $[U_E E_R]$, the marginal negative effect on production [$\omega Q_E E_R$], and the marginal stock-pollution effect of accumulating CO_2 that negatively affects the next generation [λM_R]. Second, the resulting net price should determine resource use in production and—with an increasing net price—adjust total extraction and the burning of fossil resources downwards. Third, there are various instruments that can be used to implement this price adjustment. The best-known policies are the Pigou tax (an eco-tax)[8] and tradable permits.[9] Both instruments lift the price so that resource inputs and damage are reduced.[10]

In a world with no differences and asymmetries where policy instruments are enforceable by a governmental authority, a global environmental policy would not be much of a problem. In fact, there are many examples of countries where such environmental problems have been solved.[11] However, little theoretical modelling has been done so far concerning highly asymmetric countries.[12]

11.3.3 *A global environmental policy in an asymmetric world*

In the asymmetric world described above the policy conditions are fundamentally different. The theoretical approach underlying the following discussion extends the above model (see Appendix 11.2). As it primarily serves to explain the different perspectives and the associated factors that strongly influence the optimization problem, we have not yet tried to suggest a global optimal policy strategy. Our objective is to suggest a starting point to address the issue rather than to provide a comprehensive solution.

To include the impact of global asymmetries on decision making from different perspectives we assume that there are two separate world regions, the North and the South. Each of these regions constitutes its own world, in which it produces, consumes, and develops independently. The central link between these two world regions is the effect of pollution. Pollution, both accumulated (stock) and current pollution (flow), impacts negatively on welfare in the whole world, in the South as much as in the North. To focus on the problem of pollution and to identify an efficient global solution, the only asymmetry between the North and the South is the technological capability of avoiding pollution when using fossil resources. The existing pollution-reducing technologies in the North mean that this region generates significantly less pollution with the same resource input. Even if the North produces heavy

[8] The idea of internalizing external effects of public goods goes back to Pigou (1920). His approach was later extended in the context of environmental economics by Baumol and Oates (1971, 1988).

[9] See, for example, Dales (1968); Cansier (1996); and Dorn (1996).

[10] For a comparison, see e.g. Giraudet and Quirion (2008) or Oikonomou et al. (2008). For accumulated pollution, see also the discussion in Hoel and Karp (2002).

[11] See, for example, Christiansen et al. (2005) or Convery (2009).

[12] See, for example, Rose et al. (1998).

pollutant emissions due to a high level of production and income, the marginal efficiency of pollution per resource and per output unit is significantly higher in the North. From this simple asymmetry[13] we can already draw some early conclusions concerning an efficient control of polluting resources and an efficient environmental policy. From the very simple model in Appendix 11.2 we can derive environmental uncoordinated policies of the North and the South, respectively, or if acting in a coordinated way and simultaneously. The first and most important principle of an efficient policy is that pollution reduction has to start where it can be achieved most easily (with the lowest possible marginal opportunity costs). As more and more pollution is reduced, pollution-reducing technologies will become more and more expensive (decreasing marginal efficiency), so we have to begin with the technologies that are the most effective. Since the technologies used in the South have low energy efficiency we have to begin in the South, because here maximum reductions are possible with very little investment, whereas the North would incur very high expenditures to improve what are already efficient technologies. From a global point of view the most efficient measure is to implement efficiency-improving technologies until the South has reached the level of marginal resource efficiency of the North. Looking at this efficiency condition says nothing about the issue of bearing the burden of implementation costs. We discuss the question of burdens and their fair distribution in Section 11.4. To make our point as clearly as possible we separate the two issues of efficiency and fair distribution at this stage, initially focusing solely on efficiency before coming back to the problem of fair distribution.

How can a global government execute this kind of efficient environmental policy? From our theoretical model in Appendix 11.2 it is apparent that the inefficient use of resources in the South has to become more expensive relative to the North, until marginal environmental damage reaches the same level. Rising prices would be an incentive for preventing damage, until an equal efficiency level in the North and South is reached. This relative price increase can be implemented theoretically via a Pigou tax or an optimal number of tradable permits. In any case, these instruments would be a necessary incentive for implementing resource-saving technologies. Furthermore, thinking about implementing resource-efficient technologies in the South requires a more detailed insight into the characteristics of pollution-reducing technologies that partly already exist in the North. We can distinguish three cases.

1 The technology of the North is a blueprint technology, i.e. it represents an improvement in efficiency due to a pure increase in expertise. The

[13] In reality asymmetries are even more complex. Further interdependencies like trade (e.g. Bommer and Schulze (1999) and Neary (2006)) would not simplify the problem.

implementation of this expertise allows for high reduction of emissions in the production process at no cost. A first straightforward example for this kind of efficiency improvement is a simple increasing awareness of environmental inefficiency. Preventing waste of resources is an easy step towards a de facto more efficient technology. Another example of such a blueprint technology could be a simple filtering technology where the chemical composition and engineering of the filter, and not the expensive components of filter production, generate the filter effect. The physical components of the filter demand no serious resource input. Hence the value of this technology is solely generated through the knowledge of filter engineering expertise. It could be freely available or protected by a patent that generates license fees.

2 A second kind of technology would be similar to the first, except its implementation would incur major costs. These could consist of potential license fees, but also of setup and installation costs. These costs need to be considered when evaluating efficient policy instruments.

3 The third case involves a technology embodied in real capital. In this case the production process requires a substitution of the presently implemented real capital by another more energy-efficient capital stock with an integrated energy-saving technology. Under these conditions, not only would a power plant need filters in its smokestacks, it would also have to make major changes to the power generation process and hence replace a substantial share of the existing capital. Pollution could only be reduced as intended with massive investments in physical capital.

Depending on the empirical relevance of these three cases, the design of environmental and industrial policies need to take account of various aspects. Furthermore, as the three scenarios imply very different financial requirements, the issues of global efficiency and the fair distribution of burdens are affected in different ways.

11.3.3.1 ENVIRONMENTAL AND INDUSTRIAL POLICY BASED ON A BLUEPRINT TECHNOLOGY

This scenario would be the simplest and affect the cost and distribution issue the least. As this kind of technology would imply no rivalry in usage the only problem is the appropriate treatment of property rights of the technology owner. A blueprint technology that is used in one power plant can be simultaneously used in any number of other power plants without resource rivalry. As this kind of technology is characterized as a 'public good' it can be used simultaneously by several users with almost no direct costs. The optimal policy strategy in this case is for the 'global government' to pay appropriate compensation to the technology owner and supply the technology to the world for free. Like a public good, this technology would be available to all potential polluters at no cost. This would have a maximum impact on potential sources of pollution. The details of financing the appropriate compensation would have to be negotiated between the North, the likely owner of this technology, and the South. The result of these negotiations is not part of the efficiency problem, but a part of the distribution problem discussed below. The efficiency problem would be solved through deprivatization in the North and the transformation of a privately-owned technology to a global public good.

11.3.3.2 BLUEPRINT TECHNOLOGIES WITH CONSIDERABLE IMPLEMENTATION COSTS

The second case links the extremely positive characteristic of a 'public good technology' with the problem that in reality this technology is not available for free. Even if emissions filters were available at virtually no cost, installation and adjustments in the power plants would require a considerable amount of resources. Hence a considerable investment would be required to implement a low-carbon economy. The implementation costs alone would lead to investment activity and capital accumulation that would not be directed towards the output of private goods. In this respect industrial policies may face a partial trade-off between implementing low-carbon technologies and a resource allocation promoting a higher speed of capital accumulation. Hence these investments would conflict with other development goals like growth in private goods. Depending on who provides the resources, the North or the South, one party would have to carry a burden.

First, collecting these resources in the South would slow down private output growth due to a slowdown in capital accumulation. Resources allocated to pollution-reducing technologies simultaneously reduce the funds available for investment in classic production processes. Hence the speed of capital accumulation for private production and in turn, the speed of development, decelerates. Because Southern countries are poor and have a huge backlog in development this would conflict with the United Nations' Millennium Development Goals.

Second and alternatively, resources could be collected in the North leading to a real North to South transfer. Even if the necessary investment goods or implementation services were purchased in the North, which would positively affect production and employment in the North, funds still have to be raised. For a real North to South transfer taxes have to be levied in the North leading to a reduction in disposable income and consumption. Put simply, the North needs to raise taxes to buy resource-efficient investment goods from its own economy and send these goods to Southern countries.

Obviously, implementation costs lead to a reduction in private consumption in the South or the North. So aside from the ideal case of a technology that is one hundred per cent a public good, climate protection clearly generates costs.

However, these burdens are the opportunity cost of the gains we obtain by curbing global warming. These opportunity costs are the reasonable (and efficient) investment that is necessary to prevent damage through global warming. Both the South and the North have to develop an awareness that these costs exist and that it is necessary to distribute the burdens in an efficiently organized global economy.

11.3.3.3 THE TECHNOLOGY IS A SUBSTANTIAL PART OF THE CAPITAL GOOD

This third scenario is the most difficult one. Here, the technology cannot be installed within the existing capital stock. The technology is directly embodied in capital goods and hence the current capital stock cannot be upgraded. Countries need to build a completely new or a supplementary capital stock with the adequate pollution-efficient technologies. Theoretically this is comparable to scenario 2 (section 11.3.3.2). The difference is that implementation costs are not just small once and for all flows of payment, but require a substitution of existing capital by a long-term accumulation of a new and presumably even higher-valued capital stock. Industrial and environmental policies face an even more serious trade-off between fast consumption growth and low-carbon production. Again, who is capable of bearing this even greater burden? If the South mobilizes these resources, traditional production and development processes would be affected and the South would sustain a slowdown in consumption. Similar effects would occur in the North if there were a real transfer from North to South. For a real resource transfer the Northern governments, similar to scenario 2 above, would have to raise taxes in order to fund the efficient investment goods even if they were produced in the North. Raising taxes would reduce private income in the North and hence negatively influence the consumption path in the North. Nevertheless, this would increase welfare because the installation of pollution-efficient capital stocks in the South would overcompensate for the costs of global warming despite impacting on the current consumption path.

While this discussion makes clear that an efficient solution to the global climate problem is possible, it also emerges that a reallocation of resources is necessary and that there is extreme uncertainty with respect to estimating total costs and benefits and the distribution of these benefits and burdens. For example assuming that the introduction of a global carbon market could keep the temperature increase below 3°C, this policy would, according to OECD estimates, cost about 0.1 per cent of average global GDP growth between 2012 and 2050.[14] According to the UNFCCC (2007) investments of more than

[14] See OECD (2009b).

US$200 billion are necessary each year in order to maintain global greenhouse gas emissions at current levels until 2030. Even if the total value seems huge, this amount is less than US$1 per day for each citizen of the North. The Intergovernmental Panel on Climate Change estimates these costs to be around 3 per cent of world GDP (IPCC 2007).[15]

Closely connected to the required resources is a finance problem,[16] which incorporates a large-scale conflict concerning the distribution of burdens. Therefore, we have tried to make clear that in addition to the issue of an efficient solution any policy strategy that aims to solve the global efficiency problem necessarily has to ensure a fair distribution of burdens. This holds as long as a reduction in global warming is linked by technological characteristics to a reduction of the classic consumption path, and no ideal and freely accessible public-good blueprint technology is available. Industrial policy must be aware of the fact that low-carbon growth is not for free. Hence it is important to realize that, even though our model treats them separately, both problems—efficiency and a fair distribution of burdens—are closely linked.

11.4 A fair distribution of burdens

Solving the efficiency problem will most likely incur substantial implementation costs and even accumulating investment costs. Therefore, we also have to answer the question of how to distribute these burdens fairly.[17] Finding a response to this is particularly difficult because there are two components to consider. First, there is no global government that is able to decide on any kind of reasonable policy strategy on a global scale, let alone implement such a strategy effectively. So far most discussions about implementation have focused on policies within countries.[18] Second, the considerable asymmetries and heterogeneities in the world, as described in Section 11.2, make it even harder to decide what constitutes a 'fair' distribution of burdens. Both of these points are hardly discussed in the present debate, even if they are crucial to finding an effective solution. Since our chapter focuses on asymmetries we place the distribution problem, which is an intra- and an inter-generational problem, at the centre of the debate.

The *intra-generational distribution* problem is a result of the huge global disparities in the current level of development and consumption. The UN has stated clear goals concerning the elimination of poverty and the

[15] See Ott et al. (2009: 11).

[16] For a discussion on finance, see, for example, Harmeling et al. (2009) and Ott et al. (2009).

[17] Suggestions are discussed, for example, in Harmeling et al. (2009).

[18] See, OECD (2009a), even if OECD (2009b) incorporates the possibilities of international cooperation assistance, and no global coordinated programmes are discussed.

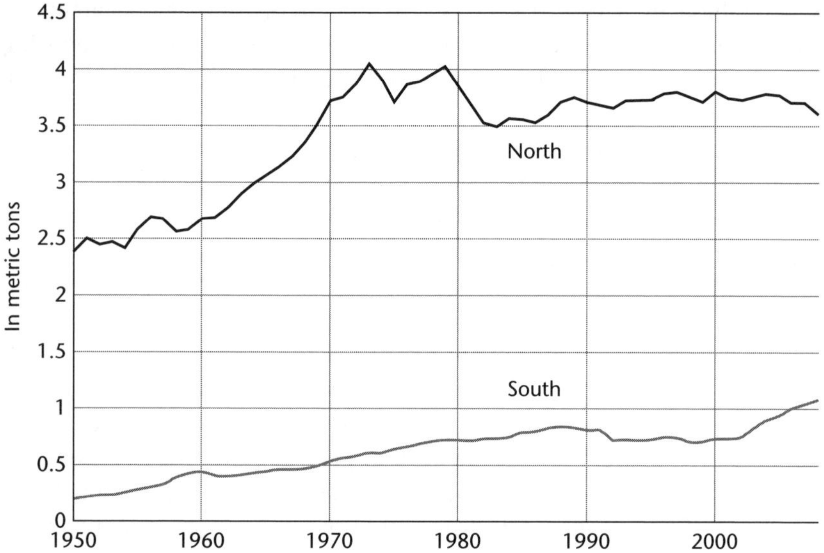

Figure 11.7a. CO_2 emissions per capita, North and South

Note: *For a definition of the country sets 'North' and 'South', see Figure 11.1a; and for a note on specific difficulties with the data, see Figure 11.5a.

Source: Boden, Marland, and Andres (2011); UN (2011).

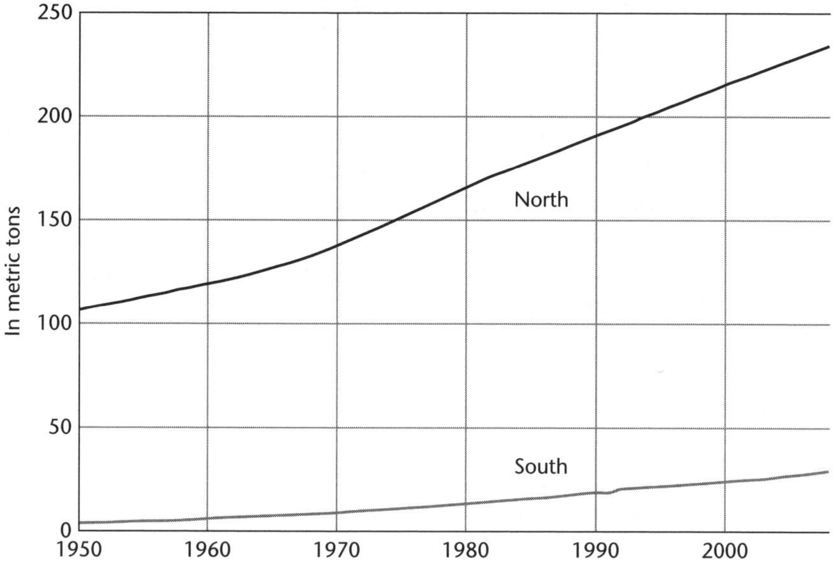

Figure 11.7b. Accumulated CO_2 emissions per capita, North and South

Note: *For a definition of the country sets 'North' and 'South', see Figure 11.1a; and for a note on specific difficulties with the data, see Figure 11.5a.

Source: Boden, Marland, and Andres (2011); UN (2011).

promotion of development in developing countries. Assuming these are common goals for the benefit of the global population, then it must be determined which principle of distribution can best achieve them.

1. According to the *ability-to-pay principle* a major share of burden would have to be carried by the North. If this principle is applied, the much higher income per capita of the North would suggest allocating a substantial share of burdens to the North. This would mean a tax increase in the North and a transfer in favour of Southern countries.

2. According to the *principle of equal distribution* a worldwide tax per head would have to be levied under the assumption that everyone is affected in the same way. However, in reality this would not be feasible because most of the population would not be capable of paying this tax due to their low income. Furthermore, it would blatantly violate the ability-to-pay principle.

3. The third possibility is the *polluter pays principle,* under which the producer of the pollution is expected to pay. The North would be most affected by this because it still produces high emissions in absolute terms. However, the South would also be affected since it includes successful emerging markets like China, India, Indonesia, and Brazil (Figure 11.5a). When calculating a measure of per capita equality—which seems reasonable—the burden on the South would decrease significantly, because in per capita terms the North still emits far more pollution than the South (Figure 11.7a). The burden on the South would drop further if we account for decreasing marginal utility of consumable income, as is often done in economic models (see Appendix11.2). In this context the marginal utility of consumption in the South would be substantially higher due to its lower per capita income. Hence the opportunity costs of tax burdens are much higher in the South than in the North. This, too, would lead to a clear and considerable additional burden on the North compared to that on the South.

So far we have only discussed fair distribution in the context of current emissions and the current world population; that is, we have looked at conditions within a generation. The phrase 'fair distribution' has another important dimension, namely *inter-generational distribution.* Looking at the emissions stocks in Figure 11.5b, this dimension becomes very obvious. The model, which is described in the Appendix, has been deliberately chosen as an emissions-stock accumulating model. The current level of global warming has evolved almost entirely through accumulated pollution generated in the past in the North. Only 20 per cent of today's accumulated pollution can be traced back to China and other Southern countries. This becomes even more obvious when looking at accumulated pollution per capita (Figure 11.7b). Hence today's need for action can be almost solely attributed to past activities in the North. Even if an efficient solution of the whole problem is not possible without incorporating the South, the issue of fair intergenerational distribution plays a major role when examining the fair distribution of burdens in the shape of investment in climate protection. While past generations in the North were able to pollute at no cost and in turn undergo development without any regard for emissions and the resulting burden on future generations, the South, while still underdeveloped, may now be held liable for additional damage prevention. Therefore, current global asymmetries, but also intergenerational asymmetry, will be important components in the debate surrounding a strategy for a global low-carbon economy.

11.5 Conclusions

The search for a global climate protection policy is a central economic problem. An efficient global strategy that incorporates a fair distribution of burdens is needed. In this respect an essential problem of searching for an efficient and fair climate and industrial policy is the massive economic and technical asymmetry between the rich advanced North and the mostly less developed poor South.

The first and most important aspect of an efficient climate and industrial policy is that pollution reduction has to start where it can be carried out most effectively (with a minimum of resources). If the highest pollution reduction can be achieved in a developing or emerging country with low resource input, then a global strategy should invest in these countries first. It is far more difficult and expensive to continue improving the already efficient technologies of the North. From a global point of view the most efficient measure would be to equip the South with efficiency-improving technologies until such time as similar marginal efficiency levels have been reached. Policy makers also have to be aware that there is a trade-off between the speed of general capital accumulation for the speed of consumption growth and low-carbon development. A global low-carbon growth path is most likely not for free.

Hence a globally fair distribution of the burden generated by these investments is the most serious problem. Because most of the historically accumulated total pollution that affects today's climate has been caused by the North, the ability-to-pay principle and the polluter pays principle would allocate the main burden to the advanced Northern economies.

In a way this is an academic discussion. Some weeks ago, my family watched the news and my children saw pictures of a great flood in Pakistan and asked if this flood had to do with climate change. 'We don't know exactly, but maybe', was my answer. Then, they asked, 'what could be done to stop it?' I said 'spend US$200 billion per year on low-carbon emission technologies'. 'What does that mean?' they asked, and I answered, 'An ice cream a day for each of us'. They looked surprised and said 'That is easy . . . .'.

Appendix 11.1 Optimal price path: homogeneous world

A global government or representative agent solves the optimal control problem:
Present value Hamiltonian:

$$H = U(C,E) + P(-R) + \omega[Q(R,K,E) - C - V] + \lambda[M(R) - \alpha A - F(V)]$$

First-order condition
Consumption and capital accumulation:

$$\frac{\partial H}{\partial C} = U_C - \omega = 0$$

Resource utilization:

$$\frac{\partial H}{\partial R} = U_E E_R + \omega Q_E E_R - P + \omega Q_R + \lambda M_R = 0$$

Clean-up efforts:

$$\frac{\partial H}{\partial V} = -\omega - \lambda F_V = 0$$

Shadow prices:

$$\dot{P} = -\frac{\partial H}{\partial S} + \rho P \Leftrightarrow \dot{P} = \rho P$$

$$\dot{\omega} = -\frac{\partial H}{\partial K} + \rho\omega \Leftrightarrow \dot{\omega} = \rho\omega - Q_K\omega$$

$$\dot{\lambda} = -\frac{\partial H}{\partial A} + \rho\lambda \Leftrightarrow \dot{\lambda} = \alpha\lambda + \rho\lambda - U_E E_A$$

Appendix 11.2 A simple model of global pollution and environmental policy (with asymmetric dynamics of pollution)

Only a small number of papers have considered heterogeneous regions with respect to stocks of accumulated pollution. For a discussion see, for example, Xabadia, Goetz, and Zilberman (2005, 2008) or Hoel and Karp (2009). For a better illustration we introduce a simple model.

Representative agents in two world regions

The world consists of two regions. On the one hand there is the technologically developed North with high income; on the other there is the technologically backward South with low levels of income. Both regions produce and consume separately. The only good that is used by both sides is the shared environment (atmosphere). Hence we have two representative agents, one that consumes the Southern product and another that consumes the Northern product. Environmental pollution is global and the resulting environmental damage E has to be borne by both sides.

$$U^N = U(C^N, E)\ U_{C^N} > 0\ U_E < 0$$
$$U^S = U(C^S, E)\ U_{C^S} > 0\ U_E < 0$$

Welfare in both regions (when considering future generations) is

$$W^N = \int_0^\infty U(C^N, E)e^{-\rho\tau}d\tau$$
$$W^S = \int_0^\infty U(C^S, E)e^{-\rho\tau}d\tau$$

Environmental damage

Local environmental damage arises from the local use of fossil resources and is linked to the existing level of environmental damage A. Because the North has better technologies it is assumed that the North pollutes less than the South. To simplify the model this differential can be interpreted such that the North emits no pollution at all while the South does. Even if this is clearly not the case in reality, this extreme scenario illustrates the asymmetries between the North and the South, which is the focus of this chapter.

$$E^N = 0 \text{ meaning clean technologies in the north}$$
$$E = E^S = E^S(R^S) + E(A)\ E^S_R > 0,\ E_A > 0$$

Production

Aggregated good Q is produced with exhaustible resource R and accumulated capital K. Asymmetric conditions are reflected in the production process. While the filter technologies of the North will, in extreme cases, have no direct negative impact on their own local production, the locally produced environmental damage in the South will affect its own production process as a negative externality.

$$Q^N = Q^N(R^N, K^N)$$
$$Q^S = Q^S(R^S, K^S, E^S).$$

Damage removal technologies

Damage removal is not damage prevention. While damage prevention technologies directly prevent damage in the first place, local technologies for damage removal F^i are capable of reducing already existing damage. Because the North does not create damage in our model it does not need any damage removal technologies. Because V_N represents the costs of damage protection, damage reduction improves with more effort.

$$F^N = F^N(V^N) = 0 \text{ not required, no local demage}$$
$$F^S = F^S(V^S)$$
$$F = F^s$$

Resource stocks and pollution stocks

Resource stocks S decrease with extraction and usage as a factor of production R.

$$\dot{S} = -R$$

$$R = R^N + R^S$$

Pollution stocks (e.g. CO_2) change with pollution through current usage M^S *(R)* less natural reduction through regeneration at the rate of regeneration α and less the reduced damage from damage removal technologies.

$$\dot{A} = M^S(R) - \alpha A - F^S(V)$$
$$A(t) = \int_0^t \left(M^S(R) - \alpha A - F^S(V)\right) d\tau$$

Restricted consumer budgets

As both regions are completely separate with the exception of a shared environment (shared pollution) they also make their own decisions with respect to accumulation and consumption.

$$\dot{K}^N = Q^N - C^N$$
$$\dot{K}^S = Q^S - C^S - V^S$$

The optimal control problem and solution

Present value Hamiltonian

North and South are completely separate with only one common problem (variable), namely shared pollution.

$$N)\quad H^N = U^N(C^N, E) + P(-R^N) + \omega^N[Q^N(R^N, K^N) - C^N]$$

$$S)\quad H^S = U^S(C^S, E) + P(-R^S) + \omega^S[Q^S(R^S, K^S) - C^S - V^S] + \lambda[M^S(R^S) - \alpha A - F^S(V^S)]$$

$$\begin{aligned} World)\quad H^W = {} & U^N\left(C^N, E(R^S, A)\right) + U^S\left(C^s, E(R^S, A)\right) + P(-R) \\ & + \omega^N[Q^N(R^N, K^N) - C^N] + \omega^S[Q^S(R^S, K^S) - C^s - V^S] \\ & + \lambda[M^S(R^S, A) - \alpha A - F^S(V^S)] \end{aligned}$$

First-order requirement

Requirement of consumption and accumulation:

$$N, S, W)\quad \frac{\partial H}{\partial C^i} = U_C^i - \omega^i = 0, \quad i = N, S$$

$$N)\quad \frac{\partial H^N}{\partial R^N} = -P + \omega^N Q^N_{R^N} = 0$$

$$S)\quad \frac{\partial H^S}{\partial R^S} = U^S_E E_{R^S} - P + \omega^S Q^S_{R^S} + \lambda M^S_{R^S} = 0$$

$$W)\quad \frac{\partial H^W}{\partial R^W} = -P + \omega^N Q^N_{R^N} = 0$$

$$W)\quad \frac{\partial H^W}{\partial R^S} = U^S_E E_{R^S} + U^N_E E_{R^S} - P + \omega^S Q^S_{R^S} + \lambda M^S_{R^S} = 0$$

Resource use

Pollution clean-up:

N) no damage removal because there is no locally produced pollution

$$S, W)\quad \frac{\partial H^S}{\partial V^S} = -\omega^S - \lambda F^S_V = 0$$

Shadow-price developments:

$$\dot{P} = -\frac{\partial H}{\partial S} + \rho P, \Leftrightarrow \dot{P} = \rho P$$

$$\dot{\omega}^N = -\frac{\partial H}{\partial K^N} + \rho\omega^N, \Leftrightarrow \dot{\omega}^N = \rho\omega^N - Q_K\omega^N$$

$$\dot{\omega}^S = -\frac{\partial H}{\partial K^S} + \rho\omega^S, \Leftrightarrow \dot{\omega}^S = \rho\omega^S - Q_K\omega^S$$

$$\dot{\lambda} = -\frac{\partial H}{\partial A} + \rho\lambda, \Leftrightarrow \dot{\lambda} = \alpha\lambda + \rho\lambda - U_E E_A$$

From these first-order conditions we can develop optimal policy strategies for each problem. This should especially be done for the price path of the resource. An optimal solution for the whole system is identified in three steps.

Price path in the North and in South without considering pollution

Bear in mind that we assume that the North emits no pollution at all (unrealistically) in order to point out the effects of the asymmetries.

$$N)\quad \frac{\partial H^N}{\partial R^N} = -P + \omega^N Q^N_{R^N} = 0$$

$$S)\quad \frac{\partial H^S}{\partial R^S} = U^S_E E_{R^S} - P + \omega^S Q^S_{R^S} + \lambda M^S_{R^S} = 0$$

$$N)\ P = \omega^N Q^N_{R^N}$$

$$S)\ P^{net,S} = \omega^S Q^S_{R^S} = P$$

Price path when only considering the South

$$N) \quad \frac{\partial H^N}{\partial R^N} = -P + \omega^N Q^N_{R^N} = 0$$

$$S) \quad \frac{\partial H^S}{\partial R^S} = U^S_E E_{R^S} - P + \omega^S Q^S_{R^S} + \lambda M^S_{R^S} = 0$$

$$N) P = \omega^N \quad Q^N_{R^N}$$

$$S) \quad P^{net,S} = \omega^S \quad Q^S_{R^S} = P - U^S_E E_{R^S} - \lambda M^S_{R^S}$$

Price path from a global point of view, optimal pricing for the world

$$W) \quad \frac{\partial H^W}{\partial R^N} = -P + \omega^N Q^N_{R^N} = 0$$

$$W) \frac{\partial H^W}{\partial R^S} = U^S_E E_{R^S} + U^N_E E_{R^S} - P + \omega^S Q^S_{R^S} + \lambda M^S_{R^S} = 0$$

$$N) P = \omega^N Q^N_{R^N}$$

$$S) \quad P^{net,S} = \omega^S Q^S_{R^S} = P - U^S_E E_{R^S} - U^N_E E_{R^S} - \lambda M^S_{R^S}$$

One world policy could be a Pigou tax, which would only be levied on the resources used by the polluting South. This tax covers the components $-U^S_E E_{R^S} - U^N_E E_{R^S} - \lambda M^S_{R^S}$. However, this price segmentation is a considerable incentive for illegal arbitrage (smuggling), which in turn can only be prevented at high cost. A smuggling-free alternative could be a tax levied at source on resource extraction. Under this system the North, too, would pay the efficient resource price of the South. The result would be that the price charged in the North would be too high, considering the damaging effects, and resource use in the North would be too small.

References

Agrawala, S., (ed) (2005). *Bridge Over Troubled Waters: Linking Climate Change and Development.* Paris: OECD.

Baumol, W. J., and W. E. Oates (1971). 'The Use of Standards and Prices for Protection of the Environment', *Swedish Journal of Economics*, 73: 42–54.

——(1988). *The Theory of Environmental Policy*, 2nd edition. Cambridge: Cambridge University Press.

Boden, T. A., G. Marland, and R. J. Andres (2011). 'Global, Regional, and National Fossil-Fuel CO2 Emissions'. Oak Ridge, TN: Carbon Dioxide Information Analysis Center, Oak Ridge National Laboratory. Available at: doi 10.3334/CDIAC/00001_V2011 (accessed November 7, 2011).

Bommer, R., and G. G. Schulze (1999). 'Environmental Improvement with Trade Liberalization', *European Journal of Political Economy*, 15: 639–61.

Cansier, D. (1996). *Umweltökonomie,* 2nd edition. Stuttgart: UTB für Wissenschaft, Lucius & Lucius.

Christiansen, A. C., A. Arvanitakis, K. Tangen, and H. Hasselknippe (2005). 'Price Determinants in the EU Emissions Trading Scheme', *Climate Policy,* 5: 15–30.

Convery, F. J. (2009). 'Reflections—The Emerging Literature on Emissions Trading in Europe', *Review of Environmental Economics and Policy,* 3: 121–37.

Dales, J. H. (1968). *Pollution, Property and Prices.* Toronto: University of Toronto Press.

Dorn, R. (1996). *Effizienz Umweltpolitischer Instrumente zur Emissionshinderung. Technische und ökonomische Kriterien.* Berlin: Erich Schmidt Verlag.

Farzin, Y. H. (1996). 'Optimal Pricing of Environmental and Natural Resource use with Stock Externalities', *Journal of Public Economics,* 62: 31–57.

Giraudet, L.-G., and P. Quirion (2008). 'Efficiency and Distributional Impacts of Tradable White Certificates Compared to Taxes, Subsidies and Regulations'. Nota di Lavoro 88. Milan: Fondazione Eni Enrico Mattei, International Energy Markets.

Gries, T. (1995). *Wachstum, Humankapital und die Dynamik der komparativen Vorteile.* Tübingen: Mohr Siebeck.

——(2007). 'Global Shift—The European Union, the United States, and the Emergence of China'. In R. Tilly, P. J. J Welfens, and M. Heise (eds), *50 Years of EU Economic Dynamics.* Berlin: Springer.

Gries, T., and S. Jungblut (1997a). 'Catching-up and Structural Change', *Economia Internationale,* 50 (4): 3–24.

——(1997b). 'Catching-up of Economies in Transformation'. In P. J. J. Welfens, and H. C. Wolf (eds), *Banking, International Capital Flows and Growth in Europe.* Berlin: Springer.

Harmeling, S., C. Bals, W. Sterk, and R. Watanabe (2009). 'Funding Sources for International Climate Policy'. Briefing Papers. Bonn/Berlin: Germanwatch.

Heston, A., R. Summers, and B. Aten (Penn World Tables) (2011). Version 7.0 Philadelphia, PA: University of Pennsylvania, Center for International Comparisons of Production, Income and Prices. Available at: http://pwt.econ.upenn.edu/php_site/pwt_index.php (accessed on 20 April 2012).

Hoel, M., and L. Karp (2002). 'Taxes versus Quotas for a Stock Pollutant', *Resource and Energy Economics,* 24: 367–84.

Lieb, C. M. (2004). 'The Environmental Kuznets Curve and Flow versus Stock Pollution: The Neglect of Future Damages', *Environmental & Resource Economics,* 29, 483–506.

Milanovic, B., and S. Yitzhaki (2002). 'Decomposing World Income Distribution: Does the World have a Middle Class?'. *Review of Income and Wealth,* 48 (2): 155–78.

Neary, J. P. (2006). 'International Trade and the Environment: Theoretical and Policy Linkages', *Environmental & Resource Economics,* 33: 95–118.

OECD (2009a). *Integrating Climate Change Adaptation into Development Co-operation: Policy Guidance.* Paris: OECD.

——(2009b). *The Economics of Climate Change Mitigation—Policies and Options for Global Action beyond 2012.* Paris: OECD.

Oikonomou, V., C. Jepma, F. Becchis, and D. Russolillo (2008). 'White Certificates for Energy Efficiency Improvement with Energy Taxes: A Theoretical Economic Model', *Energy Economics,* 30: 3044–62.

Ott, H., F. Mersmann, W. Sterk, R. Watanabe, B. Wegmann, and H. Curtius (2009). 'Internationale Finanzmittel für den Klimaschutz', Wuppertal Papers 181. Berlin: Wuppertal Institut für Klima, Umwelt, Energie GmbH.

Perman, R., Y. Ma, J. McGilvray, and M. Common (2003). *Natural Resource and Environment Economics*, 3rd edition. Essex: Pearson Education Limited.

Pigou, A. C. (1920). *The Economics of Welfare. Basingstoke*: Palgrave McMillan.

Rose, A., B. Stevens, J. Edmonds, and M. Wise (1998). 'International Equity and Differentiation in Global Warming Policy—An Application to Tradable Emission Permits, *Environmental and Resource Economics*, 12: 25–51.

Stern, N. (2006). *The Economics of Climate Change*. Cambridge: Cambridge University Press.

United Nations (UN) (2011). 'World Population Prospects: The 2010 Revision'. CD-ROM edition. New York: UN, Department of Economic and Social Affairs, Population Division.

Xabadia, A., R. U. Goetz, and D. Zilberman, (2005). 'Control of Accumulating Stock Pollution by Heterogeneous Producers', *Journal of Economic Dynamics & Control*, 30: 1105–30.

——(2008). 'The Gains from Differentiated Policies to Control Stock Pollution when Producers are Heterogeneous', *American Journal of Agricultural Economics*, 90 (4): 1059–73.

12

Global Supply Chains in Chinese Industrialization: Impact on Waste Scavenging in Developing Countries

Martin Medina

12.1 Introduction

Recycling in developing countries relies on the activities carried out informally by scavengers or waste pickers. These activities have existed for centuries, supplying raw materials that industry recycles (Medina 2007). But over the past two decades, globalization has encouraged the development of global supply chains that link scavengers in many developing countries with industrial activities in China and India. These new supply chains have received scant attention from researchers. This chapter intends to fill some knowledge gaps about these supply chains.

Over the past two decades China, and, to a lesser extent India, has undergone a remarkable economic transformation. This transformation has been spearheaded by industrialization. Between 2003 and 2007, the increase of China's industrial production grew at an annual rate of 11.5–12.8 per cent. In 2006, the added value of industrial activities accounted for 43.1 per cent of the national economy.

Industrial activities require a wide variety of inputs, such as energy, water, metals, plastics, wood, textiles, glass, and so on. China is now an important global player in the international commodities markets. The country is a significant producer and consumer of commodities and other industrial inputs.

China now tops the world in the production of steel, coal, cement, TVs, and cotton fabric, and ranks second in power generation, third in sugar output, and fifth in crude oil output. But the country is not self sufficient in a number of raw materials, such as crude oil, coke, paper, metals, and plastics. In order to close the gap between demand and domestic production, China must import large amounts of raw materials, and this encouraged the development of global supply chains and the world's largest recycling efforts. Some of the industrial inputs are recyclable materials recovered from waste in many countries. It can be argued that Chinese industrialization has been fuelled by waste from the USA and other countries. China is the world's largest consumer and largest importer of recyclable materials. In 2008, the USA sold China over US $7.7 billion in recyclable materials.

China's recycling supply chains are more global than those of other countries. Waste pickers also play an important role in the domestic supply chains in many developing countries. In Brazil, for instance, about 90 per cent of the materials recycled by industry are recovered by Brazilian scavengers (Medina 2010).

These supply chains have received little attention from researchers and thus our knowledge of them is incomplete.

12.2 Why industry in emerging countries recycles

Industry in developing countries shows a strong demand for recyclable materials due to their low cost. The main factors that account for the lower prices of secondary materials are the following. First, materials recovered from waste often include impurities. Even when materials are segregated at the source, extraneous items can be found, such as tags, traces of glue, and moisture. Virgin materials are thus more homogeneous than secondary materials. Second, most developed countries have created recycling programmes that produce large amounts of secondary materials. But supply of these materials usually exceeds domestic demand, so a large percentage of materials must be exported and sold in international markets. Third, many materials can be easily recycled and transformed into new products. But there are constraints on recycling some materials, such as paper. Paper is made from vegetable fibres, most commonly wood. Each time paper is recycled the fibres break and get increasingly shorter. As a result, paper and cardboard can only be recycled two to four times before the fibres get too short. A ton of wood pulp has more fibre than a ton of recovered paper. Fourth, recycling requires less energy and water than processing virgin materials (see Table 12.1), thus lowering industry's operating costs. Fifth, the recovery of materials in developing countries relies on large numbers of scavengers, who lack the organization and power to have an impact on prices (Bartone 1988; Medina 2007).

These factors translate into lower prices for recyclable materials. For example, in Mexico the price per ton of wood pulp imported from the USA

Table 12.1. Environmental benefits from substituting secondary materials for virgin resources

Environmental benefit	Aluminum%	Steel%	Paper%	Glass%
Reduction of energy use	90–97	47–74	23–74	4–32
Reduction of air pollution	95	85	74	20
Reduction of water pollution	97	76	35	—
Reduction of mining wastes	—	97	—	80
Reduction of water use	—	40	58	50
Savings CO2 emissions	5–12*	1*	1–2*	1*

Notes: *Savings in ton/ton.

Sources: Based on Cowles Letcher (1986) and ISWA (2009).

is seven times that of recovered waste paper. And in China, in 2008 the price of scrap copper was 8 per cent lower than virgin copper. In May 2009, the price of virgin polyethylene terephthalate (PET) was US$0.87/lb while secondary PET was US$0.65 (25 per cent lower).

Recycling can render social, economic, and environmental benefits. It provides an income to scavengers who recover recyclable materials. Factories that consume recyclable materials can be built for a fraction of the cost of building plants that consume virgin materials. Recycling lowers industry's operating costs and reduces the amount of waste that needs to be collected, transported, and disposed of, thus extending the life of disposal facilities. This translates into savings to municipalities (Vogler 1984). Recycling can result in a more competitive economy and a cleaner environment, and can contribute to a more sustainable development.

12.3 The development of global supply chains for raw materials

The current supply chains for China, India, and other developing countries differ in important respects from those in the developed world today and when they underwent industrialization. Chinese industrial supply chains show a more circular pattern, with more intensive recycling of materials:

Obviously, these loops are not completely closed. Chinese production and consumption activities generate large amounts of waste of all kinds that does not enter these recycling loops. In fact, in 2005, China surpassed the USA as the world's largest generator of solid waste. No other country in history has generated as much waste in such a short period as China. Chinese industrial activities have created serious environmental problems in terms of air, water, and land pollution (Yardley 2005).

China's use of coal and lack of pollution-prevention measures translates into highly polluted air. The country has become the worst atmospheric

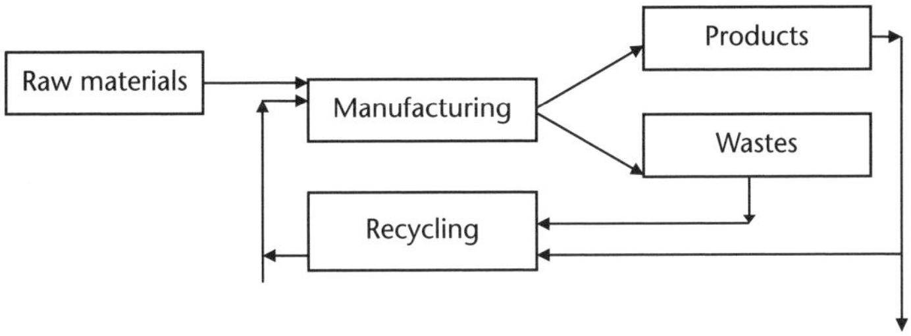

Figure 12.1. A more environmentally sustainable model of production and consumption
Source: Based on Medina (2007).

polluter in the world in terms of sulphur dioxide (SO_2) and nitrogen oxides (NO_x). But the recycling of materials is widespread throughout the Chinese economy. And Chinese demand has encouraged the development of global supply chains to provide recycled materials to its industry, and in the process it has encouraged the development of perhaps the largest recycling effort in the history of the world. These new supply chains span the globe and their underlying cause is economics (Branigan 2009).

Chinese industry discovered that the use of recycled raw materials is much cheaper than the use of virgin materials. Historically, the prices of materials recovered from waste (also known as 'recyclables' and 'secondary materials') are lower than their virgin counterparts. But the prices of secondary materials usually move in tandem with the prices of raw materials.

The prices of commodities in international markets are determined by the interplay of factors that affect global demand and supply, such as economic growth, interest rates, currency exchange rates, natural disasters, labour strikes or political crises in important producing regions, exploitation of new mines, and so forth (Medina 2007).

Periods of strong economic growth tend to push up demand for commodities, as well as their prices. Over the past ten years, the economies of China and India have grown at a fast pace, which in turn has put upward pressure on commodities. The price of copper, for instance, tripled between 2002 and 2007, the price of zinc doubled, and wheat and soybean rose 70 per cent in 2007. Futures prices of crude oil, gold, silver, lead, uranium, cattle, cocoa, and corn were all at or near record levels at the end of 2008. The biggest single factor increasing commodity prices is China's rush to construct factories, other buildings, and roads to satisfy a growing, increasingly middle-class urban population with a taste for cars and other consumer goods.

China today has over 7,000 steel factories, double the number in 2002. Every new factory needs electricity, which means that power plants must be built.

More diesel-powered trains are required to get the coal to the power plants, and more trucks and expanded ports are needed to move the steel to market.

China's Industrial Revolution caused an increase in crude oil consumption from 5.5 million barrels in 2003 to 8 million in 2008, according to the International Energy Agency, representing 31 per cent of the total rise in global demand (Anon. 2011). Over the same period, China was responsible for 64 per cent of the increased global demand for copper, 70 per cent of that for aluminium, and 82 per cent for zinc (Fagone 2011).

The relatively recent globalization of the supply chain has a greater impact on international trade than it used to. According to some estimates, in the 1960s and 1970s, if global GDP increased (or decreased) by 1 per cent, trade would grow (or shrink) by about 2 per cent, but in the 1990s, the change in trade was 3.4 per cent. A globalized supply chain has a direct impact on the prices that scavengers throughout the developing world get paid for the recyclables they recover. During the boom years of 2006–8, the high prices of recyclables encouraged the development of an active international trade. High prices translated into higher incomes for millions of scavengers worldwide, and probably allowed many to escape poverty.

China is now a major global player in the commodities markets, as well as in the international trade of recyclables. The greater impact of a globalized supply chain encouraged international trade in recyclables. In 2001 China became the world's largest importer of scrap metal. Most of China's imports of recyclable materials originally comes from developed countries. But about 15 per cent came from developing countries, which arguably has benefitted millions of scavengers worldwide (Pollack and Bradsher 2004). Recovery of recyclables within China is intensive, and has led to the development of the world's largest informal recycling sector, with as many as 6 million scavengers (Medina 2008).

But in 2008 the international economic crisis that began in the USA had a dramatic impact on those same scavengers that had benefitted from Chinese demand in earlier years. Lower demand for all kinds of products in the USA and other countries reduced the demand for commodities and recyclables, depressing their prices (see Figure 12.1). Prices of recyclables dropped by more than 50 per cent, reducing scavengers' incomes, thus forcing many of them back into poverty.

China's demand for recyclables is well-documented, as are its imports from various countries. What is not well-documented is how much the informal sector in developing countries accounts for in Chinese imports of recyclables. Newspaper articles have presented evidence that scavengers from many developing countries contribute significantly to China's imports (see for instance, Brooke 2004; Pollack and Bradsher 2004; Branigan 2009). In field work I have conducted in Africa, Asia, Latin America, and the Middle East

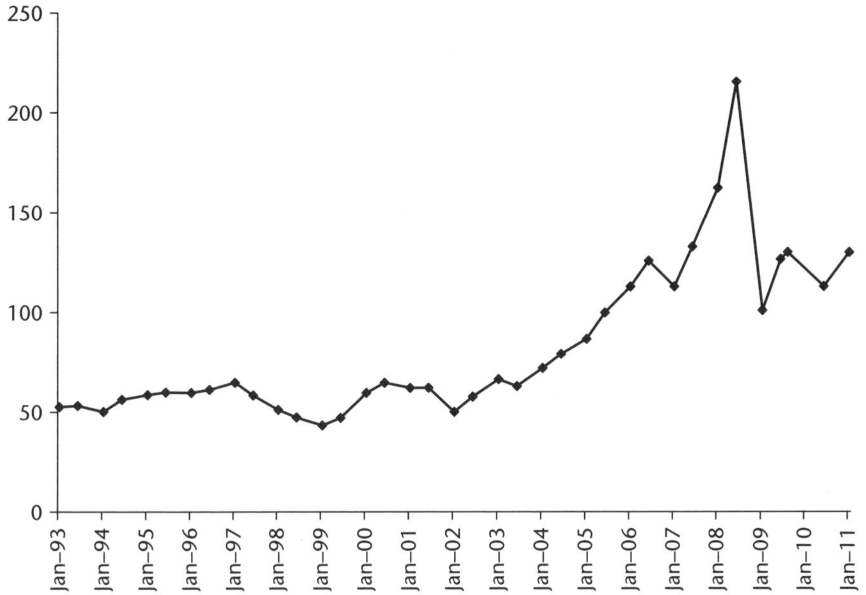

Figure 12.2. Commodity price index, 1993–2011
Source: prepared using IMF data (http://www.imf.org/external/np/res/commod/index.aspx).

respondents report that some of the materials recovered by local scavengers are exported to China. Current import and export statistics of recyclable materials do not distinguish whether the materials were recovered by scavengers or not. Research in this area is necessary to quantify scavengers' contribution to the international trade in recyclables.

In early 2009, prices of recyclables started to rebound due to economic recovery in several Asian countries, as Figure 12.2 illustrates.

12.4 Features of global supply chains for secondary materials

Recycling activities in developing countries rely largely on the informal recovery by scavengers of materials from waste. It has been estimated that in African, Asian, and Latin American cities about 1 per cent of the urban population survives by scavenging. This translates into a potential scavenger population of about 15 million worldwide. Scavengers recover materials to sell for reuse or recycling, as well as diverse items for their own consumption. These individuals are generally known as 'scavengers' 'waste pickers', or 'rag pickers' in English-speaking areas, but they also receive different names, depending on the local language, on the place they work, and on the material(s) they collect. In Mexico, for example, dumpsite scavengers are known as *pepenadores*, in Brazil they are known as *catadores*, while the term *cartoneros* applies to the cardboard collectors, *buscabotes* to the aluminum can collectors, and *traperos* to rag collectors. And Colombians use the generic term *basuriegos*, with scrap metal collectors known as *chatarreros*, glass bottle collectors as *frasqueros*, and so on (Medina 2007).

The underlying factors that created the current recycling system are fundamentally economic. The developing world is becoming more urban, which translates into a concentration of generation of large amounts of waste materials. Depending on the composition of industrial activities, industry demands inexpensive raw materials recovered from waste. Given the widespread poverty prevalent in developing countries, the inability of the economy to generate enough jobs, and the lack of a safety net for the poor, many people are forced into scavenging.

Most studies report that scavengers constitute disadvantaged and vulnerable segments of the population. Scavengers face multiple hazards and problems. Due to their daily contact with garbage, scavengers are usually associated with dirt, disease, squalor, and are perceived as a nuisance, a symbol of backwardness, and even as criminals. They survive in a hostile physical and social environment (see Furedy 1984, 1991; Castillo 1990; Fundacion Social 1990, 1991; Abad 1991; Chapin 1995).

Figure 12.3 shows the typical flow of recyclable materials in the informal recycling sector. Because industry demands large volumes of materials that are processed—sorted, baled, crushed, or granulated—it does not buy directly from individual waste pickers. Instead, middlemen purchase recyclables recovered by waste pickers, then sell the materials—after some sorting, cleaning, and processing—to scrap dealers, who in turn sell to industry. In these circumstances, middlemen often earn large profits, while waste pickers are paid much too little to escape poverty. The existence of middlemen allows the possibility of exploitation and/or political control of scavengers (see Figure 12.3).

Scavengers usually specialize in recovering one or a few types of materials from waste. This depends on the availability of a vehicle to transport materials. For example, anyone with a sack or plastic bag can recover aluminium cans on the streets, but some kind of vehicle is necessary to carry cardboard, which is bulky and heavy. Upper-income neighbourhoods, as well as hotels and business and commercial districts are the most desirable areas for scavengers because they generate more recyclables.

12.4.1 *Scavenger characteristics*

Based on a review of studies, both academic and policy-oriented, as well as on anecdotal evidence, it is possible to enumerate the following generalizations about scavengers (see Figure 12.4).

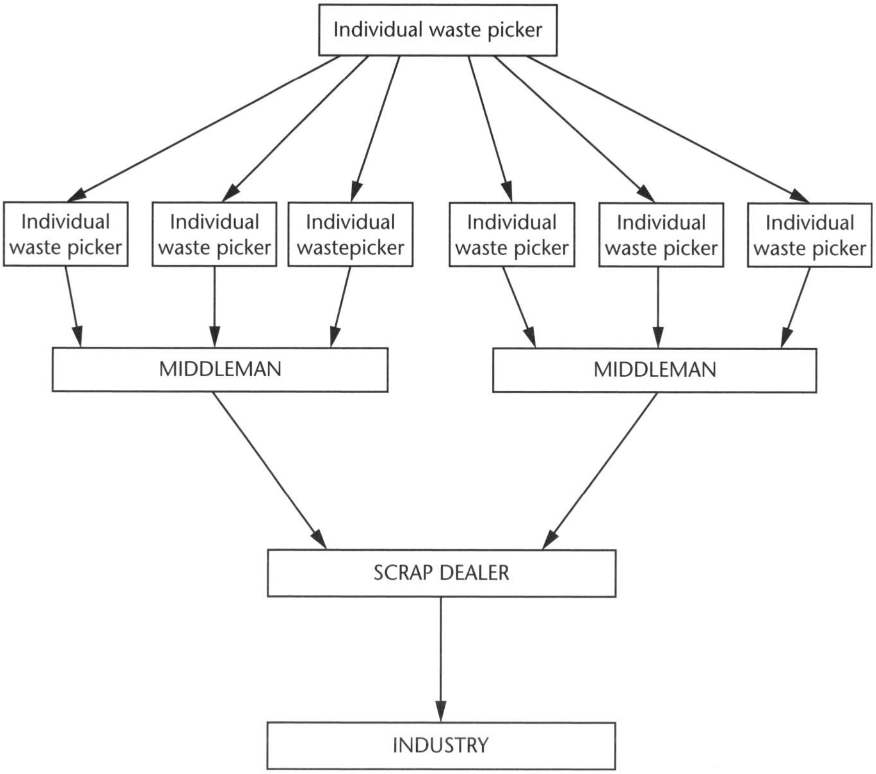

Figure 12.3. Typical supply chain for recyclable materials
Source: Based on Medina (1997).

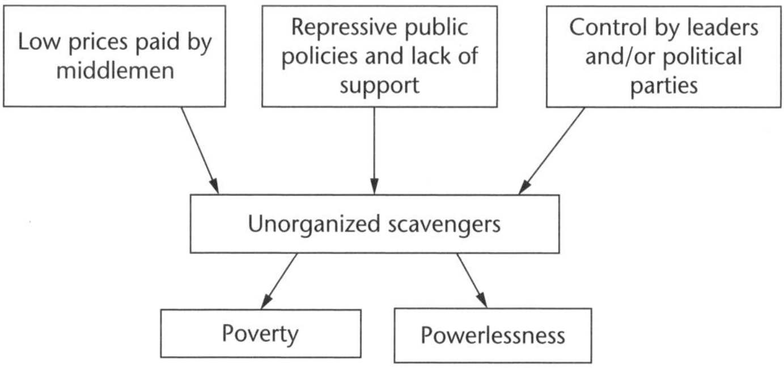

Figure 12.4. Typical power relations in scavenging in developing countries
Source: Based on Medina (1997).

(i) Scavenger individuals tend to be poor relative to the rest of society. Many studies have found that scavenger earnings fall below the minimum wage. When scavenging activities are supported or at least tolerated, however, scavengers can earn decent incomes.

(ii) Due to their daily contact with waste materials, their low incomes, and their often ragged appearance, society ascribes a low status to scavengers. Their scavenging activities frequently face a hostile and sometimes violent environment.

(iii) Immigrants, often from rural areas, comprise an important percentage of scavenger populations.

(iv) Scavenging epitomizes the informal sector: it constitutes a labour-intensive, low-technology, low-paid, unrecorded, and unregulated activity.

(v) Scavenging can render economic and environmental benefits, such as work for unemployed individuals, supplies raw materials for industry, reducing the demand for collection, transport, and disposal equipment and facilities. Furthermore, recycling has a lower environmental impact than use of virgin resources.

(vi) Scavenging not only generates benefits to society, it may also have social costs, such as scattering waste on the streets.

(vii) Scavenging represents an adaptive response to the chronic poverty prevalent in developing countries. However, scavenging also appears during particularly stressful situations that beget extraordinary circumstances and scarcity, such as war and severe economic crises. In the aftermath of the collapse of the Soviet Union in 1989, and the ensuing economic crisis and unemployment, street and dumpsite scavenging became widespread in Hungary, Russia, Ukraine, Yugoslavia, and Romania.

(viii) Depending on the degree of industrialization of a country, scavenging supplies raw materials largely to either artisans or to industry. In regions where industrialization is relatively more advanced, such as in China, Latin America, and South East Asia, the materials recovered by scavengers are consumed by industry. Various studies have documented industrial use and demand for inexpensive materials recovered by scavengers. On the other hand, in regions where use of industrial consumer products is not widespread, such as in Africa and the non-oil-producing countries of the Middle East, scavengers supply artisans with materials. In these countries, artisans manufacture a wide variety of consumer goods from materials collected by scavengers, such as sandals and water bags from old tires, oil lamps that use burnt-out light bulbs as fuel reservoirs, children's toys, musical instruments, and household utensils from metal scrap (Medina 1997, 2007).

12.4.2 *Recovery patterns*

The recovery of materials from waste by scavengers in developing countries takes place in a wide variety of settings. Although the circumstances under which materials are recovered in a particular place may be unique, scavenging patterns do exist. According to where they occur along the waste management system, scavenging activities can be classified into the following:

1. *Source separation.* Individuals at homes, small businesses, and offices recover materials, such as food leftovers and aluminium cans. These materials are then reused, sold or given away (Medina 1993).

2. *Sorting of recyclables by collection crews while on their collection routes.* This activity is common in Mexican, Colombian, Thai, and Philippine localities. Collection crews later sell the materials on their way to transfer or disposal facilities and divide the proceeds among them. Sorting of recyclables by collection crews can double their salaries, providing a strong incentive to engage in it (Medina 1997).

3. *Recovery of recyclables by informal refuse collectors.* The *zabbaleen* of Cairo constitute an effective refuse collection and recycling system. A pair of *zabbaleen* working with a pickup truck can collect garbage from 350 households in a day. After sorting the garbage, the collectors feed the edible portion to pigs, sell pig droppings and human excrement to farmers as fertilizer, and scrap metal, glass, paper, and plastics to middlemen, who then sell the materials to craftsmen or to industry for recycling. They can reuse or recycle 80 per cent of the waste they collect. Thus only the residual 20 per cent needs final disposal. This high diversion rate from landfills renders social, economic, and environmental benefits (CID 2001).

4. *Itinerant buyers purchase recyclables from residents.* In many cities, itinerant buyers purchase from residents various types of items for reuse and recycling, such as cans, bottles, paper, old appliances, and old mattresses. They use pushcarts, animal-drawn carts, and pick-up trucks to transport these items.

5. *Scavengers salvage materials from dumpsters.* Scavengers consider refuse from high-income neighbourhoods, hotels, and stores as particularly valuable, since wealthy individuals tend to discard more recyclables and items that can be repaired or reused. They can often be seen near dumpsters, looking for items and materials they can salvage.

6. *Scavenging on the streets or public spaces*: Scavengers pick up recyclables from litter, for example in Pune, India, where the approximately 10,000 'rag pickers' in the city recover materials from garbage thrown into the streets. This type of recovery activity is perhaps the most common in the world, because virtually anyone equipped with a bag or sack can do it (Chapin 1995).

7. *Recovery in canals and rivers that cross urban areas.* Canals and rivers that run through urban areas in developing countries often transport waste materials thrown in by residents or litter carried by run-off water. This type of scavenging activity is common in cities such as Manila and Bangkok, where canals and rivers run through their cities. Scavengers generally recover recyclables from small boats, which they also use to transport the materials for sale. Recyclables present in canals and rivers tend to be more abundant during the rainy season, as run-off water carries materials littered on the streets.

8. *Recovery at composting plants.* Recovery of recyclables also exists at composting plants, such as the one in Monterrey, Mexico, which allows scavenging activities in its premises. This does not interfere with composting operations and reduces the presence of inorganic materials in the compost. Inorganic materials are contaminants if present in the compost, and thus scavenging improves the quality of the final product.

9. *Recovery at municipal open dumps.* Large scavenging communities have developed around open dumps in many developing country cities. As many as 20,000 scavengers live and work in Calcutta's municipal dumps: 12,000 in Manila, and 15,000 in Mexico City. By settling around the dumps, scavengers minimize their transportation costs, occupy land that may be undesirable to others, have access to discarded materials that can be used as construction materials for their homes—usually shacks—and thus save on housing costs. Living around a dump allows entire families to recover materials there by simply claiming an area and salvaging materials while mothers keep an eye on their children. Street scavenging, on the other hand, requires walking several miles a day searching for materials, making it harder for families with small children to recover materials. Settling around a dump also enables families to raise pigs by feeding them discarded organic materials found at the dumps.

10. *Recovery at landfills.* Prior to the compaction and burial of waste, scavengers recover materials at landfills, at least where these activities are allowed, as in Mexico City. At these sites, scavenging activities have been integrated into the normal operation of the landfills. As soon as the refuse is dumped on the ground, scavengers pick over the piles of mixed waste, searching for any items that can be reused or recycled. Later during the day, bulldozers compact the refuse and cover it with a layer of dirt (Medina 1997).

12.4.3 *Formalization of scavenging*

Scavengers are not always the poorest of the poor. In fact, scavengers sometimes earn more than factory workers. When scavengers organize themselves in micro-enterprises, scavenger cooperatives, or form public–private partnerships with municipalities, they can achieve a decent standard of living and improve their working conditions, resulting in grassroots development. In

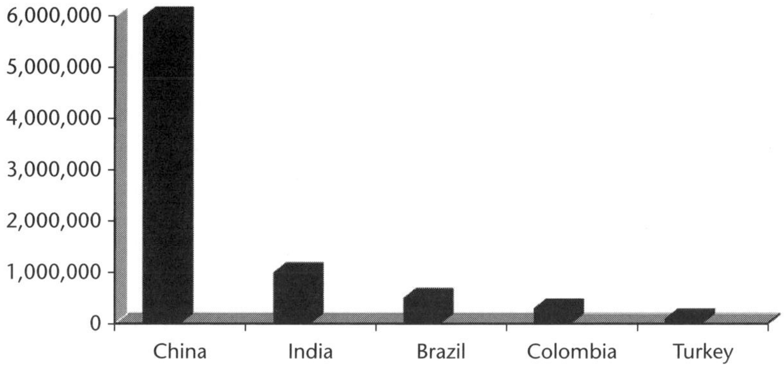

Figure 12.5. Estimated number of waste-pickers in selected countries
Source: Based on Medina (2007, 2008).

African, Asian, and Latin American cities there is a growing number of successful micro-enterprises, scavenger cooperatives and public–private partnerships that provide low-cost waste management services to municipalities.

The structural causes of scavenging are under-development, poverty, unemployment, the lack of a safety net for the poor, as well as industrial demand for inexpensive raw materials. These factors are likely to continue to exist. Therefore, a public policy that supports scavenging activities would be humane, as well as make social, economic, and environmental sense.

Figure 12.5 presents estimates of the number of scavengers in selected countries.

A growing number of experiences in Africa, Asia, and Latin America demonstrate that formalization of scavenging can promote grassroots development, empowerment, poverty reduction, as well as protect the environment and improve industrial competitiveness. The most common models are:

1. *Scavenger cooperatives*: By getting organized, waste pickers become empowered. They can strengthen their bargaining position with industry and government, become actors in the development process, and overcome poverty through grassroots development. Working together, they can gain stability, higher incomes, and legalization of their activities. They can obtain better prices by circumventing middlemen and adding value to materials sold. And organized into cooperatives, they can enter into contracts with industry or grant agreements with donors. In South America alone, there are about 1,000 scavenger cooperatives, mostly in Argentina, Brazil, and Colombia.

2. *Micro-enterprises*: Scavengers can also create their own micro-enterprises to perform waste collection, recycling, and various manufacturing activities that use waste as raw materials.

3. *Public–private partnerships*: Public–private partnerships can combine the energy, creativity, and low-operating costs of scavengers in the waste management sector. Public–private partnerships for collecting waste and recyclables can be beneficial to waste picker groups as well as to broader society. In partnerships in several Colombian cities, the municipality provides infrastructure and equipment while waste pickers provide labour. In Bogotá a partnership has been formed to operate a recycling plant, managed by the Bogotá Association of Waste Pickers, to which the municipality takes recyclables separated at source.

As Figure 12.6 illustrates, cooperatives that have access to source-separated materials, such as the one in Juarez, Mexico, can earn ten times the country's poverty line income. Cairo micro-entrepreneurs that collect waste, sell recyclables, and manufacture products from recyclable materials earn nearly eight times the poverty line income, and therefore have been able to escape poverty (Medina 2008).

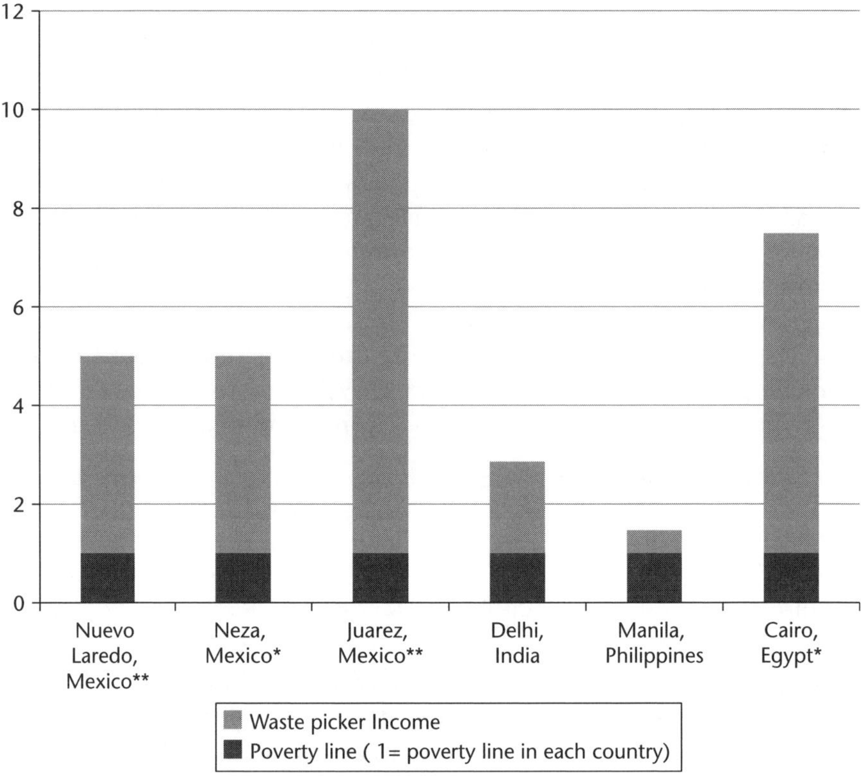

Figure 12.6. Scavenger income in selected cities

Note: *includes income from waste collection and recycling activities. **includes income from collection of source-separated recyclables.
Source: Based on Medina (2007).

12.4.4 *Economic and environmental impact of scavenging*

Scavenging renders economic and environmental benefits, for example providing an income to unemployed individuals, supplying inexpensive raw materials to industry, reducing the demand for collection, transport, and disposal equipment and facilities. Furthermore, recycling has a lower environmental impact than the use of virgin resources.

Despite the lack of reliable data at the national level, various studies have highlighted the economic importance of scavenging activities. In Bangkok, Jakarta, Kanpur, Karachi, and Manila, scavenging saves each city at least US$23 million a year in the shape of lower imports of raw materials, and reduced need for collection, transport, and disposal equipment, personnel, and facilities. In Mumbai the economic impact of recycling activities has been estimated at nearly US$1 billion per year in the recovery of materials and the manufacture of products from them. According to some estimates, Indonesian scavengers reduce the amount of waste that needs final disposal by one third, which has significant environmental and economic benefits. In the city of Nuevo Laredo, on the USA–Mexican border, the economic impact of scavenging activities has been estimated at nearly half a million dollars a month. Table 12.2 shows estimates on the economic impact of several cities.

12.4.5 *Scavenging and climate change*

When organic waste—mostly food leftovers, kitchen and garden waste—is sent to open dumps and landfills it gets buried under layers of waste or dirt. Eventually, all oxygen is consumed and organic matter decomposes in anaerobic conditions. Anaerobic decomposition generates methane, a greenhouse gas that is 20 times more potent than CO_2 in trapping the sun's heat. Garbage dumps and landfills generate about 11 per cent of anthropogenic emissions of greenhouse gases.

Table 12.2. Estimated economic impact of scavenging in selected cities, 2007 (US$/year)

City	Economic impact
Mexico City*	95 million
Bogotá, Colombia*	56 million
Buenos Aires, Argentina*	50 million
Manila, Philippines*	40 million
Cairo, Egypt**	281 million
New Delhi, India*	54 million

Notes: *includes only the recovery of recyclable materials and not the manufacturing of products made from waste materials. ** includes income from waste collection, sale of recyclables, and manufacturing activities.

Source: Based on Medina (2007).

Diverting organic waste from dumps and landfills can prevent the generation of methane and reduce greenhouse emissions. There are two ways to accomplish this: composting and pig farming. Composting is the biological decomposition of organic matter in aerobic conditions, which generates little or no methane. The resulting compost can be used in landscaping, horticulture, and as a soil conditioner in agriculture. Organic waste, such as food leftovers can be recovered and used to feed pigs. Composting and pig farming can also create jobs and reduce poverty for the scavengers who recover those materials. In southern Bali, Indonesia, 50 pig farms generate enough demand for organic waste to provide income opportunities for hundreds of scavengers. This practice, however, requires additional research to make sure it does not pose risks to public health from consuming the meat from these farms.

The recovery and recycling of inorganic materials by scavengers saves energy. Power generation is one of the largest sources of greenhouse gases. Assuming that everything else remains the same, recycling also reduces the emissions of greenhouse gases.

12.5 Public policy issues that need to be addressed

The informal recycling sector and the international trade in recyclables can benefit millions of low-income and vulnerable individuals worldwide, as well as contributing to a more competitive economy and environmental protection. It can be argued that scavenging can be a perfect example of sustainable development. Only supportive efforts can unlock their development potential. But there are several important issues that need to be addressed:

1. Public-policy. Authorities in developing countries display a wide variety of policies that deal with scavengers. Those policies can be classified into the following:
    a. Repression. The dominant view of scavenging, which still prevails in many developing countries, sees scavenging as inhuman, a symbol of backwardness, and a source of embarrassment and shame for the city or country. Scavenging has been declared illegal and punished in many cities of Asia and Latin America.
    b. Neglect. In other cases, authorities simply ignore scavengers and their operations, leaving them alone, without persecuting or helping them. African cities such as Dakar, (Senegal), Bamako (Mali), and Cotonou (Benin), illustrate the policy of neglect towards scavengers.
    c. Collusion. Government officials sometimes develop with scavengers relationships that are exploitative but also allow for mutual profit and mutual assistance; that is, relationships of political clientelism.

d. Stimulation. When scavengers get organized and receive external support, it can result in grassroots development. It can be argued that only supportive policies can unlock the development potential of the informal recycling sector.

2. Exploitation. Due to the existence of intermediaries—middlemen and scrap dealers—as well as their limited organization and education, scavengers are often subject to exploitation, being paid as little as 5 per cent of the prices paid by industry. Growing evidence demonstrates that supportive policies and scavenger organizations can end this exploitation.

3. Scavengers' health. Daily contact with waste has a serious impact on scavengers' health. Mexico City scavengers have a life expectancy of 53 years, while the general population's is 67 years. The prevalence of infectious diseases is high. And a study of the zabbaleen in Port Said, Egypt, showed that the infant mortality rate was 1/3 (i.e. one death of an infant under one year of age out of every 3 live births). This is several times higher than the rate for the region as a whole. The prevalence of enteric and parasitic diseases among the zabbaleen is much higher than the one for the region. And in Cairo, one in four babies born in the scavenger communities dies before reaching their first year. In Manila, more than 35 diseases have been identified in scavenger communities and slums, including diarrhoea, typhoid fever, cholera, dysentery, tuberculosis, anthrax, poliomyelitis, skin disorders, pneumonia, and malaria. Most health risks derive from scavengers' contact with waste of all kinds while recovering and sorting materials. Health risks can be minimized by involving scavengers in source-segregation programmes in which residents and businesses used different bins for recyclable and non-recyclable materials (Meyer 1987; Cointreau 2006).

4. Organization and empowerment. Many scavengers are illiterate or have a low educational levels. Only when they get organized they can alter the unfavourable power relations and repressive public policies that affect them.

5. Child labour issues. Scavenging is one of the worst forms of child labour. Yet scavenging is a common activity throughout the developing world. Brazil has had the most remarkable success in minimizing child labour in scavenging by including scavenger families in the *Bolsa Familia*, a conditional cash transfer programme that requires children to attend school (Medina 2010).

6. Smuggling of hazardous and e-waste: Unscrupulous individuals and businesses from developed countries sometimes smuggle municipal, hazardous, and electronic waste under the guise of exporting recyclables to countries in Africa, Asia, and Latin America. Most developed countries have enacted stringent regulations for the handling and disposal of hazardous and electronic waste. This translates into high costs for their processing, recycling, or disposal. Simply dumping this waste in developing countries is much cheaper.

Current practices for the dismantling and recovery of recyclable materials from e-waste entail serious risks to the health of those engaging in it.

12.6 Scavenging and international development agencies

Scavengers or waste pickers have been largely ignored by researchers and international development agencies. Despite the fact that there are about 15 million scavengers worldwide with an economic impact of several billion dollars, and the fact that scavenging has the potential to create jobs, reduce poverty, and improve industrial competitiveness, there is not a single academic programme that studies the informal recycling sector. Table 12.3 demonstrates that major development organizations are behind the curve and mostly ignore scavenging.

12.7 Concluding remarks

The industrialization of China and India has been fuelled by recycling waste from around the world, creating the world's largest recycling effort. In the process, global supply chains have developed, providing recyclable materials to the Chinese and Indian industry. The significance of recycling activities and their truly global character differ from supply chains when the West industrialized. China, India, and other emerging countries recycle because it makes economic sense: it is profitable for everyone in the supply chain. The fact that recycling also renders environmental benefits is incidental and does not figure in industry's decision to recycle in emerging countries.

Table 12.3. International development agencies and scavengers

Organization	Initiative to support scavengers	Actions to support scavengers
The World Bank	No	Several and growing
Asian Development Bank	No	One project in Vietnam
InterAmerican Development Bank	No	One project in Colombia
African Development Bank	No	No
UNEP	No	No
ILO	No	Campaign to eliminate child labour in scavenging
UNIDO	No	No
USAID	No	No
AVINA Foundation	Yes	Several and growing

Source: Based on Medina (2009).

Scavengers recover most of the recyclables in developing countries. There are big gaps in our knowledge of scavenging, but we know it is an activity that provides an income to at least 15 million people worldwide, with an economic impact of billions of dollars each year. Many scavengers are subject to exploitation by middlemen and affected by repressive/unsupportive public policies. Scavengers' low incomes are often the result of this exploitation and lack of support.

When scavengers are supported they can change the unfavourable power relations. The results can constitute a perfect example of sustainable development: jobs can be created, poverty can be reduced, industry can be supplied with inexpensive raw materials, natural resources can be conserved, and the environment can be protected. Scavenger cooperatives, micro-enterprises, and public–private partnerships can be successful models to formalize and incorporate scavengers into domestic and global supply chains.

External support is necessary in order to unlock the development potential of scavenging. Unfortunately, scavenging is ignored by most multilateral, bilateral, and international non-governmental agencies that work in international development and environmental protection. Scavenging has also received scant attention from scholars.

Scavengers do suffer from serious problems that need to be addressed, particularly the risks to their health and the prevalence of child labour. Nevertheless, growing evidence demonstrates that formalization and organization can solve or greatly minimize these problems. In Brazil, for instance, scavengers have been given legal status as a legitimate stakeholder in the waste management system and they can receive loans, grants, and training. As a result there has been a reduction in child labour and Brazilian scavengers now enjoy benefits such as empowerment, increased earnings, a reduction in police harassment, and better working and living conditions.

Industrial policy in developing countries should include active support for the informal recycling sector. Working with the informal sector can create jobs, reduce poverty, improve industrial competitiveness, conserve natural resources, protect the environment, and save cities money by reducing the amount of waste that needs to be collected, transported, and disposed of.

References

Abad, R. (1991). 'Squatting and Scavenging in Smokey Mountain', *Ateneo de Manila: Philippine Studies*, 39: 267–85.

Anon. (2011). 'Oil and Gasoline', *The New York Times*, 23 August.

Bartone, C. (1988). 'The Value in Wastes', *Decade Watch*, September: 3–4.

Branigan, T. (2009). 'From East to West, a Chain Collapses', *The Guardian*, 8 January.

Brooke, J. (2004). 'Asian Scavengers Feed China's Hunger for Steel', *The New York Times*, 11 June.

Castillo, H. (1990). *La Sociedad de la Basura: Caciquismo Urbano en la Ciudad de México*, 2nd edition. Mexico City: UNAM.

Chapin, C. (1995). 'The Rag-Pickers of Pune', *UNESCO Courier*, March: 18–19.

Community and Institutional Development (CID) (2001). *The Informal Solid Waste Sector in Egypt: Prospects for Formalization*. Cairo: CID.

Cointreau, S. (2006). 'Occupational and Environmental Health Issues of Solid Waste Management: Special Emphasis on Middle-and Lower-Income Countries'. Urban Papers 2. Washington, DC: World Bank.

Cowles Letcher, R. (1986). 'Source Separation and Citizen Recycling'. In W. Robinson (ed.), *The Solid Waste Handbook*. New York: John Wiley & Sons.

Fagone, J. (2011). 'There's Gold in that Scrap', *The New York Times*, 12 August.

Fundación Social (1990). *Memorias del Primer Encuentro Nacional de Recicladores*. Bogotá: Fundación Social, Programa Nacional de Reciclaje.

——(1991). *Tecnología, Diseño Industrial y Factores Humanos en el Reciclaje de Basuras*. Bogotá: Fundación Social, Programa Nacional de Reciclaje.

Furedy, C. (1984). 'Resource-Conserving Traditions and Waste Disposal: The Garbage Farms and Sewage-Fed Fisheries of Calcutta, *Conservation & Recycling*, 7: 181–90.

——(1991). 'Social Aspects of Solid Waste Recovery in Asian Cities'. Environmental Sanitation Reviews 30. Bangkok: Environmental Sanitation Centre.

International Solid Wastes Association (ISWA) (2009). 'Background Document for the 2009 ISWA and DAKOFA Conference on Waste and Climate Change'. Copenhagen: ISWA.

Medina, M. (1993). 'Collecting Recyclables in Metro Manila'. *BioCycle*, June: 43–45.

——(1997). Informal Recycling and Collection of Solid Wastes in Developing Countries: Issues and Opportunities'. Working Paper 24. Tokyo: United Nations University, Institute of Advanced Studies.

——(2007). *The World's Scavengers: Salvaging for Sustainable Consumption and Production*. Lanham, MD: AltaMira Press.

——(2008). 'The Informal Recycling Sector in Developing Countries: Asset or Liability?', *GRIDLINES*. Washington, DC: World Bank.

——(2009). 'Global Supply Chains in Chinese and Indian Industrialization: Impact at the Grassroots in Developing Countries'. Paper presented at the UNU-WIDER, UNU-MERIT, and UNIDO Workshop on 'Pathways to Industrialization in the 21st Century: New Challenges and Emerging Paradigms', Maastricht, 22–23 October.

——(2010). 'Brazil: The World's Largest and Most Dynamic Scavenger Movement', *BioCycle*, 51 (10): 32–33.

Meyer, G. (1987). 'Waste Recycling as a Livelihood in the Informal Sector—The Example of Refuse Collectors in Cairo', *Applied Geography and Development*, 30: 78–94.

Pollack, A. and K. Bradsher (2004). China's Need for Metal Keeps US Scrap Dealers Scrounging. *The New York Times*, 13 March.

Vogler, J. (1984). 'Waste Recycling in Developing Countries: A Review of the Social, Technological, and Market Forces'. In J. Holmes (ed.), *Managing Solid Wastes in Developing Countries*. New York: John Wiley & Sons.

Yardley, J. (2005). China's Big Next Boom Could Be the Foul Air. *The New York Times*, 30 October.

Part V
Challenges to Industrial Policy

13

Can Industrial Policy Work under Neopatrimonial Rule?

Tilman Altenburg

13.1 Introduction[1]

Technological latecomer countries suffer from more pervasive market failure than early industrialized countries. Their business environments lack most of the cluster synergies that more advanced locations offer. Sectorally targeted industrial policies are needed to overcome these disadvantages and create the preconditions for economic diversification and technological development. Industrial policies, however, affect the productivity of economic activities and thus create rents and, consequently, incentives for political capture. The development challenge is to manage rent creation in a way that maximizes public welfare and keeps political capture to the minimum. Yet this is difficult when the ruling elites employ patronage and political clientelism systematically to create and preserve their legitimacy. This is the core of neopatrimonialism, a common characteristic of most developing countries. Industrial policies in particular can easily be employed to gain political support from specific constituencies, given that the criteria for establishing which activities merit protection and subsidies, and which ones do not, can be interpreted creatively.

Hence latecomer countries face a dilemma. They need industrial policies more urgently than mature economies do, but they are also the most likely candidates for political capture. This section explores the practical implications of this problem. Do the risks of misallocation outweigh the benefits of correcting market failure? Should these countries confine their economic

[1] The author would like to thank Steffen Erdle. The section on Tunisia is summarized from Erdle (2011).

policies to sector-neutral measures for improving their investment climates, or can industrial policy work under neopatrimonial rule?

Section 13.2 carves out why technological latecomer countries suffer from more pervasive market failure than early industrialized countries, and which particular problems call for industrial-policy solutions. It argues that, even when industrial policies are needed, governments may have insufficient capabilities and inappropriate incentives for implementing them efficiently. Neopatrimonialism is then introduced as a concept to explain the behaviour of interest groups in industrial development. We argue that neopatrimonialism greatly enhances the risks of political capture, but we also highlight the fact that some countries with strong neopatrimonial traits have made extraordinary economic progress. Section 13.3 provides empirical evidence of industrial policy-making in four sub-Saharan African (SSA) countries and three countries in the Middle East and North Africa (MENA) region. It shows that neopatrimonialism is indeed pervasive in these countries and affects the way industrial policies are designed and implemented. Overall, industrial policy effectiveness is fairly weak, although some programmes have succeeded in developing new activities. Ethiopia and Tunisia stand out for pursuing long-term strategies of industrial transformation and implementing them fairly effectively, and are therefore described in greater detail. Section 13.4 then draws general conclusions about industrial policy under neopatrimonial rule and discusses why the policy performance varies so significantly among the countries.

13.2 Theoretical considerations: industrial policy, latecomer development, and neopatrimonialism

13.2.1 *The case for industrial policy in latecomer countries*

Developing countries are latecomers to industrial development and other forms of knowledge-based production. In a globalizing world, their economies have to compete with others that initiated their industrial development decades or even centuries earlier. Catching up with the frontrunners becomes more and more difficult, because products and processes turn out to be increasingly complex and dependent on complementary assets provided by other companies and institutions. Early industrializing countries have been able to create many of these assets through a cumulative process of business specialization and sophistication of supporting institutions. Their firms can thus build on a range of network externalities that give them a substantial competitive edge over isolated newcomers in other locations. This makes it very difficult for the latter to compete in any kind of tradable goods—not only in export markets, but also at home, given that international investors and traders are penetrating their domestic markets. Referring to Africa, Collier and Venables (2007: 1) illustrate the disadvantages of latecomer development in the following way:

> Africa has lagged behind partly because its economic reforms lagged those of Asia. When export diversification started to boom in Asia in the 1980s, no mainland African country provided a comparable investment climate. Now a number of African cities . . . offer reasonable investment climates, but they cannot compete with Asian cities that have comparable investment climates since the Asian cities have established clusters of firms in the new export sectors. Such clusters provide firms in the cluster with the advantages of shared knowledge, availability of specialist inputs and a developing pool of experienced labour . . . Until African cities can establish such clusters, firms located in Africa face costs that will be above those of Asian competitors, but because costs are currently higher individual firms have no incentive to relocate.

The larger the gap vis-à-vis more advanced countries, the more difficult it is to build competitive industries. Of course, poor countries may build on comparative advantages in natural resource endowments and/or low wages, but industrial upgrading towards more productive and profitable activities is not easy. In low-cost manufacturing it is difficult to compete against China and other established (mainly Asian) export locations that benefit from economies of scale and network synergies *cum* low wages, and growth paths built on exports of natural resources imply a range of well documented economic and political challenges.[2] Latecomers thus face a number of competitive disadvantages that can hardly be overcome without pro-active government action. Low-income countries in particular suffer from severe market failure, as the following three examples illustrate:

First, *coordination failure* is far more frequent than it is in mature economies. Coordination failure occurs when market actors refrain from investing because activities are interdependent. In order to become viable, any new branch requires simultaneous investments in complementary activities, so that no investor dares take the first step unless they can be sure that others will provide the interrelated assets. This, of course, is a very common situation at the beginning of a country's industrial development. The quote from Collier and Venables illustrates the problem. Thus latecomers need a coordinated 'big push'—e.g. simultaneously attracting and/or nurturing providers of key inputs and investing in infrastructure, skills, and technological services—if they want to establish cluster synergies in order to make up for the advantage of established competitors.

[2] See the 'resource curse' literature, e.g. Auty (2001) and Mehlum, Moene, and Torvik (2006).

Second, there is typically a *lack of opportunity entrepreneurship*. While Naudé (2011) suggests that poor countries may have as many citizens with the necessary personal traits for entrepreneurship as any other country, the institutional set-up of pre-capitalist societies typically discourages entrepreneurial behaviour in a number of ways. This holds for social norms as much as for economic incentives. Social norms, as reflected inter alia in school curricula, may not be supportive of curiosity, creativity, and search. Some societies do not promote the pursuit of personal achievements; for example, they may have built-in social norms that oblige those who have earned an extraordinary income to share it with their community, thereby discouraging the search for business ideas and constraining capital accumulation. Also, the weakness of institutions providing risk assurance leads to risk-averse attitudes. Last but not least, would-be entrepreneurs in poor countries live in an information-scarce environment where managerial role models, sophisticated customers, and new business ideas are in short supply.

Thus governments have an important role in nurturing entrepreneurship. They need to foster a societal consensus on the desirability of entrepreneurship for the society at large, to create a cultural and business environment that encourages risk-taking behaviour and fosters an 'achievement culture', and to facilitate training of entrepreneurial and managerial skills. Moreover, they need to create a learning environment that balances protection and competitive challenge: on the one hand, the nascent entrepreneurial class needs a certain degree of protection to avoid imports and direct investments from more advanced economies asphyxiating the emerging companies; on the other hand, competition needs to augment gradually to ensure that national enterprises continuously improve their performance.

Even in mature capitalist societies with advanced entrepreneurial and managerial skills, there is a case for subsidizing the search for new business options, because the social value of discovering new products or processes can be far greater than the return on investment for the innovator. Developing a new business idea is costly and involves the risk of failure. When the idea materializes, however, competitors may quickly copy it. While this may offer enormous advantages to the local economy, the copycats dissipate the rents that the risk-taking innovator could have obtained from his innovation. Due to this non-appropriability, innovative business models are typically undersupplied. This calls for government programmes to stimulate the discovery of new business opportunities (Hausmann and Rodrik 2003).

Third, the *enterprise structure* of latecomer countries is typically fragmented. In well-functioning market economies, companies that bring a superior product or process to the market oblige their competitors either to make comparable improvements or to exit the market. This process of 'creative destruction' (Schumpeter 1942) homogenizes factor productivity across all surviving companies. In developing countries, however, it does not work well. Here, the initial productivity gap between modern enterprises (e.g. foreign corporations) and traditional cottage industries is so huge that the latter cannot simply emulate the sophisticated business models of the former. At the same time, the latter employ the bulk of the workforce (OECD 2009), and it is impossible for the more efficient firms to absorb additional workers at the same rate at which inefficient firms disappear (unless GDP grows at very high rates over several decades). As a consequence, owners and workers of these firms typically retain their economic activities even at minimal levels of productivity. Contrary to Schumpeter's assumption, the productivity of newly established firms does not exceed that of exiting firms (Tybout 2000). As a result, a large, mostly unregistered, survivalist economy persists alongside modern firms, and the productivity spread is much greater than it is in mature market economies. Moreover, due to low productivity, low quality, and lack of proper registration, modern, scale-intensive and registered firms only rarely engage in business transactions with small informal enterprises. Governments have an important role in narrowing the productivity gap and reducing fragmentation. This implies helping micro and small enterprises to increase their productivity, linking them to clusters and value chains, and improving the employability of those engaged in survivalist activities.

13.2.2 *The necessary capabilities for successful industrial policy-making*

In sum, standard neoclassical assumptions about the allocative efficiency of markets apply much less to low-income countries than they do to rich countries with their more sophisticated institutions. It is therefore hard to imagine a catching up process without a pro-active government that helps to manage structural change, supporting diversification, and the development of new activities that promise to generate more and better paid jobs and other social benefits. This is what industrial policy is about. For the purpose of this section, we define industrial policy as any government measure or set of measures intended to shape structural change in ways that the government views as desirable. This implies selectivity, i.e. certain economic activities are favoured over others that are regarded as less promising for national development.

Neoclassical theorists criticize such selectivity for distorting the allocative efficiency of markets. Bureaucrats, they argue, should not 'pick winners'. In practice, however, all governments provide differential support in favour of particular new technologies, regions, or sectors. More interventionist governments even support selected groups of firms at the micro-level, which greatly increases the risks of collusive behaviour.

In any case, making the right policy choices is not an easy task, and implementing policies in ways that help to overcome market failures rather than creating new costs of doing business is equally demanding. For the following analysis we distinguish two key capabilities that the political leadership needs to have to shape structural change in a welfare-enhancing way.

First, policy makers need *strategic capability* to develop a 'national project' of productive transformation that is viable and widely accepted and supported by the society. Such a 'project' includes strategic choices about investment priorities, which in turn implies value-based judgements, for example determining how much international competition is desirable, whether growth takes precedence over distribution, and who deserves protection for how much time. Furthermore, it presupposes a good understanding of the changing requirements of the global economy, the ability to observe industrial developments at home and abroad in order to identify 'latent' comparative advantages,[3] and to translate the observed phenomena into a strategy of incremental socioeconomic transformation. It further requires the ability to create a social contract in support of this strategy. Where external actors, such as large foreign investors or donor agencies, play key roles it is important to align them with the strategy. Ohno (2009) has highlighted how important the ability to define a clear policy vision and strategy has been in the industrialization of Asian countries.

Second, policy makers must be able to set up service agencies and devise incentive schemes and verifiable performance measurement systems for them to ensure effective and customer-oriented implementation of regulatory and supporting services. Meritocratic recruitment and promotion systems are key to improving such *implementing capability*. Furthermore, 'embedded autonomy' (Evans 1995) is needed: policy makers need to interact closely with the private sector to gain a thorough understanding of business opportunities and constraints and identify market failure, but they must also have the autonomy to withdraw or reallocate rents before they become unproductive—often against the resistance of incumbents.

13.2.3 *The risks of industrial policy*

Industrial policy increases the profitability of some activities and reduces the profitability of others. This necessarily involves risks of government failure. Such failure may come from two sources: *inability* and/or *intentional political capture* of rents.

With regard to *inability*, critics of industrial policy frequently claim that governments are unlikely to identify promising future investments that market

[3] The term is borrowed from Lin and Monga (2010). It refers to advantages that are principally in line with the existing factor endowments but have not yet been fully exploited by market actors due to existing information, coordination or externality problems.

actors do not recognize (Pack and Saggi 2006). This critique is plausible as far as immediate business opportunities are concerned. Governments should therefore not intervene in micro-level investment decisions. They may, however, have a facilitating role in organizing sector groups, pulling information together, and initiating participatory search processes to identify market failures that hamper the long-term development of a particular activity. Moreover, they may advocate public interests, such as the quest for socially inclusive and environmentally sustainable patterns of production. As regards the implementation of policies, reviews have shown that the services that state agencies are expected to deliver to the private sector are often quite inefficient, mainly because their incentive systems do not stimulate them to operate in a business-like and customer-oriented manner (Committee of Donor Agencies 2001). The challenge is thus to reform the incentive systems for these agencies, for example allowing for more competition among service providers, privatizing certain services, or introducing results-based management.

The issue of incentives takes us to the next point: the existence of political interests and power relations, and the related risk of *intentional political capture* of rents. As Chang (1996) observed, it would be naïve to assume that governments always and only try to maximize public welfare. Three interest groups typically try to make use of industrial policies for their own interests:

- *Beneficiaries in the private sector* are interested in influencing rules and regulations in such a way that economic rents are increased, for example via subsidies, restriction of market entry for competitors, and decreasing contributions to the society (taxes, severance payments, etc.);
- *Politicians* may use industrial policies as an instrument of patronage in order to enhance their legitimacy and win elections;
- *State agencies* are interested in maximizing their budgets, hiring more employees, and paying them higher salaries. Hence they have an incentive to implement programmes, regardless of their efficiency.

Industrial policy effectiveness is thus not primarily a technical issue that can be solved with education and training of stakeholders; the main challenge is political, namely how to create and withdraw economic rents with a view to technological capacity building and productivity enhancement. These mechanisms can easily be captured by interest groups, unless a strong system of checks and balances is in place.

13.2.4 *When political systems build on political capture: neopatrimonialism*

Both problems—the inability to design and implement appropriate policies as well as political capture—can be expected to be particularly serious in poor countries. Those countries' *ability* is more limited, ceteris paribus, due to resource constraints. Therefore, subsidies tend to be modest, agencies understaffed, and the outreach of programmes low. The fact that public pay scales are usually not competitive implies that the best trained personnel often prefer to work for private companies or international (donor) organizations.

There are also good reasons to assume that *political capture* occurs more frequently in developing countries, because these typically lack many of the checks and balances that hold politicians and executive organs accountable in mature democracies—including electoral competition, an independent judiciary, an autonomous central auditing authority, critical feedback from independent media, as well as monitoring and evaluation routines. As an example, 80 per cent of all low- and lower-middle-income countries rank below the median on the topic of 'judicial independence' (Kaufmann, Kraay, and Mastruzzi 2008). Public officials thus have more discretionary power. The combination of low salaries in the public sector—officials usually depend on additional sources of income—and considerable discretionary power stimulates favouritism and bribery. Governance indicators in fact confirm that these phenomena are especially pervasive in low- and lower-middle-income countries. According to the same source, 71 per cent of these countries rank in the bottom half regarding 'favouritism in decisions of government officials'. The Corruption Perception Index (Transparency International 2008)[4] ranks 82 per cent of low- and lower-middle-income countries in the bottom half with regard to 'control of corruption'.

To gain a better understanding of the way policies are designed and implemented in developing countries, we refer to the concept of 'neopatrimonialism'. The last few decades have witnessed remarkable transitions from non-democratic to democratic regimes and from centrally planned to market economies. This has occurred in all developing regions. In most cases, however, the new political and economic institutions did not fully replace those that existed before the transition. Instead, 'hybrid regimes' (Diamond 2002) emerged, in which the state is often formally shaped after the principles of modern statehood, but permeated to a high degree by informal institutions that are based on arbitrary decision making or at least on non-codified and non-actionable rules. Over the last twenty years, many attempts have been made to analyse and classify these hybrid regime types.[5] While the authors mostly agree on the increasing relevance of such hybrids between modern rule-based democracies and traditional political systems, no consensus has been reached in terms of terminology and classification. Instead, new

[4] Available at: http://www.infoplease.com/world/statistics/2008-transparency-international-corruption-perceptions.html

[5] See e.g. Croissant and Merkel (2004).

concepts have proliferated, such as 'partial' (Epstein et al. 2006), 'illiberal' (Zakaria 2003), or 'defective democracies' (Croissant and Merkel 2004).

For the purpose of this section, the concept of neopatrimonialism captures the most important elements that help to explain the phenomenon of political capture in industrial policy-making. While some authors conceptualize neopatrimonialism as a subcategory of hybrid regimes (and thus distinct from democratic and authoritarian regimes), this section follows Erdmann and Engel (2006), who identify elements of neopatrimonial rule in different regime types, including 'illiberal' democracies and authoritarian regimes.

The following characterization integrates the main characteristics of neopatrimonialism identified in the work of Bratton and van de Walle (1997) and Erdmann and Engel (2006). According to them, neopatrimonialism is a mixture of two systems:

1. *A patrimonial system of personal relations* in which the private and the public realm are not separated, with the effect that 'obedience is owed not to enacted rules but to the person who occupies a position of authority or tradition or who has been chosen for it by the traditional master' (Weber 1978: 227, cited in Erdmann and Engel 2006: 8).
2. *A legal-rational system* that clearly separates the two realms and consistently applies codified and actionable rules. Building on Weber (1978), legal-rational bureaucratic rule is characterized, among other things, by the following elements: officials are hired and promoted according to proven technical qualifications; they receive a fixed salary according to their rank in the hierarchy; promotion is dependent on the judgement of superiors; each office has a clearly defined sphere of competence; the office is the only or primary occupation of the employee and they are controlled in the conduct of their office. In neopatrimonial systems, such norms may *formally* also be valid, but their *social practice* is often personalized and informal.

The following elements characterize neopatrimonialism:

1. *Presidentialism with strong concentration of power,* whereby the ruler and inner circles of power partly exercise power in a privatized and discretionary way. Decision making is thus frequently not based on laws and regulations, and only few institutional checks and balances exist to hold decision makers accountable. The president is a 'strongman' and the 'centrifugal force around which all else revolves' (Sandbrook 1986: 323).
2. *Political clientelism and patronage. Clientelism* refers to the award of personal favours, such as public employment, personal promotion, or preferential treatment in the bureaucracy, in exchange for votes or other forms of loyalty. Rulers appoint members of the political elite to hold key positions in the bureaucracy and the state economy. These in turn assign positions or give

other favours to their personal clients and so on, thus creating a cascading system of patron–client relationships that ensures loyalty with the political elite. While clientelism refers to personalized relations, *patronage* means the strategic use of state resources to win the electoral and other political support from larger, anonymous societal groups, but also to enhance political cohesion among regions, social and/or ethnic groups.

The concept of neopatrimonialism suggests that two different spheres of government—politicians and the state bureaucracy—may employ state resources to buy political support. Even though both are part of an encompassing system of patron–client relationships, they may pursue different, even contrary, aims. For example, politicians may have an interest in making services for the general public cheaper and better, whereas bureaucracies may prefer to maximize their budgets and focus support on their personal clients.

Industrial policy plays an important role in stabilizing neopatrimonialism as it creates political space for politicians and bureaucrats to allocate government resources to specific groups of beneficiaries. These can be employed to strengthen ties of loyalty between individual politicians or bureaucrats and private beneficiaries, but also to buy political support from specific social and ethnic groups that are considered important for the survival of the incumbent regime. As we have argued in the previous section, governments of industrial-latecomer countries need to create, protect, and nurture a national entrepreneurial class. This implies the creation of rents for a selected social group. If governments derive their legitimacy systematically from patronage and clientelism, it greatly increases the risk that rents are created for political supporters rather than to maximize welfare. This risk is further aggravated because policy choices among sub-sectors and technologies build on assumptions about dynamic scale economies and future knowledge spillovers that are necessarily subjective and debatable. Consequently, politicians and bureaucrats who want to employ industrial policy for patronage and clientelism can easily find technical justifications to mask their political objectives.

For these reasons, many researchers and practitioners doubt that industrial policies can work under neopatrimonial rule. Proponents of public choice theory especially make this claim, as they assume that the relevant stakeholders—governments, bureaucrats, business people—act simply as self-interested individuals who create rents for their own material interests or to increase their legitimacy and political power. Hence the public sector will try to expand activities that increase its discretionary power for rent creation, using differential trade and tax regimes, direct subsidies, licenses, and so on, whereas the private sector will lobby for access to such rents, and those who benefit would oppose any liberalization that might reduce those rents (for instance, Krueger 1974). Political systems that owe their legitimacy to the distribution of specific benefits to their clients are of course especially susceptible to rent-seeking behaviour, especially when the number of large enterprises is fairly small, relationships between politics and business are highly personalized, and checks and balances are weak (Bräutigam 2000). Even scholars who defend the need for industrial policies in principle are often sceptical about their applicability at early stages of industrialization. Soludo and Ogbu (2004: 27), for example, state that 'only when the state is capable and developmental, and has a vibrant capitalist class can industrial policies be effective'.

The assumption that all stakeholders simply pursue self-interest, however, needs to be qualified on two grounds. First, politicians and bureaucrats are not only driven by short-term interests of revenue maximization. They are, to different degrees, also motivated by elements of social responsibility, personal reputation, and professionalism. Altruistic considerations, the quest for social recognition, the need to ensure legitimacy in the longer term as well as prevailing ideologies and paradigms all play important roles. Second, the assumptions of public choice theory are challenged by empirical evidence. Some Asian countries with strong neopatrimonial traits—such as Indonesia under Suharto and Malaysia under Mahathir—have extensively applied industrial policies and achieved rapid industrialization combined with considerable welfare gains (Khan and Jomo 2000; Moore and Schmitz 2008). Such success can hardly be explained under the assumption of indiscriminate pursuit of self-interest.

13.3 Evidence: industrial policy in sub-Saharan Africa and the MENA region

This section explores the performance of industrial policies in SSA and the MENA region. These two regions are most frequently associated with neopatrimonialism (e.g. Pawelka 1985; Bratton and van de Walle 1997; Bank and Richter 2010), and both are among the least competitive regions in non-resource-based industries. Not surprisingly, the (unfortunately scarce) literature on industrial policy in these regions is mostly very critical with regard to the effects and prospects of industrial policy.[6] Recently, however, some dissenting voices have started to reinterpret informal public–private ties as being (partly) functional for development. Kelsall et al. (2010: 26) published a paper on 'developmental patrimonialism' in SSA, arguing that 'centralized, long-horizon rent-seeking, when combined with broadly pro-capitalist policies, can generate dynamic growth'. Along similar lines, Abdel-Latif and Schmitz (2010) discover public–private 'growth coalitions' in Egypt.

[6] See e.g. Soludo, Ogbu, and Chang (2004) for SSA, and Galal (2008) for the MENA region.

Against the backdrop of these inconsistent findings, the German Development Institute (DIE) conducted a comparative analysis of industrial policy performance in four SSA and three MENA countries; a synopsis of overall findings follows. For most countries, the analysis confirms the critical views on industrial policy under neopatrimonial rule. Two countries, however, challenge the standard assumptions about the inability of neopatrimonial systems to contain rent-seeking and manage successful productive transformation: Tunisia and Ethiopia. These cases are therefore presented in some detail.

13.3.1 *Industrial policy in seven countries: main findings*

The following analysis includes the sub-Saharan countries Ethiopia, Mozambique, Namibia, and Nigeria as well as Egypt, Syria, and Tunisia in the MENA region.[7] All of these countries apply selective support programmes for particular technologies and groups of firms, defined either by subsector, value chain, region, or target market. The research explored to what extent neopatrimonial patterns impinge on industrial policy decisions and what this implies for their effectiveness.

The case studies confirm that neopatrimonialism is indeed pervasive in industrial policy-making. Interview partners frequently mentioned cases where decisions regarding public contracts, credit allocation, jobs in the public sectors etc., had been taken on the basis of arrangements that did not correspond to the stipulated rules and regulations. It goes without saying that these informal practices cannot be corroborated easily, precisely because neopatrimonialism implies the coexistence of formally valid legal-rational norms with informal social practices that function beyond the legal surface. The following observations are therefore based upon qualitative information gathered from experts, published case studies, grey literature, and own observations. All these sources mainly capture perceptions rather than hard evidence. To avoid mistakes or unfair judgements, information has been carefully cross-checked with country experts in different positions.

Presidentialism with a high degree of concentration of power is a common element in all seven countries. Decisions about industrial policies can often be directly attributed to the president, with a fairly limited influence of the parliament. Presidents often personally preside over the most important committees related to industrial development, use personal media appearances to promote industrialization programmes, and personally visit business associations to urge their members to join government initiatives. In

[7] See Altenburg (2011) for a synthesis report (which excludes the case of Nigeria and includes Vietnam). Most country case studies have been, or will soon be, published as DIE Discussion Papers: www.die-gdi.de

some cases they intervene directly in industry-specific decisions. Ethiopia's President Meles Zenawi, for example, stepped in to resolve problems in the emerging cut flower industry, including the negotiation of more favourable freight tariffs with the national airline and the allotment of land under favourable leasing conditions. Business tycoons often directly approach the presidents if they need to solve a specific problem rather than using formal channels. Furthermore, members of elites with trustful personal relations with the president are appointed to key positions of the public administration and state-owned enterprises or parastatals. In some cases, the presidents and intimates are directly involved as shareholders in large national investment projects, for example in the case of Mozambique's president Guebuza.

In all seven countries, institutional checks and balances are weak. They all rank clearly below OECD standards on governance indicators, although with substantial differences between countries. Namibia and Mozambique rank remarkably higher on the relevant indicators of 'voice and accountability', 'political participation', and 'rule of law' than Egypt, Ethiopia, Nigeria, Tunisia, and Syria. With regard to the World Bank indicator for 'voice and accountability', for example, the latter five all rank below the 25th percentile (2009).[8] Looking at industrial policy in particular, programmes are not rigorously evaluated in any of the countries, with the exception of some programmes with strong financial involvement of donors. Some countries do conduct regular and detailed indicative planning, for example to prepare five year plans, which may entail mid-term and final reviews (e.g. in Ethiopia). These, however, tend to monitor activities, rather than outcomes or impacts. Moreover, they are not carried out by independent parties and rarely challenge the fundamentals of how programmes and institutions are organized.

The case studies also revealed widespread clientelism and patronage in industrial policy operating through a variety of channels. One important channel is the assignment of jobs in the public administration and state-owned enterprises on the basis of political loyalty rather than professional merit. In Mozambique, it is well-known that positions in the civil service are almost entirely reserved for members of the ruling FRELIMO party. In some cases, organizations affiliated with the ruling party, such as the National Union of Namibian Workers, also have considerable influence on the award of jobs. Typically, those employed in the public sector and state-owned enterprises receive a range of benefits, such as higher wages, pension and insurance

[8] See: http://info.worldbank.org/governance/wgi/index.asp The Bertelsmann Transformation Index (BTI) for 'political participation' (2010) more or less confirms this picture (see: http://www.bertelsmann-transformation-index.de/bti/). With regard to 'rule of law' World Bank and BTI data are inconsistent. Here, the World Bank ranks the MENA countries fairly high, similar to Namibia and Mozambique, whereas the BTI gives the lowest scores to the three MENA countries and Ethiopia, but ranks Nigeria fairly high.

schemes, severance payments, and public holidays, which are not granted to other citizens.

Another mechanism of clientelism is privatization of state enterprises. In Mozambique after the civil war, FRELIMO transferred privatized companies to politically associated persons and supported them with subsidized credit, with the dual objective of creating a national class of entrepreneurs and enhancing political loyalty. In Egypt, state enterprises, for example in the steel and cement industries, have been transferred to intimates of President Mubarak who have been able to reap considerable rents from these protected industries.

In addition to such collusive practices of privatization, politically connected companies have often taken many of the business opportunities left for private engagement. Examples include companies owned by members of the ruling party (e.g. in Mozambique), the military (as in Egypt and Syria), or party-affiliated endowment funds (as in Ethiopia). As a result, the borderline between business and politics is often blurred. Entrepreneurs who compete with state-owned and politically connected enterprises frequently claim that those enterprises get preferential treatment when it comes to operating and import licences, public purchasing, and credit from the state banking system, or that they are bailed out in times of crisis. As government decisions in these fields are often not transparent and may not be subject to checks and balances, however, it is very difficult to verify such allegations. Moreover, the case studies suggest an overall shift towards economic liberalization, albeit not necessarily with increased political freedom. Most notably in the three MENA countries, new technocratic and industrial elites have emerged that depend less on oil and gas revenues, international aid, and other rents.

How do these neopatrimonial practices influence the effectiveness of industrial policies? In this regard we found remarkable differences. This is particularly true for strategic capability. All countries have formally laid down their industrial development objectives in plans or 'vision' documents that outline medium-term targets until 2025 or 2030, but the practical relevance of these plans varies greatly. In most cases, the national strategies express overall targets (e.g. to increase value added or to develop new export activities) and in some cases identify priority sectors (such as agro-industries or the textile industry), but they do not provide a clear perspective with regard to where the countries may have a latent comparative advantage, what the most binding constraints are, and what concrete steps should be taken to gradually move into more rewarding activities. Moreover, plans are often not well harmonized with the budgeting process. In smaller countries, planning documents are sometimes drafted by international consultants rather than developed in a participatory national planning process. In several cases, not even the main implementing agencies and competent private sector associations attributed any importance to these strategies. The two exceptional cases are Ethiopia and

Tunisia.[9] As the following sections show, both countries have operationalized strategies for industrial upgrading and diversification, and the top leadership is clearly committed to following up on these agendas.

With regard to implementing capability, the project encountered numerous examples of poor performance in all countries, but also some fairly successful projects. Due to attribution gaps and lack of counterfactual evidence it is generally difficult to assess the effectiveness of industrial policies. In many cases, however, failure was obvious. For example, most programmes aimed at promoting investment in export processing zones fell clearly short of their targets and often failed to attract more than a handful of investors (e.g. in Nigeria and Namibia). Similarly, several investment promotion agencies performed miserably, not only because they failed to attract much foreign investment, but also because many companies that did invest stated that they did not make use of any of their services except for compulsory licensing issues (e.g. in the case of Ethiopia). In Mozambique, efforts to transfer state-owned enterprises to private entrepreneurs and support them with subsidized credits largely failed, and large parts of the credits were never paid back. SME promotion agencies were generally rated as highly inefficient in terms of impact and outreach,[10] and several SME development funds were discontinued due to dissatisfactory performance.[11] In some cases, government sources admit policy failure. A Nigerian government report assessed the country's system of fiscal incentives as lacking in focus and poorly administered. Overall, industrial development programmes are typically initiated without defining an exit strategy, which may make it difficult to withdraw rents when they are no longer needed.

Some industrial policies, however, seem to have been quite successful. Tunisia's industrial upgrading programme is a case in point. The long-term effort to support the competitiveness of enterprises with the aim of tapping into outsourcing opportunities from Europe successfully strengthened and diversified the export industry. Increases in manufacturing investment in Egypt and improved export performance could also be traced back to industry modernization and investment promotion programmes. In the SSA countries, the case studies identified a handful of successful initiatives in particular subsectors. These were usually related to areas of latent comparative advantage, where powerful investors pushed for supporting measures and regulatory

[9] The research referred to Tunisia under Ben Ali, who was ousted in January 2011. It is not clear to what extent the new government will take new directions from the authoritarian regime.

[10] Such as the Instituto de Desenvolvimento da Industria Local in Mozambique, the Small Scale Enterprise Development Agency in Nigeria, and the Federation of Medium and Small Enterprise Development Agencies in Ethiopia.

[11] Including the Fundo de Fomento a Pequena Industria in Mozambique and the Small and Medium Enterprises Equity Investment Scheme in Nigeria.

reforms. Examples include the development of the aluminium smelter and supporting industries cluster in Mozambique and the Ethiopian cut-flower industry. In some cases, donor support facilitated successful initiatives, for example supporting incipient clusters of pharmaceutical and leather industries in Ethiopia and Namibian exporters of plant products for the cosmetics and pharmaceutical industries.

Tunisia and Ethiopia are particularly interesting due to their clear commitment to an agenda of industrial transformation and reasonably effective implementation. In Tunisia, this commitment resulted in sustained economic growth relative to the rest of the Maghreb/Mashriq region, an increasing share of manufacturing in GDP, and a rapidly growing urban middle class. Tunisia today scores far higher on the global competitiveness index than any other country of its region. Ethiopia achieved sustained growth of over 10 per cent annually in the period 2005 to 2010 and is one of the few SSA countries on track to achieve the Millennium Development Goals. Its industrial development and economic diversification are not satisfactory, but progress in terms of human capital formation and firm productivity are expected to spur industrial development in the near future.

The strong development commitment and above-average performance of Tunisia and Ethiopia is somewhat unexpected, because both governments are quite authoritarian and score particularly low on political participation.[12] Ethiopia, furthermore, ranks clearly below the average of SSA on indicators of rule of law and regulatory quality.[13] Why did these two countries—despite weak governance and characteristics typical of neopatrimonialism—manage to foster productive transformation better than the other countries? According to almost any governance indicator, policy processes should be much more effective in Namibia and Mozambique, but none of these countries has made visible progress in terms of industrialization, enterprise upgrading, and diversification.

The following sections summarize the industrial policies and the performance of Ethiopia and Tunisia. The two countries are at very different stages of economic and institutional development. Ethiopia is one of the poorest countries in the world, ranking 119th in terms of global competitiveness (2010–11). Its challenge is to create the very basic preconditions for industrial development in an agrarian post-war society. Tunisia is a middle-income country ranking 32nd on global competitiveness, and it is in the middle of a transformation from a rent-based, state-driven, and inward-looking economy

[12] On the BTI 2010 ranking of political participation, Tunisia scores 2.5 and Ethiopia 3.0 (against a maximum of 10 points).

[13] World Bank Governance Indicators for 2009.

to a modern industrial market economy that is increasingly integrated into European value chains.

13.3.2 *Ethiopia: creating conditions for industrial development in an agrarian post-war society*[14]

Ethiopia is one of the world's least developed countries. The country is still largely agrarian, with 85 per cent of the workforce engaged in the rural economy. Its main resources are agrarian, but the potential for commercial crop production is limited as only small areas are irrigated and rainfall is irregular. From 1974 until 1991, the country was ruled by a pro-Soviet military junta that nationalized most industries and private urban real-estate holdings. Mismanagement and the junta's violent rule provoked a protracted civil war.

When the civil war ended in 1991, the incoming government under President Meles Zenawi was confronted with multiple market failures; it recognized the private sector as the main driver of economic growth, but there was very little private sector to build upon, as the better educated and entrepreneurial persons had mostly fled the country during the years of socialist dictatorship and civil war. Moreover, the new regime distrusted the old elites, which it regarded as rent-seekers interested in making quick money from trade and financial transactions rather than investing in industrial infrastructure and technological capabilities. Also, the main potential lay in improved agricultural productivity and agro-processing, but the rural areas lacked irrigation and roads, let alone cold chains to market perishable products. After the previous socialist government's failed effort to collectivise farmers, land had been returned to smallholders, which also made it difficult to attract large-scale investment in agriculture. Finally, the education system was unable to supply the skills needed both in government and the private sector.

In this situation, the government embarked on an ambitious top-down transformation project. Its aim was to industrialize the country with a focus on export-led growth. Big public investments were made in infrastructure and education, including the foundation of about twenty new universities and the establishment of a system of technical and vocational education and training (TVET) which, by 2010, had 815,000 enrolled students. Specialized institutions for sector-specific technology development were created. Simultaneously, the government pushed for technological upgrading and export-orientation of national industries that would absorb the skilled workforce once it had graduated from the university and TVET systems.

[14] Altenburg (2010) provides more background information on Ethiopia's industrial policy.

Leading companies were involved in an upgrading programme in which the government set export targets and offered consulting and credit on the basis of performance.

While encouraging private investment, the government made sure that it kept control of the economy and established clear limits to liberalization. It privatized many state-owned enterprises, but defined narrow boundaries for private engagement in the financial sector and maintained its monopoly in telecommunications. It facilitated long-term lease contracts for investors in agriculture, but refrained from liberalizing rural land markets; it invites donor support while carefully avoiding aid dependency, so as to retain control over its economic policies.

The government applies an authoritarian command-and-control style of policy-making. It distinguishes 'developmental entrepreneurs' from 'rent-seekers' and interferes to support the former and limit the scope for the latter; it favours producers over traders and exporters over producers for the local market; and it handpicks companies for its enterprise upgrading programmes. Business associations are used to convey the government's messages and educate their members rather than to engage in an open dialogue. When opposition forces gained influence in the 2005 elections and started to seriously challenge the government, the leadership of the Ethiopian Chamber of Commerce was replaced. The overall attitude towards the private sector is to educate, guide, and train, rather than to encourage creativity and competition. The ambiguity of government policy is also reflected in its public sector reform. A business-process re-engineering programme has been implemented to strengthen meritocracy and improve performance; below the surface of this programme, however, critics claim that the restructuring process was used to remove political dissenters from office.

Hence Ethiopia's policy can be characterized as an authoritarian, politically controlled, and state-led attempt to create a competitive economy. In this attempt, informal ties with parts of the business community have an important role. Following the civil war, endowment funds were created from remaining war funds and incoming aid, and these were allocated to ex-combatants. Their dual purpose was to reward and reintegrate combatants and to reconstruct the country. As the liberation fronts were organized along ethnic lines, so are the endowment funds. How exactly these funds were allocated, and how big they are, is not transparent. Although they operate as non-governmental public charity organizations, they have never been audited and there is no transparency with regard to management structure or profits and losses. Private competitors claim that endowment companies have preferential access to credit facilities of the state-owned Commercial Bank of Ethiopia and that indebted companies have been bailed out, but due to the discretionary character of many government policies it is not possible to verify these allegations. In any case, due to their head start, the endowment companies seized many unfilled business opportunities and are now among the largest investors.

Industrial policies often provide support on a case-by-case basis. Leading agro-industries, textile, garment, and leather-product companies are targeted to become role models for their respective sectors and make inroads in export markets. Beneficiaries may receive land, buildings, or consultancies at highly subsidized rates. While subsidy allocation is discretionary, it generally seems to be based on assumptions about spillover effects and benefits different types of enterprises. While state-owned and endowment companies are among the beneficiaries, there is no strong bias in their favour. In exchange for support, the government expects companies to support its development programmes. This is particularly true for endowment companies. When the government launched a cooperative vocational training programme, for example, these companies were expected to accommodate students.

Ethiopia is now starting to reap the benefits of its coordinated effort to develop infrastructure, human capital, and the private sector. It achieved extraordinary economic growth of over 10 per cent annually in the period 2005 to 2010, increasing per capita GDP from US$682 to US$1,120 (PPP). In 2010, 29 per cent of the about 81 million population were estimated to live below the poverty line of US$1.25 a day (PPP)—a considerable improvement compared to the 61 per cent reported in 1995. Industrial development is stagnating at a low level, and export competitiveness and diversification are increasing only slowly. However, progress has been made in terms of human capital formation and productivity of its larger enterprises, which is likely to spur industrial development in the near future.

Ethiopia's industrial development strategy blends different ideological elements. As in Western market economies, the private sector is recognized as the main driver of growth. At the same time, carrots and sticks are used to develop specific groups of enterprises and push them towards exporting. Korea, Taiwan, and Japan are Ethiopia's role models in this regard. Moreover, the preference for manufacturing industries and disdain of trade and commerce can be seen as a legacy of the Marxist roots of the liberation movement. Overall, the regime deserves to be characterized as 'developmental'. Government interference in the economy is strong, but generally with the intention of achieving government targets rather than for personal enrichment. Enterprise surveys confirm that corruption is clearly below normal SSA levels. Still, non-transparent state–business relations and the lack of institutional checks and balances give cause for serious concern and may derail the developmental course of the government any time.

13.3.3 *Tunisia: managing the transition from a state-led pre-industrial society to an export-driven market economy*[15]

When Tunisia became independent in 1956, it hosted only 290 enterprises of more than 50 employees; 85 per cent of the firms were owned by foreigners. The incipient national entrepreneurial class was mainly engaged in small agricultural and commercial activities. Industry employed only 2 per cent of the workforce. Aside from some phosphates and iron ore, Tunisia did not possess significant fossil and mineral resources, and its farming sector was heavily dependent on seasonal rainfall. The country had inherited an educated middle class and a fairly professional civil service from the French, but it lacked many of the skills needed for industrial development. At the time of independence, Tunisia did not have a single institution of higher education. Hence although Tunisia at independence was not as poor as Ethiopia after the civil war, it was confronted with similarly adverse conditions for economic development.

Today, the country has an export-led market economy based on competitive private companies. Over the last 15 years, Tunisia has achieved sustainable economic growth of about 5 per cent annually, which compares favourably with other countries of the region. In 2010, industry accounted for 34.6 per cent of GDP, up from 11.9 per cent in 1980. Manufacturing exports are gradually shifting from simple garment assembly to more demanding electronic and mechanical products. Recently, the country has intensified its efforts to advance towards an innovation-oriented economy, with new support schemes, including 'techno-cities' and business incubators, and considerable investments in new activities, such as information and communication technologies and solar energy. Tunisia's industrial development programme was labour-intensive and relatively inclusive, enabling the emergence of a considerable middle class; 80 per cent of the Tunisian population are officially rated 'middle class'. The US$2/day poverty rate fell to 3.8 per cent (2005).

This success was achieved on the basis of an authoritarian system. From 1956 until 2011, only two presidents ruled the country—Bourguiba until 1987 and Ben Ali until 2011. Their power was close to being absolute, building in particular on a dominant party system, a professional palace administration, and a repressive security apparatus. While their rule is best characterized as authoritarian, both presidents used neopatrimonial politics to reinforce their power. Leading positions within state institutions were reserved for party members (and, under Ben Ali, increasingly also loyal technocrats). Important policy decisions were taken by a very small circle of top decision makers from

[15] This section summarizes the DIE project's country case study by Erdle (2011).

the ruling party and the key institutions of the central state. Bourguiba had created a largely uncontrolled presidential 'shadow' budget, which allowed him to create personal links to key social actors, including the country's business elites. An extended clientelist network clustered around the presidential family itself. Furthermore, the social security schemes and subsidized commodities and utilities were used to grant privileges to state officials and public sector employees. Patronage resource was employed to buy support from specific societal groups. Examples include preferential customs rates for small cars, subsidized personal computers for low-income families, and subsidies for the interior provinces. Some of these schemes operated outside the state budget and were granted in an ad hoc fashion.

Tunisia is thus another interesting case of successful structural change under neopatrimonial rule. This development, however, was not straightforward. Following independence, president Bouguiba initially tried to avoid every step that could possibly scare away investors, many of them still foreigners. It soon became apparent, however, that it would not be possible to unleash economic growth and create sufficient employment for the rapidly growing population unless the government would undertake pro-active measures to develop indigenous productive capabilities. In the early 1960s, the government therefore embarked on an import-substitution strategy. In parallel, Bourguiba enacted social reforms, for example liberating women from their religiously sanctioned dependency on male family members and enabling them to participate in the modern labour market. As a result of this new policy, the number of state-owned enterprises and public sector organizations increased from less than 25 in 1960 to about 185 in 1970, and their share of national investment grew from 2 to 34 per cent.

As in many other countries, import-substituting industrialization proved to be financially unsustainable. In the early 1970s, Tunisia therefore started to complement import-substitution with export promotion, with a focus on labour-intensive manufacturing. About 800 new industrial ventures emerged in the following years, effectively doubling industrial capacity. The private share in industrial investment, which was only 22 per cent in the 1960s, rose to 43 per cent in the mid-1980s. Still, loss-making state enterprises and the negative trade balance of import-substituting industries increased the external debt. When droughts, decreasing remittances, and an increasing dollar price exacerbated the debt crisis and austerity measures provoked public rioting, Bourguiba was finally deposed in 1987.

The incoming president Ben Ali recognized the need to create new employment opportunities in order to absorb the country's growing workforce and maintain socio-political stability. The crisis had consolidated a consensus among the 'inner circle elites' that economic development should be achieved through market forces rather than state planning. Ben Ali increasingly brought technocrats into leading positions; they would have the expertise to manage the necessary transition but were also loyal followers. In the absence of easily extractable natural resources, the future was seen in increasing the insertion of Tunisian business in European value chains. Industrial policies reallocated resources from import-substituting production to export industries as well as the foreign-exchange-earning services, mainly tourism. The domestic market was increasingly liberalized, and most 'strategic' sectors were opened for privatization, including transport, energy, telecoms, and banks. WTO accession and agreements with the European Union (Euro-Mediterranean Partnership in 1995; Euro-Mediterranean Association Agreement in 1996) made economic liberalization virtually irreversible, enhancing the legal security of private investors. In parallel, an ambitious export-industry upgrading programme—the *programme de mise à niveau*—was launched. To date, about 4400 enterprises have received consultancies and financial support to enhance their productivity. In 2009, manufacturing accounted for 75.4 per cent of exports (up from 36 per cent in 1980).

Tunisia's industrial transition is a remarkable success story, especially when compared with the slow increase of manufacturing competitiveness in most other Maghreb and Mashriq countries. Although the national transformation project of export-led industrialization was implemented under authoritarian rule, it was not only about shifting from an agrarian to an industrial society; it also changed the composition of the elites, with increasing power of private entrepreneurs and technocrats; it created a broad urban middle class; and it changed the pattern of economic governance from informal to increasingly rules-based decision making. Political liberalization, however, did not keep up with the economic transformation. Also, jobs could not be created at the pace necessary to employ the rapidly growing workforce and conform to the social aspirations of the emerging middle class. Public discontent with the economic situation and political repression led to a revolution in early 2011.

13.4 Conclusions

Latecomer countries face more severe market failure than mature market economies. Many of them still have to create a societal consensus on the need for industrial transformation and diversification; they need to encourage entrepreneurship and economic experimentation, nurture a nascent national entrepreneurial class, invest in skills development at all levels, set up regulatory institutions and quality assurance systems, and develop many other aspects that investors can already build on in established market economies. It is difficult to imagine how latecomers should be able to build new and internationally competitive industries unless their governments adopt pro-active policies to tackle some of the most problematic development constraints in a coordinated way. With limited state resources, such activities necessarily have to focus on the most binding constraints in the most promising sectors.

At the same time, our case studies corroborate the pervasiveness of neopatrimonialism in industrial policy-making. The risks of making industry-specific choices under these circumstances are well-known. Where decision making is informal and personalized, where institutional checks and balances are weak and the whole political system is built on granting favours in exchange for loyalty, political capture is unavoidable. Lack of enforceable property rights creates uncertainty and thereby discourages private investment. Innovation is held back, because the alliance between governments and incumbent economic elites discourages competition with outsiders, and engaging in rent-seeking is often more lucrative for incumbents than concentrating on productive investments. Also, clientelism in the assignment of public employment runs counter to the principles of a meritocratic civil service, thereby reducing the effectiveness of policy implementation. In fact, the case studies confirm the pervasiveness of anti-competitive alliances between government and economic elites as well as principal-agent problems leading to ineffective policy implementation.

While these observations confirm conventional wisdom, two remarkable research findings call for a more differentiated consideration of the effects of neopatrimonialism. First, all of the seven economies considered attract substantial, and generally increasing, private investment and achieved considerable economic growth—ranging from 4.3 per cent (Syria) to 7.9 per cent (Ethiopia) annually in the 2000–8 period. Many investors have obviously not been scared away by the informality of policy-making and limited enforceability of contracts, suggesting that it is possible to make arrangements with the authorities that provide sufficient investment guarantee. This is perfectly rational, because patron–client relations usually imply *mutual* commitments; politicians provide investment guarantees in exchange for political support or job-creating investments that help to enhance their legitimacy. In Egypt, Abdel-Latif and Schmitz (2010) found that informal 'growth alliances' between policy makers and specific groups of investors in fact lowered barriers to investment. In the same vein, clientelism and patronage may strengthen social ties in larger groups and thereby facilitate collective action among firms. In the Arab world, the term *wasta* ('favouritism') therefore has a partly positive connotation.[16] By definition, these arrangements are exclusive and therefore neither fair nor very efficient in terms of stimulating innovation, but the

[16] See the discussion of favouritism in Loewe et al. (2007).

interesting finding is that they may still be able to bring about private-sector-led economic growth.

Second, while the concentration of political power in the hands of strong presidents with considerable discretionary power may stimulate nepotism and corruption, the cases of Tunisia and Ethiopia suggest that this does not rule out the possibility of rulers pursuing ambitious projects of productive transformation. On the contrary, a neopatrimonial leader may need to make fewer compromises than a government in a mature democracy with complex political checks and balances, and thus be better able to organize big targeted investment programmes or to grant lavish subsidies to industrial-upgrading programmes for the existing economic elites. The fact that power is exercised in a personalized way further increases the scope of political leaders to engage in arm's length relations with key investors; for example by negotiating tailor-made subsidies for particular strategically relevant investors and to demand their moral commitment to actively support the governments' development programmes.

More research is needed to understand why some neopatrimonial leaders, in Leftwich's (2009) terms, become 'developmental' and create growth coalitions with the private sector, whereas others become 'predatory or collusive'. Our country case studies point to three important interrelated determinants:

1. The *endowment with easily extractable natural resources* seems to be one important determinant. The fact that the governments of countries with high oil, gas, or mineral resource rents—Nigeria, Egypt, Syria[17]—do not seem to be as highly committed to a national project of productive transformation as those in resource-poor Tunisia and Ethiopia supports the resource curse hypothesis. Governments in resource-poor countries have only few patronage resources at their disposal and therefore need to offer a convincing perspective of economic growth that benefits the population at large in order to ensure their legitimacy. Rents need to be created through productive sectors before they can be distributed.

2. The *ruler's time horizon* seems to be another differentiating factor. As Olson (1993) analysed in his seminal paper on dictatorship, democracy, and development, purely self-interested rulers would have an incentive to immediately extract as many rents as possible if they assumed their tenure to be short. When they expect a long tenure, in contrast, they have more incentive to invest in economic development that would pay off in future rents and simultaneously buy political support from the electorate. The long reign of the authoritarian rulers Ben Ali in Tunisia (1987–2011) and Meles Zenawi in

[17] Mozambique receives considerable rents from the Cabora Bassa hydro-electric power project which in turn attracted an aluminium smelter industry.

Ethiopia (1995–2012) enabled them to invest in long-term transformation projects that would inevitably take more than a decade to produce economic growth—such as the creation of a new system of technical universities and vocational training almost from scratch in Ethiopia, and the creation of a new export-oriented light manufacturing industry complex in Tunisia. Both presidents pushed their projects with an explicit long-term perspective in mind, and both started from a position of authoritarian rulership that was (with the exception of Ethiopia's 2005 election) never seriously challenged by electoral competition. Nigeria is a counter-example, where presidential terms have been much shorter and no societal agreement on national transformation strategies was achieved. It should be noted, however, that long tenures by no means guarantee developmental attitudes of the rulers, as the large number of long-lasting predatory regimes in the region shows.

3. Hence, the *intrinsic development orientation* of the national leadership makes a big difference. The assumption of purely self-interested surplus-extracting leaders Olson (1993: 574) makes for analytical purposes is obviously simplistic, as he himself recognizes. In practice, individuals act out of very different motives. Political leaders are, to different degrees, also guided by values and convictions that include elements of altruism and nationalist convictions, and are influenced by the predominant development ideas of their times. As shown for the example of Ethiopia, different ideological components can be traced back to specific historical lessons and international role models that impressed the top leadership.

The above factors are highly interrelated and dependent on many other context variables. The case studies point out, however, that the political convictions of the presidents and the top leaderships as well as the way they seek to create legitimacy and secure their power are key determinants of the quality of industrial policy-making and explain more of the country variation than structural characteristics of the economy or the administration. This is why a thorough understanding of the political logic of neopatrimonialism and its specific local manifestations are important to predict whether and how industrial policy may function.

At the same time, it needs to be stressed that an enlightened, developmental leadership that is not subject to political checks and balances provides a fragile basis for sustainable development. As Kelsall et al. (2010: 27) point out, developmental experiments were not sustained in any of the African cases they studied, and they raise the question 'to what extent degeneration is an evitable consequence' of a model that encourages rent-seeking and lacks institutionalized controls. The recent revolutions in Arab countries confirm the latent instability of authoritarian regimes, even when they have been able to manage a fairly successful economic transition, as in the case of Tunisia.

References

Abdel-Latif, A., and H. Schmitz (2010). 'Growth Alliances: Insights from Egypt'. *Business and Politics*, 12 (4): 1–27. Berkeley: Berkeley Electronic Press. Available at: http://www.bepress.com/bap/vol12/iss4/art4

Altenburg, T. (2010). 'Industrial Policy in Ethiopia'. Discussion Paper 2/2010. Bonn: German Development Institute.

——(2011). 'Industrial Policy in Developing Countries. Overview and Lessons from Seven Country Cases'. Discussion Paper 4/2011. Bonn: German Development Institute.

Auty, R. M. (ed.) (2001). *Resource Abundance and Economic Development*. UNU-WIDER Studies in Development Economics. Oxford and New York: Oxford University Press.

Bank, A., and T. Richter (2010). 'Neopatrimonialism in the Middle East and North Africa: Overview, Critique and Alternative Conceptualization'. Paper presented at the GIGA Workshop 'Neopatrimonialism in Various World Regions', Hamburg, 23 August.

Bratton, M., and N. van de Walle (1997). *Democratic Experiments in Africa. Regime Transitions in Comparative Perspective*. Cambridge: Cambridge University Press.

Bräutigam, D. (2000). 'Interest Groups, Economic Policy, and Growth in Sub-Saharan Africa'. African Economic Policy Discussion Paper 40. Washington, DC: USAID.

Chang, H.-J. (1996). *The Political Economy of Industrial Policy*, 2nd edition. Basingstoke: Palgrave Macmillan.

Collier, P., and A. J. Venables (2007). 'Rethinking Trade Preferences to Help Diversify African Exports'. Policy Insight 2. Oxford: Centre for Economic Policy Research.

Committee of Donor Agencies for Small Enterprise Development (2001). 'Business Development Services for Small Enterprises: Guiding Principles for Donor Intervention'. Washington, DC: Committee of Donor Agencies for Small Enterprise Development.

Croissant, A., and W. Merkel (2004). 'Introduction: Democratization in the Early Twenty-First Century', *Democratization*, 11 (5): 1–9.

Diamond, L. (2002). 'Elections Without Democracy: Thinking about Hybrid Regimes', *Journal of Democracy*, 13 (2): 21–35.

Epstein, D. L., R. Bates, J. A. Goldstone, I. Kristensen, and S. O'Halloran. (2006). 'Democratic Transitions', *American Journal of Political Science*, 50 (3): 551–69.

Erdle, S. (2011). 'Industrial Policy in Tunisia'. Discussion Paper 1/2011. Bonn: German Development Institute.

Erdmann, G., and U. Engel (2006). 'Neopatrimonialism Revisited: Beyond a Catch-All Concept'. Working Paper 16. Hamburg: German Institute of Global and Area Studies.

Evans, P. (1995). *Embedded Autonomy: States and Industrial Transformation*. Princeton: Princeton University Press.

Galal, A. (2008). *Industrial Policy in the Middle East and North Africa. Rethinking the Role of the State*. Cairo and New York: The American University in Cairo Press.

Hausmann, R., and D. Rodrik (2003). 'Economic Development as Self-Discovery', *Journal of Development Economics*, 72 (2): 603–33.

Kaufmann, D., A. Kraay, and M. Mastruzzi (2008). 'Governance Matters VII: Governance Indicators for 1996–2007. Policy Research Working Paper 4654. Washington DC: World Bank.

Kelsall, T., and D. Booth, with D. Cammack and F. Golooba-Mutebi (2010). 'Developmental Patrimonialism? Questioning the Orthodoxy on Political Governance and Economic Progress in Africa. Working Paper 9. London: Overseas Development Institute.

Khan, M., and K. S. Jomo (eds) (2000). *Rents, Rent-Seeking and Economic Development: Theory and Evidence in Asia*. Cambridge: Cambridge University Press.

Krueger, A. O. (1974). 'The Political Economy of the Rent-Seeking Society', *American Economic Review*, 64 (3): 291–303.

Leftwich. A. (2009). 'Bringing Agency Back In: Politics and Human Agency in Building Institutions and States'. Research Paper 6. New York: University of York, Department of Politics.

Lin, J., and C. Monga (2010). 'Growth Identification and Facilitation. The Role of the State in the Dynamics of Structural Change'. Policy Research Working Paper 5313. Washington, DC: World Bank.

Loewe, M., J. Blume, V. Schönleber, S. Seibert, J. Speer, and C. Voss (2007). 'The Impact of Favouritism on the Business Climate: A Study of *Wasta* in Jordan'. DIE Studies 30. Bonn: German Development Institute.

Mehlum, H., K. Moene, and R. Torvik (2006). 'Institutions and the Resource Curse', *The Economic Journal*, 116: 1–20.

Moore, M., and H. Schmitz (2008). 'Idealism, Realism and the Investment Climate in Developing Countries'. Working Paper 307. Brighton: Institute of Development Studies.

Naudé, W. (2011). 'Entrepreneurship is not a Binding Constraint on Growth and Development in the Poorest Countries', *World Development*, 39 (1): 33–44.

OECD (2009). *Is Informal Normal? Towards More and Better Jobs in Developing Countries*. Paris: OECD.

Ohno, K. (2009). *The Middle Income Trap. Implications for Industrialization Strategies in East Asia and Africa*. Tokyo: GRIPS Development Forum.

Olson, M. (1993). 'Dictatorship, Democracy, and Development', *American Political Science Review*, 87 (3): 567–76.

Pack, H., and K. Saggi (2006). 'The Case for Industrial Policy: A Critical Survey'. Policy Research Working Paper 3839. Washington, DC: World Bank.

Pawelka, P. (1985). *Herrschaft und Entwicklung im Nahen Osten: Ägypten*. Heidelberg: C. F. Müller Juristischer Verlag.

Sandbrook, R. (1986). 'The State and Economic Stagnation in Tropical Africa', *World Development*, 14 (3): 319–22.

Schumpeter, J. A. (1942). *Capitalism, Socialism, and Democracy*. New York and London: Harper & Brothers.

Soludo, C., and O. Ogbu (2004). 'A Synthesis of Major Themes in the Political Economy of Trade and Industrialization in Africa'. In C. Soludo, O. Ogbu, and H.-J. Chang (eds), *The Politics of Trade and Industrial Policy in Africa: Forced Consensus*? Trenton, NJ: Africa World Press.

Soludo, C., O. Ogbu, and H.-J. Chang (eds) (2004). *The Politics of Trade and Industrial Policy in Africa: Forced Consensus*? Trenton, NJ: Africa World Press.
Tybout, J. R. (2000). 'Manufacturing Firms in Developing Countries: How Well do They Do, and Why?', *Journal of Economic Literature*, 38: 11–44.
Weber, M. (1978 [1968]). *Economy and Society. An Outline of Interpretative Sociology*, ed. G. Roth and C. Wittich. New York: Bedminster Press.
Zakaria, F. (2003). *The Future of Freedom: Illiberal Democracy at Home and Abroad*. New York: W. W. Norton and Company.

14

Entrepreneurship, Stages of Development, and Industrialization

Zoltan J. Ács and Wim Naudé

14.1 Introduction

Entrepreneurs play an important part in economic growth and development. This has been a key insight since the contribution of Schumpeter (1911) and others (for a discussion, see Naudé 2011a). Entrepreneurs are also vital in the process of structural change or industrialization (Gries and Naudé 2010), a process without which development is not possible, as many of the contributions in Part I of this book have explained. As formalized in Gries and Naudé's (2010) model of entrepreneurship and structural change, entrepreneurial innovation leads to the reallocation of resources from the traditional (agricultural) sector to the modern (manufacturing) sector. There is substantial agreement that recovery after the 2008–9 global financial and economic crises[1] and the challenge of climate change will require more, not less, of such entrepreneurial innovation. What is needed are quality jobs through low-carbon industrialization (Mayer 2010; Naudé 2010b). As was made clear in Chapter 1 there is now a growing rediscovery of industrial policy as being necessary to overcome a number of market failures that inhibit entrepreneurial innovation in job creation and low-carbon industrialization. This implies an industrial policy where the relationship between government and entrepreneurs (the private sector) is important. Unlike in the past where industrial policy was either focused on creation and growth of state-owned firms or alternatively consisted merely of broadly functional policies without consideration for firm or entrepreneurial specifics, the requirement now is that future

[1] As put by *The Economist* (14 March 2009: 3) 'The lights may have gone out on Wall Street, but Silicon Valley continues to burn bright'.

industrial policy ought to be a nuanced partnership between entrepreneurs and the state.

In this chapter we outline some considerations for such an industrial policy where the entrepreneur–state nexus is paramount. Moreover, we argue that such an industrial policy will need to take into consideration that the entrepreneur–state nexus is evolving, and that it depends on the stage of development of a particular country. This builds on the recent contributions of Ács and Szerb (2009) and Ács (2010), in which the different roles of entrepreneurship across a country's stages of development is recognized.

In the next section we discuss the role of entrepreneurs in industrialization. Then in Section 14.3 we analyse the role of entrepreneurship across various stages of development, with particular consideration of the empirical evidence and on using the Global Entrepreneurship Development Index (GEDI) as a guide to inform industrial policy aimed at entrepreneurial innovation. This section relies heavily on Ács and Szerb (2009) and Ács (2010). In Section 144 we bring together these two strands of thinking and tease out the implications for industrial policy across various stages of development. Section 14.5 concludes.

14.2 Entrepreneurship and industrialization

Gries and Naudé (2010) provide a model to illustrate the role of the entrepreneurial innovation in industrialization. Here entrepreneurs fulfil essential roles. First, they create new firms outside the household, offering new products and introducing new processes that provide information as a 'lead' activity. Second, they increase the size of firms (and wage employment) by making use of scale economies. Such larger firms tend to specialize, and the clustering of specialized firms can give rise to localization economies, further encouraging innovation and specialization. Third, entrepreneurs can raise the returns to human and physical capital and so provide incentives for further investment and education.

Entrepreneurs may not automatically provide these functions, as they will be constrained by market failures. Industrial policy may thus be justified. Rodrik (2007), recognizing this, discusses a number of such entrepreneurship-inhibiting market failures. This can occur in financial, labour, product, and knowledge markets. He remarked that in developing countries 'the deck is stacked against entrepreneurs who contemplate diversifying into non-traditional areas' (ibid.: 7).

Consider first the creation of new firms and the market failures due to the information it generates. Early or lead entrants into a market or production process reduce the uncertainty for followers by providing information as to its profitability (Hoff 1997). It has been described as a 'cost-discovery' function by Hausmann and Rodrik (2003).[2] An industrial policy that facilitates this cost-discovery function of entrepreneurs needs to be flexible and moreover to encourage experimentation. According to Aghion (2009: 15) entrepreneurially consistent industrial policy needs to be able to facilitate experimental state intervention, but must be able to 'stop the intervention if it turns out not to be efficient'. There is wide opposition to industrial policies that, by eschewing an approach consistent with entrepreneurship, have few mechanisms to get rid of inefficient firms. Just as firm entry is important, assuming new opportunities, providing higher returns to human capital, and signalling what an economy may be good at producing, so firm exit, once a firm has failed, is important too. According to Campbell (2009: 1), citing the case of Pakistan, industrial policy can fail when governments lack the strength 'to cut support to unsuccessful companies and industries' that are politically well-connected.

Second, market failures often prevent firms from growing. An empirical regularity associated with the failure of industrialization in much of Africa is the failure of small firms to grow—Page in this volume argues that these firms need to 'learn to compete'. In contrast, the growth in firm size as a country industrializes is a 'stylized fact' of economic development. It depends, however, crucially on entrepreneurship and specifically entrepreneurial talent or ability, as illustrated by Murphy, Shleifer, and Vishny (1991). Market failures result in the misallocation of entrepreneurial talent.

The role of entrepreneurial ability in the industrial success of the newly industrialized economies (NIEs) has been emphasized by Nelson and Pack (1999). They offer a dual-economy model to explain the structural transformation of economies, such as Korea and Taiwan, from being characterized by a 'craft' sector to a 'modern' economy. They assign a key role to the 'effectiveness of entrepreneurship' (or entrepreneurial ability), which they see as a vital determinant of the rate of assimilation of technology (ibid.: 420). They stress the imitative role of entrepreneurship as well as its role in taking on uncertainty, given that the adoption of (mostly) foreign technology by entrepreneurs in these countries entails significant risk-taking (ibid.: 418). By performing this task, the entrepreneur is the essential mechanism causing new knowledge, as embodied for instance in foreign technology, to 'spill over' (Braunerhjelm, Ács, and Audretsch 2010).

[2] The current European industrial policy (EC 2005, 2007) recognizes this role of lead entrants. For example it has adopted a 'lead market initiative' which consists of 'legal and regulatory frameworks, fostering of open-innovation mechanisms, standards, public procurement practices, intellectual property protection, or the availability of venture capital' with the aim to 'lift obstacles that hinder the development of new markets' (EC 2007: 7–8).

The third role of entrepreneurship inhibited by market failures is that of creating incentives for further investments in human-capital formation. Since the process of industrial catching up requires a higher level of skilled labour, entrepreneurs cause an increase in the demand for educated labour. This leads to an overall improvement in human capital in a country, in turn facilitating the imitation and adoption of foreign technology.[3] Nelson and Pack's model implies that a 'rapid' expansion of skilled labour can only be absorbed if entrepreneurial ability is high, and that without entrepreneurial ability the returns to physical and human capital are low (Nelson and Pack 1999: 423). Entrepreneurial ability therefore has positive externalities that could justify support for it within industrial policies.

14.3 Entrepreneurship across the stages of development

In his classic text, Rostow (1960) suggested that countries go through five stages of economic growth:

(i) the traditional society
(ii) the preconditions for take-off
(iii) the take-off
(iv) the drive to maturity
(v) the age of high mass consumption.

While these stages are a simplified way of looking at the development of modern economies, they identify critical events. When the Soviet Union did not develop into a mass consumption society (in part due to a lack of total factor productivity), the stages approach to economic growth went out of fashion.

However, influenced by recent developments in economics, Porter, Sachs, and McArthur (2002) have provided a modern rendition of this approach by identifying three stages of *development* as opposed to growth and two transitions. The three stages are:

(i) a factor-driven stage
(ii) an efficiency-driven stage
(iii) an innovation-driven stage.

While Rostow (1990) focused on the *age of high mass consumption*, Porter, Sachs, and McArthur (2002) following recent developments in the economics of innovation focuses on the *innovation-driven stage*. Historically, an elite

[3] Keller (2004: 752) points out that for most countries, foreign sources of technology account for 90 per cent or more of local productivity growth.

entrepreneurial class appears to have played a leading role in economic development. Today we believe that they are also crucial for the innovation-driven stage. The transition to the innovation-driven stage is characterized by increased activity by individual agents. In the innovation-driven stage knowledge provides the key input. In this stage the focus shifts from firms to agents in possession of new knowledge. The agent decides to start a new firm based on expected net returns from a new product. The innovation-driven stage is biased towards high value-added industries in which entrepreneurial activity is important.

Institutions dominate the first two stages of development. In fact, innovation accounts for only about 5 per cent of economic activity in factor-driven economies and rises to 10 per cent in the efficiency driven stage. However, in the innovation-driven stage, when opportunities have been exhausted in factors and efficiency, innovation accounts for 30 per cent of economic activity. We see an S-shaped relationship between entrepreneurship and economic development because in the first transition stage entrepreneurship plays a minimal role in productive transformation. It increases in the efficiency-driven stage. However, as we move from the efficiency-driven stage to the innovation-driven stage (the knowledge-driven stage) entrepreneurship plays a more important role, at an increasing rate but then leveling off as economies become fully developed.

Figure 14.1 shows the relationship between entrepreneurship and economic development. Entrepreneurship is considered to be an important mechanism

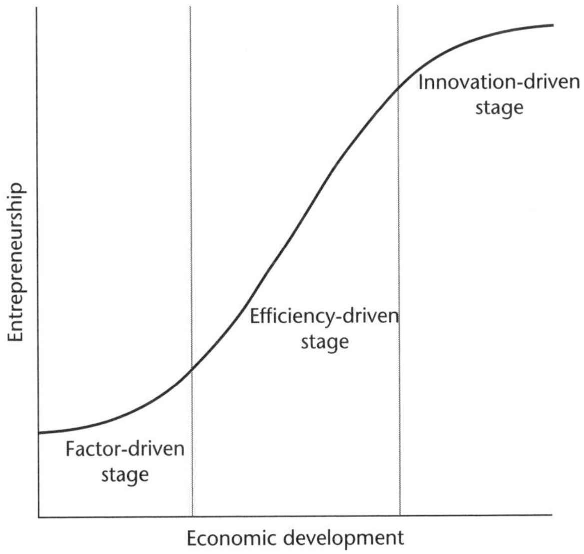

Figure 14.1. Entrepreneurship and the corresponding stages of development
Source: Ács and Szerb (2009).

for economic development through employment, innovation, and welfare. The intersection of the S-curve on the vertical axis is consistent with Baumol's (1990) observation that entrepreneurship is also a resource, and that all societies have some amount of economic activity, but that activity is distributed between productive, unproductive, and destructive entrepreneurship.

What is crucial is to determine how much productive entrepreneurship we have in countries at different stages of development?' The S-curve suggests that in the factor-driven stage a relatively small amount of entrepreneurial activity is productive; that is, it creates economic and/or social value. As mentioned earlier, this increases sharply through the efficiency-driven stage and levels off in the innovation-driven stage of development. As institutions are strengthened, more and more entrepreneurial activity is shifted towards productive entrepreneurship strengthening economic development. We will discuss the implications of this for industrial policy in the next section.

A related question is 'What are the other entrepreneurs doing?' The answer is that if the supply of entrepreneurship is constant, then the majority of entrepreneurs are engaged in either destructive entrepreneurship (destroying social value) or unproductive entrepreneurship (not increasing social value). For example entrepreneurship may thrive on and encourage the existence of a black market, the best and the most talented may be engaged in bureaucratic rent-seeking or risky and (at times) illegal ventures that destroy social value even when adding to the wealth of the individual in concern. If a constant proportion *X* of the population is engaged in entrepreneurship and only a small fraction of this is in productive entrepreneurship, the rest are destroying value. Building better institutions and changing the incentive structure of the society can only eliminate this valley of backwardness above the S-curve. All of this requires good government and governance, and industrial policy focusing on the broader institutional environment may play a crucial role in this case.

To identify the level of entrepreneurial activity in a country corresponding to the stage of development and its role in industrial policy we need good measures for entrepreneurship. The existing measures do not fully capture the essence of entrepreneurship, empirically or conceptually. GEDI is an independent index that provides a comprehensive measure of entrepreneurship. The index draws on previous measures of economic freedom, competitiveness, and entrepreneurial activity but improves on each of these by providing a more focused and quality-oriented approach.

As illustrated in Table 14.1 three sub-indexes of activity, aspiration, and attitudes combine to constitute the entrepreneurship super-index. While other indices have focused on entrepreneurship at the innovation-drive stage, the newly created GEDI takes into account entrepreneurship at all stages of development. First, the three entrepreneurial sub-indices are not of equal importance. The attitude sub index measures society's basic attitudes toward

Table 14.1. The global entrepreneurship and development index

Global entrepreneurship and development index (GEDI)		
Entrepreneurial Attitudes sub-index	Opportunity Perception	*Opportunity*
		Marketagglom
	Startup skills	*Skill*
		Educpostsec
	Nonfear of failure	*Nonfear*
		Business risk
	Networking	*Knowent*
		Internetusage
	Cultural support	*Carstat*
		Corruption
Entrepreneurial activities sub-index	Opportunity startup	*Teaopport*
		Freedom
	Technology sector	*Techsect*
		Techabsorp
	Quality of human Resources	*Higheduc*
		Stafftrain
	Competition	*Compet*
		Markdom
Entrepreneurial Aspirations sub-index	New product	*Newp*
		Gerd
	New tech	*Newt*
		Innov
	High growth	*Gazelle*
		Buss strategy
	Internationalization	*Export*
		Glob
	Risk capital	*Infinv*
		Ventcap

Source: Ács (2010).

entrepreneurship through education and social stability. The activity sub-index measures what individuals are actually doing to improve the quality of human resources and technological efficiency. The aspiration sub-index measures how much of the entrepreneurial activity is being directed toward innovation, high-impact entrepreneurship, and globalization. The sub-indexes are based on their constituent pillar scores. The pillars, in turn, are based on the interaction between their constituent individual and institutional variables. The incorporation of institutional variables is a unique feature of the GEDI and reflects the qualitative aspect of entrepreneurship. Understanding the sub-indexes and their changing importance towards entrepreneurial development across stages of development provides a useful approach towards informing a more appropriate set of industrial policies.

14.4 Entrepreneurship and industrial policy across stages of development

Despite the threefold important role played by individual entrepreneurs as was discussed in Section 14.2, and despite the clear evidence that the role of the entrepreneur differs across stages of development, many earlier industrial policies largely failed to explicitly incorporate the entrepreneur and to pay attention to the developmental stage of a country. This is especially the case in Africa where industrial policy is now seen to be largely unsuccessful (see Chapter 9 in this volume)—with the possible exception of South Africa.[4] In Africa market and government failures resulted in a much larger misallocation of entrepreneurial ability towards unproductive and even destructive activities (as mentioned earlier; see also e.g. Baumol 1990; Baumol, Litan, and Schramm 2007) and in an inappropriate emphasis on stimulating economic activity and growth in a manner that was not optimal for entrepreneurship given these countries' levels of development.

In contrast, there is considerable evidence that in the countries where industrial policies have been more successful—such as the NIEs and China—that industrial policy more properly considered the nature of a country's entrepreneurs and their relation to the state. Thus for instance in Singapore and Korea, where the entrepreneurial base was judged to be lacking, industrial policy was at first aimed at complementing and strengthening the domestic entrepreneurial base, through allowing in much more foreign entrepreneurship and by

[4] Central in the country's industrial policy was the state-owned creation of the largest venture capital fund for manufacturing on the African continent, the Industrial Development Corporation (IDC) of South Africa in 1940. In the following sections we will stress the potential importance of an entrepreneurial approach to industrial policy of promoting venture capital in developing countries.

providing financial support to allow entrepreneurs to take on more risk in imitating and adopting foreign technology (Nelson and Pack 1999). And in Taiwan and Japan, where the entrepreneurial base was fairly strong to begin with, more limitations were placed on foreign entrepreneurs.

China's economic transformation since the late 1970s also shows a measure of consideration of entrepreneurship. Thus, for instance, Siebert (2007: 899) remarks that 'the Chinese now show a larger acceptance of the market economy than the three large continental countries of Europe'. He describes how the Chinese reforms fostered the emergence of more productive enterprises, not by dismantling or privatizing state-owned enterprises upfront (as in Eastern Europe or some African countries), but of maintaining these and 'simply by letting new economic activities develop outside the government controlled sector' (ibid.: 900). China also allowed the growing class of private sector entrepreneurs to influence the evolution of the institutional framework shaping its industrial policy—a process described as 'institutional entrepreneurship'.

Reasons for the neglect of the entrepreneur in industrial policy in the past may be due to the likelihood that the nature of the firm was not always adequately understood (Lazonick 2009), in other words that early development economics did not see entrepreneurship as a binding constraint on economic development (Naudé 2011b). We can also add to this the argument of this chapter, namely that the measurement of entrepreneurship was a neglected area, and that the nature of the contribution of entrepreneurship across various stages of development was not properly recognized.

Understanding the nature of the firm as described should be seen in conjunction with the advances in recent years of distinguishing the role of entrepreneurship across various stages of development. This recognizes that different types of industry develop or evolve over the course of a country's development path (Lin and Chang 2009) and that different types of industry and firm heterogeneity entail different types of entrepreneurship, which in turn requires different types of support from the government. Hart (2001), for instance, makes a distinction between a 'developmental state' and a 'regulatory state', arguing that a developmental state, which is more hands-on and leading in the process of industrialization, is more suited when a country's industry will benefit from centralization and intervention—i.e. where the firm and the entrepreneur is still operating well within the technological frontier. A similar argument is made by Phan, Venkataraman, and Velamuri (2008) in a study of entrepreneurship in emerging countries. They conclude:

> ...studies of entrepreneurial regions across the world...have underscored the critical role of governments at different levels in the emergence of these regions... the magnitude of government influence, which is significant in the early stages of development, seems to decline in later stages relative to other factors...The

> explanations for this vary from the traditional factor substitution wherein government kick-starts the development of a sector, which then becomes attractive for private capital to accumulate, to the post-modern institutionalization, in which the development of such institutions as intellectual property regimes engender capital accumulation. (ibid.: 325)

Thus they find that in early stages of development government intervention is needed to address market failures and to kick-start growth. They see this intervention as a prerequisite for the later development of an entrepreneurial economy.

The discussion so far suggests very strongly that there is no 'one size fits all' as far as industrial policy is concerned. This is in line with Chapter 5, where Hobday argues that instead of trying to ape the successful Asian industrializing countries, poor countries should adopt appropriate, home-grown industrial policies based on their resources, capabilities, and stage of development. Because innovation, as the fundamental driver of economic growth makes a different contribution across stages, industrial policy should be closely aligned (consistent) with innovation policy. Indeed it is recognized in the innovation literature that 'innovation ambitions and policies have to be adapted to levels of development' (Aubert 2004: 14).

The relationship between entrepreneurs and government and the implications for industrial policy and innovation (also informed by the GEDI) through various phases of development are summarized in Table 14.2.

In the table the left-hand column refers to three stages of development: the factor-driven stage, the efficiency-driven stage, and the innovation-driven stage—as described in the previous section. In the second column this is set against the dominant private sector mode, in the third column against the characteristics of the innovation system (given that industrial policy should primarily support innovative entrepreneurship) and on the final column against the type of state orientation most conducive for the development of the private sector mode.

The table indicates that at an early stage of development the entrepreneurial base is still small, and that private sector activity is mainly in dispersed, low-productivity traditional activities. In such a stage of development, states are very often fragile (see Naudé, McGillivray, and Santos-Paulino 2011) and the major development challenge is to move the state from being fragile to being facilitating. In other words, the state establishes legitimacy, authority, and capacity, and starts to put in place basic framework conditions for investment and productivity growth. This will enable a core of entrepreneurship to emerge, most often in accordance with the country's comparative advantage,[5] and will prepare the economy for the efficiency-driven path.

[5] Indeed, Lin defines a 'facilitating state', as a 'state that facilitates the private sector's ability to exploit the country's areas of comparative advantage' (Lin and Chang 2009: 484).

Table 14.2. Stages of country development, entrepreneurship, and industrial policies

Stage of country development	Private sector mode	Innovation system characteristics	Industrial policy orientation
Factor-driven	*Traditional economy*	*Low science and technology capabilities*	*Fragile or facilitating*
Production most intensive in unskilled labour and natural resources	Dominance of primary sectors	Innovation may account for only 5 per cent of economic activity	Establishing authority, capacity and/or legitimacy important to move from fragile to facilitating
	Specialization in cash crops, mineral extraction	Adoption of existing technology to local conditions main challenge	Facilitating state aims at establishing conducive business environment (property rights, stability, rule of law, accessibility)
	Spatially dispersed production	'Brain drain' and outflow of skills	Demonstration of 'basic innovations' that can contribute to development
	Small entrepreneurial base	Low technology absorption capability	Basic investment in technology infrastructure
	Largely small, informal and low and minimal technology SMEs	Little private sector R&D	Start addressing broader environment for innovation (education, trade, finance) and industrialization
		Little incentive for indigenous knowledge commercialization	Gather data on local indigenous knowledge. Promote positive *attitudes* towards entrepreneurship
Efficiency-driven	*Managerial economy*	*Medium science and technology capabilities*	*Developmental or Facilitating*
Production more efficient, and movement towards technology frontier starts.	Manufacturing sector grows	Innovation becomes more important and could contribute to around 10 per cent of economic activity	Developmental state to use policies to encourage domestic technological capability formation
	Greater product diversification	Growth in private and public sector R&D	Use of government procurement for innovation capability
	Larger firms, SOE and MNEs start to dominate	IPR protection becomes more important	building and industrial capacity
	'Fordist' production by obtaining productivity growth through economies of scale		Attract appropriate FDI
	Growing spatial clustering and urbanization		Develop autonomous innovation promotion institutions/improve the science base
	More technologically competent enterprises		Policies aimed at high-technological innovation

(continued)

Table 14.2. Continued

Stage of country development	Private sector mode	Innovation system characteristics	Industrial policy orientation
			Promote entrepreneurial *activities* broadly, including through starting to promote venture capital
			Public R&D to complement and crowd-in private R&D
			Trade liberalization, openness, international research collaboration
			Use of diasporas (and reverse the brain drain)
			Indigenous knowledge utilize, protect
Innovation-driven	*Entrepreneurial economy*	*High science and technology capabilities*	*Facilitating*
Production of high-tech goods and innovative to expand the technological frontier	Rise in services sector share in GDP	Knowledge becomes the main driver of growth	The state promotes basic framework conditions
	High value-added manufacturing activities dominate, with greater specialization	Innovation can contribute to more than 30 per cent of economic activity	Substantial focus on innovation, technology, also regional focus
	High-tech clusters stabilize and R&D-rich firms to be found		Strengthen research base
	Reemergence of (advanced) small businesses on both national and international markets		Promote entrepreneurial *aspirations*
			Market competition, market development through entry of new entrepreneurial firms important
			Ensure well-functioning venture capital markets
			Careful selectivity on potential high-growth entrepreneurship

Source: author's compilation based on the discussions in Aubert (2004); Porter (2004); Ács and Szerb (2009); and Altenburg (2009).

To fully embark on this path of efficiency-driven growth, however, the state needs to expand its intervention in the economy to 'defy' the comparative advantage through selective industrial policies. This will, for instance, allow economies of scale to be reaped, which will encourage self-reinforcing agglomerations, facilitate growth in firms' size, and will see a greater role, for instance, for state-owned enterprises (SOEs) and multinational enterprises (MNEs) as the latter makes use of special economic zones and other incentives.

During the efficiency-driven stage, innovation policies as subset of industrial policy increase in importance. Thus for instance as suggested in column 4, row 2, intellectual property protection is often not seen as being of such great importance in earlier stages of development, only becoming more important when a country has already entered a rather more advanced stage of development (Aubert 2004). Thus, as shown in the efficiency-driven stage of development, public R&D starts to play a more important role but it is less important in the factor-driven stage. Impact evaluations have found that public R&D can stimulate total investment in R&D and can thus crowd-in private R&D (Taymaz and Üçdoğruk 2009).

In earlier phases of development, the adoption and eventual adaptation of technologies are important to encourage. Policies that can do this include those that improve skills, organizational learning, and attitudes and culture (Lindahl 2005).

Aubert (2004) focuses on the obstacles to entrepreneurial innovation in developing countries in earlier stages of development. He recommends measures and reforms to address broad or 'functional' obstacles, such as business environment constraints. This is indeed what typical private-sector development initiatives attempt to improve.

At some point, the country's sectoral development will be such that it needs a flexible industrial policy, so as to shift again towards being less interventionist, more functional but also, perhaps surprisingly, more selective. Many countries embark on trade liberalization during this phase of their development. Examples given in this chapter include the EU, the USA, and India. China's two-track approach since 1978 can be seen as a variant of this shift, whereby the change is gradually introduced by allowing a more liberalized private-sector economy to develop whilst not disbanding state-owned enterprises.

As is also shown in column 4 of Table 14.2, and based on the GEDI, entrepreneurially oriented industrial policies should at different stages focus differently on attitudes, activities, and aspirations. Attitudes are an essential prerequisite for either activity or aspirations. This is in part cultural, as certain societies (e.g. communism and feudalism) outlawed entrepreneurship. Attitude is followed by activity, and after activity, aspirations become important. In some sense, this process is cumulative over time, but it has large overlaps as well. In a factor-driven (agricultural economy) the focus needs to be on entrepreneurial attitudes in the population. In an efficiency-driven (manufacturing) economy individual entrepreneurs need to be encouraged to start businesses. In an innovation-driven (knowledge-based) economy some people need to create very large and successful businesses. The role of institutional and individual variables used in the construction of the indices is also an important aspect of the development process. While institutional improvement is vital for factor-driven countries to advance to the next level of development, the enhancement of individual characteristics is increasingly critical for innovation-driven economies.

Thus important policy implications for the countries at different levels of development emerge from the GEDI rankings.

Factor-driven economies need to focus on entrepreneurial attitudes, start to develop activity, and begin the process of enabling entrepreneurial aspirations. Here an instructive example is from India, where entrepreneurship has been resurgent since the early 1990s. It has made strong contributions to growth through innovation—as has been demonstrated by the country's vibrantly growing ICT sector. A number of policy initiatives have been important in facilitating this growth. Das (2009) identifies in this regard most importantly a change in culture and attitudes towards entrepreneurs.

The key focus of efficiency-driven economies should be on entrepreneurial activity. Here it is also important that entrepreneurs start to be more socially responsible—making increasing contributions to health, education, and welfare, so that 'the business community sees development issues as their problem, too' (Das 2009: 3), and that governments start to provide more supported entrepreneurship and innovation through creation of venture capital funds as they did for instance in India (Mani 2011).

However, continuous improvement of attitudes and the development of entrepreneurial aspirations are also important. In innovation-driven economies, the key focus should be on aspirations. However, both attitudes and activity need to be improved to maintain balance across the three sub-indices. This is also highlighted in Table 14.3.

These policy recommendations are reflected in column 4 of Table 14.2. It is important to note that there is a bidirectional causality between innovation, industrialization, and stages of development. At a high level of per capita GDP, governments spend more on R&D and universities, creating a supporting environment for creative pursuits, including technological innovation, which spurs further industrial sophistication.

The greater selectivity during the innovation stage (and to an extent already during the efficiency-driven growth stage) stems from the requirement of focusing on the small subset of firms that are really innovative. Not all firms are innovative. Innovative entrepreneurship is sometimes also seen as

Table 14.3: Industrial policy emphasis for economies at different stages of development

Stage of Economic Development	Sub-Index		
	Attitudes	Activity	Aspirations
Factor-driven economy	Key focus	Develop	Start enabling
Efficiency-driven economy	Continuous improvement	Key focus	Develop
Innovation-driven economy	Continuous improvement	Continuous improvement	Key focus

Source: Ács and Szerb (2010).

synonymous with high-impact or high-growth entrepreneurship (HGE; Wong, Ho, and Autio 2005; Lerner 2009; Shane 2009, and their firms are described as 'gazelles' (Stam et al. 2009; Teruel and De Wit 2011). These HGE firms are disproportionately important for economic growth and development—as put by Shane (2009: 145) 'a tiny sliver of companies accounts for the vast majority of the contribution to job creation and economic growth'. Selectivity and targeting have the benefits of overcoming shortcomings of past efforts, raising the effectiveness and sustainability of industrial policies, and conserving resources (Stam et al. 2009).

For countries in the factor-driven and efficiency-driven stages of development it is often reckoned that the informational requirements for selective industrial policy is too great—and that government failure will result if they do attempt such selectivity (Coad and Rao 2008; Stam et al. 2009). For advanced economies on the production-possibility frontier, the challenge is also how high-growth potential firms can be identified *ex ante* (Hölzl 2009).

Shane (2009) also cautions against targeting potentially HGE firms, but points out that these types of firms very often tend, at least in advanced economies, to be financed disproportionately by venture capital. He refers to data that show that in the USA in 2003 firms that were supported by venture capital employed almost 10 per cent of all the private sector. Of course the difficulty is that venture capital funding is still very underdeveloped in developing and emerging economies in the first stages of development, where innovative entrepreneurs rely more on internal funding and where many donor and other entrepreneurship programmes have aimed at expanding debt financing to firms. This implies that if in future the benefits of selectivity are to be gained, that perhaps support for the emergence of venture capital across the developing world should be a priority.

If specific firms are difficult to target due to informational problems, some have argued that a second best option is to target not firms but clusters or agglomerations of firms, noting that knowledge generation, learning, innovation, and economic activity tend to be localized processes (Braunerhjelm 2010: 6). Hence cluster approaches to entrepreneurship are important. The groundwork for such an approach needs to have started already by the factor-driven stage of development, as Table 14.2 implies.

Entrepreneurs are the essential drivers of innovation as Schumpeter recognized, and the 'filters' through which knowledge externalities spill over. It therefore makes sense for industrial-policy support for entrepreneurship to consider the formation and function of regional clusters (because of the localization of spillovers), and their linkages with the rest of the economy—and to ensure venture capital support at clusters. In such an environment an open economy that stimulates creativity and attracts the 'best and the brightest' receives priority in industrial policy.

14.5 Concluding remarks

A perennial challenge for industrial policy concerns not the 'why' but the 'how' (Rodrik 2007). In this chapter we have argued that an entrepreneurial approach to industrial policy offers an answer to the 'how' of industrial policy. This stands in contrast to past approaches, which have been characterized by heavy government interference and management of the economy, which have been characterized by the adoption of policies and strategies that were inappropriate for a country's level of development, and which ignored the important role of innovation in economic growth and catching up.

There is as yet no substantial literature on the relationship between the stages of development, the evolving nature of entrepreneurship, and the orientation of the state—indeed this chapter is one of the first to make this link and to argue that this as yet emerging paradigm is essential in any future pathways to industrialization. However, we recognize that it is likely to be confounded by the difficulties that governments and international development organizations will encounter in identifying their stage of development, by the fact that stages overlap (as the third column in Table 14.2 suggests), that some countries may leapfrog stages, and that the instruments and measurements to guide industrial policy in each stage are not well understood. We have argued that the GEDI, which we described in Section 14.3, may be instructive in this regard.

Where a country ranks on the GEDI and what scores it has on the different institutional and individual level pillars can be indicators of the relative strengths and weaknesses that face the country. These scores can be used to design industrial policy, shifting away from weaker pillars and concentrating on features that respond better, given the stage of development that country is in. The sequence of the sub-indices of the GEDI in the development process is important to note and offers suggestions for the aims of industrial policy.

We believe that industrial policy can play a role in fostering entrepreneurship for economic development. It can be used as a tool to overcome the market failures that concern entrepreneurs by ensuring that inefficient forms exit the market, by helping small firms grow, and by ensuring investment in human-capital development. The GEDI illustrates the quantitative and qualitative levels of entrepreneurial activity across the nations and countries at different stages of development. The different policy requirements needed to boost entrepreneurship and to generate growth at the three stages of development necessitate industrial policies that recognize the different kinds of entrepreneurial activity that may exist at different stages of development. The examples of countries like Korea, Singapore, and China are illustrative in this regard. The GEDI rankings can be an indicator of whether a country needs to focus on improving its entrepreneurial attitudes, activities, or aspirations.

The distinction made between various stages of development is of course one that should be made carefully, as a watertight demarcation or classification of countries is difficult. As the OECD (2011: 39) remarks 'development has become more compressed, not only in terms of a higher pace but also because different development stages are pursued concurrently by emerging economies'. This means that care has to be taken to understand the way in which a particular economy is characterized in terms of these stages, where its industries and sectors are in terms of sources of growth, and how to ensure a policy differentiation. The demarcation of stage is thus still useful because it provides a basis for this demarcation of policy, which would otherwise have been difficult. It allows various stages of development and firm growth to be considered in the fine-tuning of industrial policy.

References

Ács, Z. J. (2010). 'Entrepreneurship and Economic Development: The Valley of Backwardness', *Annals of Innovation and Entrepreneurship*, 1 (1). Available at: www.innovationandentrepreneurship.net/index.php/aie/article/view/5641 (accessed 15 December 2010).

Ács, Z. J., and L. Szerb (2009). 'The Global Entrepreneurship Index (GEINDEX)'. Jena Economic Research Papers 2009-028. Jena: Friedrich Schiller University and the Max Planck Institute of Economics.

Ács, Z. J., and L. Szerb (2010). 'Global Entrepreneurship and the United States'. Washington, DC: SBA Office of Advocacy. Available at: archive.sba.gov/advo/research/rs370tot.pdf (accessed 30 July 2012).

Aghion, P. (2009). 'Some Thoughts on Industrial Policy and Growth'. Working Paper 2009-09. Paris: OFCE.

Altenburg, T. (2009). 'Industrial Policy for Low and Lower-Middle Income Countries'. Paper presented at the UNU-WIDER, UNU-MERIT, and UNIDO Workshop on 'Pathways to Industrialization in the 21st Century: New Challenges and Emerging Paradigms', Maastricht, The Netherlands, 22–23 October.

Aubert, J. E. (2004). *Promoting Innovation in Developing Countries: A Conceptual Framework*. Washington, DC: The World Bank Institute.

Baumol, W. J. (1990). 'Entrepreneurship: Productive, Unproductive and Destructive', *The Journal of Political Economy*, 98 (5): 893–921.

Baumol, W. J., R. E. Litan, and C. J. Schramm (2007). *Good Capitalism, Bad Capitalism and the Economics of Growth and Prosperity*. New Haven, CT: Yale University Press.

Braunerhjelm, P. (2010). 'Entrepreneurship, Innovation and Economic Growth: Past Experience, Current Knowledge and Policy Implications', Working Paper 224, Royal Institute of Technology – CESIS, Stockholm.

Braunerhjelm, P., Z. J. Ács, and D. B. Audretsch (2010). 'The Missing Link: Knowledge Diffusion and Entrepreneurship', *Small Business Economics*, 34: 105–25.

Campbell, K. (2009). 'Industrial Policy: Kick the Losers', *Engineering News Online*, 31 July. http://www.engineeringnews.co.za/article/industrial-policy-kick-losers-2009-07-31 (accessed 16 August 2012).

Coad, A., and R. Rao (2008). 'Innovation and Firm Growth in High-Tech Sectors: A Quantile Regression Approach', *Research Policy*, 37: 633–48.

Das, T. (2009). 'Keynote Address'. In J. Y. Lin and B. Pleskovic (eds), *Private Sector and Development*. Washington DC: World Bank.

European Commission (EC) (2005). *Implementing the Community Lisbon Programme: More Research and Innovation*. Brussels, EC.

——(2007). *Mid-term Review of Industrial Policy*. Brussels: EC.

Gries, T., and W. A. Naudé (2010). *Small Business Economics*, 34 (1): 13–29.

Hart, J. A. (2001). 'Can Industrial Policy be Good Policy?'. Paper prepared for the Conference on 'The Political Economy of Policy Reform', Tulane University, New Orleans, Louisiana, 9–10 November.

Hausmann, R., and D. Rodrik (2003). 'Economic Development as Self-Discovery', *Journal of Development Economics*, 72 (2): 603–33.

Hoff, K. (1997). 'Bayesian Learning in an Infant Industry Model,' *Journal of International Economics*, 43 (1): 409–436.

Hölzl, W. (2009). 'Is the R&D Behaviour of Fast-Growing SMEs Different? Evidence from CIS III Data for 16 Countries', *Small Business Economics*, 33: 59–75.

Keller, W. (2004). 'International Technology Diffusion', *Journal of Economic Literature*, 42 (3): 752–82.

Lazonick, W. (2009). 'How American Capitalism Really Works: Some Lessons for Developing Countries'. WIDER Angle April 2009. Helsinki: UNU-WIDER. Available at:

http://www.wider.unu.edu/publications/newsletter/articles/en_GB/07-04-09/ (accessed 30 July 2012).

Lerner, J. (2009). *Boulevard of Broken Dreams*. Princeton: Princeton University Press.

Lin, J., and H.-J. Chang (2009). 'Should Industrial Policy in Developing Countries Conform to Comparative Advantage or Defy it? A Debate between Justin Lin and Ha-Joon Chang', *Development Policy Review*, 27 (5): 483–502.

Lindahl, C. (2005). 'Wealth of the Poor: Eliminating Poverty through Market and Private Sector Development'. Sida Studies 14. Stockholm: Sida.

Mani, S. (2011). 'Promoting Knowledge-intensive Entrepreneurship in India'. In Szirmai, A. Naude, W.A. and Goedhuys, M. (eds), *Entrepreneurship, Innovation and Economic Development*. Oxford: Oxford University Press.

Mayer, J. (2010). 'Global Rebalancing: Effects on Trade Flows and Employment'. Discussion Paper 200. Geneva: UNCTAD.

Murphy, K., A. Shleifer, and R. Vishny (1991). 'The Allocation of Talent: Implications for Growth', *Quarterly Journal of Economics*, 106 (2): 503–30.

Naudé, W. A. (2010). 'Industrial Policy: New Challenges'. Working Paper 2010/107. Helsinki: UNU-WIDER.

——(ed.) (2011a). *Entrepreneurship and Economic Development*. Basingstoke: Palgrave Macmillan.

——. (2011b).'Entrepreneurship is not a Binding Constraint on Economic Growth and Development in the Poorest Countries', *World Development*, 39 (1): 33–44.

Naudé, W. A., M. McGillivray, and A. U. Santos-Paulino (eds) (2011). *Fragile States: Causes, Costs and Responses*. Oxford: Oxford University Press.

Nelson, R. R. and H. Pack (1999). 'The Asian Miracle and Modern Growth Theory', *The Economic Journal*, 109 (457): 416–36.

Organisation for Economic Co-operation and Development (OECD) (2011). 'Global Value Chains: Preliminary Evidence and Policy Issues', Discussion Paper DSTI/IND (2011)3. Paris: OECD.

Phan, P. P., S. Venkataraman, and S. R. Velamuri (2008). *Entrepreneurship in Emerging Regions around the World: Theory, Evidence and Implications*. Cheltenham: Edward Elgar.

Porter, M. E. (2004). *Competitive Strategy: Techniques for Analyzing Industries and Competitors*. London, New York : Free Press.

Porter, M., J. Sachs, and J. McArthur (2002). 'Executive Summary: Competitiveness and Stages of Economic Development'. In M. Porter, J. Sachs, P. K. Cornelius, J. McArthur, and K. Schwab (eds), *The Global Competitiveness Report 2001–2002*. New York: Oxford University Press.

Rodrik, D. (2007). 'Normalizing Industrial Policy'. Mimeo. Paper prepared for the Commission on Growth and Development. Cambridge, MA: Harvard University, John F. Kennedy School of Government.

Rostow, W. W. (1960). *The Stages of Economic Growth: A Non-Communist Manifesto*. Cambridge: Cambridge University Press.

Schumpeter, J. A. (1911). *The Theory of Economic Development*. Cambridge, MA: Harvard University Press (1934 trans. R. Opie).

Siebert, H. (2007). 'China: Coming to Grips with the New Global Player', *The World Economy*, 30 (6): 893–922.

Stam, E., K. Suddle, J. Hessels, A. and Van Stel (2009). 'High-Growth Entrepreneurs, Public Policies, and Economic Growth'. In J. Leitao and R Baptista (eds), *Public Policies for Fostering Entrepreneurship. International Studies in Entrepreneurship*. Berlin: Springer.

Shane, S. (2009). 'Why Encouraging More People to Become Entrepreneurs is Bad Public Policy', *Small Business Economics*, 33: 141–9.

Taymaz, E., and Y. Üçdoğruk (2009). 'Overcoming the Double Hurdles to Investing in Technology: R&D Activities of Small Firms in Developing Countries', *Small Business Economics*, 33: 109–28.

Teruel, M., and de Wit, G. (2011). 'Determinants of High-Growth Firms: Why Have Some Countries More High-Growth Firms than Others?'. Research Report H201107. Zoetermeer: EIM.

Wong, P. K., Y. P Ho, and E. Autio (2005). 'Entrepreneurship, Innovation and Economic Growth. Evidence from GEM Data', *Small Business Economics*, 24: 335–50.

15

Industrial Policy in the Twenty-First Century: Challenges for the Future

John Weiss

15.1 Introduction

Industrial policy has attracted considerable controversy in the development context, possibly out of all proportion to its potential impact (either positive or negative). Arguably, the intensity of the debate stems from the fact that here the structuralist and neoclassical traditions of development studies meet head on, with the former seeing industrial policy as a means of correcting for the limitations of markets and the latter seeing it as the highpoint of 'government failure'. This chapter makes a case for a pragmatic and limited approach to intervention as a means of stimulating industrialization in the context of current and future challenges facing newly industrializing economies. It begins with a simple definition of industrial policy, a brief survey of the theoretical case and a taxonomy of different possible interventions. The second section considers how far government policy per se has contributed to manufacturing success, drawing on the very extensive literature in this area. The third highlights a series of key issues for today's industrializing economies that industrial policy needs to address, and the final section concludes.

15.2 What is the case for industrial policy?

The term industrial policy is used here in the sense of policy interventions designed to affect the allocation of resources in favour of industry (principally manufacturing) as distinct from other sectors. Such interventions may also affect resource allocation within industry in favour of either particular branches or sub-sectors or particular firms (so they may be 'selective' rather than 'functional'). Interventions can involve either the price mechanism or direct controls and be focused on export as well as the domestic market. Industrial policy in this definition is thus much wider than import-substitution trade policies with which it is often associated.

Industrial policy has three dimensions, which are sometimes confused in the literature:

- the overall vision or strategic direction the government wishes to set.
- the process whereby a dialogue is established with the key actors in the private and public sectors.
- the policy instruments used to affect change.

Even if there can be broad agreement on the vision—a competitive and dynamic industrial sector—there can be different paths to achieving this, with varying degrees of public ownership, consultation with the private sector, direct controls, fiscal incentives, and openness to trade.[1]

The theoretical basis for industrial policy as defined here focuses on two propositions, the first relatively uncontroversial and the latter rather more so.

i) Markets (particularly in developing countries) fail to produce a social optimum due to factors like externalities, lack of information, monopolization or social barriers.
ii) Manufacturing industry has a special role in growth due to its greater scope for generating high levels of and growth in productivity (at least at relatively early stages of development) and externalities.[2]

The early development literature was full of analyses of how market failures could be overcome by government intervention; through coordinating investments to overcome demand constraints (the big push/balanced growth analyses of Rosenstein-Rodan and Nurkse), through encouraging the absorption of the labour surplus in manufacturing (the Lewis model), and through building learning-by-doing (through infant industry protection). Significantly, the original neoclassical tradition of the development literature equally embraced market failure and acknowledged the need for intervention to address this. The difference was that in this analysis optimal interventions were to be designed to minimize by-product costs and thus should be based on the price mechanism

[1] Hausmann, Rodrik, and Sabel (2007b) highlight the process aspect of industrial policy and illustrate it in relation to South Africa.

[2] Rodrik (2007) associates industrial policy with any form of selective intervention not just that favouring manufacturing. Arguably this broadens the concept too far to be very useful. He also adopts the broad definition of industrial policy used here to cover both functional and selective and market-based as well as direct measures.

through tax subsidy measures.[3] Unlike later policy interpretations, in this analysis subsidies to compensate for market failures were wholly acceptable. The rationale for interventions based on market failure logically implies that support should be offered equally to all participants in the market ('functional' support). The functional-versus-selective distinction is never precise, since only certain firms will benefit from even broad changes in policy. For example, only producers of internationally tradable goods gain from an exchange rate devaluation and only firms large enough to conduct R&D gain from tax credits related to this type of expenditure.

The clearest statement of the original case for manufacturing as a special 'engine of growth' though its capacity for productivity growth and externalities comes from the work of Nicholas Kaldor, who highlighted the capacity of manufacturing to generate 'dynamic increasing returns'; that is, rising productivity through the expansion of production. This is in contrast to agriculture, where productivity growth was seen as arising through labour-saving technical change and the movement of workers off the land, and to services, which respond passively to increases in other sectors (although it is now understood that this analysis underestimated the potential for new branches of services linked with the computer-based technology to generate sustained productivity growth and behave in the same way as manufacturing).[4] More recent theorizing following Krugman has extended this analysis of dynamic sectors by building increasing returns into trade theory models and thus highlighting the importance of 'first mover advantages'. Once established (perhaps behind tariff barriers) an activity can build on its productivity growth to become internationally competitive. Similarly more recent economic geography models have stressed the importance of location externalities ('agglomeration effects') arising through labour-market effects, networks of suppliers, or various knowledge spillovers. Not all of these agglomeration effects need arise from manufacturing but many will, and arguably the sector has greater capacity to produce these externalities than does services.[5]

The 'self-discovery' model of Hausmann and Rodrik (2003) sets out the case for subsidizing risk-taking activity in the introduction of new products and technologies, arguing that all potential followers gain from the actions of

[3] Corden (1974) is the classic statement of this 'policy hierarchy' approach. For example, instead of compensating new manufacturing activity for paying a wage above the opportunity cost of rural labour by granting tariff protection (and thus penalizing consumers), compensation should be through an employment subsidy (whose cost could be spread over all tax payers, not just consumers of the product in question).

[4] Weiss (2002: chapter 4) sets out the Kaldor case. The introduction of the selective employment tax (to tax service sector employment) in the UK in the late-1960s designed by Kaldor was a dramatic (and highly controversial) example of industrial policy in a developed-economy context.

[5] UNIDO (2009) presents data on the empirical significance of agglomeration effects from manufacturing. Collier and Venables (2007) have a useful discussion of their significance in modern manufacturing.

innovators. Manufacturing need not be the only activity where this type of externality occurs but, provided innovation is more prevalent there, the model again provides a justification for its special place in growth. If increasing returns and externalities are the rationale for intervention, logically this implies selectivity in support, since the scope for these effects will vary both between branches and between firms in branches.

In brief there is no shortage of theoretical arguments that can be utilized to make a case for industrial policy. The objections relate to its feasibility and the possibility of policy 'capture'.

15.3 Different perspectives on industrial policy

In the literature two competing perspectives have emerged on the role and application of industrial policy. One can be characterized as a 'promotional' approach. Here governments are recommended to think big and to support and promote either subsectors or firms within these. The aim is to shift fairly rapidly into new, dynamic, and technologically sophisticated activities. Some of these may be quite different from the goods in which the economy is currently specialized. Since by definition some will be new activities for the economy, firms may need financial incentives to justify the risk involved. Governments are perceived as promoters who act as catalysts, who provide the financial support needed during the learning period of the new firms, and who assist in the process of industrial start-up with training, export marketing, and the general coordination of support activities.

The other perspective, which can be characterized as a 'market-based' approach, sees governments as facilitators whose role is to address the malfunctioning of markets, either to correct for externalities or to provide the information and infrastructure needed by firms. Although this role may seem modest, it can be substantial where governments interpret market failure in a broad sense, for example providing credit where the financial sector is risk averse, or training where firms underinvest due to the risk of workers leaving. From this latter perspective the facilitating government corrects for failures, whilst leaving firms to decide how far they wish to innovate and upgrade their production; support is available to all firms affected by the market failure, not to a selected few.

These distinctions can be linked with the concept of 'economic distance', defined in terms of the similarity between the skills and technological capabilities required to produce different sets of goods. Thus distance is low where similar capabilities are required to produce two goods and high where markedly different capabilities are involved. The promotional approach can be thought of as an attempt to move into the production of dissimilar or distant goods and the market-based one to a closer or similar set of goods to those in which the economy is already specialized. Quantification of economic distance is complex, although there have been recent efforts based on the probability that pairs of countries have a comparative advantage in the same two goods.[6] The difference in approach to economic distance underlies the debate on industrial policy between Lin and Chang (2009). When Lin writes of a facilitating state that supports activities with a comparative advantage and Chang of a more interventionist state that funds technological upgrading, they are, in effect, discussing different strategies towards distance, with Lin advocating a move to closer and Chang to more distant product lines to those in which an economy is currently specialized.

Practical advice can of course draw on both approaches. The most recent academic interpretation of industrial policy, as developed by the Hausmann–Rodrik team at Harvard University, has been applied to a number of countries and draws on both perspectives. For example, in their analysis of the policy options for South Africa Hausmann, Rodrik, and Sabel (2008) argue that industrial policy should work at two levels. At the first, micro level (what they term 'in the small') this involves a regular dialogue between the government and the private sector, where bottlenecks and market failures are identified and the government plays a coordinating and facilitating role to remove these. The second level (what they term 'in the large') involves a more ambitious role for government in providing funds in the form of risk capital for innovative ventures through a public venture capital fund or a development bank. The aim is to support risk-taking activities that are genuinely new to a country and represent a major shift away from current specialization. The rationale for public support is that risk takers who innovate provide a path for others to follow and thus create a form of external benefit for which they are not compensated, so in the absence of public support there will be too little risk-taking and innovation. Since, as noted above, a lack of funds for new activities can be interpreted as a credit-market failure, this is compatible with the market-based perspective. However, aspects of their recommendations suggest elements of a promotional approach where the government selects a priority area and then looks for and supports private investors to develop it. Since the support that can be offered will be limited, in practice either explicitly or implicitly governments will be favouring some areas over others.[7]

What sort of intervention is likely to be involved with industrial policy under the broad definition used here? Table 15.1 sets out a simple taxonomy

[6] Distance is calculated for pairs of individual products (*i* and *j*) based on the probability that countries in the world have a specialization (revealed comparative advantage ratio above unity) in both. Goods thus are similar where there is a high probability that if a country is specialized in *i* it will also be specialized in *j*; see Hausmann and Klinger (2006).

[7] Hausmann and Rodrik (2006) describe this dilemma dramatically as being 'doomed to choose'.

distinguishing between 'market-based' and 'promotional', where, as noted above, roughly the former aim to correct for market failures as they affect existing activity and the latter to promote or create new activities with the potential for productivity growth and externalities (or to restructure activities with potential). 'Functional' means widely available, as opposed to 'selective', which refers to favoured activities or firms (although as noted above the distinction is never precise). Although the correspondence is not exact, the selective measures associated with past industrial policies in many low- and middle-income countries roughly equate to promotional measures and the market-based measures correspond to what is seen as legitimate market corrections in conventional policy-thinking.

Each measure has its advantages and disadvantages. Government expenditure on infrastructure provision, for example, may lower production and transport costs and boost the incentive to invest in industry. However, it has to be financed and thus places strong demands on fiscal policy. Tax concessions of various types do not involve direct expenditure, but only benefit firms after investment decisions have been made. The availability of credit will be important to investors where the commercial banking system is not playing

Table 15.1. Industrial policy taxonomy

Market-based measures	Coverage	Rationale
R&D tax credits	Functional	Technology spillovers and risk-taking externalities
State industrial research and education	Functional	Creation of national technological capability
Labour training subsidy	Functional	Labour training externality
State venture capital funds	Selective	Risk-taking externality
State export promotion agency	Functional	Lack of information and provision of a public good
Infrastructure provision for special economic zones	Functional	Encouragement of clustering and agglomeration effects
Profits tax holidays	Functional	Encouragement of manufacturing investment
Undervaluation of exchange rate	Functional	Encouragement of internationally traded activities, including manufacturing
Promotional measures		
Temporary financial assistance	Selective	Funding to allow restructuring of uncompetitive activities
Temporary import tariff protection	Selective	Protection of uncompetitive activities requiring restructuring
State procurement policy	Selective	Priority in access to public sector contracts
Export subsidy	Selective	Differential rates of subsidy based on productivity potential
Import tariffs	Selective	Differential rates of protection based on productivity potential
Directed credit	Selective	Priority allocation of credit based on productivity potential
Profits tax holidays (selective)	Selective	Favourable tax treatment for foreign investors
Incentive packages of tax, loans and infrastructure	Selective	Favourable treatment for foreign investors

Source: Weiss (2011: box 7.1).

its financial intermediation role effectively, but where domestic savings are insufficient external funds will have to be found. How far credit should be available at a concessional or subsidized interest rate is highly controversial. Low-interest loans raise the incentive to invest, but run the risk of encouraging low-return activities, since investors do not need to cover the opportunity cost of the funds. In addition, they may, if used widely, shift the choice of technology in a capital-intensive, labour-saving direction. Import protection has the great attraction of not requiring additional revenue, since support for investors is provided by domestic consumers of the protected goods. However, whilst the theoretical case for protecting infant industries is well-established, protection can also create the wrong incentives through an anti-export bias and the sheltering of high-cost producers.

As set out here, the degree of controversy over these measures is meant to increase moving down the table. Thus most governments subsidise private R&D, provide some state investment in research with industrial potential, and fund labour training. The market-based measures have been described in many countries as 'competitiveness policy' and most countries apply some or all of them. On the other hand developing-country governments are typically warned against selective promotional measures, particularly because of the risk of rent-seeking. Moreover, WTO rules and those of regional trading agreements limit the scope for promotional measures.[8]

15.4 Industrial policy and growth

Empirical evidence suggests that the arguments from the early development literature on the role of manufacturing have broadly stood the test of time. Particularly at relatively low-income levels, a dynamic manufacturing sector will be important in raising income, creating jobs, and diversifying exports. It is well-established that as countries grow up to a threshold income level the share of manufacturing in GDP rises. Recent work has linked a rising share of manufacturing with growth acceleration and with a diversification of exports, which in turn has a positive effect on growth.[9] However, the evidence that

[8] Chang (2009) makes the point that the freedom of discretion is greater than might be thought since although some selective subsidy measures are in principle 'actionable' at WTO, this does not mean complaints will be made (particularly where a country plays a small role in world or regional trade) and restrictions do not apply to domestic as opposed to trade-related subsidies.

[9] ADB (2007) examines these issues for developing Asia, finding support for the special role of manufacturing in growth; Hausmann, Hwang, and Rodrik (2007a) make the case that what you export matters and that high-value (chiefly manufactured) exports generate more rapid GDP growth, controlling for other factors. However, there is also emerging evidence that in some countries (most notably India) parts of the service sector are also playing this role; see Szirmai in this volume.

manufacturing remains an important sector, particularly for relatively low-income economies that are well below the threshold at which the manufacturing share in GDP stabilizes, does not demonstrate that earlier industrial policy interventions per se have had a positive effect. Because of the diversity of experience it is difficult to establish major generalizations from what is a vast literature. However, there are some things we do know.

It is well-established that today's industrialized economies offered various support to their industries at their take-off stages (Chang 2002). Post-1945 success with versions of industrial policy in developed economies has been claimed in, amongst others, France (through indicative planning), Finland (through technology policy), and Ireland (through targeting of high-technology foreign investment). In terms of foreign trade, it is clear that free trade has been a policy of the economically strong, adopted when their economies were competitive enough to benefit from opening to foreign competition. This generalization applies, for example to the UK and USA in the nineteenth century and to Japan in the 1960s, Korea and Taiwan in the 1980s, and more recently China in the 1990s. None of these economies were 'early trade liberalizers', although all have benefited greatly from liberalization when it came.

East Asia is the region of the developing world where there is the most plausible case for the successful application of industrial policy. Hobday (in this volume) discusses the East Asian case in more detail. Japanese experience with state financial support for selected industries though subsidized directed credit programmes, and the use of 'administrative guidance' and control over licenses for technology imports to influence industrial structure greatly influenced policy in Korea and to a lesser degree Taiwan (Weiss 1986). Although all economies in the region applied some or all of the measures listed in Table 15.1 there was never a unique East Asian model (when one is mentioned it is usually a simplified version of policy in Korea circa 1970) with the emphasis on different measures varying between countries and changing over time within the same country. Broadly speaking this change reflected a shift between the early promotional measures to the market-based ones. At the early stages of industrialization key subsectors were highlighted and promoted strongly with directed credit, import protection, and favours in licensing. As manufacturing became more sophisticated and the technologies used more complex this selective approach was gradually replaced by a functional one more supportive of the decisions of firms themselves. The distinction is roughly between initially creating winners and later letting them emerge. The mix of policy measures was sometimes complex. China, for example, has employed a twin track approach of liberalizing the economy to foreign trade, through special economic zones and later WTO entry and encouraging foreign investment and the transfer of foreign technology. At the same time it has employed measures to support large national conglomerate firms and to encourage local R&D (Nolan 2001).[10]

However, the record with industrial policy, even within East Asia, is both mixed and controversial. It is seen as much more effective in Korea, Taiwan, and Singapore than elsewhere. In Indonesia, the Philippines, and Malaysia, for example, it is viewed principally as driven by cronyism and patronage rather than rational economic calculation and it is associated with high-cost protectionist trade policy.[11] Where it worked well, key characteristics of policy appear to be:

- flexibility, so measures changed over time in line with economic conditions
- use of performance requirements, where special support was time-limited and conditional on achieving specified targets
- a focus on exporting.

Also where it worked well governments were strong enough to avoid capture by producer interests and could take decisions on a national not sectional basis. This independence of the planning bureaucracy seems to have been more important than their technical calibre (at least in Korea and Taiwan, but possibly not in Singapore).[12]

However, even in the acknowledged success stories empirical studies have had difficulty in demonstrating that industrial policy made a difference. This is partly because much of the theoretical case rests on externalities of various types, which are difficult to pin down empirically, particularly when they are of the technological type and operate at the sector or economy-wide levels. In addition, any counterfactual test of what would have happened without policy intervention is little more than speculative.[13] Given this empirical ambiguity, advocates of industrial policy largely base their case on the association between government support of various types, which raised the profitability of manufacturing, and subsequent export success from the promoted activities. As Stiglitz (2001: 19) puts it:

[10] In an otherwise excellent book on Chinese economic development Bramall (2009) argues that by entering WTO China has abandoned the tools of industrial policy that created the successful industrialization of Korea and Taiwan. This fails to recognise that trade liberalization on its own terms and at its own pace has been an integral part of industrial strategy in China. WTO entry ensured China's most favoured nation status, which was critical for its manufactured exports. Exchange rate protection, through deliberate undervaluation, has been retained as a key policy measure.

[11] Weiss (2005) surveys the evidence in more detail.

[12] Chang (2009) stresses this and points as evidence to the fact that in the early 1960s Korea sent civil servants to attend training programmes in the Philippines and Pakistan, two countries not known for the success of their measures to support industry.

[13] Detailed work reported in Pack (2001) and Noland and Pack (2003) based on input-output relations and assumptions about productivity growth and knowledge transfers suggests positive, but modest impacts on GDP growth from industrial policy in Korea and Taiwan, respectively.

> The fact that almost *all* economies of the region had industrial policies (with the exception of Hong Kong, China which benefited from the industrial policies of its neighbour, Mainland China) *suggests* that such polices were an important part of their growth strategies, whether or not the highly imperfect econometric techniques for quantifying such impacts succeeded in verifying such claims. (emphasis in the original)

Elsewhere in the developing world, evidence on the success of industrial policy is far more difficult to find. In India, for example, the import substitution programme of the 1960s and 1970s has been associated with high-cost, uncompetitive production, and the system of licensing controls (the 'Licence Raj') that began to be dismantled gradually in the 1980s is seen as a major obstacle to private-sector initiative. The most that can be claimed for industrial policy over a period of thirty years is that through its learning effects it may have laid the ground for the growth acceleration after the liberalization of the early 1990s (Rodrik and Subramaniam 2005). In sub-Saharan Africa (SSA) most industrial policy in the early post-colonial period was a version of import substitution, largely leading to high-cost, low-quality production for small domestic markets. The shift towards manufactured exports in the 1990s after the reforms of the structural adjustment era has been modest and African economies suffer from serious deficiencies in infrastructure, service provision, and access to credit, which make it difficult for them to overcome entry barriers into export markets (UNCTAD 2008).

The region where the contrast with East Asia is made most frequently is Latin America. In 1960 the latter was by far the more industrialized region, with a tradition of government intervention and a technically skilled bureaucracy. However, in terms of manufacturing it has long since been left behind by East Asia and it is difficult to find case studies of the successful impact of industrial policy in the region (Weiss and Jalilian 2004).[14] Arguably, none of the explanations of the much poorer performance of industrial policy in Latin America as compared with East Asia are wholly convincing on their own; they include lack of performance requirements ('too much carrot and too few sticks'), greater corruption and bureaucratic capture, a premature shift to 'secondary import substitution', and a lack of incentive to focus on manufactured exports due to either larger domestic markets or greater availability of natural resources than in East Asia.

In short, the recent track record of industrial policy in the developing (as opposed to the developed) world suggests that it was too often associated with

[14] The fact that the examples cited for the success of industrial policy in the region are typically Embraer aircraft in Brazil and the salmon industry in Chile, supported by Fundacion Chile, shows the limited range of options. One might add the automobile sector in Mexico, supported by a special programme to raise local content and generate exports (Ros 1994).

import substitution policies that failed to deliver internationally competitive production and that, whilst in principle it can work effectively (and has done so in a few countries), it is difficult to implement. Furthermore, the shifting use of industrial policy in the successful cases (from what is termed here promotional to market-based measures) indicates the need for flexibility and for tailoring interventions to the state of the economy and the broader international environment. International experience, drawing particularly from East Asia, suggests that the precise mix of instruments used in the application of industrial policy is less important than the pursuit of several broad principles to ensure that these lead to genuine industrial development as opposed to increasing the profits of the recipients (Weiss 2005). These conclusions can be summarized as:

- a regular dialogue with the private sector, through industry associations or chambers of commerce to identify problems is important provided governments can avoid capture by producer interests
- establishment of clear performance criteria so the success or otherwise of an intervention can be judged and there should be transparency regarding who receives government support
- support that is time-limited, not open-ended, so recipients have an incentive to improve efficiency by the end of the period specified
- support as far as possible for broad activities (such as R&D or labour training) or sectors (like electronics) rather than to individual firms to avoid distorting competition and establishing monopolies[15]
- encouragement of exporting as a means of introducing competition and opening a sector to foreign technology.

15.5 Challenges for the future

There are many possible future challenges ahead that a version of industrial policy can help to address and five are identified here.

15.5.1 *Financial sector reform*

In many countries a key aspect of industrial policy will be to create or sustain an adequate system of financial intermediation that ensures that the long-term funds needed for industrial investment are forthcoming. In many

[15] There is some dispute as to whether sector targeting is sensible, with some preferring to stress support to activities that generate externalities and may span several sectors; see Hausmann and Rodrik (2005: 79).

countries it is still difficult to access long-term credits, and where these are available a high-risk premium is built into lending rates of interest. Poor corporate governance and lack of transparency in business operations are said to have made it difficult for banks to assess credit risk and forced them to rely on collateral-based lending with high-risk premiums, particularly for small and medium enterprises. Alternative models of financial intermediation include lending through a commercial banking sector with a sufficiently long-term horizon, the use of equity through venture capital schemes, and a state-owned industrial development bank. In many lower and middle-income countries the commercial banking sector is not sufficiently developed to play this intermediation role adequately, which opens up a key role for public intervention.

Where there is a reasonably well-developed stock exchange, state-funded venture capital schemes provide a mechanism to support innovation with a ready exit strategy through the sale of the government equity stake once a company is on a sound footing. Alternatively, public funds can be channelled through a state industrial development bank. State-owned development banks have gone out of fashion in recent years, with many advising that a preferable option is the development of a commercial banking sector that can provide long-run finance on a more efficient basis. The case against development banks is that by attempting to combine commercial, economic, and social objectives they can fund unviable projects, which squander national resources. To avoid such risks clear criteria need to be established before projects are accepted. These must focus on the demonstrated potential net benefits to the economy from the projects concerned, as well as their financial viability. Techniques for assessing both economic and financial returns of projects are readily available and have been applied by international development agencies for many years.[16] To avoid the risk of multiple objectives confusing decision-taking it is preferable not to incorporate employment generation or distributional change as separate criteria for project acceptance, leaving policy instruments other than development bank funding (such as labour training or social sector expenditure) to address these important considerations directly.

15.5.2 *Breaking into global production networks*

As is well-known, globalization has meant that in many branches of manufacturing—with low weight-to-value ratios and technical divisibility of production—there has been a growing trend to fragmentation of production. This has allowed low-wage economies to be integrated into global production networks either as supply contractors or 'own equipment manufacturers'. The

[16] Textbooks such as Curry and Weiss (2000) or Potts (2002) make clear the distinction between economic and financial effects.

parts of the developing world that have been least successful in integrating their producers into these networks—chiefly SSA and Latin America—are where manufacturing export growth has been slowest. In future decades the evolution of these networks is likely to be driven by two factors: the continued decline in 'trade costs' (the cost of doing business globally, including transport and communication costs) and the increasing global concentration of production amongst lead firms and their first-tier suppliers (Nolan, Zhang, and Liu 2008). These factors will be expected to work in contrary directions, with the former making it easier and the latter more difficult for inexperienced developing country firms to break into these networks. However, the expectation must be that niches still exist for newcomer firms and that state support will be helpful in accessing these. Potential industrial policy measures range from export-marketing facilities and trade credit (and possibly time-limited export subsidies, which are allowable for least developed countries) for small local firms to investment incentive packages and supportive infrastructure investment for foreign investors. In dealing with foreign investors there are now clear restrictions imposed by WTO rules and it is no longer possible to link incentives with export or local-content targets, as was done in the past, although non-trade-related targets (like employment or output growth) can be used. Other wider aspects of the 'investment climate' relating to governance and institutional issues will also need to be addressed.[17]

15.5.3 *Facing competition from the reemerging giants*

Most forecasts suggest that China, and to a lesser degree India, will have a major impact on the pattern of global growth.[18] For developing countries with a competitive manufacturing sector this poses a great opportunity to export to these large, rapidly expanding markets. Neighbouring economies in East Asia have already seen a significant rise in their exports of equipment, parts, and components (often as part of trade within regional production networks), with these economies running trade surpluses with China. In addition, with the increasingly affluent consumer markets in the two giant economies there is an opportunity for the export of competitively priced consumer goods, of a product quality and style unsuited to the markets of higher-income economies.

On the other hand middle-income developing economies with well-established manufacturing sectors face a major competitive threat from China, in particular, both in their traditional export markets of North America and Europe and potentially in their home markets as well. China has been

[17] Boardman (2007) gives a detailed assessment of investment climate issues holding back African manufacturing.

[18] See the detailed analyses in Winters and Yusuf (2007).

competing at both the low-technology unskilled labour-intensive and high-technology skill-intensive ends of the product spectrum, and its gains in export market share at the expense initially of other East Asian economies and more recently of Latin and Central American economies have been well documented.[19] Greater competition in domestic markets may come if there are further reductions in tariffs for manufactures, as part of the WTO negotiating process. Average applied tariffs for non-agricultural goods are now relatively low (10–15 per cent) in most middle-income economies, but there are peaks for sensitive items so average bound tariffs in India, Brazil and Mexico, for example, are 30–35 per cent.[20] Reductions in these will create competitive pressure on domestic firms.

To meet this competitive pressure middle-income developing economies need to upgrade their technological capability. This is likely to require state support, for example in the form of training initiatives, publicly funded research centres, incentives for private sector R&D, and venture capital funding to support risk-taking. The case for boosting the higher technology segment of manufactured exports is strengthened if the long-term trend—whereby these types of manufactures have been the fastest growing element of world trade—is continued.[21]

Similarly, at lower levels of technological sophistication low-wage economies in Africa may also see their domestic markets threatened by cheaper goods from China. In many products higher productivity allows Chinese goods to be produced at lower unit costs than in most African economies despite significantly higher wages in China. In Chapter 9 of this volume, Page discusses African manufacturing in more detail, but there is a fear in many countries that the route to industrialization through the production and subsequent export of labour-intensive manufactures like textiles, clothing, footwear, and toys may be blocked by Chinese competition. How far this threat will be ameliorated in the medium-term by appreciation of the Chinese currency is unclear and there is a significant agenda for African governments wishing to address lack of local competitiveness through a supportive industrial policy.

15.5.4 *Addressing climate change*

One certainty is that future industrialization will be strongly influenced by governments' reaction to climate change, and the chapters by Gries and

[19] See for example Lall and Albaladejo (2004); and Jenkins, Dussel Peters, and Mesquita Morreira (2008).

[20] Data are from the WTO website.

[21] UNIDO (2009) reports that in the short period 2000–5 it is resource-based manufactures that have grown most rapidly, although over longer period 1990–2005 the higher technology goods have had the most rapid growth.

Naudé in this volume discuss in more detail the implications of climate change for industrial policy. The key issue here is the energy, and therefore carbon-emission, content of different manufacturing outputs and the future cost that is imposed on producers of such emissions. Estimates of the damage caused per ton of carbon emission provide a value for the 'social cost of carbon', which in theory should form the basis of an optimal carbon tax to be levied by national governments.[22] Whether future carbon charges are through taxation or through the price emerging from a market in permits to use carbon, the expectation must be that in the longer term there will be a major impact on both sources of energy and the location of energy-using industries. There will be a further migration of energy-intensive heavy industries, like steel, chemicals, non-ferrous metals, petrochemicals, cement, and pulp and paper to the developing world, assuming similar carbon charges are not adopted there. To some extent this migration is already taking place, driven by differences in wage and raw material costs, but an additional cost of carbon would accelerate the process.

If there is a global ceiling on emissions, then global welfare will be unaffected by this migration, but the recipient country would benefit from the national value added created by the migrating industry. However, if the notion of a global ceiling is unrealistic then there will be a trade-off between the national gain and the negative global externality created by the contribution to global warming. Insofar as individual countries sign up to post-Kyoto emissions targets, it will be necessary for government policy to support the adoption of best-practice energy-efficient technologies. From a global perspective if breakthrough technology (such as carbon capture and storage) becomes commercially viable there is a strong case that it should be transferred to poorer countries as part of overseas development assistance at its marginal (not full) cost.

15.5.5 *Avoiding jobless growth*

Manufacturing industry can play a key role in growth, as discussed above, through creating high-productivity jobs. Historically in the developed economies, and more recently in the successful newly industrialized economies, this wage income has helped greatly in pulling large sections of the population out of poverty. Experience of poverty reduction in China in the 1990s, with millions of workers migrating from the central and western parts of the

[22] Tol (2009) gives a comprehensive survey of estimates of the social cost of carbon. He points out that substantial reduction in carbon emissions requires a carbon tax of at least US$50/ton of carbon.

country to take up manufacturing jobs in the coastal areas and special zones, is dramatic evidence of this.

It is well known that as the manufacturing sector grows in technological sophistication and in the level of labour productivity the employment elasticity with respect to output declines, sometimes steeply.[23] What has become a concern more recently has been the slow rate of job creation in manufacturing in economies with relatively low income levels. In most of Latin America, for example, manufacturing share in income and employment is now very similar to that in Europe and North America whilst the income per capita level is much lower, creating what has been termed 'premature deindustrialization', with the risk that new entrants to the labour market end up in low-productivity activities in services or informal parts of manufacturing; Tregenna in this volume has a fuller discussion of deindustrialization.

In part, such trends may reflect the direction of global technical change that may continue in the future, but low-employment growth may also be due to factors that industrial policy needs to address. In some countries, particularly India, it has been argued that inflexible labour markets with significant employment protection rights dissuade employers from taking on new workers. There is some evidence supporting this claim from analysis across states in India with different labour laws, but it remains controversial, particularly since a skilled and permanent workforce (as opposed to one that is a low-cost and transitory) should offer a superior longer-term route to international competitiveness.[24]

Slow overall employment growth in manufacturing may also be due to the coexistence of expanding and declining branches of the sector. This has emerged as a major issue in China, for example, with a dramatic fall in the number of workers employed in the state-owned enterprise sector in the last ten years and only a modest increase in overall manufacturing employment.[25] The role of industrial policy here will be to accelerate the assimilation of retrenched workers through retraining and to support temporarily the

[23] For example for the period 1980–2004 Felipe et al. (2007: table 2) calculate employment elasticities in manufacturing of 0.81 and 0.55 for the Philippines and Thailand, respectively and of 0.14 for both Korea and Taiwan. Aswicahyono, Hill, and Narjoko in this volume provide evidence from Indonesia.

[24] This has been debated intensely in the Indian context. Overall since the early 1970s formal sector employment in manufacturing in India has been growing at little more than 1 per cent annually (with no acceleration in the post-1991 period), although growth in informal sector employment appears to have been considerably higher (Gupta, Hasan, and Kumar 2008).

[25] Official figures suggest only a very modest rise of 3.4 million extra workers employed in manufacturing between 1991 and 2003 (when the data series stops; see www.adb.org). Corrections to this data to account for the omission of workers from what was the township and village enterprises sector and migrant workers suggest total manufacturing employment in 109 million in 2002 (as compared with the official figures of 83 million), but still suggest the same trend of a slow overall growth with employment peaking at 130 million in 1996 and declining subsequently with the changes in ownership and restructuring (Bramall 2009: 426).

restructuring of failing activities that are judged to have a long-term future. As the impact of globalization and freer trade spreads across the developing world we can expect acceleration in the reallocation of resources within and between sectors and the case for state guidance of this process will be strengthened.

15.6 Conclusions

The case argued here is that industrialization remains an important objective for most developing countries and that there are numerous theoretical reasons why well-designed industrial policy interventions, whilst no panacea, can help. Paradoxically, one can argue that where such interventions are most needed (in the lowest-income countries with thin markets and a small private sector) the capacity to introduce them is weakest. There are plenty of practical problems that can be identified and what will be feasible will be context-specific. Broadly speaking the challenges for governments to address in middle-income economies relate to competitiveness and the development of technological capability. For poorer countries, well within the international technology frontier, support will have to focus on export upgrading using imported technology, location within global production networks, and the removal of key bottlenecks to successful investment.

How governments can help with specific policy interventions will need to be identified as part of a regular dialogue with the private sector through industry or trade associations, so critical aspects of the business environment can be highlighted. Constraints identified in this way, whether lack of long-term credit, shortage of power, lack of labour skills, or 'dumping' by foreign competitors or temporary import surges, can set the agenda for policy interventions.

This chapter has argued that industrial policy should be viewed as widely as possible, encompassing the range of measures in Table 15.1 (and other possible ones not included there). In terms of past debates the inward- versus outward-looking debate is now largely resolved. There is scope for 'natural' import substitution, created by large domestic markets and trade costs, but new policy-induced programmes make little sense aside from the larger countries and even there on only a temporary and selective basis. Current bound tariff rates in many countries allow this sort of temporary protection, and whilst it may provide a short-term boost to profitability, it has to be combined with initiatives to support productivity growth and exports.

In terms of the promotional versus market-based distinction used in Table 15.1, at lower-income levels when markets are thin and options are limited, promoting a number of key activities may make sense. This is likely to require dealing with major foreign investors with a negotiated package of special incentives. As economies grow and the manufacturing sector becomes more complex the case for such selectivity weakens because of the difficulty of setting priorities. If too many activities are treated as priorities the system becomes ineffectual.[26] This is where the availability of functional support available to all who wish to take it up becomes relevant. Support for risk-taking though public-sector venture capital funds is an important aspect of this strategy that has a sound basis in economic theory.

In summary, there is much that can and needs to be done without a reversion to failed, relatively closed-economy interpretations of industrial intervention.

References

Asian Development Bank (ADB) (2007). *Asian Development Outlook 2007*. Manila: ADB.

Boardman, H. (2007). *Africa's Silk Road: China and India's New Economic Frontier*. Washington, DC: World Bank.

Bramall, C. (2009). *Chinese Economic Development*. Milton Park: Routledge.

Chang, H.-J. (2002). *Kicking Away the Ladder: Development Strategy in Historical Perspective*. London: Anthem Press.

——(2009). 'Industrial Policy: Can We Go Beyond an Unproductive Confrontation?'. Plenary Paper at World Bank ABCDE Conference, Seoul, 22–24 June.

Collier, P., and A. Venables (2007). 'Rethinking Trade Preferences: How Africa can Diversify its Exports', *World Economy*, 30 (8): 1326–45.

Corden, W. M. (1974). *Trade Policy and Economic Welfare*. Oxford: Clarendon Press.

Curry, S., and J. Weiss (2000). *Project Analysis in Developing Countries*. Basingstoke: Palgrave Macmillan.

Felipe, J., M. Leon-Ledesma, M. Lanzafame, and G. Estrada (2007). 'Sectoral Engines of Growth in Developing Asia: Stylized Facts and Implications. ERD Working Paper 107. Manila: ADB.

Gupta, P., R. Hasan, and U. Kumar (2008). 'What Constrains Indian Manufacturing?'. ERD Working Paper 119. Manila: ADB.

Hausmann, R., and B. Klinger (2006). 'Structural Transformation and Patterns of Comparative Advantage'. CID Working Paper 128. Cambridge, MA: Harvard University.

Hausmann, R., and D. Rodrik (2003). 'Economic Development as Self-Discovery', *Journal of Development Economics*, 72 (2): 603–33.

——(2005). 'Self-Discovery in Development Strategy for El Salvador', *Economia*, 6 (1): 43–101.

——(2006). 'Doomed to Choose: Industrial Policy as Predicament'. Mimeo. Cambridge, MA: Harvard University. Available at: www.ricardohausmann.com

[26] As evidence of the difficulty of setting priorities in an era of rapid technical change nearly 200 products were listed as 'strategic' in Taiwan in the late 1980s as part of its targeting high-technology activities, although less than half of these had asked for special assistance (Smith 2000: appendix D).

Hausmann, R., J. Hwang, and D. Rodrik (2007). 'What you Export Matters', *Journal of Economic Growth*, 12 (1): 1–25.

Hausmann, R., D. Rodrik, and C. Sabel (2007). 'Reconfiguring Industrial Policy: A Framework with Application to South Africa'. Mimeo. Cambridge, MA: Harvard University. Available at: www.hks.harvard.edu/fs/drodrik/

——(2008) 'Reconfiguring Industrial Policy: A Framework with an Application to South Africa'. CID Working Paper 168. Harvard University, Centre for International Development.

Jenkins, R., E. Dussel Peters, and M. Mesquita Morreira (2008). 'The Impact of China on Latin America and the Caribbean', *World Development*, 36 (2): 235–53.

Lall, S., and M. Albaladejo (2004). 'China's Competitive Performance: A Threat to East Asian Manufactured Exports?', *World Development*, 32: 1441–66.

Lin, J., and H.-J. Chang (2009). 'Should Industrial Policy in Developing Countries Conform to Comparative Advantage or Defy It?', *Development Policy Review*, 27 (5): 483–502.

Nolan, P. (2001). *China and the Global Economy*. Basingstoke: Palgrave Macmillan.

Noland, M., and H. Pack (2003). *Industrial Policy in an Era of Globalization*. Washington, DC: Institute for International Economics.

Nolan, P., J. Zhang, and C. Liu (2008). 'The Global Business Revolution, the Cascade Effect and the Challenge for Firms from Developing Countries', *Cambridge Journal of Economics*, 32: 29–47.

Pack, H. (2001). 'Technological Change and Growth in East Asia: Macro versus Micro Perspectives'. In J. Stiglitz and S. Yusuf (eds), *Rethinking the East Asian Miracle*: New York: OUP for the World Bank.

Potts, D. (2002). *Project Planning and Analysis for Development*. Boulder: Lynne Rienner.

Rodrik, D. (2007). 'Normalizing Industrial Policy'. Mimeo. Cambridge, MA: Harvard University. Available at: www.hks.harvard.edu/fs/drodrik/

Rodrik, D., and A. Subramanian (2004). 'From Hindu Growth to Productivity Surge: The Mystery of the Indian Growth Transition'. Mimeo. Cambridge, MA: Harvard University. Available at: www.hks.harvard.edu/fs/drodrik/

Ros, J. (1994). 'Mexico's Trade and Industrialization Experience Since 1960'. In G. Helleiner (ed.), *Trade Policy and Industrialisation in Turbulent Times*. Milton Park: Routledge.

Smith, H. (2000). *Industrial Policy in Taiwan and Korea in the 1980's*. Cheltenham: Edward Elgar.

Stiglitz, J. (2001). 'From Miracle to Crisis to Recovery: Lessons from Four Decades of East Asian Experience'. In J. Stiglitz and S. Yusuf (eds), *Rethinking the East Asian Miracle*: New York: OUP for the World Bank.

Tol, R. (2009). 'The Economic Effects of Climate Change', *Journal of Economic Perspectives*, 23 (2): 29–51.

UNCTAD (2008). *Economic Development in Africa, 2008 Export Performance Following Trade Liberalization: Some Patterns and Policy Perspectives*. New York and Geneva: UNCTAD.

UNIDO (2009). *Industrial Development Report 2009*. Vienna: UNIDO.

Weiss, J. (1986). 'Japan's Post-war Protection Policy: Some Implications for Less Developed Countries', *Journal of Development Studies*, 22 (2): 385–406.

——(2002). *Industrialisation and Globalisation: Theory and Evidence from Developing Countries*. Milton Park: Routledge.

——(2005). 'Export Growth and Industrial Policy: Lessons from the East Asian Miracle Experience'. Discussion Paper 26. Manila: Asian Development Institute.

——(2011). *The Economics of Industrial Development*. Milton Park: Routledge.

Weiss, J., and H. Jalilian (2004). 'Industrialisation in an Age of Globalisation: Some Comparisons between East and South East Asia and Latin America', *Oxford Development Studies*, 32 (2): 283–307.

Winters, A., and S. Yusuf (eds) (2007). *Dancing with Giants*. Singapore/Washington, DC: World Bank and Institute of Policy Studies.

Part VI
Conclusion

16

Pathways to Industrialization: Summary and Overview

Wim Naudé and Adam Szirmai

16.1 Introduction

Not so long ago Rodrik (2007: 46) described the debate about industrial policy as having become 'stale' and languishing in an 'impoverished state'. The various chapters in this book show that this is no longer the case. New challenges and emerging paradigms have turned industrialization and industrial policy into one of the most hotly debated and interesting issues of the early twenty-first century.

In the first chapter we explained that this book is an attempt to answer some of the questions characterizing this new debate. To recapitulate, we identified the following questions.

- Is industrialization (and specifically manufacturing) still an engine of growth in light of the rise of the service sectors? To what extent should manufacturing be the main focus of industrial policy in developing countries?
- What are the recent patterns of manufacturing structural change in the world economy?
- How big a threat to economic development is deindustrialization?
- What lessons can be learned from already successful industrializing countries in Asia?
- What lessons can be learned from past policy failures?
- What are the challenges facing industrial policy in Africa and Latin America?
- Can developing countries still industrialize after the rise of China?

- What about the least developed countries—can industrial policy be successful when good governance is lacking?
- How should industrial policy take global climate change into account?
- What are new directions and paradigms in thinking about industrial policy?
- How do the relationships between the state and entrepreneurs evolve across different stages of development and how does the nature of state-entrepreneurship relationships influence the choice of industrial policies?

In this final chapter we offer a summary and synthesis of the answers to these questions that were given by the authors contributing to this volume and offer a novel view of their collective message. We conclude by pointing to some new questions that were raised—questions that frame the future research agenda.

16.2 Answers to the questions posed in Chapter 1

We can group the questions listed in Section 1 into three categories that correspond to the main sections of this book. The first set of questions relates to the need for industrialization in general, and the *specific role of the manufacturing sector*; Chapters 2 to 4 dealt with these issues. The second set of questions focuses on what can be learned from the *comparative experiences* of countries across time and space. Chapters 5 to 9 addressed these issues. Finally, the third set of questions relates to *new challenges* such as global catching-up, climate change, and entrepreneurship. The challenges were discussed in Chapters 10 to 15. In the following paragraphs we reflect on what we have learned about these questions and where more research is required.

16.2.1 *The role of manufacturing*

As we explained in Chapter 1, manufacturing has historically been the driver of economic growth, structural change, and catch-up. In recent decades, from 1950 to 2005, the pattern of industrialization has closely reflected changes in global patterns of development. Thus over this period the share of manufacturing in GDP in the rising economies of Asia has doubled, while the share has been stagnant in Latin America and sub-Saharan Africa (SSA). In the advanced economies productivity in manufacturing has continued to be high, but the share of manufacturing in value added declined dramatically in the long run. Services have become by far the largest sector, which means that their weight in explaining growth has increased.

These global patterns of change suggest that manufacturing continues to be a potential engine for growth and catch-up—even for the poorest countries. As John Page (Chapter 9) emphasized in the case of SSA, African countries should continue to strive for industrialization—indeed without manufacturing growth the region will face limited growth prospects and will remain vulnerable to external shocks, adverse changes in terms of trade, and the challenges of avoiding the 'natural resource curse' when commodity prices boom.

Manufacturing brings with it, as Adam Szirmai wrote in Chapter 2, special opportunities for reaping economies of scale, engaging in technological progress and learning, profiting from spillovers to other sectors and providing job opportunities for variously skilled levels of labour.

In this light, premature deindustrialization is a potential threat to development, especially in Latin America and Africa. In Chapter 3, Fiona Tregenna made an important distinction between different types of deindustrialization focusing on the difference between declines in manufacturing employment due to increasing productivity of manufacturing and declines due to declining levels and GDP shares of manufacturing output. If productivity improvements are the main cause of declines in the employment shares, this decline should not be considered as deindustrialization and need not have a negative impact on growth prospects of a country. Deindustrialization becomes a major problem in a developing country if there is a sustained decline in both the share of manufacturing in total employment and the share of manufacturing in GDP. If that occurs at lower levels of income, we have premature industrialization.

Between 1985 and 2005 several developing countries experienced premature deindustrialization. In Africa especially, deindustrialization has been a disappointing feature of the post-1990 period. The problem—missing out on the benefits of a growing manufacturing sector—is compounded by the fact that reindustrialization may be more difficult to achieve than getting industrialization going in the first place. Hence there is a need for industrial policy to promote manufacturing in industrially lagging countries (ILCs).

It is important to emphasize, however, that this does not mean that other sectors such as agriculture and services are not important in economic development. There are a great variety of inter-sectoral linkages between agriculture and manufacturing and between services and manufacturing, which should not be neglected in the long-run development strategy. As was mentioned in Chapter 2, in many advanced and developing countries agricultural productivity growth has exceeded productivity growth in manufacturing. Without a dynamic and healthy agricultural sector the prospects for industrial development in many countries—most notably African countries—may remain limited.

It should also be noted that the recent empirical evidence on the role of manufacturing is somewhat mixed. On historical grounds, it seems that the importance of the manufacturing sector as the driver of catch-up in the post-war period is overwhelming, and as we just concluded, manufacturing remains a key sector in development. But one should beware of industrial bias and a disregard of the role of other sectors in economic development. There are indications that the service sector may be becoming more important over time as a driver of growth in developing countries. The share of the service sectors is increasing and some countries, such as India, owe parts of their recent growth acceleration to dynamic service sectors such as software. This strengthens the case for industrial policies that are broader in scope than manufacturing alone, and requires more research to deepen our understanding of the relationship between manufacturing and services, particularly in the structural transformation process of industrially lagging countries.

16.2.2 *Comparative experiences*

This book offered a variety of comparative experiences to draw on. What these experiences suggest is that (i) industrialization is not an automatic process—history, policies, and luck matter; and (ii) that different types of industrial policies are necessary in different contexts and different times. Drawing 'lessons' from country experiences may therefore be difficult, as a number of contributors to this volume have made clear.

Indeed, from various country analyses in Part III a number of aspects of 'received wisdom' of industrialization were challenged. For instance, Asian development took off in the 1950s and 1960s 'largely in the dark through trial and error learning' (Mike Hobday in Chapter 5) and not through careful and artful prospective central planning; China's famous rise as a manufacturing giant involved a key role for the state, which long predates the communist period, as shown by Harry X. Wu in Chapter 6. But post-war development has involved high costs of 'disastrous policy mistakes' as Wu illustrated. In Indonesia, seen by many as a miracle economy that confounded expectations in the 1960s when it was an 'economic basket case', industrial success was less due to selective and sectoral policies than a 'broad set of orthodox policies' (Aswicahyono, Hill, and Narjoko, Chapter 7). For Latin America, Wilson Peres (Chapter 8) pointed out that industrial policy has been making a comeback despite the apparent shortcomings of important substitution industrialization policies in the 1960s and 1970s and the general rejection of industrial policy during the 1980s and 1990s. This comeback has occurred in 'open economies with orthodox macroeconomic policies—contrary to the previous conventional wisdom that they were incompatible'.

In the current debates about industrial policy one can distinguish two polar positions. The first position is the neo-liberal position, which continues to focus on the shortcomings and inefficiencies of the inward-looking orthodox industrial policies in the developing world in the period 1950 to 1980. This approach is generally critical of industrial policy. At the other extreme stand the neostructuralists who argue for a revival of industrial policies including the option of protection for infant industries in industrially lagging countries. The neostructuralists point to the pervasiveness of selective industrial policies and government interventions in the successful Asian development experiences. They emphasize the disappointing experiences of Latin America and Africa in the period of structural adjustment, liberalization, and deregulation.

Based on the chapters in this book we believe that both of these positions are wrong, and that the most appropriate policy with respect to industrial policy today is somewhere between these two polar opposites. A more pragmatic, middle-ground position towards industrial policy requires that we should take into account the lessons to be learned from recent experiences, but without forgetting the critical lessons of the post-war period of 1950 to 1980. There can be no return to policies of the past. Rather, policy design should focus on the new challenges and new circumstances, as was set out in this book.

In Chapter 5, Mike Hobday has emphasized the difficulty of drawing general lessons from the Asian experience, because of the great variety of conditions and challenges facing different countries. Nevertheless one should not be despondent about the possibilities for industrially lagging countries to catch up through manufacturing growth. Industrialization remains a possibility for these countries despite the rise of Asia as a manufacturing giant. As Hobday suggested, industrially lagging countries should complement rather than imitate the Asian economies. Their policies should respond to new trends and new opportunities. Among others, this might mean that South–South trade could play a more dominant role in future industrialization than it played in the past—at least for African and Latin American countries, and that such South–South-led industrialization may need close scrutiny by researchers and policy makers in future. In Latin America resource-based industrialization may offer new opportunities. Finally, industrial policies need to be combined with strategies prioritizing sound macroeconomic management and improvements in governance—also in Africa, where John Page has argued (Chapter 9) in particular for business climate reforms to underpin industrialization.

16.2.3 *New challenges*

In Chapter 15, John Weiss discusses a number of new challenges that industrially lagging countries face. These include the need for global financial reform, the difficulties of breaking into global value chains, the competition they face from China and India, and the need to avoid jobless growth. The employment challenge can be addressed in different ways. Fiona Tregenna has shown that in some of the dynamic Asian economies growth of manufacturing value added and value added shares can compensate for the employment-reducing effects of productivity growth. Haryo Aswicahyono, Hal Hill, and Dionisius Narjoko argued in Chapter 7 that in a dynamic economy other sectors can absorb excess labour. But the lack of sufficient employment creation in manufacturing in countries with a youth bulge remains a serious challenge for researchers and policy makers.

One of the challenges discussed in the chapter by Peres (and also noted in Chapter 1) is the loss of policy space due to globalization and the current architecture of international institutions. We have learned from past experiences that there are few examples of successful industrialization which did not involve a phase of protection of new industrial activities. Whatever the inefficiencies of import substituting industrialization policies, especially when continued for too long, it seems that they have indeed contributed to capability building in economies such as Korea, India, Indonesia, and China. This enabled (existing or new) firms to compete in later, more liberal policy environments when policy turned outwards. One response to current policy constraints is to engage in more regional and decentralized policy initiatives. Another possible response is to revisit the notion of non-reciprocity, which under the General Agreement on Tariffs and Trade allowed poor countries latitude for protection, while reducing barriers to trade in the global economy. This might be relevant for the poorest developing countries embarking on structural change in the face of Chinese and advanced-economy competition. The notion of non-reciprocity emphasizes the important point that we want to avoid creating obstacles to the growth of world trade—one of the obvious dangers of resurgent protectionism—while creating opportunities for poor developing countries to embark on structural change and entry into global trade.

In his chapter on African industrialization, John Page discussed the notion of agriculture-led industrialization. This strategy is a response to the earlier neglect of agriculture in post-war industrialization. Its proponents argue that a dynamic and more commercialized agricultural sector is one of the preconditions for successful industrialization. Page criticized the notion of agriculture-led industrialization strategy, because globalization means that industry no longer depends on a domestic market for its growth. But in countries where a very large part of the labour force is still employed in agriculture, it is important not to neglect this sector, as Page himself emphasized. He also noted that agro-processing offers new opportunities to poor African countries, even though global standards and product quality requirements create new challenges and difficulties. In this regard we have therefore argued for more research into ways in which small businesses and farmers can be assisted to become part of global value chains—see also below.

An interesting insight derived especially from Chapter 13 by Tilman Altenburg is that industrial policies should be well-aligned with administrative and governance capabilities of the state apparatus. In a neo-patrimonial setting, industrial policies are easily subordinated to political interests. The more discretionary and selective policies are, the greater the danger of abuse. Nevertheless, even in Africa, some countries—such as Ethiopia and Tunisia—do much better than others, depending on the developmental drive of the government. In other settings, where administrative capabilities are well-developed and the bureaucracy is more insulated from political pressure groups and factions, more selective policies can be implemented.

One of the most important new challenges—new in the sense of not being an issue when the existing industrial countries first engaged in industrialization—is posed by climate change. As the chapters in Part IV argue, both mitigation of and adaptation to climate change will require greater global co-ordination of industrial policies as well as more emphasis on innovation within the content of industrial policies. In particular Thomas Gries argued in Chapter 11 that the global asymmetries between advanced and developing countries make global policy co-ordination essential. Pollution reduction should start in developing countries, where environmental efficiency is low and the greatest gains could be realized at the lowest cost. At least part of the funding for such efforts should be provided by the advanced economies, which have contributed so much more to the global pollution stocks in the past.

Both of these required shifts in industrial policies will have to aim first at reducing waste—both on the output side (through greater recycling) and on the input side (through greater energy efficiency and the development and use of more sustainable energy sources)—and second, on utilizing the opportunities for different patterns of industrialization inherent in 'green' or 'low-carbon' industrialization. Achieving these difficult objectives may require a different approach to industrial policy than in the past, requiring such policies to being more entrepreneur-focused, rather than state-focused (we will discuss this implication in greater detail below). It will also require much more research than is available at present to identify opportunities and risks for green industrialization, to learn how to generate the entrepreneurial innovations—both radical and incremental—that may be required to utilize the opportunities and minimize the risks, and to better understand the when and how of regulation of industry and technology.

What we have learned in this book is that one of the rapidly growing sectors in both advanced and developing countries is the recycling sector. In his

Chapter 12 on waste scavengers, Martin Medina made us aware that there are worldwide some 15 million workers engaged in waste collection. This poses a major policy challenge: to improve their livelihoods. It also offers new economic opportunities but requires much further research on how appropriate mechanisms for support, formalization, and regulation of the recycling sector can be put in place, especially given that this sector is the responsibility of the global community.

The chapters on climate change have brought to the fore the need for innovation. As Zoltan Ács and Wim Naudé discussed in Chapter 14, the design of industrial policies to support innovative entrepreneurship is an underresearched and complex challenge. It is, however, a challenge that is possibly central to the way in which successful industrial policy will be conducted in future. Entrepreneurial innovation is important for the reallocation of resources from the traditional (agricultural) sector to the modern (manufacturing) sector. As they put it 'there is substantial agreement that recovery after the 2008 global financial and economic crises and the challenge of climate change will require more, not less, of such entrepreneurial innovation'. This implies industrial policies where the relationship between government and entrepreneurs (the private sector) is important.

According to Hausmann and Rodrik (2003), entrepreneurial entry in developing countries generates information on the possible latent comparative advantage of a country. Thus industrial policy becomes a process of 'self-discovery' of what the economy might be good at producing. Because leading/early entrants absorb the costs (but not necessarily the benefits) of early entry, entry itself may be sub-optimal. Policies to promote such 'self-discovery' could be support for innovation, including the establishment and promotion of national innovation systems; support for new firm start-ups (e.g. by reducing regulations and requirements and/or providing subsidized credit), and by supporting the integration of domestic small firms into global value chains. More research is needed in this regard, for instance on establishing national innovation systems given the nature of firms' positions in global value chains and linking national innovation systems with multinational firms and their outsourcing to indigenous firms.

These considerations imply that one should be careful in arguing for industrial policy to be merely focused on an industrially lagging country's specialization based on its comparative advantage. They also imply that unlike in the past, where industrial policies were either focused on creation and growth of state-owned firms or alternatively consisted merely of broadly functional policies without consideration for firm or entrepreneurial specifics, the requirement now is for industrial policy to be a nuanced partnership between entrepreneurs and the state. The difficulty is that such industrial policies will require heterogeneity at the country, firm, and regional level to be incorporated into policy. It implies that one-size-fits-all policies for industrial development are unlikely to work, and require more research on development and the use of better tools for measuring and studying entrepreneurship across various levels of development.

The focus on entrepreneurship draws our attention to important new elements in the industrial policy debate, namely the orientation towards learning, experimentation, and self-discovery. In the past, industrial policy was often heavily state-oriented and based on top-down planning. Today industrial policy needs to be interactive and experimental. Entrepreneurial effort, innovation, and the knowledge sector fulfill pivotal roles. Hence policy should seek to create a learning environment in which capabilities are upgraded and complemented. Policies also need to be more experimental, willing to quickly phase out activities that turn out not to be promising, while expanding support to activities that turn out to be successful.

The renewed debate about latent comparative advantage (see Lin and Monga 2010) fits well within this new approach to policy-making. It criticizes the older emphasis on static comparative advantage. This is replaced by a search for latent comparative advantage: activities in which a country will have a comparative advantage in the future. The state has an important role in identifying and supporting these new activities and sectors. One of the ways in which this can be done is by making comparisons with experiences of countries with similar characteristics at later stages of development, as elaborated in the chapter by Haraguchi and Rezonja (Chapter 4). We may conclude by emphasizing two important roles for an entrepreneurship-oriented state within the challenges discussed in this book. Both of these are still fundamentally based on classic reasons for state intervention—information deficiencies, externalities, and co-ordination failures in markets.

The first, based on information deficiencies (and partly co-ordination problems and externalities) is the challenge of supporting developing country producers to become part of global value chains. As discussed in Chapter 1, and also by John Weiss in Chapter 15, global value chains have been fragmented—or 'sliced up'—in recent years. Providing their entrepreneurs with the competencies to be able to take part in these global value chains and with the information on, for instance, how to conform to the standards set by leading firms, can help developing country producers to grow and develop through exporting—especially where domestic markets are small. It is no longer necessary to develop complete domestic value chains encompassing all stages of production. The challenge for policy is not only to enter global value chains but to upgrade the position of a country in these chains over time. How governments can do this—for instance through multi-stakeholder platforms or other institutional innovations—remains an important area for future research (see also Van Wijk, Vellema, and Van Wijk 2010).

There is a strong case for assisting domestic firms to become part of global value chains, or to attract foreign firms that are already part of these chains. A considerable literature documents that export-oriented and foreign-owned firms are more productive than others and industrial policies have been found to be useful in this regard (e.g. Rose 2007). Many of the least developed countries do have some policy scope under the World Trade Organisation to promote their exports. Furthermore, extending trade preferences can make an important contribution to stimulate exports from these countries. Trade preferences to African manufacturers, such as the Multifibre Agreement's impact on Mauritius's industrialization, or the USA's African Growth and Opportunity Act promotion of clothing and textile manufacturers in Lesotho, Swaziland, and Kenya (Collier and Venables 2007) have illustrated their potential role. For such trade preferences to be successful it has been argued that they ought not to impose too stringent rules of origin and, according to Collier and Venables (2007), would need local competencies in terms of skills and infrastructure—areas that will require industrial policies, and also areas requiring more research.

A second and related area for the state to support latent comparative advantages is in terms of co-ordination. The classic case for co-ordination failures was made by Rosenstein-Rodan (1943), who argues that industrialization in Eastern Europe after the Second World War would not have occurred automatically, as these countries were caught in a low-level equilibrium trap,[1] resulting from co-ordination failures. The notion of co-ordination failures is still with us as many believe that industrially lagging countries are still caught in a low-level equilibrium trap due to co-ordination failures. Altenburg (2009) observes that co-ordination is particularly difficult for the latecomers to industrialization. He illustrates these difficulties with a good example:

> Take the example of a country with promising location and agro-ecological conditions for horticultural exports. Even if the country offers excellent investment climate and investors recognize the potential of the country, they typically start off with lacking irrigation; bad roads; no cooling facilities in place; no high quality inputs and specialized technical support services available; inefficient ports and airport facilities; high freight rates due to low trade volumes, etc. Developing all the necessary infrastructure facilities and services simultaneously usually far exceeds the possibility of individual investors. Unless a major co-ordinated effort is organized to develop complimentary assets ... the potential for horticultural exports will remain unexploited. (ibid.: 30–1)

[1] 'If the industrialization of depressed international areas were to rely entirely on the normal incentive of private entrepreneurs, the process would not only be very much slower, the rate of investment smaller ... the whole economic structure of the region would be different' (Rosenstein-Rodan 1943: 206–7).

Several early development economists also recognized co-ordination failure as an important obstacle to industrialization, but did not consider a balanced-growth 'big push' approach as necessary or feasible. Fleming (1955) and Hirschman (1958), for instance, saw the promotion of key sectors (those with forward and backward linkages) as being sufficient to get industrialization going. In more recent years, these concepts have been formalized within the new economic geography literature (Mayer 2004; see also, e.g. Krugman 1995; Ottaviano and Puga 1998; Deichmann et al. 2008). Here forward and backward linkages in manufacturing lead to increasing returns to scale with positive externalities resulting in higher output growth and higher productivity growth. Common pools of labour in agglomerations stimulate knowledge spillovers. When there are trade costs, firms will locate or cluster in large markets (Mayer 2004), which become self-reinforcing (cumulative causation). Because of this self-reinforcing nature, industrially lagging countries may need to kick-start the process, with the government stimulating the agglomeration or cluster of manufacturing activities through policy support. How this can best be done in developing countries where state capacity is lagging remains an important challenge for researchers and policy makers.

More recently, both Rodrik (2004), Ulltveit-Moe (2008), and Lin and Monga (2010) have re-emphasized the importance of co-ordination failure as a hindrance to industrialization. Rodrik (2004), in particular, argues that co-ordination failures constitute one of the strongest cases for industrial policy, as co-ordination failures are more 'rampant' than other types of market failures. He points to the fact that co-ordination measures are specific to each industry, so that setting up a horticultural industry will require different co-ordinating activities than establishing, for example, a motor vehicle industry. This is a far cry from the original big-push notions.

Ulltveit-Moe (2008) also stresses the continued importance of using industrial policy to overcome co-ordination failures. Her concerns emanate from the significance of agglomerations (clusters) of economic and industrial activity for productivity. Globalization makes the possibility of co-ordination failure more acute through the fragmentation of value chains, because the latter determines the spatial location of industry (see also Mayer 2004; Forslid and Midelfart 2005). However, Collier and Venables (2007) presume the clustering of economic activity to mean that government co-ordination of supporting infrastructure and services can be focused in a particular geographic area without being provided across the entire country, thus making it potentially less costly. And as Rodrik (2004) points out, co-ordination can be achieved without the need for large financial outlays for direct subsidies. Often government information, communication, persuasion, and guarantees can unlock the simultaneously needed entrepreneurial investment.

The roles described for the state in the above imply a partnership with entrepreneurs. Such an industrial policy cannot and should not be done in a top-down fashion. Discovering new possibilities for structural change and export indeed requires the intensive interaction between the state and firms and entrepreneurs, which was one of the characteristics of the East Asian experience. It also involves the support of environments in which learning takes place such as export zones, incubators, and science parks, and industrial clusters and agglomerations. Here, industrial policy and innovation policy converges (see also Cimoli, Dosi, and Stiglitz 2009) and points to a fruitful area for future research.

16.3 Concluding remarks

The development prospects of developing countries in the early twenty-first century depend on a type of industrialization that can deliver high quality employment, which is aligned with the international division of labour, and which would not take place in autarky. We believe that industrial policy can make valuable contributions to structural change and industrialization if the lessons of the past and the challenges of the future are sufficiently taken into consideration. Developing countries can benefit from the debates on industrial policy and on the amassed literature on the topic. The debate should focus less on whether or not there should be any industrial policy and more on making existing policy instruments more effective and crafting new policy instruments that take into account entrepreneurship, level of development of a country or region, and the changing relationship between state and private sector. Policy makers and academics need to be aware of the recent trends, challenges, and emerging paradigms in the world economy and to understand how these shape the crafting of new industrial policy instruments and the effective application of existing instruments. While industrial policy is perhaps even more urgent than ever, it may also be more difficult to practically implement than before. These aspects should not be overlooked in the policy dialogue and should increasingly form part of the scholarly agenda. Hopefully this volume makes a contribution to this dialogue.

References

Altenburg, T. (2009). 'Industrial Policy for Low and Lower-Middle Income Countries'. Paper presented at the UNU-WIDER, UNU-MERIT, and UNIDO Workshop on 'Pathways to Industrialization in the 21st Century: New Challenges and Emerging Paradigms', Maastricht, The Netherlands, 22–23 October.

Cimoli, M., G. Dosi, and J. E Stiglitz (eds) (2009). *Industrial Policy and Development.* Oxford: Oxford University Press.

Collier, P., and A. J. Venables (2007). 'Rethinking Trade Preferences: How Africa can Diversify its Exports', *The World Economy*, 30: 1326–45.

Deichmann, U., S. V. Lall, S. J. Redding, and A. J. Venables (2008). 'Industrial Location in Developing Countries', *World Bank Research Observer*, 23 (2): 219–46.

Fleming, M. (1955). 'External Economies and the Doctrine of Balanced Growth', *Economic Journal*, 65: 241–56.

Forslid, R., and K. H. Midelfart (2005). 'Globalization, Industrial Policy and Clusters', *Journal of International Economics*, 66: 197–213.

Hausmann, R., and D. Rodrik (2003). 'Economic Development as Self-Discovery', *Journal of Development Economics*, 72 (2): 603–33.

Hirschman, A. O. (1958). *The Strategy of Economic Development.* New Haven, CT: Yale University Press.

Krugman, P. (1995). *Development, Geography, and Economic Theory*. Cambridge, MA: MIT Press.

Lin, J. Y., and C. Monga (2010). 'Growth Identification and Facilitation: The Role of the State in the Dynamics of Structural Change'. Policy Research Working Paper 5313. Washington, DC: World Bank.

Mayer, J. (2004). 'Industrialization in Developing Countries: Some Evidence from a New Economic Geography Perspective'. Discussion Papers 174. Geneva: UNCTAD.

Ottaviano, G., and D. Puga (1998). 'Agglomeration in the Global Economy: A Survey of the New Economic Geography', *The World Economy*, 21: 707–31.

Rodrik, D. (2004). 'Industrial Policy for the Twenty-First Century'. Discussion Paper 4767. London: Centre for Economic Policy Research.

——(2007). 'Normalizing Industrial Policy'. Mimeo. Cambridge, MA: Harvard University, John F Kennedy School of Government.

Rose, A. K. (2007). 'The Foreign Service and Foreign Trade: Embassies as Export Promotion', *The World Economy*, 30 (1): 22–38.

Rosenstein-Rodan, P. (1943). 'Problems of Industrialisation of Eastern and South-Eastern Europe', *Economic Journal*, 53: 202–11.

Ulltveit-Moe, K. (2008). 'Live and Let Die: Industrial Policy in a Globalised World'. Expert Report 22. Sweden's Globalisation Council.

Van Wijk, J., Vellema, S. and Van Wijk, J. (2010). 'Institutions, Partnerships and Institutional Change: Towards a Theoretical Framework', Working Paper 009. Rotterdam: The Partnerships Resource Centre.

Index

Note : Bold entries refer to Figures or Tables

Index